THE DISAPPEARING F\

The standard account of the First Amendment presupposes that the Supreme Court consistently has expanded the scope of free speech rights over time. This account holds true in some areas, but not in others. In this illuminating work, Ronald J. Krotoszynski, Jr. acknowledges that the contemporary Supreme Court rigorously enforces the rules against content and viewpoint discrimination for those who possess the wherewithal to speak but when citizens need the government's assistance to speak – for example, access to public property for protest – free speech rights have declined. Instead of using open-ended balancing tests, the Roberts and Rehnquist Courts have opted for bright line, categorical rules that minimize judicial discretion. Opportunities for democratic engagement could be enhanced, however, if the federal courts returned to the Warren Court's balancing approach and vested federal judges with discretionary authority to require government to assist would-be speakers. This book should be read by anyone concerned with free speech and its place in democratic self-government.

Ronald J. Krotoszynski, Jr. teaches and writes about constitutional law, administrative law, First Amendment, and comparative constitutional law, with a particular focus on the First Amendment and freedom of expression. He is the author of three books, including *Privacy Revisited* (2016), *Reclaiming the Petition Clause* (2012), and *The First Amendment in Cross-Cultural Perspective* (2006). He has published works in leading law reviews and is the co-author of two casebooks, *First Amendment: Cases and Theory* (3rd ed. 2017) and *Administrative Law* (4th ed. 2017).

The Disappearing First Amendment

RONALD J. KROTOSZYNSKI, JR.
University of Alabama School of Law

CAMBRIDGE
UNIVERSITY PRESS

CAMBRIDGE
UNIVERSITY PRESS

University Printing House, Cambridge CB2 8BS, United Kingdom

One Liberty Plaza, 20th Floor, New York, NY 10006, USA

477 Williamstown Road, Port Melbourne, VIC 3207, Australia

314–321, 3rd Floor, Plot 3, Splendor Forum, Jasola District Centre,
New Delhi – 110025, India

79 Anson Road, #06–04/06, Singapore 079906

Cambridge University Press is part of the University of Cambridge.

It furthers the University's mission by disseminating knowledge in the pursuit of
education, learning, and research at the highest international levels of excellence.

www.cambridge.org
Information on this title: www.cambridge.org/9781108481540
DOI: 10.1017/9781108674188

First published 2019

Printed in the United Kingdom by TJ International Ltd, Padstow Cornwall

A catalogue record for this publication is available from the British Library.

Library of Congress Cataloging-in-Publication Data
NAMES: Krotoszynski, Ronald J., 1967– author.
TITLE: The disappearing First Amendment / Ronald J. Krotoszynski, Jr. University
of Alabama School of Law.
DESCRIPTION: Cambridge, United Kingdom ; New York, NY : Cambridge University
Press, [2019]
IDENTIFIERS: LCCN 2019008718 | ISBN 9781108481540
SUBJECTS: LCSH: United States. Constitution. 1st Amendment. | Civil rights – United States. |
Freedom of speech – United States. | Freedom of the press – United States.
CLASSIFICATION: LCC KF4770 .K735 2019 | DDC 342.7308/5–dc23
LC record available at https://lccn.loc.gov/2019008718

ISBN 978-1-108-48154-0 Hardback
ISBN 978-1-108-72291-9 Paperback

For my father, Ronald J. Krotoszynski, Sr.

Contents

Preface

The Free Speech Clause has enjoyed quite a good run and presently has a rather remarkable – and robust – scope of application. Since the firm ascendency of the Holmes-Brandeis vision of the First Amendment in the mid-twentieth century,[1] the First Amendment has been something of a growth stock. Over time, and with great predictability, the Supreme Court has expanded the First Amendment's scope of coverage. This is particularly true of the Free Speech Clause and the unenumerated right of free association; admittedly, this proposition holds somewhat less true for the First Amendment rights of assembly, petition, and press.

In light of these considerations, one would stand on firm jurisprudential ground to posit that, as a general matter, the scope of expressive freedom in the United States has moved in a single direction – toward an ever broader scope of potential application. The Free Speech Clause has come to encompass more varied kinds of speech (commercial speech, sexually explicit speech, offensive speech, intentionally false speech) and even conduct (for example, selling data related to the prescription practices of physicians in Vermont) with the passage of time. However, there is another story to be told – a story of doctrinal evolution followed by doctrinal retrenchment. And this story reflects a very different trend line involving the consistent diminution of certain First Amendment rights over time.

Of course, other legal scholars have shown how First Amendment rights in some specific areas have declined, rather than expanded, with the passage of time. Steven Gey, for example, called attention to the shrinking public space available for speech activity in the mid-1990s. Erwin Chemerinsky has posited that the Roberts Court is not a "free speech" court at all, citing the Roberts Court's decisions invalidating campaign finance reform measures, withdrawing First Amendment protection from government employees who speak out about a matter of public concern, and the imposition of new limits on the First Amendment rights of faculty and students at the nation's public schools, colleges, and universities.

---

[1]   For a history of the First Amendment before the Supreme Court came to accept the Holmes/Brandeis understanding, see DAVID M. RABBAN, FREE SPEECH IN ITS FORGOTTEN YEARS (1997).

So too, Helen Norton and Mary-Rose Papandrea have written lucidly, and repeatedly, about the federal courts' failure reliably to protect the speech rights of government workers. Caroline Mala Corbin and Claudia Haupt have all called attention to the growing problem of government compelled speech (particularly for those in licensed professions). Tim Zick has demonstrated how the protection afforded to transborder speech activity has contracted over time. Joseph Blocher, Danielle Citron Keats, Gia Lee, and Lyrissa Lidsky have cautioned about the potential distortionary effects of misattributed government speech on the process of democratic deliberation. Robert Post and Owen Fiss have written quite persuasively and lucidly on growing threats to academic freedom and the formation of collective knowledge.

I have benefited greatly from the important work of these academic colleagues and fellow First Amendment travelers. These names – accompanied by a good number of citations and quotations, both above and below the line – will appear in the pages that follow.

So, what does this book bring to the table? How does it add to our understanding of the areas and ways in which expressive freedoms in the United States have declined, rather than expanded, over the years? In other words (and stated more directly): Why should anyone bother to read this book?

The Disappearing First Amendment does something new – it offers a novel overarching thesis for why speech rights have contracted, rather than expanded, in some, but not all, areas of First Amendment jurisprudence over time under the Burger, Rehnquist, and Roberts Courts. On a first look, the areas in which First Amendment rights have declined seem to be entirely unrelated to each other: access to public property for speech activity, access to private property for speech activity, the speech rights of government employees, the speech rights of faculty and students in public schools, colleges, and universities, transborder speech, newsgathering and reporting activities, professional speech, and limitations on government speech. A common thread exists – a thread that links these disparate areas of First Amendment law, theory, and practice.

The Warren Court decisions that pioneered protection for government employee speech, student speech, and its overall approach to requiring access to government property for speech activity all adopted open-ended balancing tests to weigh a would-be speaker's interest in the government's assistance in speaking, against the government's claim of a managerial necessity in withholding the requested support. These open-ended balancing tests created more speech net. On the other hand, however, the tests also certainly produced inconsistent results across the decentralized system of federal and state courts that would engage in the requisite balancing exercise. Consistency and predictability would suffer when different judges, facing cases with largely identical facts, rendered inconsistent decisions. Inconsistency in the context of free speech cases gives rise, at least potentially, to a risk of content, or even viewpoint, discrimination.

By way of contrast, bright-line, categorical rules generally protect less speech on balance than more open-ended balancing tests but will produce more consistent results across the run of cases requiring judicial decision. For example, a rule that provides that a government employee's speech enjoys no First Amendment protection if it falls within the scope of her employment will generate more consistent results than a balancing exercise that weights the employee's interest in speaking against the government employer's interest in managing the workplace. In sum, a categorical approach to applying the First Amendment will often protect less speech net, but will ensure that litigants receive the same outcome on the same facts. To be somewhat more precise, many of the categorical rules that the Rehnquist and Roberts Courts have adopted in cases where a would-be speaker needs the government's assistance in order to speak actually protect less speech than the open-ended balancing tests that they replaced.

As a normative matter, one can make the case for consistency and predictability over more net speech. After all, fundamental fairness (justice) arguably requires that judges render the same decision in cases presenting substantially identical facts.

In my view, however, the Warren Court has the better of this argument. If, as Alexander Meiklejohn so famously argued, it is essential to the process of democratic self-government "that everything worth saying shall be said,"[2] an approach that empowers more ordinary citizens to speak – and thereby to contribute to the process of democratic deliberation – should be preferred to an approach that generates predictable results but less speech. I will advance this argument, in a sustained way, over the course of the pages that follow.

Categorical rules will often tend to favor the rich and the powerful over the poor and the marginal; rules against speaker, content, and viewpoint-based discrimination all empower those with the means to speak to do so at will – and at whatever volume they wish. In this regard, Greg Magarian characterizes the Roberts Court's freedom of expression jurisprudence as reflecting and incorporating a "managed speech" approach that routinely favors the government and the powerful over the ordinary (much less the marginal).[3] Kathleen Sullivan objects to a "Lochnerian" vision of the First Amendment that presumptively treats any and all government interventions in speech markets as distortionary and misguided.[4]

These class-based critiques of the Roberts and Rehnquist Courts are not wide of the mark – the results in major contemporary First Amendment cases do tend to favor those with the wherewithal to speak over those who require the government's assistance to speak. I am not certain, however, that dislike for ordinary Americans, or a robust regard for the privileged, actually drives the Justices to reach these decisions. Rather than a conscious effort to link property and speech (admittedly a plausible

---

[2] ALEXANDER MEIKLEJOHN, FREE SPEECH AND ITS RELATION TO SELF-GOVERNMENT 25 (1948).

[3] GREGORY P. MAGARIAN, MANAGED SPEECH: THE ROBERTS COURT'S FIRST AMENDMENT 252–53 (2017).

[4] Kathleen Sullivan, Comment, *Two Concepts of Freedom of Speech*, 124 HARV. L. REV. 143, 143–46, 155–63 (2010).

explanation), I believe that a fear of transparent exercises of judicial discretion in First Amendment cases animates decisions that reject balancing in favor of categorical rules.

If the appearance of judicial discretion in First Amendment cases is distressing, any approach that incorporates "balancing" or proportionality analysis (to use the term more widely in vogue in the rest of the world[5]) forces judges to pick free speech winners and losers. Moreover, they must do so in a very open and transparent fashion. By way of contrast, bright-line, categorical rules hide judicial discretion more effectively – the rule produces the outcome (not the judge). Of course, this is nonsense – because the Justices of the Supreme Court are themselves responsible for both creation of a legal rule and also for its application, or non-application, in any given case, any judicial decision deciding a contested question of constitutional law involves, of necessity, an exercise of judicial discretion.[6]

The exercise of discretion is far less transparent when a judge cites and mechanically applies a categorical rule than when she engages in a balancing exercise. For conservative jurists, the appearance of consistency in First Amendment cases is a cardinal virtue in fashioning a doctrinal test for assessing the merits of constitutional arguments – and the obvious and transparent exercise of discretion is a mortal sin. The Warren Court, and to some extent, the Burger Court, were far more comfortable living with doctrinal approaches that self-evidently vested discretion with judges than the Rehnquist and Roberts Courts. And cases presenting demands for the government's assistance in exercising First Amendment rights will, of necessity, entail the adoption and application of balancing devices.

Free speech rights have contracted, rather than expanded, in areas where the decision of First Amendment claims requires open-ended balancing of the interests of would-be speakers, on the one hand, and the government, on the other. That is, in any case, the main thesis of this book. Whether or not the pages that follow adequately prove it out will be up to its readers to decide for themselves.

Having shown my hand, allow me to briefly outline how I intend to prove out my main thesis – which, restated and simplified, consists of three main points: (1) Judicial discretion in First Amendment doctrine has the potential to enhance, rather than degrade, the process of democratic deliberation essential to the process of democratic self-government; (2) the Warren Court understood this and, although not always in forceful or maximalist ways, worked to innovate in First Amendment theory and doctrine to enhance opportunities for ordinary citizens to engage in public debate; and (3) the Roberts and Rehnquist Courts consistently have favored certainty, predictability, and consistency over speech when deciding First Amendment questions. After an introduction and overview, set forth in Chapter 1, Chapters 2–8 prove out an empirical claim, namely that First Amendment rights

---

[5] See Vicki C. Jackson, *Constitutional Law in an Age of Proportionality*, 124 YALE L.J. 3094 (2015).

[6] *See generally* Frederick Schauer, *Giving Reasons*, 47 STAN. L. REV. 633 (1995) (discussing a judge's role in creating, maintaining, and applying a legal rule in a particular case).

have declined, rather than expanded, in some important areas implicating expressive freedom.

Chapter 9, which considers the importance of non-judicial actors to the scope and vibrancy of expressive freedoms, admittedly departs from the general approach of the area-specific seven chapters that precede it. The Warren and Burger Courts were not particularly successful in using the First Amendment to curb the pretextual use of admittedly constitutional discretionary police and prosecutor authority to squelch public discourse. To be sure, the Warren and Burger Courts weeded out breach of peace laws that facially targeted speech or made a hostile audience reaction the gravamen of a crime. They did not, however, find a reliable solution to the problem of the misuse of perfectly constitutional criminal laws, such as unlawful assembly, breach of peace, impeding pedestrian or vehicular traffic, and failure to obey a lawful police order. Nevertheless, Chapter 9 fits into the larger overall project of demonstrating how First Amendment rights, at least in some areas, have shrunk rather than grown over the years.

The Disappearing First Amendment also has a doctrinal objective. Even if the current three and four part tests do not empower judges to reliably facilitate, rather than impede, the exercise of First Amendment rights, the existing doctrinal tests could be refined and improved. Even if a return to the open-ended balancing tests favored by the Warren Court is an unrealistic proposal, we can and should make existing doctrinal rules function in more free speech-friendly ways when possible. Accordingly, each substantive chapter offers some concrete ideas and suggestions for modest reforms that would enhance the scope and vibrancy of First Amendment rights in the contemporary United States.

The empirical and doctrinal critiques, however, are in the service of my larger, normative thesis, which is that play in the joints works to facilitate more speech, and in a mass participatory democracy with universal suffrage, more speech is not merely a good thing, it's an essential thing. The 2016 election, with many voters believing blatant falsehoods, demonstrates the critical importance of a freely-operating and vibrant political marketplace of ideas that successfully engages our body politic in the process of democratic deliberation. For example, claims that Pope Francis endorsed Donald Trump for president and that Hillary Clinton ran a child sex-slave ring out of a Washington, DC pizzeria, influenced more than a few voters. With a margin of only 72,000 votes, in three states (Michigan, Pennsylvania, and Wisconsin) out of over 126 million ballots cast deciding the outcome of the Electoral College, it is entirely plausible that false speech, in conjunction with Russian trolling in support of Donald Trump, led to Trump's Electoral College victory. Voters who credit blatant, objective falsehoods – for example, that climate change does not exist – will go on to cast badly misinformed ballots. Democratic self-government will suffer as a result.

The 2016 presidential election clearly proves – if proof were needed – that democratic discourse is crucial to the proper functioning of a democratic polity.

The process of democratic deliberation benefits when more voices, rather than fewer voices, are heard. The First Amendment, properly understood and applied, should provide a constitutional basis for imposing affirmative duties on the state to enable ordinary citizens to be heard and seen – and to engage in a meaningful way with each other about the candidates, the issues, and the values that our government should both reflect and respect. Whatever the faults and limitations of the Warren Court's efforts to use the First Amendment as a source of affirmative duties on the government to facilitate the speech of private citizens, the Warren Court was actively and creatively engaged in trying to identify and sustain the conditions that make effective and successful democratic self-government possible.

Our democracy needs a First Amendment that empowers more people to speak to and with each other – and to do so with greater frequency. In a mass participatory democracy, more speech and more speakers are better than less speech and fewer speakers. The imposition of positive, or affirmative, obligations on government to facilitate private speech will require balancing – and balancing will require judges to embrace discretion. For better or worse, enabling ordinary voters to engage in the process of democratic discourse will require judges to render difficult decisions in close cases.

Balancing exercises, by their very nature, are messy and will not yield consistent results on a predictable basis. In other areas of constitutional law, however, the Supreme Court has learned to live with discretion and the indeterminacy that accompanies it. For example, the main test for ascertaining the adequacy of procedural due process considers the citizen's interests, the government's interests, and the probability of improving the accuracy of factual determinations if the government provided additional process.[7] The *Mathews v. Eldridge* test has all of the infirmities of an open-ended balancing test; it does not, and cannot, produce consistent results on a reliable basis. However, it has the virtue of permitting judges to consider, in any given context, whether the procedures the government used could have been, and should have been, more robust to ensure a factually accurate determination of the claimant's interest in life, liberty, or property.

We should not expect, or demand, perfect play from judges. But open and honest wrestling with how best to accommodate First Amendment claims with the government's legitimate managerial needs constitutes an unavoidable task.[8] We also have learned to live with "play in the joints" in the context of mass benefits programs. The government is not going to decide every claim correctly – but we can live with a certain number of blown calls if, in the vast run of cases, the government usually reaches the correct decision.[9]

Concerns about stealth content and viewpoint discrimination should make us worry a bit about *too much* play in the joints in First Amendment jurisprudence. But

[7]   Mathews v. Eldridge, 424 U.S. 319 (1976).
[8]   *See* ROBERT C. POST, CONSTITUTIONAL DOMAINS: DEMOCRACY, COMMUNITY, MANAGEMENT (1995).
[9]   *See* JERRY MASHAW, BUREAUCRATIC JUSTICE: MANAGING SOCIAL SECURITY DISABILITY CLAIMS (1983).

in the wider world, where proportionality analysis is quotidian, judges seem to be able to balance private interests, government interests, and general concerns about fairness and means/end fit without endangering the institutional legitimacy of the courts. If Canada's Supreme Court and the German Federal Constitutional Court can balance in free speech cases, without bringing their work into disrepute, then the Supreme Court of the United States should be able to embrace balancing, and the discretion inherent in it, as well.

In sum, and for the record, I do not suggest that the Warren Court was perfect or that the Supreme Court's efforts since Chief Justice Earl Warren left the bench have been terrible. That kind of simplistic "Warren good/Roberts bad" analysis would do very little, if anything, to advance or improve our understanding of how expressive freedoms should work in a polity dedicated to maintaining an ongoing project of democratic self-government. I do believe, and will argue in the pages that follow, that the Warren Court was more willing to innovate, to create, to bend First Amendment rules and theory to support the process of democratic self-government, than its successors have proven to be.

The Warren Court's willingness to engage with difficult questions related to maintaining a public discourse of the quality and depth capable of supporting self-government for the long-term constituted a signal virtue of its (admittedly imperfect) efforts. If our governing institutions derive their legitimacy through the imprimatur of "We the People," provided at regular intervals via the ballot box, that imprimatur can only be as meaningful as the process that informs the act of voting. Accordingly, the quality, scope, and vibrancy of democratic deliberation are essential inputs to a meaningful electoral process.

In sum, the First Amendment should certainly stand as a bulwark against ham-fisted government efforts to suppress particular speakers, ideas, or ideologies that the government dislikes. But, properly understood and applied, the First Amendment also should serve as a basis for imposing duties on the government to empower, rather than impede, citizens who wish to speak and to participate in the ongoing democratic dialectic that informs the act of voting on election day.

Acknowledgments

In order to be successful, a scholarly project of this scale and scope requires the active support – and encouragement – of many persons and institutions. *The Disappearing First Amendment* has benefited from the insights and ideas of many friends and colleagues – at my home institution (Alabama), as well as at other law schools in the United States and abroad. Accordingly, I owe a deep debt of gratitude for the active support and assistance that so many friends and colleagues have provided to me while I have been researching and writing this book.

At the top of the list: Dean Mark Brandon, of the University of Alabama School of Law. Mark has supplied consistent and unwavering support for my work on this project – including financial support and, no less important, affirmative and consistent institutional efforts to ensure that I enjoyed the necessary time and space to write and edit this book. In addition, *The Disappearing First Amendment* would not have been possible without the generous financial assistance of the University of Alabama Law School Foundation, which has provided summer research grants to support my work on this project for the last several years.

I also should acknowledge, with gratitude, the active support of the Seattle University School of Law, which has hosted me as a visiting scholar in residence for the past several summers. Dean Annette Clark, and the administrators, faculty, and staff at Seattle University, all helped to facilitate this project by providing comprehensive research support during my periods in residence in Seattle, Washington – and were also kind enough to host multiple faculty workshops associated with this book. Ms. Lori Lamb, my assistant at SUSL, always goes out of her way to ensure that my time in Seattle is as productive as it can possibly be.

Over a dozen law school faculties contributed significantly to *The Disappearing First Amendment* by hosting workshops at which I have presented one (or more) draft chapters. In fact, I have workshopped each and every chapter at least twice. The kind of sustained, well-informed, and engaged feedback that an author receives at a faculty workshop is simply invaluable to a project of this sort. I am very grateful to the law faculties at the University of Alabama School of Law, Cornell Law School, University of California Hastings College of the Law, Emory University School of Law, Indiana University-Indianapolis McKinney School of Law, Lewis & Clark Law School, Ohio State University Moritz College of Law, University of Oregon School of Law, Santa Clara University School of Law, Seattle University School of Law, Syracuse University College of Law, Texas A & M University School of Law, University of Texas School of Law, University of Washington School of Law, University of Utah S. J. Quinney College of Law, and University of Windsor School of Law for helping me to refine my claims and arguments.

In addition, I presented *The Disappearing First Amendment* at the Freedom of Expression Scholars Conference, hosted by the Yale Law School; at the First Amendment Discussion Group, hosted by Pázmány Péter Catholic University School of Law (in Budapest, Hungary); at a colloquium hosted by the faculty and graduate students at the University of Oregon School of Journalism and Communication; at the *Ohio State Law Journal*'s symposium on "The Expanding First Amendment," hosted by the Ohio State University Moritz College of Law; and at a "Meet the Author" workshop organized by the student editors of the *Michigan Law Review*. The participants at these events provided highly constructive and useful comments on this book.

I also owe a debt of gratitude to many friends and colleagues who generously read and offered comments and insights on draft chapters. Although I hesitate to mention them all by name – for fear of omitting someone whose assistance merits mention – I should acknowledge the assistance of the following legal academics: David Anderson, Ash Bhagwat, Vince Blasi, Joseph Blocher, Mark Brandon, Caroline Mala Corbin, Scott Dodson, Mike Dorf, Tabatha Abu El-Haj, Bruce Elman, Bill Funk, Charlotte Garden, Erika George, Lauryn Gouldin, Aziz Huq, John Inazu, Lily Kahng, Margot Kaminski, András Koltay, Sandy Levinson, Lyrissa Lidsky, Clark Lombardi, Barry McDonald, Andy Morriss, Jonathan Nash, Helen Norton, Jim Oleske, Zach Price, Scot Powe, Aziz Rana, Marty Redish, Joel Schumm, Steve Shiffrin, David Sloss, Gary Spitko, Frank Sullivan, David Super, Mark Tushnet, Chris Walker, Danielle Weatherby, Chris Wells, Sonja West, George Wright, Kyu Ho Youm, and Tim Zick. *The Disappearing First Amendment* reflects the benefit of their ideas, comments, and reactions.

Finally, portions of *The Disappearing First Amendment* first appeared in print as:

(1) Ronald J. Krotoszynski, Jr., *Whistleblowing Speech and the First Amendment*, 93 INDIANA LAW JOURNAL 267 (2018) (Chapter 4).
(2) Ronald J. Krotoszynski, Jr., *Transborder Speech*, 94 NOTRE DAME LAW REVIEW 473 (2018) (Chapter 6).
(3) Ronald J. Krotoszynski, Jr., *Our Shrinking First Amendment: On the Growing Problem of Reduced Access to Public Property for Speech Activity and Some*

Suggestions for a Better Way Forward, 78 OHIO STATE LAW JOURNAL 779 (2017) (Chapter 2).

It bears noting that the material drawn from these earlier published works has been revised and expanded for inclusion in this book.

Table of Cases

Two Steps Forward, One Step Back

On the Decline of Expressive Freedoms under the Roberts and Rehnquist Courts

"All right," said the Cat; and this time it vanished quite slowly, beginning with the end of the tail, and ending with the grin, which remained some time after the rest of it had gone.

"Well! I've often seen a cat without a grin," thought Alice; "but a grin without a cat! It's the most curious thing I saw in all my life!"[1]

– Lewis Carroll, Alice in Wonderland (1869)

The contemporary Supreme Court's approach to enforcing the First Amendment is not unlike Lewis Carroll's Cheshire Cat: Over time, the Justices have rendered the Free Speech Clause a "grin without a cat," at least if one believes that the First Amendment, properly construed and applied, encompasses not merely freedom from government censorship, particularly in the form of content and viewpoint discrimination, but also the right to government support for expressive activities related to the project of democratic self-government. By way of contrast, during the Warren Court and Burger Court eras, federal judges routinely required government to facilitate private speech activity. This support came in a variety of forms – including access to government property for speech activity, government employment, extending expressive freedoms to students, faculty, and staff at public educational institutions (including public schools, colleges, and universities), and requiring the government to facilitate, rather than impede or disrupt, newsgathering activities by the press.

In times past, the government, unlike a private citizen or corporation, could not pick and choose which speakers, and what kinds of speech, it would lend its assistance.[2] Instead, the federal courts generally assumed a duty on the part of government to facilitate speech activity – unless it could justify with convincing clarity that its decision to withhold its assistance from a would-be speaker was based on considerations founded on the necessity of reserving government resources for their intended purposes in order to achieve them.[3] Something less than impossibility would suffice as a justification – but the government had an obligation to explain refusals to assist would-be speakers.[4] Today, however, the federal courts no longer reliably require the government to facilitate private speech.[5] Instead, the Supreme Court increasingly has permitted government to pick and choose which messages, and messengers, it will lend its assistance – or even tolerate.[6]

Nevertheless, the Cheshire Cat's grin clearly remains. Even as the Supreme Court has reduced government obligations to facilitate private speech, the Justices have been increasingly protective of the rights of private speakers who possess the resources necessary to speak.[7] Although the Supreme Court has not formally tethered speech rights to the ownership of private property, the end results of doctrinal changes over the past forty years have more-or-less led to this outcome.

Thus, if one can speak without the government's assistance, the Supreme Court has aggressively scrutinized government efforts to control – or even shape – the marketplace of ideas.[8] On the other hand, if one requires the government's assistance in order to speak, the government is increasingly free to grant or withhold its assistance as it sees fit.[9] As Kathleen Sullivan has suggested, the Roberts Court's strongly libertarian vision for the First Amendment "emphasizes that freedom of speech is a negative command that protects a system of speech, not individual speakers, and thus invalidates government interference with the background system of expression no matter whether a speaker is individual or collective, for-profit or nonprofit, powerful or marginal."[10]

Several possible explanations exist for this trend toward greater receptivity to a system of "managed speech,"[11] or, alternatively, judicial regard for the government's "managerial domain" over its assets.[12] The most obvious thesis would be to posit that conservative Justices favor a system of speech rights that tethers the ability to exercise such rights to the ownership of property and limits the ability of government to attempt to level the playing field.[13] As the materials that follow will demonstrate, this thesis is entirely plausible. However, I have come to believe that the actual reason for the decline of some speech rights, even as others have expanded radically, is more complicated than judicial class consciousness.

As I will explain in the chapters that follow, the Roberts and Rehnquist Courts seem to detest open-ended balancing tests that involve obvious exercises of judicial discretion to select free speech winners – and free speech losers. The Warren Court, in particular, and to a lesser extent, the Burger Court, both adopted and applied First Amendment tests that involved a kind of proportionality analysis;[14] the reviewing court would weigh the interest of the would-be speaker against the government's interest in denying its support to proposed speech activity. The outcome in any given case would depend on how the scale came to rest.

Of course, this balancing of interests (or proportionality) approach meant that litigants presenting First Amendment cases with very similar facts would, from time to time, and place to place, receive different judicial outcomes. On the other hand, however, this open-ended balancing of interests approach led to the net protection of more speech activity than would have been possible under a system of more rigid, categorical rules. By way of contrast, however, the Roberts Court and Rehnquist Court consistently have abjured balancing tests in favor of bright-line rules that limit, to the extent feasible, judicial discretion to pick and choose free speech winners and losers. One could mount serious normative and policy arguments in favor of either approach – but one cannot deny that the approach of the Warren and Burger Courts – to embrace judicial discretion in First Amendment cases – created more opportunities for the kind of civic engagement that contributes to the process of democratic deliberation than the rule-based, categorical approach favored by the Roberts and Rehnquist Courts.

This chapter begins, in Part 1.1, by considering the important and underappreciated ways in which speech rights have declined, or eroded, rather than expanded over time. In Part 1.2, it continues by considering the significantly more speech-friendly baselines that existed under the Warren and Burger Courts. Using the Selma-to-Montgomery March as an exemplar of the potential breadth of the government's obligation to facilitate private speech activity, this Part argues that, not too long ago, the federal courts were considerably more willing to use the First Amendment as a basis for imposing positive obligations on the government to facilitate expressive activities.

Part 1.3 posits that the contemporary Supreme Court has increasingly linked the ability to speak to the ownership of property sufficient to support speech activity. Moreover, this trend tends to undermine significantly the equality of citizens within the process of democratic deliberation. If we are truly committed to the principle of equal citizenship and "one person, one vote," then we should be just as concerned about the openness and inclusiveness of the deliberative process that informs voting as we are with the relative weight or strength of a person's vote. Part 1.4 traces the Supreme Court's increasing resistance over time to using open-ended balancing tests to decide First Amendment cases – even at the significant price of providing less net protection to expressive activity. Part 1.5 provides a general overview of the remainder of this book. Finally, Part 1.6 concludes by providing a brief overview and synthesis of both this chapter and the book as a whole.

1.1 THE CONTRACTION UNDER THE ROBERTS AND REHNQUIST COURTS OF THE GOVERNMENT'S FIRST AMENDMENT DUTY TO FACILITATE PRIVATE SPEECH RELATED TO DEMOCRATIC SELF-GOVERNMENT

Notwithstanding a general narrative that emphasizes the ways in which the protection of expressive freedoms has increased over time in the United States,[15] in some important contexts contemporary First Amendment rights have contracted, rather than expanded. In fact, First Amendment analysis increasingly seems to reflect the views and approach expressed by Oliver Wendell Holmes, Jr., in *Davis v. Commonwealth*.[16] One could characterize the approach as reflecting "managed speech" or a "managerial domain" that vests the government with broad discretion to grant, or withhold, its support to those who seek its assistance in order to speak.

Professor Greg Magarian posits that the Roberts Court has embraced a system of "managed speech"[7] that favors some institutional speakers (including the government) and certain messages. He explains that "[m]anaged speech describes a mode of First Amendment jurisprudence that seeks to reconcile substantial First Amendment protection for expressive freedom with aggressive preservation of social and political stability."[8] The "managed speech" approach conveys "a strong measure of managerial control over public discussion," tends to marginalize the "First Amendment claims of *outsider speakers*," including "less powerful, and lesser-financed speakers, political dissenters, and others outside the social mainstream," and a bias in favor of "modes of public discussion that promote social and political stability" and against "modes of discussion that threaten to destabilize existing arrangements of social and political power."[9] Essentially, managed speech involves the federal courts vesting the government and powerful private entities with the discretion to marshal and deploy their resources to shape, if not control, the marketplace of ideas.

Professor Robert Post has advanced a quite similar argument that emphasizes the importance – and difficulty – of disentangling the legitimate managerial claims of the government as a manager from its exercise of more general regulatory authority as a sovereign.[20] As he explains the point, "[i]f government action is viewed as a matter of internal management, the attainment of institutional ends is taken as an unquestioned priority."[21] In the sphere of governance, however, "the significan[ce] and force of all potential objectives are taken as a legitimate subject of inquiry."[22] Accordingly, the distinction between "management" and "governance" is crucially important because the characterization of a particular undertaking as one or the other will prefigure the appropriate degree of judicial skepticism (or solicitude).

When federal judges expand the scope of the managerial domain, the government enjoys a much freer hand to take actions that adversely affect speech activity – when speech activity requires access to government property or other kinds of support.[23] Alternatively, and using Magarian's nomenclature, to the extent that the federal courts embrace a system of managed speech, those who require the government's assistance in order to speak are out of luck – if the government prefers not to facilitate the exercise of First Amendment rights.

Justice Holmes, while serving on the Supreme Judicial Court of Massachusetts, arguably pioneered the concept of "managed speech." Holmes squarely rejected a claim of a right of access to the Boston Common for the purpose of engaging in speech activity, explaining that "[f]or the Legislature absolutely or conditionally to forbid public speaking in a highway or public park is no more an infringement of rights of a member of the public than for the owner of a private house to forbid it in the house."[24] The Supreme Court of the United States affirmed, with Justice Edward Douglass White positing that "[t]he right to absolutely exclude all right to use necessarily includes the authority to determine under what circumstances such use may be availed of, as the greater power contains the lesser."[25] In other words, citizens have a right to speak, but not necessarily a right to speak using government-owned property in order to do so. The government may exercise managerial prerogatives over public property – granting or declining access to particular government property for speech activity as it sees fit.[26]

In the United States, we maintain a strong commitment to the theoretical equality of all speakers, and all speech, but contemporary First Amendment doctrine ignores the gross disparities that exist in practice between those with the ability to use money to advance an agenda and those without it. In other places, such as much of Europe, a similar commitment to equality exists, but it is operationalized to advance the actual equality of speakers on the ground, rather than as a merely theoretical commitment to formal equality of opportunity. Substantive equality, not procedural equality, is what counts.

Thus, in France or Germany, limits on campaign contributions and expenditures are quotidian – necessary government policies that seek to keep the playing field of democratic politics level (or reasonably so).[27] In these jurisdictions, the idea that government efforts to equalize the voice of speakers are inconsistent with a meaningful commitment to freedom of expression simply doesn't wash.[28] By way of contrast, modern First Amendment jurisprudence all too often takes the view that if a would-be protestor cannot use a public park, street, or sidewalk for speech activity, that person should instead buy advertising time on a commercial radio or television station or rent a billboard adjacent to a major road or highway.[29]

As Anatole France wryly observed, "the majestic equality of the law forbids the rich as well as the poor to sleep under bridges, to beg in the streets, and to steal bread."[30] In the context of speech rights, those with property have an enhanced ability to speak relative to those without it. Yet, as a formal matter, we claim to observe a rule of one person, one vote, and to embrace the formal legal equality of all citizens as voters.[31] Obviously, government efforts to create a level playing field by silencing some voices and enhancing others would present serious normative and doctrinal difficulties.[32] The First Amendment serves as a strong bulwark against both content and viewpoint-based government efforts to regulate speech.[33]

Yet, surely it is possible to imagine a world in which the government may not silence speakers with the means to speak even though it also affirmatively facilitates – by subsidizing those without means – speech related to the project of democratic self-government.[34] Using public resources to facilitate the exercise of expressive freedoms need not imply a generalized power to squelch speech by persons and entities that are able to speak without any government support. An important, and related, question involves whether government support of speech activity should be entirely discretionary – or whether the federal courts might use the First Amendment as a basis for requiring public subsidies of speech activity (particularly if the speech relates to democratic self-government).

I fully appreciate the legal fact that, as a general matter, constitutional rights in the United States are negative, not positive, in nature. Consistent with this general approach, the federal courts do not usually impose positive duties on the government to facilitate the exercise of constitutionally-protected rights by individual citizens.[35] The First Amendment, at least since the 1930s, has been different; the Supreme Court has regularly and consistently required government to facilitate speech even when it would prefer not to do so.[36]

As Justice Owen Roberts explained the proposition in *Hague*:

> Wherever the title of the streets and parks may rest, they have immemorially been held in trust for the use of the public, and, time out of mind, have been used for purposes of assembly, communicating thoughts between citizens, and discussing public questions. Such use of the streets and public places has, from ancient times, been a part of the privileges, immunities, rights, and liberties of citizens.[37]

Thus, the First Amendment does impose *positive* obligations on the government to use its resources to facilitate speech activity – unlike most constitutional rights in the United States, it possesses both a negative and a positive aspect.

The very same constitutional logic requires the government to protect unpopular speakers from being silenced by a hostile audience – even at considerable and unforeseen public expense.[38] It also prohibits the government from attempting to shift the cost of protecting unpopular speakers to those speakers.[39] Thus, existing doctrinal rules *already require* the government to use its resources to support speech activity – even when it would prefer not to do so. The question, then, is the *scope* of this duty, rather than the *existence* of such a constitutional duty.

The existing jurisprudential trendline is worrisome because it reflects a turn away from the Warren Court's speech-protective stance and back toward an approach that places undue weight on the government's managerial domain.[40] A case upholding a protest ban at the Jefferson Memorial, in Washington, DC, is highly instructive and demonstrates this approach in action.

Would-be speakers sought to use the Jefferson Memorial for collective, public speech activity – but were rebuffed by the National Park Service.[41] In upholding the National Park Service's speech ban, Judge Thomas Griffith, of the US Court of Appeals for the District of Columbia Circuit, unironically observed that "[o]utside the Jefferson Memorial, of course, Oberwetter and her friends [would-be protestors] have always been free to dance to their hearts' content."[42] This sentiment plainly echoes Anatole France's trenchant observation about how formal legal equality can constitute an empty, if not meaningless, form of equality. Moreover, suppose that on the facts presented – as was the case in *Williams v. Wallace*,[43] Judge Frank M. Johnson, Jr.'s bold decision that facilitated the iconic Selma-to-Montgomery March – the only property available to facilitate the protest activity happens to be government-owned property?[44]

Government arguably has both a duty to facilitate speech about democratic self-government and an interest in ensuring that democratic politics function on an inclusive basis. To the extent that the government's legitimacy flows from the consent of the governed, that consent must result from a free, open, and inclusive debate.[45]

1.2 THE PROBLEM DEFINED: COULD THE SELMA MARCH TAKE PLACE TODAY?

In March 2015, major celebrations took place to mark the fiftieth anniversary of the Selma-to-Montgomery March. To be sure, Selma was a defining moment in the nation's long road to equal citizenship for all.[46] The NAACP's Selma Project, including the March 21–25, 1965 protest march from Selma, Alabama to Montgomery, Alabama, and March 25, 1965 mass protest rally on the steps of the Alabama state capitol, helped to secure the enactment of the Voting Rights Act of 1965.[47] As legal historian Jack Bass observes, "[t]he drama of the Selma march produced a sense of national outrage that energized Congress to join the other two branches of government in recognizing the historical dimensions of the problem," and the Voting Rights Act "brought spectacular results."[48]

Speaking at the Selma March's concluding rally, the Rev. Martin Luther King, Jr., observed that "Selma, Alabama, has become a shining moment in the conscience of man."[49] He added that, "[t]he confrontation of good and evil compressed in the tiny community of Selma, generated the massive power that turned the whole nation to a new course."[50] It was, without question, both fitting and proper to take note of this important civil rights milestone on the event's fiftieth anniversary.

Yet, to celebrate Selma as an important historical milestone, and as an exemplar of the systemic legal and social change that peaceful protest activity can bring about, rings somewhat hollow because, under existing First Amendment law, a march of the same majestic scale and scope could not take place – at least if the government now, like Alabama's state government then, did not wish to permit such a large-scale protest event using a main regional transportation artery. This state of affairs should be a matter of some general concern because the process of democratic self-government requires an active and ongoing dialogue within the body politic. Just as government may not condition voting on wealth or property,[51] it should not be permitted to shepherd its considerable resources in ways that limit participation in the process of democratic self-government to those who can afford to purchase access to the political marketplace of ideas.

The active intervention of the federal courts was needed in order to make the Selma March possible. The Selma March took place under an injunction issued by US District Judge Frank M. Johnson, Jr., who creatively read and applied the First Amendment to justify the court's remarkably broad remedial order.

The crux of Judge Johnson's opinion in *Williams v. Wallace*[52] rested on the proposition that the right to protest on public property should be commensurate with the scope of the constitutional wrongs being protested.[53] Johnson reasoned that:

[I]t seems basic to our constitutional principles that the extent of the right to assemble, demonstrate and march peaceably along the highways and streets in an orderly manner should be commensurate with the enormity of the wrongs that are being protested and petitioned against. In this case, the wrongs are enormous. The extent of the right to demonstrate against these wrongs should be determined accordingly.[54]

Given the gravity of the constitutional wrongs that the plaintiffs established in open court, Judge Johnson issued an injunction of extraordinary scope; his order required state and federal officials to facilitate a five-day march, using the main highway in the region, and culminated with a mass voting rights rally at the Alabama state capitol attended by over 25,000 marchers.[55]

Then and now, Judge Johnson's "proportionality principle" was controversial. Burke Marshall, who headed the Civil Rights Division of the Department of Justice during the early 1960s, characterized Judge Johnson's opinion as a novelty in the law.[56] Nicholas de Belleville Katzenbach, who served as Attorney General under President Lyndon Johnson, also criticized Judge Johnson's reasoning in the Selma March case. He described the *Williams* decision as an "unusual opinion" and as "interpret[ing] existing doctrine imaginatively."[57] Katzenbach also "question[ed] that rule [the proportionality principle] as a practical measure of the applicability of the first amendment."[58] To be sure, the "proportionality principle" constituted something of a doctrinal innovation.[59] However, if viewed against the larger warp and weft of existing First Amendment law in the 1960s, it was not quite as radical as it might seem today.

Consider, for example, *Brown v. Louisiana*,[60] a 1966 case involving a silent protest against racial discrimination that took place in a local public library. Holding a civil rights protest in a public library might, at first blush, seem incongruous with the very purposes that lead governments to establish and to maintain public libraries in the first place. In fact, Justice Abe Fortas noted this anomaly in his majority opinion: "It is an unhappy circumstance that the locus of these events was a public library – a place dedicated to quiet, to knowledge, and to beauty."[61]

Nevertheless, in *Brown*, the Supreme Court overturned the protestors' criminal trespass convictions, holding the silent protest to be protected under the First Amendment. The Justices did so because the use of the library for the silent protest was not fundamentally inconsistent with its more regular uses:

Fortunately, the circumstances here were such that no claim can be made that use of the library by others was disturbed by the demonstration. Perhaps the time and method were carefully chosen with this in mind. Were it otherwise, a factor not present in this case would have to be considered. Here, there was no disturbance of others, no disruption of library activities, and no violation of any library regulations.[62]

Moreover, this outcome obtained because the facts at bar squarely implicated "a basic constitutional right – the right under the First and Fourteenth Amendments guaranteeing freedom of speech and of assembly, and freedom to petition the Government for a redress of grievances."[63]

Brown v. Louisiana, like *Williams v. Wallace*, starts from a baseline assumption that government property that can be used for First Amendment activity should be available for such activity, absent a very good reason – a reason, moreover, entirely unrelated to antipathy toward the viewpoint of the would-be speakers or the content of their message. Thus, in the 1960s, federal courts assumed that government had a duty to facilitate peaceful protest by making public space available for First Amendment activity – even non-obvious venues like public libraries and major US highways were potentially available for expressive activities.

However, times have changed since then. Under the public forum doctrine, government may restrict the use of government-owned property for peaceful protest if the specific property at issue does not constitute a public forum.[64] In other words, the analytical baseline has shifted significantly from one that puts the burden on the government to justify excluding expressive activities from its property, to one that requires persons wishing to use government property for speech activity to first establish that the property at issue constitutes either a public forum or a designated public forum.[65]

This development has provoked well-stated criticism from important and highly-regarded legal scholars – including Steven Gey[66] and Tim Zick.[67] Professor Greg Magarian's sustained critique of the contemporary Supreme Court's "managed speech" approach to enforcing the First Amendment offers a related, and equally dyspeptic, assessment of current trends.[68] To date, however, the federal courts have not heeded these calls for a return to a more functional approach to making public property available for the collective exercise of First Amendment rights. In this respect, the scope of public property available for First Amendment activity has contracted, rather than expanded, over time.

1.3 THE EVER-EXPANDING FIRST AMENDMENT UNIVERSE THEORY RECONSIDERED: THE IMPORTANT, BUT UNDERAPPRECIATED, GROWING RELATIONSHIP OF PROPERTY TO SPEECH

Of course, the standard account of the modern First Amendment is one of the triumphs of free speech, and expressive freedoms, including assembly, association, and petition, over a wide variety of government interests.[69] As Professor Marty Redish has argued, "democracy invariably involves an adversarial competition among competing personal, social, or economic interests."[70] The Supreme Court's efforts to disallow content-based and viewpoint-based speech restrictions, creating and facilitating a marketplace of ideas, permits this "adversarial competition" to take place, largely, if not completely, free of government control or manipulation.[71] Moreover, in many material respects, this generally-accepted narrative holds true: The Supreme Court has vindicated free speech interests in a wide variety of contexts. Moreover, the Justices have done so even when the government offers important interests to justify restricting speech.

For example, in *Snyder v. Phelps*,[72] the Supreme Court held that the First Amendment protected a highly offensive, targeted protest of Marine Lance Corporal Matthew Snyder's funeral. Snyder had been killed while on active duty in Iraq and the Westboro Baptist Church picketed Snyder's funeral to call attention to the church's opposition to homosexuality.[73] Despite the outrageous and highly offensive nature of the church's protest, and the entirely plausible arguments for restricting the protest in order to secure the privacy and dignity interests of the grieving family,[74] the Supreme Court held the church's protest was protected under the First Amendment.[75] Chief Justice John G. Roberts, Jr. explained that "[a]s a Nation we have chosen a different course – to protect even hurtful speech on public issues to ensure that we do not stifle public debate."[76]

Snyder represented an expansion and extension of an earlier precedent, *Hustler Magazine, Inc. v. Falwell*,[77] which held an intentionally outrageous parody to be protected under the First Amendment.[78] Chief Justice William H. Rehnquist, writing for a unanimous Supreme Court in *Falwell*, explained that "[a]t the heart of the First Amendment is the recognition of the fundamental importance of the free flow of ideas and opinions on matters of public interest and concern."[79] Despite the fact that Hustler Magazine intentionally had designed the parody to inflict maximum emotional harm on its target, the Rev. Jerry Falwell, Sr., the Supreme Court squarely held that neither a bad motive nor the inherent "outrageousness" of the parody could serve as a basis for imposing civil liability on Hustler Magazine under the law of tort. This was so because "[s]uch criticism, inevitably, will not always be reasoned or moderate; public figures as well as public officials will be subject to 'vehement, caustic, and sometimes unpleasantly sharp attacks.'"[80]

Moreover, *Snyder* is only one of a whole series of recent Supreme Court decisions that vindicate a wide variety of free speech claims. The contemporary Supreme Court has protected false speech about military honors,[81] violent video games,[82] and depictions of animal cruelty.[83] So too, the Justices have held that data constitutes speech and that a Vermont privacy statute that prohibited the transfer of physicians' prescription data for marketing purposes constituted an impermissible content-based speech regulation.[84]

Perhaps most famously, in *Citizens United v. Federal Election Commission*,[85] the Supreme Court, by a 5-4 vote, invalidated key provisions of the Bipartisan Campaign Reform Act of 2002 because the law prohibited political speech by corporate entities. In holding that strict limits on uncoordinated political advocacy by corporations violate the First Amendment, Justice Anthony Kennedy explained that "the First Amendment protects speech and speaker, and the ideas that flow from each."[86] In consequence, "political speech must prevail against laws that would suppress it, whether by design or inadvertence."[87]

Thus, the generally accepted view, which posits that the First Amendment has flourished under the Roberts and Rehnquist Courts, has a strong factual basis. In myriad contexts, and with great regularity, the Supreme Court has broadly interpreted and applied the First Amendment and invalidated both federal and state laws in order to advance the freedom of speech. However, even as the Supreme Court has *expanded* the scope of the First Amendment's application in some contexts, it concurrently has *reduced* its scope of application in others. Moreover, this trend of reducing some expressive freedoms while expanding others has not received sufficient scholarly attention.[88] Instances of the federal courts contracting First Amendment rights constitute an important countertrend to the more generally observed, and often celebrated, ever-expanding First Amendment universe meme.

The speech rights of government employees, including constitutional protection for whistle-blowers, provide an illustrative example of the Supreme Court reducing First Amendment protection rather than expanding it.[89] To be sure, First Amendment protection for government employees who speak out about matters of public concern has never been particularly robust. The original, unmodified *Connick/Pickering*[90] standard protected a public employee who spoke out about a matter of public concern, but *only* if the employee's continued presence in the government workplace after blowing the whistle was not unduly disruptive. Thus, the *Connick/Pickering* test, even at is zenith, plainly sanctioned a kind of heckler's veto[91] by hostile coworkers.

In 2006, the Supreme Court held that government employee speech is not protected, despite relating to a matter of public concern, if the speech at issue falls within the scope of an employee's official duties.[92] *Garcetti* involved a police warrant officer making false statements containing "serious misrepresentations"[93] to a judge in order to obtain a search warrant. Richard Ceballos, a supervising deputy district attorney in Los Angeles, California, discovered evidence that false testimony might have been used to secure a search warrant and investigated the matter. Despite the obvious public interest in preventing police from obtaining search warrants using false representations of fact, the Supreme Court held that the First Amendment offered Ceballos no protection for his actions because his speech related to his official duties.

We protect most government workers from being fired over their partisan identity, thereby constitutionalizing civil service protection in order to safeguard government workers from retaliation based on their partisan commitments and beliefs.[94] This same principle should apply with full force with respect to whistle-blowers. This is particularly important because the Supreme Court also has held that the press has no special right of access to information held by the government.[95] Thus, if government misconduct is to out, so that public officials may be held democratically accountable, the electorate must have information that only government employees can provide. First Amendment protection of whistle-blowers is necessary to facilitate and enable the process of democratic self-government – a core purpose of the First Amendment.[96]

Of course, the contraction of expressive freedom is not solely a function of the federal and state courts failing to enforce the First Amendment with sufficient vigor. The actions of police and prosecutors also significantly burden the exercise of First Amendment rights. Simply put, First Amendment rights are not only a function of the actions of judges and courts; the vibrancy of expressive freedoms in the United States significantly depends on the willingness of police, prosecutors, and other local officials to respect the right of ordinary citizens to express dissenting viewpoints.[97]

For example, in Ferguson, Missouri, police used a wide variety of tactics to impede peaceful protests, including tear gas, rubber bullets, Tasers, flash grenades, and snipers.[98] Moreover, local officials imposed a requirement that the protests be "respectful" and police implemented a "five-second rule" that required protesters to keep moving and not to congregate.[99] Although US District Judge Catharine D. Perry enjoined the five-second rule, and ordered local law enforcement officers to respect the right of the plaintiffs to peacefully protest the death of Michael Brown,[100] she could not enjoin the use of routine law enforcement practices, such as arrests for failure to follow a lawful police order, that can be and are used to impede public protests.[101]

These trends also support a larger thesis involving the reduction, if not complete loss, of an obligation on the part of government to expend public resources to facilitate speech. We seem to have evolved from the position that government must provide the support necessary to enable all persons, rich and poor alike, to take an active, meaningful role in the process of democratic self-government[102] to a model premised on a highly abstract concept of equality that promotes the formal equality of opportunity rather than the actual reality of equality on the ground level.[103] One could also characterize the modern approach as pursuing procedural – rather than substantive – equality among speakers.

The reduction in the scope of First Amendment protection for government workers who speak out about official misconduct is only one example of a larger trend – a trend that also includes reduced access to public property for speech activity. In myriad ways, in the contemporary United States, freedom of expression faces serious challenges and threats.

Other salient examples of contracting speech rights in the United States include:

- Bans on hate speech on college and university campuses.
- Police and prosecutor actions against demonstrators, including pretextual arrests designed to impede and harass protest efforts, and the filing and subsequent dropping of charges by public prosecutors to impede or prevent protest activities.

- More generalized restrictions on government workers' speech, including efforts by Florida and Wisconsin to prevent employees from discussing climate change in official documents.
- Restrictions on citizen investigations and reportage, such as Iowa's "ag gag" statutory prohibition on video recording by employees in meat processing facilities and similar state laws prohibiting photographing or reporting on industrial farming operations.
- Forced speech, including state regulations that require medical care professionals to give (mis)information about various treatments and their effects, particularly in the context of abortion service providers.
- Failure to reliably protect journalists engaged in newsgathering activities integral to reporting on matters of public concern.
- Reduced speech rights for students attending the public schools, including restrictions on student speech both on campus and off campus.

These developments, although occurring independently of each other, suggest that the contemporary commitment to safeguarding the freedom of speech is far from absolute (despite fairly regular suggestions to the contrary in the academic literature).[104]

Another troubling trend that emerges from the Supreme Court's most recent First Amendment decisions: First Amendment law increasingly links the ownership of property to the ability to exercise free speech rights. Accordingly, if you lack property, your speech rights have been in decline for many years, and at least since the 1970s, when the Supreme Court first started to deploy the public forum doctrine.[105] This doctrine, as developed and applied over time, has permitted government officials to restrict large swathes of government-owned property from being used for protest.[106] Citizens have a right to speak and protest – but only if they can do so without any direct support from the government.[107]

If you have property, then your speech rights have never been more robust – the world is your oyster. On the other hand, however, if you lack property, your speech rights are subject to very broad forms of government discretion to make public property available for the use of impecunious citizens – or to withhold access. All citizens have a theoretical right to speak, but enjoy the ability to speak in practice only if they possess the means of doing so without any government aid or support. This unregulated free-market approach to allocating First Amendment rights has profound, and quite negative, implications for the political marketplace of ideas – and especially for democracy and democratic participation by ordinary citizens.

The Supreme Court tends to frame equal citizenship in highly formal terms that relate to the equal voting power of all citizens at the ballot box.[108] However, if we actually care about a meaningful form of substantive equal citizenship, formal equality at the ballot box is simply not sufficient. Instead, citizens must also possess a meaningful ability to participate in the process of democratic deliberation that culminates in the act of casting a ballot on election day. Moreover, persons who lack dignity are usually not capable of acting as equals in the process of democratic deliberation. Government policies and practices that reduce professionals to being the mere mouthpieces of the government degrade these individuals and undermine their agency as authentic speakers – not only in their professional lives, but more generally, as well.[109] The Constitutional Court of the Republic of South Africa has directly embraced this proposition – dignity is the precondition to the democratic equality of all persons.[110] Government programs that coerce speech accordingly undermine the equality of citizens as speakers.

The equal dignity of citizens requires an equal ability to speak freely and openly – to share thoughts, ideas, and concerns with other citizens. However, equal citizenship must also encompass autonomy, or agency, as a speaker.[111] We could think of this as the ability to be an authentic citizen; a citizen whose decisions to speak, or not to speak, are the product of an entirely voluntary choice.[112] Both compelled speech and coerced silence are inconsistent with the authenticity of a speaker, and hence degrade or destroy the agency – and dignity – of the speaker.[113]

Wealthy citizens invariably have the ability to speak authentically because they use their financial resources to buy or contract around whatever efforts government might make to compromise their agency as speakers. For example, the Koch Brothers are authentic speakers; they enjoy a full measure of citizenship. Whether or not one agrees with their point of view, it possesses a greater persuasive force precisely because it is self-evidently genuine. Moreover, as citizens, the Koch Brothers are not compromised by being forced to say something that they do not mean or believe – or prevented from sharing thoughts, ideas, and concerns because the government threatens to impose a burden or withhold a benefit if they speak their minds freely.

The problem with compelled speech and compelled silence is not simply – or only – that it distorts the marketplace of political ideas. (Although, for the record, it certainly has this effect.) When the government forces speakers to say things that they do not believe – or prevents individuals from saying things that they *do* believe – democracy suffers. Only a democratic discourse conducted by citizens who possess equal dignity as citizens will ensure that, as Meiklejohn puts it, everything that needs to be said *is* said.[114] Democracy, over the longer term, requires something more than verisimilitude – it requires genuinely honest and open democratic engagement.[115]

As Justice Robert H. Jackson so astutely noted in *Barnette*, "[i]f there is any fixed star in our constitutional constellation, it is that no official, high or petty, can prescribe what shall be orthodox in politics, nationalism, religion, or other matters of opinion, or force citizens to confess by word or act their faith therein."[116] This is because a citizenry that lacks meaningful agency and autonomy will not prove capable of sustaining democratic self-government over time.[117] Thus, if we truly embrace the concept of the equality of all citizens, this concept has to encompass a real, meaningful, and sustained commitment to intellectual freedom – the freedom to think – just as it encompasses the freedom to to vote. Simply stated: Intellectual freedom must be an implied premise of a full, participatory democracy.[118]

The First Amendment, if considered from this vantage point, should be no less concerned with indirect efforts to command and control citizens as speakers and thinkers than it is about more obvious and direct forms of coercion – such as bans on particular ideas or ideologies. Direct forms of coercion are perhaps the easiest to ferret out and eradicate, but indirect forms of coercion – the use of government power to force speakers to act inauthentically – are no less harmful to the vibrancy of the marketplace of ideas. A speaker forced to compromise her agency as a speaker is simply not an equal citizen. And the effects of this compromised agency will not begin and end with the particular context in which the coercion occurs.[119] Thus, silencing a high school student who wishes to use social media to post comments critical of his teachers, or forcing a medical professional to tell patients things she believes to be medically false, degrades the speakers, denies their agency, and erodes their ability to participate as equals in the process of democratic deliberation.[120]

Of course, the promise of an election is change. For elections to be free and fair, however, everything has to be on the table (at least in theory). Government speech controls that deny the equal dignity of citizens compromise the freedom, and the fairness, of elections by making citizens comprehensively less able, and less willing, to engage actively in the process of democratic self-government. It might be less obvious than a wealth or religious requirement for exercising the right of suffrage; to be sure, the effects are certainly more subtle. But the effects are nevertheless real and fundamentally inconsistent with the underlying first principles of why we hold regular elections in the first place and use voting to legitimize the policies that elected officials adopt once in office.

We can and should take justifiable pride in the scope of expressive freedoms in the contemporary United States. US citizens enjoy the broadest, and deepest, protection of freedom of expression in the world. At the same time, however, a meaningful commitment to democracy and equal citizenship requires that government not be permitted to act like a private citizen or corporation when deciding whether to permit the use of its property, workplaces, and schools for expressive activities and protest.[121]

Although the Supreme Court has been vigilant in preventing government from using its authority to censor private speech, it has been considerably less vigilant in requiring government to facilitate speech using public property or taking place in the context of a government-operated enterprise, such as a public school, university, or workplace, in which the government may claim a managerial role or function.[122] Nor has the Supreme Court moved with sufficient dispatch to check government efforts to coerce private speech as a condition of obtaining a government benefit or holding a government-issued professional license. Equal citizenship requires the ability of each and every person to speak autonomously and authentically.

But why has this been happening? Why have the federal courts failed to use the First Amendment to check government efforts to compel speech or coerce silence? The general trend, across specific doctrinal terrain, has been away from open-ended balancing tests and toward bright-line categorical rules that diminish the potential scope of judicial discretion in selecting free speech winners and losers. The Warren Court embraced open-ended balancing tests – which, applied across a decentralized system of lower federal and state courts,[123] would certainly lead to conflicting results in cases presenting similar facts. The Warren Court's rules, which usually consisted of general framing devices, facilitated more speech by a wider variety of speakers. This trend abated during the Burger Court years, but in some areas, such as freedom of the press, it largely continued.[124] By way of contrast, the Roberts and Rehnquist Courts have designed and applied relatively rigid doctrinal rules that will produce consistent results – but result in less protection for speech activity overall.

1.4 THE EVOLUTION IN FIRST AMENDMENT THEORY AND DOCTRINE FROM FACILITATING SPEECH TO CONSTRAINING JUDICIAL DISCRETION IN FIRST AMENDMENT CASES

The Warren Court greatly expanded the First Amendment's scope of application. Nevertheless, one should take care not to overstate the Warren Court's overall record of First Amendment expansion. In many areas, the Warren Court's innovations were tentative, halting, and limited – the protection of transborder speech provides a salient example.[125] The extension of First Amendment protection to government employees provides another.[126] Extending First Amendment rights to students and faculty at the nation's public schools, colleges, and universities furnishes a third.

In all three instances, prior to the Warren Court's doctrinal innovations, the First Amendment's application in a particular context was at best uncertain. The Warren Court issued innovative decisions that extended First Amendment protection – but the scope of these decisions was more often than not relatively narrow. Of course, the Warren Court's approach had the important effect of expanding the universe of protected speech – even if did not do so in a maximal fashion.

The Burger Court, by way of contrast, was more institutionally cautious. In many, but not all, instances, it limited the scope of the Warren Court's precedents and consistently declined to extend or expand them. First Amendment protection for newsgathering activities, however, provides an important counterexample to this general trend.[127] To be sure, Justice Potter Stewart was responsible for some of the Burger Court's more expansive Press Clause opinions.[128] However, the Chief Justice himself wrote several major majority opinions securing the right of the press to engage in newsgathering activities related to press access to and reportage about trials and the criminal process.[129] In general terms, however, the Burger Court was considerably more cautious than its predecessor.

The Rehnquist Court and Roberts Court, however, rejected both specific Warren Court precedents and also the Warren Court's more general jurisprudential approach (which usually relied on open-ended balancing tests rather than on bright-line, categorical rules). In some contexts, this more categorical approach better secured expressive freedoms than a more open-ended balancing approach.

For example, the Rehnquist and Roberts Courts have both strictly enforced the First Amendment's proscriptions against content and viewpoint discrimination – consistently, vigorously, and unstintingly. On the other hand, however, protections for government employees, students and faculty at the nation's public schools, colleges, and universities, and for those seeking access to government property for speech activity, have all *decreased* as the Rehnquist and Roberts Courts have rejected balancing tests in favor of bright-line rules that strictly cabin judicial discretion.

In sum, one should certainly resist the urge to overstate the Warren Court's commitment to using the First Amendment as a font of positive duties on the government to facilitate private speech related to democratic self-government. At the same time, one cannot gainsay that the Warren Court pioneered many important doctrinal innovations that greatly expanded the scope of the First Amendment's application and significantly enhanced the vibrancy of expressive freedoms in the United States. Its decisions generally rejected the government's unproven claims of a managerial necessity as a justification for speech-hostile actions and policies. Could the Warren Court have done more? Certainly. But the First Amendment's scope of application was considerably more robust in June 1969, when Chief Justice Earl Warren retired from the bench, than it was in October 1953, when Warren first became Chief Justice of the United States.

The Roberts Court, and its immediate predecessor, the Rehnquist Court, have been far less inclined to use the First Amendment as a source of affirmative duties on the government. Indeed, in several important contexts, the Roberts Court and Rehnquist Court have significantly limited (if not overruled in part) major Warren Court precedents that adopted balancing tests. As this book will explain in greater detail, and through the use of specific examples, this trend does not reflect antipathy toward particular speakers and viewpoints so much as a general rejection of doctrinal approaches that vest federal judges with broad discretion to select free speech winners and losers.

Categorical rules constrain discretion, and generate predictable results, more reliably than open-ended balancing tests. On the other hand, however, the use of balancing tests can and does protect more speech activity – and for more speakers. The Warren Court recognized this trade-off and embraced open-ended balancing tests that attempted to strike a sensible balance between the legitimate managerial necessities of the government and the ability of ordinary citizens to speak out about matters of public concern.

1.5 TRACING THE EVOLVING BOUNDARIES OF THE FIRST AMENDMENT: AN OVERVIEW OF THE ARGUMENTS AND PROOFS THAT FOLLOW

The chapters that follow will explore the ways in which expressive freedoms have become less, rather than more, secure since the days of the Warren and Burger Courts. The first four chapters consider areas in which government – or even *private* – subsidies are necessary to facilitate speech. Chapter 2 takes up a critically important question: access to public space for speech activity. The public forum doctrine, coupled with an increasingly lax application of the rules governing regulations of the use of public forums, have together worked to limit significantly access to public places for speech activity. As noted earlier, it is highly doubtful that a protest of the size and scale of the Selma March could take place today if government officials objected to it. Chapter 2 argues that less rigid rules, of the sort used during the Warren Court and Burger Court years, would enhance the scope and vibrancy of the political marketplace of ideas.

Although the Warren Court greatly expanded access to public property for speech activity, as discussed in Chapter 2, it also created First Amendment easements to *private property* for expressive activities – at least when access to particular private property, such as a large-scale shopping center that effectively functioned as a town's central square, was essential to the process of democratic deliberation. Chapter 3 considers the Warren Court's creation of First Amendment easements to private property. *Amalgamated Food Employees Union Local 590 v. Logan Valley Plaza, Inc.*[130] demonstrates that the Warren Court's decisions securing access to public property for speech activity actually reflect a deep-seated commitment to deploying the First Amendment to facilitate the ability of citizens to engage with one another about matters of public concern effectively, in real time, and in person.

Chapter 4 examines how the government can and does leverage its power as an employer to restrict the exercise of First Amendment rights by its employees. Although the unconstitutional conditions doctrine generally prohibits the government from conditioning benefits on the surrender of constitutional rights,[131] in the context of government employee speech, however, the federal courts have generally accepted the imperatives of the government as a manager over unconstitutional conditions-based objections by government employees.[132] The speech rights of government employees provides a highly salient example of an area where the Warren and Burger Courts were far more solicitous of First Amendment claims than their successors, the Rehnquist and Roberts Courts.

Chapter 5 continues and expands the theme of disappearing First Amendment rights in the context of public education – both at the K-12 level and in the context of higher education. To be sure, federal courts have generally rejected campus speech codes when litigation occurs, but university officials at public colleges and universities still routinely adopt very broadly crafted speech restrictions – and apply them aggressively to banish disfavored content and viewpoints.[133] Federal court interventions have failed to secure expressive freedoms reliably on the ground level; this, in turn, raises some serious questions about the merits and efficacy of the federal courts' efforts to secure First Amendment rights more generally.

Chapter 6 considers the problem of transborder speech and regulations that limit the ability of speakers to enter the United States and the ability of US citizens to exercise First Amendment rights when abroad. This chapter also considers the problems presented by pervasive forms of government surveillance aimed at preventing crime. Simply put, government dragnet surveillance programs based on Big Data present serious threats to the vibrancy of the marketplace of ideas.[134] At the same time, however, the federal courts have been very reticent to apply First Amendment values to these national security programs – particularly in the face of a widely held perception that the risk of terroristic attacks is both real and growing.[135]

Chapter 7 analyzes the failure of the federal courts to deploy the First Amendment to protect newsgathering. To be sure, threats to the ability of journalists to report on matters of public concern initially arise from the actions of non-judicial actors – namely federal and state prosecutors who seek to force journalists to disclose confidential sources incident to criminal proceedings. However, the federal courts also bear some responsibility for the failure to protect newsgathering. The Supreme Court has consistently refused to give independent force and effect to the Press Clause of the First Amendment, which could easily be interpreted to convey some level of constitutional protection to newsgathering activites.[136]

Chapter 8 considers the ways in which government compels speech, misidentifies its identity as a speaker, and attempts to limit speech that could be embarrassing to the government itself (such as recording police officers when in public). In some instances, federal courts disallow government efforts to compel or mislabel speech – but the federal courts have not been consistent in disallowing forced speech (even by medical professionals treating patients) nor have they required the government to abjure efforts to use sock puppets to hide its identity as a speaker.[137] As Professors Helen Norton and Danielle Citron have warned, "[i]f a message's governmental source is obscured ... political accountability mechanisms provide no meaningful safeguard."[138]

In Chapter 9, the analysis turns to nonjudicial government actors, including police and prosecutors, who can use their discretion to squelch the exercise of First Amendment rights. Because the powers at issue are essential to the discharge of their official law enforcement duties, the federal courts are not particularly well positioned to prevent their abuse to suppress dissent. The vibrancy of expressive freedom within a community very much depends on the commitment of local police and prosecutors to respect the right of citizens to express dissenting viewpoints. (Police and public prosecutors do not, as a general rule, target protests that express politically popular viewpoints – precisely because both police and prosecutors are directly, or indirectly, democratically accountable.)[139] Any effort to assess the health and vibrancy of First Amendment freedoms in the contemporary United States must take account of non-judicial actors who can facilitate – or constrain – public protest. Simply put, judges are not the only government officers with responsibility for securing First Amendment rights.

Chapter 10 offers a brief summary and overview of the preceding chapters, in addition to some concluding thoughts. If one takes seriously the concept of equal citizenship, then the government's obligation to support the machinery and mechanics of voting must extend beyond the ballot box itself[140] to encompass processes integral to making the act of voting meaningful. This will require recasting the First Amendment as not merely a source of negative rights, but as a source of affirmative government obligations as well. What's more, if more speech is better, as the Supreme Court argued with such evangelical zeal in *Citizens United*,[141] then First Amendment jurisprudence should be theorized and operationalized to facilitate more – rather than less – speech.

This concluding chapter provides an overview and synthesis of the preceding chapters and identifies three main points: first, an empirical claim that in many important areas of First Amendment law, expressive freedoms have declined rather than expanded under the Roberts and Rehnquist Courts. Second, a doctrinal claim that even if the federal courts are unlikely to embrace a strong, but novel, positive right account of the First Amendment, they could improve the vibrancy of the marketplace of ideas and better protect the process of democratic deliberation by undertaking targeted doctrinal reforms that will empower more citizens to speak with fewer impediments. Third, and finally, a normative claim that a meaningful form of equal citizenship requires easier and broader access to the political marketplace of ideas for ordinary citizens possessed of relatively modest financial means and that rules that vest the lower federal courts with the discretion to balance requests for the government's assistance in speaking against the government's legitimate managerial imperatives would better secure core First Amendment values.

1.6 CONCLUSION

The standard account of the modern First Amendment, which posits that the Supreme Court consistently has broadened the scope of First Amendment protections since the Warren Court era, has much to recommend it. In contexts involving viewpoint-based, content-based, and speaker-based government restrictions on speech, the standard account largely holds true. It also holds true with respect to commercial speech and commercial speakers. In these contexts, the Supreme Court has been both vigilant and consistent in enforcing the First Amendment.

On the other hand, however, the contemporary Supreme Court has been less inclined to require government to facilitate private speech with its resources than were its predecessors. Whether would-be speakers seek to use government property for expressive activity, to speak while holding government employment, to speak while enrolled in a public school, college, or university, or to speak while receiving government subsidies or holding a professional license, the Supreme Court has been significantly more sympathetic to the government's managerial claims than it has been to the First Amendment objections of would-be speakers. The federal courts also have done little to respond to the risks presented by police and prosecutor tactics designed to suppress expressive activity. Because of these developments, the ability to exercise First Amendment rights increasingly depends on a would-be speaker possessing the financial wherewithal to buy or rent the property necessary to support expressive activity.

As I will explain in following chapters, the Warren Court engaged in creative doctrinal experimentation in multiple contexts – and almost always expanded the First Amendment's scope of application to empower both individuals and groups to participate in the process of democratic deliberation. Many of these innovations involved the adoption of open-ended balancing tests that required government to justify refusals to facilitate private speech activity. By way of contrast, the Burger Court was, in general, less open to jurisprudential innovations of this sort. The Rehnquist and Roberts Courts, on the other hand, consistently have rejected open-ended balancing tests that vest discretion with federal judges to select free speech winners and losers – in favor of more formal approaches that use bright-line rules that minimize judicial discretion.

Plausible normative arguments exist to support both general approaches. However, if democracy benefits from more speech, rather than less speech, then the Warren Court's approach should be preferred because it will result in more net speech than the more rules-oriented, categorical approach favored by the Rehnquist and Roberts Courts.

The overall picture of freedom of expression in the contemporary United States is mixed. In many respects, the First Amendment's scope of application has never been broader or more robust. In other respects, however, First Amendment rights have receded in important ways because the federal courts have narrowed expressive freedoms in contexts where would-be speakers need government support in order to engage in First Amendment activity. If the First Amendment exists to facilitate democratic self-government, then the federal courts should consider more carefully the government's affirmative constitutional duty to facilitate expressive activities – and to refrain from conditioning access to government-controlled benefits on either compelled speech or coerced silence. Moreover, we should be willing to accept some play in the joints of our First Amendment rules and doctrines if the effect of such judicial discretion is a more open, and more vibrant, political marketplace of ideas.

The Public Forum Doctrine and Reduced Access to Government Property for Speech Activity

Over time, the federal courts have become predictably and consistently less willing to force government – at all levels – to make public property available for First Amendment activities.[1] For would-be speakers who do not own property suitable for holding a mass protest or rally – or even for a peaceful picket or leafletting exercise – access to government-owned property is simply essential to their ability to speak.

Moreover, this holds true even in the age of the internet. As I will explain in greater detail, public protests, featuring face-to-face, real time interactions, remain essential to the process of democratic deliberation because real time, in person encounters permit the effective targeting of a particular audience and also because the mass media's coverage of public protests opens up a wider dialogue within the body politic as a whole. A Facebook post or Twitter "tweet" lacks these important characteristics. In addition, social media platforms are privately owned and, accordingly, need not permit speech that they would prefer to censor or suppress. The usual suspects offered as the new (virtual) town square are not cabined by constitutional proscriptions against viewpoint or content discrimination. Simply put, some speakers and some speech are not welcome on Facebook, Twitter, YouTube, and Instagram.

Thus, collective public protest retains salience – it still matters. Public, collective protest activity in public places and spaces constitutes an essential modality of our democratic politics. Unfortunately, under the Roberts and Rehnquist Courts, the general public's access to public property for collective speech activity has consistently diminished. What's more, to the extent that government may ban expressive activity from its property, just like the owner of a private speech forum (whether physical or virtual), would-be speakers will face the unenviable task of finding a private property owner who is willing to make space available to them for their protest.[2]

For a variety of reasons, however, private property owners are not apt to respond with alacrity to requests to use their property for various forms of social, economic, or political protest activity.[3] It should not be surprising that private companies operating shopping malls, hotels, theaters, amusement parks and the like generally would prefer to avoid the potential controversy of being associated with highly unpopular causes and speakers.[4]

Of course, if one owns property suitable for speech activity, or has the ability to rent property to engage in speech activity, lack of access to government-owned property does not matter. So too, if the speech activity in question is highly popular and uncontroversial, both government and private property owners are likely to be willing to host it voluntarily. For example, the organizers of a mass participation event to raise funds for breast cancer research will have a much easier time finding public or private space for a rally than the Ku Klux Klan or Nazi Party. Accordingly, the burden of declining access to public property for speech activity falls much more heavily on some speakers than on others – and will correlate strongly with the popularity or unpopularity of both speakers and messages.[5]

But it was not always thus.[6] To be sure, some scholarly commentators have posited that the broadly speech-protective decisions of the Warren Court might well have had as much to do with the identity of the speakers seeking access to public property for speech activity as with the generic requirements of the First Amendment.[7] Although the Supreme Court consistently has embraced viewpoint and content neutrality as central aspects of the nation's commitment to safeguarding the freedom of speech,[8] it would require almost willful blindness to ignore the fact that many of the Warren Court's most generous applications of the First Amendment invariably involved civil rights protests in the Deep South.

Nevertheless, as the anti-war protests of the Vietnam era exploded in the late 1960s and 1970s, the Supreme Court did not resile from its general approach – an approach that started with the presumption that public spaces suitable for expressive activity should be available for such activity.[9] Moreover, arguably the Warren Court's most speech-protective decision, *Brandenburg v. Ohio*,[10] deployed the First Amendment to protect the speech of racists who, at a Ku Klux Klan rally held on a farm outside Cincinnati, Ohio, called for a race war.[11] The Warren Court, in a *per curiam* opinion, tossed out Ohio criminal syndicalism charges, holding that the First Amendment's Free Speech Clause "do[es] not permit a State to forbid or proscribe advocacy of the use of force or of law violation except where such advocacy is directed to inciting or producing imminent lawless action and is likely to incite or produce such action."[12]

It would be difficult to imagine a protest less consonant with the goals and objectives of the civil rights movement. The Klansmen in *Brandenburg* were not civil rights protesters, yet the Justices afforded their racist hate speech – speech calling for unlawful action – very broad protection under the First Amendment.[13]

Going back to the Supreme Court's landmark decision in *Hague v. C.I.O.*,[14] decided in 1939, the federal courts have required government entities to make public property available for speech activity. As late as the 1960s, the federal courts generally held that government property should be presumptively available for speech activity. Under the contemporary public forum doctrine, however, the ability of government to restrict access to public property for speech activity has increased significantly;[15] simply put, the strong presumption of access to government property for speech activity no longer exists.[16] Thus, during the Warren and Burger Court eras, federal courts more often than not began their First Amendment analysis in cases involving denials of access to government property by assuming a general duty on the part of government to make public property available for First Amendment activity – provided that the proposed use was otherwise compatible with the property's more regular uses. Today, by way of contrast, the burden has shifted to would-be speakers to show that government property constitutes a traditional public forum or a designated public forum. This shift in the burden of proof means that Warren Court decisions involving the use of public property for speech activity would not be decided in favor of would-be speakers today.[17]

Under the Warren Court's approach, a public library could be used for a silent protest against segregation; it is doubtful that federal courts would reach the same result under the public forum doctrine.[18] So too, during the Burger Court era, a military base could be used as a place to protest the Vietnam War.[19] The Roberts Court almost certainly would not reach these results under today's public forum doctrine. During the Warren and Burger Court eras, the First Amendment analysis generally required government to justify proscribing or restricting speech on its property – rather than requiring a would-be speaker to establish that the particular real property at issue constituted either a traditional or designated public forum.[20]

For example, it would be easy to characterize a prison, in categorical terms, as a kind of First Amendment dead zone. Yet, the Burger Court did not take this approach. Instead of holding that prison officials may ban or restrict speech activities without being responsible for respecting First Amendment values because a prison is neither a public forum nor a designated public forum, the Supreme Court instead held that "a prison inmate retains those First Amendment rights that are not inconsistent with his status as a prisoner or with the legitimate penological objectives of the corrections system."[21]

Under this approach, "challenges to prison restrictions that are asserted to inhibit First Amendment interests must be analyzed in terms of the legitimate policies and goals of the corrections system."[22] In other words, a functional test applies and prison administrators must respect free speech rights absent a good reason based on either maintaining order within the prison or otherwise advancing a permissible penological objective. To be sure, the majority in *Pell* rejected the specific claim at bar – the right of a prisoner to participate in an in person face-to-face interview with a journalist.[23] Nevertheless, the locus of the expressive conduct – a prison – did not entirely foreclose the First Amendment claim from being considered on the merits and the government had to shoulder a significant burden of justification to prohibit otherwise protected First Amendment activity.[24]

In other words, as Professor Michael Seidman has observed, "the Court has read the First Amendment as requiring a kind of free speech subsidy in the form of constitutionally mandatory private use of government property for speech purposes."[25] Today, however, the baseline has shifted – and shifted rather dramatically. Would-be speakers are largely limited to using property of the government's own choosing for their speech activity – and must do so at a time when the government deems it convenient to make the property available for speech activity.[26] If the government designates particular public property a non-public forum, any speech regulations that can be characterized as "reasonable" are perfectly constitutional.[27] Government may also create spaces that are reserved either for particular speakers or particular messages (or both). Limited purpose public forums, such as a theater dedicated to presenting theatrical performances suitable for children, may exclude categorically proposed speech that falls outside the designated users or purposes.[28] A forum created for a particular group of speakers, for example current students at a state-operated college or university, may be entirely closed to local townsfolk.[29] Thus, the government as property owner often enjoys a freedom of action that mirrors that of a private land owner.

It is easy enough to say, "But if it is the government's property, why shouldn't the government be permitted to decide by whom it may be used and for what purposes it may be used?" The answer to this question is both simple and straightforward: Government as a property owner should not be able to leverage its ownership of property to burden or prevent the expression of dissenting voices.[30] First Amendment doctrine should reflect a fundamental social commitment to facilitating the process of democratic self-government in order to ensure that "everything worth saying shall be said."[31] If, as Professor Alexander Meiklejohn posited, "[t]he principle of the freedom of speech springs from the necessities of the program of self-government,"[32] then courts committed to enforcing First Amendment values should analyze government actions through the prism of whether they advance, or impede, the ongoing process of democratic deliberation. My thesis in this chapter is that the open-ended balancing approach used by the Warren and Burger Courts advanced these values, whereas the categorical, bright-line rules approach currently in vogue, and which came to full flower during the Rehnquist and Roberts Courts, does not.[33]

This chapter proceeds in three main parts. It begins, in Part 2.1, by considering some iconic decisions of the Warren and Burger Courts. Because the Warren Court decisions often involved speech associated with the civil rights movement, it would be reasonable to question whether or not the outcomes reflect a generalized commitment to making public property available for speech activity or rather targeted support of a cause that most of the incumbent Justices subjectively supported. However, later judicial decisions, issued during the Burger Court era, did not involve civil rights protesters or efforts to end Jim Crow and racial segregation and, yet, still generally used the same open-ended balancing approach to resolve disputes about access to government property for speech activity – with the government having to shoulder the burden of justifying denials of access to public property for speech activity. Indeed, even in cases involving locations such as prisons and military bases, the

Burger Court used a functional balancing approach – rather than a categorical approach – to determine whether government has a First Amendment obligation to make its property available for speech activity.[34]

In Part 2.2, the chapter continues by contrasting the more categorical approach of the Rehnquist and Roberts Courts, which relies on an initial characterization of particular government-owned property to prefigure the extent to which government must make it available for private speech activity. Moreover, even if this initial analysis leads to the conclusion that property should generally be available for speech activity, a second level of analysis considers whether government restrictions on expressive activity using the property are content and viewpoint neutral and constitute reasonable time, place, and manner restrictions.[35] To state the matter simply, the tables have turned and the burden has shifted from the government to justify restricting speech on its property to would-be speakers to prove that they have a legal right to use the property for speech activity.

Part 2.3 considers how First Amendment values could be better secured and advanced if the federal courts were to move the analytical baseline back toward the more speech-friendly approach of the Warren and Burger Courts. Simply put, government should always have to shoulder the burden of justifying why public property cannot be made available for private speech activity.[36] I do not suggest that no categorical rules should exist – some government spaces, for example, a judge's chambers, should be subject to categorical exclusions from use for expressive activities. However, the governing doctrinal framework should presume a generalized duty on the government's part to facilitate, rather than impede, activities protected under the First Amendment.[37] More specifically, federal courts should not use a historical approach to determine whether a particular kind of government property should be available for private speech activity but instead should revert back to the functional approach that the Warren and Burger Courts routinely deployed.[38] Part 2.4 offers a brief summary and conclusion.

Today, government enjoys broad discretion to ban protest from public property – even from property like national parks and public memorials that, if not traditional public forums in a strict sense, nevertheless usually possess all the functional characteristics of a traditional public forum.[39] Moreover, even in a traditional public forum, the federal courts routinely have sustained content neutral, reasonable time, place, and manner restrictions that significantly restrict the availability of public property for speech activity.[40]

If we truly believe that a well-functioning democratic polity requires a vibrant ongoing dialogue among citizens about government and its officers,[41] including a strong, if not unyielding, commitment to protecting the freedom of political speech,[42] then the federal courts must require government to make more public spaces available for public protest and to do so more reliably. Simply put, ownership of property should not be a de facto precondition of participating in the process of democratic deliberation.

2.1 FACILITATING DEMOCRATIC DELIBERATION BY PROVIDING WOULD-BE SPEAKERS WITH ACCESS TO PUBLIC PROPERTY FOR EXPRESSIVE ACTIVITIES: A POSITIVE FIRST AMENDMENT RIGHT OF ACCESS TO GOVERNMENT PROPERTY UNDER THE WARREN AND BURGER COURTS

The Supreme Court, in the nineteenth century, took the view that government, as the owner of a property interest, could regulate the use of its property more-or-less exactly as a private property owner could manage its property.[43] Consistent with this logic, if government possesses the power to close property that it owns entirely to speech activity, then it should hold a concomitant power to decide what kinds of expressive activity it will tolerate on its property. As then-Justice, and later Chief Justice, Edward D. White explained in *Davis*, "The right to absolutely exclude all right to use necessarily includes the authority to determine under what circumstances such use may be availed of, as the greater power contains the lesser."[44] This perspective reflects the view that the government, as the owner of real property, has the constitutional power to decide what uses it will permit on what is, after all, the government's property.[45]

Over time, however, the Supreme Court came to reject the analogy of the government to a private property owner and began to require government to make public spaces available for First Amendment activities. Thus, in *Hague v. Committee for Industrial Organization*,[46] the Justices squarely rejected a claim more or less identical to the government's claim in *Davis* and, if not expressly overruling it, signaled that *Davis*'s approach no longer commanded a majority of the Court.

Writing for a plurality, but with a majority supporting this portion of his opinion, Justice Owen Roberts explained that the First Amendment limits the government's authority to regulate its real property in ways that impede expressive activities protected by the First Amendment. He explained that:

> We have no occasion to determine whether, on the facts disclosed, the *Davis* case was rightly decided, but we cannot agree that it rules the instant case. Wherever the title of streets and parks may rest, they have immemorially been held in trust for the use of the public and, time out of mind, have been used for purposes of assembly, communicating thoughts between citizens, and discussing public questions. Such use of the streets and public places has, from ancient times, been a part of the privileges, immunities, rights, and liberties of citizens. The privilege of a citizen of the United States to use the streets and parks for communication of views on national questions may be regulated in the interest of all; it is not absolute, but relative, and must be exercised in subordination to the general comfort and convenience, and in consonance with peace and good order; but it must not, in the guise of regulation, be abridged or denied.[47]

In other words, the government, in its capacity as a property owner, must make real property available for expressive activities – even if it would prefer not to do so. This approach clearly gives the First Amendment a significant affirmative, or positive aspect; the Free Speech and Assembly Clauses do not merely prevent government from acting to prohibit speech and assembly, but also require government to lend its affirmative assistance to such activities.

Thus, unlike other provisions of the Bill of Rights – indeed, even other provisions of the First Amendment itself, such as the Press Clause – the Free Speech and Assembly Clauses empower citizens to make positive demands for assistance, in the form of access to government-owned property, to facilitate speech activity. Although Justice Roberts does not directly link this obligation to provide affirmative support to expressive activities to the project of democratic self-government, his language plainly acknowledges the relationship between speech and assembly, on the one hand, and democratic self-government, on the other. After all "views on national questions" and discussion of "public questions" plainly relate to the process of democratic deliberation that is necessary to sustain democratic self-government. Under the animating theory of *Hague*, the government must afford the general public access to public spaces for the purpose of exercising their First Amendment rights.

Subsequent cases make clear that the right to use public property for expressive activities is not without boundaries. To redeploy a phrase first used in the Supreme Court's seminal regulatory takings precedent, "[g]overnment hardly could go on"[48] if any and every citizen could demand, at will, access to public property for the purpose of engaging in speech activity. *Hague* cannot mean that the imperatives of the government as a manager can never take precedence over the interests of would-be speakers who seek access to public property for speech activity. However, the question is where the burden in such cases should fall. Should it rest with the government, to show that particular property cannot be used for speech activity without impeding the legitimate managerial imperatives of the government?[49] Or rather on a would-be speaker to show that the government has traditionally permitted particular property to be used for First Amendment activities?

Throughout the civil rights movement, the Supreme Court generally vindicated the use of government property for speech activity – even if the property did not constitute what contemporary jurisprudence would call a "traditional public forum."[50] For example, a public library is not self-evidently a place that, since time immemorial, has been available for protest activity. Yet, the Supreme Court rejected a claim that a local government could seek to enforce a trespass claim against civil rights protesters who held a protest in a racially segregated local public library.[51] So too, South Carolina had a duty to make available the grounds surrounding the state capitol building, even though these grounds were not routinely used for mass protests.[52] The Supreme Court also invalidated criminal convictions against civil rights protesters who marched from Louisiana's old state capitol building to the local parish (county) courthouse to protest the arrest of student activists who had sought to desegregate local lunch counters in Baton Rouge, Louisiana.[53]

Cox v. Louisiana is highly instructive because the majority opinion, authored by Justice Arthur Goldberg, considers the ability of government to ensure the smooth functioning of the public courts of law, but concludes that, as applied, a law aimed at protecting courts from the influence of fixed pickets violated the First Amendment. The protesters' facial challenge to the Louisiana law failed because the state possessed a strong interest in preventing political pressures from being brought to bear on the administration of justice.

Justice Goldberg explained that:

> There can be no question that a State has a legitimate interest in protecting its judicial system from the pressures which picketing near a courthouse might create. Since we are committed to a government of laws, and not of men, it is of the utmost importance that the administration of justice be absolutely fair and orderly. This Court has recognized that the unhindered and untrammeled functioning of our courts is part of the very foundation of our constitutional democracy.[54]

Accordingly, the state could, consistent with the First Amendment, enact a general proscription against fixed pickets at courthouses, so long as the measures adopted are "necessary and appropriate to assure that the administration of justice at all stages is free from outside control and influence," and provided that the statute is "narrowly drawn" to achieve these objectives.[55]

Justice Goldberg's analysis, however, involves an open-ended balancing of the government's interest in safeguarding the impartial administration of justice and the interest of would-be protesters in maintaining a fixed picket near a courthouse. In considering an "as-applied" challenge to the application of the statute on the facts at bar, Justice Goldberg rejected the argument that any and every protest proximate to a courthouse will be prejudicial to the fair and orderly administration of justice. He also carefully considered precisely how and when the protest took place: "It is undisputed that the demonstration took place on the west sidewalk, the far side of the street, exactly 101 feet from the courthouse steps and, judging from the pictures in the record, approximately 125 feet from the courthouse itself."[56] Thus, the demonstration was merely "near" and not "in" the courthouse.[57] Government officials also had specifically authorized a protest directly across the street from the courthouse grounds.[58] These factors, considered together and in context, required reversal of the convictions on an as-applied basis.[59]

Justice Hugo L. Black, by way of contrast, agreed that the breach of peace convictions were invalid, but dissented from the majority's conclusion that the as-applied challenge to Louisiana's ban on protests near courthouses possessed merit. He noted that the statute in question, section 14:401, made it unlawful for any person to stage a demonstration proximate to a courthouse with the intent of influencing judges and other court officials regarding a pending judicial matter.[60] Justice Black emphasized that this statute prohibited "anyone, under any conditions, [from] picket[ing] or parad[ing] near a courthouse, residence or other building used by a judge, juror, witness or court officer, 'with the intent of influencing' any of them."[61] He emphasized that the law sought to protect the judicial process itself "from the intimidation and dangers that inhere in huge gatherings at courthouse doors and jail doors to protest arrests and to influence court officials in performing their duties."[62]

Thus, Justice Black argued for a more categorical approach to making government property available for protest activity – and, in Black's view, a courthouse, and environs surrounding it, could be constitutionally declared "off limits" for speech activity. Justice Black would have upheld this regulation even though the protest at issue took place near a local courthouse but outside regular business hours – and therefore did not pose much of a threat of undue influence.[63] And, even though other forms of expressive conduct, such as buying television ads, radio spots, or outdoor billboards attacking a particular judge or urging a particular result in a pending case, could present no less direct a threat to the integrity of the judicial process but would have fallen outside the letter of the Louisiana statute. The Louisiana law was plainly both overinclusive (because it prohibited protests when judicial personnel were absent) and underinclusive (because it did not regulate other speech activity that might unduly influence judges or court personnel regarding pending judicial business).

The majority's approach, unlike Justice Black's approach, uses an open-ended balancing test to resolve the relative equities on the facts presented. Because local government officials had approved a location for the protest almost identical to the location actually used, the government's claim that it had a pressing need to banish the protest from the area near the courthouse rang entirely hollow.[64] After all, if one side of the street was appropriate for a mass meeting and protest featuring 2,000 participants, then so too was the other. Justice Goldberg's approach obviously suffers from the risk of subjective application of the balancing test – if a judge were hostile to the message protesters sought to propagate, she could put her thumb on the scale when assessing the risk the protest presented.

This is, to be sure, a non-trivial shortcoming of an open-ended balancing test to determine the suitability of public property for First Amendment activities.[65] A less categorical approach to determining whether public property should be available for would-be protesters presents a risk of enabling stealth content- or viewpoint-based discrimination by federal judges. This problem of judicial discretion is no greater, however, than in other contexts, such as how to categorize speech for purposes of applying the First Amendment.

For example, the categorization of speech as "political," "commercial," or "obscene" often prefigures its protected or unprotected status under the First Amendment. Applying categorical labels to particular examples of speech activity involves no less judicial discretion than would the task of assessing whether proposed speech activity is consistent, or inconsistent, with the more regular uses of the particular public property at issue.[66] A balancing approach that weighs the interests of would-be speakers against the interests of the government in reserving property for its more regular uses means that any and all government property could, at least in theory, be available to support expressive activities.[67]

To be sure, the government's interest in reserving some public property exclusively for the government's use will be impossible to overcome – for example, a judge's chambers or a district attorney's office. Even so, however, a balancing exercise could work. As I have argued previously, "[a]lthough this exercise creates the possibility of unfairness in individual cases," the potential benefits of this approach, "more than offset this opportunity cost."[68] In sum, the distinct virtue of Justice Goldberg's approach is that it forces the government to make a convincing case that it has a good reason for denying access to the property that the protesters seek to use; the burden rests on the state to justify a denial of access, rather than on would-be protesters to establish an affirmative and general right to use the public property for speech activity.[69]

Other properties will obviously be off limits during some periods of time – for example, the government's interest in using a high school building for educational activities would outweigh the interest of would-be protesters in using the building for a political rally during periods when classes are actually in session. But what about periods, such as the summer break, when the high school is not being used for classes – and sits more or less empty and unused? Or periods of the day during the school year when the high school isn't being used for instructional activities – such as in the evenings or during the weekend? Should a local school board be able to say "our high school auditorium is a non-public forum" and deny access to anyone seeking to use it for First Amendment activities? Even if it constitutes the only facility of its kind in a remote, rural community? And even if the school board permits its use for non-educational functions, such as serving as an official polling place for primary and general elections?

Under the Warren Court's functional approach mandating access to public property for speech activity, would-be speakers would have a First Amendment right of access to use such a facility for collective speech activity. Under the public forum doctrine that replaced it, however, the would-be speakers would find themselves out of luck – they would face the unenviable task of finding an alternative forum removed from the community that they seek to engage. Democratic discourse would be the poorer for the forced relocation of their collective expressive activity.

2.2 THE PUBLIC FORUM AND TIME, PLACE, AND MANNER DOCTRINES VEST GOVERNMENT WITH BROAD DISCRETION TO LIMIT OR PROHIBIT SPEECH ACTIVITY ON PUBLIC PROPERTY

In the 1970s, even as a majority of the Burger Court continued to use an open-ended balancing test to determine whether government property should be available for First Amendment activities, then-Associate Justice William H. Rehnquist argued, initially in dissent, but eventually in majority opinions, that a more categorical approach was needed to vindicate the government's legitimate managerial interests.[70] By the 1980s, and his promotion to the Chief Justice's office, these views came to command regularly a majority of the Justices.[71] Instead of squarely placing a burden of justification on the government when it denied access to public property for speech activity, the Supreme Court instead required would-be speakers to establish that the property that they wished to use constituted either a public forum or a designated public forum.[72]

By the 1990s, spaces that clearly could be used for expressive activities, such as airport concourses, were judicially declared to be off limits – non-public forums – and closed to speech activity.[73] In addition to an increasingly restrictive definition of public forums, the Supreme Court also adopted a test for analyzing restrictions on the use of public forums that allowed very broad restrictions on speech activity within traditional and designated public forums.[74] The combined screening effects of a very limited universe of highly regulated public forums and designated public forums significantly restricted the public property potentially available to host First Amendment activities.

In fairness, a turn toward a more categorical approach to determining whether the First Amendment requires government to make public property available for speech activity first appeared during the Burger Court's later years[75] and continued to gain jurisprudential traction into the 1980s.[76] By the early 1980s, the public forum doctrine was sufficiently well-established that Justice Byron White, in *Perry Educators Association*,[77] was able to read existing precedents as creating three, and possibly four, typologies of government property.[78] Nevertheless, the public forum doctrine did not reach full flower until the Rehnquist Court.

Although some legal scholars point to decisions such as *Southeastern Promotions Ltd. v. Conrad*[79] and *Lehman v. City of Shaker Heights*,[80] as constituting the Supreme Court's initial embrace of the public forum doctrine, these decisions, in point of fact, did not establish the rigid public forum doctrine enforced by the federal courts today.[81] Later decisions, such as *Greer v. Spock*,[82] reverted to the more open-ended balancing test used in cases like *Brown v. Louisiana*.[83] Until the 1980s, the suggestion that government could categorically exclude speech from its property unless the property constituted a traditional public forum or a designated public forum appeared exclusively in *dissenting* opinions.

Justice Hugo L. Black pioneered the argument that government could exclude speech from public property if the property did not constitute a traditional public forum. He made this argument, in very strong terms, in *Cox* – but in dissent. Black argued in *Cox* that a categorical proscription against protest activity proximate to courthouses did not offend the First Amendment: "Justice cannot be rightly administered, nor are the lives and safety of prisoners secure, where throngs of people clamor against the processes of justice right outside the courthouse or jailhouse doors."[84]

Similarly, Justice Rehnquist advocated a categorical approach to evaluating denials of access to government property in cases presenting government efforts to prohibit speech activity on public property. He began to sketch his vision of the public forum doctrine in his dissenting opinion in *Flower*,[85] a case that invalidated a ban against leafletting on a portion of a military base in San Antonio, Texas, that was generally open to the public.[86]

Then-Justice, and later Chief Justice, Rehnquist argued that:

> [C]ivilian authorities may draw reasonable distinctions, based on the purpose for which public buildings and grounds are used, in according the right to exercise First Amendment freedoms in such buildings and on such grounds. Simply because some activities and individuals are allowed on government property does not require the abandonment of otherwise allowable restrictions on its use.[87]

Harking back to the reasoning of *Davis*, government as a property owner may select the kinds and scope of expressive activity that it will permit on its property.[88]

Two years later, Justice Rehnquist renewed his effort to reduce the imposition of involuntary First Amendment easements on government-owned property. His dissenting opinion in *Southeastern Promotions* makes a largely identical argument to his *Flower* dissent, namely that "if it is the desire of the citizens of Chattanooga, who presumably have paid for and own the facilities, that the attractions to be shown there should not be of the kind which would offend any substantial number of potential theatergoers," then the city should be able to refuse to rent the venue for the purpose of mounting a racy, adult-oriented traveling production of the musical *Hair*.[89] In other words, if government creates a forum for expressive activity, then government may decide both who may use the forum and the expressive purposes for which it may be used.

It was not until 1983, and Justice Byron White's opinion for a 5–4 majority in *Perry Education Association*, that the public forum doctrine enjoyed a full explication and the clear support of a majority. Justice White's *Perry* opinion organizes earlier cases into categories and posits the existence of three, or perhaps four, distinct classes of public property: (1) traditional public forums, (2) designated public forums, and (3) non-public forums.[90] Justice White hints at a fourth category – a limited purpose public forum – and subsequent cases have made clear that this constitutes a distinct subcategory comprised of forums, whether physical or intangible, that the government creates and designates for the exclusive use of particular speakers, content, or both.[91] In *Perry*, however, Justice White lumps limited purpose public forums in with designated public forums;[92] subsequent cases, however, have distinguished them and given the government broad authority to subsidize particular speakers or speech.[93]

The specific forum at issue in *Perry*, an internal mail system created and maintained by a public school district,[94] was not generally open to the public and although not reserved exclusively for internal school district communications, was used primarily for official communications between the school district's administration and the district's employees.[95] Even under the more open-ended balancing test of *Brown v. Louisiana*,[96] it is doubtful that the First Amendment would have supported a generalized right of access by the public to the school district's internal mail system. The dissenting Justices in *Perry* did not posit a universal right of public access, but instead argued that an association of teachers seeking to challenge the incumbent collective bargaining representative should be granted the same access to the school district's internal mail system that the incumbent teachers' union already enjoyed.[97]

Thus, Justice William J. Brennan, Jr.'s dissent did not posit that the internal mail system should be generically available to any and all comers, but instead characterized the exclusion of a rival employees' union as a form of viewpoint discrimination in a forum that had been made available for speech of the sort that the rival union wished to propagate.[98] Justice Brennan's dissent also used a functional analysis that assessed the compatibility of the proposed speech with the particular government-created forum and found that the proposed speech came within the subject matter of the forum and would not unduly burden its use for its more regular purposes.[99]

Perry represented a near-complete victory for the Black/Rehnquist categorical approach to assessing whether particular public property should, in general, be available to the public for the exercise of First Amendment rights. Subsequent cases, decided under the Rehnquist Court, quickly consolidated this doctrinal innovation and ossified it. The Supreme Court narrowly defined the concept of a public forum and used a very strict, tradition- and history-based approach to exclude new kinds of forums – such as charitable fundraising drives among government workers,[100] a sidewalk and parking lot at a post office,[101] and airports.[102] Taking quite literally *Hague*'s language about places that had, since time immemorial, been available for use for expressive activities,[103] the conservative majority granted government very broad discretion to prohibit speech activities on publicly-owned property.[104]

In short, the Supreme Court increasingly held that the government possesses broad authority to determine for itself whether or not its property would be generally available for speech activity. It did so, as Chief Justice Rehnquist explained, because "[w]here the government is acting as a proprietor, managing its internal operations, rather than acting as lawmaker with the power to regulate or license, its action will not be subjected to the heightened review to which its actions as a lawmaker may be subject."[105] In other words, managerial imperatives justify limiting or even proscribing the use of government property for speech activity.[106] Under this approach, the government does not operate under any general duty to create free speech easements on its property unless it chooses to do so voluntarily (by creating a designated public forum)[107] or the property at issue constitutes a traditional public forum using a history-based test (which categorically excludes new types of government property from ever becoming a traditional public forum).[108]

Concurrently, with respect to a public forum, the Rehnquist Court adopted a policy of sustaining against First Amendment challenges content and viewpoint-neutral reasonable time, place, and manner (TPM) regulations.[109] Thus, even if a would-be speaker was able to prevail on the preliminary question of whether particular government property should be available for speech activity, clearing this initial hurdle was merely a necessary, and not sufficient, condition for obtaining access to government property for protest activity. Government retained broad discretion to regulate the terms and conditions under which a traditional public forum (or designated public forum) could be used for speech activity.[110]

Justice Anthony Kennedy, writing for the majority in *Ward*, explained that "even in a public forum the government may impose reasonable restrictions on the time, place, or manner of protected speech, provided the restrictions 'are justified without reference to the content of the regulated speech, that they are narrowly tailored to serve a significant governmental interest, and that they leave open ample alternative channels for communication of the information.'"[111] The *Ward* test sounds considerably more demanding in theory than it proves to be in practice.

First, the federal courts do not look very deeply into the government's actual motives for enacting TPM regulations; thus, the adoption of limits on protest activity near abortion clinics after Operation Rescue comes to town does not make TPM regulations content-based.[112] Second, the federal courts are not terribly demanding regarding either the government's purpose or the fit between the means used to achieve the government's substantial goal and actual attainment of the goal itself.[113] Third, and finally, the "ample alternative channels for communication" requirement may be satisfied if one could upload a blog post to the internet or hand out leaflets somewhere else.[114] Thus, "[p]rovided that government is willing to restrict all speakers alike, the time, place, and manner doctrine, as explicated in *Ward* and subsequent cases, imposes relatively few absolute limits on such regulations."[115] The end result is a regime that makes it quite easy – indeed too easy – for government to relegate dissenting voices to the margins of contemporary political discourse.[116]

2.3 TOWARD A RENEWED COMMITMENT TO MAKING PUBLIC SPACE RELIABLY AVAILABLE FOR SPEECH ACTIVITY

The Supreme Court's motive in adopting a categorical approach to define and structure the public's right to use government-owned property for speech activity is easy to understand: The public forum doctrine provides bright-line rules that are easy to state and relatively easy to apply. Accordingly, lower federal and state courts will usually reach the same results regarding the nature of a particular forum – whether traditional, designated, limited purpose, or non-public. The TPM doctrine also provides an easy to state, and relatively easy to apply, framework for determining whether government limits on public, designated, and limited purpose public forums trench too deeply on the exercise of expressive freedoms. Both the categorization exercise and the TPM doctrine vest government with substantial managerial discretion to reserve public property for the specific purposes that led government to acquire the property in the first place. Given the challenges government faces in running vast bureaucracies, the random use of government property by private citizens for speech activity could easily lead to chaos and disruption.[117]

In sum, the public forum and TPM doctrines both protect the government's ability to operate its myriad programs on a day-to-day basis. The federal courts also have disallowed government efforts to parcel out access to public property for speech activity based on the viewpoint or content of the proposed speech activity.[118] Government officials also must apply TPM regulations with an even hand and such regulations must advance an important government interest and leave open ample alternative channels of communication.[119] It would be wildly wide of the mark to suggest that the Rehnquist and Roberts Courts have returned the First Amendment baseline to *Davis v. Commonwealth*.[120] Under the existing doctrinal rules, government clearly may not restrict speech on public property with as free a hand as a private citizen or corporation may restrict speech on privately-owned property.

Nevertheless, the Rehnquist and Roberts Courts have reset the balance in the government's favor and have done so to a significant degree. Access to government property for expressive activities is considerably more circumscribed today than it was in the 1960s or 1970s. Persons seeking access to government property for speech activity now have to meet an initial burden of convincing a court that the specific property they seek to use constitutes a traditional or designated public forum – or that it is a limited purpose public forum and the proposed speakers or speech activities fall within the class of speakers or speech authorized to use the forum.[121] Even if a plaintiff meets this initial burden, the government will still prevail if the denial of access results from viewpoint- and content-neutral reasonable time, place, and manner restrictions. TPM restrictions, aggressively applied, can reduce the space available quite considerably – to a small circle or two within a major public park, such as the St. Louis Arch, in downtown St. Louis, Missouri.[122]

Thus, the problem is two-fold: Federal courts too easily permit government to adopt self-serving classifications of public property that banish protesters and protest activity. And, even with respect to public property that cannot be entirely closed to speech activity, government may adopt burdensome, and highly effective, regulations that severely limit the availability of the property for First Amendment activities. In the days of the Warren and Burger Courts, neither of these propositions held true. Government property was presumptively available for speech activity, and government had to establish why its proposed use for speech activity constituted too great a burden for the government to shoulder.[123] Moreover, federal courts viewed with skepticism efforts to aggressively limit use of traditional public forums to prevent speech activity. *Cox v. Louisiana*[124] provides a good example – if government officials authorized a protest on one side of a public street proximate to a county courthouse, then they could not object to the use of sidewalks on the opposite side of the street.[125]

To permit a mass protest near a courthouse, on an as-applied basis in the context of a state law that sought to protect judges and court officials from improper influences, constitutes a remarkable commitment to securing and advancing First Amendment values. So too, ordering military officials to permit protest activity on a military base represents a strikingly broad, and deep, commitment to facilitating the process of democratic deliberation that is essential to the maintenance of democratic self-government.[126] Although the Burger Court ultimately declined to extend its initial ruling mandating access to military bases for speech activity,[127] it did so in an opinion that did not declare, in categorical terms, that such facilities may be closed entirely to the public and declared free speech-free zones.[128] Indeed, the Burger Court even declined to adopt a categorical approach to declaring a prison off limits to any and all forms of expressive activity.[129]

The Warren and Burger Courts essentially treated the First Amendment as a font of affirmative, positive obligations on the government to lend its assistance to would-be speakers through selective access to government owned property. Government could not pick and choose which speakers and messages it would lend its support in the form of access to public property – instead it had a duty to facilitate all comers. To be sure, this approach had the effect of significantly increasing the social cost of speech activity on public property.[130] When half of a major US highway is used for a major civil rights protest, rather than for vehicular traffic, drivers seeking to use the highway to get from Point A to Point B incur a non-trivial cost.[131] So too, the use of public spaces for speech activity makes the space less available for other activities – if a group of New Age women descend upon the interior of the Jefferson Memorial to dance, the quietude of the interior space is disrupted for those who wish simply to contemplate the neo-classical interior and massive sculpture of Jefferson.[132]

The same, however, could be said of having Dr. Martin Luther King, Jr. speak at the rally associated with the iconic August 27–28, 1963, March on Washington for Jobs and Freedom, from the interior space of the Lincoln Memorial to the mass audience attending the rally on the National Mall and also those persons watching King's speech live on broadcast television.[133] Should government be free to banish protests from both spaces? On the theory that they exist solely for reverential contemplation of Jefferson and Lincoln – rather than expressive activities associated with political, ideological, or religious beliefs?

The Warren and Burger Courts were willing to force government entities to justify refusals of access to public property with persuasive reasons that demonstrated the incompatibility of speech activity with the more regular uses of public property. Moreover, during this era, the Supreme Court also entertained "as-applied" challenges to speech restrictions that were otherwise valid on their face – such as proscriptions against efforts to bring extra-judicial pressure to bear on state court judges and court personnel.[134] In sum, the federal courts routinely pushed government to facilitate speech by making public property available for First Amendment activities.

The contemporary First Amendment demands much less of government with respect to making public property available for private speech. To be sure, government is free to make property available for speech activity, but it has a much narrower obligation to do so – both with respect to the kind of property it must open to expressive activities and with respect to the terms and conditions it imposes on private citizens who wish to use public property for protest.[135] Of course, if a would-be speaker owns the property necessary to speak, and therefore does not require access to government property as a locus for their speech, the Rehnquist and Roberts Courts have aggressively protected the right of private property owners to use their property for expressive purposes.[136]

The public forum doctrine was firmly established by the final years of the Burger Court[137] and ossified quickly under the Rehnquist Court.[138] Over forty years later, calling for the Supreme Court to abandon completely the public forum doctrine is likely to be unsuccessful. Moreover, it is hardly surprising that the federal courts would prefer categorical rules that permit the easy and consistent disposition of litigation that seeks access to government property for speech activity to an open-ended balancing test that requires courts to reconsider the availability of public property for speech activity on a case-by-case and ad hoc basis. Accordingly, calling for a return to the open-ended balancing approach of *Brown v. Louisiana* will not prove to be a successful strategy for making more public property reliably available for First Amendment activities.[139]

A more realistic alternative to a wholesale repudiation of the public forum doctrine would entail finding a mechanism for improving on the existing public forum framework. Happily, there are some potential improvements that could shift the burden from would-be protesters to prove a constitutional right of access to public property to the government to establish a clear legal right to deny access to particular property. Indeed, some areas of First Amendment law already work in this fashion – for example, government generally must prove that the risk of violence associated with speech activity is so clear and present a danger that it justifies silencing an unpopular speaker.[140] We do not allow the government to establish categorical, content-based rules that render highly unpopular speech proscribable because of a risk of unrest or violence;[141] by parity of reasoning we should be more willing to require government to show that providing access to particular kinds of government property would be unduly disruptive to government operations.[142]

It also bears noting that the rule against silencing an unpopular speaker because of the potential for public disorder or even violence also imposes significant financial burdens on the government, on an entirely involuntary basis, and effectively forces government to expend scarce resources in order to facilitate speech activity in public spaces.[143] Police budgets are not infinite and the costs of policing public events featuring radically unpopular speakers could be quite significant. Yet, under the First Amendment, government may not invoke the cost of providing protection to unpopular speakers as a basis for requiring them to cease speaking.[144] In this sense, the First Amendment creates a positive duty on government to facilitate private speech.

Moreover, this aspect of the First Amendment constitutes well-settled law.[145] Access to public property through a free speech easement is simply another form of involuntary speech subsidy – the question that federal judges must ask and answer is the degree to which government entities should possess discretion to deny this subsidy to would-be speakers.

The main virtue of the pre-public forum doctrine era cases was a functional approach to determining whether public property could be used for First Amendment activities.[146] Rather than relying on the government's (potentially self-serving) labels for particular property or even on the government's declared purpose for owning property, the federal courts would instead consider the kinds of activities the government permitted voluntarily and the consistency, or inconsistency, of speech, assembly, petition, and association-related activities in those spaces.[147] Even if the Supreme Court retains the public forum framework, the question of whether a space constitutes a traditional or designated public forum could be determined using a functional approach, rather than a formalistic historical approach that would exclude many important public spaces from use for protest simply because the spaces did not exist in 1791 (for example, an airport or train station).[148]

First Amendment values would be better advanced if more government property were available for use by private citizens seeking to engage their fellow citizens over matters of public concern. A more contextualized, functional approach to identifying public forums would open up more public property for speech activity without forcing federal judges to reinvent the wheel every time a would-be protester seeks access to government property that cannot be regularly used for speech activity without undermining or precluding the government from maintaining its regular operations. I do not propose returning generically to an open-ended balancing exercise – instead, consistent with the reform proposals persuasively advocated by Professor Steven Gey,[149] I propose revising the definitional exercise to consider more carefully actual uses of government property rather than the label affixed to a particular place.

To the extent that government permits property to be used by the public for activities that are not much different from leafletting or fixed pickets, it should not be permitted to close the property to would-be speakers who seek to engage in expressive activity protected under the First Amendment. For example, if a government building features a courtyard generally open to the public, and through which members of the general public may pass, linger, or sit, it seems easy enough to permit someone to linger or sit while wearing a t-shirt with a political message or holding a sign. The disruption caused by someone occupying space within the courtyard while drinking a cup of coffee or reading a newspaper is essentially, if not exactly, the same. Thus, if a government-owned space is otherwise open to the public for one set of activities (i.e., drinking coffee or reading a newspaper), the public space also should be open for speech activity that is no more disruptive.

Declaring public property otherwise open to any and all members of the public to be a non-public forum, and thereby closing it to all forms of expressive activity, should not be an available option.[150] The federal courts should deny the government the power to pick and choose arbitrarily what public property will be deemed suitable for speech activity regardless of the actual characteristics, and regular day-to-day uses of the property, that the government actually permits.[151] If the Boston Common is open to those who wish to stroll, exercise, or read, then it should be equally open to those who wish to brandish political signs.[152]

On the other hand, and by way of contrast, a city water treatment plan is closed to the public for all purposes and, accordingly, closing it to speech activity would be constitutionally unobjectionable. If the government closes property to the public for all purposes, it is far less likely to be engaged in an effort to burden or squelch protected speech activity based on the viewpoint or content of the would-be speaker's message. When government targets expressive activity for disfavored treatment, however, the federal courts should react with a healthy degree of skepticism about the government's motives – and their consistency with the First Amendment.[153] If assessing motive seems a difficult task for courts,[154] simply applying a functional approach would avoid difficult exercises in ascertaining the government's actual purpose in closing public property to speech activity. To state the point more directly, the regular and everyday uses of government property, rather than a government-affixed label or the historical origins of the particular kind of property, should control the First Amendment analysis – and outcome.

Second, federal courts should be more receptive to as-applied challenges to denials of access to particular property and also to TPM regulations. Even if government may constitutionally close certain categories of public property to speech activity, federal courts should nevertheless consider whether, on a particular set of facts, the First Amendment requires mandated access for a particular group of speakers because of a nexus between the speakers and their message and the space at issue.[155]

Indeed, one could read *Brown v. Louisiana* narrowly as permitting the particular protest in the local library because a silent protest did not disrupt other uses of the library and because the protest targeted the operation of the library on a racially segregated basis.[156] In other words, a different kind of protest, seeking to call attention to a different cause wholly unrelated to the public library, might not enjoy First Amendment protection.[157] The government's ability to deny access to its property depended on the burden the protest imposed on the government's ability to achieve its objectives and also on the relationship of the speech to the venue. Even if most forms of protest, and most protesters, could not demand to use a public library's circulation desk area for a political protest, the civil rights protesters, engaged in a silent protest of the racially segregated operation of that specific public library, stood on different First Amendment ground.

So too, Judge Frank M. Johnson, Jr.'s order in *Williams v. Wallace*[158] plainly takes into account the nature of the protest and the nexus between the forum and the speakers. Even if most protesters could not routinely commandeer a federal highway for a multi-day, 52-mile march, the SCLC, in the context of a massive state-wide effort to suppress the voting rights of African-American citizens, possessed a qualitatively different kind of claim that justified greater access to public property than the First Amendment would ordinarily require.[159] Simply put, a different First Amendment analysis – and outcome – should and did obtain.[160]

Judge Johnson considered carefully the petitioning cast of the proposed speech activity and the legal responsibility of state and local officials for serious constitutional deprivations of basic civil and political rights before issuing an injunctive order permitting the march to proceed as proposed.[161] Both the identity of the speakers and the relationship of the speech to the particular forum factored very heavily into Judge Johnson's First Amendment analysis.[162]

To be sure, considering a speaker's identity and message does involve content-, and perhaps even viewpoint-, based factors. It might seem counterintuitive to use a speaker and content-based screen to determine access to public property for speech activity. However, upon more careful reflection, these objections are not fatal flaws and do not doom this approach to granting targeted access to public property to some speakers but not to others. In the context of *Williams v. Wallace*, "Judge Johnson was correct to recognize enhanced rights of access to public property for petitioning speech seeking a redress of grievances from the government entity being both petitioned and protested against through the same hybrid petitioning activity."[163]

First, and most important, the public forum doctrine already permits the government itself to limit access to public property for speech based on the would-be speaker and her message.[164] The entire concept of a limited-purpose public forum entails government creating a forum accessible by some speakers, and for some messages, but not others.[165] If government may limit access to forums based on the would-be speakers' identities and the content of their proposed speech, and federal courts are competent to assess the fair enforcement of such restrictions, it seems implausible to say that "as-applied" access to public property cannot work. If courts are capable of superintending forum access limits in the context of limited purpose public forums, then they are also capable of considering "as-applied" requests for access to non-public forums or under terms and conditions that violate otherwise constitutionally valid TPM regulations. The federal courts have not signaled any problems with the creation of limited purpose public forums; if speaker-based and message-based limits are capable of judicial implementation in this context, then identical considerations in the context of non-public forums should be equally feasible.

Second, First Amendment doctrine is rife with content-based distinctions. Pornography and commercial speech receive less robust First Amendment protection than political speech.[166] In order to apply content-based rules of this sort, federal judges must ascertain the content of the speech and place it within one category or another.[167] If federal courts can determine whether speech is commercial or political in nature,[168] then they are also quite capable of determining whether a nexus exists between a particular government-owned property and a proposed protest that would take place on that property.[169]

Suppose, for example, that MPs on a military base shoot and kill an unarmed intruder found on base property. Suppose further that allegations of racial bias arise within the community as a possible motive for the shooting. Is it unthinkable that the base commander might have to make base property available for protest activity on these facts, even if the base is not otherwise available as a locus for expressive activities? Moreover, would it vest federal judges with too much discretion to engage in the kind of analysis that would allow a local civil rights organization to stage a march that crosses base property without requiring the base to be open to any and all would-be protesters? The answers to these questions are quite obvious – if we truly view freedom of speech as integral to the process of democratic deliberation and government accountability, then a federal court faced with a lawsuit seeking an injunction that orders the base commander to facilitate a protest march on base property should not be resolved with a two-line order that tersely states that a military base is not a public forum.

Finally, one might reasonably ask, in the era of the internet, if "silence on the street corner," to use Professor Owen Fiss's wonderful and apt metaphor, really matters.[170] The short answer: It does. A speaker who wishes to use one modality of speech should not be relegated to another; just as the government may not order speakers to engage – or refrain from engaging – in speech featuring a particular viewpoint or content,[171] the First Amendment should also prohibit government from regulating the particular modality of speech that a would-be speaker may use to communicate her message.[172]

Moreover, several legal scholars have explained why in-person speech still matters in the age of the internet.[173] Without doubt, Professor Tim Zick has mounted the most sustained defense of the continuing relevance of mass protests in public spaces. Zick argues that "despite the proliferation of electronic speech fora, providing material public space for speech remains critical to the health of our expressive culture."[174]

This is so because of the so-called "siloing" of audiences on the web.[175] Simply put, it is quite easy to ignore messages that one dislikes on the web; as Zick puts it, listeners and viewers can "filter speech they do not wish to hear," making public spaces "one of the last locales where the undecided listener might be reached."[176] Thus, collective speech activity in public spaces provides would-be speakers with a meaningful opportunity to reach otherwise unwilling listeners – and democratic deliberation requires these kinds of unfiltered interactions between citizens about matters of public concern.

Equally important, public protest provides a forum for collective public action. As Zick puts it, "[t]hings such as movement, volume, mass, and emotion do not exist in online settings."[77] Collective public protest tends to garner mass media attention – which permits a message to be disseminated to a wider, even more diverse, audience.[78] The fact of mass action is in and of itself news – which means that a mass public protest's impact on the citizenry will often extend far beyond the physical precincts in which it takes place.

Collective public protest also has an important symbolic value. As Zick explains, "[t]he symbolic significance of public speech does not lie in its success at persuasion or in its erudition," but rather "in the fact that public speech events are part of a distinct expressive culture."[79] Thus, "there is something to being *there* that makes other alternatives, however *ample*, still *inadequate*, in light of the specific expressive interests at stake."[80] Collective speech activity has a cultural meaning and salience that is simply of a different kind and scope than a blog post or tweet.

In sum, even in the age of the internet, "[p]rotection of access to the streets, sidewalks, and parks remains critical to expressive and associational freedoms."[81] For all of the wonders of reaching a mass audience with the click of a mouse, "cyberspace, for all of its innovations, simply cannot replace or imitate live protests and other forms of expression."[82] This is so because *"being there*, and *with others*, are critical aspects of public dissent."[83] In sum, public protest still matters and helps to sustain the process of democratic engagement that makes it possible for elections to serve as an effective and reliable means of securing government accountability.

Despite the central importance of public protest, for these reasons and others, we face a legal landscape in which the federal courts require less and less of the government with respect to facilitating the exercise of First Amendment expressive rights. As Zick notes, "[o]ur expressive topography is increasingly inhospitable to the very speech that merits the greatest protection, namely speech on matters of public concern, including political speech."[84] The Warren Court's approach, which effectively forced government to make public space available to would-be dissenters, far better advanced these core constitutional values than the considerably more restrictive approach of the Roberts and Rehnquist Courts (whose decisions increasingly treat the government more or less like a private property owner entitled to pick and choose who may use its property for speech activity). However, reforming the public forum doctrine would constitute a partial, incomplete, and less than fully effective response to the growing problem of a lack of public space for the expression of dissenting speech.

Other doctrinal reforms in the Supreme Court's jurisprudence of access to public space for speech activity are also needed. In particular, reform of the application of the TPM doctrine could help to create and sustain needed breathing room for the exercise of expressive freedoms in public places. The federal courts should apply the content-neutrality requirement in a more demanding fashion and not simply accept the facial neutrality of a speech regulation as sufficient to establish that the regulation passes the first prong of the *Ward* test. In cases like *Hill v. Colorado*,[185] the federal courts have been highly credulous of government claims that speech regulations were content-neutral, even when the facts and circumstances surrounding the adoption of the TPM regulations strongly suggest a government purpose to silence a particular speaker or message.[186] In other contexts, such as ferreting out discrimination based on race[187] or religious belief,[188] the federal courts make a serious effort to ascertain the real or actual purpose of a facially neutral enactment. This same rigorous methodological approach to assessing the government's purpose should be deployed when assessing content-neutrality under the *Ward* test.[189]

Second, the federal courts should press the government to provide an actual reason for the creation and enforcement of TPM regulations – rather than simply accept vague assertions that particular TPM regulations advance an important government interest. In this regard, federal judges should not blithely credit highly generalized invocations of security concerns as a basis for banishing dissent from public spaces.[190] At present, however, courts are inclined to be extremely deferential to government invocations of security and public safety rationales for speech bans on public property and to require very little in the way of "narrow tailoring" to achieve the government's important or substantial purpose.[191]

Third, and finally, the ample alternative channels for the communication prong of the *Ward* test should take into account whether the available alternative means of communication are likely to permit the would-be speaker to reach the same audience no less reliably, effectively, and efficiently than through a public protest. For example, a protest of a NATO meeting proximate to the meeting venue for a group of NATO officials is far more likely to be heard and seen by NATO officials than a random blog post or tweet.[192] At present, however, this aspect of the *Ward* test does not take into account the efficacy of the alternative means of communication in reaching the speaker's preferred audience.[193] As the saying goes, if a tree falls in the forest, and no one sees it, the event might as well not have happened. What is true of trees falling in forests holds doubly true of public protest aimed at engaging the general citizenry to support or oppose particular government policies and actions.[194]

These reforms in the application of the *Ward* test for TPM regulations would substantially improve the application of existing doctrine and would materially shift the burden to the government to justify refusals to make public property that admittedly comprises a public forum available for speech activity. However, a more general and systematic reorientation of First Amendment theory and doctrine is plainly needed in this important area of law.[195]

Simply put, the Roberts and Rehnquist Courts have been far too solicitous of the government's unsubstantiated claims of managerial necessity[196] – and have credited weak, to the point of spurious, claims that speech bans or TPM regulations are necessary in order for government to function efficiently. Resetting the balance in favor of greater access to public property for speech activity would not seriously endanger or prevent government from achieving its legitimate purposes. Nor would it mean that public parks, streets, and sidewalks would devolve into total chaos as protesters commandeered such spaces at will. Instead, adopting such theoretical and doctrinal innovations would help to advance and facilitate broad-based participation in the process of democratic self-government by ordinary people who lack the ability to use their own private property to access the political marketplace of ideas.

2.4 CONCLUSION

The right of ordinary citizens to use public property for First Amendment activities has declined over time from the 1980s to the present. During the Warren and Burger Court eras, the federal courts were far more willing to require government to facilitate private speech by ordering access to government-owned property for First Amendment activities. The First Amendment gave rise to a positive right of access – a free speech easement – to public property. Beginning in the early 1980s, and accelerating into the 1990s, the Supreme Court retreated from this commitment in favor of granting the government considerably broader discretion to manage public property as it thinks best.

To be sure, the Supreme Court is unlikely to jettison the public forum doctrine at this point in time. Simply put, too much water has flowed under the doctrinal bridge. But we should not make the merely better the enemy of the best – it would be possible to modify the operation of the public forum doctrine to shift the balance away from unfettered government discretion to grant or withhold access to public property toward a model in which the government has to shoulder a higher burden of justification for refusing to make public property available for protest activity. Defining "public forums" in functional terms, rather than historical terms, would constitute a good first start.[197] In addition, the federal courts should signal a greater willingness to consider "as-applied" challenges both to denials of access to non-public forums and also to otherwise-valid TPM regulations of public forums.

If freedom of speech is a necessary condition for the maintenance of democratic self-government, then government, at all levels, should be required to incur costs and inconveniences in order to facilitate democratic deliberation among the citizenry. Just as government cannot limit voting rights to those with a minimum amount of property, government should not have the discretion to leave access to the political marketplace of ideas entirely to private market ordering. I do not suggest that government should be able to limit, or level-down, the ability of those with property to use their property for speech activity. But, citizens who wish to protest government policies, like Cindy Sheehan,[198] should not be forced to purchase real property in order to do so effectively.

It is possible to imagine a limited, affirmative right to use government property for speech and to adopt a doctrinal framework that fully honors this baseline commitment to safeguarding democratic deliberation. The Warren and Burger Courts' open-ended balancing approach might have vested too much discretion with trial courts and undoubtedly produced inconsistent results in cases presenting similar facts. Even so, it would be possible to move toward an Aristotelean "virtuous mean"[199] between the extremes of treating the government as if it were just another private property owner and permitting citizens to appropriate government property for First Amendment activities whenever and wherever they choose.

In sum, under the Rehnquist and Roberts Courts, the balance has shifted too far in favor of government discretion to deny would-be speakers access to public property for protest. A course correction that places a higher burden of justification on the government for resisting free speech easements on public property would better serve our core commitment to freedom of expression as an essential condition for democratic self-government to flourish.

3

The First Amendment As a Source of Positive Rights

The Warren Court and First Amendment Easements to Private Property

The Warren Court's creative use of the First Amendment as a font of affirmative governmental duties to facilitate speech related to the process of democratic self-government began, but did not end, with its decisions requiring the government to make public property available for speech activities.[1] In addition, the Warren Court extended First Amendment rights of access to *private property* if particular privately owned property served as an essential locus of democratic deliberation[2] – the contemporary equivalent of the municipal park at issue in *Hague*.[3] Accordingly, even if a skeptical reader remains unconvinced by my claim that the Warren Court conceived of the First Amendment as a source of both positive and negative rights, its approach to mandating access to *private* property for First Amendment activity provides further, and quite striking, support for this argument.[4]

Simply put, the Warren Court not only required government to justify refusals of access to its property for expressive activity (a pattern that continued into the Burger Court era), but also mandated access to private property when doing so was necessary to facilitate the process of democratic deliberation. On such facts, the First Amendment created a kind of free speech easement applicable to privately owned property for expressive activities.[5]

Moreover, the jurisprudential pattern that exists with respect to access to public property for speech activity holds true in this First Amendment context too. The Warren Court pioneered a novel application of the First Amendment, quite literally to provide breathing space for speech activity, but the Burger, Rehnquist, and Roberts Courts either limited or rejected the Warren Court's doctrinal innovations. Indeed, it fits the pattern more or less exactly: The Burger Court arrested the further development of the Warren Court's jurisprudential innovation in *Amalgamated Food Employees Union Local 590 v. Logan Valley Plaza, Inc.*[6] – but did sustain the application of a state constitution's free speech guarantee to create a free speech easement to private property that was otherwise open to the general public.[7] The Rehnquist and Roberts Courts, by way of contrast, have done nothing either to use the First Amendment to create free speech easements on private property or to encourage local and state governments to redefine the law of trespass to permit such use of private property on an involuntary basis.[8]

On the contrary, and as explained in the last chapter, the Rehnquist and Roberts Courts have moved the doctrinal needle involving *government* property back toward recognizing a broader form of managerial discretion for the government to control its property as it wishes.[9] As Professor Gregory Magarian observes (with respect to the Roberts Court), "[t]he public forum decisions ... advance managed speech by resisting calls to distribute expressive access."[10] In other words, the modern Supreme Court has been far more inclined to treat government more like a private entity than to treat private entities like the government with respect to access to property for expressive activities.

Logan Valley arguably has new relevance in the age of the internet. Today, neither the town square nor the suburban shopping mall reliably serves as the central locus for the process of democratic deliberation. As we know from the Russian meddling scandal in the 2016 US presidential election, much of our democratic discourse now takes place on the internet, on social media platforms such as Facebook, Twitter, YouTube, and Instagram, and through the modality of search engine providers such as Google and Bing. These social media platforms are, of course, privately owned and the owners are not state actors – they do not perform an exclusive government function, they do not exist in a symbiotic relationship with the government, the government has not encouraged, much less compelled, the terms of service polices that these companies have adopted, and these companies and the government are not otherwise "entwined" with each other.[11] Accordingly, it is not plausible to argue that private companies such as Facebook, Twitter, and Google should be deemed state actors under the existing tests for state action.

On the other hand, however, the reasoning and constitutional logic of *Logan Valley* would support the recognition and enforcement of First Amendment easements that facilitate access to these social media platforms and search engines on a nondiscriminatory basis.[12] Professor Michael Seidman has argued persuasively that state action decisions, such as *Marsh v. Alabama*[13] and *Terry v. Adams*,[14] reflect the view that "[a] private entity might be engaged in a public function when it is able to exert extraordinary coercive power comparable to state power over individuals."[15] Alternatively, he posits that these decisions might be understood to mean that "an entity might be engaged in a 'public function' when it voluntarily opens itself to the public in a fashion that made its claims to immunity from government regulation implausible."[16] Both observations reflect and incorporate plausible readings of decisions like *Marsh, Terry*, and *Logan Valley*, that impose limited constitutional obligations on nongovernmental actors.

My own view, however, is that the Warren Court was engaged in a broader, multifaceted effort to secure access to the space required for democratic deliberation to flourish. At the same time it was holding that the First Amendment created a free speech easement to use private property for speech activity,[17] it was also holding that government employees have a right to speak out about matters of public concern without being subject to arbitrary discharge for insubordination,[18] that teachers and students in the nation's public schools do not "shed their constitutional rights to freedom of speech or expression at the schoolhouse gate,"[19] that government has a duty to make public property available for speech activity if such activity is otherwise consistent with its ordinary and everyday uses,[20] and that the US Postal Service has a constitutional duty to deliver communist political propaganda produced by foreign governments to US residents who wish to peruse such materials.[21] If one reads these decisions conjunctively, rather than disjunctively, it becomes reasonably clear that the Warren Court had undertaken a broad jurisprudential effort to deploy the First Amendment as a tool to require government to facilitate, rather than impede, the process of democratic deliberation. Not only on government property, such as libraries and public schools, or by government employees, whether on or off the clock, but also on *privately owned property*.

In all of these cases, potential choke points existed that, if left unaddressed, would have suppressed, in some cases completely, potentially important contributions to the process of democratic deliberation.[22] Professor Alexander Meiklejohn made this point expressly and forcefully: "As the self-governing community seeks, by the method of voting, to gain wisdom in action, it can find it only in the minds of its individual citizens. If they fail, it fails. That is why freedom of discussion for those minds may not be abridged."[23] Democracy requires an ongoing deliberative process, a dialogue among and between voters, that informs electoral choices and renders the citizenry capable of rendering wise decisions on a predictable basis.[24] Accordingly, as Meiklejohn posits, "[t]o be afraid of ideas, any idea, is to be unfit for self-government."[25]

"And what," one might ask, "does this have to do with forced access to Facebook or suburban shopping malls?" A great deal, as I will explain in some detail. If a private company comes to possess control over an essential modality of democratic deliberation, the federal courts arguably have a duty to bring the First Amendment to bear to ensure that control over that modality is not used to disrupt or prevent the deliberative process. In any given case, the question should be whether a particular resource is integral to the process of democratic deliberation. And, in 1968, in the era of post-*Brown* white flight to suburbia, the privately owned shopping mall had come to completely eclipse the publicly owned town square. Accordingly, the Warren Court held that suburban shopping mall owners had to make such properties available for First Amendment activity – whether or not they wished to do so.

Today, shopping centers are far less relevant to the process of democratic deliberation; just as they displaced the town square, they have in turn been displaced themselves as a central locus for community gatherings and collective activity.[26] Instead, some academics argue that "[g]rass roots campaigns are now carried out on social media," which constitute "the new poor man's mass medium."[27] Professors Loren Selznick and Carolyn LaMacchia suggest that "[s]ocial media offer activists free platforms for mass expression,"[28] rendering access to both public and private real property for collective expressive activities increasingly irrelevant.

The problem, of course, is that unlike the town square or a public park, Facebook, Twitter, YouTube, and Instagram are all privately owned and maintain terms of service rules that sharply limit permissible content.[29] In other words, not all ideas and viewpoints may be expressed on these social media platforms. Yet, if they have come to take the place of the town square, as a kind of *agora* for public discourse, an unlimited private power to silence some voices while accommodating other voices should be seen as deeply problematic.[30]

To be sure, this is not an entirely new problem. Iconic First Amendment scholars, such as Professors Owen Fiss[31] and Jerome Barron,[32] have expressed concern that the increasingly consolidated ownership of mass media outlets could present a threat to the process of democratic deliberation. Fiss, for example, has suggested that the state must "safeguard the conditions for true and free collective self-determination."[33] In other words, state regulatory interventions in speech markets are not invariably distortionary efforts to tilt the political marketplace of ideas – in some instances, they are entirely necessary efforts to redress a pre-existing tilt (or perhaps "stranglehold") that arises from concentrated private power over the mass media.

Professor Cass Sunstein has made similar arguments, expressing concern that the shift of the locus of democratic deliberation from the town square to the internet might lead to undue self-filtering of ideas and information through a process of informational self-isolation.[34] He has also expressed serious concern about the dangers that would arise from a poorly informed citizenry incapable of making prudent electoral choices.[35]

Professor Sunstein admits that some of his ideas for ensuring an electorate capable of self-government might seem unduly paternalistic, observing that "[i]t may seem controversial or strange to say that there is a problem for the Madisonian system if people do not seek serious coverage of serious issues" and musing "perhaps we should take people however we find them."[36] On the other hand, however, the "system of deliberative democracy" does not exist "simply to implement existing desires," and instead aims "to create the preconditions for a well-functioning demo-cratic process."[37]

In sum, a lack of the knowledge and information necessary to hold government accountable through the electoral process constitutes a serious problem, and a problem that we cannot simply ignore. This is so, Sunstein argues, because "a polity that does not show the requisite attention cannot create or benefit from genuine citizenship."[38] In the absence of a robust and engaged electorate, armed with facts, "public deliberation will be far less successful, and the Madisonian conception will be badly compromised."[39] This is an oblique way of saying that voters will render bad decisions – decisions that will lead to terrible consequences for the well-being of the nation.

So, how does this all relate back to the Warren Court's creation of First Amendment easements to use privately owned shopping malls for expressive activity? By a rather direct route, as I will explain in the balance of this chapter. Justice Thurgood Marshall's approach in *Logan Valley* takes seriously the idea that democratic engagement is an essential condition for democracy to function – no less central or important than the act of voting itself – and if a private entity controls a forum essential to the process of democratic deliberation, then the First Amendment requires an easement to ensure that it is open to all would-be speakers on equal terms.[40]

In other words, as Justice Marshall posited, it is imperative "that traditional public channels of communication remain free, regardless of the incidence of ownership."[41] This concern might be more persuasive if articulated in a slightly different fashion: If a private company comes to possess monopoly power over an *essential* (rather than merely "traditional") forum for democratic discourse, the First Amendment should impose limits on how and when the forum's owner may exercise the power to deny access to the forum for speech activity. Just as undertaking to perform a task integral to the electoral process renders an entity that self-identifies itself as "private" a state actor for purposes of the Equal Protection Clause of the Fourteenth Amendment, as well as the Fifteenth Amendment,[42] if a private company comes to control an essential means of conducting democratic discourse, the process that shapes and filters voting decisions, then that private company should not be heard to complain when federal courts impose First Amendment easements to its social media platform or search engine.[43]

Logan Valley, and its underlying theory that control of the places in which democratic deliberation occurs should be accompanied with duties to facilitate, rather than impede, the process of democratic deliberation, would support the recognition and enforcement of First Amendment easements against private companies such as Facebook, Twitter, YouTube, Instagram, Google, and Bing that control social media platforms or search engines that are now integral virtual spaces for the conduct of our elections and electioneering.[44]

This chapter proceeds in four main parts. Part 3.1 considers the emergence of a First Amendment easement to use private property for First Amendment activity under the Warren Court and its subsequent – and speedy – demise under the Burger Court. It also notes the subsequent failure of both the Rehnquist and Roberts Courts to resurrect the *Logan Valley* doctrine – or to show any interest (at all) in taking this step. Part 3.2 considers the normative and doctrinal implications of "free speech easements" to private property when private property, whether real or intangible, serves as a principal locus for the process of democratic deliberation. Social media platforms have come to serve as the modern-day equivalent of the town square; simply put, Facebook, Twitter, YouTube, and Instagram serve as primary modalities of contemporary political discourse and, as such, play a crucial role in the process of democratic self-government – a role not dissimilar from that played by the political parties themselves.

Part 3.3 argues that continued reliance on self-regulation by social media companies and search engine providers is both unwise and ineffective. Just as the political parties were required to observe certain constitutional rules, because of their stranglehold on the electoral process,[45] so too, these private entities should be required to honor certain constitutional guarantees because they *voluntarily* play an integral role in the electoral process. Finally, Part 3.4 briefly summarizes and concludes.

Starting in the 1950s and 1960s, large-scale, suburban shopping malls started to displace the traditional town square or city park as a locus of community engagement.[46] Over time, the relative importance of these retail developments has waxed and waned. The real point is not requiring access to "shopping malls" as such, for speech activity, but avoiding the privatization of the political marketplace of ideas. The Warren Court, and Justice Thurgood Marshall, recognized the risk that the privatization of public space presented to the process of democratic deliberation – indeed, to democracy itself – and moved to deploy the First Amendment to arrest this trend. Today, the same threat to democratic discourse exists, but from the many important intangible forums for political speech that have proliferated on the internet. The same solution can and should be used to address this problem – the judicial creation of free speech easements to privately owned property to safeguard the process of democratic deliberation.

3.1 THE WARREN COURT'S RECOGNITION OF FREE SPEECH EASEMENTS TO PRIVATE PROPERTY UNDER THE FIRST AMENDMENT

The Warren Court pioneered the recognition of free speech easements to private property for speech activity. However, the *Logan Valley* decision was not the first Supreme Court precedent to impose a free speech easement on private property. Rather, in *Marsh v. Alabama*,[47] the Supreme Court initially held that the First Amendment creates mandatory access to private property for speech activity. This part considers the line of cases that begins with *Marsh* and ends with *PruneYard*,[48] a Burger Court precedent that holds that local, state, or the federal government may create free speech easements to private property generally open to the public without violating either the First Amendment or the Takings Clause. As in other areas where the Warren Court required government to facilitate private speech activity, the *Logan Valley* line of precedents follows the same general pattern: The Warren Court deployed the First Amendment creatively to empower ordinary citizens to speak; the Burger Court arrested the growth in the Warren Court's jurisprudential innovations; and the Rehnquist and Roberts Courts either ratified or expanded on the Burger Court's speech-restricting precedents.

As this part will show, the Warren Court not only required the government to make its own property available for speech activity – it also required private property owners to permit the use of their property for expressive activities. The animating theory of *Logan Valley*, if applied today, would support the imposition of free speech easements on entities like Facebook, Twitter, YouTube, Instagram, and Google. Moreover, the Burger Court's *PruneYard* precedent would support the creation of such easements through positive law – whether at the local, state, or federal level of government.

The story begins, however, in Chickasaw, Alabama, a company town located a few miles north of Mobile, Alabama. In the 1940s, the town was owned, lock, stock, and barrel, by the Gulf Shipbuilding Corporation.[49] Both business and residential properties within Chickasaw were rented or leased to the occupants – title to the property remained with the company. Ms. Grace Marsh, a member of the Jehovah's Witnesses, wished to proselytize on the streets of the commercial district of Chickasaw. An off-duty deputy sheriff working for the company as a town security officer warned Marsh that she was trespassing and should cease and desist her distribution of tracts; she refused to comply with this order. The deputy sheriff then arrested her for trespassing.[50] At trial and in the state appellate courts, Marsh argued that her arrest violated the First Amendment – to no avail.[51]

The Supreme Court reversed Marsh's conviction on First Amendment grounds. Writing for a 5–3 majority,[52] Justice Hugo L. Black observed that "[h]ad the title to Chickasaw belonged not to a private but to a municipal corporation[,] and had appellant been arrested for violating a municipal ordinance rather than a ruling by those appointed by the corporation to manage a company town it would have been clear that appellant's conviction must be reversed."[53] The fact remained that the property in question was *not* public property – but rather private property. The Supreme Court nevertheless held that "[w]e do not agree that the corporation's property interests settle the question" of access to the company town's business district for the purposes of engaging in First Amendment activities.[54]

The Supreme Court concluded that privately owned property or not, the First Amendment applied in the central business district of Chickasaw, Alabama. This result obtained because "[o]wnership does not always mean absolute dominion."[55] Instead, because the Gulf Shipbuilding Corporation had created a civic space critical to democratic discourse, it incurred the same obligation as the state government to permit the property's use for leafletting with tracts. Justice Black explained that "[w]hether a corporation or municipality owns or possesses the town the public in either case has an identical interest in the functioning of the community in such manner that the channels of communication remain free."[56]

Democratic discourse requires that ordinary people be able meet, talk, and debate the issues of the day. Moreover, this holds true regardless of whether or not they live in a company town:

> Many people in the United States live in company-owned towns. These people, just like residents of municipalities, are free citizens of their State and country. Just as all other citizens they must make decisions which affect the welfare of the community

and the nation. To act as good citizens, they must be informed. In order to enable them to be properly informed their information must be uncensored. There is no more reason for depriving these people of the liberties guaranteed by the First and Fourteenth Amendments than there is for curtailing these freedoms with respect to any other citizens.[57]

In other words, the interest of the company in controlling its property had to give way to the imperatives of the democratic discourse necessary to maintaining the project of democratic self-government.[58]

As Professor Robert Post has observed, "[a]t its core, First Amendment doctrine is designed to restrict government regulation of public discourse."[59] Democratic discourse is essential "because such participation makes democratic legitimation possible" and "[d]emocratic legitimation is necessary for self-government."[60] Justice Black's opinion in *Marsh* incorporates and reflects these considerations. On the facts at bar, the "balance" of constitutional interests favored Ms. Marsh over the Gulf Shipbuilding Company – the company's property interest was "not sufficient to justify the State's permitting a corporation to govern a community of citizens so as to restrict their fundamental liberties and the enforcement of such restraint by the application of a state statute."[61]

To be sure, Justice Stanley F. Reed authored a dissenting opinion in *Marsh*, expressing his view (joined by Chief Justice Harlan F. Stone and Justice Harold H. Burton), that "[t]he rights of the owner, which the Constitution protects as well as the right of free speech, are not outweighed by the interests of the trespasser, even though he trespasses in behalf of religious speech."[62] In his view, merely opening private property to the public for some purposes did not justify the creation of a free speech easement for other, unrelated purposes.[63]

In *Logan Valley*, Justice Marshall, writing for a 6–3 majority, found that the First Amendment created a right of access to a privately owned shopping center for First Amendment activity. The case involved a picket of a non-union grocery store near Altoona, Pennsylvania. Logan Valley Plaza, Inc., built and operated a large retail development, the Logan Valley Mall.[64] Members of a local labor union sought to picket the Weis Market, a grocery store located in the Logan Valley Mall and staffed with non-union employees. The pickets took place "entirely in the parcel pickup area and that portion of the parking lot immediately adjacent thereto."[65] Although the union's picketing activity caused "some congestion" in the pickup area of the parking lot, the grocery store's operations were not materially affected and would-be customers were free to enter and leave the store without any impediments. Finally, "[t]he picketing was peaceful at all times and unaccompanied by either threats or violence."[66]

The mall and grocery store owners sought and obtained in the local state trial court (the Court of Common Pleas) an injunction against the union's picketing activity on the mall's property – first on a temporary basis after an *ex parte* hearing and, later, on a permanent basis after a contested hearing before the court. The union appealed the adverse decision to the Pennsylvania Supreme Court – but lost on appeal.[67]

A badly divided state supreme court, by a 4–3 vote, affirmed the trial court's decision, observing "that the Commonwealth has not only the power but the duty to protect and preserve the property of its citizens from invasion by way of trespass is clear beyond question."[68] To be sure, both Logan Valley Plaza, Inc. and Weis Markets, Inc. had invited the public to visit their property. However, "that invitation to the public was not without restriction and limitation; it was not an invitation to the general public to utilize the area for whatever purpose it deemed advisable but only to those members of the public who would be potential customers and possibly would contribute to the financial success of the venture."[69] Thus, "[w]hile both Weis and Logan granted to a segment of the public certain rights in connection with the use of their property, such cession of rights did not constitute a grant of all their rights to all the public."[70]

Writing in dissent, Justice Herbert B. Cohen drew a strong and direct analogy between the Logan Valley Mall and the company town at issue in *Marsh*. He argued that "[i]n the sense that both are freely accessible to the public, a company town and a shopping center are analogous arrangements, and for purposes of considering possible constitutional abridgments should be similarly analyzed."[71] The conflict between the mall and grocery store owners' property rights, on the one hand, and the labor union picketers, on the other, required a careful balancing of the equities and "[o]nly by a thorough consideration of these conflicting values" could the constitutionally correct balance be struck.[72] Accordingly, he "deem[ed] unincisive the majority's failure to recognize any conflict between the rights of private ownership and the constitutionally guaranteed freedoms of speech and of the press."[73] For Justice Cohen, the fact that the mall and grocery store were privately owned constituted a relevant factor to be considered – but not the only relevant factor to be considered.

The Supreme Court granted review and reversed the Pennsylvania Supreme Court. Justice Marshall started his analysis "from the premise that peaceful picketing carried on in a location open generally to the public is, absent other factors involving the purpose or manner of the picketing, protected by the First Amendment."[74] Marshall also found Justice Cohen's analogy to *Marsh* both apt and persuasive: "The similarities between the business block in *Marsh* and the shopping center in the present case are striking."[75] Accordingly, the *Logan Valley* majority saw "no reason why access to a business district in a company town for the purpose of exercising First Amendment rights should be constitutionally required, while access for the same purpose to property functioning as a business district should be limited simply because the property surrounding the 'business district' is not under the same ownership."[76]

In light of these principles, the labor union had a right to use a free speech easement on the private property.[77] As Justice Marshall explained, "Logan Valley

Mall is the functional equivalent of a 'business block' and for First Amendment purposes must be treated in substantially the same manner."[78]

Marshall's use of "substantially" was more than accidental – Marshall did not have in mind treating private property as identical to public property. The mall and store owners, for example, possessed a legitimate and cognizable constitutional interest in safeguarding the "normal business operation of the property" and were legally entitled to take steps to protect the regular, commercial uses of the shopping center.[79] Because the Logan Valley Mall was privately owned property, rather than public property, the owners enjoyed the right "to limit the use of that property by members of the public in a manner that would not be permissible were the property owned by a municipality."[80] Regulation of use for expressive purposes would be perfectly consistent with the limited First Amendment rights at issue. Even so, however, "the State may not delegate the power, through the use of its trespass laws, wholly to exclude those members of the public wishing to exercise their First Amendment rights on the premises in a manner and for a purpose generally consonant with the use to the which the property is actually put."[81]

Accordingly, property owners are perfectly free "to make reasonable regulations governing the exercise of First Amendment rights on their property."[82] Such regulations are particularly appropriate when expressive activity on mall property "will unduly interfere with the normal use of the public property by other members of the public with an equal right of access to it."[83] Time, place, and manner regulations that delimit how, when, and where expressive activity takes place in a privately owned mall complex do not violate the First Amendment. The holding is also expressly limited to privately owned shopping malls that function as the equivalent of a town square – it has no application to either a single, stand-alone business or a private home.[84]

Justice Black dissented vigorously in *Logan Valley*. He emphatically rejected the analogy to *Marsh* (which he authored) because "the basis on which the *Marsh* decision rested was that the property involved encompassed an area that for all practical purposes had been turned into a town."[85] Chickasaw, Alabama, "had all the attributes of a town and was exactly like any other town in Alabama."[86] He could "find very little resemblance between the shopping center involved in this case and Chickasaw, Alabama."[87] Only if a private entity "has taken on *all* the attributes of a town" should private property be subject to court-created First Amendment easements.[88]

Black characterized the majority's creation of a First Amendment easement to use Logan Valley Plaza's property for speech activity as a kind of "confiscation" in which property rights were unreasonably transferred from the property's rightful owner "to people who want to picket on it."[89] To be sure, the labor union possessed a constitutional right to protest the Weis Market's employment practices – but, in Justice Black's view, "they do not have a constitutional right to compel Weis to furnish them a place to do so on its property."[90]

Logan Valley is a bold, creative decision that reads *Marsh* quite broadly to justify imposing First Amendment obligations on the owners of large, multi-store shopping centers and malls. The majority opinion uses the First Amendment to create not only a positive, or affirmative, right to access property for speech activity, but applies this right to a private actor.

The best argument in favor of taking this approach is that access to the shopping mall was essential for the would-be speakers in *Logan Valley* to reach their intended audience. This is a fact that Justice Marshall forthrightly acknowledges: "The picketing carried on by petitioners was directed specifically at patrons of the Weis Market located within the shopping center and the message sought to be conveyed to the public concerned the manner in which that particular market was being operated."[91] As in *Marsh* itself, a claim of necessity undergirds the constitutional analysis. If another forum, on public property, had been available and equally efficacious in permitting the labor union to communicate with its intended audience, then perhaps access to the Logan Valley Mall would not have been necessary to vindicate core First Amendment interests. The recognition of a First Amendment easement should be an exception, not a rule – but when the invocation of private property rights would unduly limit or prevent the process of democratic deliberation, property rights must give way to the imperatives of the First Amendment.

Logan Valley was, and remains, a controversial decision.[92] Whether or not one agrees or disagrees with the constitutional and factual predicates for Justice Marshall's majority opinion, it cannot be seriously disputed that the Supreme Court used the First Amendment as a tool to create an affirmative right of access to certain kinds of private property so that members of the public could more easily and efficaciously exercise their First Amendment expressive freedoms.

Lloyd Corporation, Ltd. v. Tanner[93] constitutes the Burger Court's first engagement with *Logan Valley*. It did not go well for *Logan Valley*. Although the *Lloyd Corp.* majority did not squarely overrule *Logan Valley*, the decision limited the precedent to circumstances in which a nexus exists between a protest and particular private property. To be sure, *Logan Valley* does contain a footnote that cautioned that its ruling might not be generally applicable to any and all private property for any and all speech activity.[94] However, the logic of both *Logan Valley* and *Marsh* would plainly make private property that functions as a town square available for private speech activity – regardless of whether or not the property's owners wished to permit the speech activity.

No nexus between the property and the proposed private speech activity existed in *Lloyd Corp.*, and Justice Lewis F. Powell, Jr., seized upon this distinction to reject the would-be protesters' claim of a First Amendment-based free speech easement to a large, multi-building commercial, shopping, and professional services complex in Portland, Oregon.[95] On November 14, 1968, the would-be protestors attempted to distribute anti-Vietnam War leaflets in the Lloyd Center, a large, indoor mall that, then and now, features stores, restaurants, and even an indoor ice-skating rink.[96] The anti-war protesters were quiet and non-disruptive – but were nevertheless told to leave the premises on pain of arrest (which they did). Both the US District Court for the District of Oregon and the US Court of Appeals for the Ninth Circuit, applying *Logan Valley*, found that the would-be protestors had a right to leaflet in the Lloyd Center.[97] The district court issued an injunction requiring the mall to permit them to engage in peaceful, non-disruptive leafletting activity,[98] which the Ninth Circuit affirmed.[99]

In many ways, recognizing a free speech easement to the Lloyd Center complex would have been easier than with respect to the shopping center at issue in *Logan Valley*. The Lloyd Center comprised "66 linear blocks"[100] in the heart of a major US city. For Justice Powell, however, the private ownership of the land was the controlling factor: "In addressing this issue, it must be remembered that the First and Fourteenth Amendments safeguard the rights of free speech and assembly by limitations on *state* action, not on action by the owner of private property used nondiscriminatorily for private purposes only."[101] In light of this fact, the analogy to running a city "reaches too far" because "[t]he Constitution by no means requires such an attenuated doctrine of dedication of private property to public use."[102] *Marsh*, Justice Powell explained, involved a private company assuming *all* the obligations of a municipal government – not merely some of them: "In effect, the owner of the company town was performing the full spectrum of municipal powers and stood in the shoes of the State."[103]

This is certainly a plausible reading of *Marsh*. But it is not the *only* plausible reading of *Marsh*. Justice Black's *Marsh* opinion emphasizes the practical necessity of making the shopping district of Chickasaw, Alabama, available for speech activity if the citizens of the town were to be able to engage with each other as part of the process of democratic discourse.[104] The opinion does not suggest, for example, that the Gulf Shipbuilding Company has a duty to provide procedural due process before firing "city" employees[105] or that the company cannot prefer to hire men over women.[106] In other words, the *Marsh* opinion, as written, seems rather speech specific – the *Lloyd Corp.* gloss on the decision, as being primarily about the assumption of an exclusive government function, is entirely plausible. But so too would a gloss that reads *Marsh* as being less about the Gulf Shipbuilding Company as a generic state actor and more about the problems of a private land owner having the power to exercise an effective monopoly over the political marketplace of ideas in Chickasaw, Alabama.

In *Lloyd Corp.*, the majority effectively rebalanced the relative importance of a corporation's property rights against the speech rights of the would-be protesters – with the majority finding in favor of the former rather than the latter. The principal argument seems to be that a private property owner does not cede the right to exclude simply by opening its property to the general public for other purposes. As Justice Powell states the proposition, "private property [does not] lose its private character merely because the public is generally invited to use it for designated purposes."[107]

Justice Marshall, joined by three members of the Court, dissented vigorously from the majority's restrictive interpretation of *Logan Valley*. Although he forthrightly acknowledged that the *Logan Valley* majority had limited the scope of the decision's holding to protests with a nexus to a business located in a privately owned shopping center, he emphasized that the logic of the decision supported a more general recognition of a free speech easement to privately owned property for public protest activity. Accordingly, in Justice Marshall's view, "the distinction that the Court sees between the cases does not exist."[108]

Marshall viewed the Lloyd Center district as being clearly the equivalent of a town square in an earlier time. Given the city's support for the project, including the transfer of title of property and relocation of streets and sidewalks, "[i]t is plain . . . that Lloyd Center is the equivalent of a public 'business district' within the meaning of *Marsh* and *Logan Valley*."[109] Moreover, the Lloyd Corporation had opened up its property to the general public, routinely hosting "football rallies," "presidential candidates," "service organizations," and other civic events.[110]

In light of its functional characteristics and general use by the public for expressive activities, Marshall argued that the Lloyd Center's owner could not selectively exclude would-be speakers from its property.[111] This was so because no "logical reason [exists] to treat differently speech that is related to subjects other than the Center and its member stores."[112]

Justice Marshall's central argument, however, is that access to the Lloyd Center for First Amendment activities is essential for the process of democratic deliberation to function. Because it provides a comprehensive basket of services, "[f]or many Portland citizens, Lloyd Center will so completely satisfy their wants that they will have no reason to go elsewhere for goods or services."[113] Accordingly, the only practical way to reach at least some Portland voters would involve in-person interaction in the Lloyd Center's public spaces: "The only hope that these people have to be able to communicate effectively is to be permitted to speak in those areas in which most of their fellow citizens can be found."[114] When "private property expands to the point where it becomes, in reality, the business district of a community, the rights of the owners to proscribe speech on the part of those invited to use the property diminish."[115]

In any given case involving a claim to a free speech easement to access private property for expressive activities, "[t]he critical issue [will be] whether the private property ha[s] sufficient 'public' qualities to warrant a holding that the Fourteenth Amendment reached it."[116] In Marshall's view, the private property at issue in both *Lloyd Corp.* and *Logan Valley* was sufficiently "public" in character to justify the imposition of a First Amendment easement permitting at least some forms of collective expressive activity – regardless of whether the owners wished to permit such activity to take place on their property.

Justice Marshall predicted that, over time, city governments would work with developers to privatize ever larger swathes of previously public space. He warned that "[i]t would not be surprising in the future to see cities rely more and more on private businesses to perform functions once performed by governmental agencies."[117] As this process moves forward, "public property decreases in favor of privately owned property."[118] Over time, creeping privatization will make it "harder and harder for citizens to find means to communicate with other citizens" and "[o]nly the wealthy may find effective communication possible."[119] And, in the end, "[w]hen there are no effective means of communication" open to any and all citizens, "free speech [will be] a mere shibboleth."[120]

The other shoe dropped in *Hudgens v. National Labor Relations Board*,[121] in which a 5–4 majority voted to squarely overrule entirely *Logan Valley*. The case involved a union's effort to access the North DeKalb Shopping Center, a private shopping center near Atlanta, Georgia, in order to picket a store, Butler's Shoe Company, that was located in the mall. The labor union was involved in a contract dispute with Butler and sought to picket both its warehouse and retail stores.[122] The National Labor Relations Board (NLRB) found that the National Labor Relations Act (NLRA) secured a right of access to the mall for purposes of a peaceful picket; the US Court of Appeals for the Fifth Circuit enforced the NLRB's order, ruling that the First Amendment, as interpreted and applied in *Lloyd Corp.*, secured the union a right of access to the privately owned mall for the purpose of conducting its picket.[123] The Supreme Court reversed, with the *Hudgens* Court rejecting the attempted distinction that *Lloyd Corp.* established between protest activity with a nexus to a business located within a privately owned shopping center and protest activity that lacked such a nexus.

Writing for the majority, Justice Potter Stewart observed that "[i]t is, of course, commonplace that the constitutional right of free speech is a guarantee only against abridgment by government, federal or state."[124] When state action is absent, "statutory or common law" can "provide redress against a private corporation or person who seeks to abridge the free expression of others," but the Constitution itself does not provide "protection or redress."[125] Justice Stewart candidly acknowledged that *Lloyd Corp.* did not overrule either *Logan Valley* or *Marsh*.[126] Nevertheless, he concluded that "the reasoning of the Court's opinion in *Lloyd* cannot be squared with the reasoning of the Court's opinion in *Logan Valley*."[127] This was so because "the ultimate holding in *Lloyd* amounted to a total rejection of the holding in *Logan Valley*."[128] In consequence, "the rationale of *Logan Valley* did not survive the Court's decision in the *Lloyd* case."[129]

Justice Marshall again dissented, arguing that if "the owner of the modern shopping center complex, by dedicating his property to public use as a business district, to some extent displaces the 'State' from control of historical First Amendment forums," and thereby acquires "a virtual monopoly of places suitable for effective communication," then the federal courts must deploy the First Amendment to create mandatory free speech easements to such quasi-public property.[130] Where particular private property, otherwise open to the public, serves as an essential locus of collective public deliberation, the First Amendment requires that the owner's ability to control the property by censoring speech be circumscribed.[131] Property rights "must be accommodated with the interests of the public"[132] because the interest of would-be speakers to communicate with each other on this type of privately owned property is "substantial."[133]

Hudgens essentially completes the Burger Court's rejection of the underlying theory of the First Amendment that animates *Logan Valley*: If an essential modality of communication is privately owned, in the absence of some positive law that limits the owner's right to exclude others from its property, the property owner may decide for itself whether or not to permit speech activity to take place on its property. The decision expressly holds that a statutory right of access to private property for union-related speech activity might arise under the NLRA.[134] The majority remanded the case to the NLRB so that the agency could consider and decide whether a statutory right of access to the privately owned work site at issue in *Hudgens* existed under the NLRA.[135]

The logic of this position suggests that even if the First Amendment does not create easements to private property for speech activity, a statute or common law doctrine could require a property owner to permit speech activity on its property. In *PruneYard Shopping Center v. Robins*,[136] the Supreme Court made this implicit ruling in *Hudgens* explicit, by sustaining a California state supreme court precedent that interpreted the state constitution's free speech guarantee to require a private shopping mall to permit on-site protest activities.

The facts involved are straightforward. A group of high school students sought to protest the United Nation's treatment of Israel by distributing leaflets and soliciting signatures on a petition supporting Israel from a card table located in a Sacramento, California shopping mall called "The PruneYard."[137] A mall security officer informed the students that their leafletting and petitioning activity were not permitted on mall property – and that they would have to relocate their activities to a public sidewalk on the perimeter of the complex.[138] After losing in the state trial and intermediate appellate courts, the California Supreme Court held that the state constitution[139] guaranteed a right of access to private property otherwise open to the public for peaceful speech activity.[140]

Justice Frank C. Newman, writing for the 4–3 California state supreme court majority, found that the state constitution's protection of expressive freedom was more expansive than the First Amendment's scope of application. He explained that "[t]he California Constitution broadly proclaims speech and petition rights" and that "[s]hopping centers to which the public is invited can provide an essential and invaluable forum for exercising those rights."[141] Newman went on to hold that the state constitution's free speech guarantee protects peaceful, non-disruptive leafletting and petitioning in a large, commercial shopping center otherwise open to the public.[142] The shopping mall's owner sought and obtained review of this decision before the US Supreme Court, arguing that the involuntary creation of a free speech easement on privately owned property violated both the First Amendment and the Takings Clause of the Fifth Amendment.[143]

Writing for a unanimous Supreme Court, then-Justice, and later Chief Justice, William H. Rehnquist held that the California free speech easement on private property did not violate either the First Amendment or the Takings Clause. He explained that "[o]ur reasoning in *Lloyd* ... does not *ex proprio vigore* limit the authority of the State to exercise its police power or its sovereign right to adopt in its own Constitution individual liberties more expansive than those conferred by the Federal Constitution."[144] Moreover, "[i]t is, of course, well established that a State in the exercise of its police power may adopt reasonable restrictions on private property so long as the restrictions do not amount to a taking without just compensation or contravene any other federal constitutional provision."[145]

Here, the burden placed on private property owners was reasonable and did not violate either the First Amendment or the Takings Clause. This was so because "[t]he decision of the California Supreme Court makes it clear that the PruneYard may restrict expressive activity by adopting time, place, and manner regulations that will minimize any interference with its commercial functions."[146] The availability of other property – publicly owned property – which could be used to exercise First Amendment rights did not alter the analysis. The state supreme court could constitutionally conclude "that access to appellants' property in the manner required here is necessary to the promotion of state-protected rights of free speech and petition."[147]

Professor Seidman posits that the *PruneYard* ruling makes plain that, at least to some extent, "shifts in property rights were constitutionally discretionary rather than mandatory."[148] Thus, although the Constitution itself does not create free speech easements to private property, a statute that "obligated shopping malls to permit picketing" would be constitutional.[149] *PruneYard* vests discretion with the local, state, and federal governments to mandate access to private property, to some extent at least, for activities protected by the First Amendment.

To date, however, relatively few jurisdictions have elected to exercise this discretionary authority to mandate access to private property for expressive activities – in addition to California, Colorado, New Jersey, and Oregon currently maintain judicially created rights of access to large shopping centers and malls for expressive activities.[150] Massachusetts has recognized a limited right of access to privately owned shopping center property for the purpose of collecting signatures for ballot access.[151] Finally, Washington State's Supreme Court initially recognized free speech easements to mall property,[152] but subsequently resiled from this ruling, holding that the state constitution did *not* mandate access to private property for speech activities.[153] By way of contrast, around twenty state supreme courts have declined to recognize a right of access to privately owned shopping mall property for the purpose of engaging in First Amendment activities.[154]

Subsequent federal Supreme Court decisions under the Rehnquist Court make clear that if a right of access to private property for speech activity arises by operation of a local or state law, the burden on the private property owner is constitutional provided it does not unduly hamper the ability of the property's owner to use it for its regular commercial purposes.[155] Neither the Rehnquist Court nor the Roberts Court have even *hinted* at any interest in returning to *Logan Valley*'s application of the First Amendment to create mandatory free speech easements to secure access to private property for speech activity integral to democratic self-government. Thus, even though the First Amendment does not create free speech easements to privately owned property after *Hudgens*, local, state, or federal law can restrict the right of a private property owner to close its property to speech activity.[156]

In sum, the Warren Court recognized a free speech easement to private property in *Logan Valley*, but the Burger Court first limited, and then rejected, this creative use of the First Amendment to create a positive right of access to private property that functioned as a town square. The Burger Court did authorize the imposition of such free speech easements through statutory law, common law, or incident to a state constitution's free speech guarantee, but took the federal courts out of the business of forcing private property owners to accommodate First Amendment activity on their property. Finally, the Rehnquist and Roberts Courts have not revisited the question of whether the First Amendment, properly interpreted and applied, secures a right of access to certain kinds of private property for speech activity. Accordingly, *PruneYard* is and remains the Supreme Court's final word on this question to date.

3.2 IN DEFENSE OF *LOGAN VALLEY*: THE AFFIRMATIVE CASE FOR DEPLOYING THE FIRST AMENDMENT TO CREATE MANDATORY FREE SPEECH EASEMENTS TO CERTAIN KINDS OF TANGIBLE AND INTANGIBLE PRIVATE PROPERTY

Does access to private property for speech activity matter in the age of the internet? Some commentators argue that it does not – and, accordingly, that *PruneYard* should be overruled. Professors Selznick and LaMacchia, for example, suggest that "the decline of shopping malls" and "the widespread availability and use of social media" render access to shopping malls for expressive activities irrelevant and anachronistic.[157] They argue that "[u]nder current conditions, it may be time to reconsider the rationale for forcing mall owners to accommodate expression in those states" that have followed California's lead in *PruneYard*.[158] Selznick and LaMacchia ask, "If protesters now have free access to an effective means of mass communication in social media and malls are no longer the town square substitutes they were becoming in the latter half of the 1900s, should mall owners still be forced to use their property as a forum for expression?"[159]

Other scholars are not yet convinced that access to public spaces is irrelevant today. For example, Professor Gerry Korngold observes that "[s]ome have wondered whether physical spaces are still necessary for the exchange of ideas in the digital and social media era."[160] Like Selznick and LaMacchia, Korngold points to the existence of internet-based social media platforms, such as "Facebook, Google, Twitter, LinkedIn, Instagram, and other vehicles" that "allow for a robust and open discussion of political, social, economic, and other ideas."[161] Korngold, however, posits that face-to-face, in-person encounters retain importance because of their unique characteristics.

Professor Korngold suggests that "[f]ace-to-face meetings remove the anonymity of the internet, perhaps making speakers more responsible, accountable, and thoughtful for their words."[162] In turn, the higher credibility of an in-person speaker "may make listeners more open to listening."[163] In addition, collective action in real time provides opportunities for organizing that are "missing on a computer screen."[164] Finally, in-person interactions permit a would-be speaker to deliver a message to a particular audience – something that usually is not possible on most social media platforms.

Korngold notes that major retail developments often require the active assistance and support of local government – he argues that municipal governments should leverage this discretionary authority to ensure that quasi-public spaces remain open for speech activity.[165] More specifically, he suggests conditional use of eminent domain, incentive zoning, and community benefits agreements to secure access to privately owned spaces open to the public and perfectly suitable for collective expressive activity. Such steps are necessary, Professor Korngold argues, because "[m]alls and large shopping centers in the twenty-first century are not dead, reports to the contrary notwithstanding."[166]

Malls have evolved over time into destination "lifestyle centers" and "town centers" that are the modern-day equivalent of the classic town square.[167] Moreover, these developments have effectively "supplanted the traditional business district, consuming vital civic capital [by banishing] free speech and expression that [once] took place in those public spaces."[168] In the contemporary United States, outdoor, open air, destination "town center" shopping center developments are entirely commonplace – quotidian, in fact – and these new retail developments routinely ban protest and other forms of speech activity on site. In sum, access to public spaces in the United States continues to shrink and this trend toward the privatization of public spaces is also accelerating over time.

In light of all of this, Professor Korngold has the better argument regarding the continuing relevance of access to privately owned malls and shopping centers for expressive activities. Moreover, the framing device he chooses – which happens to be the same framing device that Justice Marshall adopted in *Logan Valley* – seems spot on: When a large-scale private retail development serves as an essential locus for the process of democratic deliberation, the First Amendment should impose public access obligations on the entity that owns and operates that development. When the political parties undertake tasks essential to the election process, they incur constitutional obligations, including a duty not to discriminate based on race.[169]

By parity of constitutional logic, when a retail developer, with the assistance of the local government, opens a large-scale "town center" style shopping district, the First Amendment should create a free speech easement guaranteeing access to would-be speakers and a concomitant right of would-be listeners to interact with such speakers.

More than a little irony exists with respect to municipal policies that support and accelerate the creeping privatization of public spaces. Both local and state governments often provide direct and indirect forms of support for new "lifestyle" shopping developments and thus bear a significant measure of responsibility for the creeping privatization of the town square. Given the interrelationship of government to the creation of these quasi-public spaces – "public" by both design and operation – the imposition of First Amendment-based free speech easements constitutes a perfectly defensible legal, and quite constitutional, rule.

The question, in any case, must be whether the private property at issue functions as an essential locus for the process of democratic deliberation. If it does, then the recognition of a First Amendment easement to the property, under the theory of *Logan Valley*, becomes plausible. If not, however, then the property owner's interests should be controlling. In this sense, then, a single mom-and-pop soda shop would not be subject to a free speech easement under the First Amendment, whereas the Mall of America, in suburban Minneapolis, Minnesota would be. The Mall of America encompasses over five million square feet of shopping space, has over 10,000 parking spaces, and includes an indoor amusement park. The development's management boasts that "seven Yankee stadiums" would fit within the mall's metes and bounds.[170]

Quite obviously, for people living in Bloomington, Minnesota and Minneapolis-St. Paul, Minnesota, more generally the Mall of America constitutes a central hub of community life that has displaced the traditional town square as a place to meet and interact.[171] Imposing a free speech easement on such a property would not interfere in any significant way with the mall owner's commercial interests, given that even under *Logan Valley*, the mall owners would be entirely free to impose reasonable time, place, and manner regulations on expressive activities within the facility. The question really reduces to this: Is our commitment to democratic deliberation, as a self-governing people, sufficient to impose social costs on private property owners in order to facilitate the kind of in-person civic engagement required for democracy to function?

The Warren Court used the First Amendment to literally create breathing space for expressive activity – as a source of affirmative rights of access to property for the purpose of engaging in protest. Government, of course, had an obligation to make public property available for speech activity, if the property was otherwise suitable for such activity and the proposed use did not preclude the government from achieving its own legitimate objectives.[172] But, this was not enough. As suburbanization and post-*Brown* white flight from the nation's urban centers accelerated, commercial developments such as the Logan Valley Plaza and Lloyd Center came to be no less relevant to the process of civic engagement than the town center of Chickasaw, Alabama.

Moreover, at least initially, the Burger Court followed this expansive approach – for example, by ordering the US Army to provide access to a San Antonio, Texas military base so that leafletters could promote, on base property that both resembled and functioned as a traditional town central shopping district, an anti-Vietnam War protest event.[173] The government's constitutional obligation to make property available for speech activity was broad and wide – much broader, in fact, than the limited right of access recognized in *Logan Valley*. The key fact in *Logan Valley* was that the shopping center served as an essential nexus for community members to meet and interact; the loss of this venue for democratic discourse would have imposed an unacceptable burden on the free flow of information and ideas within the community. Thus, the Warren Court demanded less of a private property owner than of the government itself – but even a private property owner had an obligation to facilitate, rather than impede, the process of democratic deliberation.[174]

The opposite approach – allowing government to use its powers to facilitate large-scale, private developments that come to serve as central hubs of community life, but then permitting the business owners to operate such public spaces as closed private property, is "to subordinate public citizenship to the allegedly inflexible rights claimed by private property owners."[175] As one commentator observes, the widespread judicial rejection of *Logan Valley* facilitates the "subordination of public discourse to private ownership," and results in "the further obliteration of any arena for 'public citizenship.'"[176] Another commentator observes, quite accurately, that "[m]any Americans are already living in communities that are literally composed entirely of private space."[177]

The Supreme Court has emphasized that "[a] State enjoys broad authority to create rights of public access on behalf of citizens,"[178] and a handful of state supreme courts have taken this step, under the constitutional license the US Supreme Court provided in *PruneYard*.[179] But leaving this question to the discretion of local and state governments puts speech integral to the operation of democratic self-government at risk. What is more, if a physical location truly serves as the hub of the community's public life, permitting its private owners to close it to expressive activities shuts off an integral venue for democratic discourse.

As Professor Tim Zick has observed in the context of access to government property, "there is something to being *there* that makes other alternatives, however *ample*, still *inadequate* in light of the specific expressive interests at stake."[180] This observation holds true regardless of whether particular property happens to be held in government or private hands. Moreover, and as Zick argues, "[r]econsidering, locating, engaging, and systematically reading places can produce not only a more robust and wide-open macrogeography, but a more speech-facilitative microgeography, as well."[181] If "expressive place" is as important to effective and meaningful democratic discourse as Zick posits, then the accident of public or private ownership of that space should not prefigure the First Amendment analysis. *Logan Valley* recognized and incorporated these important First Amendment values, whereas *Hudgens* did not.

We should also recognize, in the age of the internet, that "place" is not limited to physical locations. Intangible spaces, such as social media platforms, can and do constitute essential locations for the process of democratic deliberation. Professor Zick emphasizes the importance of physical spaces for expressive activity: "[D]espite the proliferation of electronic speech fora, providing material public space for speech remains critical to the health of our expressive culture."[182] As Chapter 2 explains in some detail, I agree wholeheartedly that in person, collective speech activity in public spaces remains essential to the process of democratic deliberation. However, in thinking about free speech easements and a positive role for the First Amendment in creating opportunities for voters to engage with each other, we cannot ignore the fact that social media platforms currently serve as central locations for democratic discourse.[183]

Logan Valley, at least arguably, could serve as a justification for imposing common carrier duties on dominant social media platforms, such as Facebook, Twitter, YouTube, and Instagram, that serve as essential conduits for the exchange of ideas and opinions about public officials, public figures, and matters of public concern. Indeed, one could conceive of *New York Times Co. v. Sullivan*[184] as creating a kind of free speech easement to degrade the reputation and standing of public officials, public figures, and those involved in matters of public concern within the community. It does not require much of a stretch to conceive of an interest in personal reputation as an intangible property interest[185] – if this is so, then *Sullivan* has the effect of essentially permitting critics to "trespass" on this property, and to do so without incurring any obligation to make the subject of the factually erroneous criticism whole through an award of money damages (at least in the absence of clear and convincing proof that the defendant published the false statement of fact with malice aforethought, meaning with actual knowledge of its falsity or with reckless disregard for the statement's truth or falsity[186]).

If we renormalize *Sullivan* in this way, the decision essentially involves a transfer of property rights from the would-be plaintiff in a defamation action to the media defendant. It functions more or less identically to *Logan Valley* in forcing a private entity to incur non-trivial costs in order to facilitate democratic discourse. In other words, *Sullivan* deploys the First Amendment to require private entities to give up something of value in order to facilitate an "uninhibited, robust, and wide-open" public discourse that "may well include vehement, caustic, and sometimes unpleasantly sharp attacks on government and public officials."[187] *Logan Valley*, in turn, burdened a different kind of property interest – the right to prohibit persons otherwise invited to visit a private shopping center from engaging in collective expressive activities – but did so for more or less identical reasons.

Thus, the same constitutional logic that undergirds *Sullivan* would support the recognition of free speech easements to dominant social media platforms. It is not clear why a modality of speech, like Facebook or Twitter, should be permitted to censor third-party speech in the same way as the *Miami Herald*.[188] These platforms serve to distribute the speech of others – not the speech of the proprietors. In this sense, social media platforms and search engine providers are more like American Telephone & Telegraph (AT & T) in the 1920s and 1930s – a modality of communication. And, the federal government imposed common carrier duties on AT & T that required the company to service any and all persons and entities that could pay the tariffed rates for telephonic services.

Cable system operators provide another potentially useful analogy. In the Cable Act of 1992,[189] Congress imposed common carrier duties on local cable system operators to ensure that they did not use their monopoly power to banish content providers – whether for ideological reasons or because the cable system operator lacked a financial stake in a particular broadcast or cable station. Because cable system operators constituted a critical choke point to the marketplace of ideas, and were not distributing their own speech like a newspaper, the Supreme Court permitted Congress to impose free speech easements on their local channel line-ups[190] – including a duty to make leased access channels available, limitations on the carriage of stations in which the cable system operator maintained a financial interest, the obligation to provide "PEG" (public, educational, and government) channels on the local cable line-up incident to franchise agreements with local governments, and a "must carry" duty with respect to all local terrestrial broadcast stations that elect must carry status.[191]

To be sure, Congress, and not the federal courts, imposed common carrier duties on AT & T and also on cable system operators. And, under the logic of *PruneYard*, Congress, a state legislature, or a city council, could presumably impose such duties on social media platforms, search engine providers, or even internet service providers (ISPs). If the Supreme Court were to embrace the constitutional reasoning of *Logan Valley*, however, it would be possible for the First Amendment itself to directly impose common carrier duties on entities like Facebook or Twitter.

In this brief chapter, it is simply not possible to develop and defend a complete program of action for imposing such duties on social media platforms, search engines, and ISPs – such an undertaking lies beyond the scope of my immediate project, which is to show how First Amendment rights have declined, rather than expanded, over time and to posit persuasive reasons that help to explain this phenomenon. Nevertheless, if we truly believe that the locus of democratic politics has shifted from the physical world to the virtual world, permitting private companies to exercise an unfettered discretion to censor makes no sense if democratic deliberation really is essential to a successful program of democratic self-government.

3.3 THE PROFOUND DANGERS OF CASTING A BLIND EYE ON THE UNLIMITED POWER OF SOCIAL MEDIA AND INTERNET SEARCH ENGINE PROVIDERS TO CENSOR SPEECH: WHY CONTINUED RELIANCE ON SELF-REGULATION PRESENTS A CLEAR AND PRESENT DANGER TO THE PROCESS OF DEMOCRATIC DELIBERATION – AND HENCE TO DEMOCRATIC SELF-GOVERNMENT ITSELF

Our current approach to the regulation of dominant social media platforms and search engine providers reflects a remarkable degree of trust in these companies to follow their own rules – and to do so predictably. Based on recent revelations about the practices of companies like Facebook, this trust seems entirely unwarranted. Social media companies routinely fail to follow their own stated policies when doing so seems to convey a sufficiently attractive financial benefit. Thus, despite repeated promises to the contrary, Facebook permitted app developers to access freely users' personal data.[192] Even after Facebook came clean about its lax protection of users' personal data, it misrepresented when the company actually stopped providing app developers with access to it.[193] Facebook also tried to pressure financial institutions and credit card companies to share users' financial data – in order to exploit the data "for a range of purposes, including advertising."[194] In other words, one should take Facebook's promises of self-restraint in exploiting users' data with several grains of salt.

Of course, social media companies are highly likely to argue that they are entitled to First Amendment protection because they "speak" via their platforms. If the Supreme Court credits these claims, and applies the newspaper paradigm to social media companies, the prospects for either judicially-created or legislatively-created free speech easements to such platforms would be, at best, bleak. Some legal scholars have posited that the collection and aggregation of data constitutes "speech."[195] Prominent First Amendment scholars also have argued that artificial intelligence programs, like Siri, should enjoy First Amendment protection as a speaker.[196] Accordingly, social media platform companies are highly likely to attempt to characterize themselves as more akin to a newspaper, magazine, or television news room than a common carrier information service provider, such as AT & T or a cable system operator.

Professor Jack Balkin has proposed relatively modest regulatory reforms that would encourage competition among social media and search engine providers and the imposition of "procedural due process" duties that would protect users from arbitrary content-based decisions by these companies.[197] At the same time, he strongly opposes the application of First Amendment principles to dominant social media and search engine companies.[198] Balkin's reform proposals are well stated and quite sensible – but their prospects for adoption in Congress are bleak. In addition, they might well not be sufficiently strong medicine to safeguard the process of democratic deliberation on private platforms such as Facebook, Twitter, and YouTube.

Starting with the first point, the political economy of legislative or regulatory efforts to create more competition are open to serious doubt. Simply put, companies like Facebook and Google can afford K Street's best Gucci-clad lobbyists. Accordingly, however salutary a proposal for efforts to subject dominant social media companies to competition might be, securing adoption and implementation of such proposals would constitute a very heavy lift.

Even if such programs were adopted, precisely who would invest in a venture seeking to compete head-to-head with the likes of Facebook, YouTube, Twitter, or Google? The willingness of investors with venture capital to place such financial bets against companies like Facebook and Google is highly questionable. Telecommunications history also has some lessons to teach about the plausibility of opening up a natural monopoly to meaningful competition.

In fact, Alphabet, Google's parent company, attempted to dethrone Facebook's hegemony as the dominant online social media network, introducing Google+ in 2016.[199] Despite the vast resources and expertise of Google, Google+ was a dismal failure; it failed to secure many users and Facebook effectively and efficiently swatted away Google's challenge.[200] Recently, after disclosing a major data breach involving Google+ users, Google shut down the social network entirely, effectively running up the white flag in its effort to displace Facebook's market dominance.[201] As one industry analyst explained, "[w]ith these business models, it's really winner takes all" and, as a practical matter, "it's almost impossible to displace the incumbent."[202] If a sophisticated, well-resourced industry player like Google cannot mount a successful challenge to Facebook, the obvious question is: Who can?

AT & T enjoyed a monopoly for generations not because of a government grant of exclusivity, but rather because the cost of building a rival network would have been entirely prohibitive (and likely futile). AT & T's ability to refuse to interconnect calls with rival networks made competition effectively impossible. It was not until the 1982 break-up order,[203] and AT & T being subject to mandatory interconnection obligations that benefitted competitive long-distance carriers, that meaningful competition came into existence.

Could the federal government require social media companies to interconnect with rivals? This was the regulatory solution that permitted competition to emerge for interstate and international telephony. However, forcing Facebook, YouTube, and Twitter to redistribute content from rivals' platforms is probably unconstitutional (on First Amendment and Takings Clause grounds) and would be unlikely to change users' behavior in any event. After all, MySpace still exists – but is, quite literally, a virtual ghost town. Creating an effective competitor presents serious, probably insurmountable, problems involving transaction costs, collective action, and path dependence.

For example, a long-term Facebook user will probably view with utter dismay the prospect of reloading a decade's worth of photographs, posts, and links. The labor involved would be quite considerable – and to what end? If the people that a person wants to interact with all use Facebook, migration to a competitor's service would involve a great loss of utility and functionality, at the cost of a considerable investment of time, money, and energy. Google tried and failed – which provides an important lesson about the plausibility of mounting a successful challenge to Facebook's dominance.

Moreover, Bing currently finds it necessary to offer financial incentives for new users; it does so because most people who have relied on Google as their primary internet search engine are not much inclined to migrate to a new service provider. As the saying goes, "if it ain't broke, don't fix it." If a user is satisfied with an existing social media platform, search engine, or ISP, they are unlikely to migrate to a competitor absent some sort of significant financial – or other – incentive. Most people are highly path dependent and have to be "nudged" to change their ways.[204]

As for Professor Balkin's call for due process rights against social media companies, it is highly likely that these companies would insist on arbitration as a means of resolving disputes about content-based decisions. Certainly, the Federal Arbitration Act[205] would seem to be available to companies like Facebook, YouTube, and Twitter, absent some sort of statutory amendment that prohibits them from requiring users to agree to arbitrate disputes. Arbitration would provide a fast, efficient forum – but one that almost certainly would systematically favor the social media companies' interests over those of users. Arbitral panels usually do not issue formal written decisions, giving reasons, and even when they do issue written decisions that explain a ruling, these rulings are usually not available to the public.

Either solution, frankly, is highly unlikely to be adopted by Congress. Social media companies will spend freely to engage the lobbying firepower necessary to block the enactment of legislation that would disrupt their businesses. A legislative solution, accordingly, is not likely to be forthcoming any time soon.

Another problem with Professor Balkin's argument is his assumption that the application of the First Amendment to social media companies, search engines, and ISPs would have to be an all-or-nothing affair.[206] We could imagine a world in which the federal courts impose some, but not all, First Amendment obligations applicable to the government to dominant social media platforms, search engine providers, and ISPs. As it happens, we even have a potential jurisprudential road map for implementing such an approach.

When the Supreme Court was considering whether to apply provisions of the Bill of Rights to the states, members of the Supreme Court proposed a variety of solutions. For example, Justice Black proposed "total incorporation" of the first eight amendments (but not the Ninth Amendment).[207] Under this approach, the first eight amendments in the Bill of Rights would apply "line for line, and jot for jot" in the same way against the state governments as they did against the federal government. Under this approach, California would no longer have the option of initiating criminal charges by information rather than grand jury indictment.

The principal competing approach to the incorporation of the Bill of Rights was to use the rubric of "due process" to identify rights sufficiently basic and essential to any civilized system of justice as to rank as being fundamental. Such rights arose not from the Bill of Rights at all, but from the concept of ordered liberty safeguarded against encroachments by the state governments under the Due Process Clause of the Fourteenth Amendment.[208] Justice John Marshall Harlan was a principal and fierce advocate of this approach.[209] Using this methodology, the Free Speech Clause of the First Amendment does not apply against the states at all – rather, a right to freedom of expression is implicit in the concept of ordered liberty and therefore may be asserted against the states. In any given case, the outcome of a free speech claim arising under the Due Process right of freedom of expression might – or might not – correspond to the result that would obtain under the Free Speech Clause, which, strictly speaking, applies only to the federal government.[210]

Justice Harlan's approach would have permitted some variation in practices regarding things like the size of criminal petit juries and whether a jury verdict in a criminal trial had to be unanimous. The federal criminal jury requirement, which called for a unanimous verdict by a twelve person jury, would not necessarily apply to the states – and the fact that the states used smaller, non-unanimous juries would not affect, at all, the federal right to a jury trial under the Sixth Amendment[211] and Article III, Section 2, Clause 3.[212] Thus, in any given context, the federal right and the state Due Process Clause analogue might, or might not, feature a coextensive scope of coverage.[213]

The owners of private property, whether real or virtual, obviously possess constitutionally protected property interests and also interests in avoiding coerced speech.[214] Accordingly, the imposition of free speech easements to privately owned property cannot be coextensive with the First Amendment duties of the federal, state, and local governments. The application of First Amendment principles to private property owners, including social media platforms, search engines, and ISPs, could be less than total and complete. Moreover, if the federal courts were to impose limited First Amendment duties on private actors, a powerful incentive would arise for these companies to support reasonable legislation that defines their duties to facilitate third party communications. In other words, the federal courts might issue judicial decisions that would apply in the absence of legislation that draws with greater precision the rights and obligations of social media platforms, search engines, and ISPs.

As Professor Curtis Berger has argued, "[a]ccess to a public space in which politicians and citizens may air their views lies at the very foundation of American politics."[215] Moreover, "[w]hether one believes that democracy draws strength from an engaged citizenry or from a robust 'marketplace of [political] ideas,' participation in politics is essential."[216] If we possess a genuine commitment to these two propositions, we cannot allow the accident of private ownership to prefigure the availability of essential forums for public discourse. Consistent with the First Amendment, state law may not vest an absolute and unreviewable power to censor in the hands of private corporations that are wholly unaccountable for how they choose to exercise their censorial powers to silence the speech of others. One should also keep in mind that a general duty to provide reasonable access to all comers on equal terms would not imply that a forum's owner lacks the authority to establish and enforce reasonable restrictions on such access (including content controls).[217]

With the creeping privatization of the spaces and modalities of democratic discourse, continuing to rely on a traditional application of state action principles will put the process of democratic deliberation at considerable risk. Professor Jody Freeman observes that "[i]nstead of seeing privatization as a means of shrinking government, I imagine it as a mechanism for expanding government's reach into realms traditionally thought private."[218] Freeman suggests that private entities might voluntarily embrace public-oriented duties, observing that "privatization can be a means of 'publicization,' through which private actors increasingly commit themselves to traditionally public goals as the price of access to lucrative opportunities to deliver goods and services that might otherwise be directly provided by the state."[219] However, with respect to social media platforms and internet search engine providers, voluntary compliance with public-regarding norms is unlikely – nor does the government possess any obvious carrots to dangle to secure such cooperation.[220]

In a similar vein, Professor Sarah Schindler argues that courts should push the envelope by "review[ing] and potentially expand[ing] their First Amendment and state action jurisprudence," in order to "impos[e] public space laws on private actors."[221] She argues that "[b]y treating private actors as state actors, courts might also require them to adhere to norms of democratic accountability."[222] In fairness, Schindler readily acknowledges that "[t]his currently seems highly unlikely."[223]

We need not embrace an "all-or-nothing" approach to imposing First Amendment easements on private property – whether real or virtual. Instead, we could imagine a virtuous mean between the two extremes of unfettered deference to the managerial preferences of private property owners and the unthinking application of constitutional values, across the board, to entities that perform a function integral to the process of democratic self-government. Justice Thurgood Marshall's opinion in *Logan Valley*, read in conjunction with his dissents in *Lloyd Corp.* and *Hudgens*, and Justice Black's opinion in *Marsh*, point the way toward a sensible solution that has the federal courts impose limited, but still meaningful, First Amendment obligations on certain private property owners.

3.4 CONCLUSION

In order to facilitate the process of democratic deliberation, the Warren Court deployed the First Amendment to create an easement for would-be speakers who wished to use privately owned shopping centers and malls for protest activity. *Logan Valley* demonstrates that the Warren Court's decisions granting access to government property for First Amendment activity were, in fact, part of a larger, broader effort to use the First Amendment to create positive rights of access to public spaces for the exercise of expressive freedoms. Moreover, the Warren Court interpreted the First Amendment to create affirmative, positive rights of access to both public and private property for protest activity.

To be sure, the Warren Court made clear that the First Amendment did not displace a private property owner's ability to ensure that its property could be used for its primary commercial purposes. In this respect, then, a kind of "junior varsity" version of the First Amendment applied to private shopping centers and malls – regulations limiting the scope of access to private property for speech activity could be broader and more restrictive than the rules that the government itself might be able to adopt and enforce on public property. This is a crucial point: In thinking about creating First Amendment easements to dominant social media platforms and search engines, we need not assume that the First Amendment rules applicable to the government itself would apply lock, stock, and barrel to private social media and search engine companies. We could imagine a more limited, circumscribed, set of First Amendment rights applicable to such entities – even if we remain committed to applying the full strength First Amendment to the government itself.

If private companies control critical choke points that limit, or prohibit, access to the political marketplace of ideas, democratic deliberation will suffer if the absence of state action means that the First Amendment has no application whatsoever to such entities. If the monopoly power of the political parties to serve as gatekeepers for holding public office justified applying the Equal Protection Clause and Fifteenth Amendment to them – institutions that deemed themselves non-governmental, "private" associations – then the exact same constitutional logic would justify the recognition and enforcement of free speech easements to private property that serves as a central locus for democratic deliberation.

A return to *Logan Valley*, however, is highly unlikely under the Roberts Court. A jurisprudential recommitment to *Logan Valley* would require the federal courts to embrace a First Amendment doctrine that involves open-ended balancing of the interests of private property owners, on the one hand, and would-be speakers seeking to use private property (whether real or intangible), on the other. Both the Rehnquist and Roberts Court have abjured such tests on a very consistent, and predictable, basis.[224] The Warren Court, by way of contrast, repeatedly embraced doctrinal innovations that enhanced speech rights even if they also expanded the role of federal judges in selecting free speech winners – and free speech losers.[225]

4

Whistleblowing Speech and Democratic Accountability

The Growing Problem of Reduced First Amendment Protection for Government Employee Speech

Democratic self-government relies on regular elections to ensure that government remains accountable and responsible to the body politic. However, for elections to serve as a reliable means of securing government accountability, the voters must have access to relevant information about the successes – and failures – of those who currently hold office.[1] Without information, the electoral process cannot serve as an effective means of ensuring government accountability for both its actions and its failures to act.[2] This holds true as a general matter, but holds doubly true in a period when the incumbent White House administration openly and brazenly embraces the concept of "alternative facts."[3]

Professor David Anderson observes that for James Madison and the other proponents of the Bill of Rights, "freedom of the press was inextricably related to the new republican form of government and would have to be protected if their vision of government by the people was to succeed."[4] The press obviously plays a crucial role in facilitating the process of democratic deliberation and government accountability.[5] But the press can play this role only if journalists are able to obtain and disseminate accurate information about the government's activities.[6]

Since time immemorial, however, government officers will race to claim responsibility for successes but are far more reticent to acknowledge – much less take responsibility for – government failures.[7] All of the relevant incentives run toward attempting to hide or cover up instances of corruption, malfeasance, or ineptitude. And, yet, democratic accountability requires that information that incumbent government officers would prefer to suppress be made available to the voters – who express a collective judgment on the success, or failure, of the incumbent officers on election day through their ballots.[8]

Government employees are obviously quite often in the best position to know about government engaging in questionable, if not entirely illegal or unconstitutional, activity. Edward Snowden's revelations about the existence of a massive domestic spying program set off a national debate about the relative importance of national security, and anti-terrorism efforts, versus informational privacy.[9] Because intelligence agencies invariably operate in largely non-transparent ways, only an insider – a whistleblower – could credibly confirm the existence of government domestic spying programs like PRISM.[10]

What's more, domestic surveillance programs could easily be used in ways that thwart or inhibit democratic accountability – for example, by using embarrassing personal information to discredit political opponents of the incumbent president,[11] or by aiding or inhibiting the election of a sitting member of Congress – or even a presidential candidate – through selective data dumps.[12] Truly, information is power – particularly when the information is purloined from smart phones, email accounts, and web surfing habits.[13] Very few people would want to share with God and country all of their most intimate communications and online activities.[14]

In sum, for elections to secure government accountability, the electorate must have the information required to reach sensible conclusions about what government is doing well and what government is doing poorly.[15] As Professor Alexander Meiklejohn stated the proposition, "[w]hen a free man is voting, it is not enough that the truth is known by someone else, by some scholar or administrator or legislator."[16] Instead, "[t]he voters must have it, all of them."[17]

The question then becomes: How precisely will the electorate come to possess the information that it requires to make accurate determinations about the current government's wisdom – or lack of it? It is easy enough to say, "Well, the mass media will report on the activities of the government." But, this only kicks the can down the road a bit further – precisely how will the media come to possess the information necessary for voters to make wise electoral decisions?

Quite obviously, government employees will play a regular and important role in facilitating the ability of citizens to hold government accountable through the electoral process.[18] A government employee who possesses information relevant to government misconduct has a choice to make: She could release the information to the press, in order to facilitate reform and electoral accountability or, as the alternative, she could remain silent in order to protect a government office from public embarrassment. If we want government employees to facilitate accountability by sharing critical information about the government's activities with the body politic, we should consider carefully the incentives – and disincentives – that we provide for choosing speech over silence.[19] For example, if we wish to encourage strongly public disclosure about matters of public concern,[20] we would provide very robust legal protections against a government employer retaliating against a government employee who engages in whistleblowing activity.[21] Simply put, ambiguity in the scope of such protection is a strong incentive for government employees to remain silent. A rational government employee will not disseminate information about wrongdoing within her department or agency if a not improbable consequence will be the loss of her employment.[22] Given the importance of accurate information about the government's activities to holding government accountable for its actions, the federal courts should deploy the First Amendment as a shield for whistleblowing speech.[23]

The First Amendment's protection of speech integral to the political process could logically encompass speech by government employees that relates to matters of public concern that involve the government office in which the employee works. Targeted protection for "whistleblowing speech" could be justified in normative terms because such speech is essential to the proper functioning of the political process. The Supreme Court, however, has not provided robust protection for government employees who engage in whistleblowing activities.[24] Nor has Congress enacted legislation that provides comprehensive and reliable protection to government employees who disclose truthful, but embarrassing, information about significant failures in the operation of government programs.[25]

This chapter proceeds in five parts. Part 4.1 examines the Supreme Court's initial efforts to protect government employees who speak out about matters of public concern under the *Connick/Pickering* doctrine.[26] Part 4.2 then contrasts the approach of the Rehnquist and Roberts Courts, which have declined to extend *Connick/Pickering*. Indeed, although the Rehnquist and Roberts Courts have never mustered a majority to overrule expressly *Connick* and *Pickering*, the Supreme Court's most recent decisions have narrowed significantly the First Amendment protections afforded to government employees' speech.

Part 4.3 considers the paradox of the near-absolute protection that the Supreme Court has afforded government employees to be free of a spoils system in which elected government officials condition government employment on partisan loyalty. To be clear, I do not suggest that the Supreme Court has erred in constitutionalizing civil service protections through First Amendment precedents that prohibit the use of a political patronage system for government employment (at least for non-confidential and non-policymaking positions). The point is more subtle: If the potential disruption of a government office is not a sufficient predicate for firing an employee based on her partisan identity, the same logic would suggest that government should be equally debarred from firing a government employee who speaks out on a matter of public concern.

Part 4.4 proposes the creation of a new First Amendment speech category: namely, "whistleblowing" speech. The *Connick/Pickering* line of precedent does not adequately take into account the value of a government employee's speech to the process of democratic deliberation; whistleblowing speech conveys important benefits on the body politic that transcend the government employee's personal autonomy interests in speaking out on matters of public concern. Part 4.5 provides a brief summary and conclusion of the arguments set forth in this chapter.

Government employees are often uniquely situated to provide voters with information essential to holding government accountable.[27] First Amendment doctrine, under the existing *Connick/Pickering* doctrine, fails to take this consideration into account.[28] To be sure, government employees should not be required to relinquish their right to speak more generally as citizens regarding matters of public concern as a consequence of working for a government employer. At the same time, however, whistleblowing speech, an important subset of government employee speech, clearly facilitates the process of holding government democratically accountable through the electoral process.

Just as political speech enjoys enhanced First Amendment protection vis á vis other kinds of speech, such as commercial speech[29] and sexually explicit speech,[30] so too, government employee speech that empowers voters to assess accurately government successes and failures should be specially and specifically protected because of its essential nexus with the process of democratic deliberation. Although not all government employee speech is whistleblowing speech,[31] only government employee speakers can engage in whistleblowing speech because they are uniquely situated to provide the body politic with the information it must have to ensure government accountability through the democratic process. In sum, such speech merits targeted protection under the First Amendment, but contemporary First Amendment jurisprudence fails to distinguish whistleblowing speech from more generic, less socially valuable, kinds of government employee speech.

4.1 THE WARREN AND BURGER COURTS' CONTINGENT PROTECTION OF GOVERNMENT EMPLOYEES AS CITIZEN-PARTICIPANTS IN THE PROCESS OF DEMOCRATIC SELF-GOVERNMENT

Government employees have never enjoyed strong First Amendment protection for their speech activity – whether on the job or off the clock.[32] Nothing even remotely close to a First Amendment privilege for whistleblowing speech has ever existed in the governing constitutional precedents. To be sure, the Warren Court did take some tepid steps toward affording government employees who speak out about matters of public concern some measure of First Amendment protection. In *Pickering*, decided in 1968, the Supreme Court held that government employers could not punish employees for exercising their First Amendment rights – at least when an employee speaks out on a matter of public concern.[33] The *Pickering* test, however, was never particularly robust – it involves a balancing exercise that considers the employee's interest in speaking out about a matter of public concern and then weighs this private interest against a government employer's interest in maintaining a well-functioning workplace.[34]

Marvin L. Pickering was a high school teacher in Will County, Illinois.[35] He published a letter to the editor of the local newspaper criticizing the local school board's handling of efforts to secure public approval of new school taxes.[36] Pickering's letter challenged some of the local school board's claims about existing school district expenses and its financial support for the district's athletic programs.[37] The school district promptly fired Pickering after the newspaper published his letter criticizing both their management of the district, particularly with respect to athletics programs, and the board's efforts to secure public approval of an increase in local school taxes through a public referendum.[38] The district did so because it concluded that, in the words of the governing state law, his continued employment would be "detrimental to the efficient operation and administration of the schools of the district."[39] The Illinois state courts upheld the school district's discharge of Pickering as an appropriate action to rein in an insubordinate school district employee.[40]

The Supreme Court of the United States granted review and reversed the Illinois Supreme Court.[41] Writing for the majority, Justice Thurgood Marshall explained that public school employees do not relinquish their ability to speak out as citizens regarding matters of public concern.[42] He observed that

> [t]o the extent that the Illinois Supreme Court's opinion may be read to suggest that teachers may constitutionally be compelled to relinquish the First Amendment rights they would otherwise enjoy as citizens to comment on matters of public interest in connection with the operation of the public schools in which they work, it proceeds on a premise that has been unequivocally rejected in numerous prior decisions of this Court.[43]

On the other hand, however, Justice Marshall emphasized that "it cannot be gainsaid that the State has interests as an employer in regulating the speech of its employees that differ significantly from those it possesses in connection with regulation of the speech of the citizenry in general."[44] Accordingly, "[t]he problem in any case is to arrive at a balance between the interests of the teacher, as a citizen, in commenting upon matters of public concern and the interest of the State, as an employer, in promoting the efficiency of the public services it performs through its employees."[45]

From its inception, the *Pickering* doctrine thus required federal courts to weigh the disruption associated with the continued employment of a whistleblower against the interest of the employee in exercising her First Amendment rights. At least arguably, an important third interest exists and should have been directly factored into the balance – namely, the value of the information that the government employee provides to the body politic. Plainly, the value of information provided by government employees about the operation of a government office varies – particularly with respect to the information's potential relevance to the ability of voters to enforce democratic accountability at the next election.[46] Moreover, the value of information to voters will often correlate positively with the potential disruption that release of the information might cause to the government office about which it relates.[47] Explosive revelations of serious and ongoing wrongdoing will cause more workplace disruption than a complaint about the occasional misuse of a government-owned copier by certain coworkers.[48]

In other words, revelations that do not seriously embarrass the head of a government agency are less likely to be deemed "disruptive" than revelations that lead to criminal investigations or demands for resignations of principal officers within the agency.[49] The *Pickering* test, however, focuses not on the value of the information to the community, but rather on the abstract interest of the employee in exercising her First Amendment rights as a citizen. I do not suggest that an employee's interest in exercising her First Amendment rights should be deemed irrelevant to the analysis – but I would suggest that the importance of the information and the availability of the information (or lack of it) from other sources should also be considered in the decisional matrix used to determine if a government employer may constitutionally fire an employee who engages in whistleblowing activity.

To be sure, Justice Marshall did emphasize the importance and value of having government employees participate in the process of democratic deliberation.[50] In the context of a referendum of school district voters to approve or reject new taxes to support the school district, "free and open debate is vital to informed decision-making by the electorate."[51] Moreover, "[t]eachers are, as a class, the members of a community most likely to have informed and definite opinions as to how funds allotted to the operation of the schools should be spent" and "it is essential that they be able to speak out freely on such questions without fear of retaliatory dismissal."[52] In this regard, one should bear in mind that Marvin Pickering was less a crusading whistleblower than an angry crank; his claims about the school district's policies were poorly informed and, in fact, contained numerous inaccuracies.[53]

This aspect of the *Pickering* majority opinion *hints* at the relevance of information to the body politic as a relevant consideration in affording a government employee who engages in whistleblowing activity protection under the First Amendment. However, the formal balancing test – which weighs a government employee's autonomy interest in speaking out about a matter of public concern against the disruptions that such action might cause going forward in a government workplace – does not take this factor into consideration at all.

Nevertheless, Pickering prevailed because on the facts at bar his speech related to a matter of public concern and did not cause significant workplace disruption.[54] Moreover, he prevailed even though his letter to the editor contained some factual errors. Pickering made the errors in good faith, the board could easily have corrected the public record, if it wished to do so, and Pickering's letter, the inaccuracies notwithstanding, plainly related to a matter of public concern. Critically, however, Pickering's authorship and subsequent publication of the negative letter did not "in any way either impede[] the teacher's proper performance of his daily duties in the classroom or – interfere[] with the regular operation of the schools generally."[55] On these facts, the Supreme Court "conclude[d] that the interest of the school administration in limiting teachers' opportunities to contribute to public debate [was] not significantly greater than its interest in limiting a similar contribution by any member of the general public."[56]

Subsequent cases involving the free speech rights of government employees decided during the Warren and Burger Court eras generally followed *Pickering* and afforded a government employee who spoke out on a matter of public concern

First Amendment protection, provided that the employee's continued presence in the government workplace was not unduly disruptive.[57] To be sure, in *Connick v. Myers*, the Burger Court narrowed *Pickering*'s scope by requiring that the speech at issue relate to a matter of public, rather than private, concern.[58] This decision also defined "public concern" in relatively narrow terms to exclude internal workplace management disputes.[59]

Sheila Myers, an assistant district attorney working in New Orleans, Louisiana, was unhappy with being reassigned within the district attorney's office.[60] After learning of her reassignment, she circulated a questionnaire "concerning internal office affairs."[61] Her survey asked employees about various office personnel policies, including transfers, morale, the lack of a formal grievance committee, confidence in office managers, and "whether employees felt pressured to work in political campaigns."[62] She was promptly fired because the distribution of her survey allegedly caused a "mini-insurrection" within the district attorney's office.[63] After being discharged, Myers brought a federal lawsuit alleging a *Pickering* violation; she prevailed on this claim in the lower federal courts.[64] The Supreme Court granted review and reversed.[65]

The *Connick* Court found that most of the questions on the survey, save for Question 11 on whether office employees felt pressured to work on political campaigns, related to matters of private, rather than public, concern.[66] Writing for the majority, Justice Byron White explained that "*Pickering*, its antecedents, and its progeny lead us to conclude that if Myers's questionnaire cannot be fairly characterized as constituting speech on a matter of public concern, it is unnecessary for us to scrutinize the reasons for her discharge."[67] This result obtained because "[w]hen employee expression cannot be fairly considered as relating to any matter of political, social, or other concern to the community, government officials should enjoy wide latitude in managing their offices, without intrusive oversight by the judiciary in the name of the First Amendment."[68]

The *Connick* majority feared that reading *Pickering* more broadly would turn the First Amendment into a means of seeking routine federal court review of "ordinary dismissals from government service which violate no fixed tenure or applicable statute or regulation."[69] Routine dismissals of government employees wholly unrelated to an employee's speech about a matter of public concern "are not subject to judicial review even if the reasons for the dismissal are alleged to be mistaken or unreasonable."[70]

Justice White strongly argued that speech primarily related to internal employment disputes does not seriously implicate core First Amendment values.[71] He explained that

> when a public employee speaks not as a citizen upon matters of public concern, but instead as an employee upon matters only of personal interest, absent the most unusual circumstances, a federal court is not the appropriate forum in which to

review the wisdom of a personnel decision taken by a public agency allegedly in reaction to the employee's behavior.[72]

Employee speech about a matter of public concern enjoys First Amendment protection, but speech related to a matter of private concern does not. *Connick* sets forth an open-ended test for determining whether a government employee's speech relates to a matter of public or private concern and the relevant considerations include "the content, form, and context of a given statement, as revealed by the whole record."[73]

Even though the *Connick* Court read *Pickering* narrowly and confined its scope of protection to speech that implicates interests beyond the immediate workplace environment, *Connick* did not undercut *Pickering*'s protective force when a government employee's speech squarely related to a matter of public concern. And, the Burger Court was relatively generous in construing speech as relating to a matter of public concern – including, for example, a Mississippi county constable office clerk's declaration, while at work, following the unsuccessful assassination attempt on President Ronald Reagan's life, "If they go for him again, I hope they get him."[74] In fairness to Ms. Ardith McPherson, the office clerk who made the off-color remark, the record clearly established that, if considered in context, her comments plainly related to the Reagan administration's efforts to reduce or wholly eliminate various public assistance programs – rather than her personal support for John Hinckley, Jr.'s effort to murder President Reagan.[75]

It also bears noting that *Rankin v. McPherson*, decided in 1987, is technically a decision from the Rehnquist Court, rather than the Burger Court. However, *Rankin* fits more comfortably with the Warren and Burger Court precedents that permitted government employees to invoke the First Amendment to contest allegedly retaliatory discharges from government employment.[76] By the early 2000s, the Rehnquist Court, with a firm conservative majority in place, proceeded to erode the *Pickering* line of cases by creating ever-broader general exceptions to its application. If the process of democratic deliberation requires information held only by government employees, the First Amendment must provide an effective shield for government employees who choose speech over silence.

4.2 REDUCED PROTECTION FOR GOVERNMENT WORKERS' SPEECH ACTIVITY UNDER THE REHNQUIST AND ROBERTS COURTS

Whatever the limitations and shortcomings of the *Connick/Pickering* doctrine, the Warren and Burger Courts applied the doctrine more generously than did their successors. The Rehnquist and Roberts Courts, although never squarely overruling the *Connick/Pickering* doctrine, moved to strictly cabin its potential scope of application. In so doing, the Rehnquist and Roberts Courts made an already weak framework for protecting government employee speech even less robust. To be sure, the *Connick/Pickering* doctrine affords only a modest degree of protection to government employees who speak within the government workplace. The doctrine's most objectionable feature is the "heckler['s] veto"[77] that it embraces.[78] The protection of government employee speech is *always* contingent on the reaction of other employees within the workplace. If a whistleblower's mere presence in the government office produces significant disruption that impedes the office's work, then the government employer may fire the whistleblowing employee without violating the First Amendment.[79]

Despite the relatively weak protection that the *Connick/Pickering* doctrine confers on government employees, it represented a major improvement from the approach it replaced – namely that the government as an employer enjoys the same freedom of action to fire a troublesome employee that a private employer would enjoy.[80] To state the matter simply, imperfect protection of government employee speech is preferable to no protection of government employee speech; the perfect solution should not be the enemy of the merely good.

The Rehnquist and Roberts Courts have weakened significantly even the modest protection of government employee speech that the *Connick/Pickering* doctrine conveys on government workers. For example, in *Waters v. Churchill*,[81] the Supreme Court held that if a government employer fires an employee based on speech mistakenly attributed to the employee, *Pickering* does not provide any basis for contesting the discharge.[82] Rather than emphasizing the autonomy interests of the speaker and the potential value of a government employee's speech to the process of democratic deliberation, *Waters* emphasizes the importance of the government's managerial interest in maintaining order within government workplaces.[83]

Justice Sandra Day O'Connor, writing for the *Waters* plurality, observed that "practical realities of government employment" require that in "many situations . . . the government must be able to restrict its employees' speech."[84] Moreover, "when an employee counsels her co-workers to do their job in a way with which the public employer disagrees, her managers may tell her to stop, rather than relying on counterspeech."[85] The "practical realities" of supervising government employees permit a government employer to fire an employee based on a mistaken belief that the employee made either an unprotected statement or a disruptive statement about a matter of public concern.[86] This result obtains because "[m]anagement can spend only so much of their time on any one employment decision."[87] In sum, managerial necessities permit government employers to act in good faith, but mistakenly, based on a reasonable belief about an employee engaging in either unprotected or protected-but-disruptive workplace speech.

The Supreme Court further curtailed its protection of government employee speech in *Garcetti v. Ceballos*.[88] In *Garcetti*, Richard Ceballos, a deputy district attorney working in the LA County District Attorney's Office, was subjected to discipline for testifying in open court his belief that a police officer submitted an affidavit in support of a request for a search warrant that contained "serious misrepresentations."[89] Ceballos did this even though his supervisors had decided not to amend or correct the police officer's affidavit in support of the warrant request.[90] Following his testimony, Ceballos claimed that he was reassigned and subjected to other forms of retaliatory action by his government employer.[91]

Writing for the *Garcetti* majority, Justice Anthony M. Kennedy found that even if speech relates to a matter of public concern, a government employee may not claim the protection of the First Amendment if the speech falls within the scope of the employee's work-related duties.[92] He explained that "[a] government entity has broader discretion to restrict speech when it acts in its role as employer, but the restrictions it imposes must be directed at speech that has some potential to affect the entity's operations."[93] Consistent with this view, the *Garcetti* majority held that "when public employees make statements pursuant to their official duties, the employees are not speaking as citizens for First Amendment purposes, and the Constitution does not insulate their communications from employer discipline."[94]

The Supreme Court subsequently limited the scope of *Garcetti* in *Lane v. Franks*,[95] by finding that testimony offered under subpoena does not automatically constitute employment-related speech.[96] Instead, a government employee who offers sworn testimony in a civil or criminal judicial proceeding usually speaks as a "citizen" rather than as an "employee."[97] Moreover, "[t]hat is so even when the testimony relates to his public employment or concerns information learned during that employment."[98] Accordingly, a public university employee who testified about financial irregularities within the university spoke as a citizen, not as an employee, about a matter of public concern – and could therefore claim the benefit of *Pickering*.[99] But *Lane* is hardly a broad repudiation of *Garcetti* – after all, testimony in open court is citizen speech only when it is "outside the scope of his ordinary job duties."[100]

Accordingly, a public employee in a district attorney's office, like Richard Ceballos, whose job includes regular court appearances, would still be speaking as a government employee, rather than as a citizen, when in court. *Lane* certainly cabins *Garcetti*, but it still requires employees who speak out about matters related to their employment to do so at their own peril.[101] Under *Garcetti*, if a government employer fires an employee based on antipathy toward comments regarding a matter of public concern, the employee enjoys no First Amendment protection if the speech arguably falls within the scope of the employee's duties.[102] Moreover, under *Waters*, the same outcome also applies if a government employer disciplines or fires an employee based on the mistaken belief that a particular employee made comments about a matter of public concern that come within the scope of her employment.[103]

Thus, the contemporary Supreme Court has limited quite significantly the constitutional protections available to government employees who wish to call attention to misconduct or inefficiency in government operations.[104] The *Connick/Pickering* doctrine conveyed modest protection – at best – to government employees who engage in whistleblowing speech. But modest protection is better than *no* protection for whistleblowing speech.

In sum, the absence of reliable protection for government employees who engage in whistleblowing speech makes it less likely that the people best able to inform the public about misconduct in public institutions will come forward. The result will be that government officials' bad behavior will go undiscovered and, in consequence, uncorrected. A better approach would link the importance of a government employee's speech and the scope of the First Amendment protection afforded to the speaker.[105] Moreover, enhanced First Amendment protection for whistleblowing speech would neither imply nor require any reduced *Connick/Pickering* protection for government employee speech about a matter of public concern that does not constitute whistleblowing speech.[106]

4.3 THE PARADOX OF CONFERRING COMPREHENSIVE FIRST AMENDMENT PROTECTION AGAINST GOVERNMENT EMPLOYERS RETALIATING AGAINST A GOVERNMENT EMPLOYEE BASED ON THE EMPLOYEE'S PARTISAN AFFILIATION

Professor Robert Post has written lucidly and persuasively about the importance of affording government the ability to manage workplaces to ensure that government offices function efficiently and achieve their objectives.[107] For example, Departments of Motor Vehicles (DMVs) are already widely thought to be highly dysfunctional places;[108] were DMV employees free to engage in speech activity at will, while on the job, DMVs would be even less functional.[109] The problem, however, is distinguishing between legitimate government efforts to manage and supervise government offices and illegitimate efforts to use the accident of government employment to squelch a government employee's speech.

The line is, at best, an ephemeral one. In this regard, Professor Post observes that "the allocation of speech to managerial domains is a question of normative characterization."[110] Yet, if federal courts fail to make serious efforts to maintain meaningful boundaries that cabin effectively the scope of this "managerial domain," government employees can be either silenced or coerced into speech that has nothing to do with the legitimate managerial imperatives of the government as an employer.

An additional paradox exists: Since the 1970s, the Supreme Court has vigorously prohibited punishing government employees based on their partisan affiliations.[111] If an employee does not hold either a policymaking position or have access to confidential information, a government office may not use either the employee's partisan affiliation – or lack of one – as a basis for discharging her.[112] Indeed, since deciding *Elrod v. Burns*,[113] the first case in this line of precedents, the Supreme

Court consistently has expanded this rule's scope of application to encompass even the termination of a contract with a government agency over a business owner's partisan affiliation.[114] In a kind of mirror-image of *Waters v. Churchill*, the Supreme Court has held that the First Amendment disallows a government agency from firing a government employee based on a *mistaken appraisal* of an employee's partisan commitments and associations.[115]

In other words, even if an employee does not actually hold a particular partisan commitment or associational link, a government employer that uses partisan affiliation in error has a chilling effect on the ability of government employees to participate in the political process – a chilling effect[116] that violates the First Amendment.[117] As Justice Stephen G. Breyer explains, "[t]he constitutional harm at issue in the ordinary case consists in large part of discouraging employees – both the employee discharged (or demoted) and his or her colleagues – from engaging in protected activities."[118] Moreover, in terms of a potential chilling effect on the exercise of First Amendment rights, "[t]he discharge of one [employee] tells the others that they engage in protected activity at their peril."[119] This chilling effect simply does not depend on whether the employer accurately perceives the employee's partisan beliefs and commitments – it is the act of punishing an employee based on her political commitments, whether real or imagined, that produces the chilling effect on the exercise of First Amendment rights.[120]

Perhaps most significant, the potential disruption that an employee's partisan affiliation might cause to the smooth operation and managerial efforts of a government agency are quite irrelevant to the proscription against a government employer retaliating against an employee based on her partisan identity. These concerns are included in the Supreme Court's framework – but only in a highly formalized way.[121] The exclusion of positions that involve policymaking or confidential office information reflect a balancing of interests that assumes that for such positions, the government's managerial interests will usually overbear the First Amendment interests of an employee in freedom of speech, association, and assembly.[122]

As Justice John Paul Stevens explained in *Branti*, "the ultimate inquiry is not whether the label 'policymaker' or 'confidential' fits a particular position; rather, the question is whether the hiring authority can demonstrate that party affiliation is an appropriate requirement for the effective performance of the public office involved."[123] In this respect, the *Elrod* line of cases does take some account of the potential for disruption that employing a political opponent of the office's elected supervisor might cause. But, if the position is merely clerical in nature, and does not involve either policymaking duties or processing confidential information, the fact that the person's presence in the office is highly disruptive is entirely irrelevant.[124]

Thus, as *Heffernan* explains, as a general matter, "[w]hen an employer demotes an employee out of a desire to prevent the employee from engaging in political activity that the First Amendment protects, the employee is entitled to challenge that unlawful action under the First Amendment."[125] This result obtains because to permit a government employer to retaliate against an employee – whether based on real or imagined partisan commitments – would "discourag[e] employees – both the employee discharged (or demoted) and his or her colleagues – from engaging in protected activities" because "[t]he discharge of one tells the others that they engage in protected activity at their peril."[126] Moreover, when an employer acts on a mistaken belief in the context of a partisan firing, the First Amendment still confers protection because "[t]he upshot is that a discharge or demotion based upon an employer's belief that the employee has engaged in protected activity can cause the same kind, and degree, of constitutional harm whether that belief does or does not rest upon a factual mistake."[127]

In other words, the potential chilling effect of partisan discharges justifies a broad and almost categorical rule of First Amendment protection. Whatever dysfunction or disruption results from the employee's continued presence in the office is a cost that the First Amendment requires the government employer to bear. Unlike a *Pickering* case involving a government employee who merely speaks out as a citizen about a matter of public concern, the government may not invoke managerial necessities to justify sacking a person who wears the wrong partisan label. Yet, it is quite obvious that the problem of a chilling effect is identical; whether an employee speaks out on a matter of public concern or engages in partisan activity outside the office, other employees will get the message that if they wish to retain their employment, they should avoid attracting negative attention from their elected boss.

The juxtaposition of these lines of precedent is puzzling. The First Amendment prohibits the operation of government workplaces on a spoils system basis; the Supreme Court has held that this kind of retaliatory motive is flatly unconstitutional even if the employee's continued presence proves to be highly disruptive.[128] The *Elrod/Branti* doctrine creates a prophylactic rule that treats partisan antipathy as a constitutionally impermissible basis for adverse employment decisions. By way of contrast, however, the *Pickering/Connick* doctrine permits employers to use potentially pretextual claims of possible workplace disruption as a basis for firing government employees who speak out on matters of public concern.[129]

As the next Part explains in some detail, this differential First Amendment protection of government employees' partisan identities, on the one hand, and public ideological and policy commitments, on the other, is not self-evidently justified. These lines of precedent should – but do not – reflect a great degree of alignment with respect to the relative importance of government employees' First Amendment rights and the managerial imperatives of public employers.

4.4 THE NEED TO PROVIDE ENHANCED PROTECTION TO GOVERNMENT WORKERS WHO FACILITATE DEMOCRATIC ACCOUNTABILITY BY ENGAGING IN WHISTLEBLOWING ACTIVITY

The Supreme Court's *Elrod* line of cases plainly seeks to prevent the government, as an employer, from imposing an unconstitutional condition on its employees – namely, that they refrain from partisan activity that the elected head of the government agency dislikes.[130] Protecting the right of government workers to avoid coerced silence – or coerced partisan activity – is clearly an important, and justifiable, First Amendment objective. After all, Justice Robert Jackson famously posited:

> If there is any fixed star in our constitutional constellation, it is that no official, high or petty, can prescribe what shall be orthodox in politics, nationalism, religion, or other matters of opinion or force citizens to confess by word or act their faith therein. If there are any circumstances which permit an exception, they do not now occur to us.[131]

Consistent with this approach, the mere accident of a citizen holding a position with a government employer should not zero out the application of this constitutional verity.[132] Accordingly, I do not suggest that cases like *Heffernan*, *Branti*, and *Elrod* reach the wrong outcome on the merits – a government employer should not be able to demand partisan loyalty as a condition of employment if the position does not involve either policymaking functions or regular receipt of confidences. However, it does seem exceedingly strange to protect partisan identity in almost absolute terms, and generally without much regard for the potential disruption that will be associated with a person's presence in a government workplace, while permitting a "heckler's veto"[133] in the context of truthful, non-misleading speech about a matter of public concern. Indeed, many public employees probably care much more deeply about particular public policy issues or ideological commitments than they do about their ability to wear their party preference on their sleeves.[134]

In sum, it cannot be gainsaid that the protection of government employees' speech about matters of public concern has waned, rather than expanded, under the Rehnquist and Roberts Courts. Moreover, a strong case can be made that the Warren Court's initial effort to reconcile the managerial imperatives of government employers with the rights of government employees to speak as citizens was insufficiently protective in *Pickering* itself. To the extent that an employee speaks out on a matter involving serious wrongdoing within her government agency, it is more likely rather than less likely that her continued presence will cause disruption in the workplace.

The *Pickering* test thus seems to endorse a de facto heckler's veto: Insubordinate agency employees who are disruptive in the presence of a whistleblower should be subject to discipline. Firing the employee who calls public attention to serious government wrongdoing or misconduct is to punish the wrong party. Yet, this is precisely how the *Connick/Pickering* analysis works.[135] Unruly coworkers who behave badly in the wake of whistleblowing activity provide the government employer with a constitutionally acceptable predicate for firing the worker who called problems within the government agency to the attention of the body politic.[136] In strong contrast with the near absolute protection conveyed on a government employee with respect to her partisan identity and activity, government employees who speak out about matters of public concern risk serious adverse consequences – up to and including potential discharge from their government employment.

On the other hand, however, the Supreme Court has held, repeatedly, that government almost never acts legitimately when it seeks to punish an employee because of the presence, or absence, of a commitment to a particular political party.[137] If an employee does not have policymaking responsibilities or access to confidential information, no matter how potentially disruptive her partisan activities outside the workplace, the government employer must simply absorb these costs. The contrast with the level of protection afforded to employees who choose to speak out about a matter of public concern is both dramatic and, it seems to me, inexplicable.

Simply put, if potential disruption to a government workplace is the evil which justifies a government employer in disciplining or discharging an employee, the precise source of the workplace disruption should be quite irrelevant to the analysis. From a Post "managerial necessity" perspective,[138] keeping a government office functioning should be a sufficient justification either in both cases or in neither case. The better course of action, it seems to me, would be to afford broader and more robust protection to government employees who speak out about a matter of public concern.

Moreover, to date the federal courts have not taken into account the value of information to the public when fixing the precise scope of First Amendment protection to be afforded a government employee's speech. Not all government employee speech has equal worth in the marketplace of ideas. More specifically, not all government employee speech is integral to facilitating government accountability through the electoral process.

For example, Edward Snowden's shocking revelations about massive government domestic spying programs galvanized a broad-based response – both within the government itself and also within the larger political community.[139] Snowden certainly exercised his individual autonomy as a speaker by leaking classified information about PRISM; but his speech also conveyed particularized knowledge that we should care about collectively because it facilitated the citizenry's ability to hold government accountable (or not).[140] In some instances, the efficacy of democratic elections to serve as an effective brake on bad government behavior necessarily rests on information that only a government employee possesses.[141] If we do not effectively protect government employees who share such information with the body politic, then the body politic is far less likely to have access to relevant information about the government and its operations.

Government employee speech that constitutes whistleblowing should be afforded broader constitutional protection under the First Amendment than more generic government employee speech that merely relates to a matter of public concern. The Supreme Court has given a remarkably broad scope to the concept of a "matter of public concern." Precedents like *Snyder v. Phelps*[142] seem to hold that a matter of public concern lies, more or less, in the eye of the beholder.[143]

If Westboro Baptist Church's lunacy[144] comprises speech about a matter of public concern, then virtually *any speech* that relates to any question that implicates, or could implicate, government policy constitutes speech related to a matter of public concern.[145] To state the matter bluntly, if the phrase "God Hates Fags" is speech about a matter of public concern, then what isn't? As I have observed previously,

> the protean nature of the public concern test in the United States essentially makes the press itself the judge of what constitutes reportage of a matter of public concern; courts are highly unlikely to second-guess even a marginally plausible claim that speech relates to a matter of public concern.[146]

As the social cost of protecting speech increases, it becomes correspondingly easier to deem the government's interest in restricting the speech compelling.[147] If everything is speech about a matter of public concern, then government regulations that limit or restrict such speech by government employees will be inevitable. More specifically, if virtually all government employee speech could conceivably relate to a matter of public concern, then the net amount of workplace disruption that such speech could occasion is very high indeed – and potentially crippling to the ability of a government office to function. At the same time, the Supreme Court's strong commitment to respecting a First Amendment that disallows content and viewpoint discrimination[148] makes this liberal approach to defining – or, more aptly, refusing to define – a matter of public concern quite understandable (indeed, even predictable).[149] However, the value of information to the public ought to be part of the constitutional metric that we use to assess how much disruption government must tolerate in order to facilitate government employee speech.[150]

The problem arises because when all speech is deemed equally worthy of First Amendment protection, federal courts are not unlikely to level down the scope of constitutional solicitude that they afford to non-commercial, core political speech.[151] This has happened in other areas of constitutional law, such as the right to a jury trial in criminal cases under the Sixth Amendment.[152] Before the Supreme Court held the Sixth Amendment right to a jury trial incorporated, via the doctrine of substantive due process, against the states,[153] the Sixth Amendment required that a person be convicted of criminal charges by the unanimous vote of a twelve-person jury. In order to accommodate variations in state criminal procedure regarding a petit jury's size and operation, however, the Supreme Court post-*Duncan* quickly permitted the states to allow convictions based on non-unanimous jury votes,[154] and to use a jury comprised of as few as six members.[155] To be sure, the Supreme Court did disallow a jury comprised of only five members.[156] Thus, the Supreme Court's incorporation of the right to a jury trial to state criminal proceedings – in theory broadening the scope of application of the right – had the perverse effect of watering-down the right to a jury trial in federal criminal trials. In sum, as the scope of a right's application expands, it becomes correspondingly easier to justify imposing limits or restrictions on the exercise of that right.[157]

We protect partisan identity in nearly absolute terms in order to avoid the unconstitutional conditions problem that would arise if we permitted government as an employer to cage its employees as citizens.[158] But government employees act no less as citizens when they contribute to the process of democratic deliberation by providing information relevant to the function of elections in securing government accountability. If we assume, with some good cause, that government entities seek to tout good news and suppress bad news, then we need to create sufficient First Amendment breathing room for courageous government employees who choose speech over silence.[159]

First Amendment theory and doctrine should be sufficiently supple to take account of this important contextual consideration.[160] Government employee speech certainly implicates the individual autonomy interest of the government employee as a citizen and speaker; but government employee speech also has important value to its audience when the content relates to official wrongdoing, inefficiency, or misconduct.[161] To state the matter simply, whistleblowing speech is not merely a private good, but also constitutes a public good, and First Amendment doctrine should reflect this fact; we should encourage civic courage in such circumstances by effectively protecting it against targeted forms of retaliation.[162]

Like radically unpopular dissenters in periods of perceived national crisis, government workers who engage in whistleblowing speech risk swift and sure retributive action by their employer and coworkers alike; accordingly, the doctrinal standards applied under the First Amendment to such speech must be more robust and constrain judicial discretion more effectively than the current *Pickering/ Connick* doctrine.[163] My proposal to afford whistleblowing speech targeted First Amendment protection simply seeks to apply Professor Vince Blasi's "pathological perspective" approach in the context of government employee speech integral to the process of democratic self-government.[164]

Accordingly, the Supreme Court should adopt a kind of modified Hand formula[165] to govern the analysis of whistleblowing speech by a government employee. Speech that facilitates securing government accountability through the electoral process has social value not merely because of the speaker's autonomy interest in speaking, but also because of the importance of the information to the electoral process and the associated democratic deliberation that informs it. It would not require much of an extension of existing doctrine to carve out a separate category of employee speech, namely "whistleblowing speech," that would be eligible for more robust protection under the First Amendment than more generic government employee speech related to a matter of public concern.

One might object that the protection of whistleblowers is a matter for Congress and state legislatures to consider and decide. It is certainly true that the federal government and most state governments afford statutory protection to at least some forms of whistleblowing activity by government employees.[166] But these statutes often contain serious gaps and omissions.[167] More often than not, an employee who engages in whistleblowing speech will quickly find herself standing in the unemployment line.[168] If I am correct to posit that whistleblowing speech has a particularized and identifiable social value, because of its ability to facilitate government accountability through the democratic process, then the scope of its protection should not be solely a matter of legislative grace.

In fact, the same potential objection could be leveled at the Supreme Court's use of the First Amendment to constitutionalize civil service protections and, in so doing, protect government employees from retaliation for partisan activity (or the lack of it). The existence of the Hatch Act,[169] and similar state laws, did not prevent or deter the Justices from applying the First Amendment vigorously to protect government employees from being compelled to engage – or to refrain from engaging – in partisan activity.[170]

In fact, Justice William J. Brennan, Jr.'s *Elrod* opinion relies directly on the existence of civil service protections to support the conclusion that the First Amendment generally disallows the creation and maintenance of a partisan spoils system.[171] Rather than giving preemptive effect to federal and state civil service laws, the *Elrod* Court cited the existence of such laws to help establish the illegitimacy of patronage systems.[172] Under the same analytical logic, the existence of laws conveying limited protection on whistleblowers should support, rather than undermine, the creation of a constitutional privilege, grounded in the First Amendment's Free Speech Clause, that shields whistleblowers from retaliation by their public employers.

Provided that speech occurs outside the workplace (as Pickering's did), there is little that separates partisan activity/speech and citizen speech related to democratic accountability. If anything, speech that facilitates democratic accountability is more important to the process of democratic self-government than partisan activity or speech by government employees. Non-government employees can engage in partisan activity; it is not essential to have government employees engaged as partisan agents for political parties to function – but it is arguably necessary to remove politics from the operation of the civil service in order for it to function.[173] By way of contrast, voters must have information that only government employees can provide in order to cast well-informed ballots on election day. If elections are to function as an effective means of securing democratic accountability from the government, then the electorate must have accurate, truthful information about areas in which the government's efforts are falling short of the relevant mark.[174]

4.5 CONCLUSION

Existing First Amendment theory and practice underprotects government employee speech in general and grossly underprotects whistleblowing speech by government employees. The *Connick/Pickering* doctrine leaves the protected status of a government employee's speech largely, if not entirely, in the hands of their coworkers and supervisors. If a government employee engages in highly unpopular speech, the *Connick/Pickering* doctrine authorizes government workplace managers to invoke a heckler's veto as a basis for dismissing the troublesome employee – even though, viewed from a different vantage point, the insubordination of the speaker's coworkers might present a better (stronger) case for discipline. Given that the First Amendment, as a general matter, prohibits viewpoint discrimination,[175] it is unfortunate that government employee speech is essentially subject to viewpoint-based regulation in the guise of a balancing test. Government employees, as citizen-speakers, merit more robust protection for their autonomy as speakers.

Of course, some protection as a citizen-speaker is better than no protection. The Warren and Burger Courts deployed the First Amendment to convey modest protection on government employee speech under a test that favors the government as a manager over the government employee as a speaker and citizen. Whatever the shortcomings of the *Connick/Pickering* test prior to the Rehnquist and Roberts Courts, the most recent decisions on the speech rights of government employees have exacerbated, rather than reduced, them. Allowing a government employer to fire an employee based on misattributed speech – or even speech that did not happen – hardly protects the government employee as a citizen-speaker.[176] Nor does denying protection to government workers who speak on a matter of public concern within the context of their employment duties.[177] The Rehnquist and Roberts Courts took an already weak doctrinal framework for protecting government employee speech and rendered it even less protective.[178] Thus, in this important context, First Amendment rights have contracted, rather than expanded, over time.[179]

To be sure, some government employee speech contributes little, perhaps nothing, to the process of democratic deliberation. Nevertheless, it should be protected because government employees do not lose their status as citizens and voters simply because they work for the state. Like other citizens who do not hold government employment, government employees have a right to participate in the process of democratic deliberation; this autonomy interest certainly merits First Amendment protection. However, a subset of government employee speech, whistleblowing speech, possesses an essential nexus to the electoral process's core function of holding government accountable to the electorate for its actions. The failure of the federal courts to take into account this critically important informational value of whistleblowing speech constitutes a major failure of judicial vision (if not judicial courage).

In sum, the Supreme Court has failed to recognize and incorporate an important First Amendment value in the context of government employee speech: the clear relationship of government employee speech to holding government accountable through the democratic process. In many circumstances, relevant information about government misconduct will be known only by government employees. Accordingly, if government employees do not speak, the information simply will not come to the attention of the electorate, and government accountability to the people will be impeded as a result. If one of the principal animating purposes of the First Amendment is to facilitate the process of democratic deliberation,[180] precisely to facilitate the ability of ordinary citizens to enforce government accountability, then stronger constitutional medicine is clearly needed.[181] First Amendment theory and doctrine can and should take account of these values by conveying targeted and robust protection to whistleblowing speech by government employees.

5

Shedding Their Constitutional Rights at the Schoolhouse Gate

The Decline of Freedom of Speech for Students and Teachers in the Nation's Public Schools, Colleges, and Universities

Under existing Supreme Court precedents, and as Professor Peter Byrne observes, "[t]he First Amendment protects academic freedom."[1] The argument in favor of recognizing academic freedom in the context of a government-sponsored college or university is relatively easy to make.[2] The case for academic freedom in K-12 public schools is considerably more complicated because government historically has exercised very broad authority over the curriculum in the public schools (notably including specific learning requirements for promotion and graduation). Moreover, the notion that public school teachers and students can exercise substantial autonomy as speakers in the context of curricular activities exists in substantial tension with the traditional powers of the state governments to regulate comprehensively the public schools.[3]

The Warren Court first recognized academic freedom in the college and university context – and then extended this protection to the public school context. Although it did not expand on these precedents, the Burger Court did not resile from them.[4] The Rehnquist and Roberts Courts, however, have significantly reduced the scope of First Amendment protection available to faculty and students alike in the nation's public schools, colleges, and universities.[5]

In *Tinker v. Des Moines Independent Community School District*, Justice Abe Fortas famously observed that "It can hardly be argued that either students or teachers shed their constitutional rights to freedom of speech or expression at the schoolhouse gate."[6] Although Justice Fortas asserted that "[t]his has been the unmistakable holding of this Court for almost 50 years,"[7] in point of fact *Tinker* broke important new First Amendment ground by bringing the First Amendment into the nation's K-12 public schools. Of course, to say that *Tinker* was novel is not to say that it was wrongly decided. On the contrary, the decision constitutes a robust, and entirely plausible, view of the First Amendment – an ungrudging vindication of the speech rights of public school students and their teachers.

The Supreme Court previously had recognized that parents enjoy substantial autonomy in directing their children's education[8] and also that students possess a right to be free from compelled political speech in the public schools.[9] *Tinker's* recognition of a general right to freedom of speech for students while on campus, however, went well beyond these prior, more limited precedents and established that school children have constitutionally protected autonomy as speakers under the First Amendment. In this respect, *Tinker* significantly broadened the scope of the First Amendment's application to a context in which government previously had enjoyed a relatively free hand to regulate speech by students and teachers alike.

By way of contrast, the Supreme Court had clearly recognized academic freedom in the college and university context prior to its 1969 decision in *Tinker*. In 1957, the Warren Court held that faculty members at state-sponsored colleges and universities enjoy a right of academic freedom as a penumbra of the Free Speech Clause of the First Amendment.[10] The Supreme Court restated and reaffirmed that principle in 1967.[11]

Times have changed since the days of the Warren and Burger Courts. Two trends have significantly reduced the scope of expressive freedom in the nation's public schools, colleges, and universities. The first relates to a cultural shift within the institutions themselves – motivated by benign reasons related to checking bullying, harassment, and targeted forms of discrimination, educational institutions have adopted comprehensive antidiscrimination policies that restrict freedom of expression both on and off campus.[12] As one commentator observes, "American college campuses have become the focus of increasing public unrest as the arrival of provocative speakers sparks violent protests, political debates unsettle classrooms, and designated free-speech zones and codes threaten the concept of free and unfettered speech."[13]

In addition, federal and state courts have declined to extend and thereby expand the scope of Warren Court decisions like *Tinker* and *Keyishian*. Thus, educational institutions regulate speech on campus more comprehensively now than they did forty or fifty years ago and federal and state courts are less inclined to second guess policies aimed at providing a safe and secure learning environment.

With respect to the first trend, public universities regulate speech and protest on campus much more heavily today than was the case a few decades ago – during the era of massive Vietnam War and civil rights protests. Evidence also suggests that academic freedom is less robust now than it was during the Red Scare years.[14] Public universities generally defended faculty alleged to subscribe to Marxist or Socialist ideologies in the McCarthy years, but today professors, like Gene Nichol at the University of North Carolina School of Law, who speak out on issues of public concern can and often do face retaliation (both personally and with respect to their institutions as a whole).[15] In addition, in response to student demands to be protected from offensive and hurtful expression while on campus, an increasing number of public colleges and universities have adopted "bureaucratic solutions, such as safe spaces, speech codes, and free-speech zones."[16]

When university administrators elect to vindicate First Amendment values by making it possible for radically unpopular speakers to appear on campus, they often face extraordinary – and unbudgeted – security expenses.[17] In 2017, the University of

California, Berkeley, spent more than $2 million for security at special events; the University of Florida incurred an expense of over $500,000 for security at a single campus event featuring white nationalist Richard Spencer.[18] These exorbitant costs have pressured the nation's colleges and universities to balance free speech rights, campus security, and cost in order "to come up with a consistent answer to requests to speak."[19] It should not come as a surprise that many universities, including the Ohio State University, the University of California, Berkeley, and Texas A & M University, have actively considered adopting more restrictive campus speaker policies.

Students also have been subjected to discipline for exercising their First Amendment rights. For example, President David Boren, at the University of Oklahoma, summarily expelled undergraduate students who led a racist sing-along event on a bus to an off-campus fraternity event – apparently without any sort of formal hearing or process.[20] So too, the University of South Carolina has expelled a student for writing a racist epithet on a white board in a university library conference room and then posting a picture to the social media platform Snapchat.[21] And, a contretemps arose at the University of Michigan regarding a screening of *American Sniper* – with the screening being canceled and then rescheduled.[22] Although anecdotes are not a data set, the commitment of public colleges and universities to protect vigorously unpopular or controversial speech by students, faculty, and staff seems to be on the decline.

This brings us to the second important trend under the Roberts and Rehnquist Courts: To date, the federal courts' response has been, at best, tepid. Despite regulatory creep, the federal courts have not responded reliably to protect students' speech rights not only while on campus, but off campus as well if the speech in question targets an audience comprised of students, faculty, or staff members.[23] At the K-12 level, a broad-based movement exists to encourage state governments to ban the use of social media by students if posts to sites like Facebook would upset or "torment" school teachers or administrators. (This is direct language from a model statute that has been proposed in several states.) These laws are so broadly written that even fair public criticism of a teacher or school administrator could be the basis of *criminal* proceedings against juvenile offenders or their parents.

In sum, the Supreme Court has been less than vigilant in protecting student speech rights since its landmark decision in *Tinker* and the lower federal courts have issued conflicting decisions regarding the scope of student speech rights outside the classroom.[24] Although the ability of school administrators and teachers to maintain good order and discipline in our public schools undoubtedly constitutes a pressing and important government objective – perhaps even a "compelling" government interest – the legitimate pedagogical goals and objectives of public school officials cannot serve as a blank check that justifies any and all forms of censorship of student speakers, both on and off campus.[25]

The Warren and Burger Courts were, in general, more aggressive in requiring university and public school administrators to tolerate risk in order to facilitate speech than the Roberts and Rehnquist Courts. In this, the contemporary Supreme Court is more tolerant of speech regulations on campus than its predecessors. Moreover, this comprises part of a larger overall trend: Government enjoys a relatively freer hand today than in the past to leverage its control over public resources and institutions as a basis for regulating speech.[26] Because students and faculty require a government boon – an association with a public school, college, or university – they may be required to observe limitations on the scope of their speech rights not only when on campus, but off campus as well.[27]

This chapter will proceed to consider the scope and vibrancy of speech rights in public colleges and universities and also in the nation's primary and secondary schools. Because the Supreme Court initially recognized academic freedom in the context of public colleges and universities, Part 5.1 considers how the Warren and Burger Courts brought the Free Speech Clause of the First Amendment to bear to protect the academic freedom of professors and, to a lesser extent, their students. Part 5.2 then examines the First Amendment rights of teachers and students in the nation's public schools. Part 5.3 argues that social and cultural trends have created considerable pressure on public school and university administrators to regulate speech both on and off campus to advance concerns rooted in diversity, multi-culturalism, and in avoiding violence on the nation's campuses. To date, the federal courts have responded cautiously to these developments, leaving speech rights on campus less protected than was the case under the Warren and Burger Courts. Part 5.4 offers a brief overview of my main arguments and a conclusion.

I do not argue that the concerns that have led public school and university administrators to regulate speech on campus more aggressively today than in times past are facially illegitimate – or that the First Amendment should render government powerless to advance these objectives. Even if one views these objectives as sufficiently weighty to justify serious incursions into the scope and vibrancy of speech rights enjoyed by faculty and students, the fact remains that speech rights on the nation's campuses are more circumscribed now than they were thirty or forty years ago. Simply put, public school and university officials are less reticent to assert their regulatory authority and courts are more deferential to such regulatory efforts.[28] That said, the federal courts should be more aggressive in requiring administrators to demonstrate that speech regulations, particularly regulations applicable to off-campus speech activity, are necessary in order to avoid disruption; merely theoretical or abstract fears that "there could be trouble" should not serve as a constitutionally sufficient basis for proscribing students' and faculty members' speech.[29]

5.1 THE FIRST AMENDMENT AS A GUARANTOR OF ACADEMIC FREEDOM IN PUBLIC COLLEGES AND UNIVERSITIES

Since the 1950s, the Supreme Court has recognized that the First Amendment secures academic freedom to faculty members at state-supported colleges and universities as a penumbral First Amendment right. Although Justice Felix Frankfurter wrote a concurring opinion that broadly recognized academic freedom in the university context that predates the Warren Court by two years,[30] the principle that academic freedom enjoys robust First Amendment protection came into full flower under the Warren Court. The Supreme Court first endorsed First Amendment protection for college and university professors in 1957[31] and reiterated and reaffirmed this principle two years later.[32] Accordingly, by the late 1950s, the notion that the First Amendment protects academic freedom for university professors had been firmly established.[33]

However, *Keyishian v. Board of Regents*, decided in 1967, contains the Warren Court's broadest endorsement of academic freedom. *Keyisihian*, like *Sweezy* and *Barenblatt*, involved an anti-communist enactment, the Feinberg Law, as amended, which required a loyalty oath coupled with a promise to abstain from teaching the doctrines of Marxism and Leninism.[34] More specifically, the Feinberg Law, as implemented by the Board of Regents for New York's public colleges and universities, required professors working at state-sponsored colleges and universities to represent under oath that they were not members of the Communist Party and did not advocate its doctrines.[35] Professor Byrne explains that "[t]he Court read certain sections of the law outlawing advocacy of forceful overthrow of the government to embrace potentially sympathetic classroom treatment of Marxist or other revolutionary works or ideas."[36] The Supreme Court's earlier decisions involved loyalty oaths that presumed guilt by association with organizations deemed "subversive" by the federal or state governments; *Keyishian*, by way of contrast, involved extending constitutional protection to the teaching of the abstract need for violent revolution.

Writing for the majority, Justice William J. Brennan, Jr., observed that "Our Nation is deeply committed to safeguarding academic freedom, which is of transcendent value to all of us and not merely to the teachers concerned. That freedom is therefore a special concern of the First Amendment, which does not tolerate laws that cast a pall of orthodoxy over the classroom."[37] Applying these principles to the facts at bar, the *Keyishian* majority invalidated the ban on teaching Marxism and Leninism and also invalidated the ban against employing faculty members who were members of the Communist Party.[38] Unlike *Sweezy* and *Barenblatt*, however, *Keyishian* badly divided the Justices, and was decided on a 5–4 vote.

Justice Brennan's rejection of the Feinberg Law represents the high watermark for judicial protection of academic freedom. To be sure, the Supreme Court has not resiled from *Keyishian*, *Barenblatt*, and *Sweezy*. The erosion of protection for academic freedom in the contemporary United States has more to do with university practices that do not, strictly speaking, seek to punish academics for their speech but rather use other, constitutionally permissible policies to discipline or fire academics who prove troublesome. In this sense, then, the diminution of academic freedom in the college and university context has not been because of subsequent judicial decisions that have reversed or limited the relevant Warren Court precedents, but rather because of a failure to expand on them to ferret out pretextual uses of otherwise-constitutional university policies.

The line of precedent ending in *Keyishian* constitutes an important extension of First Amendment protections to academic endeavors by public college and university professors. As Professor Byrne explains, "[d]espite their analytical shortcomings, *Sweezy* and *Keyishian* contributed substantially to the virtual extinction of *overt* efforts by non-academic government officials to prescribe political orthodoxy in university teaching and research."[39] He also posits, however, that "[t]he Court has been far more generous in its praise of academic freedom than in providing a precise analysis of its meaning."[40] Thus, "[a] gross imbalance between encomium and rule suggests an extreme reluctance by or difficulty for a court to find any particular practice to be a violation of academic freedom."[41]

For example, controversial university professors, like Ward Churchill, are almost never fired because of their scholarly writings or lectures.[42] Instead, academic activity that gives rise to sustained and intense negative publicity more often than not will lead to a careful and comprehensive review of the employee's behavior more generally; if the university discovers that its troublesome professor has engaged in activity that violates the terms of his employment, the violation of university policies will serve as the formal predicate for the discharge.[43] Thus, and as Byrne explains, "[e]ven when courts agree in principle that a teacher's behavior is constitutionally protected, they often find that antagonism to the protected behavior was not the effective motivation for a teacher's dismissal."[44]

As a general rule, if an employer can establish that it would have legal cause to fire an employee based on evidence discovered after an employee files a complaint, for example alleging age or sex discrimination, the employer can avoid an order requiring either front pay or reinstatement.[45] Even though the evidence would not have been discovered absent the retaliatory motive, the Supreme Court has held that "[t]he employee's wrongdoing must be taken into account ... lest the employer's legitimate concerns be ignored."[46] This approach takes "due account of the lawful prerogatives of the employer in the usual course of its business and the corresponding equities that it has arising from the employee's wrongdoing."[47]

Thus, even if the review that leads to the discovery of the evidence used to justify discharge is motivated by antipathy toward a faculty member's exercise of her academic freedom, after-acquired evidence can serve as a basis for denying front pay and reinstatement and for limiting damages for back pay to the point at which the university employer discovers the information that justifies the discharge.[48] Thus, "[o]nce an employer learns about employee wrongdoing that would lead to a legitimate discharge, we cannot require the employer to ignore the information, even if it is acquired during the course of discovery in a suit against the employer and even if the information might have gone undiscovered absent the suit."[49]

The employer does have to shoulder the burden of persuasion with respect to whether the misconduct constitutes a firing offense. Accordingly, "[w]here an employer seeks to rely upon after-acquired evidence of wrongdoing, it must first establish that the wrongdoing was of such severity that the employee in fact would have been terminated on those grounds alone if the employer had known of it at the time of the discharge."[50]

When one applies the principles of *Nashville Banner Publishing Co.* in the context of discipline or dismissal of a faculty member at a state-sponsored institution of higher learning, the inherent weakness of the *Keyishian/Barenblatt/Sweezy* line of precedent comes into very clear focus. Even though the state cannot directly regulate a professor's reading list or lecture notes,[51] the university, as an employer, may attempt to find a constitutionally permissible basis for discipline or discharge if a faculty member draws unwanted attention to herself and her home institution.[52] Thus, and as Professor Katheryn Katz observes, "[p]rofessors are not immune from suffering the unfavorable consequences of their speech."[53] An academic will prevail in resisting discharge based on after-acquired evidence "only if the court finds that 'but for' the protected activity, the employee would not have been removed."[54]

Provided that the misconduct would, as a general matter, justify discipline or discharge, the university may dismiss the employee – again, not for exercising her constitutionally-protected right to academic freedom, but because of the misconduct discovered incident to a general investigation of the employee's background and actions while serving on the public college's or university's faculty. In sum, the scope of protection afforded academic freedom can be astonishingly narrow – if antipathy toward the employee's exercise of her First Amendment rights serves as the "but for" cause of the review of the professor's activities, then the evidence adduced would not have existed absent a bad motive on the part of the university employer.

Other kinds of retaliation are also available and, in the main, perfectly constitutional. When Gene R. Nichol, a University of North Carolina law professor, wrote a series of highly critical editorials making unflattering comparisons between the incumbent governor, Pat McCrory, and racist Southern governors during Jim Crow, the state legislature responded by pressuring the university's board of regents to abolish the Center on Poverty, Work, and Opportunity, a privately-funded center on poverty law and policy based at UNC's law school that Professor Nichol helmed.[55] In addition, not entirely satisfied with abolishing Nichol's center, the legislature also imposed a punitive $3 million cut to the law school's annual appropriation. Even though hostility to the exercise of Professor Nichol's academic freedom clearly motivated both the board's action and the legislature's action, the Supreme Court's academic freedom precedents would not have provided a sound basis for seeking judicial relief.

A cynical person might even posit that the First Amendment merely prohibits any prior restraints against college and university professors teaching or advocating ideas that they find professionally appropriate or, in the alternative, commandeering a professor's syllabus as a means of disseminating the state's preferred point of view on controversial subjects like abortion, same-sex marriage, or drug policy. However, existing First Amendment doctrine does relatively little to protect faculty members from subsequent retaliatory government actions involving their employment status or funding for their subdivision of the college or university.[56] The Supreme Court's existing jurisprudence protects against direct assaults on academic freedom – but not all actions that constitute adverse reactions to unpopular faculty writing or speaking.

A recent case involving the speech rights of government employees who speak out about a matter of public concern as part of their official duties adds further uncertainty about the current status of academic freedom in public colleges and universities. Under *Garcetti v. Ceballos*, it is not clear that speech undertaken in the context of a university/professor employment relationship enjoys *any* targeted First Amendment protection.[57] As noted earlier in Chapter 4,[58] *Garcetti* holds that the First Amendment does not protect a government employee who speaks out about a matter of public concern if the employee's speech constitutes part of her official employment duties.[59]

Justice Anthony M. Kennedy, writing for the *Garcetti* majority, did observe that "[t]here is some argument that expression related to academic scholarship or classroom instruction implicates additional constitutional interests that are not fully accounted for by this Court's customary employee-speech jurisprudence."[60] Accordingly, the majority did not "decide whether the analysis we conduct today would apply in the same manner to a case involving speech related to scholarship or teaching."[61] Application of the *Garcetti* rule to faculty members at institutions of higher learning would have the effect of stripping their academic teaching and writing of any meaningful First Amendment protection.[62]

Indeed, some lower federal courts quickly held that *Garcetti* governs the speech of public school teachers hired to provide particular kinds of instruction. Writing in 2007, a year after the Supreme Court decided *Garcetti*, Chief Judge Frank Easterbrook, of the US Court of Appeals for the Seventh Circuit, explained that "[e]xpression is a teacher's stock in trade, the commodity she sells to her employer in exchange for a salary"[63] and, accordingly, a school system "does not 'regulate' teachers' speech as much as it *hires* that speech."[64] In fact, Judge Easterbrook argues that "[c]hildren who attend school because they must ought not be subject to teachers' idiosyncratic perspectives."[65]

To be sure, Judge Easterbrook notes that "[h]ow much room is left for constitutional protection of scholarly viewpoints in post-secondary education was left open in *Garcetti* ... and need not be resolved today."[66] So too, out-of-the classroom writings and publications might not come under the *Garcetti* rule.[67] However, with these limited caveats, the *Mayer* panel held that "the first amendment does not entitle primary and secondary teachers, when conducting the education of captive audiences, to cover topics, or advocate viewpoints, that depart from the curriculum adopted by the school system."[68]

The logic of this reasoning would easily extend to the classroom duties of a college or university professor.[69] Moreover, a larger, important question arises: Does academic freedom protect the university as an *institution* or, rather, an *individual faculty member* teaching and pursuing research at a public university?[70] Professor Katz explains that "[w]hile there is federal protection against interference with classroom speech by governmental bodies external to the institution, the institution itself can impose and enforce restraints almost at will."[71] In light of this fact, the scope of an individual faculty member's academic freedom vis á vis her employer, a public college or university, "is extremely limited in scope."[72]

Consistent with these principles, the lower federal courts generally have held that a college or university enjoys substantial control over the curriculum and course coverage questions.[73] In consequence, the application or non-application of *Garcetti* will answer one important question, namely, do instructors at public schools, colleges, and universities continue to enjoy a First Amendment interest in academic freedom while teaching in the classroom? However, even if the federal courts resolve this question in favor of the continuing validity of *Keyishian* and *Sweezy*, this simply kicks the can down the road to the rules that will govern competing invocations of academic freedom by institutions of higher learning and individual faculty members.[74]

Regardless of how the conflict between institutional and personal claims to academic freedom are resolved, the *Garcetti* majority's failure to address directly and forthrightly the application of the government employee speech doctrine to faculty at public colleges and universities provides concrete evidence of how speech rights on campus have declined, rather than expanded, over time. By failing to decide whether the Supreme Court's prior academic freedom precedents survived the development and growth of the government employee speech doctrine, the Supreme Court introduced unnecessary ambiguity in an area where ambiguity has a predictable and serious chilling effect on speech. Failing to expand the baseline established in decisions like *Keyishian*, *Barenblatt*, and *Sweezy* is one thing – but inviting government employers to directly regulate faculty speech undertaken as part of a faculty member's official duties represents not merely a failure to expand the speech rights of faculty members, but a clear contraction of those rights.

5.2 ONE STEP FORWARD, TWO STEPS BACK: THE SUPREME COURT'S JURISPRUDENTIAL EFFORTS TO EXTEND ACADEMIC FREEDOM PRINCIPLES TO PRIMARY, MIDDLE, AND SECONDARY PUBLIC SCHOOLS

The Warren Court pioneered general First Amendment protection for public school students while on campus. Although earlier precedents recognized a right to be free from coerced political speech in the public schools, to seek instruction in a foreign language, and to enroll in a parochial or otherwise religiously-identified K-12 school rather than a public school, it was not until 1969, and the *Tinker* decision, that the Supreme Court recognized that public school students possess a general right to freedom of speech during the school day.

The Supreme Court's decision in *Tinker* constitutes the Supreme Court's boldest and broadest vindication of student speech rights while on campus.[75] In *Tinker*, a 7–2 majority recognized the constitutional right of middle and high school students to protest the Vietnam War by wearing black armbands while on campus during regular school hours. Justice Fortas, writing for the majority, explained that "[s]chool officials do not possess absolute authority over their students."[76] Unless school authorities can establish that student speech activity on a public school campus presents a credible risk of "substantial disruption of or material interference with school activities,"[77] students in the nation's public schools "are entitled to freedom of expression of their views."[78] On the facts at bar, the wearing of black armbands at Des Moines, Iowa, public schools did not cause material disruptions to the academic program; in consequence, "our Constitution does not permit officials of the State to deny their form of expression."[79]

The Burger Court, however, quickly created important exceptions and limitations to the potentially broad *Tinker* rule. In *Bethel School District No. 403 v. Fraser*,[80] the Supreme Court declined to apply *Tinker* to a ribald nominating speech in support of a candidate for student government office. Like *Tinker*, *Fraser* was a 7–2 decision. Chief Justice Warren E. Burger emphasized that ribald, or arguably indecent, speech in public schools stood on different First Amendment ground from core political speech. He posited that a "marked distinction" existed "between the political 'message' of the armbands in *Tinker* and the sexual content of [Fraser's] speech in this case."[81]

According to Chief Justice Burger, Matthew Fraser's nominating speech violated viewpoint-neutral school rules aimed at proscribing inappropriate content from school-sanctioned curricular activities. He explained that "[t]he First Amendment does not prevent the school officials from determining that to permit a vulgar and lewd speech such as respondent's would undermine the school's basic educational mission."[82] *Tinker* notwithstanding, "it was perfectly appropriate for the school to disassociate itself to make the point to the pupils that vulgar speech and lewd conduct is wholly inconsistent with the 'fundamental values' of public school education."[83] After *Fraser*, school officials may regulate lewd speech on campus – and the decision broadly hints that school authorities enjoy wide discretion to regulate speech related to the curriculum and curricular activities.

Under the Rehnquist Court, the Supreme Court made explicit the implied authority of school officials over all things curricular in *Hazelwood School District v. Kuhlmeier*.[84] *Kuhlmeier* further limits *Tinker's* scope of application, squarely holding that the First Amendment does not prohibit public school authorities from exercising wide discretion over the curriculum – including even the power to censor a high school student newspaper.[85] Writing for the 6–3 majority, Justice Byron White opined that public school officials are "entitled to regulate the contents of [a high school newspaper] in any reasonable manner."[86] With respect to curricular speech, public school educators and administrators may regulate "student expression to assure that participants learn whatever lessons the activity is designed to teach, that readers or listeners are not exposed to material that may be inappropriate for their level of maturity, and that the views of the individual speaker are not erroneously attributed to the school."[87] Consistent with these principles, the *Kuhlmeier* Court held that "educators do not offend the First Amendment by exercising editorial control over the style and content of student speech in school-sponsored expressive activities so long as their actions are related to legitimate pedagogical concerns."[88]

The *Kuhlmeier* test is obviously almost toothless; it is a test of mere reasonableness (or rationality), not a form of strict or even heightened scrutiny. Provided that school officials can proffer *any* credible reason for censoring student speech that occurs in the context of the curriculum, a First Amendment claim challenging a school district's censorship will fail. In conjunction with *Fraser*, *Kuhlmeier* extends the censorial powers of public school teachers and administrators. Moreover, *Tinker* itself vests broad discretion in school officials to censor non-curricular speech, that is not lewd or indecent, provided that the school authorities can make a plausible case that the student's speech would be disruptive to school operations.

The Roberts Court continued the Supreme Court's project of limiting, but not overruling, *Tinker* by extending the authority of public school authorities to regulate off-campus speech if it is arguably related to a school-sponsored activity. Joseph Frederick, a high school student enrolled in a public school in Juneau, Alaska, attended the Olympic Torch Relay on January 24, 2002, in downtown Juneau, Alaska. Frederick, along with a group of classmates, unfurled a banner bearing the message "BONG HiTS 4 JESUS" while standing on a sidewalk across the street from the high school building.[89] The school's principal, Deborah Morse, demanded the banner be taken down and confiscated it; she subsequently suspended Frederick for ten days for displaying it.[90] Frederick challenged his suspension and discipline, arguing that the school district had violated his First Amendment right to freedom of expression. The trial court found for the school district, but the US Court of Appeals for the Ninth Circuit reversed, finding that the school district failed to show a risk of substantial disruption to the school's operations (as required under *Tinker*).[91]

The Supreme Court reversed the Ninth Circuit's decision, holding that "the school officials in this case did not violate the First Amendment by confiscating the pro-drug banner and suspending the student responsible for it."[92] The majority opinion, written by Chief Justice John G. Roberts, Jr., characterized the torch relay as a school sanctioned event that took place "during normal school hours."[93] It is doubtful that the school authorities could constitutionally have sought to censor

Frederick's speech or punish him for advocating marijuana use from his personal laptop at home (if that is, indeed, what the nonsense message actually did). By characterizing the speech as having clear curricular characteristics, Roberts arguably brought the case within the ambit of *Fraser* and *Kuhlmeier*. However, Frederick's expressive activity was quite clearly not part of the formal educational curriculum in the high school, did not take place on public school grounds, and would not have been attributed to the high school or the school district by a reasonable observer. Even so, the majority concluded that Frederick's speech was curricular in nature.[94]

Chief Justice Roberts characterized Frederick's speech as "speech reasonably viewed as promoting illegal drug use,"[95] reasoning that "the government interest in stopping student drug use ... allow[s] schools to restrict student expression that they reasonably regard as promoting illegal drug use."[96] Unlike the abstract fear of disruption in *Tinker*, "[t]he danger here is far more serious and palpable"[97] and "the First Amendment does not require schools to tolerate at school events student expression that contributes to those dangers."[98] *Morse*, to use the language of Justice Clarence Thomas's concurring opinion, "add[s] to the patchwork of exceptions to the *Tinker* standard,"[99] without actually overruling *Tinker*.

The arc of the Supreme Court's protection of student speech in the nation's public schools is easy to make out. After the Warren Court provided limited protection to non-disruptive student speech on campus in *Tinker*, the Burger, Rehnquist, and Roberts Courts proceeded to limit *Tinker's* potential scope of application by creating categorical exclusions for curricular speech, lewd or indecent speech, and speech advocating the use of illegal drugs. Moreover, *Tinker* itself did not provide particularly robust protection for student speech – and even that decision has been limited to non-curricular speech.

It bears noting that immediately after the Supreme Court decided *Tinker*, some lower federal courts held that high school *teachers* possess a limited scope of academic freedom to make pedagogical choices within the prescribed public school curriculum.[100] To be clear, these decisions certainly recognized that the school district possessed the constitutional authority to determine the subject matter to be taught and even the lesson plan to be used – but the ability to define the curricular objectives did not necessarily extend to regulating the precise means an instructor would use to achieve them. As Professor William Van Alstyne – writing just after *Tinker* – observed, "[w]ithin the very classrooms where the nation's future leaders are trained, no robust exchange at all would be possible if the State were constitutionally free to select just one view of any given subject and to instruct its teachers to avoid mention or consideration of any other."[101]

Judge Frank M. Johnson, Jr.'s opinion in *Parducci v. Rutland*[102] provides an illustrative example of how it would be possible to recognize a limited scope of academic freedom even in a public high school. Marilyn Parducci taught high school English classes at Jefferson Davis High School, a public high school located in Montgomery, Alabama. Parducci assigned *Welcome to the Monkey House*, a short story authored by Kurt Vonnegut, Jr., to her junior English class; the assignment generated parental complaints to the high school principal and to school district officials.[103] The principal and associate superintendent met with Ms. Parducci to discuss the assignment; during this meeting, they described Vonnegut's short story as "literary garbage" that featured themes related to "the killing of elderly people and free sex."[104]

Parducci refused to fall on her sword and vigorously defended the reading assignment as age-appropriate for her students. The school board subsequently declined to renew her employment contract because Parducci assigned material that had a "'disruptive' effect on the school and for refusing 'the counseling and advice of the school principal.'"[105] Parducci promptly filed a complaint in federal district court, alleging that the non-renewal of her employment contract was an unconstitutional violation of her First Amendment rights.

Judge Johnson's analysis of Parducci's legal claims begins by acknowledging "that teachers are entitled to First Amendment freedoms is an issue no longer in dispute," citing to *Tinker*.[106] Johnson considered the materials being taught in other sections of junior English and found that *Welcome to the Monkey House* was no more vulgar than other books being assigned.[107] Moreover, based on the record, the assignment was not, in fact disruptive: "Rather than there being threatened or actual substantial disruption to the educational processes of the school, the evidence reflects that the assigning of the story was greeted with apathy by most of the students."[108]

In light of these factual conclusions, and in conjunction with *Tinker*, Johnson held that Parducci's discharge violated the First Amendment.[109] He warned that "[t]his situation illustrates how easily arbitrary discrimination can occur when public officials are given unfettered discretion to decide what books should be taught and what books should be banned," and observed that the public school district's approach to approved reading lists was "not only enigmatic but grossly unfair."[110] Thus, having created space for individual teacher autonomy in making specific reading assignments in high school English classes, the school district could not then fault an instructor for making a pedagogical choice that fell squarely within the parameters of approved books, such as J. D. Salinger's *The Catcher in the Rye*.[111]

To be clear, Judge Johnson does not remotely suggest that Parducci would have been within her rights to talk about abstract art in her junior English class – much less give the time over to proselytizing for fundamentalist Christian beliefs. His reasoning and judgment are considerably more narrow; the idea is that if a school district creates discretion with respect to specific curricular matters, it cannot subsequently enforce a rigid form of viewpoint-based discipline on an instructor who reasonably exercises this discretion. Had Jefferson Davis High School required all 11th grade English instructors to teach *The Catcher in the Rye*, and nothing else, then Parducci would not have been free to select and assign a text by Kurt Vonnegut, Jr. in its place. However, this was not what the school district had done. Moreover, even if the school district had selected a particular text and made coverage of it mandatory, the logic of Judge Johnson's opinion suggests that a teacher, like Parducci, would still be free to express her view that *The Catcher in the Rye* is not a very good or deep book – and to criticize it and Salinger's writing sharply rather than praise it.

To adopt Judge Frank Easterbrook's approach in *Mayer*,[112] and hold that a high school teacher is nothing more than the school district's mouthpiece, is to put public school teachers in an impossible situation. They are not automatons and cannot consistently guess what the principal, superintendent, or noisy parents will think about Shakespeare's *Othello* or Chaucer's *Canterbury Tales*. What is more, if the purpose of the enterprise is teaching and learning – pedagogy – then there has to be some breathing room for instructors to make informed professional judgments about how to approach the material set forth in the prescribed curriculum.

Warren Court-era decisions like *Parducci* recognize this fact and require school district officials to respect a limited zone of instructor autonomy – a zone of autonomy that would seem to be inherent in the act of teaching.[113] Simply put, teaching *The Catcher in the Rye* to high school students necessarily involves a complex series of interpersonal interactions that renders the exercise radically different from changing the oil in an automobile. One cannot simply equate the state paying a high school teacher to lead sustained study of a novel in a public high school with tasks that do not, of necessity, involve a large of number of subjective, professionally-informed considerations and decisions.

At a minimum, requiring a public school or university to behave in a consistent fashion in regulating curricular speech would provide at least a modicum of protection for academic freedom. For example, if an instructor distributes a reading assignment that otherwise falls within the ambit of the course in question, but it contains an offensive word ("motherfucker"), the school's decision to discipline the instructor for this pedagogical decision should align with its other curricular decisions.

In 1969, the US Court of Appeals for the First Circuit held that a school district could not fire a teacher for assigning an essay with the word "motherfucker" in it when other curricular materials, approved by the same school district, contained the same exact word.[114] Moreover, the punishment – discharge of a tenured high school teacher – did not fit the crime. Judge Bailey Aldrich, writing for the *Keefe* majority, found that the social studies materials at issue were age-appropriate and demonstrably related to the curriculum.

Judge Aldrich explained that, even if some parents were offended by the word in question, this consideration could not be given controlling constitutional weight:

> Hence the question in this case is whether a teacher may, for demonstrated educational purposes, quote a "dirty" word currently used in order to give special offense, or whether the shock is too great for high school seniors to stand. If the

answer were that the students must be protected from such exposure, we would fear for their future. We do not question the good faith of the defendants in believing that some parents have been offended. With the greatest of respect to such parents, their sensibilities are not the full measure of what is proper education."[115]

The presence of multiple books in the high school library that contained the same word buttressed the court's conclusion that Mr. Keefe had acted within the scope of his academic freedom under the First Amendment.[116] The school district undoubtedly possessed some authority to regulate the curriculum more aggressively – but having vested residual pedagogical authority in individual instructors, the school district could not treat the reasonable exercise of this discretion as a firing offense.

To be sure, cases like *Parducci* and *Keefe* were relatively rare even in the 1960s. Then and now, most federal courts, most of the time, will sustain broad assertions of authority over the curriculum in the public schools.[117] Writing just after *Parducci* and *Keefe*, Professor Stephen Goldstein observed that "[t]hese two decisions were the first attempts to create a theory of constitutional protection of a public school teacher's choice of teaching material."[118] Goldstein objected that "[t]he courts never adequately explained … the basis for such a doctrine," and described the *Parducci* and *Keefe* courts' reasons for extending academic freedom to public school teachers as "quite weak."[119] He concluded that "[n]either sound constitutional analysis nor authoritative precedent support a federal constitutional right of teachers to determine what they teach" and, instead, "in a democratic society, it would seem desirable that politically responsive groups have the power to effect the public will concerning the structure and content of public education."[120] The federal courts have essentially followed this path.

Because the development and deployment of a public school curriculum of necessity involves myriad decisions involving the content and viewpoint of instructional materials, the reticence of federal judges to displace school administrators and elected school boards is quite easy to understand and appreciate.[121] On the other hand, however, as Professor Marty Redish posits, although "[t]he idea that educational officials could not constrain teachers in making curricular choices could lead to disastrous results," it is "not feasible to confine the teacher's right only to those situations in which the teacher is exercising good judgment."[122] Thus, some breathing room for professional pedagogical decision-making in the classroom must exist – even if larger questions of the curriculum are subject to relatively direct forms of political control.

Within the bounds of the curricular choices made by school administrators and school board members, individual instructors have to retain some measure of professional discretion if they are to be effective as teachers.[123] Else why bother to require field-specific training and certification as a precondition to employment as a public school teacher? A public school teacher invests and imbues her classroom lectures and lessons with her informed professional judgment, an aspect of academic freedom, and the First Amendment should afford some protection to an activity that is inherently and intrinsically expressive.[124]

Finally, it bears noting that the federal courts' reticence to extend serious First Amendment protection to public school teachers may be less problematic than one would otherwise expect because of statutory tenure provisions that protect many public school teachers. Even if the Supreme Court and lower federal courts declined to build on *Tinker* and *Keyihisian's* promise of First Amendment-based protection for the academic freedom of public school teachers, state laws and school district policies often convey security of position on public school teachers.[125] In addition, public school teacher union contracts can and do impose meaningful limits on the ability of school administrators to fire or discipline instructors for making reasonable, but controversial, pedagogical choices. In many cases, rights associated with procedural due process, statutory tenure provisions, and public employee union contracts will provide more substantive and procedural protection for public school teachers' pedagogical choices than the First Amendment.

Without question, procedural protections arising from statutes, contracts, and the Fourteenth Amendment's Due Process Clause all impose important limits on the ability of a school district to take arbitrary action against faculty members. As Professor Van Alstyne argues, "[w]ithout question, therefore, the effective protection of the substantive constitutional rights of teachers and professors may critically depend upon the availability of pretermination procedural due process."[126] He posits that post-termination substantive remedies are "often simply too little and too late."[127] These observations obviously ring true; the First Amendment is not the only source of effective protection for reasonable pedagogical choices by public school teachers and university faculty members.[128]

On the other hand, however, we should take care not to accept the proposition that educators lack any meaningful claim on the First Amendment when pedagogical choices intersect with the curriculum. Even if procedural protections, tenure, and union grievance procedures meaningfully limit the ability of public schools, colleges, and universities to arbitrarily punish a faculty member for her pedagogical choices, there is still a role for the First Amendment to play. The creation and dissemination of knowledge has a direct relationship to the process of democratic self-government, and the ability to impose orthodoxy in the classroom substantially and materially burdens both the maintenance and operation of democratic self-government.[129]

As Professor Post argues, "[a] state that controls our knowledge controls our minds."[130] Moreover, "[t]he value of democratic competence is undermined whenever the state acts to interrupt the communication of disciplinary knowledge that might inform the creation of public opinion." In light of these considerations, the federal courts must "safeguard the value of democratic competence by extending First Amendment coverage ... to state actions that inhibit the *creation* of expert knowledge."[131]

The transmission of information, knowledge, and ideas in the nation's public schools, colleges, and universities therefore requires First Amendment protection because this process plays an integral role in creating a citizenry capable of democratic self-government. As Thomas Jefferson once noted in a letter to Charles Yancey, of January 6, 1816, "[i]f a nation expects to be ignorant and free, in a state of civilisation, it expects what never was and will never be."[132] The process of education, then, requires more than a modicum of protection under the First Amendment and classroom instruction cannot be subject to complete and total political control.[133]

From this vantage point, *Tinker, Parducci,* and *Keefe* better protect and advance important First Amendment values than more modern cases that emphasize the importance of democratic controls over the nation's system of public education. To be sure, faculty members cannot be free agents and define the curriculum for themselves. However, there is plainly room for play in the joints between the ability of school boards and provosts to shape and define the curriculum and the discretion of individual faculty members to implement it in the classroom.

5.3 THE DIFFICULTY OF CALIBRATING "DISRUPTION" TO THE LEARNING ENVIRONMENT AS A LEGAL TEST AND THE CONCOMITANT RISK OF REGULATORY CREEP

Even as state and federal courts began to sustain ever-broader assertions of regulatory authority by university administrators and public school authorities, the underlying legal test remained entirely unchanged – students and faculty enjoy a general right to freedom of expression both on and off campus, but speech rights may be curtailed if necessary to avoid disruption of the institution's core pedagogical mission. The question in any given case is whether speech will disrupt the educational activities of the institution. And, like "reasonableness,"[134] a test based on disruption could be highly protective of speech activity or convey only very modest protection on speech. The outcome in any given case – in the absence of proof that speech was actually disruptive – will depend on how much risk the federal courts will require school and university administrators to tolerate.

Indeed, it is highly questionable whether the Justices would decide *Tinker* the same way in 2019 as they did in 1969. Wearing black armbands to protest an ongoing war effort clearly presents a risk of disruption within a public middle or high school. The *Tinker* Court observed that the local school officials had tolerated a wide variety of potentially fraught symbols on campus, including the Iron Cross,[135] and used the school district's tolerance for other potentially controversial political symbols to conclude that the proscription against John Tinker, Mary Beth Tinker, and Christopher Eckhardt wearing black armbands to protest the Vietnam War while on campus constituted a form of viewpoint-based discrimination.[136]

As Justice Fortas explained, "the prohibition of expression of one particular opinion, at least without evidence that it is necessary to avoid material and substantial interference with schoolwork or discipline, is not constitutionally permissible."[137] Taking a position, for example, on monuments to Confederate military officers and government officials, in a public school constitutes speech about a matter of public concern – yet a federal district judge faced today with a *Tinker* claim associated with a ban on such speech on campus will likely credit the risk of disruption.[138]

The logic of *Tinker* also seems to encourage school officials to resort to broad, content-based speech bans to avoid the appearance of engaging in viewpoint-based discrimination. Had the Des Moines school district enacted and enforced a ban against "offensive, indecent, or discriminatory speech" on campus, a school administrator could reasonably claim that a black armband to protest the Vietnam War falls within the proscription and does not constitute viewpoint discrimination. The more broadly crafted a public school district's speech regulation, the harder it will be for a would-be student speaker to assert successfully that the regulation constitutes viewpoint discrimination – and content-based speech restrictions are not inherently inconsistent with a disruption-based standard.

In fact, any speech about a matter of public concern has at least some potential for causing disruption.[139] For example, during the 2016 presidential campaign, anonymous students at Emory University "chalked" the campus with pro-Trump messages.[140] Nothing could more clearly constitute core political speech than advocacy for or against a major party candidate for the presidency. On the other hand, however, given Donald Trump's outrageous and offensive personal statements and behavior, particularly with respect to women, immigrants, Muslims, and other minorities, advocacy of his election also arguably conveyed messages of hate and exclusion.[141] Any reasonable person would credit the idea that a woman, an immigrant, or an adherent of Islam would find anonymous, pro-Trump messages on campus sidewalks disquieting – even affirmatively threatening. The question then becomes: May a public university administrator, taking this fact into account, prohibit or punish the dissemination of such messages if the university can successfully identify the message's author?[142]

Nor is the motivation to regulate such speech particularly difficult to understand or appreciate – both public school and university administrators seek to avoid the creation of a hostile learning environment that adversely affects the ability of all students to achieve their educational objectives.[143] The Department of Education, charged with enforcing Title IX, has taken the position that "Title IX grantees have the responsibility to investigate complaints of and remedy, if appropriate, 'any unwelcome conduct of a sexual nature' that creates a hostile environment on campus."[144] In order to discharge this obligation, Professors Terri Day and Danielle Weatherby claim that "[s]chools concerned about violating Title IX have felt compelled to censor and punish subjectively offensive speech or risk the loss of federal funding tied to Title IX compliance."[145]

Concerns about the potential for violence in the public schools also undergird speech-related school regulations – such as dress codes and uniform requirements. Certainly, public school administrators have a compelling interest in preventing gang-related violence on campus – fights and physical altercations constitute the epitome of "disruption" and it does not require much guesswork to recognize that emblems that communicate a gang-related affiliation will give rise to violence. But banning gang-related insignia in a New York City or Los Angeles public school presents an easy case – a mere straw man. Could a student in a racially diverse public high school, that includes a large number of Muslim immigrants, come to school daily wearing a Trump/Pence 2016 t-shirt? And how much should we expect the federal courts to second guess a school administrator's professional judgment that such a t-shirt presents too much risk of disruption to tolerate?[146]

Off-campus speech on social media platforms also presents very difficult, but pressing, issues of the permissible scope of the government's regulatory authority. If a high school or college student participates in anti-abortion protests or in NORML (the National Organization for the Reform of Marijuana Laws) rallies, may she post photographs on platforms like Facebook or Instagram that are easily accessible by classmates? It is entirely foreseeable that off-campus speech on electronic platforms could cause serious disruption inside the public schools. On the other hand, however, a student should not be required to cease being a citizen simply because she happens to attend a public high school or university. A rule that allows unpopular off-campus political activity to serve as a basis for discipline would essentially empower a heckler's veto[147] against any students or faculty members who, in their off time, engage in unpopular advocacy.

If applied in the 1950s or 1960s, the risk of campus disruption would have justified the suspension or expulsion of students who were actively engaged in the civil rights movement. From the perspective of public school and university administrators at institutions in the process of desegregating, civil rights activism off campus would have presented a non-trivial risk of disruption on campus. It should be unthinkable to posit that participation in the Southern Christian Leadership Conference (SCLC), Student Non-violent Coordinating Committee (SNCC), or Congress of Racial Equality (CORE) could serve as a basis for exclusion from a public school or university – in such a case, the student's speech rights would clearly require administrators to embrace a higher degree of risk than they might wish to shoulder.[148]

The First Amendment also clearly forbids government from adopting and enforcing content- and viewpoint-based speech regulations.[149] Consistent with the strong presumption against content- and viewpoint-based speech regulations, unpopular political advocacy that advances civil rights cannot be protected more robustly than unpopular political advocacy that seeks to impede or roll back civil rights protections. If the metric for vindicating government censorship of speech is "disruption," then the disruption associated with the speech, rather than its viewpoint or content, must drive the analysis.

Accordingly, a public school or university cannot treat an Antifa counter-demonstrator more favorably than a Nazi or Aryan Nations white supremacist demonstrator – unless the decision objectively relates to the potential disruptiveness of the speech. To borrow Professor Robert Post's highly apt turn of phrase, within the government's "managerial domain,"[150] an imperative exists for regulating speech (whether on or off campus) and relates to the probable empirical effects of particular speech activity on campus – not on a school administrator's subjective agreement or disagreement with the content or viewpoint of the speech. Of course, it may be that racist or anti-Semitic viewpoints, in point of fact, present a higher risk of disruption than speech advocating tolerance, inclusion, and mutual respect – just as sexually explicit speech presents a greater risk of disruption than advocacy of abstinence or chastity.[151]

To be sure, some kinds of speech – including particular content and specific viewpoints – will be more disruptive than other kinds of speech,[152] and a legal test that turns on disruption necessarily builds a heckler's veto into the decisional matrix. Majority-culture points of view, attitudes, and sensibilities will necessarily affect whether particular kinds of speech run a risk of disruption in a public school.[153] In this sense, then, participation in an anti-Trump rally might not be objectively disruptive in a school environment, whereas participation in a pro-Trump rally could present a significantly stronger risk of disruption. But, under *Tinker*, it is the objective risk of disruption, not the content or viewpoint of the speech, that is supposed to control the public school administrator's decision-making process.

The problem with the contemporary application of *Tinker* is that it is too deferential to school administrators' claims of managerial necessity and, accordingly, permits public school and university administrators to engage in content and viewpoint discrimination under the guise of avoiding disruption. By predicting that trouble will arise from speakers who espouse certain points of view, and not others, a university administrator can permit Peter Singer to come to campus to advocate the killing of infants born with serious birth defects[154] while prohibiting Ann Coulter, Milo Yiannopoulos, or David Duke from speaking. So too, a public school administrator might permit a high school student to wear a Jeb Bush 2016 t-shirt but disallow a Trump 2016 t-shirt on campus. To prevent the selective accommodation of speakers on public college and university campuses, a number of state legislatures have enacted laws that require public colleges and universities to facilitate, rather than impede, controversial speech on campus.[155] Even so, however, "universities still struggle with free speech issues, even when the law is clearly on the side of the speaker."[156]

What's more, the *Tinker* test strongly incents school administrators to aggressively ban entire categories of speech that include potentially disruptive speech in order to avoid the risk of being accused of viewpoint-based discrimination. A flat ban on wearing clothing that presents a political message obviates the need to defend a rule that permits a pro-John Kasisch message to be disseminated on campus – but not a pro-Donald Trump message. This insulates the public school administrator from potential liability for underpredicting disruptions (and hence appearing to engage in viewpoint-based discrimination). But this litigation insurance policy comes at a very high price indeed – the extirpation of political messages on the school's campus.

A better approach might relate the level of deference that a reviewing court should give a public school or university administrator to the precise nature of the disruption. The more self-evidently serious the threat, the more deferential a reviewing court should be.[157] Where the threat is minor, even trivial, the federal courts should require school administrators to shoulder a higher burden of justification in order to proscribe or punish student, faculty, and staff speech.[158]

To provide a concrete example, the US Court of Appeals for the Third Circuit rejected a public school district's decision to ban pink wristbands featuring the phrase "I ♥ Boobies!" as part of a breast cancer awareness month fund raiser and educational project.[159] The public school district's rationale was that the speech was indecent and, under *Morse* and *Fraser*, indecent speech is presumptively disruptive regardless of its actual effects on the school's operations. The 9–5 en banc Third Circuit did not disagree with the school district's legal claim that indecent speech is inherently disruptive, but rejected the school district's characterization of the bracelets as indecent.[160] Had the judges found the speech to be indecent, the school district would have prevailed over the students.[161]

One should also keep in mind that five members of the en banc court disagreed with this characterization – finding the message to be indecent and therefore proscribable.[162] As much as one would like to dismiss the dissenting judges' views on this point as complete and utter nonsense, the *Fraser/Morse* framework makes the characterization of the speech as "lewd" outcome determinative. The problem with this analysis is that a student wearing a breast cancer awareness wristband featuring this phrase simply does not present a serious risk of disruption to a middle school's core pedagogical mission. Cases like *Fraser* and *Morse* treat trivialities and Columbine-esque threats as more-or-less the same thing – when they plainly are not.

On the other hand, suppose a student posts a poem on Facebook that threatens a mass casualty event at his high school.[163] The student claims that the poem is nothing more than personal artistic expression.[164] At one level of analysis, this claim rings true: The poem constitutes a form of self-expression. On the other hand, the poem also constitutes a terroristic threat of violence. Viewed from this vantage point, the student's speech is inherently disruptive and renders the author's mere presence on his high school's campus too great a risk for reasonable public school officials to bear.[165]

Ribald speech presents a risk of trivial harm, whereas threats of violence, even if thinly fictionalized, and even if not seriously intended, impose much higher social costs. The *Tinker* doctrine should be subtle enough to take differences of this sort into account. I do not go so far as to propose adopting the Hand Formula in the context of analyzing the potential disruptive effect of student speech (whether uttered on or off campus).[166] But courts should take into consideration the precise nature of risk that student speech presents and school administrators should have a freer hand in regulating serious risks; a practical approach to the assessment of risk seems both appropriate and necessary. In the context of the Supreme Court's school speech jurisprudence, however, trivial threats and serious threats are more or less lumped together in an exercise that tries to ascertain whether any sort of credible risk of disruption exists to the regular pedagogical activities of the public school.

The question of the permissible constitutional scope of a school administrator's regulatory power over student speech should also be calibrated to the nature of the threat. When a public high school student authors a rap that includes violent threats such as "I'm going to hit you with my rueger [sic]," "going to get a pistol down your mouth," and "he get no mercy nigga," with the threats clearly directed toward specific members of the high school's faculty, and then posts the rap to popular social media platforms (such as Facebook and YouTube), thus plainly directing the content toward the high school community, school officials have good cause to act proactively to avoid the risk of disruption on campus by temporarily barring the author from campus. Moreover, they possess much better cause for quick action on these facts than when a puckish student posts a dirty limerick mocking the vice-principal.[167] Nor is this merely a hypothetical: Taylor Bell, a student at a Mississippi public high school, wrote and widely disseminated via social media outlets a rap laced with violent threats against identifiable school personnel – and subsequently claimed that the First Amendment protected him from any adverse disciplinary consequences.

Treating threats directed against school personnel as a form of prohibited harassment does not transgress the First Amendment.[168] Even if Taylor Bell's rap did not rise to the level of a "true threat,"[169] the ability of public school officials to react to the prospect of disruption in his high school should not be limited by the same standards that constrain the imposition of criminal liability for speech.[170] Moreover, even though Bell did not literally "speak" on campus, his speech was clearly and intentionally directed to the high school community.[171] Given the fraught nature of this kind of threat in the post-Columbine era, it should be constitutionally permissible for school administrators to treat threats of violence, even if made off campus, as justifying a swift institutional response (including discipline or removal of the student who uttered the threat).

On the other hand, efforts to regulate students' off-campus speech, in the absence of strong justifications for doing so, can easily go too far. What's more, *Tinker's* balancing test could invite thin-skinned school administrators to punish students for speech that is merely critical of the school district, school administrators, or teachers. For example, a Pennsylvania public school district attempted to punish a student, Justin Layshock, for posting a fake MySpace profile of Eric Trosch, the local high school principal.[172] Layshock's fake profile was unquestionably mean and insulting, and attempted to body-shame Trosch, whom Chief Judge Theodore McKee describes as "apparently a large man."[173] The fake post also contained transphobic and homophobic content, again likely intended to mock and humiliate Trosch.[174] Layshock's parody proved to be wildly popular with his peers and led to the creation and posting of three additional fake MySpace profiles, each even "more vulgar and offensive than Justin's."[175]

However, even if Layshock's conduct was rude, insulting, and perhaps even cruel, it did not present the same kind of threat as a social media post that threatened to harm Principal Trosch, other faculty or staff, or students. The nature of the harm associated with the fake MySpace profile, which no reasonable person would have taken as literally true, extended to hurt feelings on Trosch's part. And, if one works with teenagers, one must realize, at some level, that young people can be mean. The ability of the school district to manage student speech should be more circumscribed on these facts than in cases like *Bell* or *LaVine*. As it happens, some lower federal courts seem to intuitively grasp the necessity of this doctrinal approach.

Unsurprisingly, the school district treated Layshock's fake profile of Trosch as a form of "harassment of a school administrator," suspended Layshock for ten days, and imposed additional severe punitive sanctions (including banning Layshock from all extracurricular activities for the balance of the academic year and also prohibiting him from participating in the high school's annual commencement exercises).[176] The Third Circuit, sitting en banc, applied *Tinker* and, affirming the district court, found that the school district had violated Layshock's First Amendment rights.[177]

This outcome, however, was not a function of the nature of the speech, and the potential harm associated with it, but rather rested on the fact that Layshock's "conduct did not disrupt the school."[178] The school district had attempted to invoke *Morse* and *Fraser* to punish off-campus speech completely outside the context of the school's programs. However, the *Layshock* majority correctly refused to extend these precedents to cover off-color, off-campus speech. Had the school district litigated the case under the theory that the fake MySpace profiles of Trosch had disrupted the high school's regular operations, the constitutional analysis would likely have been quite different – and the school officials could well have prevailed.

The Supreme Court needs to make clear that something like a rule of administrative necessity cabins the ability of school administrators to regulate the off-campus speech of students. When students speak outside the context of the classroom and curriculum, even when directing speech toward their peers (classmates), they should not be subject to pervasive regulation by school administrators with thin skins. This is not to say that harassment and intimidation have any claim on the First Amendment – they do not. But if speech constitutes a crime, that is for police and prosecutors – not high school principals – to address. On the other hand, some kinds of off-campus speech are so inherently disruptive, and the disruptive effect is so easily foreseeable, that school officials should enjoy a relatively broad power to stage an administrative intervention to prevent tragedy.[179]

Given the competing and conflicting interests at stake, a test that considers the risk of material and substantial disruption might be the most speech-tolerant test that the federal courts would be willing to embrace. Even so, however, the burden of proof for establishing a clear and present danger of the requisite level of disruption should always rest on the government – would-be speakers should not be required to establish that their speech would be met with equanimity by their peers as a precondition for speaking.

The Warren Court adopted and applied this approach in *Tinker*.[180] However, the *Tinker* test has been systematically weakened – watered down – over time by the lower federal courts during the Roberts and Rehnquist Court eras. *Tinker* itself characterized the protection of speech on the nation's public school campuses as a "hazardous freedom,"[181] because "[a]ny word spoken, in class, in the lunchroom, or on the campus, that deviates from the views of another person may start an argument or cause a disturbance."[182] Despite the potential social cost, the Warren Court concluded that "our Constitution says we must take this risk."[183] Justice Fortas explained that "our history says that it is this sort of hazardous freedom – this kind of openness – that is the basis of our national strength and of the independence and vigor of Americans who grow up and live in this relatively permissive, often disputatious, society."[184] Unfortunately, we seem to have lost the national self-confidence necessary to embrace "hazardous freedoms."

The scope of application of school district speech regulations has also been expanding over time and now extends beyond the metes and bounds of a public school's campus. Federal courts should arrest this trend and properly limit regulations based on disturbance to speech with a clear and direct nexus with a public school or university campus. Accordingly, as the locus of speech activity becomes more removed from the immediate physical precincts of a public school, college, or university campus, the quantum of proof required to justify a regulation or proscription of the speech should increase. It is simply implausible to suggest that an off-campus tweet or Facebook post presents the same threat of disruption as a speech made from the high school cafeteria or on the university library steps. The federal courts should not reflexively extend *Tinker* to any and all off-campus speech by citizens who happen to study or teach at a public school, college, or university.

5.4 CONCLUSION

The importance of academic freedom cannot be gainsaid. As Professor Byrne argues, "[p]reserving the fundamental academic values of disinterested inquiry, reasoned and critical discourse, and liberal education justifies a constitutional right of academic freedom."[185] Along very similar lines, Professor Post posits that "[r]eliable expert knowledge is necessary not only for intelligent self-government, but also for the very value of democratic legitimation."[186] Academic pursuits – and the academic freedom needed in order to undertake them successfully – thus are integral to creating and maintaining a body politic capable of sustaining the project of democratic self-government. Yet, the federal courts have shown, at best, a halting and incomplete commitment to bringing First Amendment values to bear in order to protect the academic enterprise – research, writing, teaching, and learning.

Moreover, the trend line is rather unpromising – we have not seen any significant contemporary Supreme Court decisions protecting academic work.[187] To be sure, the Roberts, Rehnquist, and Burger Courts did not squarely overrule the landmark academic freedom First Amendment precedents of the Warren Court – decisions that deployed the First Amendment to protect the speech rights of faculty members and students in the nation's public schools, colleges, and universities. Nevertheless, the First Amendment's scope of application in these environs quite clearly has contracted, rather than expanded, over time.[188]

To some extent, it is not altogether surprising that federal judges would defer to public school and university administrators in the wake of horrific events, such as the mass shootings at Virginia Tech and Columbine High School. The perceived social cost of disruption on campus no longer stops at a missed lesson because of squandered instructional time; in the era of mass shooting events with semi-automatic weapons, disturbing student-authored poems featuring violent fantasies, whether presented in a high school English class or posted on Facebook, should be more than merely a cause for concern by school officials – they can and should take swift and effective action to address violent threats. The imperative of creating and sustaining an open and inclusive learning environment also incents public school and university administrators to adopt conduct regulations that have the predictable effect of chilling speech both on and off campus.

To be sure, legitimate – indeed compelling – reasons exist for regulating speech on campus. The question, however, is the level of risk that school administrators should be required to tolerate in order to create breathing room for the freedom of speech on campus. Although the legal standard for regulation – a serious risk of material and substantial disruption – has not changed since the Warren Court first recognized speech rights for students and faculty members alike, the federal courts have applied this test less rigorously under the Roberts and Rehnquist Courts. Moreover, they have done so in contexts where the potential harm to the institution's pedagogical mission was, at best, picayune. At the end of the day, a test that relies on the metric of potential disruption can easily become a mere cellophane wrapper for content- and even viewpoint-based censorship of speech.[189]

If not checked by careful and conscientious judicial oversight, the potential for disruption rationale could easily justify imposing broad-based and comprehensive speech regulations on faculty and students twenty-four hours a day, seven days a week. The First Amendment should not permit such an outcome. Accordingly, broad claims of comprehensive government authority to use the accident of either employment or enrollment at a government-sponsored educational institution should not serve as a basis for imposing comprehensive speech regulations on either faculty members or students.[190]

In sum, the managerial imperatives associated with advancing the pedagogical mission of the nation's public schools, colleges, and universities cannot be permitted to justify turning these institutions into "enclaves of totalitarianism."[191] The federal courts can and should do a better job of reconciling the competing goals of a safe and effective learning environment with the speech rights of faculty and students – both on and off campus. A posture of reflexive judicial deference puts too much weight on the managerial interests of the government and fails to afford sufficient constitutional solicitude to the First Amendment rights of those who work and study on our nation's campuses.

6

Transborder Speech

Using the Accident of Geography As a Makeweight Justification for Suppressing Expressive Freedoms

This chapter will consider an overlooked and underappreciated subset of First Amendment activity: transborder speech. Transborder speech involves the exercise of freedom of speech, assembly, association, press, and petition across national borders; it relates to the global information flows of ideas, knowledge, and argument and the various forms of interpersonal engagement among and between individuals that facilitate knowledge and understanding. Simply put, in the age of the internet, the marketplace of ideas does not respect national boundaries.[1] Even though transborder speech constitutes an increasingly important aspect of expressive freedom, it enjoys considerably less protection than purely domestic speech activity.[2]

If the value of information and ideas is not a function of its source, as the Supreme Court explained with great force in *Citizens United*,[3] then it necessarily follows, as a matter of constitutional logic, that the *locus* of speech activity should be equally irrelevant to ascertaining the value of particular speech to the marketplace of ideas – or to the process of democratic self-government.[4] Professor Timothy Zick argues that we "ought to treat American citizens' rights to engage in speech, assembly, petition, and press as fully portable."[5] Nevertheless, as Professor Burt Neuborne and his co-author, Steven R. Shapiro, observed in 1985, "[r]ecent case law hardly encourages optimism about the prospects for close judicial scrutiny of impediments to the flow of information and ideas across the national border."[6] Moreover, from the vantage point of the Reagan era, "the trend probably points in the opposite direction."[7] Subsequent judicial developments have entirely borne out this baleful prediction.

As this chapter will explain in some detail, transborder speech has never enjoyed a strong claim on the First Amendment. Moreover, despite its merely modest protection under the Warren Court, the protection of transborder speech has declined, rather than increased, over time. Even as the Rehnquist and Roberts Courts have radically expanded the protection afforded to domestic speech activity,[8] transborder speech has remained something of a First Amendment orphan.

The Warren Court pioneered the constitutional protection of transborder speech, affording such speech tentative, modest protection.[9] The Burger Court halted the further extension of First Amendment protection for transborder speech activity, but did not overrule the relevant Warren Court precedents.[10] The Rehnquist and

Roberts Courts, on the other hand, effectively have resiled from the modest protection afforded to transborder speech under the Warren Court.[11]

In the age of the internet, national boundaries should not impede the free flow of information and ideas. Yet, as Neuborne and Shapiro observe, "America's border has been permitted to evolve into a discernible impediment to the free flow of ideas."[12] The fact that speech crosses a border should not affect its status under the First Amendment. No necessary relationship exists between the geographic origin of speech or a speaker and its potential utility to the project of democratic self-government.[13]

Professor Zick, one of the few contemporary legal scholars to consider the application of the First Amendment to transborder speech in a comprehensive and sustained fashion,[14] argues that "U.S. citizens ought to enjoy protection for free speech, press, assembly and petition rights without regard to frontiers or borders."[15] Yet, in the United States and elsewhere, governments routinely use the accident of geography as a basis for regulating – or even proscribing entirely – speech activity that would enjoy robust constitutional protection but for its transborder characteristic. In the contemporary United States, federal laws and regulations use control over the border to suppress speech activity that the national government deems inimical to its diplomatic, military, and national security interests.[16] For the most part, and for reasons that the Supreme Court has never fully explained or justified, crossing the nation's borders provides a sound basis for disregarding the First Amendment's strictures.[17]

To provide one concrete example of the problem, consider that the ability of foreign speakers to enter the United States – and the ability of US citizens to travel abroad in order to inform themselves about issues of central importance to matters of public concern in the United States – are subject to pervasive regulation and control. Moreover, these controls can be used, and are used, to engage in viewpoint- and content-based censorship of speech.[18] *Holder v. Humanitarian Law Project*[19] sustained a flat ban on any contact with foreign organizations listed on a State Department terrorist-group watch list. The Humanitarian Law Project (HLP) sought to teach peaceful dispute resolution techniques, and principles of international law, to Kurdish rebels (members of the Partiya Karkeran Kurdistan or PKK).[20] The Supreme Court sustained the federal government's *criminal* ban on this entirely peaceful, non-violent, speech and associational activity.[21] Chief Justice John G. Roberts, Jr., explained that "in regulating the particular forms of support that plaintiffs seek to provide to foreign terrorist organizations, Congress has pursued that objective [national security] consistent with the limitations of the First and Fifth Amendments."[22]

Humanitarian Law Project raises very troubling questions about the rigor with which the First Amendment will be applied in circumstances where US citizens seek to exercise First Amendment freedoms outside the United States.[23] As Professor David Cole has observed, "[f]or the first time in its history, the Court upheld the criminalization of speech advocating only non-violent, lawful ends on the ground that such speech might unintentionally assist a third party in a criminal wrongdoing."[24] In an increasingly globalized marketplace of ideas, we need to ensure that First Amendment rights do not end at the water's edge. Simply put, the locus of expressive activity should not prefigure the government's ability to engage in censorship, yet good evidence exists that this is not really the case under current First Amendment law and doctrine.[25]

This chapter also considers the problems presented by national security-based surveillance programs aimed at preventing crime. Many of these programs, such as those created under the Foreign Intelligence Surveillance Act,[26] use the transborder nature of communications as a basis for engaging in surveillance of electronic communications without any individualized showing that a particular person's electronic communications might relate in some way to unlawful activities.[27]

Pervasive forms of surveillance have a predictable and significant chilling effect; simply put, surveillance programs based on Big Data present serious threats to the vibrancy of the marketplace of ideas.[28] As Professor Neil Richards observes, "[s]hadowy regimes of surveillance corrode the constitutional commitment to intellectual freedom that lies at the heart of most theories of political freedom in a democracy."[29] Nevertheless, the federal courts have been very reticent to apply First Amendment values to these national security programs that use the accident of crossing a national border as a basis for justifying comprehensive data collection – particularly in the face of a widely-held perception that the risk of terroristic attacks is both real and growing.[30]

National security efforts, such as the PRISM program[31] and other, similar activities sanctioned by section 215 of the Patriot Act,[32] present some very serious risks to the exercise of expressive freedoms. A surveillance state may be many things, but it is not likely to be a successful democracy. Surveillance produces a significant chilling effect that impedes democratic discourse – something that the Court of Justice of the European Union noted in its landmark *Digital Rights Ireland* decision.[33] Surveillance can and does function as a powerful tool for social control; programs like PRISM seriously burden the exercise of expressive freedom by incenting self-censorship.[34]

Despite the risks to democratic self-government that mass surveillance programs present, the Roberts Court has refused to even consider the constitutional status of such programs on the merits, finding that US citizens who generally engage in telecommunications activities with people and institutions located abroad lacked Article III standing to challenge the constitutionality of these mass surveillance programs because there was no present injury.[35] Because the federal government does not officially acknowledge even the existence of some of these programs, much less provide a database of persons whose electronic communications have been recorded and stored, it is not possible for a would-be plaintiff to establish that her communications have been surveilled. In the absence of discovery, it is quite impossible for a would-be plaintiff seeking judicial review of these programs to prove that Big Brother has been watching and listening to her communications.

Yet, in *Clapper*, the Supreme Court held that the inability to assert with something approaching certainty the fact of government surveillance means that a would-be plaintiff lacks a concrete and particularized injury in fact sufficient to establish constitutional standing.[36] In consequence, mass surveillance programs that target transborder communications operate free and clear of judicial review. The First Amendment obviously cannot constrain the government's spying on its citizens if the federal courts refuse to apply it.

The fact that many of these mass surveillance programs rely on the transborder nature of communications as a basis for government surveillance is telling. Clearly, the political branches of the federal government have figured out that the federal courts are unlikely to apply the First Amendment at full strength to speech activity that takes place, even in part, outside the United States.[37] Because the Supreme Court has signaled that a junior varsity version of the First Amendment applies to transborder speech, the accident of geography can be used as a basis for censoring speech that Congress and the President dislike. However, if content- and viewpoint-based speech regulations are antithetical to the freedom of speech required for democracy to function,[38] the fact that speech has a transborder element should not serve as a constitutionally sufficient basis for denying it the full protection of the First Amendment.[39]

It has not always been thus. The idea that transborder speech has at best a very weak claim on the First Amendment is of relatively recent vintage and reflects a break with precedents of the Warren Court. To be sure, the Warren Court did not vigorously move to protect transborder speech activity.[40] During the Warren Court years, however, the Justices issued opinions that invoked the First Amendment to limit government efforts to censor speech and associational activities with transborder characteristics that the political branches not only disliked, but feared.[41] These decisions were tentative and halting – but they nevertheless brought First Amendment values to bear to protect transborder First Amendment activity.

The Burger Court, by way of contrast, failed to expand on these precedents. When presented with opportunities to build on the work of its predecessor, the Burger Court declined to extend Warren Court precedents and, instead, distinguished them away.[42] When doing so, however, the Burger Court reiterated that government border regulations that burdened access to information and ideas triggered the protection of the First Amendment.[43] Thus, the Burger Court ratified prior holdings that applied the First Amendment to transborder speech, but proceeded to uphold government regulations that burdened or precluded transborder speech and association activities. It did so by finding that the government was regulating conduct, rather than speech, and that the non-speech justification for regulating conduct was consistent with the First Amendment.[44]

During the Rehnquist and Roberts Court eras, however, the Supreme Court has moved to flatly deny First Amendment protection to transborder speech activity.[45] For example, the Supreme Court has upheld regulations aimed at chilling the distribution of motion pictures produced abroad[46] and also sustained a federal law that criminalized any contact made abroad with proscribed foreign organizations.[47] In reaching these conclusions, the Justices have either declined to find the First Amendment implicated at all (*Keene*) or applied a watered-down version of the First Amendment that bears little relationship to its more rigorous, domestic first cousin (*Humanitarian Law Project*).

Accordingly, and as this chapter will demonstrate, it is not possible to gainsay that the protection afforded transborder speech has decreased, rather than increased, over time in the United States. The federal government has successfully invoked imperatives associated with diplomatic, military, and national security concerns to justify content- and viewpoint-based speech regulations that burden or completely prohibit First Amendment activity based on the locus of the speech activity being outside the United States.

As I will explain in greater detail, a perplexing asymmetry exists in the contemporary Supreme Court's approach to transborder speech and corporate speech. The Roberts Court has been remarkably protective of corporate speech activity, positing that the value of information to an audience is not a function of the identity of the speaker or the speaker's motive for speaking.[48] Thus, a corporation may claim the full protection of the First Amendment when it speaks out on a matter of public concern or about a candidate for public office.[49] It is puzzling why speaker identity and motive are irrelevant to the protected status of corporate speech about a matter of public concern but afforded central and controlling weight in the context of transborder speech.[50]

This chapter proceeds in four main parts. Part 6.1 considers the Warren Court's tentative efforts to map the First Amendment on to transborder speech activity. Even though these efforts were halting and limited, they represented a major theoretical and doctrinal innovation. Prior to the Warren Court, the Supreme Court had not suggested, much less held, that the First Amendment had extraterritorial effect.[51] Part 6.2 takes up the more cautious approach of the Burger Court, which declined to build on the jurisprudential foundations established by its predecessor. To be sure, the Burger Court acknowledged that the First Amendment applied to transborder speech, but was inclined to credit the federal government's claims that foreign relations, military affairs, and national security interests justified the imposition of significant limits on transborder speech activity.

Part 6.3 discusses the diminution of transborder speech protection under the Rehnquist and Roberts Courts. The most recent cases involving transborder speech either find no serious First Amendment interest or, worse still, sustain transborder speech restrictions under a form of "strict scrutiny" lite. Drawing on the iconic work of Alexander Meikejohn, Part 6.4 presents a sustained argument in favor of affording transborder speech activities full and robust First Amendment protection. Part 6.5 provides a brief overview and conclusion.

6.1 THE WARREN COURT AND TRANSBORDER SPEECH: TENTATIVE RECOGNITION AND MODEST, BUT INCONSISTENT, FIRST AMENDMENT PROTECTION

The Warren Court recognized constitutional protection for international travel, both as a liberty interest under the Fifth Amendment's Due Process Clause and as an aspect of the First Amendment. Travel provides opportunities that advance important First Amendment interests, including association, access to news and information, and education. Thus, denial of a passport, which has the effect of precluding international travel, implicates the First Amendment.[52] The Warren Court also held that the right to receive news and information from abroad, including foreign political material, falls within the scope of the First Amendment's protection.[53]

In *Kent v. Dulles*,[54] the Warren Court first recognized the right to travel abroad. Writing for the 5–4 majority, Justice William O. Douglas observed that "[t]he right to travel is part of the 'liberty' of which the citizen cannot be deprived without due process of law under the Fifth Amendment." Rockwell Kent sought to attend a "World Council of Peace" conference in England.[55] The State Department's Passport Office denied Kent's application for a passport because of an alleged association with the Communist Party.[56] Kent sued, arguing that the denial of a passport based on his political beliefs and associations violated the Constitution; Kent lost in both the district court and before the US Court of Appeals for the District of Columbia Circuit.

The Supreme Court granted review and reversed. Rather than reaching the broader constitutional questions,[57] the majority instead held that Congress did not authorize the State Department to refuse to issue passports based on a US citizen's political beliefs. Justice Douglas explained that it would be mistaken to infer a power "to curtail in [the Secretary of State's] discretion the free movement of citizens in order to satisfy himself about their beliefs or associations."[58] Thus, the majority held that the relevant statutory provisions did "not delegate to the Secretary the kind of authority exercised here."[59]

Strictly speaking, *Kent* does not directly hold that a constitutional right to travel internationally exists; instead, it relies on a saving construction to avoid reaching the larger constitutional question.[60] Even so, Justice Douglas's opinion strongly intimates that an express authorization to deny a passport based solely on ideological beliefs or political associations would fail to pass constitutional muster. He explained that "we deal here with a constitutional right of the citizen, a right which we must assume Congress will be faithful to respect."[61] By way of contrast, the dissenting Justices would have permitted the State Department to deny a passport when the applicant "is going abroad with the purpose of engaging in activities that would advance the Communist cause,"[62] an approach that would have denied meaningful protection to any and all transborder speech activities disapproved of by the State Department.

The Supreme Court's next major transborder speech case also involved passports – more specifically, the revocation of passports based on the holders' support of communist or socialist ideologies and organizations that advocated for such causes. In *Aptheker v. Secretary of State*,[63] the Supreme Court reaffirmed and extended its earlier ruling in *Kent*. The State Department invoked authority under the Subversive Activities Control Act of 1950 (the Act).[64] The law prohibited the issuance or use of a passport by "any member" of a Communist organization. On October 20, 1961, the federal government listed the Communist Party of the United States under the Act. Following this listing, the State Department notified Herbert Aptheker, as well as Elizabeth Gurley Flynn, "that their passports were revoked."[65]

Following the passport revocation, Aptheker and Flynn sought judicial review of the State Department's order on constitutional grounds; among other constitutional claims, they argued that the order violated both due process and First Amendment rights.[66] A three-judge district court ruled in favor of the State Department and against Aptheker and Flynn.[67] The Supreme Court granted review and reversed, holding that the Act "too broadly and indiscriminately restricts the right to travel and thereby abridges the liberty guaranteed by the Fifth Amendment."[68]

Justice Arthur Goldberg, writing for the 6–3 majority, found the provision authorizing the passport revocations "unconstitutional on its face" because it "swe[pt] too widely and too indiscriminately across the liberty guaranteed in the Fifth Amendment."[69] He explained that "[t]he prohibition against travel is supported only by a tenuous relationship between the bare fact of organizational membership and the activity that Congress sought to proscribe."[70] Because there was no requirement that the State Department assess a citizen's actual level of involvement with the Communist Party on an individualized basis, the statute was not drawn with sufficient narrow tailoring.

The Supreme Court reached this conclusion even though Aptheker was a leader of the Communist Party and the editor of *Political Affairs*, an official publication of the Communist Party of the United States, and Flynn served as Chair of the Communist Party of the United States.[71] Aptheker sought to visit Europe for "study," "recreation," and "to observe social, political and economic conditions abroad, and thereafter to write, publish, teach, and lecture in this country about his observations."[72] In addition, he sought to "attend meetings of learned societies and to fulfill invitations to lecture abroad."[73] Flynn offered similar reasons for her desire to travel outside the United States.[74]

Aptheker's reasons for traveling abroad clearly and directly implicated core First Amendment values; his proposed activities all involve the exercise of the freedom of speech, assembly, and association. Accordingly, it should not be surprising that, in addition to the due process rationale, Justice Goldberg also recognized the First Amendment implications of revoking a passport in order to prevent the exercise of protected expressive freedoms: "[S]ince freedom of travel is a constitutional liberty closely related to rights of free speech and association, we believe that appellants in this case should not be required to assume the burden of demonstrating that Congress could not have written a statute constitutionally prohibiting their travel."[75] Justice Goldberg's opinion clearly recognizes that citizens seek to go abroad in order to exercise First Amendment freedoms and that this activity enjoys some measure of constitutional protection.

Justice Douglas, in his concurring opinion, drew the link even more directly. He argued that "[f]reedom of movement is kin to the right of assembly and to the right of association."[76] In his view, "[t]hese rights may not be abridged."[77] Douglas posited that "[w]e cannot exercise and enjoy citizenship in world perspective without the right to travel abroad."[78]

The Warren Court's most sweeping transborder speech decision, *Lamont v. Postmaster General*,[79] invalidated a federal statute that required written registration with the federal government in order to receive "communist political propaganda."[80] The statute provided that foreign material mailed to the United States, and determined by the Postal Service to constitute "communist political propaganda," would not be delivered to the recipient, but instead "detained by the Postmaster General upon its arrival for delivery in the United States."[81] The recipient would be notified of its availability and, in order to receive the material, would have to notify the Post Office that the material is "desired by the addressee."[82]

Obviously, Congress intended this statute to have a predictable and profound chilling effect on the willingness of US residents to receive materials from abroad that the Postal Service deemed to constitute "communist political propaganda." Moreover, in order to receive it, the postal customer had to be willing to create a permanent record, in the form of a reply card, informing the Postal Service in writing of her desire to obtain such material.

The Supreme Court invalidated the statute as facially unconstitutional. Writing for a unanimous Supreme Court, Justice Douglas explained that "the Act as construed and applied is unconstitutional because it requires an official act (*viz.*, returning the reply card) as a limitation on the unfettered exercise of the addressee's First Amendment rights."[83] Requiring a recipient to request delivery of otherwise lawful books and periodicals "is almost certain to have a deterrent effect, especially as respects those who have sensitive positions."[84] For example, many government employees, including school teachers, "might think they would invite disaster if they read what the Federal Government says contains the seeds of treason."[85] Moreover, "any addressee is likely to feel some inhibition in sending for literature which federal officials have condemned as 'communist political propaganda.'"[86]

Concurring in the judgment, Justice William J. Brennan, Jr., joined by Justice Goldberg, observed that "[t]hese might be troublesome cases if the addressees predicated their claim for relief upon the First Amendment rights of the senders."[87] However, *Lamont* did not involve free speech claims by foreign governments; instead "the addressees assert First Amendment claims in their own right."[88] In Justice Brennan's view, "the right to receive publications" constitutes an important, indeed "fundamental" right, and "[t]he dissemination of ideas can accomplish nothing if otherwise willing addressees are not free to receive and consider them."[89] In other words, "[i]t would be a barren marketplace of ideas that had only sellers and no buyers."[90]

Unlike the passport decisions – *Aptheker*, *Kent*, and *Dayton*, which all featured a badly divided Supreme Court – *Lamont* was a unanimous decision. Not a single member of the Supreme Court dissented from the ruling. Perhaps this was so because, as Justice Douglas observed, the regulatory scheme before the Court was "at war with the 'uninhibited, robust, and wide-open' debate and discussion that are contemplated by the First Amendment."[91] Or, as Justice Brennan stated the point, "inhibition as well as prohibition against the exercise of precious First Amendment rights is a power denied to government."[92]

It is quite clear that foreign governments seeking to disseminate propaganda have no protected constitutional interest in using the US mail service to accomplish this objective. Thus, *Lamont* does not suggest, much less hold, that Russia's efforts to influence the 2016 presidential election in the United States have any purchase on the First Amendment whatsoever.[93] But, even if foreign governments lack any protected speech rights, or right to access the US marketplace of ideas, US citizens have a right to receive and consider what foreign governments have to say.[94]

As Professor Alexander Meiklejohn so forcefully explained, the foreign source of ideas and inspiration is immaterial to their potential relevance to the ongoing project of democratic self-government. For democratic self-government to work, "the citizens of the United States will be fit to govern themselves under their own institutions only if they have faced squarely and fearlessly everything that can be said in favor of those institutions, everything that can be said against them."[95] Thus, *Lamont* protects the right of US citizens to receive "communist political propaganda" through the mail because a power to censor ideas, through the expedient of censorial postal regulations, is a power to control political thought – and such a power simply cannot be reconciled with a meaningful commitment to the process of democratic self-government.[96]

The accident of the materials at issue in *Lamont* originating with a foreign government, and from outside the United States, could have been used as a basis for denying them any meaningful First Amendment protection. Under the plenary power doctrine,[97] the federal government has nearly unfettered discretion to control who may enter the United States and who may seek lawful resident status or naturalization as citizens.[98] It would not require much of a jurisprudential stretch to extend the plenary power doctrine to use the nation's border as a basis for excluding foreign material – in this instance, communist political propaganda – from the United States. Yet, *Lamont* does not feature even a single vote for this outcome; censoring what US citizens may read lies beyond the legitimate scope of the federal government's powers (even when control over the nation's borders is implicated in the speech activity).

Unfortunately, the Warren Court was not consistent in affording serious First Amendment protection to transborder First Amendment activities. In *Zemel v. Rusk*,[99] the Warren Court refused to credit a First Amendment claim that a US citizen has a right to travel to Cuba. *Zemel* constitutes an important exception to the Warren Court's generally protective approach to transborder speech claims.

In 1962, Louis Zemel sought a visa permitting him to "travel to Cuba as a tourist."[100] The State Department denied the visa application. In October 1962, Zemel renewed his request notwithstanding the State Department's denial of his initial request. Zemel elaborated on his reasons for seeking to travel to Cuba, explaining that he wanted to learn about the current state of affairs on the island in person so as to make himself "a better informed citizen."[101] The State Department again denied the visa application. Zemel responded to this second denial by filing suit in federal district court, asserting that the visa denial burdened his First Amendment rights.[102] A three-judge district court dismissed his claim and entered summary judgment for the State Department. Zemel appealed to the Supreme Court.

The Supreme Court affirmed the trial court's order. The State Department had statutory authority to deny Zemel's visa application; moreover, doing so did not violate the First Amendment. Chief Justice Earl Warren, writing for a 6–3 majority, explained that "we cannot accept the contention of appellant that it is a First Amendment right which is involved."[103] He characterized the visa denial as merely a regulation of "action" rather than "speech," observing that "[t]here are few restrictions on action which could not be clothed by ingenious argument in the garb of decreased data flow."[104] Accordingly, "[t]he right to speak and publish does not carry with it the unrestrained right to gather information."[105]

Justice Douglas dissented vigorously, positing that "[t]he ability to understand a pluralistic world, filled with clashing ideologies, is a prerequisite of citizenship if we and the other peoples of the world are to avoid the nuclear holocaust."[106] He characterized *Kent* as a freedom of speech decision, arguing that it "reflected a judgment as to the peripheral rights of the citizen under the First Amendment."[107] Travel to other nations, for the purpose of seeking information about foreign peoples and cultures, and the opportunity to learn from such experiences, "gives meaning and substance to freedom of expression and freedom of the press."[108] In light of these free speech values, "[r]estrictions on the right to travel ... should be so particularized that a First Amendment right is not precluded unless some clear countervailing national interest stands in the way of its assertion."[109]

In sum, the Warren Court applied the First Amendment to protect transborder speech, but did so in contexts where the locus of the First Amendment activity being protected was domestic. The State Department attempted to deny passports not based on concerns about what the citizen would do abroad, but instead based on purely domestic political activity – namely, membership and participation in the Communist Party. So too, *Lamont* protected the right of persons in the United States to receive foreign materials – not the right of US citizens to go abroad for the purpose of disseminating speech. Even though *Lamont*, *Aptheker*, and *Kent* implicated transborder expressive activity, the First Amendment claims at issue in all three decisions involved government actions that placed burdens on domestic speech and associational activity as well.

6.2 THE BURGER COURT AND TRANSBORDER SPEECH: RETRENCHMENT AND GRUDGING ACKNOWLEDGMENT OF THE FIRST AMENDMENT'S APPLICATION TO TRANSBORDER SPEECH

The Burger Court declined to extend the Warren Court's transborder speech precedents and instead distinguished them away to sustain government burdens on transborder speech – specifically foreign speakers entering the United States[110] and US citizens traveling abroad to speak.[111] The Burger Court's transborder speech precedents acknowledge that the First Amendment applies to such speech – but nevertheless find that the federal government had acted constitutionally and for reasons wholly unrelated to suppression of speech based on content or viewpoint (a dubious conclusion based on the facts at bar).

In *Kleindienst v. Mandel*, the Supreme Court sustained the Nixon Administration's decision to refuse Ernest E. Mandel an entry visa.[112] Mandel, a Belgian journalist, served as the editor of a socialist publication, *La Gauche* ("The Left"); he was also an accomplished Marx-Engels scholar and had published works on communist political theory.[113] In September 1969, Mandel applied for a visa for entry into the United States in order to attend an academic meeting at Stanford University, in Palo Alto, California.[114] Famed economist John Kenneth Galbraith was to serve as the keynote speaker at this conference. Mandel was to speak on a panel discussion following Galbraith's address. After Mandel's invitation to speak at Stanford University became publicly known, Mandel received additional speaking invitations, including invitations from "Princeton, Amherst, Columbia, and Vassar."[115]

The US Consulate in Brussels rejected Mandel's visa application in October 1969. The State Department, in a formal letter denying the visa application, claimed that Mandel had violated the terms of his 1968 visa by "engag[ing] in activities beyond the stated purposes" and that his extended activities "represented a flagrant abuse of the opportunities afforded him to express his views in this country."[116] Thus,

Mandel was denied lawful entry to the United States and was unable to speak in person to the various audiences that wished to hear his views.[117]

Mandel, joined by a number of US citizens, all university professors who wished to hear and interact with Mandel in person, brought suit in March 1970 to challenge the visa denial. A three-judge district court found the relevant immigration statutes invalid as applied to Mandel on these facts, and ordered the State Department to provide him with an entry visa. The ruling rested not on Mandel's right to enter the United States for the purpose of public speaking, but rather on the interest of US citizens in hearing and interacting with him.[118] Judge John F. Dooling, Jr., writing for the majority, explained that "[t]he nature of the First Amendment rights as a retained attribute of the sovereignty of the people is reflected in the emphasis that recent adjudications particularly have given to the 'the right to hear.'"[119]

Justice Harry Blackmun, writing for the *Mandel* majority, did not contest the lower court's conclusion that the First Amendment protected audience autonomy, including the right to hear and receive ideas from non-US sources and speakers.[120] Moreover, this right to receive information has particular salience in the context of "our schools and universities."[121] Justice Blackmun considered and squarely rejected the government's argument that US citizens could access Mandel's ideas and opinions through means other than in-person, real time communication. Direct personal communication involves "particular qualities inherent in sustained, face-to-face debate, discussion and questioning."[122] Thus, the "existence of other alternatives" did not "extinguish[] altogether any constitutional interest on the part of appellees in this particular form of access."[123] Thus, as one commentator has observed, *Mandel* "recognizes that a policy of ideological exclusions has important constitutional consequences for American citizens and therefore is subject to constitutional scrutiny."[124]

On the other hand, under the plenary power doctrine, Congress possesses very broad discretion to admit or exclude non-citizens from entering the United States. Congress has "plenary power to make rules for the admission of aliens and to exclude those who possess those characteristics which Congress has forbidden."[125] Moreover, "the formulation of these policies is entrusted exclusively to Congress," a principle that "has become about as firmly imbedded in the legislative and judicial tissues of our body politic as any aspect of our government."[126] Accordingly, in light of this vast discretion, Mandel's supporters did not claim that the First Amendment precluded Congress from barring issuance of a visa to Mandel, but rather that the existence of a waiver procedure meant that the Executive Branch could not exercise its discretionary authority in a way that reflected viewpoint discrimination.[127]

The Supreme Court ultimately dodged the question of whether the State Department could bar Mandel based on his political and ideological beliefs, depriving a US audience of the right to interact with him in person, because the government proffered a "facially legitimate and bona fide" alternative basis for Mandel's exclusion. The State Department denied the waiver "because [it] concluded that the previous abuses by Mandel made it inappropriate to grant a waiver again."[128] Thus, when the Executive Branch uses discretionary authority to exclude an alien "on the basis of a facially legitimate and bona fide reason, the courts will neither look behind the exercise of that discretion, nor test it by balancing its justification against the First Amendment interests of those who seek personal communication" with a visa applicant.[129] In the absence of a facially legitimate and bona fide reason unrelated to the suppression of information and ideas, a meritorious First Amendment claim *might* exist.[130]

Justice Douglas vigorously dissented, arguing that the government applied an "ideological test"[131] to deny Mandel a visa and that "[t]hought control is not within the competence of any branch of government."[132] In his view, persons living in the United States "may need exposure to the ideas of people of many faiths and many creeds to further their education," and, accordingly, the federal courts should have narrowly construed the State Department's statutory authority to deny a visa based on antipathy toward a speaker's likely message.[133]

Justice Thurgood Marshall also dissented, characterizing the stated reason for denying Mandel a waiver as completely pretextual: "There is *no* basis in the present record for concluding that Mandel's behavior on his previous visit was a 'flagrant abuse' – or even willful or knowing departure – from visa restrictions took place."[134] The State Department, in point of fact, had found that these restrictions were not communicated to Mandel, so that he could not fairly be charged with violating conditions that he did not know existed in the first place. Justice Marshall seems to have the better of this argument.

Marshall posited that the government's real reason for denying Mandel's visa application was its "desire to keep certain ideas out of circulation in this country" and "[t]his is hardly a compelling governmental interest."[135] He wryly observed that "[n]othing is served – least of all our standing in the international community – by Mandel's exclusion."[136] Mandel's exclusion constituted a departure "from the basic traditions of our country, its fearless acceptance of free discussion."[137]

Mandel thus reaffirmed the holding of *Lamont* and acknowledged that the First Amendment protects the interest of a US audience in receiving ideas and information from abroad. At the same time, however, it credited what appeared to be an entirely pretextual reason offered to support denial of entry to a world-famous Marx scholar and journalist. Justice Blackmun, and the *Mandel* majority, clearly placed a thumb on the scale in order to find that the real reason for Mandel's exclusion was his failure to comply with limitations on his speaking engagements when he was in the United States in 1968.

Mandel leaves the law more-or-less as it existed after *Lamont*: The geographic locus of ideas and information does not prefigure its protected status under the First Amendment. Audience autonomy, not the plenary power doctrine, should control with respect to the right of US citizens to read and hear news, ideas, and points of view. However, provided that the federal government does not facially target speech qua speech for regulation, it may use its plenary power over the borders to take actions that burden or preclude US would-be audiences from reading, hearing, or seeing foreign speakers.

In other words, even as the *Mandel* Court invoked *Lamont* and reaffirmed its central holding, it adopted the *Zemel* Court's approach to assessing the consistency of federal government action regarding control over the nation's borders. The visa denial was not about "speech" – it was merely about "conduct" (or "action," to use the precise language from *Zemel*[138]). To be sure, and as Professor Zick has observed, "U.S. restrictions on the cross-border movement of citizens have long affected cross-border political, intellectual, academic, social, artistic, and religious exchanges."[139] Although *Mandel* acknowledges the importance of transborder interactions between US citizens and the wider world and holds that the First Amendment affords significant protection to such interactions, the credulousness with which the majority accepted a clearly pretextual basis for denying Mandel a visa grossly disserved core First Amendment values and the process of democratic deliberation.

The Burger Court adopted a largely identical approach in *Haig v. Agee*,[140] holding that the First Amendment protected a right to travel abroad, but finding that the government's decision to revoke Philip Agee's passport was unrelated to concerns about the content or viewpoint of his speech and related solely to Agee's conduct – namely, unlawful disclosure of national security information.[141] Agee had worked for the Central Intelligence Agency (CIA) from 1957 to 1968 and had personal knowledge of "covert intelligence gathering in foreign countries."[142] In the 1970s, Agee embarked on a public campaign to "out" secret CIA operatives, as well as to release classified intelligence information to facilitate holding the agency publicly accountable for its actions.[143]

In December 1979, the State Department revoked Agee's passport based on the department's conclusion that his "activities abroad are causing or are likely to cause serious damage to the national security or foreign policy of the United States."[144] Agee brought suit in federal district court and prevailed;[145] the US Court of Appeals affirmed this decision.[146] The lower federal courts found that Congress had not authorized the regulation used to revoke Agee's passport. The US Court of Appeals for the District of Columbia Circuit acknowledged that Agee's actions "may be considered by some to border on treason,"[147] but nevertheless concluded that the State Department had exceeded its lawful statutory authority because the court was "bound by the law as we find it."[148] The Supreme Court granted review and reversed.

Agee clearly presented serious First Amendment issues – at the heart of Agee's program was an effort to disclose covert CIA operations in foreign countries, activity that certainly involved public officials and matters of public concern.[149] It might seem startling to posit that the unlawful disclosure of classified intelligence information constitutes speech about a matter of public concern, but as Professor Robert Post has explained, "[f]rom the perspective of the logic of democratic self-governance, any restriction of the domain of public discourse must necessarily constitute a forcible truncation of possible lines of democratic development."[150]

This does not mean, of course, that public discourse may never be curtailed to advance important government interests, but it does mean that the concept's "periphery will remain both ideological and vague, subject to an endless negotiation between democracy and community life."[151]

Then-Justice, and later Chief Justice, William H. Rehnquist found that the State Department had established a clear policy of revoking passports to prevent a "substantial likelihood of serious damage to the national security or foreign policy of the United States."[152] He also emphasized that the gravamen of the administrative action was "conduct" rather than speech – the State Department's policy existed to prevent "conduct likely to cause serious damage to our national security or foreign policy."[153] *Kent* was not controlling because the policy of denying US passports to members of the Communist Party had not been consistently enforced and also because "the *Kent* court had no occasion to consider whether the Executive had the power to revoke the passport of an individual whose *conduct* is damaging to the national security and foreign policy of the United States."[154] Justice Rehnquist emphasized that "*Kent* involved denials of passports solely on the basis of political beliefs entitled to First Amendment protection."[155]

Accordingly, on the facts presented, "Agee's First Amendment claim ha[d] no foundation," even assuming "that First Amendment protections reach beyond our national boundaries."[156] Agee's disclosures certainly constituted speech, but they were also conduct, conduct aimed at "obstructing intelligence operations and the recruiting of intelligence personnel," goals and objectives "clearly not protected by the Constitution."[157] Justice Rehnquist emphasized that "[t]he mere fact that Agee is also engaged in criticism of the Government does not render his conduct beyond the reach of the law."[158] Moreover, even after revocation of his passport, "Agee is as free to criticize the United States Government as he was when he held a passport – always subject, of course, to express limits on certain rights by virtue of his [employment] contract with the Government."[159] Justice Rehnquist also found no evidence of either "subterfuge to punish criticism of the Government" or "any basis for a claim of discriminatory enforcement."[160]

Justices Brennan and Marshall dissented, not on the point of whether passport revocation could occur on the facts presented, but rather on whether Congress had, in point of fact, authorized the State Department to adopt the regulation used to effect the revocation of Agee's passport.[161] Moreover, the federal government had not established that Congress had implicitly sanctioned the policy reflected in the regulations.[162] The dissent, then, was about Congress's responsibility for clearly authorizing the policy, and not whether such a policy, if plainly authorized, would violate the First Amendment.[163]

Whatever the shortcomings of *Agee*, the majority takes pains to acknowledge the Warren Court's precedents holding that the First Amendment protects the right to travel abroad for the purpose of engaging in expressive activities. *Agee*, like *Mandel*, does not resile from the Warren Court's holdings that extend First Amendment protection to transborder speech. To be sure, both cases are more broadly deferential to the federal government's use of control over visas and passports than the relevant Warren Court decisions – yet neither case suggests that First Amendment rights stop at the water's edge.

It would be quite fair to say that the Burger Court declined to build on the Warren Court's transborder speech precedents – but it would be off the mark to say that the Burger Court overruled or ignored them. One can perceive, however, a clear and discernable shift toward a posture of greater judicial deference toward the political branches with respect to efforts to regulate speech activity abroad that has the potential for undermining US foreign policy or national security objectives. This trend grew and accelerated under the Rehnquist and Roberts Courts.

6.3 RETROGRESSION: THE REHNQUIST AND ROBERTS COURTS' FAILURE TO AFFORD MEANINGFUL PROTECTION TO TRANSBORDER SPEECH ACTIVITY

The Rehnquist and Roberts Courts have plainly permitted the federal government to restrict the exercise of First Amendment rights based on the transborder character of expressive activities. For example, the Rehnquist Court declined to follow *Lamont* and permitted the federal government to discourage the dissemination within the United States of films funded in part by foreign governments.[164] In addition, it applied the plenary power doctrine to permit targeted deportations that allegedly reflected the federal government's hostility to the deportees' political associations and activities in the United States.[165] Both decisions represent clear, clean breaks with the analytical approach and precedents of the Warren and Burger Courts.

The Roberts Court continued the Rehnquist Court's de facto policy of declining to afford transborder speech significant First Amendment protection. It refused to reach the merits of a challenge to a federal government spying program that targeted all domestic communications with persons or institutions located outside the United States.[166] Even more depressing, the Roberts Court sustained a content-based ban on speech abroad with members of proscribed terrorist organizations – on pain of criminal indictment and imprisonment for lending "material support" to such organizations.[167] In fact, *Humanitarian Law Project* rests on premises fundamentally inconsistent with *Aptheker, Kent,* and even *Agee.* For the first time, the Supreme Court held that the federal government may treat otherwise peaceful, non-violent speech abroad about a matter of public concern as a crime, despite any direct connection between the transborder speech activity and unlawful activities – whether in the United States or abroad.

The Supreme Court's retrenchment project commenced in *Meese v. Keene,*[168] a case that involved coerced speech aimed at discouraging the domestic circulation of films and periodicals produced with foreign government funding. The Foreign

Agents Registration Act of 1938[169] (FARA) requires that persons who distribute films and periodicals within the United States funded by foreign governments register as "agents of foreign principals." Barry Keene, a California state senator, wished to arrange for public showings of three films produced with support from the National Film Board of Canada; two of the films addressed the adverse environmental effects of acid rain and the third was about the potential catastrophic environmental effects of nuclear war.[170]

The FARA required the films to be registered with the Department of Justice and labeled as "foreign political propaganda" distributed at the behest of a "foreign principal."[171] The law required "such political propaganda" to be "conspicuously marked at its beginning with, or prefaced or accompanied by, a true and accurate statement" describing the material's source. The statute also required the exhibitor to provide a formal statement to the recipients of the materials that identifies "such agent of a foreign principal and such political propaganda and its sources."[172] The FARA defined "political propaganda" quite broadly to encompass "any oral, visual, graphic, written, pictorial, or the other communication or expression by any person."[173] Thus, as in *Lamont*, a person seeking to obtain information from abroad had to register with the federal government and, in addition, to distribute a mandatory disclosure form when exhibiting the material to the public.[174]

The district court found that the FARA's registration and mandatory disclosure requirements had a profound chilling effect, coerced speech, and hence violated the First Amendment.[175] US District Judge Raul A. Ramirez found that branding expressive materials as "political propaganda" was clearly pejorative and that Congress adopted the measure in order to discourage the dissemination of materials subject to the registration and disclosure requirements.[176] In consequence, the court held "that the use of the phrase 'political propaganda' in the Foreign Agents Registration Act abridges plaintiff's freedom of speech within the meaning of the First Amendment."[177] The Supreme Court granted direct review of the district court's judgment and reversed.

Writing for the *Keene* majority, Justice John Paul Stevens characterized the FARA's mandatory registration and disclosure requirements as wholly unobjectionable and fully consistent with the First Amendment. He flatly rejected the district court's conclusion that the term "political propaganda" has an obvious and profound pejorative connotation. Accordingly, its compelled use to describe motion pictures, books, or magazines distributed in the United States "places no burden on protected expression."[178]

Of course, *Lamont* holds that the federal government's labeling materials from abroad as "communist political propaganda," and requiring would-be recipients in the United States to register with the government to receive such materials, have an obvious and profound chilling effect – indeed, these requirements could easily prove ruinous to those wishing to receive the information.[179] Why the operator of a movie theater would not fear serious adverse consequences flowing from being identified as the purveyor of "political propaganda" being distributed by the "agents of foreign principals" is far from obvious.[180] Justice Stevens blithely asserts that "Congress simply required the disseminators of such material to make additional disclosures that would better enable the public to evaluate the import of the propaganda."[181] This approach is fundamentally inconsistent with the Warren Court's serious concerns about the chilling effects of having to register with the federal government to receive otherwise lawful material from abroad.

It is certainly true that "Congress did not prohibit, edit, or restrain the distribution of advocacy materials in an ostensible effort to protect the public from conversion, confusion, or deceit."[182] Of course, these exact arguments could have been made in *Lamont* – but were not. Justice Stevens posits that "[b]y compelling some disclosure of information and permitting more, the Act's approach recognizes that the best remedy for misleading or inaccurate speech contained within materials subject to the Act is fair, truthful, and accurate speech."[183] However, were the materials at issue of purely domestic origin, coerced speech requiring the distributor to affix a pejorative label – for example, requiring materials distributed by a public employees labor union to be described as "political propaganda distributed at the behest of labor union agitators" – would be unthinkable. The Supreme Court would reflexively invalidate coerced speech that requires a speaker to denigrate her own speech in a way conceded to be an effort to undermine its persuasive force.[184]

Justice Stevens argued that the cure for the coerced speech problem was not invalidation of the statute imposing the pejorative "foreign propaganda" label, but rather to clarify "before, during, or after the film, or in wholly separate context – that Canada's interest in the consequences of nuclear war and acid rain does not necessarily undermine the integrity or the persuasiveness of its advocacy."[185] Thus, the remedy for coerced speech is more effectively coerced speech – the irony runs very deep.[186]

Moreover, the federal government did not have to shoulder *any* meaningful burden of justification in *Keene* – a result that seems quite remarkable. Again, the Supreme Court, in the context of domestic speech, has protected anonymous speech and invalidated efforts to force political speakers to admit publicly authorship of particular political messages.[187] In fact, Justice Stevens wrote the majority opinion *invalidating* Ohio's proscription against anonymous campaign advocacy. In the context of purely domestic political speech related to an election or ballot measure, the "more speech is better" rationale went out the window because "[u]nder our Constitution, anonymous pamphleteering is not a pernicious, fraudulent practice, but an honorable tradition of advocacy and of dissent."[188] Moreover, "[a]nonymity is a shield from the tyranny of the majority."[189]

It bears noting that not a single reference to *Meese v. Keene* appears in Justice Stevens's majority opinion in *McIntyre*. Nor is there any suggestion that mandatory information disclosures enhance and secure First Amendment values in the domestic electoral context – rather they constitute a very clear violation of the

First Amendment. The only distinction between *Keene* and *McIntyre* involves the geographic source of the expression; domestic speech cannot be subjected to mandatory disclosure requirements, whereas speech that originates abroad, that was funded in whole or in part by a foreign government, may be subjected to mandatory, pejorative labeling requirements.

To be sure, *Keene* was not a unanimous decision. In a powerful and persuasive dissent, Justice Blackmun argued that "[b]y ignoring the practical effect of the Act's classification scheme, the Court unfortunately permits Congress to accomplish by indirect means what it could not impose directly – a restriction of appellee's political speech."[190] The FARA clearly burdens speech because it "inhibits dissemination of classified films."[191] It will dissuade exhibitors from showing the films and "taints the message of a classified film by lessening its credence with viewers."[192]

In *Reno v. American-Arab Anti-Discrimination Committee*.[193] The Rehnquist Court extended its deference to Congress and the President in transborder speech cases. The majority opinion, written by Justice Antonin Scalia, dismissed as irrelevant a claim that the federal government targeted deportation proceedings against the plaintiffs "because of their affiliation with a politically unpopular group," namely the "Popular Front for the Liberation of Palestine (PFLP), a group that the Government characterize[d] as an international terrorist and communist organization."[194]

The initial deportation proceedings facially targeted the proposed deportees on "advocacy-of-communism charges," but the federal government dropped this claim in favor of speech-neutral legal justifications for the deportation proceedings.[195] At a press conference, however, the Immigration and Naturalization Service's (INS) regional counsel stated although "the charges had been changed for tactical reasons," that "the INS was still seeking respondents' deportation because of their affiliation with the PFLP."[196] Despite the ideological motivation for the deportations, the Supreme Court held that the proceedings were not subject to judicial review.

The potential "chilling effect" of targeted deportations based on political activities was irrelevant to deciding whether the deportees' selective enforcement claims were judicially cognizable.[197] The majority effectively deprived aliens seeking to contest deportation the ability to press selective enforcement claims before the federal courts.[198] This was so because judicial review of such claims, even if laced with First Amendment arguments, would require "not merely the disclosure of normal domestic law enforcement priorities and techniques, but often the disclosure of foreign-policy objectives and (as in this case) foreign-intelligence products and techniques."[199]

As with *Zemel*, *Mandel*, and *Agee*, federal court misgivings about disrupting foreign policy and national security matters clearly motivated the Supreme Court's decision to defer to the political branches:

> The Executive should not have to disclose its "real" reasons for deeming nationals of a particular country a special threat – or indeed for simply wishing to antagonize a

particular foreign country by focusing on that country's nationals – and even if it did disclose them a court would be ill equipped to determine their authenticity and utterly unable to assess their adequacy.[200]

This presumption against judicial review could perhaps be overcome in "outrageous" circumstances, but "[w]hether or not there be such exceptions, the general rule certainly applies here."[201] Accordingly, "[w]hen an alien's continuing presence in this country is in violation of the immigration laws, the Government does not offend the Constitution by deporting him for the additional reason that it believes him to be a member of an organization that supports terrorist activity."[202]

Consistent with this posture of deference, the Roberts Court also has used decision avoidance techniques to avoid reaching the merits in important transborder speech cases. *Clapper v. Amnesty International USA*[203] provides an illustrative example of this phenomenon.

Under section 702 of the Foreign Intelligence Surveillance Act (FISA), the federal government may conduct regular surveillance of persons who do not reside in the United States.[204] Such surveillance is contingent on the approval of the FISA Court. In *Clapper*, a group of U.S. persons who engage in regular electronic communications with non-US residents sued in federal district court, seeking an order declaring section 702 to be unconstitutional.

The entire predicate for surveillance under section 702 is communications activity that crosses the nation's borders. Amendments that Congress enacted in 2008 authorize the conduct "of certain foreign intelligence surveillance targeting the communications of non-U.S. persons located abroad."[205] Under current law, surveillance undertaken under section 702 does not require any showing of probable cause or targeting of the federal government's surveillance activity. Use of the data, however, is subject to substantive and procedural protections.[206]

If the federal government engaged in this sort of ongoing, dragnet surveillance with respect to entirely domestic electronic communications, the federal courts would easily find that the surveillance activity constitutes a violation of the Fourth Amendment. The chilling effect of such surveillance also would trigger serious First Amendment concerns. Accordingly, the plaintiffs' complaint alleged that the section 702 surveillance program violated the Fourth Amendment, the First Amendment, and separation of powers principles.[207]

The *Clapper* Court declined to reach the merits of the plaintiffs' claims; instead, the majority held that the plaintiffs lacked Article III standing to challenge the "foreign" surveillance program. Justice Samuel A. Alito, Jr., writing for the *Clapper* majority, explained that the plaintiffs' "theory of *future* injury is too speculative to satisfy the well-established requirement that threatened injury must be 'certainly impending.'"[208] This was so because "it is speculative whether the Government will imminently target communications to which respondents are parties."[209] Nor was "incurring costs in anticipation of nonimminent harm" sufficient to establish a constitutionally cognizable injury because self-imposed costs could easily be used to defeat the Article III standing requirement of injury in fact by permitting would-be plaintiffs to essentially manufacture standing through entirely voluntary expenditures.[210]

To be sure, *Clapper* was a 5–4 decision. Justice Stephen G. Breyer, writing for the minority, would have held that standing existed because "there is a high probability that the Government will intercept at least some electronic communication to which at least some of the plaintiffs are parties."[211] Thus, "[t]he majority is wrong when it describes the harm threatened the plaintiffs as 'speculative.'"[212]

Standing analysis should not turn on whether a constitutional harm involves transborder speech activity or wholly domestic communications. Yet, one has to wonder if the *Clapper* majority was less concerned with judicial review of the section 702 program because it targeted communications that involve at least one foreign party. If, as the preceding cases suggest, the Bill of Rights applies more weakly outside the nation's borders, it would be reasonable to use discretionary merits-avoidance doctrines, like standing[213] or the political question doctrine,[214] to avoid reaching the merits of the NSA's mass surveillance of international electronic communications. It would have been more intellectually defensible to reach this conclusion through an analysis of the merits – in other words, one could find that at least some of the plaintiffs had standing to challenge the section 702 surveillance program, but nevertheless deny relief on the merits – and on the theory that constitutional rights apply either weakly or not at all when speech activity takes place, even in part, outside the nation's territory.

Indeed, in the final major transborder speech case of the Roberts Court era, the Supreme Court essentially took this step because avoiding the merits on standing or political question grounds was not a viable option. In *Holder v. Humanitarian Law Project*,[215] the Supreme Court essentially applied a weak, tepid version of strict scrutiny to a content-based criminal restriction of the freedom of speech and association out of concern that more demanding judicial scrutiny would interfere with important foreign affairs and national security objectives. To be sure, as Professor Zick observes, "[c]ourts seem to treat any utterance or association that happens to intersect with territorial borders as activity that touches on foreign affairs and implicates national security."[216] Even so, however, *Humanitarian Law Project's* abject deference to the political branches – at the cost of proscribing core expressive activity that would be vigorously protected under the First Amendment at home – makes the decision rather remarkable.[217]

Humanitarian Law Project involved a First Amendment challenge to a federal statute that criminalized "knowingly provid[ing] material support or resources to a foreign terrorist organization."[218] Humanitarian Law Project (HLP) sought to teach peaceful dispute resolution techniques to the Partiya Karkeran Kurdistan (PKK); the federal government listed the PKK as a "foreign terrorist organization," and, accordingly, providing the PKK with "material support" constituted a crime. HLP argued that, as applied to their associational activities with the PKK, which involved instruction in peaceful dispute resolution techniques, section 2339B violated the First Amendment.

The Supreme Court rejected HLP's First Amendment claims. The statute was not impermissibly vague in proscribing "material support" because "a person of ordinary intelligence" would understand the statute's scope of application.[219] The majority also rejected HLP's more general free speech claims, holding that because "[p]roviding foreign terrorist groups with material support in any form" has the effect of furthering terrorism,[220] the federal government had "adequately substantiated [its] determination that, to serve the Government's interest in preventing terrorism, it was necessary to prohibit providing material support in the form of training, expert advice, personnel, and services to foreign terrorist groups, even if the supporters meant to promote only the groups' nonviolent ends."[221] Chief Justice Roberts, writing for the majority, observed that "[a]t bottom, plaintiffs simply disagree with the considered judgment of Congress and the Executive that providing material support to a designated foreign terrorist organization – even seemingly benign support – bolsters the terrorist activities of that organization."[222]

The sweep and scope of the decision is astonishing. In the 1950s and 1960s, the Supreme Court invalidated state and federal laws that made mere membership in the Communist Party or affiliated organizations a criminal act; the Warren Court held that criminalizing "material support" of domestic communist organizations was incompatible with the freedoms of speech, assembly, and association safeguarded by the First Amendment.[223] Even if membership in a local branch of the Soviet Communist Party might lend legitimacy and credibility to the local organization's foreign parent, the federal government could not proscribe domestic communist organizations or criminalize mere membership in them. By way of contrast, however, *Humanitarian Law Project* holds that the slightest *possibility* of lending "legitimacy" to organizations like the PKK constitutes a harm that the federal government may legislate to prevent – using the criminal law as its means of censoring speech.

Indeed, Chief Justice Roberts asserts that *any* kind of association and coordinated activity by US citizens with members of foreign terrorist organizations abroad "helps lend legitimacy to foreign terrorist groups – legitimacy that makes it easier for those groups to persist, to recruit members, and to raise funds – all of which facilitate more terrorist attacks."[224] Professor David Cole rightly objects that Roberts "engaged in only the most deferential review, and upheld the law in the absence of any argument, much less evidentiary showing, that prohibiting plaintiffs' speech was necessary or narrowly tailored to further a compelling interest."[225] Moreover, "the Court's scrutiny was ... neither strict nor fatal, nor even 'demanding'" but rather represented "only the most deferential review."[226]

Despite the Chief Justice's claims to the contrary, this kind of "parade of horribles" reasoning would apply with no less force to mere membership in local affiliates of foreign organizations (such as the Communist Party of the Soviet Union) on the theory that *any* domestic support of local affiliates lends the foreign parent organization "legitimacy." Accordingly, the distinction must rest on the transborder character of the First Amendment activity – and not on the nature of the activity itself. This has the odd effect of making the government's power to censor speech a function of its location – rather than its potential social cost.

To be sure, *Humanitarian Law Project* does not overturn the Warren Court precedents that afforded transborder speech First Amendment protection. Instead, the majority opinion distinguishes them away because the locus of the First Amendment activities protected by the Warren Court's precedents were largely domestic in character. Chief Justice Roberts emphasizes that "[w]e … do not suggest that Congress could extend the same prohibition on material support at issue here to domestic organizations."[227] Moreover, lower federal courts have relied on this caveat to reject the federal government's efforts to criminalize membership in domestic affiliates of foreign organizations deemed to have terroristic objectives.[228]

Humanitarian Law Project essentially creates an exception to the First Amendment for speech activity that takes place outside the United States.[229] It does so to avoid the prospect of the federal judiciary applying the First Amendment in ways that would potentially interfere with foreign affairs and national security objectives that Congress and the President seek to secure. For example, US foreign relations policy could be adversely affected by transborder speech because it "strain[s] the United States' relationships with its allies and undermin[es] cooperative efforts between nations to prevent terrorist attacks."[230] Moreover, the political branches are "entitled to deference" when assessing the potential adverse effects of speech activity abroad because of the "sensitive and weighty interests of national security and foreign affairs."[231]

Even though Congress imposed a content-based restriction on speech, via the criminal law, and did nothing to narrowly tailor its regulation to directly target only unlawful activity, would-be speakers must lose their ability to exercise First Amendment rights abroad because the judgment of the political branches regarding the requisite balance to be struck "is entitled to significant weight."[232] Despite purporting to apply strict scrutiny to section 2339B, the majority applied something much closer to rationality review; neither Congress nor the President labored under any obligation to prove the factual predicates that supported a flat ban on speech activity and free association with proscribed organizations abroad. By way of contrast, the legislative record supporting the Bipartisan Campaign Finance Reform Act of 2002 spanned over 100,000 pages – but failed to incent much, if any, judicial deference.[233]

Humanitarian Law Project completes the turn that began under the Burger Court in cases like *Mandel* and *Agee*. In order to avoid interfering with foreign policy and national security objectives, the federal courts will apply a junior varsity version of the First Amendment to speech activity that takes place outside the physical borders of the United States. The potential social cost of speech activity is not usually a basis for censoring speech inside the nation's borders – but it constitutes a compelling interest outside of them. This approach is mistaken – at least if the value of speech to the project of democratic self-government bears no necessary relationship to a speaker's identity or motive for speaking.[234]

6.4 MAPPING THE FIRST AMENDMENT ON TO TRANSBORDER SPEECH: THE RELEVANCE OF MEIKLEJOHN'S DEMOCRATIC SELF-GOVERNMENT THEORY OF FREEDOM OF EXPRESSION

The value of speech has nothing to do with its foreign or domestic locus. The logic of *Citizens United* and the Meiklejohn democratic self-government theory of the First Amendment requires that the federal courts afford speech meaningful First Amendment protection regardless of its transborder nature. Using the nation's borders as a basis for censoring speech is antithetical to everything that the First Amendment ostensibly stands for – and, accordingly, cannot be accepted as a persuasive interpretation of its meaning, scope, and import.

If the central insight of *Citizens United* holds true – the identity of the speaker and the speaker's motivations for entering the marketplace of ideas are irrelevant to the potential value of speech to its audience – the failure to protect cross-border speech cannot be justified in normative, policy, or doctrinal terms.[235] Simply put, either the government may regulate speech based on the identity and motive of a speaker – or it may not. Either *Citizens United* or *Humanitarian Law Project* was wrongly decided, for these decisions rest on fundamentally incompatible premises about the central meaning of the First Amendment. In short, if we truly believe that speech related to democratic self-government requires vigorous and vigilant protection against a censorial federal government, then we should embrace the constitutional logic of *Citizens United* and reject *Humanitarian Law Project*'s embarrassingly halting, weak, and grossly underprotective vision of the freedom of speech for the citizens of a democratic polity.

The facts of the case are straightforward. As part of the Bipartisan Campaign Reform Act of 2002, a comprehensive campaign finance reform package, Congress enacted a statutory provision that prohibited corporations and labor unions alike from engaging in "electioneering communication,"[236] which the statute defined as "any broadcast, cable, or satellite communication" that refers to "a clearly identified candidate for Federal office" and made thirty days before a primary election or sixty days prior to a general election.[237] Fearing that the Federal Election Commission (FEC) would find that broadcast of *Hillary: The Movie*, a film highly critical of Hillary Rodham Clinton, would constitute an "electioneering communication" falling within section 441b's proscription against such speech by corporations and labor unions, Citizens United, the movie's producer, sought a preliminary injunction holding section 441b unconstitutional as applied to the film.[238] The district court denied the injunction and the US Court of Appeals affirmed the district court's judgment.[239]

The Supreme Court granted review and reversed. In doing so, it overruled a 2003 precedent that had specifically upheld section 441b against a First Amendment challenge[240] and also a 1990 decision that had sustained limits on corporate political speech because such speech could have a distortionary effect on the political process.[241] After overruling these precedents, the *Citizens United* majority proceeded to hold that section 441b violated the First Amendment because the statute's "purpose and effect are to silence entities whose voices the Government deems to be suspect."[242]

Justice Anthony M. Kennedy posited that "[t]he First Amendment protects speech and speaker, and the ideas that flow from each."[243] He emphasized that the government may not intervene in information markets in order to handpick free speech winners and losers: "The Government may not by these means deprive the public of the right and privilege to determine for itself what speech and speakers are worthy of consideration."[244] This rule reflects the fact that the value of information and ideas does not necessarily correlate with either the speaker's identity or motive for speaking. Moreover, *Citizens United* embraces a theory of audience autonomy that permits readers, listeners, and viewers to assess for themselves the reliability and value of speech; the decision squarely rejects government paternalism as a basis for speech regulations in the political marketplace of ideas.[245] In consequence, the government may not use a speaker's identity or motive for speaking as a basis for imposing silence.[246] As Justice Kennedy stated the point, "[s]peech is an essential mechanism of democracy, for it is the means to hold officials accountable to the people."[247]

If these premises are correct – namely that the value of information and ideas is simply not a function of a speaker's identity or motive for speaking and paternalistic government interventions in the political marketplace of ideas are inherently and unacceptably distortionary – then it should also be the case that a speaker's *geographic location* is equally irrelevant to the potential value of speech to the political marketplace of ideas and to the dangers of paternalistic government censorship of core political speech. After all, if "it is inherent in the nature of the political process that voters must be free to obtain information from diverse sources in order to determine how to cast their votes,"[248] the location of information otherwise potentially relevant to the process of democratic self-government should be irrelevant to its protected status under the First Amendment.

Given that "no basis [exists] for the proposition that, in the context of political speech, the Government may impose restrictions on certain disfavored speakers," the contemporary Supreme Court's failure to provide meaningful protection to transborder speech activity is difficult, if not impossible, to reconcile with core

First Amendment values. A theory of the First Amendment premised, at least in part, on a paradigm of audience (voter) autonomy would seem to require that transborder speech be no less protected than speech that happens to take place within the metes and bounds of the United States.

If, as the *Citizens United* majority argued, "[t]he right of citizens to inquire, to hear, to speak, and to use information to reach consensus is a precondition to enlightened self-government and a necessary means to protect it,"[249] speech that originates outside the nation's borders should be no less protected than speech that originates within those borders. So too, if citizens may engage in free speech, free association, and assembly in order to advance the process of democratic self-government at home, then US citizens should be no less free to engage in such activities abroad.[250] Speech relevant to democratic self-government must enjoy the First Amendment's most robust protection. Simply put, if "political speech must prevail against laws that would suppress it, whether by design or inadvertence,"[251] then the geographic locus of the political speech should not be the controlling factor in First Amendment analysis.

Under the logic of *Humanitarian Law Project*, however, the protection of political expression depends critically on its domestic or transborder character. This outcome simply cannot be reconciled with Justice Kennedy's soaring poetics to the centrality of free and wide-open speech to the maintenance of democratic self-government and his Cassandra-esque warnings about the danger of permitting government to banish disfavored speakers from the political marketplace of ideas.[252] Moreover, *Humanitarian Law Project*'s reasoning and outcome also cannot be reconciled with a theory of freedom of expression that justifies protecting speech because of its integral relationship to the process of democratic self-government.

Professor Alexander Meiklejohn, arguably that most prominent proponent of the democratic self-government theory of the First Amendment, argued strongly that US citizens must have access to speakers and ideas regardless of their domestic or foreign origin. He inveighed against Attorney General Tom C. Clark's adoption of regulations that "restrict[ed] the freedom of speech of temporary foreign visitors to our shores" and "declare[d] that certain classes of visitors are forbidden, except by special permission, to engage in public discussion of public policy while they are among us."[253] Meiklejohn, outraged, asked "Why may we not hear what these men from other countries, other systems of government, have to say?"[254] He condemned efforts to protect voters from speakers and ideas "too 'dangerous' for us to hear."[255] To accept the exclusion of speech, speakers, and ideas based on their foreign origin "would seem to be an admission that we are intellectually and morally unfit to play our part in what Justice Holmes has called the 'experiment' of self-government."[256]

Professor Meiklejohn states the point in forceful, yet highly persuasive, terms. The First Amendment protects the distribution of books like Adolph Hitler's *Mein Kampf*, Vladimir Lenin's *The State and Revolution*, and Friedrich Engels and Karl Marx's *Communist Manifesto* not because of "the financial interests of a publisher, or a distributor, or even of a writer."[257] Instead, "[w]e are saying that the citizens of the United States will be fit to govern themselves under their own institutions only if they have faced squarely and fearlessly everything that can be said in favor of those institutions, everything that can be said against them."[258] In sum, "[t]he unabridged freedom of public discussion is the rock on which our government stands."[259]

Meiklejohn could not have been more clear, or emphatic, in his rejection of using the transborder nature of speech or speakers as a basis for restricting, much less banning, access by US citizens to people, information, ideas, and ideologies. To threaten American citizens with criminal prosecution for interacting abroad with foreign political organizations (such as the PKK)[260] or attempting to visit Cuba in order to assess the efficacy of the US policy of embargo and isolation,[261] is to undermine, if not betray, the process of wide-open public discussion of public affairs that Meiklejohn believes to be crucial to maintaining the ability of citizens to hold the institutions of government accountable through the electoral process.[262] As he explained, "[w]hen a free man is voting, it is not enough that the truth is known by someone else, by some scholar or administrator or legislator."[263] Instead, "[t]he voters must have it, all of them."[264] If we accept Meiklejohn's arguments, then US citizens must be free to interact with both foreign speakers and ideas – at home, in the United States, but also abroad.[265]

So too, trying to discourage US voters from considering ideas and arguments from abroad by labeling films "political propaganda" being distributed "by foreign principals and their agents"[266] seems fundamentally inconsistent with a theory of freedom of speech that protects expression from paternalistic government efforts to control, or even merely to tilt, the marketplace of political ideas. Just as banning a celebrated foreign Marx scholar from visiting the United States in order to lecture and speak to and with audiences comprised of US citizens eager to hear and interact with him[267] transgresses our core constitutional commitment to maintaining a public debate that is "uninhibited, robust, and wide-open."[268] This is so because, as Professor Cole posits, "[c]ommunication across borders furthers many of the values said to be served by the First Amendment."[269]

Meikejohn emphasizes, in a well-functioning democracy, that:

> The voters ... must be made as wise as possible. The welfare of the community requires that those who decide issues shall understand them. They must know what they are voting about. ... When men govern themselves, it is they – and no one else – who must pass judgment upon unwisdom and unfairness and danger. And that means that unwise ideas must have a hearing as well as wise ones, unfair as well as fair, dangerous as well as safe, un-American as well as American.[270]

Moreover, "[t]o be afraid of ideas, any idea, is to be unfit for self-government."[271]

Citizens United, whatever one's views of the desirability of limits on corporate or union speech favoring or opposing candidates for federal elective office, reflects and incorporates these insights – government simply lacks the constitutional competence to adopt paternalistic regulations that seek to protect voters from bad ideas propagated by self-interested speakers. Audience autonomy constitutes the trump card; the public can judge for itself the merit, or lack of it, in any particular instance of political speech.[272] By way of contrast, however, *Humanitarian Law Project* permits the government to proscribe First Amendment activity because it *might* impede or burden the achievement of the federal government's foreign relations or national security objectives. Under this unfortunate precedent, the federal government may suppress, through the criminal law, transborder speech that it deems too dangerous to tolerate – because it might lend "legitimacy" to foreign organizations that it opposes.[273] However, a free people in a democratic polity should be entitled to use free speech and their votes to set or amend government policy – rather than the other way around (*i.e.*, government policies controlling the scope of permissible democratic discourse).

The normative position that animates *Citizens United* rests in a fundamental tension with the theoretical basis of *Humanitarian Law Project*: It is simply not plausible to posit that government interventions in speech markets are distortionary – except when they are not. *Citizens United* posits that the First Amendment constitutes a kind of structural check on government, literally "[p]remised on mistrust of governmental power."[274] If one presumes that government attempts to regulate or control the political marketplace of ideas are inherently and invariably distortionary, it would make sense to subject such efforts to beady-eyed judicial scrutiny.

On the other hand, *Humanitarian Law Project* vests government with tremendous power to regulate even core political speech – to criminalize it, in fact – if the speech activity happens to take place abroad and *might* present an obstacle to the federal government's foreign policy or national security objectives.[275] The risk of government abusing its power to censor speech, and thereby distort the mechanisms of democratic accountability,[276] exists regardless of the domestic or foreign locus of speech. One cannot coherently take both sides on the fundamental question of whether, as a general matter, government interventions in speech markets *enhance* or *degrade* the marketplace of political ideas. Nevertheless, the constitutional logic of *Humanitarian Law Project* would support the kinds of domestic speech regulations that the *Citizens United* majority so forcefully rejected as fundamentally incompatible with the central meaning and purpose of the First Amendment.

In sum, the threat that an organization, and its ideas, presents to the public health, safety, and welfare simply does not correlate with the organization's domestic or foreign nature. If "[t]he primary purpose of the First Amendment is, then, that all the citizens shall, so far as possible, understand the issues which bear upon our common life,"[277] then the federal courts cannot permit the transborder nature of speech to prefigure its protected, or unprotected, status under the First Amendment.[278] A thorough and meaningful commitment to democratic self-government, and the process of deliberation that facilitates it, requires that "no idea, no opinion, no doubt, no belief, no counterbelief, no relevant information may be kept from [the citizenry]."[279] Yet, the Supreme Court, from the Burger Court era to the present, has failed to respect and advance these principles when transborder speech is at issue. We can and should expect more civic courage from our nation's highest constitutional court.[280]

6.5 CONCLUSION

The Warren Court pioneered First Amendment protection for transborder speech. The Burger Court failed to expand on the limited scope of protection that the Warren Court conveyed on transborder speech – but declined to expressly overrule the Warren Court's precedents. By way of contrast, however, the Rehnquist and Roberts Courts moved both existing doctrine and practice toward a more general posture of abject judicial deference to Congress and the President when the political branches seek to regulate, or even proscribe, transborder speech activity that takes place abroad.

As Professor Zick observes "the First Amendment has a critically important transborder dimension."[281] First Amendment theory and doctrine can and must take account of transborder speech as a potentially important part of the larger process of democratic deliberation. To be sure, the federal courts' consistent failure to protect transborder speech vigorously and vigilantly suggests that securing change may take time and involve incremental, rather than wholesale, improvements. Even if this is so, however, Neuborne and Shapiro are surely correct to posit that "the assumption that present judicial attitudes are immutable, or that they even reflect a coherent legal theory, is mistaken."[282]

The case for change is not difficult to make: It is impossible to reconcile the core First Amendment reasoning of *Citizens United* with that of *Humanitarian Law Project*. *Citizens United* constitutes an extended argument that the value and relevance of speech to the project of democratic self-governance does not depend on a speaker's identity or motive for speaking. The decision also reflects deep skepticism about government efforts to censor, or even to shape, the political marketplace of ideas by banishing disfavored speakers. Yet, *Humanitarian Law Project* reflects precisely the opposite attitude – a position of reflexive trust in government – and rests on the assumption that a speaker's identity and motive for speaking (at least in the transborder context) may serve as a basis for sustaining government regulations that nakedly censor even core political speech. If the Supreme Court actually meant what it said with such force in *Citizens United* about the First Amendment being premised on a profound mistrust of government interventions in speech markets,[283] then the federal courts can and should apply the First Amendment more reliably and robustly to transborder speech.

In conclusion, First Amendment activity should not go unprotected simply because it happens to possess a transborder element. Current First Amendment theory and doctrine fails – quite badly – to respect the idea that the First Amendment protects a public debate that will be "uninhibited, robust, and wide-open."[284] If the Supreme Court's efforts to prohibit the government from distorting the political marketplace of ideas reflect a meaningful and deep-seated jurisprudential commitment – rather than a merely rhetorical one – a serious course correction is both needed and long overdue.

7

Systemic Failures to Protect Newsgathering Activities by Professional Journalists and Amateur Citizen-Journalists Alike

Democratic self-government relies on the ability of citizens to make informed decisions about the government – more specifically, elections can serve as a mechanism for securing government accountability only if voters possess the necessary information to make well-informed electoral choices. As noted earlier, in Chapter 4 regarding the contributions that government employees can make to facilitating the process of democratic self-government,[1] the Fourth Estate plays a crucial role in making democracy function. In order for journalists to perform this critical role, however, it is essential that they be able to engage in newsgathering activities;[2] reportage cannot exist in the absence of the newsgathering activities that make reportage possible.[3]

Moreover, in the age of the internet, the electorate receives news and information not only from traditional media outlets, such as local and national television newscasts, and print newspapers, but also through amateur citizen-journalists who post important information to web-based platforms.[4] Even if citizen-journalists cannot, and should not, displace completely professionally trained journalists, they can and do make significant contributions to the marketplace of ideas – contributions that help voters make better informed choices on election day.

Both professional and amateur journalists must be able to engage in newsgathering activities in order to report on public officials, public figures, and matters of public concern.[5] And, even if newsgathering is not itself a communicative activity,[6] it constitutes an essential preliminary activity that merits serious First Amendment protection.[7] Yet, the federal courts have not moved with alacrity to check government efforts at the local, state, and federal level to impede legitimate newsgathering activities.[8]

One might think that the First Amendment would be potentially relevant to the ability of professional journalists and citizen-journalists alike to record activities that take place in public and to distribute such content. One would be mistaken, however, to hold such an assumption. The Supreme Court has not yet spoken to this precise question and the lower federal and state courts have issued conflicting opinions.[9] As Professors RonNell Andersen Jones and Sonja West have observed, "despite these strong textual and historical arguments, the Supreme Court has long been wary of interpreting the First Amendment's Press Clause as an active and vibrant defender of press freedom – at least in any manner that might distinguish it from the Speech Clause."[10] In the meantime, organized government efforts to suppress newsgathering activity are real and growing.

The federal courts have never recognized a First Amendment reporter's privilege. Nor has Congress enacted a federal law providing a generic press shield that protects journalists from efforts to force them to identify confidential sources.[11] Even so, however, the federal government plainly exercised more restraint in seeking to impede journalists engaged in newsgathering activities twenty or thirty years ago than today.[12] Voluntary self-restraint of this sort, which greatly facilitated the press's role in making democracy work, has demonstrably eroded in recent years.

Things were better in the era of the Warren and Burger Courts. For example, in the context of access to judicial proceedings, and the freedom to report on them, the Burger Court issued landmark decisions that recognized the importance of press coverage of judicial proceedings to the legitimacy of such proceedings – despite the risk that such coverage could potentially burden the ability of the judicial system to provide a fair and impartial trial process.[13] Even if the Warren and Burger Courts did not issue sweeping First Amendment decisions that broadly vindicated the right of the press to engage in newsgathering activity, surely limited constitutional protection for some aspects of journalistic activity is better than no protection at all.

The Rehnquist and Roberts Courts, however, have failed to extend these earlier precedents or to establish new ones that recognize that the First Amendment protects newsgathering activity. As Professor Jocelyn Simonson aptly observes, although "it has become routine to hear experts and lay people alike declare that there is a First Amendment 'right to record' the police," such a right "is not yet settled law."[14] Several US Courts of Appeals have questioned whether such a right exists – as have multiple district courts.[15] What's more, even if the federal courts reach a consensus that such a right exists,[16] a right to record the police in public would have to be reconciled successfully with more general laws against impeding or interfering with police work.

These adverse lower court rulings simply reflect the fact that the Supreme Court has never recognized a general right to engage in newsgathering.[17] On the other hand, however, some First Amendment decisions of the Warren and Burger Courts checked efforts to impede newsgathering as such in specific contexts. And, if one cobbles together the concurring opinions – and votes – in decisions such as *Branzburg v. Hayes*[18] and *Houchins v. KQED*,[19] it is possible to argue that newsgathering activities had some claim on the First Amendment in the 1970s and 1980s.

Professors Jones and West, both thoughtful scholars of the First Amendment, and particularly the Press Clause, accurately observe that in the contemporary United States, "[t]he First Amendment provides only limited protection for the press."[20] Constitutional protections for newsgathering activities "are far feebler than you may think" and "[e]ven more worrisome, they have been weakening in recent years."[21]

Jones and West warn that in the contemporary United States, "the courts cannot be relied on – at least not as they once could be – for forceful protection of press liberties."[22] This remains so despite the open and frequent attacks that President Trump and his administration have mounted against the institutional press.[23]

Unfortunately, Professors Jones and West are quite correct to offer a Cassandra-like warning about the state of constitutional solicitude presently afforded newsgathering activities. Today, the federal courts have proven less willing to deploy the Press Clause to protect journalists engaged in newsgathering activities – activities essential to the ability of the press to report on matters of public concern – than they have in the not-so-distant past.[24] Police and prosecutors also have adopted practices aimed at harassing journalists in order to impede reporting – such as targeted mass arrests of working journalists covering events such as the Occupy Protests and the protests in Ferguson, Missouri.[25] In order to report the news, journalists must be able to gather the facts. Thus, impeding newsgathering activities effectively burdens, and in some cases precludes, reporting the news.[26] However, as Jones and West argue, "[w]ithout First Amendment protections for newsgathering, the press is left quite vulnerable while in the process of pursuing information."[27]

The failure of the federal courts to check efforts to impede newsgathering and reporting obviously creates serious risks to the process of democratic self-government – which relies on the Fourth Estate in order to function.[28] Even so, however, the contemporary Supreme Court has demonstrated little interest in deploying the Press Clause, or the Speech Clause, to convey more meaningful and robust protection on the institutional press.[29] As Professor Barry P. McDonald has noted, the Supreme Court "has declined to recognize the existence of a First Amendment right to gather information from government sources outside the discrete area of criminal judicial proceedings."[30] But the problem is broader and deeper than just denials of access to information within the government's possession – various government agencies attempt to impede newsgathering, which goes beyond simply declining to facilitate it.

Moreover, government efforts to impede newsgathering activities extend beyond efforts to prevent or merely frustrate professional journalists and include efforts to suppress newsgathering activities by would-be citizen journalists. For example, despite an ongoing problem with police misconduct, state governments have legislated to prohibit the filming of government officials, including police, when in public.

Part of the problem is that "information gathering frequently consists of predominantly non-expressive conduct that is unable to lay claim to the core of the First Amendment's protection accorded to expression itself."[31] But to say that newsgathering is not at the core of the First Amendment, because it is not communicative but antecedent to communication, is not to say that the activity should be entirely unprotected under the First Amendment. As Professor McDonald observes, "the fact that information gathering generally consists of non-expressive activity cannot be totally dispositive of the First Amendment question" because "many forms of non-expressive conduct receive such protection given a sufficient link to expressive activity."[32]

This chapter will also consider other contemporary threats to newsgathering and journalism, such as efforts to use federal anti-espionage laws, contempt proceedings, and laws against filming industrial farming operations as a means of impeding or preventing newsgathering activity.[33] It will also describe and critique the systematic failure of the federal courts to move aggressively to deploy the First Amendment to constrain, if not prevent, these efforts to block journalists from reporting the news. Simply put, the Press Clause,[34] either alone or in conjunction with the Speech Clause, should be read to convey meaningful constitutional protection on activities integral to journalistic reporting.

Importantly, the chapter will acknowledge the competing value of privacy and the importance of achieving a reasonable balance between the right to report and the right to avoid unwanted intrusion into one's home and private life.[35] In reconciling these competing and conflicting values, the federal courts should draw from the *New York Times Co. v. Sullivan*[36] line of cases, which significantly reduces the protective scope of defamation law for public officials, public figures, and persons involved in matters of public concern.[37] In sum, even if US courts should consider embracing a right to be "private in public," along the lines of the privacy interest recognized by domestic courts in Canada, Germany, the United Kingdom, and within the jurisprudence of the European Court of Human Rights,[38] public officials, public figures, and persons involved in matters of public concern must enjoy more limited rights of privacy in public places in order to facilitate democratic accountability.[39]

This chapter proceeds in five parts. Part 7.1 examines the limited, but meaningful, protection that the Warren and Burger Courts afforded to journalistic activities under the rubric of the First Amendment. Part 7.2 will then consider and critique the failure of the Rehnquist and Roberts Courts to build on the work of their predecessors to safeguard the newsgathering process. Part 7.3 describes and critiques the current ongoing assault on journalists and journalism, and argues that the emergence of more regularized government efforts to impede newsgathering require a stronger judicial response from the federal courts – at least if the press is to play its important role in the process of democratic self-government.

In Part 7.4, I argue that a viable solution will require finding and holding a sensible balance between the need to protect legitimate governmental interests and the ability of both professional and amateur journalists to engage in their craft. Even if absolute protection for newsgathering activity is not plausible because of the social cost (including the burden such an approach would place on legitimate privacy interests), more constitutional solicitude for journalistic activity is both necessary and feasible. Finally, Part 7.5 offers a brief summary and conclusion.

In sum, the federal courts should apply the First Amendment more vigorously to protect newsgathering activities – whether undertaken by full-time, professional journalists or amateur citizen-journalists. If government may constitutionally suppress newsgathering activities, then it may suppress the news itself. Just as free speech is integral to democracy because elections cannot be deemed free and fair in the absence of an open and vigorous political marketplace of ideas, it is also the case that democracy cannot flourish in the absence of a free press ready and able to provide the voters with the information required to make well-informed electoral choices on election day.[40]

7.1 THE WARREN AND BURGER COURTS: LIMITED BUT MEANINGFUL PROTECTION FOR NEWSGATHERING ACTIVITIES

Although the Warren and Burger Courts did not extend broad protection to newsgathering activities under the First Amendment, the decisions of the Warren and Burger Court eras regularly acknowledged the critical role of a free press in a democracy and took important steps to ensure that journalists could perform this role effectively. Without doubt, the Warren Court's most significant contribution to the freedom of the press involved defanging tort law's potential to chill reporting about public officials, public figures, and matters of public concern. It is simply not possible to overstate the constitutional significance of *New York Times Company v. Sullivan* to the ability of the press to report the news.[41]

Despite the fundamental importance of the *Sullivan* decision, it was actually the Burger Court that deployed the First Amendment most creatively to protect the press's ability to engage in newsgathering and reporting activity. The Burger Court held that the First Amendment secures press access to state and federal court proceedings; it prohibited prior restraints against the press; it disallowed potentially punitive taxation of the press. To be sure, the Burger Court declined to recognize a First Amendment-based reporter's privilege that would ensure the ability of reporters to honor promises of confidentiality to sources;[42] it also declined to use the Press Clause to require government to provide access or information to the press that it does not provide to the general public.[43]

On the other hand, however, the Burger Court consistently demonstrated solicitude for the role of the Fourth Estate in maintaining the project of democratic self-government. The First Amendment's protection for the press reached its zenith under the Burger Court. The Justices regularly entertained Press Clause claims and, in general, required government to facilitate newsgathering and reporting. Could the Burger Court have been even bolder? Certainly. But to say that it could have done more is not to say that it did not do anything.

Any serious consideration of press freedom in the United States must begin with *Sullivan*. In *Sullivan*, the Supreme Court held that in order for a public official to recover against a media defendant for defamation (libel), the plaintiff must show that the media defendant published damaging false statements of fact with "malice aforethought," which means with actual knowledge of falsity or reckless indifference to truth or falsity.[44] Professor Alexander Meiklejohn, arguably the principal proponent of the democratic self-government theory of the First Amendment, considered the Supreme Court's *Sullivan* decision "an occasion for dancing in the streets."[45]

Harry Kalven, Jr., another iconic First Amendment scholar, emphasized the importance of the case because of its holding that "[t]he touchstone of the First Amendment [is] the abolition of seditious libel and what that implies about the function of free speech on public issues in American democracy."[46] He argued that *Sullivan* is a foundational First Amendment decision because it makes plain that "[t]he central meaning of the Amendment is that seditious libel cannot be made the subject of government sanction."[47] In other words, the press is free to criticize the government, and thin-skinned government officials cannot use legal process, whether criminal or civil in nature, to silence the press.

Prior to *Sullivan*'s constitutional surgery on the common law of tort, a media defendant could avoid liability only by proving the truth of the defamatory statement or privilege. This provided scant breathing room for the press – which, like the *New York Times* in *Sullivan* itself, could face significant damage awards for publishing material that contained minor factual inaccuracies. L. B. Sullivan, one of three elected commissioners in Montgomery, Alabama, obtained a damages award of $500,000 against the newspaper based on very minor errors in an advertisement supporting the civil rights movement in Alabama.[48] It bears noting that four other Alabama public officials also had sued the *New York Times*, seeking another $2.5 million in damages.[49] The traditional common law rule – embraced by Alabama – required the defendant to prove truth in order to avoid liability, and thus essentially empowered civil juries to bankrupt news organizations that published largely accurate stories that happened to contain picayune factual errors.[50]

In retrospect, given the Warren Court's landmark opinions making government property available for speech activity,[51] extending First Amendment protection to government employees,[52] as well as to students and faculty members at the nation's public schools, colleges, and universities,[53] and protecting transborder speech,[54] it is somewhat puzzling that the Warren Court did not do more to animate the Press Clause of the First Amendment. This is not to detract from *Sullivan*'s central importance or the significance of the decision to First Amendment law and theory. However, it was the Burger Court – rather than the Warren Court – that pioneered First Amendment protections for newsgathering activities by the press under the rubric of the Press Clause.

The Burger Court's most iconic press case, *Branzburg v. Hayes*,[55] is often criticized for what it failed to do – namely, create a broad First Amendment-based reporter's privilege that would shield journalists from offering involuntary testimony about their confidential news sources (whether before a grand jury or petit jury). *Branzburg* consolidated for Supreme Court review three cases involving prosecutors' efforts to force journalists to identify confidential sources incident to ongoing criminal investigations.[56] All three lower courts had rejected the reporters' motions to quash the subpoenas and ordered them to testify – or face contempt sanctions. The Supreme Court affirmed all three lower courts – effectively requiring the reporters to appear and testify.[57]

Based on the outcome, it is entirely reasonable to view *Branzburg* as a dramatic loss for the press. However, the Supreme Court divided 4–1–4 on whether to recognize a reporter's privilege that would permit a reporter to refuse to identify her sources. Justice Lewis F. Powell, Jr., authored a short concurring opinion that significantly undercut the plurality opinion's effort to reject a constitutional reporter's privilege.

Justice Powell observed that "[t]he Court does not hold that newsmen, subpoenaed to testify before a grand jury, are without constitutional rights with respect to the gathering of news or in safeguarding their sources."[58] Powell opined that absent a "legitimate need of law enforcement," a reporter should not be forced to testify against her will; instead, in the absence of a clear need, a reporter can file a motion to quash a subpoena "and an appropriate protective order may be entered."[59] He explained that "[t]he asserted claim to privilege should be judged on its facts by the striking of a proper balance between freedom of the press and the obligation of all citizens to give relevant testimony with respect to criminal conduct."[60]

Powell argued that such a "case-by-case" approach to determining whether a reporter may be compelled to testify "accords with the tried and traditional way of adjudicating such questions."[61] In sum, "the courts will be available to newsmen under circumstances where legitimate First Amendment interests require protection."[62] Powell's approach clearly requires the government to shoulder a burden of justification when it attempts to force a reporter to identify a confidential source. His approach is less protective than the legal standard that Justice Potter Stewart, writing in dissent, propounded: a strict rule of absolute necessity that requires a "clear showing of a compelling and overriding national interest that cannot be served by any alternative means."[63] Even so, however, Powell's opinion prohibits prosecutors from forcing journalists to divulge confidential sources or investigative materials as a first resort – even if his approach would not limit such tactics to being only a last resort in extremely important cases.

Justice Byron White's plurality opinion, by way of contrast, would limit relief to circumstances where the government sought testimony from a reporter "other than in good faith."[64] Justice White acknowledged that "news gathering is not without its First Amendment protections," but would not provide relief to journalists seeking to avoid testifying about their methods or sources absent serious government misbehavior.[65]

To be sure, Justice White expressly disavowed the proposition "that news gathering does not qualify for First Amendment protection" because "without some protection for seeking out the news, freedom of the press could be eviscerated."[66] Nevertheless, his test for excusing a reporter from testifying in a criminal proceeding is considerably narrower than either Justice Powell's or Justice Stewart's test: "Official harassment of the press undertaken not for purposes of law enforcement but to disrupt a reporter's relationship with his news sources would have no justification."[67] If a reporter can establish bad faith on the government's part, "[g]rand juries are subject to judicial control and subpoenas to motions to quash."[68]

The Powell opinion, as in *Bakke*, would appear to be controlling. His standard is more demanding than White's, but considerably less demanding than Stewart's proposed test. Powell's approach, which requires the government to establish "legitimate need" for a reporter's testimony, has the effect of providing a limited, First Amendment-based press shield against involuntary disclosure of confidential sources. The "proper balance" analysis also seems to suggest that the gravity of the crime at issue might have some bearing on whether a reporter could be compelled to identify a confidential news source or face contempt sanctions for refusing to do so.

Certainly, Justice Stewart's standard, which requires clear and convincing evidence of absolute necessity in the context of an "overriding national interest" would have conveyed a much more robust shield for the press's newsgathering efforts. But Justice Powell's opinion makes clear that forcing reporters to name confidential sources should be closer to a last resort than a first resort. In this sense, then, *Branzburg* advances, rather than impedes, the newsgathering process. Although the decision provides only partial First Amendment protection, *Branzburg* plainly conveys some measure of protection on reporters to protect the identities of confidential news sources.

Given the 4–1–4 split among the Justices, it would have been desirable for the Supreme Court to revisit these questions and provide clearer guidance to the lower federal and state courts. Yet, almost fifty years later, *Branzburg* remains the most important First Amendment precedent on the ability of prosecutors to compel testimony from reporters in criminal proceedings.

The Burger Court's protection of press access to civil and criminal trial proceedings was both less opaque and more robust. In *Nebraska Press Association v. Stuart*,[69] the Supreme Court held that efforts to ensure a fair and impartial criminal trial cannot extend to closing trial proceedings to the press – absent a clear showing that less drastic measures would be ineffective. Chief Justice Warren E. Burger, writing for the majority, explained that "[w]e cannot say on this record that alternatives to a prior restraint on petitioners would not have sufficiently mitigated the adverse effects of pretrial publicity so as to make prior restraint unnecessary."[70]

A trial court should apply a multi-factor test before entering a gag order against press coverage of a criminal trial. The relevant factors include "the nature and extent of pretrial news coverage," "whether other measures would be likely to mitigate the effects of unrestrained pretrial publicity," "how effectively a restraining order would operate to prevent the threatened danger," and "[t]he precise terms of the restraining order."[71] In sum, a prior restraint against publication of news stories about a criminal trial, "one of the most extraordinary remedies known to our jurisprudence,"[72] should be used only as a last resort and after other, less draconian, measures have been tried and failed to secure a fair trial process for the defendant.

To be sure, *Nebraska Press Association's* protection of the right of reporters to attend a trial, in order to report on it, was indirect. Strictly speaking, the decision invalidated a press gag order in the context of a trial otherwise open to the public. The larger question of whether a criminal trial must be open to the public arguably remained an open one. Four years later, however, in *Richmond Newspapers v. Virginia*,[73] seven members of the Supreme Court, over the course of six opinions, concluded that "that the right to attend criminal trials is implicit in the guarantees of the First Amendment."[74] Moreover, although *Richmond Newspapers* involved only criminal trials, Chief Justice Burger's plurality opinion observes that "[w]hether the public has a right to attend trials of civil cases is a question not raised by this case, but we note that historically both civil and criminal trials have been presumptively open."[75]

In *Globe Newspaper Co. v. Superior Court*,[76] the Supreme Court reaffirmed the result and reasoning of *Richmond Newspapers* with a single opinion securing a clean majority.[77] *Globe Newspaper Company* was a particularly fraught case, in that it involved a Massachusetts trial court closing a trial involving a sexual offense against a child victim. Massachusetts law categorically closed trials for sex offenses against minors; the Supreme Court invalidated the statute because the state's interest in protecting minors "could be served just as well by requiring the trial court to determine on a case-by-case basis whether the State's legitimate concern for the well-being of the minor victim necessitates closure."[78] A case-by-case approach "ensures that the constitutional right of the press and public to gain access to criminal trials will not be restricted except where necessary to protect the State's interest."[79]

The Burger Court thus safeguarded the right of the press to attend and report on judicial proceedings – even when presiding judges and the litigants themselves would prefer to close judicial proceedings to the public. These decisions constitute important building blocks in the ability of the press to safeguard the integrity of the judicial process in the nation's state and federal courts.

As Justice Brennan stated the point in *Globe Newspaper Company*:

Public scrutiny of a criminal trial enhances the quality and safeguards the integrity of the factfinding process, with benefits to both the defendant and to society as a whole. Moreover, public access to the criminal trial fosters an appearance of fairness, thereby heightening public respect for the judicial process. And in the broadest terms, public access to criminal trials permits the public to participate in and serve as a check upon the judicial process – an essential component in our structure of self-government. In sum, the institutional value of the open criminal trial is recognized in both logic and experience.[80]

These decisions recognize and validate the Fourth Estate's important checking role in keeping government honest. As such, they constitute important efforts to give force and effect to the Press Clause of the First Amendment. They are also less ambiguous than *Branzburg*, plainly holding that trials must be open to the public and reporters free to attend and write about them.

Other Burger Court opinions vindicate, at least in part, the right of reporters to engage in newsgathering activity and the press to report on matters of public concern. For example, although the Supreme Court declined to constitutionalize Freedom of Information Act[81] principles by deploying the First Amendment as a means of forcing government to disclose information within its possession to the press, the Supreme Court did take into account the institutional needs of the press.

In *Houchins v. KQED*,[82] the plurality opinion rejects the proposition that the press enjoys a special right of access to a county jail. Writing for himself and Justices Stevens and Rehnquist, Chief Justice Burger opined that "[t]his Court has never intimated a First Amendment guarantee of a right of access to all sources of information within government control."[83] He posited that "[n]either the First Amendment nor the Fourteenth Amendment mandates a right of access to government information or sources of information within the government's control."[84]

Alameda County, California, provided public tours of some parts of the county jail (but not others); the press, including KQED's reporters, had a right to take those tours, but could not demand access to parts of the facility not included on the public tour.[85] Burger concluded, emphatically, that "the media have no special right of access to the Alameda County Jail different from or greater than that accorded the public generally."[86]

Houchins featured a seven-member bench – Justices Marshall and Blackmun did not participate in the decision. The Chief Justice's opinion failed to command a majority because Justice Stewart did not join it. Instead, Stewart, writing for himself, argued that for the press "equal access" had to take into account the ability of reporters to use the tools of the trade when on the public tour. He explained that "I believe that the concept of equal access must be accorded more flexibility in order to accommodate the practical distinctions between the press and the general public."[87]

More specifically, "terms of access that are reasonably imposed on individual members of the public may, if they impede effective reporting without sufficient justification, be unreasonable as applied to journalists who are there to convey to the general public what the visitors see."[88] Thus, members of the public might not be permitted to carry cameras or pens and notepads while on the tour – whereas journalists would enjoy some ability, under the First Amendment, to make contemporaneous visual and written records of their visit to the jail. Consistent with these views, "KQED was clearly entitled to some form of preliminary injunctive relief" and he would "not foreclose the possibility of further relief for KQED on remand."[89] The injunctive relief must take into account both "the constitutional role of the press and the institutional requirements of the jail."[90]

Thus, like *Branzburg*, although the Supreme Court declined to offer maximal protection to the press, *Houchins* clearly deploys the First Amendment to secure meaningful breathing room for the press. The Press Clause requires government to refrain from taking actions that would impede or preclude newsgathering and reporting activity – even if the government does not have a more general duty to provide the press with greater rights of access to a county jail than it provides to the general public.

The Burger Court's important free press decisions also include *New York Times Co. v. United States,* commonly known as *The Pentagon Papers Case.*[91] The Nixon Administration sought an injunction against publication of Department of Defense materials related to the conduct of the Vietnam War – a "massive, classified study of this Nation's involvement in the Vietnam conflict, going back to the end of the Second World War."[92] In a terse, three paragraph *per curiam* opinion, the Supreme Court rejected the Nixon Administration's request for an injunction against publication of the Pentagon Papers because the federal government had failed to overcome "the heavy presumption against" prior restraints against the press.[93] *New York Times Company* has come to stand for the proposition that neither the state nor federal courts should grant injunctions against publication of news stories; the decision serves as a bedrock of freedom of the press in the contemporary United States.

Finally, the Burger Court also prohibited efforts to burden press operations indirectly through the adoption and enforcement of targeted taxes on newspapers and other periodicals. In *Minneapolis Star & Tribune Company v. Minnesota Commissioner of Revenue,*[94] the Supreme Court invalidated a Minnesota special tax applicable to the paper and ink used to produce newspapers and magazines.[95] Writing for the 7–2 majority, Justice Sandra Day O'Connor explained that "[a] tax that singles out the press, or targets individual publications within the press, places heavy burden on the State to justify its action" – a burden that Minnesota failed to meet.[96]

Because "the power to tax involves the power to destroy,"[97] differential taxation of newspapers and magazines raises a very clear and palpable risk of viewpoint discrimination. Legislators could reward friendly editorial boards – and punish hostile ones – through the selective application of taxes (or targeted tax exemptions). Indeed, although perhaps not as draconian as requiring a license from the government in order to publish a newspaper, differential taxation of press entities functions not unlike a press licensing scheme by imposing costs on some news outlets and not others. It creates a system of targeted subsidies that make it easier – literally less expensive – for favored press entities to conduct business while imposing a targeted burden on those subject to the tax, making it harder for them to remain commercially viable.

In sum, the Burger Court era did not constitute a kind of Shangri-La for the institutional press; the Burger Court's major press decisions are, in the main, tepid and halting in conveying meaningful First Amendment protection on gathering and reporting the news. Nevertheless, virtually all of the Supreme Court's most important precedents involving freedom of the press issued during the Burger Court years. It might not have a been a "free press" Court – but it was certainly a "freer" press Court.

Moreover, the Burger Court's willingness to hear and decide cases involving the rights of the institutional press also sent an important signal to journalists that the federal courts would take seriously the First Amendment claims of working journalists. This, in turn, provided a clear warning to the political branches of the federal and state governments that targeted efforts to burden newsgathering and reporting would be subject to meaningful judicial review and require more than mere rationality in order to pass First Amendment muster.[98] Decisions such as *Branzburg, Richmond Newspapers, Houchins, Pentagon Papers,* and *Minneapolis Star & Tribune* individually and collectively sent a clear message that government could not constitutionally attempt to silence the Fourth Estate or even significantly impede its work absent a very strong, if not quite compelling, justification for so doing.

7.2 THE ABJECT FAILURE OF THE REHNQUIST AND ROBERTS COURTS TO DEPLOY THE FIRST AMENDMENT TO PROTECT NEWSGATHERING ACTIVITIES

Whatever the shortcomings of the decisions of the Warren and Burger Courts regarding the ability of the press to invoke the First Amendment as a source of protection for journalistic activities, the Supreme Court regularly heard and decided cases involving such claims. And, although the scope of press protections was admittedly modest, it was not non-existent. Over the past thirty years, by way of contrast, the Supreme Court has failed to issue any landmark decisions addressing the ability of journalists to use the First Amendment as a protective shield for newsgathering activities.

Neither the Rehnquist Court nor the Roberts Court has addressed directly the First Amendment's application to newsgathering activities that are essential to subsequent reportage. To be sure, some decisions, such as *Bartnicki v. Vopper,*[99] address news reporting by implication. Indirect consideration certainly constitutes a form of consideration – but the utter and complete absence of major Supreme Court decisions addressing newsgathering as a protected First Amendment activity is both telling and problematic. Whatever the shortcomings of *Branzburg*[100] and *Houchins,*[101] at least the Justices were actively engaged in thinking about how the First Amendment might be relevant to the professional work of journalists.

Today, this is simply not the case. As Professors Jones and West observe, "[t]he Supreme Court has not decided a major press case in more than a decade, in part because it has declined to do so, and in part because media companies, inferring the court's relative lack of interest, have decided not to waste their resources pressing cases."[102] Moreover, current members of the Supreme Court "have spoken negatively of the press in opinions or speeches."[103] Thus, the Supreme Court is not considering and rejecting First Amendment-based claims that newsgathering activities should be protected from government interference – it is not considering such claims at all.

Part of the problem inheres in the difficulty of defining "the press" for purposes of conveying targeted First Amendment protection to newsgathering and reporting activities. In the age of the internet, anyone with a smartphone is potentially "the press." And, yet, if everyone is the press, the social cost of recognizing special First Amendment rights for journalists becomes significantly higher. On the other hand, however, declining to offer any constitutional protection to newsgathering and reporting activities because of the definitional difficulties of determining whom should qualify for such protections does not constitute a satisfactory solution.

The Rehnquist and Roberts Courts failed to expand on the precedents of its predecessors – and, in fact, reduced the scope of First Amendment protection for media entities. The Supreme Court's treatment of differential taxes on the press provides a salient example of this trend. As noted earlier,[104] in *Minneapolis Star and Tribune Company v. Minnesota Commissioner of Revenue*,[105] the Burger Court applied and extended *Grosjean*[106] to invalidate a state tax that imposed a selective tax burden on some, but not all, newspapers in Minnesota.[107]

Initially, the Rehnquist Court followed the Burger Court's approach and invalidated a state law that imposed taxation on some, but not all, print periodicals.[108] Arkansas adopted a scheme of targeted sales tax exemptions that excluded all newspapers and certain magazines from the states sales tax (including magazines featuring "religious, professional, trade, and sports" content).[109] The state courts declined to apply *Minneapolis Star*, reasoning that the general sales tax could be applied to certain print publications but not others without violating the First Amendment.[110]

The Supreme Court granted review, and in a 7–2 opinion by Justice Thurgood Marshall, reversed the Arkansas Supreme Court.[111] Marshall emphasized that "[o]ur cases establish that a discriminatory tax on the press burdens rights protected by the First Amendment."[112] The First Amendment requires such a rule because "selective taxation of the press – either singling out the press as a whole or targeting individual members of the press – poses a particular danger of abuse by the State."[113] A scheme of press-specific exemptions to a general sales tax functions identically as the targeted imposition of a tax on those periodicals excluded from the exemption. Moreover, the Arkansas statute was "particularly repugnant to First Amendment principles" because "a magazine's tax status depends entirely on its *content*."[114]

To be sure, Justice Marshall did not address the argument that favoring newspapers over magazines, based on the format of the periodical, also violated the First Amendment. He observed that the Court's holding "eliminates the differential treatment of newspapers and magazines," and, in consequence, "we need not decide whether a distinction between different types of periodicals presents an additional basis for invalidating the sales tax, as applied to the press."[115] The logic of Justice Marshall's opinion – namely, that differential taxation of press entities raises a serious specter of government censorship – strongly suggested that preferring one kind of periodical over another would be constitutionally problematic.

Four years later, however, the Rehnquist Court reversed course and *sustained* the differential treatment of media for purposes of applying a state's sales tax. In *Leathers v. Medlock*,[116] Justice O'Connor wrote for a 7–2 majority and upheld the imposition of the Arkansas state sales tax on cable television services – even though state law exempted from the state sales tax satellite television services.[117] Thus, Arkansas imposed a sales tax on the provision of cable television service, while exempting from the sales tax satellite television service, in addition to newspapers and magazines. O'Connor explained that the imposition of a general sales tax on all cable system services did not present a case of discrimination against particular speakers, nor did it "single out the press."[118]

The outcome would have been different if the law differentiated among cable system operators – but it did not. The fact that one medium of expression – cable television – was systematically subjected to unfavorable tax treatment did not alter the First Amendment analysis because "the Arkansas sales tax presents none of the First Amendment difficulties that have led us to strike down differential taxation in the past."[119] Justice O'Connor observed that "[t]he Arkansas Legislature has chosen simply to exclude or exempt certain media from a generally applicable tax" and "the State's extension of its generally applicable sales tax to cable television services alone, or to cable and satellite services, while exempting the print media, does not violate the First Amendment."[120]

Justice Thurgood Marshall, writing for himself and Justice Blackmun, authored a powerful dissent that argued that differential tax treatment of media enterprises invariably raises the possibility of government censorship. He emphasized that "[o]ur decisions on selective taxation establish a nondiscrimination principle for like-situated members of the press," a principle that disallows targeted tax breaks for preferred speakers.[121] This prophylactic rule is meant to ensure that government does not "interfere with the press as an institution."[122]

Justice Marshall explained that "[b]ecause cable competes with members of the print and electronic media in the larger information market, the power to discriminate between these media triggers the central concern underlying the nondiscrimination principle," namely "the risk of covert censorship."[123] The First Amendment, properly understood and applied, prohibits government from "interfering with the process by which citizens' preferences for information formats evolve."[124]

To be sure, the majority opinion in *Leathers* draws a plausible distinction between government taxes that target specific speakers within a medium, and taxes that favor some forms of media over others. Yet, the fact remains that Justice Marshall's dissenting opinion reflects a more robust vision for press freedom. Because ascertaining legislative motive can be difficult, a differential tax on one provider of a communications service ought to be constitutionally impermissible – to tax cable service, but not satellite service, is to push consumers toward satellite service providers and away from cable system operators. Because the product being sold is, essentially, speech itself, the government should be required to offer a substantial reason to support differential tax treatment of information formats; the same risk of a censorial motive exists on these facts as when a state exempts some, but not all, print periodicals from a general sales tax. In sum, *Leathers* reflects considerably less solicitude for protecting media entities from targeted forms of adverse government treatment than the Supreme Court's earlier precedents.

In fairness, the Rehnquist Court did vindicate the press's interest in reporting on matters of public concern, essentially reaffirming and ratifying the *Pentagon Papers*[125] decision. In *Bartnicki v. Vopper*,[126] the Supreme Court held that a federal statute imposing criminal penalties on the unauthorized recording of cellular telephone communications could not be applied to a radio station that innocently acquired an unlawfully taped conversation.[127] Despite the harm to legitimate privacy interests, "privacy concerns give way when balanced against the interest in publishing on matters of public importance."[128] Accordingly, "a stranger's illegal conduct does not suffice to remove the First Amendment shield from speech about a matter of public concern."[129]

Justice John Paul Stevens's plurality opinion in *Bartnicki* constitutes a robust vindication of the right of the press to publish truthful information about a matter of public concern free and clear of the potential chilling effect of criminal liability for being an after-the-fact accessory to wire tapping. On the other hand, however, Justice Stevens's opinion obtained only four clean votes; Justice Stephen Breyer, joined by Justice O'Connor, concurred in order to emphasize "the narrow holding limited to the special circumstances here."[130] Breyer characterized the information broadcast by the radio station as "a matter of unusual public concern,"[131] and cautioned that "we should avoid adopting overly broad or rigid constitutional rules, which would unnecessarily restrict legislative flexibility."[132] In light of these considerations, he "agree[d] with the Court's holding that the statutes as applied here violate the Constitution," but he "would not extend that holding beyond these present circumstances."[133]

Chief Justice Rehnquist, joined by Justices Scalia and Thomas, would have upheld the imposition of criminal liability for the radio station's broadcast of the unlawfully recorded cell phone conversation.[134] Thus, they would have held the privacy interest to be controlling on the facts at bar.

In sum, the Roberts and Rehnquist Courts have failed to apply the First Amendment to protect newsgathering and news reporting activities. Their collective contribution to this area of First Amendment law constitute something of a null set – particularly when contrasted with the major free press decisions of the Burger Court.

7.3 GROWING THREATS TO NEWSGATHERING ACTIVITY AND THE CONCOMITANT NEED FOR A STRONG JUDICIAL RESPONSE TO PROTECT THE ABILITY OF JOURNALISTS TO PROVIDE THE CITIZENRY WITH THE INFORMATION NECESSARY TO HOLD GOVERNMENT ACCOUNTABLE

Government, at all levels, increasingly engages in efforts to frustrate, or prevent entirely, newsgathering activities. Even if government does not have an affirmative duty to assist journalists in their work, it surely has a duty not to seek to impede or block it. The Trump Administration has declared war, quite literally, on the traditional mass media, including both print and electronic journalists.[135] President Trump has "declared himself in 'a running war with the media' and the president's first press secretary, Sean Spicer, used his initial appearance at the White House press room podium to deliver a fiery jeremiad against the press."[136]

Clear and convincing evidence establishes that the Trump Administration seeks to vilify the press, presumably in order to undermine its credibility with the public. The White House also has barred journalists from disfavored news organizations from attending official briefings in the West Wing press room.[137] Finally, the Trump Administration seeks to use the press selectively as a means of disseminating "alternative facts" – meaning empirically verifiable falsehoods that constitute a rather obvious form of pro-administration propaganda.[138]

These public attacks on journalists and their craft have not been without consequences. Increasingly, working journalists must run a literal gauntlet to gather the information necessary to facilitate their reportage, including arbitrary arrest and assault. Since President Trump's inauguration, "journalists have been roughed up, been pinned to a wall, had their glasses broken or been arrested for exercising their right to ask questions."[139]

To provide just one illustrative example, Rep. Greg Gianforte (R-MT) physically attacked a journalist during the waning days of his 2017 special election campaign, body slamming *Guardian* reporter Ben Jacobs. Gianforte did so in the plain sight of a local television station's cameras – and, in consequence, the station's on-the-scene reporter recorded the assault in real time and proceeded to break the story.[140] Montana's main newspapers quickly withdrew their endorsements of Gianforte – but he handily won the special election anyway.[141]

One observer posits that President Trump bears substantial personal responsibility for the growing culture of violence against journalists: "We can lay the growing and increasingly dangerous hostility toward the press at the feet of President Trump, who thrives on demonizing the news media on Twitter and whenever he can."[142] If journalists are "enemies of the people," as the President publicly has characterized them,[143] it is not surprising that they face growing hostility – and even violence – as they go about their work. Whatever one thinks about the fairness and objectivity of journalists working for national media outlets, we should all be able to agree that journalists should not be subject to beatings, arrests, and even imprisonment merely for doing their jobs.

It would be all too easy to dismiss the current Trump Administration's ham-fisted efforts to suppress truthful, but critical, news reporting as aberrational and perhaps sui generis. Except that it is not – presidents of both political parties have sought to impede or prevent newsgathering activities that could lead to critical reporting about their administrations.[144] The fact of the matter is that "all presidential administrations, regardless of political party, are prone to suppress bad news whenever possible."[145]

In addition, under the Obama and George W. Bush Administrations, the Department of Justice showed little reticence about threatening to prosecute journalists for reporting truthful information about government national security programs – in addition to the aggressive use of contempt proceedings to attempt to coerce journalists into naming their confidential sources incident to federal criminal investigations.[146] Ironically, the Obama Administration, which promised to be the "most transparent" administration in US history,[147] proved much more aggressive at pursuing journalists on national security grounds than did the Bush Administration.

The problem of government efforts to suppress newsgathering activity is hardly limited to the federal government. State and local governments have been using existing laws, such as proscriptions against impeding police work, as well as measures specifically designed to prohibit recording the police in public,[148] to prevent both professional journalists and citizen-journalists from recording police officers engaged in law enforcement activity (or activity alleged to constitute lawful law enforcement activity).[149] Moreover, despite the increasing use of police body cameras in many places, the public often lacks meaningful access to the footage that these devices record. If police can use pretextual "impeding law enforcement activity" arrests to prevent the public from using smartphones to record police officers in public,[150] efforts to secure police accountability will be severely impeded – perhaps even thwarted entirely.[151]

To provide a concrete example, until the Illinois state supreme court invalidated it, Illinois maintained a state law that, in some circumstances, prohibited filming police officers, without affirmative consent, while they were in public.[152] However, more generic laws that prohibit unconsented-to recording of others can be just as efficacious in thwarting newsgathering in public places as more targeted enactments. Generic privacy laws that prohibit unconsented-to recording can be deployed to impede citizens from recording police encounters with citizens – as can more targeted enactments that prohibit interfering with the conduct of police work.[153] One should also bear in mind that government efforts to impede the recording of public officials are not limited to the police – journalists have been arrested for attempting to photograph or interview other government officials in places generally open to the public.[154]

On the other hand, however, and as Professor Margot E. Kaminski has observed, "[n]ot much ink needs to be spilled arguing for a theory of privacy harm that permits governments to protect individuals from having their solitude disrupted."[155] She goes further, however, and argues that "[t]here is considerable support for why information revealed in public should be protected from government surveillance."[156] Namely, that "[e]xtensive surveillance can produce both conformity and anxiety."[157] In consequence, "[p]rivacy laws can run into First Amendment problems, but they can also be essential to First Amendment interests."[158]

Of course, Professor Kaminski is principally writing about the privacy interest of ordinary citizens against an encroaching "Big Brother"-style government bent on mass surveillance – not police officers on patrol who exercise deadly force in questionable ways. It seems self-evident that recording events in public places, and then disseminating the footage, can greatly facilitate the process of democratic self-government.

Professor Kreimer persuasively argues that "[p]ervasive image capture enhances public discourse."[159] Moreover, "[i]mage capture can document activities that are the proper subject of public deliberation but which the protagonists would prefer to keep hidden and deniable."[160] For example, "[n]ews organizations place dubious police tactics on the public record"[161] and recordings of official misconduct "allow victims to claim their voice and to leverage widely held norms to shame violators."[162] Thus, "[j]ust as public surveillance cameras are said to reduce crime, the prospect of private image capture provides a deterrent to official actions that would evoke liability or condemnation."[163]

For image capture to facilitate government accountability, however, citizen journalists must be confident of their legal right to record the police. This condition simply does not exist under current law; a threat of arrest always accompanies recording activity. To be sure, "[m]any of these prosecutions [for recording police activity] have ultimately been dropped or dismissed."[164] Nevertheless, "the threat of arrest remains a potent deterrent to spontaneous photographers who have no deep commitment to capturing any particular image."[165] The problem is compounded by the fact that no realistic possibility exists for the federal courts invalidating generic "impeding" or "interfering" statutes on a facial basis – at most, an "as-applied" challenge might succeed. But such cases would involve very difficult credibility determinations that, in many instances, would probably favor the police officer's testimony.[166]

The ostensible purpose for applying general privacy statutes to prevent recording of police activity in public is to protect the personal privacy of the police officers,[167] which seems a rather weak justification for prohibiting image capture in public places (where, under current law, no reasonable expectation of privacy exists). But proscriptions against "impeding" or "interfering" with a law enforcement officer do not rest on this predicate and courts are unlikely to read such laws narrowly if they believe that doing so could endanger the safety of law enforcement officers. If the federal courts wish to avoid a serious chilling effect on citizen journalism, however, they must learn to embrace the risk that enforcing constitutional limits on impeding and interfering laws could make police work both more difficult and potentially more dangerous.

Citizen journalism, through the use of social media platforms, followed the tragic shooting of Walter Scott, in North Charleston, South Carolina, by police officer Michael Slager – and demonstrates compellingly how speech, in the form of citizen-journalist reportage, can help to secure other fundamental civil rights and liberties.[168] As two professional journalists commenting on this outrageous event observed, "[t]he South Carolina shooting demonstrates the power of citizen-captured video in the most salient way."[169] Without question, empowering amateur citizen-journalists, through the vigilant defense of speech rights and the antecedent newsgathering activity that is required to speak effectively, will pay important dividends with respect to securing other constitutional rights.[170] The ability to share important, relevant information with the body politic constitutes a sufficient justification for conveying serious First Amendment protection on image capture,[171] but the penumbral effects in securing other constitutional rights serve as important considerations as well.

In sum, the federal courts should flatly reject, on First Amendment grounds, legislative bans (whether targeted or general) on recording police officers in public – after all, police officers have no reasonable expectation of privacy when in public.[172] The federal courts also must be more vigilant against the pretextual use of laws prohibiting impeding or interfering with police work. The tragic spate of recent police shootings, including the deaths of African American citizens at the hands of police officers in Baton Rouge, Louisiana,[173] Cleveland, South Carolina,[174] and St. Paul, Minnesota[175] all compellingly demonstrate the need for strong, clear, and consistent First Amendment protection for image capture of police activity by citizen journalists.[176]

Other contemporary efforts to suppress journalism exist. For example, bans on reportage of industrial farming practices that animal rights activists believe constitute animal cruelty. These so-called "ag-gag" laws are specifically drafted with the purpose and intent of preventing activists from sharing the conditions under which farm animals live and die with the general public.[177] Professors Alan Chen and Justin Marceau explain that "Ag Gag laws seek to stifle whistle blowing and reporting regarding practices at commercial agricultural facilities."[178] To date, however, the federal and state courts have not acted with sufficient dispatch to invalidate these enactments.[179]

In January 2018, the US Court of Appeals for the Ninth Circuit weighed in on the constitutional status of Idaho's ag-gag statute[180] – and rendered a mixed verdict for Press Clause protection of newsgathering activity and investigative journalism more generally.[181] The decision vindicates some important First Amendment interests, including the right to record and to seek access to facilities, even by misrepresentation, in order to report on animal cruelty at industrial farming operations. On the other hand, however, important provisions of the law survived constitutional review, including bans on using misrepresentations either to gain employment at agricultural production facilities or to gain access to the records of such entities.

In 2014, Idaho's state legislature enacted a law to prevent "interference with agricultural production."[182] The legislative history of this law demonstrates with convincing clarity that state legislators wished to suppress reporting about animal cruelty associated with industrial farming practices.[183] In fact, "[o]ne senator compared animal rights investigators to 'marauding invaders centuries ago who swarmed into foreign territory and destroyed crops to starve foes into submission,'"[184] and "[a]nother supporter of the bill called the groups [seeking to film industrial farming operations] terrorists and insinuated that their investigations were defamatory."[185] More direct, relevant evidence of a viewpoint-discriminatory motive would be difficult to imagine. Calling those who report on animal cruelty in industrial farming operations "terrorists" reflects deep-seated antipathy toward both the speakers and their message.

After Idaho's enactment of section 18–7042, the Animal Legal Defense Fund (ALDF) brought suit in federal district court seeking invalidation of the statute on First Amendment and Equal Protection Clause grounds. The ALDF prevailed in federal district court on its First Amendment claims and obtained a preliminary injunction blocking enforcement of section 18–7042 in its entirety.[186] However, the Ninth Circuit reversed in part the district court's ruling and upheld two of the law's four provisions.

Writing for a unanimous panel regarding two of the law's four operative provisions, Judge Margaret McKeown upheld "Idaho's criminalization of misrepresentations to obtain records and secure employment" because such activities "are not protected speech under the First Amendment and do not violate the Equal Protection Clause."[187] She further explained that "the First Amendment right to gather news within legal bounds does not exempt journalists from laws of general applicability."[188] The Ninth Circuit found that engaging in deception to gain either employment at an industrial farming operation or access to a facility's records did not constitute "speech" but merely regulable "conduct."

On the other hand, and in an important victory for First Amendment values, the panel unanimously invalidated Idaho's ban on recording industrial farming operations because it constituted a content-based restriction on speech about a matter of public concern.[189] Perhaps most important, the panel reaffirmed the principle that the First Amendment conveys protection on newsgathering activity because "[t]he act of recording is itself an inherently expressive activity."[190] The ban on recording failed strict scrutiny because the government's interest was underinclusive (suggesting an impermissible viewpoint-based motive).[191] In addition, the state's preferred means of achieving its interests in protecting privacy and property rights were not sufficiently narrowly tailored.[192]

The *Wasden* panel majority, by a 2–1 vote, also voided the state's ban on using "misrepresentation" to gain access to agricultural production facilities.[193] It severed this provision from a portion of the statute that also criminalized gaining access to such facilities by "force," "threat," or "trespass,"[194] leaving the other provisions in force. The court did so because the provision was not necessary to protect the property rights of facility owners and also seemed to reflect viewpoint discrimination. Judge McKeown explained that if, "as a number of the legislators made clear and the dairy lobby underscored, the statute was intended to quash investigative reporting on agricultural production facilities, then the speech aspect of the statute prohibiting misrepresentations is even more problematic."[195]

The decision represents something of a mixed bag for the press. On the one hand, it strikes down legislative bans on recording and on using deception to gain permission to enter an industrial farming operation. On the other, however, it sustains as "conduct" criminal proscriptions against using misrepresentation to gain employment or access to a facility's records. It also bears noting that the panel divided 2–1 with regard to invalidating the provision of the statute that criminalized using misrepresentation to gain access to a facility. Judge Carlos T. Bea voted to sustain this proscription.[196]

The bottom line: If the press can gain access to an industrial farming facility, it may record its operations and disseminate widely those recordings. But, activists cannot seek to use deception to gain access to such facilities in order to record in the first place, at least as employees or with respect to a company's records. This might be the correct constitutional result, but the Ninth Circuit seems to have discounted the fact that Idaho adopted section 18–7042 precisely because legislators wished to block certain kinds of investigative reporting about matters of public concern related to farm animals' welfare.

It would certainly be plausible to posit that the First Amendment's Press Clause disallows the enactment of such a law, even if, in general terms, a truly neutral law aimed at protecting property or privacy might survive constitutional review.[197] When a state government uses its police powers to target investigative journalism and reporting, as such, the First Amendment requires that a reviewing court apply a more demanding standard of review. A state may not avoid meaningful First Amendment scrutiny by simply regulating "conduct" that is integral to the exercise of a First Amendment right.

Accordingly, state laws, like Idaho's section 18–7042, that seek to punish activity because of its communicative aspects – rather than despite them – should always be subjected to strict judicial scrutiny and, in virtually all instances, deemed constitutionally invalid.[198] In *Wasden*, however, the Ninth Circuit chose to characterize targeted bans on behavior integral to reporting and newsgathering as merely "conduct" regulations that did not trigger heightened scrutiny under the First Amendment. The panel also failed to give appropriate weight to the rather damning legislative history associated with the enactment of this statute. In this respect, US District Judge Lynn Winmill's opinion, which applied heightened scrutiny to all four provisions of Idaho's ag-gag law because of the impermissible legislative intent to squelch the exercise of First Amendment rights, better advanced core First Amendment values and facilitated the ability of the press to inform the public about an important matter of public concern (such as systematic forms of horrific animal cruelty).

7.4 THE INEVITABILITY OF BALANCING LEGITIMATE GOVERNMENTAL INTERESTS AND PRIVACY AGAINST THE NEED TO FACILITATE NEWSGATHERING AND REPORTING ACTIVITIES SHOULD NOT RENDER THE PRESS CLAUSE A CONSTITUTIONAL NULLITY

In many respects, the decisions of the Burger Court reflected an effort to achieve some measure of balance, or equilibrium, between the need for journalists to engage in newsgathering activities and the government's legitimate interests in matters such as national security, criminal law enforcement, securing fair and impartial trials to litigants, and maintaining good order and discipline in public institutions (such as prisons).[199] To be sure, the balancing was largely ad hoc and failed to articulate and apply a coherent vision of the role of journalists in a functioning democracy. Nevertheless, the balancing exercise constrained the power of the state to impede activities essential to free and fair reportage about public officials and public proceedings.

Justice Stewart championed the creation of a coherent and meaningful Press Clause jurisprudence,[200] but his views never achieved the support of a reliable majority. Most members of the Supreme Court, then and now, shied away from the definitional difficulties associated with recognizing constitutional privileges for "the press" not generally available to any and all persons seeking to disseminate news and information to the wider community.[201] The advent of computers, smartphones, and the internet have only compounded the difficulty of distinguishing "the press" from amateur citizen-journalists; today, anyone with a smartphone and an internet service provider is potentially capable of breaking a major news story. The challenge of distinguishing the press from everyone else has become more difficult, rather than less difficult, over time.[202]

Even if the definitional difficulties could be resolved in a satisfactory way,[203] the problem of defining the scope of First Amendment-based press rights would remain. Balancing of some sort would seem inevitable in this context. Of course, balancing is required in virtually all cases raising First Amendment claims. The standards of review – the various and sundry three- and four-part tests that the Justices propagate to frame and decide free speech, assembly, association, and petition cases – all involve striking a balance. The tests obviously impact the outcome of the balancing exercise. For example, strict scrutiny places a very strong burden of justification on the government, including the identification of a compelling interest and narrow tailoring of the means used to achieve it. But, even in cases involving strict scrutiny, if the government meets its burden, the federal courts will sustain even nakedly content- or viewpoint-based speech regulations.[204]

Perhaps overcoming the difficulty of defining the press and setting the metes and bounds of the constitutionally protected freedom of the press is not what has kept the Supreme Court from enforcing the Press Clause in a meaningful way. Instead, it is quite possible the Justices simply do not believe that the press makes a significant and distinct contribution to the process of democratic self-government. From this vantage point, constitutional protections for speech in general, rather than for the press in particular, should prove sufficient to ensure that the political marketplace of ideas works to facilitate the process of democratic self-government.[205] This approach, however, undervalues the critical function of the press in facilitating the operation of democratic self-government. In the absence of the information needed to hold government accountable, the process of voting cannot serve as a reliable means of securing government accountability.[206] Facilitating government accountability through the electoral process requires that newsgathering and reportage enjoy serious constitutional protection.[207]

The *Pentagon Papers* decision teaches that government cannot suppress truthful information – even when the government strongly argues that important military, foreign affairs, or national security concerns exist and justify the suppression of news reporting by the press.[208] The animating theory of *Pentagon Papers* needs to be put to broader and better use to protect against government efforts to suppress accurate, truthful reporting about the actions of the United States government – actions ostensibly undertaken in the name of "We the People" – both at home and abroad. In addition, the Press Clause should provide a meaningful shield against the targeted harassment of journalists. At present, however, it does little (if anything) to protect journalists from government retaliation for providing voters with the information they must have in order to render prudent electoral judgments.

In addition, just as the First Amendment requires public officials to accept less protection of their reputations, in order to ensure that public debate will remain "uninhibited, robust, and wide-open,"[209] they must also accept less protection for their personal privacy. Even if the federal and state governments might enact privacy laws that limit or proscribe image or voice capture of private citizens who are not involved in matters of public concern,[210] safeguarding the information flows required to sustain democratic self-government requires that public officials, public figures, and persons involved in matters of public concern receive less privacy protection than persons who fall outside of these categories. Just as they must tolerate "vehement, caustic, and unpleasantly sharp attacks,"[211] those involved in matters crucial to an assessment of government's actions on election day also must tolerate less protection for their personal privacy as well.

Professor Alexander Meiklejohn posits that the First Amendment protects information flows in order to ensure that "every voting member of the body politic [has] the fullest possible participation in the understanding of those problems with which the citizens of a self-governing society must deal."[212] Accordingly, "[w]hen a free man is voting, it is not enough that the truth is known by someone else, by some scholar or administrator or legislator."[213] Rather, "[t]he voters must have it, all of them."[214] Under this view, "[t]he primary purpose of the First Amendment is, then, that all citizens shall, so far as possible, understand the issues which bear upon our common life."[215]

The conditions required for a mass-participation democracy, featuring universal adult suffrage, to function include open, robust, and reliable information flows. The Press Clause exists precisely because the government has a strong, almost irresistible, impulse to seek to control those information flows in order to disrupt the mechanisms of democratic accountability and thereby avoid being held responsible for its failures and misadventures. Because of this law of political nature, the federal courts should be no less skeptical of efforts to impede the press and the newsgathering activities that are essential to accurate reporting than they are of more direct efforts to manipulate the political marketplace of ideas (such as government regulations that target speech for extirpation based on its content or viewpoint).

In an era characterized by harsh attacks on the credibility of the press, featuring a president who routinely catcalls the press as the "enemy of the people" in his official speeches, statements, and tweets, a clear and present danger exists to the ability of both professional and amateur journalists alike to provide voters with the information required for them to make well-informed electoral decisions. Elected politicians have little incentive to protect the ability of the press to report truthfully on matters of public concern. The protection of the press – and activities integral to reporting on public officials, public figures, and matters of public concern – will inevitably fall to the federal courts. Accordingly, if the federal courts fail to safeguard newsgathering and reporting activities, an essential condition for the operation and maintenance of democratic self-government simply will not exist.

Even if striking the proper balance between privacy and free reportage about public officials, public figures, and matters of public concern is not an easy task for the federal courts, it is nevertheless an essential one. Uncertain legal protection for newsgathering activities has a predictable, and unacceptable, chilling effect that impedes the ability of the press to play its proper role in our democracy. The failure of the Roberts and Rehnquist Courts to deploy the First Amendment to protect newsgathering and news reporting constitutes both a serious failure of constitutional vision and an existential threat to democratic self-government.

7.5 CONCLUSION

The Warren and Burger Courts were hardly great champions of extending broad First Amendment protection to newsgathering activities; almost all of the major free press precedents of this era are incremental, halting, and grudging. But, incremental, halting, and grudging vindication of press freedoms is better than no vindication of press freedoms at all. The Rehnquist Court issued relatively few precedents on the relevance of the First Amendment to newsgathering and reporting.[216] And, to date, the Roberts Court has been largely absent from the scene – the Roberts Court has not issued decisions rejecting press claims on the First Amendment; it has not even considered them.

The contrast with the Roberts Court's bold decisions protecting corporate political speech[217] and targeted offensive speech[218] are quite telling. The Rehnquist Court, as well, did not hesitate to paint with bold strokes in cases that it deemed to implicate the core purposes and values of the First Amendment.[219] The paucity of press cases over the past thirty years is, accordingly, something of a puzzle. The Roberts Court, which has vigorously enforced the First Amendment in so many contexts, has simply ignored the Press Clause.

I do not argue that the press should be self-regulating or that the difficulties of defining the press for purposes of giving the Press Clause independent legal force and effect would be easy to overcome. The Burger Court gave us the *Branzburg* puzzle almost fifty years ago and *Houchins*, another fractured decision that failed to produce a majority opinion, over forty years ago. Even if press cases require federal courts to engage in difficult balancing exercises, this does not excuse the Supreme Court from making any serious effort to address or engage the First Amendment rights (if any) of both the institutional press and citizen journalists alike.

In sum, press rights present a clear case of an area of First Amendment law in which the contemporary Supreme Court has shown little, if any, sustained interest. In an era of expanding First Amendment rights, the press – and First Amendment protections for newsgathering activities – have not received any serious attention. The Burger Court's precedents provide a clear basis for continued consideration, and explication, of the First Amendment to the press and journalism more generally. To date, however, precedents such as *Branzburg* and *Houchins* resemble the grand saguaros of the Sonoran desert – large, clear, unmistakable, and quite easy to make out even from a distance. Yet, nothing grows beneath them.

Democratic self-government cannot function in the absence of the information needed to hold the government accountable via the ballot box. To the extent that the First Amendment's core purpose relates to facilitating the process of democratic self-government, First Amendment protection of newsgathering activity is no less integral to a healthy and dynamic marketplace of political ideas than the longstanding rules against the government adopting content- or viewpoint-based speech regulations.[220] The First Amendment should preclude government efforts to suppress the gathering and dissemination of the information voters need to make wise electoral choices.[221]

8

The Citizen As Government Sock Puppet and the State Masquerading As a Citizen

The Problem of Coerced and Misattributed Speech

Increasingly, some state governments have used their ability to regulate the professions in order to compel professional speech (arguably false and misleading professional speech), while other state governments have regulated professional speech to force licensed professionals into involuntary silence (even when standards of professional ethics would require a licensed professional to speak).[1] For example, South Dakota and Texas have required medical service providers to provide medically unnecessary information and also to provide information that most physicians believe to be medically false.[2] Other states, like Florida, have prohibited medical professionals from engaging in speech related to topics, such as gun ownership, that the state would prefer them to avoid.[3]

Professor Tim Zick observes that "[a] new generation of professional speech regulations is placing considerable pressure on doctrinal, theoretical, and professional boundaries."[4] Using the "cellophane wrapper" of professional regulation,[5] government seeks to use private citizens to deliver ideologically-charged messages of its choosing. If the government itself wishes to enter the marketplace of ideas in order to disseminate particular messages about the dangers of abortion or the wonders of gun ownership, no significant First Amendment impediments would exist.[6] A state government may exhort its citizens to exercise their constitutional liberty against some constitutional rights (e.g., abortion or contraception) and in favor of others (e.g., gun ownership). But, surely the situation should be viewed differently when the government attempts to use a private citizen as a "sock puppet."[7]

To date, however, the federal courts have responded tepidly in bringing First Amendment scrutiny to bear on this important area of speech regulation.[8] As Professor Claudia Haupt notes, "[w]hat is strikingly – and perhaps somewhat surprisingly – still absent from the case law and the legal literature is a comprehensive theory of professional speech."[9] The Supreme Court, and lower federal courts, have simply assumed that most, if not quite all, government regulations of professional speech[10] comprise part of a larger pattern of entirely non-ideological, viewpoint-neutral economic and social regulation – rather than an effort to transform professional service providers into government mouthpieces.

The Supreme Court has breezily noted that "reasonable licensing and regulation by the State" is simply a cost of doing business and does not generally implicate core First Amendment values.[11] But this analysis presumes that government only imposes regulations on professionals for non-ideological reasons related to ensuring that professionals are properly educated and credentialed, and observe the prevailing professional norms governing their profession.

To be sure, in *National Institute of Family and Life Advocates v. Becerra,*[12] the Supreme Court invalidated, on First Amendment grounds, a California law that required crisis pregnancy centers to provide information about state-sponsored family planning services, including subsidized access to abortion, as well as truthful and accurate information about the actual (limited) scope of services that crisis pregnancy centers provide to their clients (which invariably do not include abortion services). Writing for the 5–4 majority, Justice Clarence Thomas rejected the argument that content- or viewpoint-based regulations of professional speech do not trigger strict scrutiny.[13]

To be sure, the *NIFLA* Court held that "[s]peech is not unprotected merely because it is uttered by 'professionals.'"[14] In doing so, however, it cited with approval language in *Casey*[15] that sustained a Pennsylvania law that coerced the speech of medical professionals in family planning clinics as merely a regulation of "conduct."[16] The "conduct" at issue in *Casey*, however, involved both forced professional speech and the mandatory disclosure of state-mandated anti-abortion literature as part of "informed consent" requirements designed to pressure a patient in family planning clinics not to have an abortion.[17] To characterize an obligation for a physician – in her own examination room – to engage in particular speech, including providing her patient with the "probable gestational age of the child,"[18] and the involuntary distribution of state-mandated anti-abortion tracts to her patients, as constituting merely the regulation of "conduct," rather than compelled speech, constitutes bad farce. Accordingly, *NIFLA* does not actually address the larger problem of state laws using the accident of professional licensing as a basis for imposing "conduct" regulations that reduce doctors, lawyers, and other professionals to mere mouthpieces of the government.

When government regulates the professions for reasons that use the accident of a licensure requirement to compel speech from professionals, more searching judicial review is plainly requisite and a generalized posture of judicial deference will not adequately protect the speech rights of professional speakers. As Professor Christina Wells observes, the core problem seems to be that the federal courts usually presume, on a reflexive basis, that any and all professional regulations relate to the qualifications and licensing of persons who offer professional services to the public.[19] She suggests that the Supreme Court's precedents treat speech-related professional licensing requirements as regulating "a form of activity rather than a form of speech."[20] Yet, increasingly, it is clear that state governments are regulating speech in the guise of regulating activity.[21]

At the same time, federal and state government entities have taken to social media as speakers – but have hidden their identities and masquerade as private citizens. Again, government may speak for itself without running afoul of the First Amendment.[22] As Professor Helen Norton observes, "[t]he First Amendment permits government to choose to advocate a pro-life or pro-choice view – or none at all – because these choices provide the public with valuable information about its government."[23] But the question that these new practices present is a very different one – namely, must the government speak *as itself*?[24] Or may government entities attempt to hide their identity and pass their speech off as that of a private citizen or business entity?

Misattributed government speech – "stealth" government speech – about pressing questions of the day presents a serious threat to the process of democratic deliberation.[25] When government speaks about matters of public concern, but actively conceals its identity, the electorate is prevented from discounting self-serving government-authored speech appropriately. Moreover, even if a private citizen or group enjoys a constitutional right to speak either anonymously or pseudonymously,[26] it is far from self-evident that the government itself should enjoy the same privilege.[27]

Thus, two problems exist that the federal courts have failed to address with adequate strength or clarity: (1) government attempting to put words in the mouths of private citizens who happen to need government-issued licenses in order to practice their professions, and (2) government attempting to hide its identity as the source of comments on various social media platforms, with both the intent and expectation that the speech will be more effective at moving public opinion if the audience misattributes its authorship to a non-governmental source. Both practices merit a more robust judicial response than they have received to date from the federal courts.

This chapter will consider both of these problems in some detail. With regard to the first problem, I will argue that if government licensing requirements seek to advance ideological, rather than bona fide health, safety, and public welfare goals, then the federal courts should treat the regulations as viewpoint-based speech regulations and apply strict scrutiny.[28] When government uses its regulatory powers to turn private citizens into sock puppets, it hides its responsibility for the content of speech and, in so doing, seriously distorts the marketplace of ideas.

Although the Supreme Court has not reviewed the most outrageous state regulations compelling professional speech or mandating professional silence,[29] its statements on First Amendment limits on regulating professional speech have been tepid at best. As a result of this weak-kneed judicial response to ideologically-motivated compelled professional speech and silence, state governments have grown ever bolder in exercising their regulatory power over the professions as an indirect means of regulating speech markets. The same standard of review – strict scrutiny – should also apply to government efforts to conceal or obfuscate the government's identity as a speaker. The federal courts should apply a deferential standard of review to government speech *only* when the government *clearly identifies itself as the speaker.*

This chapter begins, in Part 8.1, by considering recent legislative efforts to, quite literally, put words in the mouth of licensed physicians who provide reproductive health care services to women.[30] Two US Courts of Appeals have sustained compelled physician speech as just another quotidian form of "professional licensing,"[31] although the US Court of Appeals for the Fourth Circuit invalidated a North Carolina law of the same stripe.[32]

This part also considers efforts to silence professionals by prohibiting them from speaking when, consistent with their professional ethics, they believe that they have a duty to do so. The Supreme Court itself, in *Rust v. Sullivan*,[33] sustained a gag rule that prohibited doctors, nurses, and others working in federally-subsidized family planning clinics from speaking with patients about abortion services.[34] Lower federal courts, reasonably taking their lead from the US Supreme Court, have sustained gag rules that prohibit truthful, non-misleading speech about subjects or viewpoints that the government dislikes.[35] And, although the Supreme Court's *NIFLA* decision squarely declines to recognize a new category of "professional speech" and afford it lesser First Amendment protection, it nevertheless clearly holds that states may impose mandatory disclosure requirements on professionals as mere "conduct" regulations.[36]

To be sure, such compelled speech will relate solely to professional duties. Misattributed government speech nevertheless distorts the process of democratic deliberation because it reduces citizens to mere government sock puppets. In so doing, it has a serious and problematic distortionary effect – even when the speech at issue is not self-evidently linked to questions of politics or self-government. Simply put, government should not be permitted to leverage its power to license professionals as a means of extorting compelled speech or silence from members of the learned professions.

The chapter continues, in Part 8.2, by considering government efforts to speak without identifying itself as a speaker. Government attempting to hide its identity as a speaker, and doing so successfully, presents another serious risk to core First Amendment values. Even if one can make good First Amendment arguments for the ability of a private citizen to speak either anonymously or using a pseudonym, the government should not be free to attempt to secretly propagandize its citizens. Government should have an obligation to identify itself when it enters the marketplace of ideas as a speaker; it should not have the discretion to hide behind anonymous or pseudonymous speech.[37] Finally, Part 8.3 offers a brief overview and conclusion.

A vision of the First Amendment that protects speaker autonomy and government accountability for its own actions within the marketplace of ideas requires that the federal courts prevent government entities from coercing speech by private citizens or passing off its own speech as that of a private citizen. Just as government may not enact content- or viewpoint-based speech restrictions to skew or tilt the marketplace of ideas,[38] the federal courts should not permit the government to attempt to manipulate the persuasive force of speech by using its regulatory powers to misattribute the authorship of particular ideas and viewpoints. Democratic deliberation must reflect the actual will of the citizenry, not the government, if it is to play its crucial role in facilitating government accountability. The authentic voice of "We the People" cannot be heard if the government distorts the political marketplace of ideas through misattributed propaganda. Stealth government speech, of both stripes, has no place in a polity that guarantees its citizens the freedom of political speech and relies on the electoral process to convey legitimacy on the institutions of government.

8.1 THE GROWING PROBLEM OF STATE GOVERNMENTS USING THEIR BROAD REGULATORY POWERS OVER THE PROFESSIONS TO REGULATE PROFESSIONAL SPEECH TO ADVANCE IDEOLOGICAL, RATHER THAN BONA FIDE REGULATORY, OBJECTIVES

The state and federal governments have regulated the speech of medical professionals – particularly in the context of abortion procedures.[39] The federal courts have not reliably moved to invalidate coerced speech by medical providers – some of it demonstrably false. So too, some state governments, such as the Scott administration in Florida, have forbidden state government employees from using the words "global warming" or confirming the existence of this meteorological phenomenon.[40] The Trump administration has taken a page from former Florida Governor Scott's playbook, with the EPA refusing to fund climate change related-research,[41] and the CDC prohibiting the use of words such as "science-based" and "evidence-based" in some official reports.[42] Compelled speech by medical service providers, and speech bans limiting the scope of government employees' professional speech, both raise serious First Amendment problems.

Many recent state regulations of professional speech reflect blatant efforts to inject content- and viewpoint-based perspectives into the relationship of a patient and her treating physician. Florida, for example, has prohibited medical doctors from discussing gun ownership with their patients.[43] Ostensibly, this statute exists to protect the Second Amendment rights of patients. But, this argument is nonsensical. First, patients simply do not possess Second Amendment rights against their treating physicians. In the United States, fundamental rights bind only the government – not private citizens.[44] Because a private citizen, including a medical doctor engaged in private practice, is incapable of violating the Second Amendment, it is simply not possible to "protect" Second Amendment rights from violation by medical doctors in a clinical setting.

But more to the point, the adoption of a statute regulating a physician's clinical speech when treating a patient reflects an effort to inject both state-mandated content and a clear ideological viewpoint into the physician's treating room. Florida's government wishes to encourage and support gun ownership; it accordingly has regulated doctors by prohibiting them from asking their patients about gun ownership. Characterizing the Florida law as a regulation of the medical profession borders on bad farce – it's clearly a mere cellophane wrapper used to impose an ideologically driven *omerta* on Florida's doctors.[45]

Florida has a very large population of older, retired adults. Older people facing growing health problems might well suffer from depression and anxiety. Although a medical doctor can treat these conditions, a depressed person who owns a gun might well be tempted to use it in order to commit suicide. Or, facing the loss of a beloved long-time spouse or partner, even a murder-suicide. A patient with young children also creates a risk for those children if unsecured firearms are kept in the house. Accordingly, a pediatrician might inquire, quite reasonably, about gun ownership because when children play with firearms, bad things can and do happen.[46] In sum, there are very clearly mental health-based and general safety-based reasons for a doctor asking at least some patients about gun ownership in the home.[47]

When the government regulates a professional in the conduct of her profession, and forces her to violate professional or ethical standards, the loss of speaker autonomy has an effect on the agency and authenticity of the speaker as a citizen. Being turned into a sock puppet for the delivery of a government-mandated message has to impact, at least to some extent, the person's ability to speak authentically in other contexts. The effects of being reduced to the government's mouthpiece will carry over beyond the professional context and spill over into her role as a citizen engaged as a participant in the process of democratic deliberation.[48]

During the Warren Court era, government efforts to use regulatory power to enforce silence or coerce speech by private and public employees were – after some fits and starts – rejected as inconsistent with the First Amendment. Thus, loyalty oaths and bans on the employment of members of the Communist Party in public colleges and universities were invalidated on First Amendment grounds,[49] as were efforts to ban the teaching of Marxism or Soviet-style communism.[50]

So too, the Burger Court deployed the First Amendment's Free Speech Clause to prevent the government from coercing the political speech of private citizens. In *Wooley v. Maynard*,[51] the Supreme Court held that New Hampshire could not require the Maynards, committed Jehovah's Witnesses, to display the state's official motto "Live Free or Die,"[52] thereby "in effect requir[ing] that appellees use their private property as a 'mobile billboard' for the State's ideological message – or suffer a penalty, as Maynard already has."[53] Writing for the 6–3 majority, Chief Justice

Warren E. Burger explained that "[t]he First Amendment protects the right of individuals to hold a point of view different from the majority and to refuse to foster, in the way New Hampshire commands, an idea they find morally objectionable."[54]

Today, however, the Supreme Court and lower federal courts do not reliably enforce the rule against coerced speech in the context of licensed professionals. Starting with the Rehnquist Court's opinions in *Rust* and *Casey*, the Supreme Court has signaled that coerced speech is permissible provided that the state or federal government can characterize the regulation as one of professional conduct (rather than speech). The Roberts Court's decision in *NIFLA* reaffirms and continues this general pattern of casting a blind eye on coerced speech and silence – at least for medical professionals providing family planning services (if not for unlicensed, non-professional anti-abortion activists seeking to trick pregnant women into accepting the coercive "counseling services" provided by crisis pregnancy centers).[55] By way of contrast, however, the Warren and Burger Courts were prepared to look behind the face of government speech regulations, including professional regulations, to determine whether the purpose and effect of such regulations was to restrict or compel speech based on its viewpoint.

Contemporary government efforts to, quite literally, put words in the mouths of doctors, raise serious questions about the extent to which the First Amendment should be understood to allow government to extort speech. One could conceive of the problem as presenting simply a question of unconstitutional conditions.[56] However, the problem runs deeper than a run-of-the-mill unconstitutional conditions problem; when government forces a private citizen to serve as the government's mouthpiece as the price of holding a professional license, it denies that citizen the agency to speak authentically.

One problem with permitting government to use professionals as ventriloquist's dummies inheres in what Professor Jack Balkin calls their status as "information fiduciaries."[57] Balkin posits that "most professional relationships are fiduciary relationships" and, accordingly, "most professionals are ... information fiduciaries."[58] He then argues that "professionals like doctors and lawyers have fiduciary obligations that give them special duties with respect to personal information that they obtain in the course of their relationships with their clients."[59] These fiduciary obligations certainly include duties to keep confidences, as Balkin observes,[60] but they also include obligations to disclose truthful, relevant information necessary to empower clients or patients to make informed choices.[61] Thus, when government regulates professionals in ways that preclude them from discharging this obligation to provide full, complete, and candid professional advice, it forces them to breach a fiduciary duty to their clients and patients.

A broader issue arises, however, that relates to a more general problem with coerced speech resulting in diminished speaker autonomy with respect to non-professional speech. The relationship of professional speech to democratic self-government might not be obvious or self-evident. Nevertheless, a strong relationship exists between government efforts to use the need for a professional license either to coerce speech or to silence a potential professional speaker and a more generalized diminished capacity for that person to speak authentically as a citizen outside the office context.[62] Simply put, being reduced to a mere sock puppet for the government degrades the speaker and reduces her ability to speak authentically as a citizen in *all* contexts.

Professor Caroline Mala Corbin makes this argument in highly persuasive terms, observing that "[c]ompelled [private] speech may ... distort the marketplace of ideas and democratic or personal decision making."[63] It does so by denying the compelled professional speaker full personal agency. Properly understood, the freedom of speech "protects not only outward speech, but the inner life that it expresses" and "[a] person cannot be said to be autonomous in body if forced to speak when she would rather stay silent."[64] Nor is a citizen "autonomous in thought" if the government may force her "to state a belief with which she disagrees."[65] Moreover, "[t]his insult to the speaker's dignity is compounded if listeners misattribute the government's opinion to the speaker."[66]

Forced speech causes "cognitive dissonance" and "may exert a subtle pressure on the speaker to conform her thoughts and utterances."[67] Corbin posits that forced professional speech renders the speaker less than autonomous and compromises her ability to speak authentically not only in the professional context, but more generally as well.[68]

Professor Robert Post shares very similar concerns, observing that "[b]ecause compelled speech within public discourse compromises the self-determination of speakers, it is forbidden within public discourse."[69] What is more, "[c]ompelled public discourse undermines democratic legitimation in the same way, and to the same extent, as do restrictions on public discourse."[70] To be sure, coerced professional speech does not *directly* distort public discourse, but it surely does so indirectly by rendering citizens subject to serving as government sock puppets less capable of participating in the project of democratic deliberation on equal terms with citizens not forced into playing such a degrading and demoralizing role.

Because coerced professional speech degrades and diminishes those forced to serve as the government's mouthpiece, the First Amendment should provide a strong and reliable shield against such government regulations. Indeed, at its very core, the problem constitutes a reprise of the problem presented in the Supreme Court's iconic mandatory flag salute case, *West Virginia State Board of Education v. Barnette*.[71] In *Barnette*, the state attempted to leverage its control over the public schools, on pain of truancy, juvenile delinquency status, and even criminal charges against a child's parents, to coerce the public, outward expression of political beliefs.[72]

Modern efforts to coerce the speech of professionals use a different lever of government power to coerce the public expression of assent – namely, professional licensure – but Justice Robert H. Jackson's powerful constitutional logic in *Barnette* would seem to apply with equal force on these facts. Jackson famously argued that, "[i]f there is any fixed star in our constitutional constellation, it is that no official, high or petty, can prescribe what shall be orthodox in politics, nationalism, religion, or other matters of opinion or force citizens to confess by word or act their faith therein."[73] Moreover, "[i]f there are any circumstances which permit an exception, they do not now occur to us."[74]

Forcing pediatricians to refrain from asking the parents of young children about gun ownership in the home and requiring an OB/GYN to falsely tell her patient that, if she terminates a pregnancy, she is apt to experience suicidal ideation, constitute state efforts to prescribe political orthodoxy in the guise of prescribing professional orthodoxy. The government itself is quite free to propagate the message that guns and children mix well together or to deny the existence of climate change. But it is another thing entirely to force an individual citizen to represent these views as her own. The First Amendment should preclude the state from forcing citizens, on pain of the loss of their ability to pursue a living through an otherwise lawful profession, to serve as the government's involuntary propagandists.[75]

The Supreme Court's 2018 decision in *NIFLA*, which nominally rejects special, more lenient rules for government regulations of "professional speech," does not really change the preexisting legal landscape. Indeed, the decision primarily constitutes a win for unlicensed opponents of abortion who attempt to dissuade women from terminating their unwanted pregnancies, but probably will not have significantly broader jurisprudential effects because the majority cites and applies *Casey* with approval for the proposition that regulations of a professional's "conduct" need only be reasonable to be constitutional. Of course, the "conduct" at issue in *Casey* was forced speech – mandatory disclosures that Pennsylvania requires a treating physician or registered nurse practitioner to provide to her patient.[76]

Writing for the 5–4 majority, Justice Thomas squarely rejects a separate category of "professional speech" that enjoys diminished First Amendment protection. He observes that "this Court has not recognized 'professional speech' as a separate category of speech" and, accordingly, "[s]peech is not unprotected merely because it is uttered by 'professionals.'"[77] Two general exceptions exist. When professionals engage in commercial speech, regulations governing such speech are subject only to intermediate scrutiny: "Our precedents have applied more deferential review to some laws that require professionals to disclose factual, noncontroversial information in their 'commercial speech.'"[78] Regulations of professionals' commercial speech obviously does not provide a warrant to use professionals to propagate ideological messages.

The second exception, however, provided the basis for the lower federal courts concluding that the state and federal governments enjoy a free hand to regulate professional speech. When the government seeks to regulate "professional conduct," however, a different, more permissive, rule applies: "States may regulate professional conduct, even though that conduct incidentally involves speech."[79] Justice Thomas directly cites *Casey* in support of this proposition – but *Casey* permitted Pennsylvania to require medical personnel in family planning clinics to deliver government authored scripts in their examining rooms.[80]

Thus, even as the *NIFLA* Court purported to decline recognizing "professional speech" as a new, less protected category of speech, it endorsed *Casey*'s holding that government may regulate the professions by coercing professionals' clinical speech – provided that they do so in the guise of "conduct," rather than speech, regulations. The California law at issue in *NIFLA* did not purport to regulate the conduct of persons providing counseling services at crisis pregnancy centers. Ironically, because most persons working at crisis pregnancy centers are not medical professionals, it may well be the case that the government has less ability to regulate those who pretend to be physicians than actual physicians. Pennsylvania forced medical professionals to deliver a message of the state's choosing (involving the gestational age of the fetus) and also to distribute state-authored anti-abortion tracts to their patients – in the guise of "informed consent" regulations that plainly existed to push women toward childbirth (rather than abortion).[81]

In Justice Thomas's view, California's regulation of crisis pregnancy centers was "not an informed-consent requirement or any other regulation of professional conduct."[82] This was so because "the notice does not facilitate informed consent to a medical procedure" and "is not tied to a procedure at all."[83] One wonders, however, if the result would have been different if the clinics were providing prenatal care to women and the disclosures were directly tied to the provision of those services. The conservative majority's subjective antipathy toward abortion seems to have overridden their more general deference to state regulations of professional "conduct."

Justice Stephen G. Breyer, writing in dissent, makes this point quite effectively, asking "If a State can lawfully require a doctor to tell a woman seeking an abortion about adoption services, why should it not be able, as here, to require a medical counselor to tell a woman seeking prenatal care or other reproductive healthcare about childbirth and abortion services?"[84] *Casey* plainly permits states to enter the examining room to engage in stealth advocacy of pregnancy and childbirth over abortion. Simply put, "there is no convincing reason to distinguish between information about adoption and information about abortion in this context."[85] As Justice Breyer observes, "[a]fter all, the rule of law embodies evenhandedness, and 'what is sauce for the goose is normally sauce for the gander.'"[86]

Thus, *NIFLA* does not actually secure professional freedom of speech in a generalized way – it simply invalidates a California law that required crisis pregnancy center counselors to disseminate speech about abortion services and mandatory disclosure of the actual range of services that such centers provide (which do not include either abortion services or referrals for abortions). Provided that a state legislature ties a coerced speech regulation to "informed consent" associated with a particular professional service or procedure, *Casey*'s test of mere "reasonableness" will still provide the controlling standard of review. In this important respect, the NIFLA decision was good "for this day and train only."[87] Medical professionals who provide family planning services will not be able to invoke NIFLA to secure judicial invalidation of the kinds of laws enacted and enforced in places like South Dakota and Texas.

Although one should take care not to overstate the commitment of the Warren and Burger Courts to use the First Amendment to invalidate laws that coerced speech or compelled silence, they plainly did a better job of protecting the agency and autonomy of ordinary citizen-speakers than their successors. The Rehnquist and Roberts Courts have adopted a posture of judicial deference to government speech regulations that coerce speech or compel silence (particularly for professionals who require government licenses). The First Amendment, properly interpreted and applied, should prevent efforts by the government to reduce individual citizens to government sock puppets.

8.2 EFFORTS TO PROPAGANDIZE THE BODY POLITIC VIA SOCIAL MEDIA: THE PROBLEM OF STEALTH GOVERNMENT SPEECH

No serious person would deny that the government may constitutionally enter the marketplace of ideas in order to disseminate various messages of its own choosing – for example, the federal and state governments maintain active campaigns against cigarette smoking and unprotected sex. These campaigns seek to convince private individuals to refrain from engaging in lawful behaviors that the government opposes. When government speaks, and identifies itself as the entity responsible for a particular message, no serious First Amendment problems arise.[88] However, government increasingly seeks to speak while concealing its identity as a speaker.

The problem is a real and pressing one. In a variety of contexts, the government seeks to enter the marketplace of ideas, but also to hide or disguise its identity as a speaker.[89] The *Johanns* case, involving the Cattleman's Beef Promotion and Research Board, provides a good example of this phenomenon.[90] Government creates an entity and then uses it to convey messages to the public designed entirely by the government, but propagated as if the speech of a non-governmental entity. "Beef. It's what's for dinner." was a message designed, approved, and funded by the US Department of Agriculture.[91] Few members of the public probably knew (or know) this.[92]

Despite the probability of the general public misattributing the speaker – which was the USDA and not private cattle ranchers – the Supreme Court sustained the program against a First Amendment challenge.[93] As Professor Norton argues, "the public can hold government accountable for its expressive choices only when the public can attribute contested speech *to* the government."[94] Government plainly has a right to speak and, as matter of necessity, must do so on a wide variety of subjects and on a regular basis. But this begs the question of whether the government should be permitted to speak on an anonymous or pseudonymous basis.

Unlike the question of coerced speech, the Warren and Burger Courts did not have an occasion to consider stealth government speech. Accordingly, this area breaks from the more general narrative of this book, which is that in a variety of important areas of First Amendment law, theory, and practice, expressive freedoms have contracted, rather than expanded, over time. In this context, the federal courts have never undertaken serious efforts to limit or control the ability of the government, at all levels, to engage in stealth speech. Nevertheless, with the increasing importance of social media to the process of democratic deliberation, anonymous or pseudonymous government speech presents a growing problem that needs to be addressed by the federal courts.

Professors Norton and Citron note that "[g]overnments ... increasingly use interactive platforms where government speakers' identities may be both difficult to discern and to authenticate."[95] Professor Gia Lee adds that "[t]hough the full extent of the practice is necessarily difficult to measure, recent reports suggest that federal, state, and local government entities may engage in pseudonymous or anonymous communications more often than we might imagine."[96] Lee reports on a wide variety of instances in which government has entered the marketplace of ideas as an advocate, but sought either to conceal or disguise its identity as the author of a particular message.[97]

Moreover, this failure to self-identify itself to its potential audience is far from accidental. Government actively attempts to obscure its identity precisely because the government's authorship of the message could adversely affect its persuasive force. Thus, the government conceals its identity as a speaker in order to "make its views appear to be held by more esteemed or authoritative sources than they necessarily are, and more widely accepted than they really are."[98]

In a similar vein, Professor Blocher cautions that when government engages in stealth speech, "voters will not necessarily even know when the government is speaking, and therefore cannot hold it accountable for whatever message it is conveying."[99] In order to address this problem, he argues in favor of "a functional transparency requirement, which would enable voters to respond to, and control, government speech."[100] In his view, "[t]his kind of political process solution has much to recommend it" and "would surely go a long way towards ensuring that messages the government claims to be expressing in the name of voters are messages the voters actually support."[101]

Professor Robert Post also shares concerns about the dangers of both unattributed and misattributed government speech. He observes that "when government speaks in its own voice, we are alert to the possibility that it may be attempting to manipulate public opinion."[102] However, when the government speaks through a private intermediary, the processes of democratic discourse could be disrupted and public opinion could be "corrupt[ed]" by "views manufactured by government requirements."[103] Government efforts to "conscript the expression of ideas" create a serious risk of distortion of the political marketplace of ideas – the operation of which is the principal means the electorate uses to hold the institutions of government accountable.[104] Accordingly, government "stealth speech" and "ventriloquism" create risks to the democracy itself.[105]

Echoing Professor Corbin's concerns,[106] Professor Jack Balkin emphasizes the importance of speaker autonomy to the functioning of democratic discourse. He argues that "[w]hen people engage in public discourse, either as speakers or as audiences, the law presumes that they are free, independent, and autonomous, even if they are really not."[107] Consistent with this approach, "[a]ll persons (or at the very least, all adults) are treated as equally competent and equally able to fend for themselves in the realm of public discourse."[108] When government undermines the autonomy of a speaker in one context (professional speech), it fails to treat certain citizens as either equally autonomous or equally competent.[109]

To be sure government has a constitutionally valid interest in communicating directly with the body politic. But, as Professor Abner Greene has argued, "[g]overnment speech is most defensible when it does not monopolize (i.e., it is one view among many and citizen choice is based on full knowledge), when it does not coerce (i.e., it is merely persuasive), and *when it is clearly identified as that of the government.*"[110] The transparency of government speech obviously bears on both these concerns.

Greene argues that the lack of transparency presents the greatest risk of distortion to the political marketplace of ideas because it (1) reduces the government's accountability for the positions, ideas, and viewpoints that it propagates[111] and (2) creates a risk of hidden government monopolization of the marketplace because masked government speech can easily impede the audience's process of "value assessment and search for competing speakers and viewpoints."[112] When the government "buy[s] citizens to do its dirty work" a risk arises that "the public will not see clearly enough the connection between law and resulting speech to hold the government properly accountable and a monopolization danger from failure to identify the source of speech."[113] By way of contrast, the proper attribution of government-authored speech addresses both concerns effectively and ensures that government speech does not have a distortionary effect on the process of democratic deliberation because voters will not misattribute the message's source.

Accordingly, even if the First Amendment secures a right for private citizens to speak on an anonymous or pseudonymous basis,[114] the same rule simply should not apply to the government itself. Truth in advertising requires government to self-identify itself when it speaks.[115] Big Brother watching presents one set of issues, but Big Brother speaking, while attempting to hide its identity, presents another set of issues that merit sustained and critical attention from the federal courts.[116] As Lee suggests, "the constitutional commitment to political accountability counsels governmental actors to ensure the transparency of government communications and that those actors may avoid the principle of transparency only in exceptional cases."[117]

Professor Norton argues that the federal courts "should demand transparency from the government as a condition of recognizing the government speech defense to Free Speech Clause challenges to the government's expressive choices."[118] She observes that "[t]ransparency, in turn, requires a bit of planning and some political courage," but suggests that transparency and planning are "not too much to ask."[119] However, Professor Norton's proposal does not go far enough; it provides a remedy only when the government's authorship of the speech has been contested. In the many circumstances where surreptitious government speech goes undetected, her proposal would not constrain government from attempting to propagandize citizens on either an anonymous or pseudonymous basis.

Despite the obvious objections that exist to government attempting to propagandize its citizens, the federal courts have not acted to limit the ability of government to speak in non-transparent ways. Indeed, the Roberts Court's most recent government speech case, *Walker v. Texas Division, Sons of Confederate Veterans*,[120] permits the government to engage in stealth speech by using private citizens to convey its preferred messages – but not messages that it would prefer not to disseminate. The case involved a Texas affinity or "specialty" automobile license plate program.

Under its specialty license plate program, Texas permitted some groups, but not others, to establish affinity plates. State law authorized the issuance of specialty plates for "a non-profit entity" or "private vendor,"[121] but such plates are subject to state approval.[122] The Texas Department of Motor Vehicles Board exercises considerable editorial control over the content of the messages displayed on the affinity plates.[123]

Texas refused to issue a specialty plate for the Sons of Confederate Veterans that prominently featured a Confederate battle flag.[124] The board rejected the proposed plate design because "a significant portion of the public associate the confederate flag with organizations advocating expressions of hate directed toward people or groups that is demeaning to those people or groups."[125]

The *Walker* majority held in favor of the board's authority to refuse to issue the proposed plate, explaining that automobile license plates, even if selected by individual automobile owners, "convey government speech."[126] Because the specialty license plate program constitutes government speech, rather than private speech, Texas was free to deny the Sons of Confederate Veterans a dedicated specialty plate festooned with the Confederate battle flag.[127] Of course, this characterization of the specialty plate program facilitates naked forms of content and viewpoint discrimination – but content and viewpoint discrimination are inherent in government speech because the government advocates or opposes particular ideas or polices whenever it enters the marketplace of ideas.[128]

The problem, on these facts, is that it is not clear to persons who see an affinity license plate, or a personalized "vanity" license plate, that the speech is actually that of the government rather than the speech of the automobile's owner. Simply put, the use of private vehicles to convey the government's preferred messages obfuscates the government's shared authorship of the messages. Most citizens do not understand or appreciate the finer points of the affinity license plate approval process – much less the state's precise role in granting or refusing to issue a particular kind of affinity plate. A reasonable observer who sees an affinity plate affixed to an automobile will undoubtedly associate the message, e.g., "Choose Life," with the owner of the car as much, if not more, than with the state government.[129] In this fashion, the government may disseminate messages of its choosing to the general population, without taking direct responsibility as the principal author of the message.

Of course, an automobile license plate is, by its very nature, a government-issued means of communication – so the government's responsibility for affinity license plates, even if not completely transparent, is not entirely opaque either. When government agencies take to social media platforms, however, and post comments attributed to what appear to be private individuals, rather than the government, the hand of the government as the author of the message is completely opaque.[130] And, it is difficult to posit a persuasive rationale that might justify government being permitted to enter the marketplace of ideas in order to speak out about controversial issues of the day without disclosing its authorship of particular views. Just as surveillance has a chilling effect on the marketplace of ideas,[131] misattributed government interventions in speech markets have, if not a chilling effect on the speech of others, then a potentially significant distortionary effect. To date, however, the application of the government speech doctrine is not contingent on the transparency or opacity of the government's speech – which presents a serious risk of the government using stealth government speech to distort the political marketplace of ideas.

The Supreme Court's initial decision recognizing the government speech doctrine, *Pleasant Grove City v. Summum,*[132] involved the placement of privately donated monuments in a municipal public park. In consequence, the problem of identifying the government as the speaker was simply not at issue. As the owner of the public park, Pleasant Grove City was, at least in part, obviously responsible for whatever messages the monuments communicated to those who viewed them.

In *Summum,* the Supreme Court held that a city government could elect to accept, or reject, monuments to be placed permanently on display in a public park.[133] Justice Samuel Alito explained that "the City's decision to accept certain privately donated monuments while rejecting respondent's is best viewed as a form of government speech,"[134] and that "government speech" need not respect rules of content or viewpoint neutrality.[135] In fact, the First Amendment simply *does not apply* to government speech.[136]

Justice Alito observed that "[p]ublic parks are often closely identified in the public mind with the government unit that owns the land."[137] Accordingly, "[t]he monuments that are accepted, therefore, are meant to convey and have the effect of conveying a government message, and they thus constitute government speech."[138] The government may speak, or not speak, through the permanent display of monuments in its park as it sees fit.

Because the government must be able to communicate freely with the citizenry about matters of public importance, government speech is not subject to *any* level of First Amendment scrutiny (at all).[139] Given that the government speech doctrine creates, literally, a First Amendment-free zone, it must be carefully limited and circumscribed to avoid the risk of government entering the marketplace of political ideas in order to distort it through propaganda. Yet, in *Summum* and again in *Walker*, the Supreme Court failed to insist that government speech be obviously and self-evidently *only* the government's speech.[140] Moreover, notwithstanding a steady and loud chorus of scholarly objections,[141] neither the Rehnquist Court nor the Roberts Court have insisted that the government be transparent when engaging in "government speech."[142]

It is, of course, much easier to describe the problem of stealth government speech than to offer an effective solution – ideally one that would have a strong deterrent effect. Professor Norton suggests simply withholding the deferential standard of review that federal courts invariably apply in government speech cases;[143] instead, she suggests that the federal courts should simply apply regular First Amendment principles in cases involving stealth government speech.[144] This solution would constitute a good start, but is incomplete, because it would not sufficiently deter stealth government speech. Stronger medicine is required than simply allowing government stealth speech to be reviewed under generic First Amendment principles.

I would suggest that government stealth speech should be entirely unprotected as speech. At first blush, this proposal might seem to be somewhat radical – and perhaps it is. But, upon more careful reflection, it becomes clear that stealth government speech is inherently false and misleading – and false and misleading speech has never had much of a purchase on the First Amendment. Intentionally false speech may serve as a basis for imposing liability on press entities for libel.[145] So too, false and misleading speech about a lawful good or service enjoys no First Amendment protection under the commercial speech doctrine.[146] It is true that the Supreme Court has held that false speech that does not cause any independent harm enjoys First Amendment protection,[147] but I would posit that stealth government speech is inherently harmful because of its potential distortionary effects on the process of democratic deliberation and, therefore, should not enjoy *any* protection under the First Amendment.

If one accepts my premise that stealth government speech has no legitimate claim on the First Amendment, then the federal courts would simply deny any First Amendment protection to such speech when the speech otherwise engenders potential liability on the part of the government speaker. To be sure, this approach would not constitute an absolute deterrent to stealth government speech – but it would surely focus the mind of government officers when they must decide whether to speak transparently or opaquely. Moreover, if the federal courts simply revert to generic First Amendment principles, then stealth government speech related to public officials, public figures, and matters of public concern would likely enjoy robust First Amendment protection.[148] The road would remain more-or-less open to stealth government speech in most circumstances where the government would be incented to enter the marketplace of ideas while concealing its identity as a speaker.

One might also question whether private, for-profit corporations should be able to speak anonymously or using a pseudonym.[149] Under the state action doctrine, the First Amendment itself would not provide a basis for denying corporations, as opposed to government entities, the ability to speak anonymously or pseudonymously.[150] Instead, any limits or a flat ban on such speech activity would have to arise from positive legislation at the federal, state, or local level of government. Moreover, if enacted, such legislation would itself be subject to a First Amendment attack under the theory that for-profit corporations are no different from private citizens for purposes of applying the First Amendment's protections.[151]

Nevertheless, good arguments support the constitutionality of legislation limiting or banning mis-attributed corporate speech – at least with respect to for-profit, publicly traded corporations. First, speech by for-profit corporations arguably constitutes a form of commercial speech, insofar as all speech by for-profit corporations should be aimed at enhancing shareholder returns.[152] Second, the ability of shareholders to hold the board and management accountable requires that shareholders be able to assess precisely what the board and management have been doing. Even if, under *Citizens United*, corporations have a right to speak on matters of public concern (despite being motivated by concerns related to maximizing company profits), anonymous or pseudonymous corporate speech seriously undermines the ability of shareholders to assess fully and accurately speech activities by the corporation that they ostensibly own. Securing meaningful corporate accountability to the shareholders would require that all the corporation's actions, including speech about matters of public concern, be sufficiently transparent for shareholders to know about and assess.

8.3 CONCLUSION

The Warren and Burger Courts deployed the First Amendment to limit the government's ability to coerce speech by private citizens. The Rehnquist Court, by way of contrast, issued opinions, such as *Rust* and *Casey*, that permitted the government to coerce speech or compel silence by professionals. The Roberts Courts followed the Rehnquist Court's lead, reaffirming the idea that compelled professional speech, if a regulation of "conduct," does not violate the First Amendment. It also invented the government speech doctrine in *Summum* – which, in the age of the internet, creates a serious risk of the government using stealth speech to distort or disrupt the process of democratic deliberation essential to our project of self-government – and then extended its reach in *Walker* to encompass mixed government/private speech.

Accordingly, and unfortunately, the overall doctrinal pattern in this area of First Amendment law corresponds to other areas in which First Amendment rights have declined, rather than expanded, over time. Despite this unpromising record to date, however, the federal courts should deploy the First Amendment more aggressively and more reliably to protect professionals from coerced speech requirements that plainly relate to ideological, viewpoint-based commitments held by state governments. Although a state government is itself free to speak, and to propagate strong positions on controversial issues of the day, the ability to speak directly should not imply a power to speak indirectly through the use of dragooned speech proxies.

So too, government's ability to speak directly should not be construed to extend to government speech on an anonymous or pseudonymous basis. Simply put, if the government wishes to speak, it should speak for itself and it should be transparent about its authorship of a particular message. Stealth government speech should have no claim to protection under the First Amendment.

The government's increasing use of involuntary speech proxies and false identities should be reversed because misattributed government speech degrades, rather than enhances, the marketplace of ideas. And, even if private individuals – and also corporations – have a First Amendment right to speak using a proxy or on an anonymous or pseudonymous basis, the government itself should not enjoy the discretion to acknowledge – or decline to acknowledge – its authorship of a particular message. Under the First Amendment, government may certainly speak – but the same First Amendment that permits government to enter the marketplace of ideas should be construed to require the government to announce its presence in that marketplace. Neither the Roberts nor Rehnquist Courts have been sufficiently attentive to the potential evils and ill-effects of the government speaking while attempting to hide or obfuscate its identity as a speaker.

9

Using Constitutionally Permissible Statutes to Impede First Amendment Activity

The Supreme Court's Failure to Address the Abuse of Discretionary Authority by Police, Prosecutors, and Other Nonjudicial Actors

This chapter considers the impact of nonjudicial actors in defining and limiting the scope of First Amendment rights. The protection of First Amendment rights cannot be solely the province of the federal courts; non-judicial actors have an important role to play in securing expressive freedoms and facilitating the operation of the political marketplace of ideas. Police, prosecutors, and other public officials who exercise discretionary authority can use their discretion either to facilitate or impede the exercise of First Amendment rights.[1] The misuse of discretionary policing authority can profoundly affect the ability of ordinary citizens to gather in public spaces for the purpose of exercising their rights of speech, assembly, association, and petition – rights that remain highly salient even in the age of the internet.[2] As Professor Tabatha Abu El-Haj has argued, "[o]utdoor assembly has unique attributes as a form of political participation, even in the twenty-first century."[3]

Thus, non-judicial actors play an important role in determining the scope of protected speech rights. When police officers and prosecutors arrest and charge protesters, then drop charges that seem questionable on First Amendment grounds, the damage to First Amendment values remains. Discretionary police activity plainly can have a serious chilling effect on the expression of dissent. Even so, these tactics are an increasingly commonplace means of managing public assembly and protest.[4]

The problems associated with the abuse of otherwise constitutional discretionary police and prosecutor authority are compounded by the use of strategic maneuvers that insulate such bad behavior from judicial review – such as releasing those arrested (after precluding protest activity through the initial arrests) or via a prosecutor's decision to drop the criminal charges rather than take them to trial. When police arrest protesters and the charges are subsequently dropped – whether by police or public prosecutors – the government's actions are not readily subject to judicial review. It also bears noting that the federal courts are not well positioned to superintend the exercise of police and prosecutor discretion in the abstract.

The problem is complicated by the fact that the laws under which the arrests take place are unquestionably facially constitutional. As Professor Christina E. Wells has argued, "[u]ntil we come to grips with these types of restrictions on protestors, focusing only on strengthening judicial review within the Court's existing free speech framework is merely a temporary and unduly narrow fix."[5]

To be sure, the Warren Court intervened with some regularity to overturn criminal convictions for the breach of peace and disorderly conduct where the charges plainly rested on the government's antipathy to particular speakers and messages.[6] These precedents invalidated the most obvious and outrageous laws – facially overbroad state statutes and municipal ordinances that directly targeted speech by treating a hostile audience reaction as constituting a breach of the peace or lawful peaceful assembly as disorderly conduct.[7] The Burger Court expanded on the Warren Court's precedents by invalidating laws that imposed mandatory civility norms on public speech.[8]

Both the Warren Court's and Burger Court's lines of precedent involved laws that were substantively invalid – unconstitutional – rather than the abuse of discretionary police authority conveyed by perfectly constitutional laws. They also involved cases that the government took to trial in order to secure convictions – rather than arrests followed by dropped charges. Contemporary state and local laws proscribing trespass, breach of peace, and unlawful assembly are entirely content-neutral; they do not target speech because it offends or outrages the dominant forces within the community.[9] Simply put, direct constitutional attacks on such enactments will not succeed in the federal courts.[10]

The use of discretionary police and prosecutorial authority to burden, if not entirely squelch, First Amendment activity presents a form of speech-restricting government behavior that routinely evades judicial review. The Warren and Burger Courts' precedents overturning breach of peace and disorderly conduct convictions exist precisely because the charges were taken to trial and the government secured convictions. Neither the Warren Court nor the Burger Court issued landmark decisions aimed at reducing the risk of discretionary police and prosecutor authority being abused to harass, intimidate, or preclude expressive and associational activity in the absence of actual convictions.

The problem of pretextual arrests certainly existed during the Warren Court and Burger Court eras – and the federal courts did not do much to address it precisely because judicial superintendence of everyday policing decisions is both difficult and impractical. Assessing the constitutional validity of a statute is one thing; second-guessing a real-time policing decision to make an arrest is quite another. Thus, in this specific context, the failure of the Rehnquist and Roberts Courts to expand free speech rights by limiting police and prosecutor discretion to arrest and charge citizens engaged in public protest does not necessarily fall within the more general pattern that I have identified in other areas of First Amendment jurisprudence reflecting judicial indifference to speakers who lack the property necessary to speak.[11]

Moreover, that the problem of pretextual arrests and charges continues to exist without much judicial effort to address it should not be surprising. The underlying legal tools used to impede speech activity are self-evidently constitutional; simply put, laws against unlawful assembly, disorderly conduct, trespass, impeding police work, and resisting arrest do not violate the First Amendment. None of these rules target speech or assembly on their face and, in many circumstances, the application of statutes proscribing this kind of conduct does not present any serious constitutional concerns.

As applied, however, these legal rules can be used as instruments of content- and viewpoint-based censorship. And, in some instances, the potential scope of application of the criminal proscriptions does raise First Amendment concerns. For example, with respect to the crime of unlawful assembly, Professor John Inazu argues that "contemporary understandings of unlawful assembly cede too much discretion to law enforcement by neglecting earlier statutory and common law elements that once constrained liability."[12] But even a more narrowly drawn law proscribing unlawful assembly could be used pretextually – the police discretion itself presents a non-trivial risk of abuse, and constitutes a potential threat to the exercise of expressive freedoms.

Accordingly, to effectively secure First Amendment rights, the federal courts must devise constitutional metrics that would effectively and reliably sort valid applications of these laws from pretextual ones. This latter task, however, is not well-suited either to judges or the judicial process.[13] It is not enough for courts to invalidate or impose narrowing constructions on laws that target speech; such action is certainly important, but constitutes only a partial solution. Limiting the potential pretextual use of laws against trespass, unlawful assembly, and breach of the peace has to be part of a larger answer.

This chapter proceeds in four main parts. Part 9.1 seeks to identify the problems associated with police activity that impedes the exercise of expressive freedoms protected under the First Amendment. Given the increasingly prevalent use of these tactics, the relative paucity of scholarship addressing this problem is somewhat surprising.[14] Part 9.2 describes and discusses landmark decisions of the Warren and Burger Courts that deployed the First Amendment to invalidate breach of peace statutes and similar laws that relied primarily on an audience's offense or hostile reaction to speech as the gravamen of the offense. In Part 9.3, I discuss the theoretical and practical difficulties associated with attempting to subject abusive, speech-inhibiting police and prosecutor tactics to meaningful First Amendment scrutiny. Finally, Part 9.4 offers a brief overview and conclusion.

Police and prosecutor behavior seriously affects the scope and vibrancy of expressive freedoms. The use of arrests for minor criminal offenses to prevent public protest affects would-be protesters of all ideological stripes.[15] However, courts may lack the institutional capacity to supervise the discretionary use of police authority to enforce facially constitutional criminal laws. The problem is even harder to address because it is difficult – often impossible – to seek judicial review based on the First Amendment for arrests that do not lead to formal criminal charges. Simply put, courts cannot review arrests that are not prosecuted.[16] Even if courts have the ability to oversee day-to-day exercises of police authority, getting dropped charges before a federal court presents a serious legal problem.

At the same time, relying exclusively on police self-restraint and *political* controls on the use of arrests to squelch speech constitute at best imperfect means of addressing the problem.[17] Democratically elected government officials, and those holding government positions under appointments from such officials, will systematically undervalue public protest by unpopular dissenters and overvalue peace, order, and quietude in the community. In consequence, successfully addressing the abuse of police authority to enforce general laws against trespass, breach of peace, and unlawful assembly as a means of silencing public protest presents a difficult, and perhaps insoluble, problem.

9.1 POLICE AND PROSECUTORS ROUTINELY USE TRESPASS, BREACH OF PEACE/DISORDERLY CONDUCT, AND UNLAWFUL ASSEMBLY LAWS TO BURDEN OR PROHIBIT PUBLIC PROTEST

The problem of police abusing discretionary authority to burden or prevent public protest is not a new one, but the use of pretextual arrests to squelch dissenting voices seems to be growing over time. Professor Tabatha Abu El-Haj observes that in the contemporary United States, would-be protesters are "[f]orced to navigate a wide array of hurdles to gain permission to be out in public legally," and, even when the requisite permits and permissions have been secured, also must contend with "police officers routinely handing out citations, at their discretion, for a variety of minor public order offences," rendering the First Amendment's protection of the rights of speech, assembly, petition, and association "as something between weak and non-existent."[18]

Moreover, the problem of using aggressive police tactics to squelch public protest activity is hardly limited to the United States. As Professor Wells has noted, in many countries, including other industrial democracies, "widespread use of excessive force against peaceful demonstrators, unsupported claims that the police response was required to quell violence or incitement to violence, and mass arrests of peaceful protestors" are commonplace responses to peaceful mass protests.[19] In addition, police forces in the United States and abroad increasingly rely on "aggressive or military-style tactics" that "chill speech by instilling fear of bodily harm in protestors and by the 'intensive violations of personal integrity that [excessive force] necessarily involves.'"[20]

Police use perfectly constitutional state laws and municipal ordinances that prohibit trespass, unlawful assembly, and disorderly conduct to arrest protesters en masse – and thereby preclude them from reaching their intended audience.[21] Police officers also use other minor crimes, such as jaywalking, impeding vehicular or pedestrian traffic, and refusal to follow a lawful police order, as crimes that justify arresting protesters.[22] Professor Abu El-Haj notes that "[m]unicipalities have not been shy about arresting and prosecuting disruptive protestors."[23]

These crimes have broad definitions and police often use ambiguity in the scope of laws against unlawful assembly, disorderly conduct, and the like, to justify arresting and charging protesters on facts that do not meet all the requisite elements of the crime. Their potential breadth of scope "make them particularly useful tools for order maintenance in the context of demonstrations."[24] Moreover, reviewing courts tend to accept with equanimity the argument that the would-be protesters are quite free to disseminate their message – at some other time and place.[25] As Professor Abu El-Haj notes, "[o]ut of a fear of even a tiny risk of mayhem, the courts allow states to define unlawful assembly and riot broadly, ensuring that they can capture assemblies that once would have been considered peaceable."[26]

As explained in some detail in Chapters 1 and 2, the widespread availability of virtual forums through social media service providers should not relieve government from the obligation to make tangible, physical spaces available for democratic engagement and discourse. First and foremost, the ability to exercise expressive freedoms in a different way, perhaps at a different time, does not excuse the government from failing to make public space available for First Amendment activity. Simply put, a would-be speaker should enjoy a constitutional right to choose for herself the precise means by which she propagates her message.[27]

Second, the virtual, social media-based forums that provide access to large, mass audiences are all *privately owned by for-profit corporations* that can adopt and enforce whatever content, and even viewpoint, restrictions that they find congenial. Strictly speaking, the First Amendment – at least at present – has no application whatsoever to entities like Facebook, YouTube, Twitter, and Instagram.[28] Accordingly, it is entirely unreasonable to posit that these virtual speech forums – whose profit-seeking corporate owners can ban messages or speakers for a good reason, a bad reason, or no reason at all – now serve as comprehensive and fully adequate substitutes for access to public spaces for collective, in person, real time protest activity.

Third, and finally, obvious and important benefits arise from real time, in person communication that simply do not exist when a speaker propagates a message over a social media platform. These include the ability to ensure that a message reaches a particular audience, the ability to engage a broad and diverse cross-section of the community, and the ability to use public confrontation of public officials and public figures, through the intermediation of the mass media, to help create and sustain an ongoing dialogue within the community.[29] Accordingly, "[t]he ability of a citizen to confront power has a powerful effect in facilitating democratic discourse."[30] The use of pretextual arrest, with charges later being dropped without going to trial, imposes a significant, and unjustifiable, burden on the lawful exercise of First Amendment rights.

Unlawful assembly provides a particularly effective, and pernicious, means of suppressing dissent and would-be dissenters. This is so, as Professor Inazu explains, because "[i]n most cases, the only objective discernible element is the number of people gathered."[31] The other elements of the crime of unlawful assembly – "mens rea, the fact of an agreement, and the contemplated use of force or violence"[32] – are not objective in nature and largely rest on "subjective assessments."[33] The vague elements of unlawful assembly encourage police officers "to intervene at an earlier stage, even in the absence of a threat of severe harm perceived by a reasonable observer."[34]

Police also use military tactics to frighten protesters into abandoning their efforts to speak their version of truth to power. As one commentator explains, "[m]ilitarized police responses are now a staple of local government's response to the body politic's exercise of its right to peaceably assemble."[35] In the Ferguson, Missouri protests that erupted in the wake of Michael Brown's death, police officers from city, county, and state law enforcement agencies deployed "heavy-handed police tactics, ranging from a demand that protesters demonstrate in a 'respectful manner' to use of tear gas, rubber bullets and snipers."[36] Obviously, the use of aggressive, militarized-policing tactics will have a significant chilling effect on public protest activity.[37]

In many instances, nothing ever comes of these charges – which is the root of the problem of bringing the First Amendment to bear. Not uncommonly, prosecutors decline to prosecute these cases;[38] as a result, those arrested have no obvious means of challenging pretextual arrests on First Amendment grounds. Accordingly, and as Professor Wells has explained, "a variety of governmental tactics involving protesters – tactics that are used worldwide and not exceptional to the United States – elude effective judicial review."[39] As Professor Abu El-Haj notes, through these techniques of pretextual arrests followed by the non-prosecution of the charges, law enforcement agencies seeking to prevent public protest are able to "render protestors supplicant to the authorities they are challenging."[40]

Police also target for arrest journalists seeking to cover mass protests.[41] This has the effect of discouraging news coverage of public demonstrations and undoubtedly has a chilling effect on constitutionally-protected newsgathering activity.[42] One of the major objectives of mass, public protests is to generate a more general public discourse through the intermediation of the mass media.[43] By targeting working journalists, law enforcement agencies can render public protest invisible to the larger community, undermining the very process of democratic deliberation that is essential to the project of democratic self-government.[44]

Of course, it is possible to challenge the arrests on non-First Amendment grounds. However, cases challenging pretextual arrests arise "almost exclusively under the Fourth Amendment to the U.S. Constitution,"[45] rather than the First Amendment. More often than not, challenging an arrest for trespass, disorderly conduct, or unlawful assembly is a quixotic enterprise. This is so because "judges seek to determine whether police had 'probable cause' to arrest a protestor or whether the police used excessive force in effectuating an arrest."[46] These standards "are deferential and favor the government."[47] In such cases, the First Amendment simply does not come into play. The consequence is deeply problematic and entirely predictable: "[A]cross jurisdictions, police, rather than judges, are primarily responsible for decisions to quell peaceful protest."[48] Without doubt, "these tactics chill free expression."[49]

The mass protests in Ferguson, Missouri, following the police shooting and killing Michael Brown, provide an illustrative example of this problem. The background facts are well known but bear repeating: "Following the shooting of an unarmed black teenager, Michael Brown, by a local police officer ... community members and Americans from across the country took to the streets, the vast majority in a peaceful manner, demanding the arrest of the police officer for Michael Brown's death."[50] The local police reaction in Ferguson to these protests was not constructive. Instead of facilitating peaceful, non-violent protests, Ferguson police, augmented by officers from St. Louis County and the Missouri state police, "reacted with a great show of force through the employment of armored vehicles, military-grade rifles, and tactical raiding equipment."[51]

To be sure, some of the protests, particularly at night, turned violent. Private property, including a Marathon gas station, was attacked and destroyed. Even so, however, aggressive police tactics were not limited to efforts to cabin or control violent assemblies bent on criminal mischief. Instead, "[p]olice officers arrested many peaceful protestors, including public academics such as Cornel West, bringing much media coverage to the area."[52] Hundreds of arrests took place involving entirely peaceful, non-violent protesters, "the vast majority of which were for failure to disperse or resisting arrest."[53]

Unfortunately, and as Professor Abu El-Haj has explained, "the resort by law enforcement in Ferguson to enforcing an array of nonviolent misdemeanors, such as disorderly conduct and trespass to control and disperse crowds, is quite typical."[54] Moreover, in the end, "it does not necessarily matter whether charges will ultimately hold up in court if frontline law enforcement arrests large numbers of protestors for such crimes."[55]

The American Civil Liberties Union (ACLU) was able to secure limited judicial relief through litigation – but the thoughtful decision by US District Judge Catherine D. Perry provides important insights into the limits of judicial action to superintend discretionary law enforcement activities that impede or prevent the public expression of dissent. The Ferguson police, in concert with county and state law enforcement agencies, adopted a policing strategy that required protesters "to keep moving," and prohibiting them from "stand[ing] still on the sidewalks"[56] for more than five seconds (on pain of arrest). This "keep-moving" policy "was communicated to the officers at the regular roll calls, and the officers were told to use discretion, but were not told any particular circumstances or factors that they should consider in using that discretion."[57]

Mr. Mustafa Abdullah, a program associate with the ACLU, initiated a lawsuit challenging the "keep-moving" policy after he was threatened with arrest while peacefully, and lawfully, advising protesters of their First Amendment rights.[58] The ACLU sought an injunction prohibiting the police from enforcing the policy. The defendants attempted to defend their keep-moving policy as a lawful application of Missouri's refusal to disperse statute.[59]

Judge Perry held that the Missouri refusal to disperse statute did not provide a legal justification for the keep-moving policy for several reasons, including the fact that the police never told the protesters to disperse, the police officers applied the policy when fewer than six people were present (the minimum number required for the state statute to apply), and because the police applied the keep-moving policy in the absence of any credible evidence that those not moving intended to commit a crime.[60] She found that despite possible "confusion about the legal basis for the keep-moving rule," it was very clear that "people were ordered to keep moving in situations that could never have been covered by the refusal-to-disperse law."[61]

Judge Perry concluded that "[t]he keep-moving policy – as it was applied to plaintiff and others – prohibited citizens from peacefully assembling on the public sidewalks," an outcome that was fundamentally inconsistent with the First Amendment.[62] A "blanket-rule" prohibiting assembly on the public sidewalks swept far beyond the limits of the government's "valid interest in maintaining order on the streets and sidewalks."[63] Accordingly, the court held that "[t]he plaintiffs are entitled to the entry of a preliminary injunction enjoining defendants from telling citizens that they must keep moving, or from threatening them with arrest if they stand still, so long as those citizens are not committing a crime, engaging in violent acts, or participating in a crowd that contains other people doing those things."[64] So, to this extent, Judge Perry's decision represents a robust vindication of Abdullah's First Amendment rights.

On the other hand, however, the scope of the injunction was limited and did not "prevent defendants or other law enforcement agencies from using all lawful means to control crowds and protect against violence."[65] More specifically, "Missouri's refusal-to-disperse law is not restricted by this injunction."[66] Judge Perry took pains to emphasize that police officers in Ferguson could still make arrests for unlawful assembly and refusal-to-disperse without violating the federal court's injunction, explaining that "[i]f a crowd is becoming unruly, the police may find it necessary to order the crowd to disperse – including persons who are not committing crimes or violent acts – and the police may also tell an unruly crowd to move to a different place."[67] This necessarily means that "citizens who are themselves peaceful but who are part of a crowd that is becoming violent must obey these orders or face arrest."[68]

In short, the *Abdullah* decision represents a double-edged sword – something of a pyrrhic victory for those asserting their right to exercise expressive freedoms in public. One the one hand, the district court enjoined the "keep-walking" rule that prohibited citizens from talking with each other on the sidewalks of Ferguson – unless they continued moving while doing so. But, on the other, the court vindicated very broad police discretionary authority to use a variety of criminal laws to keep the peace. As Judge Perry observed, "[t]he police must be able to perform their jobs, and nothing in this order restricts their ability to do that."[69] Thus, although the court's injunction protected the right of peaceful protesters who are "peaceably standing, marching, or assembling on public sidewalks in Ferguson, Missouri," it also declared "that this order shall not prevent the defendants from enforcing the Missouri refusal-to-disperse statute."[70]

The Ferguson litigation clearly demonstrates the concrete limits of judicial protection of First Amendment rights. The ACLU achieved precisely the result it sought – the abolition of the five second keep-moving rule. At the same time, however, the court's decision left police with more than sufficient discretionary authority to continue impeding lawful, peaceful protests – it simply required them to be more clever about it. Securing First Amendment rights to public protest requires more than empty, pyrrhic victories that check some government abuses of discretionary authority while leaving others entirely unaffected (and, hence available to suppress the public expression of dissent).

Moreover, a pattern is at work here: It is much easier for judges to identify and invalidate, on First Amendment grounds, policies that target speech for unfavorable treatment (such as the keep-moving rule in Ferguson), than it is for them to supervise the use of discretionary authority to enforce laws that, on their face, do not violate the First Amendment. The former involves asking and resolving a question of law – courts are particularly well-suited to undertake analytical tasks of this sort.[71] By way of contrast, the latter task requires a judge effectively to second-guess the motives of a law enforcement officer, and to do so on a post-hoc basis. This is not to say that courts cannot intervene when clear patterns of abuse emerge over time that show the existence of a policy or practice of abusing discretionary policing authority. It is to say, however, that courts will prove reticent to superintend closely the exercise of arrest authority by police on a day-to-day basis because they mistrust their ability to ascertain the actual motives that led to any particular arrest for breach of peace, unlawful assembly, or impeding traffic.[72]

What is more, many arrests, as noted earlier, will never find their way into the judicial system at all – because they are dropped rather than prosecuted. The ability of judges to consider arrests independent of criminal proceedings to assess the guilt or innocence of the accused is even more attenuated. Beyond the absence of an obvious procedural mechanism for getting such disputes into court in the first place, most judges are likely to be broadly deferential to plausible exercises of police authority in circumstances where a non-trivial risk of public disorder exists.

As the next principal section explains, the precedents of the Warren and Burger Courts did important work to disallow the use of criminal law to banish public forms of dissent. But the decisions protecting civil rights and anti-Vietnam War protests invariably involved the invalidation of laws that targeted speech as such for criminal proscription. Thus, these decisions have more in common with Judge Perry's rejection of the keep-walking rule than with the larger, and harder, question of how to secure First Amendment accountability for the exercise of discretionary police arrest authority. It is far easier to assess the constitutional validity of a rule, in the abstract, than to assess the motives that animated the application of a constitutionally-permissible law or policy in a particular instance.

9.2 THE WARREN AND BURGER COURTS' EFFORTS TO USE THE FIRST AMENDMENT TO PROHIBIT THE ABUSE OF TRESPASS, BREACH OF PEACE/DISORDERLY CONDUCT, AND UNLAWFUL ASSEMBLY LAWS TO SILENCE UNPOPULAR PROTESTERS

The Warren and Burger Courts issued landmark opinions that invalidated the most egregious disorderly conduct statutes – those that directly targeted speech that was controversial. As Professor Abu El-Haj observes, "[i]n the 1960s, the Supreme Court repeatedly held that it is unconstitutional for government officials to use crimes such as disorderly conduct, breach of the peace, or obstructing public passage to suppress constitutionally protected assemblies."[73] However, the charges in cases like *Edwards v. South Carolina*[74] and *Hess v. Indiana*[75] were largely, if not completely, based on speech – rather than on risks associated with violent acts and public disorder. This made invalidating the disorderly conduct charges considerably easier because the underlying laws were constitutionally suspect and the reviewing courts did not have to review and second guess the application of the use of discretionary police authority.

Edwards provides a logical starting point for considering the Warren Court's efforts to protect public expressions of dissent. The decision also provides a clear example of the Warren Court's aggressive judicial response to police using speech-based disorderly conduct charges to suppress dissent.

The facts at issue in *Edwards* are straightforward. On March 2, 1961, high school and college students met as a group in Columbia, South Carolina, and marched to the South Carolina state capitol building to protest the state's racially discriminatory laws.[76] When the marchers arrived at the state house grounds, they were met by a large group of armed police – who did not initially interfere with the march or rally; at no time did public disorder break out, despite a large crowd of 200–300 onlookers.[77] The police eventually ordered the protesters to disperse within fifteen minutes – or face arrest for failing to do so.[78] The protesters disregarded this warning and, after fifteen minutes had expired, the police arrested and jailed them for "breach of the peace."[79] The students were tried and convicted; on direct appeal, the South Carolina supreme court affirmed their convictions.

The US Supreme Court reversed the students' criminal convictions, holding them to be inconsistent with the First Amendment. Writing for the 8–1 majority, Justice Potter Stewart explained that criminal convictions for breach of peace based on *conduct* would not implicate First Amendment values so directly: "If, for example, the petitioners had been convicted upon evidence that they had violated a law regulating traffic, or had disobeyed a law reasonably limiting the periods during which the State House grounds were open to the public, this would be a different case."[80] On the facts at bar, however, the defendants were convicted based entirely on evidence "show[ing] no more than that the opinions which they were peaceably expressing were sufficiently opposed to the views of the majority of the community to attract a crowd and necessitate police protection."[81]

The First Amendment prohibits criminalizing "the peaceful expression of unpopular views."[82] The South Carolina state supreme court had interpreted the state's breach of peace statute to cover interruptions to the "tranquility" of the community and held that violence need not actually occur for an offense to exist. Obviously, highly unpopular views can agitate members of the community and disturb its "tranquility." If breach of peace charges could be used to prevent speech that arouses anger or umbrage, then the public expression of unpopular viewpoints could be banished from the public streets and sidewalks – indeed, public expressions of dissent could be criminalized.[83]

Edwards presents a very easy First Amendment case because the South Carolina law, as authoritatively interpreted by the state supreme court, criminalized pure speech without any requirement of otherwise unlawful conduct. Other cases from the Warren Court era also invalidated state laws that made the gravamen of a crime expression itself. *Cox v. Louisiana*[84] provides a good example.

Once again, state and local police arrested peaceful civil rights protesters, this time in Baton Rouge, Louisiana. The local police made arrests under a generic "breach of the peace" state statute, which the Louisiana state courts interpreted to apply to entirely peaceful, non-violent public protest that met with public anger or hostility, thus allowing "persons to be punished merely for peacefully expressing unpopular views."[85] Because "maintenance of the opportunity for free political discussion is a basic tenet of our constitutional democracy,"[86] Louisiana's law, as interpreted and applied, was fatally overbroad in its scope.[87] Louisiana was not free to criminalize a large assembly of otherwise peaceful civil rights protesters using a traditional public forum to attempt to rally public support to their cause – the desegregation of places of public accommodation and the enjoyment of full and equal civil and political rights by all citizens without regard to race.

Again, however, the scope of the Supreme Court's holding was plainly limited to convictions that rest solely on non-violent, peaceful mass assembly in an otherwise lawful location. Like *Edwards*, *Cox* holds a breach of peace statute overbroad to the extent that it would criminalize peaceful mass public protests because the message angers or upsets others within the community. It does not preclude the use of breach of peace charges in response to actual violence – nor does it convey any general First Amendment-based exemption from other laws designed to prevent the disruption of vehicular or pedestrian traffic, trespass, or assembly in the absence of a required permit. In this sense, then, decisions like *Edwards* and *Cox* did not convey an absolute form of protection on public protests – they simply prohibited police from arresting protesters because they were propagating an unpopular message.[88]

The Burger Court extended these decisions and applied them vigorously to protect the use of vulgar or offensive language in public – and even in targeted ways to law enforcement officers. Decisions like *Cohen v. California*,[89] *Hess v. Indiana*,[90] and *Gooding v. Wilson*[91] all protect the right of a speaker to use offensive or opprobrious language in public; collectively they have the effect of making it difficult, and probably impossible, to impose mandatory civility norms on persons speaking in public places. As with *Edwards* and *Cox*, the Supreme Court invalidated the use of "breach of peace" laws to the extent that state and local governments sought to use such laws to criminalize pure speech.

Without doubt, *Cohen v. California* is the most storied of these decisions, and it is arguably one of the most sweeping defenses of freedom of speech that the Justices have offered.[92] Although the facts of the case are trivial – picayune, in fact – the larger legal principles are quite epic in their scope.[93]

On April 26, 1968, Paul Cohen wore a jacket emblazoned with the phrase "Fuck the Draft" in the Los Angeles County Courthouse; he was arrested and convicted of disturbing the peace based on his sartorial choices.[94] The California statute was written in very broad terms. In relevant part, it made it a criminal offense to "maliciously and willfully disburb[] the peace or quiet of any neighborhood or person," through either "offensive conduct" or the "use [of] any vulgar, profane, or indecent language within the presence or hearing of women or children."[95] The charges against Cohen alleged that wearing his jacket constituted offensive conduct under section 415 of the California Penal Code. The Supreme Court, by a 5–4 vote, invalidated Cohen's conviction because it "rest[ed] squarely upon his exercise of the 'freedom of speech' protected from arbitrary governmental interference by the Constitution."[96]

Justice John Marshall Harlan concluded that "absent a more particularized and compelling reason for its actions, the State may not, consistent with the First and Fourteenth Amendments, make the simple public display here involved of this single four-letter expletive a criminal offense."[97] He explained that the Supreme Court could not "sanction the view that Constitution, while solicitous of the cognitive content of individual speech, has little or no regard for that emotive function which, practically speaking, may often be the more important element of the overall message sought to be communicated."[98] Were the rule otherwise, "governments might soon seize upon the censorship of words as a convenient guise for banning the expression of unpopular views."[99]

To be clear, nothing in the *Cohen* Court's analysis suggests that use of a more targeted and particularized charge would meet the same fate. For example, had Cohen worn the jacket into a courtroom and refused to remove it on the request of the presiding judge, I harbor little doubt that the First Amendment would have prevented a contempt of court citation. The decision deploys the First Amendment to prohibit the imposition, under the criminal law, of mandatory civility norms at all places and times; it says nothing about the use of more narrowly targeted measures designed to address more concrete and particularized government interests.

The other Burger Court cases invalidating unlawful assembly and breach of the peace convictions are largely the same – they all involve attempts by state or local governments to use criminal law to punish speech directly. For example, *Hess v. Indiana*[100] involved a conviction for disorderly conduct. After law enforcement officers ordered a large crowd of peaceful anti-war demonstrators to disperse, Gregory Hess told a sheriff's deputy that "We'll take the fucking street again" or "We'll take the fucking street later."[101] This was the predicate for Hess's arrest and conviction for disorderly conduct.[102]

The Indiana statute itself, as applied to violent actions, is unquestionably constitutional. The question presented for the Supreme Court was whether talking back to a law enforcement officer, who was trying to police a large, somewhat unruly Vietnam War protest in Bloomington, Indiana, was constitutionally protected speech, rather than a criminal offense. The Supreme Court concluded that Hess's statement enjoyed constitutional protection under the First Amendment. Accordingly, because "Indiana's disorderly conduct statute was applied in this case to punish only spoken words"[103] – not unlawful actions – the conviction violated the First Amendment.

The Supreme Court had adopted this general approach a year earlier, in *Gooding v. Wilson*,[104] and reaffirmed this approach a year later, in *Lewis v. City of New Orleans*.[105] *Lewis* involved a New Orleans, Louisiana, municipal ordinance that made it unlawful "wantonly to curse or revile or to use obscene or opprobrious language toward or with reference to any member of the city police while in the actual performance of his duty."[106] *Lewis* merits considered attention because it squarely recognizes the danger inherent in vesting police with broad discretion to treat peaceful speech activity as crime.

The appellant, Ms. Mallie Lewis, perturbed over the arrest and detention of her son, Joseph, followed the arresting officer's patrol car. The patrol car stopped and the arresting office confronted Ms. Lewis. Lewis got out of her car and yelled "you Goddamn mother fucking police" at the arresting officer and also threatened to file a formal complaint against the arresting officer with the city police department.[107] The officer then arrested Ms. Lewis for directing lewd and opprobrious language toward him. She was subsequently tried and convicted of the charge; the Louisiana state supreme court affirmed her conviction. The US Supreme Court granted review and initially remanded the case to the Louisiana courts – which affirmed the conviction on remand. The US Supreme Court again granted review and reversed the conviction on First Amendment grounds.

Because the New Orleans law targeted only speech, and not conduct that impeded lawful police activity, the Supreme Court invalidated it. Justice William J. Brennan, Jr. explained that the ordinance "punishe[d] only spoken words" and found it to be "constitutionally overbroad."[108] Section 49–7 was "facially invalid" when measured against the requirements of the First Amendment.[109] In sum, Ms. Lewis's rude, profane comments to the police officer were fully protected under the First Amendment and could not serve as the basis for criminal charges.

Justice Lewis F. Powell, Jr. concurred in the result and made observations that should, at least in theory, apply with equal force to conduct-based charges used to impede or prevent public protest. Justice Powell explained that "[t]his ordinance . . . confers on police a virtually unrestrained power to arrest and charge a person with a violation."[110] Moreover, because arrests under section 49–7 "are made in 'one-on-one' situations where the only witnesses are the arresting officer and the person charged," the law permits a conviction whenever a court "accept[s] the testimony of the officer that obscene or opprobrious language had been used toward [the arresting officer] while in performance of his duties."[111] Laws of this sort are particularly pernicious because they tend to be invoked "only where there is no other valid basis for arresting an objectionable or suspicious person."[112] In consequence, "[t]he opportunity for abuse, especially where a statute has received a virtually open-ended interpretation, is self-evident."[113]

At one level of analysis, *Lewis* simply constitutes one more in the line of decisions beginning with *Cohen* that invalidated criminal laws that sought to impose liability based on the use of blue language or personal insults. At another level of analysis, however, *Lewis* is a different kind of case because the Supreme Court seemed to be critically concerned with limiting the potential abuse of discretionary police authority, where it was entirely foreseeable that this discretion would be used selectively to silence speech. From *Cohen* through *Lewis*, a majority of the Supreme Court rejected repeated efforts by state supreme courts to use breach of peace or disorderly conduct enactments to censor speech based on its content and viewpoint. However, because the gravamen of the criminal charges was pure speech, it was relatively easy for the Supreme Court to overturn these convictions and invalidate these laws (as least as applied on the facts presented).

It is obviously much harder to sort out valid and pretextual applications of laws against trespass, impeding vehicular or pedestrian traffic, breach of peace, disorderly conduct, and unlawful assembly. All of these laws rely in large part on specific types of intent and conduct – and not on speech alone. In any given instance, an arrest relates to a law enforcement officer's subjective evaluation of the facts on the ground – and it is simply impossible for a reviewing court to place itself in the police officer's shoes – even if the charges are not dropped, effectively precluding any opportunity for judicial evaluation of whether a particular arrest was pretextual.

Unlike in other areas considered in this book, the Roberts and Rehnquist Courts have not attempted to limit or overrule the Warren and Burger Court decisions that disallowed the use of breach of the peace and disorderly conduct for purely speech-based offenses. In fact, the Roberts and Rehnquist Courts have generally disallowed efforts to create purely speech-based liability – whether for intentionally false speech,[114] highly offensive protests designed to cause maximal emotional injury,[115] vicious parodies designed to humiliate and embarrass their subject,[116] and efforts to criminalize street protest as a form of harassment or assault.[117]

Accordingly, I do not claim that checking arbitrary uses of police authority to squelch public protest represents an area where speech rights have declined over time. The relevant Warren and Burger Court precedents enjoy the full support of the contemporary Supreme Court.[118] However, police and prosecutors in the twenty-first century are more clever than their predecessors were in the late twentieth century. They do not seek to punish speech directly, but target conduct that often correlates with collective, public speech activity as a basis for arrest and criminal prosecution.

Just as the Warren and Burger Courts deployed the First Amendment to protect unpopular speakers from being silenced by local governments based on bogus breach of peace and disorderly conduct charges, the contemporary Supreme Court needs to consider more carefully the creative use of minor crimes to suppress the public expression of dissent. The difficulty, however, is that in any given case, the application of an otherwise-constitutional statute or ordinance as a basis for an arrest could be based on general law enforcement policies wholly unrelated to efforts to suppress dissenting voices – or a targeted form of harassment that likely reflects antipathy toward the would-be speakers, their message, or both. As the next section explains, securing First Amendment accountability for discretionary use of police authority to enforce minor crimes commonly associated with public protest presents a very challenging problem – a problem, in fact, that does not admit of an easy or simple solution.

9.3 THE DIFFICULTIES ASSOCIATED WITH ESTABLISHING MEANINGFUL JUDICIAL REVIEW OF DISCRETIONARY POLICE AND PROSECUTOR POWERS TO CHARGE PROTESTERS WITH CONDUCT-BASED CRIMES

It is relatively easy to describe the problem of the police making pretextual use of discretionary law enforcement authority to burden or prevent the exercise of expressive freedoms; offering plausible solutions is considerably more difficult. Professor Wells suggests that "our approach to judicial review [] must explicitly account for such things as surveillance, pretextual arrests, arrests of journalists, and other tactics that interfere with protesters' expression."[119] She cautions that tinkering "with the level of review associated with the Court's current standards will solve only part of the problem."[120] Both points are entirely true and well taken. Yet, pointing out the limitations of judicial review in contexts where such review is either weak or non-existent does not constitute an effective solution to these problems. I agree entirely with Wells that our current approach to aggressive policing is not working to effectively protect core First Amendment values. But, this begs the question of what precisely is to be done.

No easy answer presents itself because federal courts, as in the Ferguson litigation, are going to be extraordinarily reticent to limit police discretion to apply facially constitutional laws that protect against violence, destruction of public and private property, and, quite literally chaos in the streets. As noted earlier, US District Judge Catherine D. Perry's opinion and injunctive order in the Ferguson, Missouri protest litigation were careful to emphasize that the injunction against the use of the five-second keep-moving rule did not affect the authority of the police to enforce laws against trespass, unlawful assembly, or disorderly conduct.[121] As she stated the point, "[t]he police must be able to perform their jobs, and nothing in this order restricts their ability to do that."[122]

Thus, even if we can readily agree that pretextual arrests for conduct that is ostensibly unrelated to expression present a real and pressing First Amendment problem, the ability of the federal courts to address these problems is highly uncertain. As Professor Abu El-Haj has observed, "[h]ow this should be accomplished doctrinally would need to be worked out."[123] A successful solution "will require some mechanism for forcing authorities to address violence only when the risk is substantial and immediate, rather than well in advance as we are prone to do."[124] She argues, persuasively, that "we need to move closer to a regime that focuses on real risks of violence rather than on disorder and illegality," including successful efforts to check "the strategic use of misdemeanor offenses to harass those exercising" their First Amendment rights.[125]

Generic admonitions to judges to do a better job of superintending the police are well-meaning. One can readily and happily endorse them. In an ideal world, federal and state court judges alike would exhibit greater skepticism toward arbitrary exercises of police discretion to burden or prevent public protest. We would "move closer to a regime that focuses on real risks of violence rather than on disorder and illegality."[126] But we know – based on the available evidence from across multiple jurisdictions – that judges are not keen to closely scrutinize arrests if doing so requires them to second-guess police officers. The 1960s decisions involving invalidation of disorderly conduct charges all involved laws that targeted speech itself, rather than conduct associated with public protest. In the post 9/11 world, judges are not apt to respond with alacrity to arguments that we must allow disruptive protests in the nation's urban centers.

It bears noting that the aggressive use of discretionary policing authority to impede or prevent mass public protest does not seem to reflect any obvious ideological trends. Deeply blue cities, such as New York, Boston, Denver, and Madison have all used aggressive policing tactics to silence dissent.[127] Cities like Boston invoke esoteric interests, such as "pristine lawns," as a basis for denying access to public spaces for mass protest activity – and courts accept these rationales as consistent with the First Amendment.[128] Evidently, trampling upon "pristine laws" can be equated with "disorderly conduct" consistent with the First Amendment. If state and federal court judges in states like Massachusetts, New York, and Colorado are unwilling to superintend the police more aggressively, it is most unlikely that judges in places like Jackson, Mississippi, and Provo, Utah will act boldly to check discretionary police authority to enforce facially valid state statutes and local ordinances.

In sum, legal academics have done a fine job of identifying and defining the problem and its scope – but have made considerably less progress in proposing concrete solutions capable of easy judicial adoption and enforcement. One commentator, in a student note, offers a constructive reform proposal, namely the suggestion that "courts should balance traditional factors such as whether or not the assembly is peaceable, whether the assembly is a minority or dissenting group, whether the group is assembled or manifesting on a traditionally public area, such as a park, or whether the state has a permit requirement, or if they are on private land," against whether the police response to the protest "was subjectively reasonable."[129] The author, Hiram Emmanuel Arnaud, posits that an open-ended balancing test would simply represent a return to an earlier approach used during the Warren Court era to weigh free speech and association claims against national security concerns.[130]

To be sure, Mr. Arnaud's balancing test proposal is not entirely implausible. And, the use of balancing tests can enhance the scope and vibrancy of First Amendment freedoms; the Warren Court adopted balancing tests to extend First Amendment protection to government employees and public school students, as well as in cases seeking access to public property for speech activity.[131] Nevertheless, I have grave doubts that, if adopted by the federal courts, a balancing test would do much good in this context. The problem relates to assessing whether police use of discretionary enforcement authority is "subjectively reasonable." In the context of public rioting and violent protests, which present a risk to life, property, and public safety, federal courts are going to proceed with a very light touch. Most federal judges will be highly inclined to give the police every reasonable benefit of the doubt. And, again, it is far from clear that the balancing test could be brought to bear as a response to an otherwise facially valid arrest for unlawful assembly, breach of the peace, or trespass – or, for that matter, impeding traffic, interfering with a police investigation, or resisting arrest. In short, the universe of potential criminal charges that could be used to disrupt or prevent public protest is wide and deep.

Professor Abu El-Haj decries the misuse of discretionary police authority to squelch public expressions of dissent and argues that "[c]ourts should ... demand that law enforcement scale back its enthusiasm for charging protesters with various minor breaches of public order or the catchall crime of disobeying a lawful order."[132] She posits that "[c]rimes of disorderly conduct and the like should be narrowly construed when applied to protected conduct."[133] Moreover, the crime of trespass should be construed narrowly to create breathing room for protest.[134] Finally, "front-line police officers should be trained to abide by black letter constructions for, as we have seen, police officers' arrest patterns can nullify the protections offered to those exercising their constitutional right to assemble peaceably."[135]

These are all quite sensible suggestions – but they reduce to admonishing the federal courts to superintend the exercise of police discretionary authority more aggressively. The problem, however, is that federal judges are naturally reticent to enjoin police tactics that are essential to maintaining public order. Simply put, looking to judges to check the abuse of police discretion to enforce laws against trespass, disorderly conduct, and unlawful assembly will probably not work. Judges defer to police decision-making because heat-of-the-moment decisions involving the public's welfare and safety involve split-second judgment calls and judges do not want to cause police to second-guess their own judgments in circumstances where life and property could be at serious risk. Just as courts have proven ineffectual at checking the unreasonable use of deadly force by the police, they are unlikely to serve as a reliable check against pretextual arrests used to prevent public protests.

Professor Inazu offers a targeted reform proposal with respect to the use of unlawful assembly charges to suppress collective public speech activity. He posits that "[a] more objectivist approach would look for some manifestation of social harm before intervening with an assembly."[136] The modern approach seeks "to find culpability prior to the manifestation of social harm,"[137] which has the effect of greatly expanding the potential scope of the crime of unlawful assembly.

Professor Inazu suggests that police should be required to establish with clearer evidence that the target offense that serves as a predicate for unlawful assembly "would be undertaken with force or violence."[138] He also proposes that only violent criminal conduct should serve as the predicate offense: "A better approach would eliminate liability under the inchoate offense of unlawful assembly but retain liability for the attempted or completed target offense."[139] Finally, he posits that creating "a civil remedy against law enforcement officials who disperse or arrest protesters without the requisite level of reasonable suspicion that all material elements of the offense have been met"[140] would help to constrain the pretextual use of unlawful assembly charges.

Professor Inazu argues that we need to "structur[e] our statutory language as carefully as possible and ask[] difficult questions about the justifications for criminalizing certain activity in the first place."[141] This is so because "inchoate offenses that implicate First Amendment interests – like unlawful assembly"[142] create unacceptable chilling effects on collective expressive activity. He is undoubtedly correct on both counts. Yet, his reform proposals will reign in police discretion only in some areas – and not at all in others.

Professor Inazu's thoughtful reform suggestions would help to tame the use of unlawful assembly charges to break up otherwise peaceful public protests.[143] But his reforms do not address the potential use of myriad other crimes that can be, and are, used to harass or prevent public protest, such as trespass, disorderly conduct, impeding vehicular or pedestrian traffic, disturbing the peace, disregarding a lawful police order, or even violations of noise restrictions.[144] I do not contest that Professor Inazu's proposed reforms would represent serious improvements over the status quo – precisely because they would not require courts to engage in subjective assessments of the good faith, or bad faith, of police officers trying to manage chaotic public protests. But, viewed more holistically, they represent a mere drop in the bucket; they will not prevent police officers from using pretextual charges to harass, intimidate, or chill would-be protesters.

Solving the problem of abuse of discretionary police authority to silence dissent necessarily involves the adoption and deployment of political, rather than legal, controls. Citizen review boards, for example, could be empowered to investigate and discipline police departments that have a pattern of using minor criminal offenses to prevent public protest.[145] Part of the difficulty relates to establishing patterns that demonstrate a de facto police department policy of using arrests for minor crimes as a means of banishing dissent. As Professor Stephen Rushin has explained, "[l]ocal police behavior is also notoriously difficult to judge because most agencies collect little data on officer behavior."[146]

Any individual person arrested for disorderly conduct, breach of peace, or unlawful assembly will find it difficult to establish that her arrest was pretextual; with longer-term patterns, however, involving arrests over time, it would be considerably easier to detect patterns of illegitimate police behavior. As Rushin argues, "[t]his is a testament to the importance of external accountability and accurate data collection in the legal regulation of law enforcement."[147] In other words, data showing patterns of police abuse are necessary to prove a claim of a systematic problem with local police department behavior, but local police departments have little, if any, incentive to gather and disseminate such data – an external authority not subject to local political pressures is requisite.[148]

Even if presented with strong, indeed compelling, evidence of patterns or practices of police misbehavior, I am skeptical that the federal courts will act to limit police authority to use facially constitutional laws in the context of mass protests in public spaces. For example, in *McCleskey*, the Supreme Court rejected strong evidence showing disturbing racial patterns in prosecutor death penalty charging behavior and in jury decisions to convict defendants of the death penalty.[149] The *McCleskey* majority reasoned that these patterns did not establish that any particular charging decision reflected impermissible racial bias – or that any particular jury verdict was motivated by unlawful racial bias.[150] The same reasoning would seem to apply to claims that a particular police department systematically uses minor crime arrests as a way of blocking public protest and that a particular arrest resulted from such a policy.

It would not be surprising if judges took a similarly skeptical approach to data showing that a local police department's arrests for certain kinds of minor crimes establishes that a constitutional violation exists. As with the death penalty, a pattern of results does not establish that any particular arrest was inappropriate or pretextual. On the other hand, however, non-judicial actors would be quite free to credit general patterns reflected in arrest data; they would be free to conclude that a systemic problem exists based on aggregate data without having to assess whether any particular arrest was bogus. In this respect, political controls, such as citizen review boards, could act in the face of convincing data that demonstrates the existence of police department policies that are inconsistent with the First Amendment.

Of course, the effective use of non-judicial, political controls would require that the general community exhibit concern about the use of policing authority to silence protest in public spaces. To the extent that protesters are disliked within the broader community, however, the abuse of police authority to silence them is unlikely to provoke much of a public outcry. Tragically, the same pattern manifests with police abuse of deadly force; to the extent that victims of police abuse of deadly force are disproportionately from poor, politically marginalized, minority communities, we cannot expect the local political process reliably to secure police accountability.

Because local democratic politics might not function reliably to secure police accountability for respecting expressive freedoms protected under the First Amendment,[151] external forms of political accountability are needed.[152] We should not expect local communities to punish their police force for acting to stop radically unpopular forms of mass protest.[153] We could, however, imagine that external, non-judicial controls vested in the hands of national (non-local) authorities might work.[154] Thus, just as the Department of Justice has been successful in using data collection and targeted interventions in communities like Los Angeles and Seattle, with long, troubling histories of abusive policing,[155] the Department of Justice could also provide meaningful oversight of the use of minor crimes to inhibit collective speech activity.

Social science data also teaches that the mere act of being observed can have a powerful constraining effect.[156] The most simple iteration involves Bentham's "panopticon," a circular prison in which the prisoners in their individual cells do not know at any given moment whether a guard is actively observing them.[157] Decision-makers with discretionary authority will use that authority more cautiously when they anticipate that their decisions will be subject to meaningful forms of review. Thus, the mere possibility of judicial review of agency action exerts a power constraining effect on agency behavior;[158] agency decision-makers are more cautious when their work product could be reviewed by an Article III court – regardless of whether it ever is judicially reviewed. Adoption of meaningful, national political controls on local police departments using minor crime offenses to silence public protest would force them to be more reticent to embrace such tactics.

Professor Wells warns that "[w]orldwide trends ... suggest that the locus of control regarding regulation of protesters has shifted from judges to law enforcement officials."[159] If her thesis is correct, non-judicial, political controls will be needed to improve accountability for respecting First Amendment rights. In short, we need to think beyond a judicial paradigm for securing First Amendment rights in the context of police discretion to enforce minor crimes.[160]

More effective non-judicial controls present the best way of addressing abusive policing tactics designed to burden or prevent peaceful public assemblies. Approaches used to address the abuse of deadly force by police departments, including mandatory data collection and reporting, would empower concerned and engaged local citizens to better oversee those who ostensibly exist "to protect and to serve." Moreover, problems of agency capture would be mitigated if federal, rather than state or local, authorities supervise the collection and analysis of the relevant data from local police departments.

9.4 CONCLUSION

The abuse of police discretion to arrest and charge would-be protesters with minor, non-violent offenses presents a clear and present danger to the vitality and vibrancy of expressive freedoms in the contemporary United States. And, unlike other areas where expressive freedoms seem to be at risk, the prospects for effective judicial interventions in this area appear to be bleak. This is so because judges are generally unwilling to second-guess the police or ascribe bad faith motives to otherwise constitutional law enforcement activity. Moreover, judges find it difficult to decide how far is too far; in general, most judges prefer legal standards that are objectively discernable because objective standards insulate judges from the appearance of unduly subjective decision-making.[161]

Distinguishing pretextual from bona fide arrests for trespass, disorderly conduct, and unlawful assembly is a task that requires subjective assessment of police motive. It is entirely foreseeable why judges would shrink from undertaking this task. Yet, the commonplace use of pretextual arrests for minor, non-violent crimes to stifle dissent constitutes a real and pressing problem. As Professor Abu El-Haj observes, "[s]uch arrests take protestors off the streets, rendering their formal constitutional rights meaningless."[162] The question then becomes: How can we render subjective police decisions to arrest would-be protesters transparent and subject to some form of meaningful First Amendment-based accountability?

An effective, comprehensive solution is needed. An approach that looks to non-judicial actors is more likely to succeed in this context because constraining police discretion, unlike invalidating laws that directly burden speech, is a task for which the judiciary is ill-suited.[163] We should instead seek the creation of non-judicial controls of discretionary police authority that, although facially constitutional, can be used – and is being used – to stifle public expressions of dissent. In sum, courts and judges can and should do a better job of securing our expressive freedoms. At the same time, however, we must be willing to look beyond judicial solutions to First Amendment problems when threats to the public exercise of speech, assembly, petition, and association rights require political controls in addition to judicial ones.

10

Conclusion

Enhancing Speech and Promoting Democracy: The Necessary Role of the State in Promoting Democratic Deliberation among Citizen-Speakers

If we genuinely believe that the First Amendment exists to facilitate the process of democratic self-government, then the federal courts need to consider more carefully and more reliably the government's duty to use public resources to support expressive activities related to democratic discourse. The Warren Court understood that equal citizenship required more than simply observing a rule of "one person, one vote" – although the Constitution certainly requires observation of this fundamental principle of political equality in designing electoral districts and conducting elections.[1] The Warren Court consistently worked to deploy the First Amendment as a tool to create and support opportunities for democratic engagement within the body politic; it did not simply embrace a *laissez faire* free market approach to allocating the practical ability to exercise expressive freedoms.

The Warren Court repeatedly used the First Amendment as a source of affirmative, or positive, obligations on the government to facilitate, rather than impede, the exercise of expressive freedoms by ordinary citizens. The Burger Court failed to advance this jurisprudential agenda – but refrained from squarely overruling the Warren Court's jurisprudential and doctrinal innovations. The Rehnquist and Roberts Courts, for the most part, have resiled from this project entirely.

In my view, the Warren Court clearly advocated the better approach and has the better of the normative argument about whether the First Amendment, properly interpreted and applied, has both positive and negative aspects. A serious and meaningful commitment to equal citizenship requires more than merely abstract, or theoretical, equality among speakers. An empty, formalistic equality of opportunity to speak will not ensure, to use Alexander Meiklejohn's wonderful turn of phrase, "that everything worth saying shall be said."[2] Moreover, as Justice William J. Brennan, Jr. posits in *Sullivan*, the process of democratic self-government requires "that debate on public issues [must] be uninhibited, robust, and wide-open."[3] A debate in which only the wealthy and privileged can be seen and heard will grossly disserve the project of democratic self-government.

The problem can be simply stated: Good ideas about governance are not exclusively the province of the wealthy and the connected. Yet, if meaningful access to the electorate requires great wealth, ideas that merit consideration by the electorate will simply not be heard – much less considered or adopted. In this regard, Meiklejohn argues that the voters must "face[] squarely and fearlessly everything that can be said in favor of [our governing] institutions, everything that can be said against them."[4] This free and open public debate is essential if "the citizens of the United States will be fit to govern themselves under their own institutions."[5]

From one vantage point, the First Amendment serves as a check against government schemes to capture or control the political marketplace of ideas. This negative-checking function constitutes an important part of the First Amendment's work to facilitate democratic deliberation (which, in turn, enables voters to secure government accountability through the electoral process). But to acknowledge this negative role for the First Amendment is not to exhaust all of the normative possibilities. The First Amendment also should protect and advance the process of democratic engagement that makes democratic accountability through regular elections possible. This function involves not merely negative, but also affirmative, duties on the part of the government.

Accordingly, the Supreme Court may well be correct to hold that the First Amendment prevents the government from seeking to equalize all speech and all speakers by leveling-down speakers with the financial wherewithal to disseminate their messages to a mass audience without the government's assistance or support. It is entirely plausible to posit that the dangers of government censorship that arise from such a program of government-mandated equality of result are simply too great to tolerate.[6] Even if this is so, however, the First Amendment, properly defined and applied, should also require that the government suffer inconvenience and shoulder financial burdens in order to empower ordinary citizens to engage in the process of democratic deliberation.[7] In short, a constitutional proscription against silencing some voices should not imply the lack of duty to ensure that other voices can be heard.

If one takes these principles into account, it becomes reasonably clear that the contemporary federal courts are both too lenient and too demanding in applying the First Amendment to safeguard the process of democratic deliberation. They are too lenient in permitting government to adopt policies that chill or prevent speech that requires some sort of government support. Yet, they are also too demanding in disallowing reasonable government efforts to ensure that democracy functions as a fair fight.[8]

A larger normative vision of the First Amendment explains this trend: The Warren and Burger Courts believed that government interventions in speech markets could enhance the marketplace of ideas, whereas the Rehnquist and Roberts Courts appear to be deeply skeptical about government regulation enhancing rather than debasing the political marketplace of ideas. In addition, and relatedly, the Warren Court, and to a lesser extent, the Burger Court, had faith in the ability of federal judges to apply First Amendment rules that featured significant play in the joints – open-ended balancing tests that would require trial judges to sift facts and weigh circumstances when deciding whether to recognize or reject a First Amendment claim.

Many, if not most, of the Warren Court opinions expanding the scope of First Amendment rights, including landmark decisions that ordered greater access to public property for protest, protected speech by government employees, secured academic freedom for faculty members and students, and safeguarded transborder speech activity, all feature rather open-ended balancing exercises that consider the need for a would-be speaker to enjoy the government's assistance against the government's legitimate managerial concerns. The decisions reflect faith in the ability of the lower federal and state courts to exercise structured discretion in ways that improve and enhance, rather than degrade, the political marketplace of ideas. This approach also has the effect of securing more speech – even if the pattern of winners and losers might entail some debatable outcomes in close cases presenting similar facts.

The Roberts and Rehnquist Courts have taken a radically different approach. Both have abjured open-ended balancing tests that vest great discretion with lower court judges in favor of very formal, categorical, bright-line rules that significantly cabin, if not eliminate, any room for the exercise of discretion to vindicate some First Amendment claims while rejecting other, similar claims. The contemporary Supreme Court consistently displays deep skepticism, if not outright hostility, toward legal tests that merely frame, rather than prefigure, how judges should decide a First Amendment claim.

This approach – favoring categorical rules over balancing tests – makes great sense if a judge believes that government interventions in speech markets generally do more harm than good. A judge who holds this point of view will work to develop hard, fast, categorical rules that, quite literally, wring out discretion from the process of adjudicating First Amendment claims.

So, it is not surprising that the Roberts and Rehnquist Courts have issued First Amendment precedents that reflect a deep-seated and abiding distrust of government, in general, and the federal courts, in particular, to improve on private market ordering of the political marketplace of ideas. In many important respects, the decisions of the Roberts and Rehnquist Courts reflect a strongly held belief that state ordering of speech markets, in any form or guise, is not only inefficient, but affirmatively harmful to the project of democratic self-government.

This larger jurisprudential posture – faith versus mistrust in the ability of federal judges to allocate speech rights wisely and fairly – explains much of the evolutionary change discussed in the preceding pages. When speech claims require judges to balance or ask "to what degree?," the Roberts and Rehnquist Courts tend to exit the field. By way of contrast, however, the Roberts and Rehnquist Courts have embraced with real brio First Amendment rules and doctrines that rely on binary, yes/no kinds of analyses. The categorical rules against content and viewpoint discrimination provide salient examples. This jurisprudential approach certainly limits judicial discretion, but it also denies the lower federal and state courts the needed flexibility to deploy the First Amendment dynamically and creatively to empower citizens who wish to engage in the process of democratic self-government – but require access to government resources (such as access to public property or government employment) in order to do so.

Over the course of the last nine chapters, this book has developed and advanced three discrete arguments, comprising an empirical claim, a doctrinal claim, and a normative claim. The empirical claim is that in areas where a would-be speaker needs the government's assistance in order to speak (in whatever form), the Roberts and Rehnquist Courts have been decidedly less free speech-friendly than their immediate predecessors, the Burger and Warren Courts. The doctrinal claim is that, in a variety of important areas, First Amendment rules could be strengthened to better facilitate the ability of would-be speakers to participate in the process of democratic deliberation. Finally, as a normative matter, the federal courts should interpret and apply the First Amendment in ways that require the government to facilitate, rather than impede, speech related to democratic self-government – at least when the government can do so without serious disruption or inconvenience to its operations. The balance of this concluding chapter will discuss and develop each of these ideas in turn.

10.1 THE EMPIRICAL CLAIM: SPEECH RIGHTS HAVE CLEARLY DECLINED IN SOME IMPORTANT AREAS OVER TIME

As the preceding chapters have demonstrated, expressive freedoms in many important areas have declined, rather than expanded, under the Roberts and Rehnquist Courts. Access to public property for speech activity provides the most obvious, and disheartening, example.[9] The public forum doctrine and time, place, and manner doctrine, as developed and applied over the past thirty years, have substantially narrowed the government's obligation to facilitate speech activity on public property. As noted before, iconic protests that helped to propel the civil rights movement forward, such as the Selma-to-Montgomery March, will no longer take place in the contemporary United States if the government declines access to public streets and highways. First Amendment law, theory, and practice have moved from an approach that presumed a generalized duty to facilitate collective speech, assembly, association, and petition in public places and spaces to an approach that places the burden on would-be speakers to prove a right of access to particular government property – and then to show that the government's restrictions on access to that property are irrational.

The emergence of dominant social media platforms and search engines, often controlled by monopoly service providers, presents another growing threat to the process of democratic deliberation.[10] The Warren Court, in its pioneering *Logan Valley* decision,[11] used the First Amendment to create easements to private property for expressive activity. Faced with the growing privatization of spaces and places essential to the process of civic engagement and discourse, the Warren Court held that the First Amendment required a limited right of public access to large-scale shopping centers and malls – places that had come to displace and replace the traditional town square.

Despite the growing threat that private ownership of some of the primary venues in which our democratic politics take place – with the concomitant power to censor speech and speakers that the private companies dislike, on a wholly non-transparent basis – it is virtually unthinkable that the Roberts Court would embrace the constitutional logic of *Logan Valley*. By way of contrast, the Warren Court would have been quite open to the idea that the First Amendment imposes limits on the power of Facebook, Twitter, YouTube, and Instagram to censor speech in their virtual forums – and also to imposing constitutional limits on the ability of dominant search engine providers, such as Google and Bing, to censor results to advance ideological or political objectives.

Unfortunately, other examples exist of receding protection for expressive freedoms. The speech rights of government employees, never particularly robust – even under the Warren Court – have diminished considerably.[12] Under *Garcetti*,[13] a government employee has no First Amendment claim with respect to work-related speech. In other words, government employees who happen to be professionals lose their ability to act as professionals by speaking if the government may both prescribe and proscribe work-related speech by its employees (including public school teachers and possibly including public college and university professors).

Faculty and students on the nation's campuses enjoy diminished claims on the First Amendment as well.[14] To be sure, the Supreme Court has never formally overruled the high watermark decisions of the Warren Court – *Tinker*[15] and *Keyishian*.[16] But, over time, the precedential force of these decisions has been whittled away.[17] They are now more aspirational statements than accurate descriptions of the government's de facto power to regulate the speech of faculty and students on campus. Moreover, regulatory creep has set in, and public school authorities seek not only to censor speech on campus, but to regulate faculty and student off-campus expression as well.

Transborder speech and association have emerged as a growing and important area of expressive freedom. Yet, the relevant precedents that address the ability of US citizens to exercise First Amendment rights abroad remain stuck in a time warp and relate back to the Warren and Burger Courts.[18] To the extent that the contemporary Supreme Court has addressed transborder speech at all, it has sustained content-based speech restrictions on the exercise of speech, assembly, and association rights outside the United States[19] and refused to consider the chilling effect of pervasive surveillance of conversations between US citizens and persons located abroad.[20]

Both professional and amateur journalists have made little headway in using the First Amendment to protect newsgathering activities.[21] At the same time, the federal government has moved aggressively against journalists in the context of leak and national security investigations. Journalists, and journalism, are quite literally under attack in the contemporary United States. Even so, however, the Supreme Court has not issued a major First Amendment decision on freedom of the press for over a decade – and arguably has failed to do so since the Burger Court era.

Under the guise of regulating the professions, state governments have rendered professionals who require government licenses to practice their discipline sock puppets – mere mouthpieces of the government.[22] The lower federal court response has been, at best, mixed, and the Supreme Court, after suggesting that a rationality test applies to such regulations, has been entirely absent from the field. Meanwhile, government enters the marketplace of ideas, using social media platforms, but fails to disclose its identity as a speaker – essentially seeking to pass off its views as those of a private citizen, rather than the state itself. Once again, the federal courts have done little to arrest this growing trend to use anonymous or pseudonymous government speech to propagandize the body politic.

In sum, the empirical claim – that in areas where a would-be speaker needs the government's assistance in order to speak, the Roberts and Rehnquist Courts have been less speech-friendly than their immediate predecessors – seems clearly established. In many important areas of First Amendment law and practice, expressive freedoms are less secure today than they were forty years ago. And, the trend line is not particularly promising for a course correction. Even if the Roberts Court has not returned to the baseline of decisions such as *Davis v. Commonwealth*[23] and *McAuliffe v. Mayor of New Bedford*,[24] contemporary First Amendment decisions are much more broadly deferential to government's claims of managerial necessity[25] than were the First Amendment decisions of the Warren and Burger Courts. The contemporary Supreme Court seldom, if ever, presses the government to facilitate, rather than impede, the exercise of expressive freedoms by ordinary citizens possessed of limited financial means.

10.2 THE DOCTRINAL CLAIM: THE FEDERAL COURTS CAN AND SHOULD DO BETTER TO ADVANCE EXPRESSIVE FREEDOMS IN THE CONTEMPORARY UNITED STATES

In a wide variety of areas, First Amendment rules could be significantly strengthened to better protect would-be speakers from government efforts to distort the marketplace of ideas. In addition, the federal courts should be wary of reflexively linking the ability to exercise First Amendment freedoms to the ownership of property. As noted, this is not to say that the federal courts should be sanguine about government efforts to silence disfavored speakers – a serious commitment to audience autonomy means that individual citizens, and not the government, should be empowered to choose for themselves what speech and speakers they wish to credit – and which speech and speakers they prefer to ignore.[26]

Unfortunately, this libertarian approach to the First Amendment appears to lead to a kind of indifference to the inability of many ordinary citizens to engage in the process of democratic deliberation. In too many areas of First Amendment jurisprudence, we see an accelerating loss of expressive freedoms in circumstances where the exercise of First Amendment rights requires access to public property or other kinds of government support. If a would-be speaker possesses the property necessary to speak, that speaker's First Amendment rights have never been more robust or secure. In a mass, participatory democracy premised on the equal citizenship, if not equal dignity, of all persons, we should be concerned about linking expressive freedom to the ownership of property.

If one compares and contrasts *City of Ladue v. Gilleo*,[27] which invalidated a city ordinance that prohibited a private land owner from displaying a political sign on her home's front lawn, with *Taxpayers for Vincent*,[28] which upheld, against a First Amendment challenge, a Los Angeles County ordinance that prohibited the use of utility polls for political speech, the centrality of property to the exercise of free speech rights comes into very clear focus. The reason for this, moreover, relates to the contemporary Supreme Court's antipathy toward adopting and enforcing balancing tests: Any requirement for government to use its resources to support private speakers will necessarily require a reviewing court to weigh the interests of the speaker against the government's legitimate managerial concerns.[29]

The rejection of balancing tests, of necessity, leads to outcomes that favor would-be speakers who possess the property (whether in the form of land, cash, or both) necessary to speak. The Roberts and Rehnquist Courts have most predictably and consistently applied the First Amendment to protect the ability to speak of those persons and institutions who can do so without any government assistance. By way of contrast, the Warren Court, and even the Burger Court, were less reticent to read affirmative obligations into the First Amendment; the government had a limited duty to facilitate speech when it had the ability to do so (but not the will).

Preventing government from engaging in content- and viewpoint-based discrimination constitutes an important First Amendment project – and one that prevents the government from distorting, perhaps even capturing, the marketplace of ideas. But only protecting the ability of those with the financial ability to speak when the government would prefer them to remain silent represents an incomplete and myopic vision of the role of expressive freedom in a participatory democracy. Again, the success of democratic self-government requires that engagement among and between citizens be both robust and inclusive. As Meiklejohn explains, "[w]hat is essential is not that everyone shall speak, but that everything worth saying shall be said."[30]

To be sure, selective government subsidies of speech activity can create significant distortionary effects on the marketplace of ideas.[31] And this is a problem that must be taken into account; after all, a system in which government does not provide any speech subsidies would ensure that all would-be speakers are treated equally (even if equally badly). As Professor Kathleen Sullivan observes, "[i]f government could freely use benefits to shift viewpoints in a direction favorable to the existing regime, democratic self-government would be undermined."[32] She persuasively posits that selective distribution of government subsidies can interfere with a "distributive concern whenever the content of a liberty includes some equality principle or entitlement to government neutrality" and that the "[t]argeting of benefits can destroy such equality and neutrality as readily as can imposition of harms."[33]

But to conclude from this quite legitimate concern about the potential distortionary effects of government speech subsidies that the obvious and only answer is for the federal courts not to require *any* government speech subsidies would be to draw the wrong conclusion. This is so because in the context of the process of democratic self-government, the absence of speech subsidies itself will inevitably produce market distortions that do not rest comfortably with the formal equality that we proclaim for all voters.[34] Speech subsidies can have distortionary effects – but so too can wholly unregulated markets in which the power to speak is a function of one's wealth.[35] As Professor Owen Fiss has argued, "[j]ust as it is no longer possible to assume that the private sector is all freedom, we can no longer assume that the state is all censorship."[36] Accordingly, "[t]he state should be allowed to intervene, and sometimes even required to do so . . . to correct for the market."[37]

In doctrinal terms, the most obvious solution would be for the federal courts to more readily recognize a positive aspect of the First Amendment; the notion that the government has an affirmative duty to facilitate speech related to the process of democratic self-government. If such a doctrinal innovation is too powerful a medicine in a constitutional culture that generally abjures the recognition of positive constitutional rights,[38] the second-best solution would be to deploy the unconstitutional conditions doctrine more aggressively to disallow government efforts to leverage control over its largesse either to squelch or to commandeer speech by private citizens.[39]

Finally, if developing and deploying an affirmative vision of the First Amendment constitutes a bridge too far, less sweeping doctrinal innovations – mere improvements to the existing doctrinal rules – could be implemented instead. More modest reforms of this stripe would not run up against the deeply-seated idea of the First Amendment as a source of negative, rather than positive, rights.

What's more, even relatively modest doctrinal reforms could create more breathing room for speech. To provide an illustrative example, the federal courts could use a functional, rather than historical, approach to determining whether government property constitutes a public forum.[40] So too, they could enforce the rules limiting time, place, and manner restrictions more vigorously – particularly when applying the ample alternative channels of communication requirement.[41]

Whistleblowing speech by government employees could be afforded specific and targeted First Amendment protection. The Press Clause could be deployed to protect the newsgathering activity so essential to accurate reporting. The Supreme Court could take seriously its claim that the identity of a speaker is irrelevant to the value of the speech to voters – and vigorously protect transborder speech and speakers.

The federal courts could make greater efforts to prevent government schemes to distort the political marketplace of ideas by using involuntary speech proxies (sock puppets) and hiding its identity as a speaker via anonymous and pseudonymous speech. Efforts to establish and enforce social norms that facilitate, rather than impede, collective speech activity in public also are needed; we cannot look exclusively to the federal courts to protect expressive freedoms in the United States. The police and public prosecutors must use discretionary authority in ways that enable, rather than prevent, collective public protest activity.[42]

Finally, it bears noting that requiring the government to facilitate, rather than impede, speech for would-be speakers of average means would not imply, much less require, leveling down the speech rights of others. To be sure, one could posit a theory of freedom of speech in which the government has the ability not only to amplify some voices, but to muffle others.[43] One can imagine a free speech floor without pairing it up with a free speech ceiling. Accordingly, it would be entirely possible for the federal courts to require the government to facilitate private speech related to the project of democratic self-government without permitting it to censor or impede other voices (voices who do not require government assistance in order to be heard).

10.3 THE NORMATIVE CLAIM: FEAR OF JUDICIAL DISCRETION IN FIRST AMENDMENT CASES AND THE SYSTEMATIC FAILURE TO ADVANCE CRITICALLY IMPORTANT FIRST AMENDMENT VALUES

The Roberts and Rehnquist Courts have moved to enhance speech rights in some areas, while failing to expand First Amendment rights in others. The federal courts have readily invalidated government regulations seeking to equalize the marketplace of ideas by leveling some would-be speakers down in order to make it possible for other speakers to be heard in the marketplace of ideas.[44] Several normative theories could potentially explain this doctrinal trend. One could simply argue that the Supreme Court has adopted a Lochnerian vision of the First Amendment; if you own property, you may use it to speak; if you require government assistance to speak, the government has discretion to lend its support or withhold it.[45]

It would be easy to ascribe a nakedly ideological motive to the contemporary Supreme Court and to suggest that its decisions reflect a commitment to the theoretical equality of opportunity, rather than a more meaningful, substantive, form of equality. One could go even further and argue that the Roberts Court's approach to the First Amendment reflects systematic bias in favor of the government, powerful private institutions, and connected individuals – a system of "managed speech" that "plac[es] a high premium on social and political stability," "encourages a public discussion where a limited number of speakers exchange a limited range of ideas," and that relies on "powerful government and private managers to keep public discussion within responsible boundaries."[46] Such a thesis would be cynical, but the thesis is an entirely plausible one.

In my view, an explanation that relies on class or institutional bias oversimplifies the Supreme Court's probable motive for abandoning the Warren Court's open-ended balancing tests (tests that tended to favor the little guy) in favor of bright-line, categorical rules (tests that tend, more often than not, to empower those who have the resources necessary to speak). A more plausible and nuanced explanation is that the Roberts and Rehnquist Courts' First Amendment decisions reflect a deep-seated and profound fear of judges exercising discretion in free speech cases in a direct and transparent fashion. The ghost of Hugo L. Black still haunts the pages of *U.S. Reports*.

In theorizing and applying the First Amendment, it is quite possible to posit that judicial discretion is problematic because it involves the government selecting free speech winners and free speech losers; such discretion creates a non-trivial risk of the appearance of content and viewpoint discrimination in deciding such cases. Moreover, and at a more general level of analysis, the Roberts and Rehnquist Courts – unlike the Warren Court – took the position, with regard to the First Amendment, that government interventions in the political marketplace of ideas invariably have a distortionary effect.[47]

The Warren and Burger Courts, by way of contrast, were much more open to the idea that government interventions in speech markets could significantly enhance, rather than degrade, the marketplace of ideas. They also seemed to be far more comfortable with lower court judges applying First Amendment rules that required rather transparent exercises of discretion. For example, allocating access to government property on an ad hoc basis clearly involves a great deal of subjective judicial decision-making.[48] So too, deciding how much protection reporters should enjoy when engaging in newsgathering activities involves a significant scope for judicial discretion.[49]

If one takes the view that government discretion – whether held in executive, legislative, or judicial hands – presents a risk to free speech and First Amendment values more generally, it would be quite logical to eschew adopting rules and doctrines that increase, rather than cabin, the role of subjective judicial assessments regarding the relative value or importance of speech. From an anti-discretion vantage point, clear First Amendment rules should be preferred – even if they can lead to arbitrary results.

In many respects, the First Amendment jurisprudence of the Roberts and Rehnquist Courts reflects an effort to severely limit, if not remove entirely, discretion from the federal courts' First Amendment toolkit. By way of contrast, the Warren Court, and to a lesser degree the Burger Court, issued First Amendment decisions that left considerable play in the joints. *Tinker* provides a relevant example,[50] as do *Brown*[51] and *Pickering*.[52] In many important respects, the reduction in the scope and vibrancy of expressive freedom over time has been collateral damage in the Supreme Court's ongoing effort to renormalize First Amendment law from a jurisprudence that relies on general principles to frame judicial consideration of constitutional claims to a more formal system of rigid rules that dictate clear outcomes.[53]

The government should have to shoulder a duty to facilitate speech related to democratic self-government when it can do so without serious disruption or inconvenience to its operations. But operationalizing this approach will require the federal courts to exercise considerable discretion – the kind of discretion that the Roberts and Rehnquist Courts seem to view as a vice, rather than a virtue, in First Amendment jurisprudence. Yet, because the legitimacy of elections as a means of securing government accountability depends critically on everything that needs saying being said,[54] courts simply must have the discretion to use the First Amendment flexibly to facilitate protest and the public expression of dissent.

Finally, and at the risk of undue repetition, it once again bears noting that requiring the government to facilitate speech for would-be speakers of average means would not imply or require leveling down the speech rights of others. The legitimacy of elections as a means of securing government accountability requires that everything that needs saying actually be said. If one takes seriously both the letter and spirit of *Baker* and *Reynolds*, then the ability to participate in the deliberative process that informs voting should matter as much, if not more, than the act of casting a ballot on election day.

10.4 CONCLUSION

Alexander Meiklejohn famously argued for state subsidies to facilitate participation on a widespread basis in the process of democratic self-government.[55] The Warren and Burger Courts, in some important contexts, took this lesson to heart and required the government to facilitate speech when it had the ability to do so without undue disruption to its own operations. The Roberts and Rehnquist Courts, by way of contrast, have generally given the government very broad discretion to provide or withhold support for private speech as it thinks best. If government may use its largesse to coerce speech or silence from those who require a boon, the marketplace of ideas will surely be the poorer for it.

The ability to speak freely and openly – to exercise agency as a citizen – should not be the exclusive prerogative of those who do not work for the government, attend a public school, college, or university, need a professional license in order to make a living, or require access to government property in order to speak. Nor should the accident of having to cross the nation's international borders present an opportunity to extort speech or silence from citizens. The ability to speak directly, truthfully, and authentically should be the birthright of each and every US citizen; government efforts to deny or abridge that birthright should be met with firm and steadfast judicial resistance.

Of course, things in the contemporary United States could be much worse. It also bears noting that the freedom of speech is more broadly protected in the contemporary United States than anywhere else in the world. Even so, however, the federal courts can and should do a better job of ensuring that all citizens have a chance to play a meaningful role in the project of self-government by making their voices heard in our collective efforts to hold government accountable through the electoral process.

The government, at the federal, state, and local level, should operate under a general obligation to facilitate, rather than impede, speech associated with the process of democratic deliberation. Taking this approach, however, will require the creation and enforcement of doctrinal tests that require open-ended balancing of competing interests – the interest of a private citizen in speaking must be weighed against the government's claim that legitimate managerial imperatives should excuse it from lending the would-be speaker its assistance. Discretion can be abused and the exercise of discretion in First Amendment cases will subject federal judges to criticism. But in many areas of contemporary constitutional law, notably including procedural due process claims,[56] federal courts seem to be capable of applying fairly open-ended balancing tests without risking the public's confidence in the legitimacy of the Article III courts. If federal judges can balance private interests and the government's interests in the context of procedural due process cases, no good reason exists for why they cannot balance interests in free speech cases too.[57]

In sum, if we are truly committed to the equality of all citizens, we need to be vitally concerned about the ability of all citizens, rich and poor alike, to participate meaningfully in the process of democratic deliberation that informs the casting of ballots on election day. Contemporary First Amendment law, theory, and practice do not adequately take into account this central purpose of the First Amendment. We can do better. The First Amendment should safeguard the essential processes of democracy not only from ham-fisted and obvious government efforts to distort the political marketplace of ideas, but also from more subtle efforts to use levers of government influence over the lives of ordinary Americans to coerce speech and silence from individual citizens.

Notes

1 TWO STEPS FORWARD, ONE STEP BACK: ON THE DECLINE OF EXPRESSIVE FREEDOMS UNDER THE ROBERTS AND REHNQUIST COURTS

1 LEWIS CARROLL, ALICE'S ADVENTURES IN WONDERLAND 93–94 (1869).
2 *See, e.g.*, Hague v. CIO, 307 U.S. 496, 515–16 (1939).
3 *Id.* at 516 (noting that the public's right to use public property for speech activity "must not, in the guise of regulation, be abridged or denied"); *see* Edwards v. South Carolina, 372 U.S. 229, 230–32, 235–37 (1963) (holding that civil rights protesters had a right to assemble and protest on the South Carolina state capitol grounds and that the government could not order them to disperse, on pain of arrest, because their protest offended some white onlookers).
4 *See, e.g.*, Tinker v. Des Moines Indep. Cmty Sch. Dist., 393 U.S. 503, 513–14 (1969) (holding that local school authorities had to tolerate expressive conduct opposing the Vietnam War unless they could establish a risk of "substantial disruption of or material interference with school activities"); Pickering v. Board of Educ., 391 U.S. 563, 568–69 (1968) (requiring a government employer to refrain from retaliating against an employee who spoke out about a matter of public concern absent a substantial risk of disruption associated with the employee's continued presence in the workplace and explaining that "[t]he problem in any case is to arrive at a balance between the interests of the teacher, as a citizen, in commenting upon matters of public concern and the interest of the State, as an employer, in promoting the efficiency of the public services it performs through its employees").
5 *See* Pleasant Grove City v. Summum, 555 U.S. 460, 464–68 (2009); *see also* Oberwetter v. Hilliard, 639 F.3d 545, 552–54 (D.C. Cir. 2011) (holding that "the government is free to establish venues for the exclusive expression of its own viewpoint").
6 *See* Walker v. Texas Division, Sons of Confederate Veterans, 135 S. Ct. 2239, 2246–52 (2015); *see also* Morse v. Frederick, 551 U.S. 393 (2007); Rust v. Sullivan, 500 U.S. 173 (1991).
7 *See* Citizens United v. Federal Elec. Comm'n, 558 U.S. 310, 339–42 (2010).
8 *See* Kathleen Sullivan, Comment, *Two Concepts of Freedom of Speech*, 124 HARV. L. REV. 143, 143–46, 155–63 (2010) (discussing the Roberts Court's libertarian gloss

on the Free Speech Clause as a proscription against government efforts to control the marketplace of ideas by regulating either speakers or their messages).

9 *See id.* at 149–50 (arguing that the Roberts Court has rejected an egalitarian theory of the freedom of speech and, accordingly, has declined to follow earlier "free-speech-as-equality cases" in which government "uses the First Amendment to redistribute speaking power" by "preventing government from conditioning grants of resources on speakers' curtailment of their speech" or "[b]y in effect requiring public subsidies for speech").

10 *Id.* at 176.

11 *See* GREGORY P. MAGARIAN, MANAGED SPEECH: THE ROBERTS COURT'S FIRST AMENDMENT 91–118, 227–39, 252–53 (2017) (describing, discussing, and critiquing the Roberts Court's embrace of a system of "managed speech" that tends to enhance the speech rights of the government itself and those who currently hold economic and political power but tends to marginalize and silence those who lack deep financial resources).

12 ROBERT C. POST, CONSTITUTIONAL DOMAINS: DEMOCRACY, COMMUNITY, MANAGEMENT 4–10, 13–16, 237–47, 261–62 (1995) (discussing the problem of respecting the government's need to use its resources for their intended purposes without permitting the government to leverage these resources, under the guise of managerial necessities, so as to disrupt or distort the political marketplace of ideas and the process of democratic deliberation that informs it).

13 *See* Sullivan, *supra* note 8, at 149–50, 155–63, 176.

14 R. v. Oakes, [1986] 1 S.C.R. 103, 112 (Can.) (setting forth the general test for proportionality analysis under Section 1 of the Canadian Charter of Rights and Freedoms); *see* AHARON BARAK, PROPORTIONALITY: CONSTITUTIONAL RIGHTS AND THEIR LIMITATIONS (Doron Kalir trans., 2012) (arguing in favor of proportionality analysis as a means of enhancing the protection of fundamental human rights); Vicki C. Jackson, *Constitutional Law in an Age of Proportionality*, 124 YALE L.J. 3094 (2015) (discussing and explaining the transnational salience of proportionality analysis in most systems of entrenched human rights protected through judicial review).

15 *See, e.g.*, Ronald K. L. Collins, *Exceptional Freedom – The Roberts Court, the First Amendment, and the New Absolutism*, 76 ALB. L. REV. 409, 413 (2012) (noting the "line of cases in which the Court has extended near absolute protection to expression," cautioning that "there are other cases in which the Roberts Court has been quite parsimonious in its protection of free speech," but concluding that "there is nonetheless something remarkable in how the Roberts Court has re-conceptualized the way we think about certain free speech issues and has likewise reinvigorated a measure of free speech liberty, albeit to the consternation of many"); Steven J. Heyman, *The Conservative-Libertarian Turn in First Amendment Jurisprudence*, 117 W.VA. L. REV. 231, 236–37, 297–99 (2014) (arguing that "conservative libertarianism has become one of the most powerful currents in First Amendment jurisprudence," noting that under this "libertarian approach to the First Amendment" the Supreme Court has "invalidate[d] laws

or policies that in [its] view threatened to subordinate individual liberty to liberal or progressive goals," and positing that "[a]t the heart of this view is a conception of individuals as free, equal, and independent of one another"); Sullivan, *supra* note 8, at 145–46, 156 (positing that the Roberts Court views freedom of speech "as serving the interest of political liberty," suggesting that this approach "represent[s] a triumph of the libertarian over the egalitarian vision of free speech," and concluding that under this libertarian approach "both governmental redistribution of speaking power and paternalistic protection of listeners from the force of speech are illegitimate ends that, as a categorical matter, cannot justify political speech regulation"). Professor Heyman generalizes contemporary First Amendment jurisprudence as "protect[ing] against government actions that invade individual liberty, interfere with the political process, or threaten to 'drive certain ideas or viewpoints from the marketplace.'" Heyman, *supra*, at 299. Professor Sullivan concurs, suggesting that under the Roberts Court's liberty-based approach to protecting freedom of expression, "government may not attempt to shift relative influence among private speakers any more than it may give relative preference to some ideas." Sullivan, *supra* note 8, at 156.

16 162 Mass. 510 (1895), *aff'd*, 167 U.S. 43 (1897).

17 MAGARIAN, *supra* note 11, at xiv–xvi.

18 *Id.* at xv.

19 *Id.*

20 POST, *supra* note 12, at 247–55.

21 *Id.* at 250.

22 *Id.*

23 *See id.* at 250–52.

24 *Davis*, 162 Mass. at 511.

25 Davis v. Massachusetts, 167 U.S. 43, 48 (1897).

26 MAGARIAN, *supra* note 11, at 91–118, 252–53.

27 *See* JUDGES IN CONTEMPORARY DEMOCRACY: AN INTERNATIONAL CONVERSATION 144–57 (2004) (Robert Badinter & Stephen Breyer eds., 2004) (discussing strict limits on candidate and issue advertising, as well as political contribution limits, in contemporary France and Germany).

28 *Id.* at 148–51.

29 To use a quote often attributed to Marie-Antoinette, but better attributed to Rousseau, "Qu'ils mangent de la brioche." JEAN-JACQUES ROUSSEAU, CONFESSIONS (1766), *reprinted and translated in* JEAN-JACQUES ROUSSEAU, THE CONFESSIONS, AND CORRESPONDENCE, INCLUDING THE LETTERS TO MALESHERBES 225 (Christopher Kelly, ed. & trans., 1995). The critically-acclaimed motion picture, *Three Billboards Outside Ebbing, Missouri* (2017), features precisely this theme, with a disgruntled citizen renting three large privately-owned billboards, at her own expense, to speak her version of truth to power and provoking the government to act by so doing.

30 ANATOLE FRANCE, LE LYS ROUGE 118 (1894) (Calmann Lévy ed., 1896).

31 *See* Reynolds v. Sims, 377 U.S. 533 (1964). As Chief Justice Earl Warren explained in *Reynolds*, "[s]imply stated, an individual's right to vote for state legislators is unconstitutionally impaired when its weight is in a substantial fashion diluted when compared with votes of citizens living in other parts of the State." *Id.* at 568. This rule obtained because "[l]egislators represent people, not trees or acres." *Id.* at 562. He also posited that "the right to elect legislators in a free and unimpaired fashion is a bedrock of our political system." *Id.* If voting is foundational – and constitutive of the legitimacy of the political institutions of government at the federal and state level – then the process of democratic deliberation, which is essential to the legitimacy of the electoral process, must be no less important or "foundational."

32 Arizona Free Enterp. Club's Freedom Club PAC v. Bennett, 564 U.S. 721, 734–40 (2011) (disallowing an Arizona public financing provision that provided public funds to off-set self-funded and third party political expenditures); Davis v. Federal Election Comm'n, 554 U.S. 724, 738–40 (2008) (disallowing a federal campaign regulation that raised the applicable federal contribution limits for opponents of self-funded candidates for federal office who spend in excess of $350,000 to support her candidacy).

33 *See* R.A.V. v. City of St. Paul, 505 U.S. 377 (1992); Texas v. Johnson, 491 U.S. 397 (1989). For a general discussion of the rule against content-based speech regulations, see Martin H. Redish, *The Content Distinction in First Amendment Analysis*, 34 STAN. L. REV. 113, 128–42 (1981).

34 *See* Alexander Meiklejohn, *The First Amendment Is Absolute*, 1961 SUP. CT. REV. 245, 260–63 [hereinafter Meiklejohn, *The First Amendment Is Absolute*]. Professor Meiklejohn forcefully argues for direct public subsidies of political speech: "In every village, in every district of every town or city, there should be established at public expense cultural centers inviting all citizens, as they may choose, to meet together for the considerations of public policy." *Id.* at 261; *see* ALEXANDER MEIKLEJOHN, FREE SPEECH AND ITS RELATION TO SELF-GOVERNMENT 21–27, 88–89 (1948).

35 *See* David P. Currie, *Positive and Negative Rights*, 53 U. CHI. L. REV. 864 (1986).

36 *See, e.g.*, Hague v. C.I.O., 307 U.S. 496 (1939) (holding that a city could not prohibit the use of a public park for speech activity).

37 *Id.* at 515.

38 *See* Gregory v. City of Chicago, 394 U.S. 111 (1969); Terminiello v. Chicago, 337 U.S. 1 (1949).

39 *See* Forsyth County v. Nationalist Movement, 505 U.S. 123, 133–34 (1995).

40 POST, *supra* note 12, at 12–18, 237–55.

41 Oberwetter v. Hilliard, 639 F.3d 545, 548–49 (D.C. Cir. 2011).

42 *Id.* at 554.

43 240 F. Supp. 100 (M.D. Ala. 1965).

44 TIMOTHY ZICK, SPEECH OUT OF DOORS: PRESERVING FIRST AMENDMENT LIBERTIES IN PUBLIC PLACES (2009).

45 Sullivan, *supra* note 8, at 144–45, 150–55.

46 *See, e.g.*, President Barack Obama, Second Inaugural Address (January 21, 2013), *available at* www.whitehouse.gov/the-press-office/2013/01/21/inaugural-address-president-barack-obama (last visited July 15, 2016) ("We, the people, declare today that the most evident of truths – that all of us are created equal – is the star that guides us still; just as it guided our forebears through Seneca Falls, and Selma, and Stonewall; just as it guided all those men and women, sung and unsung, who left footprints along this great Mall, to hear a preacher say that we cannot walk alone; to hear a King proclaim that our individual freedom is inextricably bound to the freedom of every soul on Earth.").

47 42 U.S.C. §§ 1973-1973p (2016). Historians have generally credited the Selma Project, and the Selma-to-Montgomery March, with catalyzing the legislative process and securing enactment of the Voting Rights Act. *See* DAVID J. GARROW, PROTEST AT SELMA: MARTIN LUTHER KING, JR. AND THE VOTING RIGHTS ACT OF 1965 133–78 (1978); *see also* JACK BASS, TAMING THE STORM: THE LIFE AND TIMES OF JUDGE FRANK M. JOHNSON, JR. AND THE SOUTH'S FIGHT OVER CIVIL RIGHTS 254–55 (1993) (noting the causal relationship between the Selma March and enactment of the Voting Rights Act). The Voting Rights Act led to the mass enfranchisement of minority citizens in the states of the former Confederacy. *See* U.S. COMM'N ON CIVIL RIGHTS, THE VOTING RIGHTS ACT: TEN YEARS AFTER 1–9, 29–52 (1975).

48 BASS, *supra* note 47, at 254–55.

49 Martin Luther King, Jr., Address at the Conclusion of the Selma to Montgomery March, *How Long? Not Long!*, Mar. 25, 1965 (Montgomery, Alabama), *available at* http://mlk-kpp01.stanford.edu/index.php/encyclopedia/documentsentry/doc_address_at_the_conclusion_of_selma_march/ (visited May 19, 2015).

50 *Id.*

51 *See* Harper v. Va. Bd. of Elec., 383 U.S. 663, 667–68 (1966) ("We say the same whether the citizen, otherwise qualified to vote, has $1.50 in his pocket or nothing at all, pays the fee or fails to pay it. The principle that denies the State the right to dilute a citizen's vote on account of his economic status or other such factors by analogy bars a system which excludes those unable to pay a fee to vote or who fail to pay.").

52 240 F. Supp. 100 (M.D. Ala. 1965). Although the Supreme Court did not directly review Judge Johnson's decision in *Williams*, it did cite his decision favorably in a subsequent case decided three years later. *See* Carroll v. President & Comm'rs of Princess Anne, 393 U.S. 175, 184 n.11 (1968).

53 *See Williams*, 240 F. Supp. at 106–09.

54 *Id.* at 106.

55 Roy Reed, *25,000 Go to Alabama's Capitol; Wallace Rebuffs Petitioners; White Rights Worker Is Slain*, N.Y. TIMES, Mar. 26, 1965, at A1. For a fuller account of the march and Judge Johnson's iconic opinion and order in *Williams v. Wallace*, see RONALD J. KROTOSZYNSKI, JR., RECLAIMING THE PETITION CLAUSE: SEDITIOUS LIBEL, "OFFENSIVE PROTEST," AND THE RIGHT TO PETITION FOR A REDRESS OF GRIEVANCES 185–207 (2012).

56 Burke Marshall, *The Protest Movement and the Law*, 51 VA. L. REV. 785, 788–89 (1965).

57 Nicholas DeB. Katzenbach, *Protest, Politics, and the First Amendment*, 44 TUL. L. REV. 439, 443–44 (1969).

58 *Id.* at 445.

59 *See* Ronald J. Krotoszynski, Jr., *Celebrating Selma: On the Importance of Context in Public Forum Analysis*, 104 YALE L.J. 1411, 1420–25 (1995) (describing and discussing Judge Johnson's proportionality principle).

60 383 U.S. 131 (1966).

61 *Id.* at 142.

62 *Id.*

63 *Id.* at 141; *see* Steven G. Gey, *Reopening the Public Forum – From Sidewalks to Cyberspace*, 58 OHIO ST. L.J. 1535, 1566–76 (1998) (arguing for a return to a functional approach to making government property available for speech activity). Professor Gey proposes using a "strong interference analysis" and posits that "whether an instrumentality of communication is a public forum depends on whether expressive activity would tend to interfere in a significant way with the government's own activities in that forum." *Id.* at 1576–77. If the government cannot meet its burden of production and persuasion, then "the forum is deemed 'public' and the speech must be permitted, subject only to the application of narrow time, place, and manner regulations." *Id.* at 1576.

64 *See* United States v. Kokinda, 497 U.S. 720 (1990); Perry Educ. Ass'n v. Perry Local Educators' Ass'n, 460 U.S. 37 (1983).

65 Pleasant Grove City v. Summum, 555 U.S. 460, 469–72 (2009).

66 Gey, *supra* note 63, at 1536–38, 1542–55.

67 ZICK, *supra* note 44, at 4–21.

68 MAGARIAN, *supra* note 11, at 91–118, 227–39.

69 *See* MARTIN H. REDISH, THE ADVERSARY FIRST AMENDMENT: FREE EXPRESSION AND THE FOUNDATIONS OF AMERICAN DEMOCRACY (2013).

70 *Id.* at 27.

71 *See id.* at 181 (arguing that "[e]ven at its worst, a First Amendment grounded in principles of adversary democracy is far preferable to a logically flawed or deceptively manipulative appeal to democratic and expressive theories grounded in some vague notion of the pursuit of 'the common good' as a basis for the selective suppression of unpopular ideas"); *see also* Sullivan, *supra* note 8, at 160–63 (observing that a libertarian approach to defining the First Amendment's scope involves a "central distinction between the use of public and private resources").

72 562 U.S. 443 (2011).

73 *Id.* at 448–49.

74 *See* RONALD J. KROTOSZYNSKI, JR., PRIVACY REVISITED: A GLOBAL PERSPECTIVE ON THE RIGHT TO BE LEFT ALONE 5, 26–30, 182–83 (2016) (discussing *Snyder* and the strong priority that US constitutional law affords to free speech interests over privacy interests).

75 *See Snyder*, 562 U.S. at 453–61.

76 *Id.* at 461.

77 485 U.S. 46 (1988). For a relevant and thoughtful discussion of *Falwell* and its rejection of the imposition of majoritarian civility standards on speech, *see* Robert C. Post, *The Constitutional Concept of Public Discourse: Outrageous Opinion, Democratic Deliberation, and* Hustler Magazine v. Falwell, 103 HARV. L. REV. 601, 624–32 (1990).

78 *Falwell*, 485 U.S. at 52–55.

79 *Id.* at 50.

80 *Id.* at 51 (quoting New York Times Co. v. Sullivan, 376 U.S. 254, 270 (1964)).

81 United States v. Alvarez, 567 U.S. 709, 716–20 (2012).

82 Brown v. Enm't Merchs. Ass'n, 564 U.S. 786, 793–801 (2011).

83 United States v. Stevens, 559 U.S. 460, 468–74, 481–82 (2010).

84 Sorrell v. IMS Health Inc., 564 U.S. 552, 566–70 (2011).

85 558 U.S. 310 (2010).

86 *Id.* at 341.

87 *Id.* at 340–41.

88 *But see* Erwin Chemerinsky, *Not a Free Speech Court*, 53 ARIZ. L. REV. 723 (2011). Dean Chemerinsky concedes that the Roberts Court has issued many decisions broadly protective of freedom of speech, *see id.* at 723–34, but argues that other First Amendment decisions are not protective of First Amendment values, *see id.* at 725–34. He posits that "a look at the overall pattern of Roberts Court rulings on speech yields a clear and disturbing conclusion: it is not a free speech Court." *Id.* at 734. With all due respect to Dean Chemerinsky, he misses the key distinction that separates recent Supreme Court decisions vindicating free speech claims from those failing to vindicate free speech claims: When a would-be speaker does not need a subsidy from the government in order to speak, the speaker invariably wins; however, when a speaker needs a government subsidy in order to speak, the speaker more often than not loses. *See infra* text and accompanying notes 92 to 113. Accordingly, it would be more accurate to say that the Roberts Court is not a "free speech subsidy" Court.

89 *See infra* Chapter 4.

90 *See* Connick v. Myers, 461 U.S. 183 (1983); Pickering v. Board of Educ., 391 U.S. 563 (1968).

91 *See* HARRY KALVEN, JR., THE NEGRO AND THE FIRST AMENDMENT 140–41 (1965). Professor Kalven is generally credited with coining the phrase "heckler's veto" as a way of describing the potential problem of permitting an audience's hostile reaction to serve as a basis for limiting, or even proscribing, the speech. *See* Frederick Schauer, *Harry Kalven and the Perils of Particularism*, 56 U. CHI. L. REV. 397, 400 (1989) (observing that "[i]t was Kalven who gave us the idea of the 'heckler's veto'").

92 Garcetti v. Ceballos, 547 U.S. 410 (2006). *But see* Lane v. Franks, 573 U.S. 228, 238 (2014) (holding that "[t]ruthful testimony under oath by a public employee outside the scope of his ordinary job duties is speech as a citizen for First Amendment purposes" and noting "[t]hat is so even when the testimony relates to his public employment or concerns information learned during that

employment"). *Franks* does not overrule *Garcetti*, however, and merely clarifies that sworn testimony in a judicial proceeding constitutes "citizen," rather than "employee," speech related to a matter of public concern. *See id.* at 238–41.

93 *Garcetti*, 547 U.S. at 414.

94 *See* Elrod v. Burns, 427 U.S. 347, 359 (1976) (plurality opinion); *see also* Branti v. Finkel, 445 U.S. 507, 515–18 (1980) (affirming and applying *Elrod* and holding that because "the First Amendment protects a public employee from discharge based on what he has said, it must also protect him from discharge based on what he believes"). Over time, the Supreme Court has expanded *Elrod*'s scope to disallow other aspects of the spoils system, such as using government contracts to reward political supporters and punish political opponents. *See* O'Hare Truck Serv., Inc. v. City of Northlake, 518 U.S. 712, 720–21 (1996). Under the Supreme Court's current jurisprudence, the First Amendment only permits consideration of partisan identity with respect to government employees who possess policy-making authority or enjoy regular access to confidential information. *See id.* at 718–19. In fact, this protection even applies when an employer mistakenly attributes a partisan identity to an employee and retaliates against the employee based on this mistake of fact. *See* Heffernan v. City of Paterson, 136 S. Ct. 1412, 1417–19 (2016). *But cf.* Waters v. Churchill, 511 U.S. 661, 679–80 (1994) (sustaining the discharge of a nurse employed at a public hospital based on comments that the nurse did not actually make because the erroneously-attributed comments did not relate to a matter of public concern but rather to work-related matters of private concern).

95 *See* Houchins v. KQED, 438 U.S. 1 (1978).

96 *See* MEIKLEJOHN, *supra* note 34, at 22–27, 88–91.

97 Popular viewpoints in a democracy do not usually face the prospect of censorship. *See* Terminiello v. Chicago, 337 U.S. 1, 4 (1949) (holding that the purpose of the First Amendment "is to invite dispute," that "the vitality of civil and political institutions in our society depends on free discussion," and, accordingly, this "is why freedom of speech, though not absolute … is nevertheless protected against censorship or punishment, unless shown likely to produce a clear and present danger of a serious substantive evil that rises far above public inconvenience, annoyance, or unrest").

98 *See* Abdullah v. County of St. Louis, 52 F. Supp. 3d 936 (E.D. Mo. 2014); *see also* John Nichols, *The Constitutional Crisis in Ferguson, Missouri*, THE NATION, Aug. 14, 2014, www.thenation.com/blog/181145/police-overreaction-has-become-constitutional-crisis-ferguson-missouri (last visited Mar. 27, 2019).

99 *Abdullah*, 52 F. Supp. 3d at 942.

100 *See id.* at 948–49.

101 *See id.* at 948 ("This injunction does not prevent defendants or other law enforcement agencies from using all lawful means to control crowds and protect against violence. Missouri's refusal-to-disperse law is not restricted by this injunction.").

102 *See, e.g.,* Cox v. Louisiana, 379 U.S. 536, 552 (1965) ("Maintenance of the opportunity for free political discussion is a basic tenet of our constitutional democracy."); New York Times Co. v. Sullivan, 376 U.S. 254, 270 (1964) (holding that a public official plaintiff suing a media defendant for defamation must prove malice aforethought in order to ensure that "debate on public issues [will] be uninhibited, robust, and wide-open, and that it may well include vehement, caustic, and sometimes unpleasantly sharp attacks on government and public officials"); Edwards v. South Carolina, 372 U.S. 229, 235–37 (1963) (holding that "South Carolina infringed the petitioners' constitutionally protected rights of free speech, free assembly, and freedom to petition for redress of their grievances" by arresting and convicting them for "breach of peace" based on student protestors conducting a civil rights rally at the South Carolina state capitol and noting that the government may not attempt to criminalize speech simply because the speakers' views are unpopular); Terminiello v. Chicago, 337 U.S. 1, 4 (1949) ("Accordingly, a function of free speech under our system of government is to invite dispute. It may indeed best serve its high purpose when it induces a condition of unrest, creates dissatisfaction with conditions as they are, or even stirs people to anger."); Stromberg v. California, 283 U.S. 359, 369 (1931) (holding that the First Amendment exists to safeguard "[t]he maintenance of the opportunity for free political discussion to the end that government may be responsive to the will of the people and that changes may be obtained by lawful means, an opportunity essential to the security of the Republic" and constitutes "a fundamental principle of our constitutional system").

103 *See* Ariz. Free Enter. Club's Freedom Club PAC v. Bennett, 564 U.S. 721, 750 (2011) ("The First Amendment embodies our choice as a Nation that, when it comes to such [political] speech, the guiding principle is freedom— the 'unfettered interchange of ideas' – not whatever the State may view as fair."); Citizens United v. Fed. Elec. Comm'n, 558 U.S. 310, 341 (2010) ("The First Amendment protects speech and speaker, and the ideas that flow from each."); *see also* Ofer Raban, *Between Formalism and Conservatism: The Resurgent Legal Formalism of the Roberts Court*, 8 NYU J.L. & LIBERTY 343 (2014) (arguing that the Roberts Court has adopted a highly formalist approach to defining and enforcing constitutional rights, including First Amendment rights).

104 It bears noting that Dean Erwin Chemerinsky has noted that the narrative of an ever-expanding universe of expressive freedom does not present an entirely accurate picture. Chemerinsky, *supra* note 88, at 723–25, 734. He concedes that "the Roberts Court sometimes rules favor of free speech claims," but that its record overall demonstrates "that it is not a free speech Court at all." *Id.* at 724.

105 Southeastern Productions, Ltd. v. Conrad, 420 U.S. 546 (1975).

106 United States v. Kokinda, 497 U.S. 720 (1990); Members of the City Council of the City of L.A. v. Taxpayers for Vincent, 466 U.S. 789 (1984).

107 *See, e.g.,* Oberwetter v. Hilliard, 639 F.3d 545, 552 (D.C. Cir. 2011) ("National memorials are places of public commemoration, not freewheeling forums for

open expression, and thus the government may reserve them for purposes that preclude expressive activity.").

108 Reynolds v. Sims, 377 U.S. 533 (1964); Baker v. Carr, 369 U.S. 186 (1962). Even more controversial cases involving voting rights, such as Shaw v. Reno, 509 U.S. 630 (1993), also arguably reflect a commitment to the equal rights and dignity of citizens as citizens. The *Shaw* majority characterized its holding against the placement of voters in particular districts based on their race as necessary to vindicate the equal status and dignity of all voters – which would be injured were they treated merely as members of racial voting blocs. *See* Miller v. Johnson, 515 U.S. 900, 911–12 (1995).

109 Caroline Mala Corbin, *Compelled Disclosures*, 65 Ala. L. Rev. 1277, 1298, 1334–39, 1351 (2014).

110 Krotoszynski, *supra* note 74, at 111–14. In South Africa, "[t]he inability to create subcategories of citizenship – favoring some groups and disfavoring others through a caste system – makes it significantly more difficult to backslide into a regime that subordinates some groups in order to enhance the relative status of other groups." *Id.* at 111.

111 Corbin, *supra* note 109, at 1334.

112 *See infra* Chapter 8.

113 *See* Corbin, *supra* note 109, at 1281–82, 1298, 1338–39, 1351 (discussing how coerced speech degrades the involuntary speaker, compromises her agency, and renders her less fit to participate as an equal participant in democratic discourse more generally).

114 Meiklejohn, *supra* note 34, at 25 ("What is essential is not that everyone shall speak, but that everything worth saying shall be said.").

115 *See id.* at 90–91.

116 West Virginia Bd. of Educ. v. Barnette, 319 U.S. 624, 642 (1943).

117 *See* Meiklejohn, *supra* note 34, at 21–27, 89–91.

118 *See* Neil M. Richards, *The Dangers of Surveillance*, 126 Harv. L. Rev. 1934, 1946, 1961 (2014) [hereinafter Richards, *The Dangers of Surveillance*]; Neil M. Richards, *Intellectual Privacy*, 87 Tex. L. Rev. 387, 403–04 (2008).

119 Corbin, *supra* note 109, at 1298 and 1298 n.127.

120 Moreover, being forced to serve as the mouthpiece of government – or to be silenced by the government – is profoundly disempowering. Particularly when one feels that, as a practical matter, one lacks any meaningful ability to choose. A high school student cannot simply say "keep your education." *See* Morse v. Frederick, 551 U.S. 393 (2007). Nor can a medical doctor realistically tell the government "keep your license" in order to avoid providing either medically unnecessary treatments or medically false information to a patient. *See* Texas Medical Providers Performing Abortion Servs. v. Lackey, 667 F.3d 570, 578–80 (5th Cir. 2012); Planned Parenthood v. Rounds, 530 F.3d 724, 729, 734–36 (8th Cir. 2008) (en banc). As a practical matter, many individuals do not have

a realistic option of "just saying no" to the terms the government sets as a precondition of securing a government benefit.

121 *See* Owen M. Fiss, The Irony of Free Speech 16–18 (1996) (arguing that disparities in wealth can and will create significant distortionary effects in the marketplace of ideas because the public "will, in effect, hear only" the viewpoints of the rich and warning that "the voice of the less affluent may simply be drowned out").

122 *See* Robert C. Post, *Subsidized Speech*, 106 Yale L.J. 151 (1996).

123 *See* Ronald J. Krotoszynski, Jr., *The Unitary Executive and the Plural Judiciary: On the Potential Virtues of Decentralized Judicial Power*, 89 Notre Dame L. Rev. 1021 (2014).

124 *See infra* Chapter 7.

125 *See infra* Chapter 6.

126 *See infra* Chapter 5.

127 *See infra* Chapter 7.

128 *See, e.g.*, Houchins v. KQED, 438 U.S. 1, 16 (1978) (Stewart, J., concurring); Branzburg v. Hayes, 408 U.S. 665, 725 (1972) (Stewart, J., dissenting); *see also id.* at 709–10 (Powell, J., concurring).

129 *See, e.g.*, Richmond Newspapers, Inc. v. Virginia, 448 U.S. 555 (1980); Nebraska Press Ass'n v. Stuart, 427 U.S. 539 (1976).

130 391 U.S. 308 (1968).

131 *See* Kathleen Sullivan, *Unconstitutional Conditions*, 102 Harv. L. Rev. 1413 (1988).

132 *See* Post, *supra* note 12, at 151–57, 164–71.

133 *See* Sarah Kellogg, *Free Speech: The Campus Battlefield*, Wash. Lawyer 18, 19–21 (Sept. 2017).

134 *See* Richards, *The Dangers of Surveillance*, *supra* note 118, at 1945–56.

135 *See* Christina E. Wells, *Fear and Loathing in Constitutional Decision-Making*, 2005 Wis. L. Rev. 115.

136 Branzburg v. Hayes, 408 U.S. 665 (1972); *see* Lyrissa Barnett Lidsky, *Not a Free Press Court?*, 2012 BYU L. Rev. 1819 (2012); Ashutosh Bhagwat, *Producing Speech*, 56 Wm. & Mary L. Rev. 1029 (2015).

137 Johanns v. Livestock Mktg. Ass'n, 544 U.S. 550 (2005); *see* Helen Norton & Danielle Keats Citron, *Government Speech 2.0*, 87 Den. U. L. Rev. 899, 903–10, 936–39 (2010); Gia B. Lee, *Persuasion, Transparency, and Government Speech*, 56 Hastings L.J. 983, 1009–26 (2005); Lyrissa Barnett Lidsky, *Silencing John Doe: Defamation and Discourse in Cyberspace*, 49 Duke L.J. 855, 896–97 (2000). As Professor Sarah Joseph has argued, "[t]he need for caution in promoting social media as an instrument of progressive political change must be acknowledged" because of the risk of government "subvert[ing] the utility of social media through the extensive use of 'sock puppets,' which would poison people's trust in the platforms." Sarah Joseph, *Social Media, Political Change, and Human Rights*, 35 B.C. Int'l & Comp. L. Rev. 145, 187 (2012).

138 Norton & Citron, *supra* note 137, at 909.

139 *But see* Watson v. Memphis, 373 U.S. 526, 535 (1964) (holding that "constitutional rights may not be denied simply because of hostility to their assertion or exercise").

140 *See* Bush v. Gore, 531 U.S. 98 (2000).

141 Citizens United v. Fed. Elec. Comm'n, 558 U.S. 310, 339–42 (2010).

2 THE PUBLIC FORUM DOCTRINE AND REDUCED ACCESS TO GOVERNMENT PROPERTY FOR SPEECH ACTIVITY

1 *See, e.g.*, U.S. v. Kokinda, 497 U.S. 720, 726–27 (1990) (holding that sidewalks within a US post office parking lot, adjacent to the main post office building, that were generally open to postal service customers were not a public forum and could be closed to speech activity); Hodge v. Talkin, 799 F.3d 1145, 1158–61 (D.C. Cir. 2015) (holding the open public plaza in front of the US Supreme Court building "to be a nonpublic forum" and observing that the plaza's status as a non-public forum "is unaffected by the public's unrestricted access to the plaza at virtually any time"); Oberwetter v. Hilliard, 639 F.3d 545, 552–54 (D.C. Cir. 2011) (holding that the Jefferson Memorial, in Washington, DC, is not a public forum for First Amendment activities); Boardley v. U.S. Dep't of the Interior, 615 F.3d 508, 515 (D.C. Cir. 2010) (holding that national parks are not presumptive public forums and that "to establish that a national park (in whole or part) is a traditional public forum, Boardley must show that, like a typical municipal park, it has been held open by the government for the purpose of public discourse"); United States v. Kistner, 68 F.3d 218, 222 (8th Cr. 1995) (finding that the Jefferson National Expansion Memorial, commonly known as the "St. Louis Arch," constitutes a public forum, but nevertheless sustaining the National Park Service's creation of five designated "free speech zones" within the park and limiting First Amendment activity to these areas). Two principal problems exist. Federal courts are broadly deferential to government decisions to label a park or memorial a "non-public forum," which empowers government to essentially ban expressive activities from the venue. Second, federal courts accept draconian regulations on speech activities within traditional public forums that exist to advance interests in "tranquility" and "the safety and attractiveness" of the government's property. *Kistner*, 68 F.3d at 222. Both the designation of parks and monuments as non-public forums, and the aggressive use of time, place, and manner regulations, significantly reduce the space available for speech activity.

2 For example, Cindy Sheehan wished to protest President George W. Bush's Iraq War policies in a direct and personal way – and was able to accomplish this objective when a private property owner with land adjacent to the route used by President Bush's motorcade going to and from his ranch in Crawford, Texas permitted her to use it for protest activity. *See* Elisabeth Bumiller, *Bush and the Protester: Tale of 2 Summer Camps*, N.Y. TIMES, Aug. 9, 2005, at A9. Sheehan had initially used the shoulder of a county road for her protest, but the local government enacted a ban on such activity on public property. Associated Press, *Mother's Antiwar Protest Prompts New Law*, N.Y. TIMES, Sept. 30, 2005, at A18.

The county government also prohibited parking on 22 miles of county roads to make staging protests near the President's ranch more difficult. *See id.* In response, Sheehan purchased a five-acre parcel of land, using proceeds from her deceased son's military death benefits to do so. *See* Associated Press, *Texas War Critic Buys Crawford Land*, N.Y. TIMES, July 28, 2006, at A25. The land was proximate to President Bush's ranch in Crawford, Texas, and her ownership of it enabled Sheehan to maintain her "Camp Casey" anti-war protest in honor of her deceased son, Casey Sheehan, who was killed while serving on active duty in Iraq. *See id.; see also* Associated Press, *War Protester Will Sell Land by Bush Ranch*, N.Y. TIMES, June 10, 2007, at A30. Thus, Cindy Sheehan literally had to acquire property in order to speak her version of truth to power. Moreover, she did so only after the local government used its ownership rights over public property – rights of way along county roads – to banish dissent.

3 *See, e.g.*, Hudgens v. NLRB, 424 U.S. 507, 518–20 (1976) (holding that private mall owners need not permit expressive activities on mall property); Lloyd Corp. v Tanner, 407 U.S. 551, 563–64 (1972) (sustaining a mall owner's decision to prohibit leafletting and picketing at a large shopping mall in Portland, Oregon). *But cf.* PruneYard Shopping Center v. Robbins, 447 U.S. 74, 86–87 (1980) (upholding, against a First Amendment challenge, the California Supreme Court's interpretation of the state constitution to create a right of access to privately-owned shopping centers for peaceful fixed leafletting activities); Marsh v. Alabama, 326 U.S. 501, 504–09 (1946) (holding that a private corporation that undertakes all of the duties and responsibilities of a municipal government constitutes a state actor and therefore must permit and facilitate First Amendment activities within the company-owned town).

4 *See PruneYard*, 447 U.S. at 87 (rejecting a private mall owner's constitutional objections to a California state constitutional rule requiring the owners of large-scale shopping centers to permit protest activity on their properties because (1) the protesters' messages "will not likely be identified with those of the owner" and (2) the mall's owner easily could "expressly disavow any connection with the message by simply posting signs in the area where the speakers or handbillers stand").

5 *See* HARRY KALVEN, JR., THE NEGRO AND THE FIRST AMENDMENT 140–41, 145 (1965) (discussing the problem of the "heckler's veto" and the need for federal courts to be vigilant in thwarting efforts to empower a heckler's veto over speech by unpopular speakers on public property); *see also* Owen Fiss, *Free Speech and Social Structure*, 71 IOWA L. REV. 1405, 1416–17 (1986) (citing Kalven's seminal work on the problem of a heckler's veto, discussing the problem of the heckler's veto, observing that private market power can be used to silence unpopular speakers, and positing that government efforts to limit the censorial power of non-government actors could enhance rather than inhibit the vibrancy of the marketplace of ideas).

6 *See* Brown v. Louisiana, 383 U.S. 131, 138–43 (1966) (holding that the government must regulate speech activity "in a reasonable and nondiscriminatory manner, equally applicable to all and administered with equality to all" and requiring a

local government to make the public library available for a silent civil rights protest).

7 *See, e.g.,* Cox v. Louisiana, 379 U.S. 536, 538–39 (1965); Cox v. Louisiana, 379 U.S. 559, 566–67 (1965); Edwards v. South Carolina, 372 U.S. 229, 229–30, 237 (1963).

8 Citizens United v. FEC, 558 U.S. 310, 340–41 (2010); United States v. Playboy Entm't Group, 529 U.S. 803, 813–14 (2000); Police Dep't City of Chicago v. Mosley, 408 U.S. 92, 95–96 (1972). As Justice Thurgood Marshall explained in *Mosley,* "above all else, the First Amendment means that government has no power to restrict expression because of its message, its ideas, its subject matter, or its content." *Mosley,* 408 U.S. at 95.

9 *See infra* text and accompanying notes 14 to 29 and 50 to 70.

10 395 U.S. 444 (1969). *Brandenburg,* decided on June 9, 1969, is literally one of the very last decisions of the Warren Court.

11 *Id.* at 444–47.

12 *Id.* at 448.

13 *See id.* at 448–49.

14 307 U.S. 496 (1939).

15 Timothy Zick, *Space, Place, and Speech: The Expressive Topography,* 74 Geo. Wash. L. Rev. 439 (2006) [hereinafter Zick, *Expressive Topography*]; Timothy Zick, *Speech and Spatial Tactics,* 84 Tex. L. Rev. 581 (2006) [hereinafter Zick, *Speech and Spatial Tactics*]; *see* Tabatha Abu El-Haj, *The Neglected Right of Assembly,* 56 UCLA L. Rev. 543, 548–54 (2009) (describing and critiquing various government efforts to suppress if not eliminate public dissent on government-owned property). Professor Tabatha Abu El-Haj has documented how governments (at all levels) increasingly marginalize speech in public places through burdensome regulations and argues that "[a]ll of these requirements undercut the possibility of large, spontaneous gatherings in the streets." *Id.* at 549.

16 *See, e.g.,* Hodge v. Talkin, 799 F.3d 1145, 1150, 1165 (D.C. Cir. 2015) (rejecting a First Amendment challenge to a federal law that bans protest on the large, elevated marble plaza located in front of the Supreme Court because of "the government's long-recognized interests in preserving decorum in the area of a courthouse and in assuring the appearance (and actuality) of a judiciary uninfluenced by public opinion and pressure"). However, the statute regulated considerably more speech than was necessary to secure this interest. *See* 40 U.S.C. § 6135 (2016). Section 6135 bars protest on the plaza regardless of whether the Supreme Court is actually in session. It is difficult to see how a protest on the plaza in mid-August, when the Justices are usually not even on the premises, could possibly influence, or give the appearance of undue influence, on the Justices. The statute bans virtually all expressive activity on the plaza, making it illegal to "parade, stand, or move in processions or assemblages in the Supreme Court Building or grounds, or to display in the Building and grounds a flag, banner, or device designed or adopted to bring into public notice a party, organization, or movement." *Id.* The statute is overbroad insofar as it covers the

plaza, which looks and functions as a public meeting space and, with respect to the plaza, applies regardless of whether the Supreme Court is actually in session during a particular protest. The D.C. Circuit made no effort to require the government to tailor section 6135's speech restrictions narrowly to protect the dignity and integrity of the Supreme Court's oral arguments. Judge Srikanth Srinivasan, writing for the majority, described the front plaza as the private enclave of the Supreme Court, which he characterized as a "nonpublic forum" that constitutes "the elevated front porch of the Supreme Court building." *Id.* at 1159. Judge Srinivasan also dismissed as irrelevant the fact that the Supreme Court Police do not consistently seek to enforce the speech ban, routinely permitting some speech activity (including large public protests). *See id.* at 1161–62. Obviously, the selective enforcement of a speech ban on public property raises a serious danger of content- and viewpoint-based discrimination against particular speakers and messages. I do not suggest that the federal government cannot declare the Supreme Court building itself off-limits to expressive activity, including noisy protests, but to extend the ban to a broad space generally entirely open and available to the public, and to characterize it as the Justices' private "front porch," reflects a gross disregard for the practical ability of ordinary citizens to participate in the process of democratic deliberation. *Id.* at 1159. *But cf. id.* at 1160 (noting that "the Supreme Court plaza's status as a nonpublic forum is unaffected by the public's unrestricted access to the plaza at virtually any time"). That Judge Srinivasan, a federal appellate judge often mentioned as a potential Supreme Court nominee for a presumably progressive Democratic President, could write such a speech-hostile opinion demonstrates quite clearly that contemporary judicial antipathy toward would-be speakers seeking to use public property for First Amendment activity is widespread and knows no ideological limits. *See* Julie Zauzmer, *What Would a Hindu Justice Mean for the Supreme Court?*, WASH. POST (Mar. 10, 2016), www.washingtonpost.com/news/acts-of-faith/wp/2016/03/10/what-would-a-hindu-justice-mean-for-the-supreme-court/?utm_term=.a279133bbb4d [https://perma.cc/4WZG-LW93] (last visited Mar. 29, 2019)

17 *Cf.* Williams v. Wallace, 240 F. Supp. 100, 105–09 (M.D. Ala. 1965).

18 Brown v. Louisiana, 383 U.S. 131, 138–40 (1966); *see* Zick, *Expressive Topography, supra* note 15, at 497 ("Under current forum analysis, the library, like most contested places, would most likely be considered a 'non-public' forum. This approach fails to place the library in local and more general historical perspective.").

19 Flower v. United States, 407 U.S. 197, 198 (1972). Base officials prohibited John Flower from distributing anti-Vietnam War leaflets at Fort Sam Houston, in San Antonio, Texas. *See* United States v. Flower, 452 F.2d 80, 81–82, 89 (5th Cir. 1971), *rev'd* 407 U.S. 197 (1972). The Fifth Circuit held that the government could prohibit speech activity on the base, *see id.* at 82–86, but the Supreme Court reversed, holding that Flower had a First Amendment right to use the base's property to leaflet and promote an anti-Vietnam War rally, *see Flower*, 407 U.S. at 198.

20 *See, e.g.*, United States v. Grace, 461 U.S. 171, 182–84 (1983); Tinker v. Des Moines Indep. Sch. Dist., 393 U.S. 503, 508–09 (1969).

21 Pell v. Procunier, 417 U.S. 817, 822 (1974).

22 *Id.*

23 *See id.* at 827–28. It bears noting that the prison did not bar alternative forms of communication between inmates and members of the press – such as through written letters and presumably also telephone calls. *See id.* at 827–28 & 827 n.5.

24 By way of contrast, the Supreme Court's current approach to substantive due process and equal protection-based challenges to economic and social legislation reflects a posture of abject deference to the government, which has no burden of justification whatsoever. FCC v. Beach Communications, Inc., 508 U.S. 307, 313–16 (1993). Instead, a plaintiff challenging economic or social legislation that does not burden or abridge a fundamental right must prove a negative – namely that no rational legislator could find that the law in question bears a rational relationship to any legitimate state interest. *See id.* at 313 ("In areas of social and economic policy, a statutory classification that neither proceeds along suspect lines nor infringes fundamental constitutional rights must be upheld against equal protection challenge if there is any reasonably conceivable state of facts that could provide a rational basis for the classification."). *Pell's* approach simply does not reflect a similar level of deference to prison officials with respect to the First Amendment rights of prisoners. *See Pell*, 417 U.S. at 826–28.

25 Louis Michael Seidman, *The* Dale *Problem: Property and Speech under the Regulatory State*, 75 U. CHI. L. REV. 1541, 1592 (2008).

26 Abu El-Haj, *supra* note 15, at 548–54, 586–88. Professor Abu El-Haj posits that "there is good reason to think that current regulatory choices are undermining the meaningfulness of public assemblies for participants as well as their effectiveness as a mechanism to influence and check government." *Id.* at 587.

27 *See* Ward v. Rock Against Racism, 491 U.S. 781, 791 (1989) (holding that "[t]he government may impose reasonable restrictions on the time, place, or manner of protected speech").

28 Perry Educ. Ass'n v. Perry Local Educators' Ass'n, 460 U.S. 37, 46–47 (1983). *But cf.* Southeastern Promotions, Ltd. v. Conrad, 420 U.S. 546, 555–61 (1975) (rejecting a city's effort to limit the kinds of programming that could be presented at a municipally-owned and operated performing arts space because the use restrictions constituted impermissible prior restraints).

29 Christian Legal Soc'y v. Martinez, 561 U.S. 661 (2010) (recognizing that government entities can and do create limited-purpose public forums and may limit access to such forums to certain speakers and particular kinds of speech without violating the First Amendment); *see* Lyrissa Barnett Lidsky, *Public Forum 2.0*, 91 B.U. L. REV. 1975, 1984–86 (2011) (describing and discussing the concept of a limited-purpose public forum and its application in *Christian Legal Society*).

30 *See* STEVEN H. SHIFFRIN, DISSENT, INJUSTICE, AND THE MEANINGS OF AMERICA 10–12, 33–35, 41–48 (1999) (proposing a general interpretative approach to

enforcing the First Amendment that privileges speech of a dissenting cast and arguing that dissent lies "at the heart of the First Amendment"). Professor Shiffrin explains that "[m]y suggestion will be that a free speech theory accenting protection for dissent fares better than a theory based in the protection of political speech or liberty." *Id.* at 33; *see id.* at 91 ("Free speech theory should be taken beyond protecting or tolerating dissent: the First Amendment should be taken to reflect a constitutional commitment to *promoting* dissent").

31 ALEXANDER MEIKLEJOHN, FREE SPEECH AND ITS RELATION TO SELF-GOVERNMENT 25 (1948).

32 *Id.* at 26.

33 For a history of the public forum doctrine's theoretical and doctrinal origins and development into the early years of the Rehnquist Court, see Robert C. Post, *Between Governance and Management: The History and Theory of the Public Forum*, 34 UCLA L. REV. 1713 (1987).

34 *See supra* text and accompanying notes 18 to 29.

35 Ward v. Rock Against Racism, 491 U.S. 781, 791 (1989) ("Our cases make clear, however, that even in a public forum the government may impose reasonable restrictions on the time, place, or manner of protected speech, provided the restrictions 'are justified without reference to the content of the regulated speech, that they are narrowly tailored to serve a significant governmental interest, and that they leave open ample alternative channels for communication of the information.'" (internal citations omitted)).

36 Steven G. Gey, *Reopening the Public Forum – From Sidewalks to Cyberspace*, 58 OHIO ST. L.J. 1535, 1634 (1998) (arguing that the government should be permitted to deny access to public property otherwise suitable for speech activity "only if the speech would otherwise significantly interfere with the government's ability to carry out its legitimate duties" and positing that "[r]igorous enforcement of this interference standard would stem the current trend toward a narrowing of the public forum"); Zick, *Expressive Topography, supra* note 15, at 502 (arguing that "[g]iven the intersection of speech spatiality ... the government should be required to draw spatial boundaries that inhibit or suppress *no more expressive or associative activity than necessary* to serve its purposes").

37 Gey, *supra* note 36, at 1576–78; Zick, *Expressive Topography, supra* note 15, at 502–05.

38 *Cf.* Int'l Soc'y for Krishna Consciousness, Inc. v. Lee, 505 U.S. 672, 683 (1992) (holding that an airport concourse does not constitute a public forum and, accordingly, that government may impose reasonable speech regulations that restrict or prohibit speech activity within the concourse area – even though it otherwise functions in many respects as a de facto government-owned and operated shopping mall). By way of contrast, Professor Steven G. Gey has posited that the federal courts should essentially return to the Warren Court's approach to determining whether government property should be available for speech activity – an approach that placed the burden on the government to establish that permitting the public to use particular government property for First Amendment activities would actually impede the government's legitimate

operations. *See* Gey, *supra* note 36, at 1576 (arguing that "whether an instrumentality of communication is a public forum [should] depend[ ] on whether expressive activity would tend to interfere in a significant way with the government's own activities in that forum" and "[i]f the government cannot prove the strong likelihood of significant interference, the forum [should be] deemed 'public' and the speech must be permitted, subject only to the application of narrow time, place, and manner regulations").

39 *See, e.g.*, Oberwetter v. Hilliard, 639 F.3d 545, 552–54 (D.C. Cir. 2011) (upholding a ban on protest activity at the Jefferson Memorial). For a relevant discussion, see Zick, *Expressive Topography, supra* note 15, at 487–505 (discussing the relevance of particular spaces and access to specific potential audiences to expressive activity and arguing that even though spaces are not inherently fungible, current First Amendment time, place, and manner jurisprudence presumes one space is just as good as another for expressive activity). Professor Zick argues that "[c]ourts should again be thinking in terms of the new expressive topography when assessing spatial adequacy. Places are *unique." Id.* at 504. It necessarily follows that "denying access to contested places is a substantial restraint on messages targeting those places." *Id.*

40 *See, e.g.*, United States v. Kistner, 68 F.3d 218, 222 (8th Cir. 1995) (upholding National Park Service TPM regulations that severely limited protest activity within the St. Louis Arch park).

41 New York Times Co. v. Sullivan, 376 U.S. 256, 269–70 (1964).

42 Snyder v. Phelps, 562 U.S. 443, 458–61 (2011); Hustler Magazine, Inc. v. Falwell, 485 U.S. 46, 52–56 (1988). For a general discussion of how and why contemporary First Amendment law disallows the regulation of offensive or outrageous speech, either directly or through the imposition of civil liability by juries, see Robert C. Post, *The Constitutional Concept of Public Discourse: Outrageous Opinion, Democratic Deliberation, and* Hustler Magazine v. Falwell, 103 HARV. L. REV. 601, 624–32 (1990).

43 Davis v. Commonwealth of Massachusetts, 167 U.S. 43, 47–48 (1897).

44 *Id.* at 48.

45 This view has resurfaced from time to time in majority opinions. *See, e.g.*, Lyng v. Northwest Indian Cemetery, 485 U.S. 439, 453 (1988) ("The Constitution does not permit government to discriminate against religions that treat particular physical sites as sacred, and a law prohibiting the Indian respondents from visiting the Chimney Rock area would raise a different set of constitutional questions. Whatever rights the Indians may have to the use of the area, however, those rights do not divest the Government of its right to use what is, after all, *its* land.").

46 307 U.S. 496 (1939).

47 *Id.* at 515–16.

48 Pennsylvania Coal Co. v. Mahon, 260 U.S. 393, 413 (1922); *see* Bi-Metallic Investment Co. v. State Bd. of Equalization, 239 U.S. 441, 445 (1915) ("There must be a limit to individual argument in such matters if government is to go on.").

49 Robert C. Post, Constitutional Domains: Democracy, Community, Management 4–10, 13–16, 237–47, 261–62 (1995); *see* Gregory P. Magarian, Managed Speech: The Roberts Court's First Amendment 91–118, 227–39, 252–53 (2017) (criticizing the Roberts Court's "managed speech" approach to enforcing the First Amendment in general and access to public property for speech activity in particular). Professor Magarian posits that "[m]anaged speech provides substantial protection for expressive autonomy" but "[b]y placing a high premium on social and political stability, managed speech encourages a public discussion where a limited number of speakers exchange a limited range of ideas." *Id.* at 252–53.

50 *See* U.S. v. Kokinda, 497 U.S. 720, 727 (1990) (holding that "[t]he mere physical characteristics of the property cannot dictate forum analysis" and explaining that "regulation of speech activity where the Government has not dedicated its property to First Amendment activity is examined only for reasonableness").

51 Brown v. Louisiana, 383 U.S. 131, 141–42 (1966).

52 Edwards v. South Carolina, 372 U.S. 229, 235–37 (1963).

53 Cox v. Louisiana, 379 U.S. 536, 538–44, 552, 558 (1965); Cox v. Louisiana, 379 U.S. 559, 568–75 (1965).

54 *Id.* at 562.

55 *Id.*

56 *Id.* at 568.

57 *Id.*

58 *Id.* at 569–70.

59 *See Cox*, 379 U.S. at 574–75.

60 La. Rev. Stat. § 14:401 (Cum. Supp. 1962).

61 *Cox*, 379 U.S. at 581–82 (Black, J., dissenting) (quoting La. Stat. Ann. § 14:401).

62 *Id.* at 583.

63 *Id.* at 584.

64 *Id.* at 569–72.

65 *See* Ronald J. Krotoszynski, Jr., Reclaiming the Petition Clause: Seditious Libel, "Offensive" Protest, and the Right to Petition the Government for a Redress of Grievances 204–05 (2012).

66 *See id.* at 202–05.

67 *See* Greer v. Spock, 424 U.S. 828, 859–60 (1976) (Brennan, J., dissenting) (arguing that "the notion of 'public forum' has never been the touchstone of public expression, for a contrary approach blinds the Court to any possible accommodation of First Amendment values in this case" and positing that "[t]hose cases permitting public expression without characterizing the locale involved as a public forum, together with those cases recognizing the existence of a public forum, albeit qualifiedly, evidence the desirability of a flexible approach to determining when public expression should be protected").

68 Krotoszynski, *supra* note 65, at 205.

69 *See* Gey, *supra* note 36, at 1576 (arguing for a functional approach to deciding access to public property for First Amendment activity that focuses on whether its proposed use would "interfere in a significant way with the government's own

activities in that forum" and positing that "[i]f the government cannot prove the strong likelihood of significant interference, the forum [should be] deemed 'public' and the speech must be permitted").

70 For an excellent discussion of how the government's role as a manager could justify at least some speech restrictions in government workplaces and on government property, see Robert C. Post, *Subsidized Speech*, 106 YALE L.J. 151 (1996).

71 *See, e.g.*, United States v. Kokinda, 497 U.S. 720, 725–28 (1989). Two decisions in the late Burger Court period embrace the public forum doctrine. *See* Cornelius v. NAACP Legal Def. & Ed. Fund, Inc., 473 U.S. 788, 800 (1985) (noting that "the Court has adopted a forum analysis as a means of determining when the Government's interest in limiting the use of its property to its intended purpose outweighs the interest of those wishing to use the property for other purposes"); Perry Education Ass'n v. Perry Local Educators' Ass'n, 460 U.S.37, 45–46 (1983) (observing that "[p]ublic property which is not by tradition or designation a forum for public communication is governed by different standards" and explaining that "[w]e have recognized that the First Amendment does not guarantee access to property simply because it is owned or controlled by the government" (internal quotations and citations omitted)).

72 *Kokinda*, 497 U.S. at 26–27.

73 *See, e.g.*, Int'l Soc'y for Krishna Consciousness, Inc. v. Lee, 505 U.S. 672, 678–82 (1992).

74 *See* Ward v. Rock Against Racism, 491 U.S. 781, 791 (1989).

75 *Perry*, 460 U.S. at 45–48.

76 *See Cornelius*, 473 U.S. at 800–06.

77 *See Perry* 460 U.S. at 45–49.

78 *Id.* at 45–46, 46 n.7.

79 420 U.S. 546 (1975).

80 418 U.S. 298 (1974).

81 *See, e.g.*, Post, *supra* note 33, at 1733–39. Professor Post points to Greer v. Spock, 424 U.S. 828 (1976), as "[t]he pivotal decision" in the development of the public forum doctrine. *See id.* at 1739. Viewed from the vantage point of doctrinal developments in 1987, this proposition seems quite reasonable – after all, *Greer* was the first case to invoke the metaphor of a "public forum" in a majority opinion. *Greer*, 424 U.S. at 838. Nevertheless, *Greer* actually used a balancing, rather than a categorical, approach to determine whether the government had an obligation to make particular property available for speech activity. *See infra* note 82. It is certainly fair to posit that *Greer* constitutes the first majority Supreme Court opinion that adopted the nomenclature of the "public forum" – but *Greer's* application of the doctrine, in hindsight, was considerably more demanding of the government than later applications of the more fully developed public forum doctrine. *See id.*

82 424 U.S. 828 (1976). To be sure, Justice Potter Stewart's majority opinion in *Greer* makes a passing reference to the concept of certain government property constituting a public forum. *Id.* at 836 ("The Court of Appeals was mistaken,

therefore, in thinking that the *Flower* case is to be understood as announcing a new principle of constitutional law, and mistaken specifically in thinking that *Flower* stands for the principle that whenever members of the public are permitted freely to visit a place owned or operated by the Government, then that place becomes a 'public forum' for purposes of the First Amendment. Such a principle of constitutional law has never existed, and does not exist now."). Despite on offhand reference to government property as a public forum, Justice Stewart's opinion carefully weighs the government's asserted interests for prohibiting a partisan political rally from a suburban New Jersey army base – it does not simply declare the base to be a non-public forum and sustain the government's speech restrictions. *See id.* at 837–40. Thus, although *Greer* does feature the phrase "public forum," the case itself does not actually adopt a rigid, categorical approach to analyzing whether the government has an obligation to make property available for speech activity. *But see* Post, *supra* note 33, at 1739–43 (arguing that *Greer* laid the theoretical and doctrinal foundation for the development of the public forum doctrine). Professor Post suggests that "*Greer's* resurrection of the major premise of the *Davis* syllogism was decisive for the future development of public forum doctrine, although the Court made no effort constitutionally to explain or justify its use of the premise." *Id.* This is undoubtedly true – *Greer* does not proceed from a strong presumption that government property otherwise suitable for proposed speech activity must be made available to the would-be speakers. Even so, however, *Greer* demands far more by way of government justification than later cases, such as *Cornelius*, which requires nothing more than that speech regulations in non-public forums be "reasonable." Cornelius v. NAACP Legal Def. & Ed. Fund, Inc., 473 U.S. 788, 797, 800–01, 806–07 (1985).

83 383 U.S. 131, 141–43 (1966).
84 Cox v. Louisiana, 379 U.S. 559, 583 (1965) (Black, J., concurring in part and dissenting in part).
85 Flower v. United States, 407 U.S. 197 (1972).
86 *Id.* at 198.
87 *Id.* at 200 (Rehnquist, J., dissenting).
88 *See* Davis v. Commonwealth, 167 U.S. 43, 48 (1897).
89 Southeastern Promotions, Ltd. v. Conrad, 420 U.S. 546, 572 (1975) (Rehnquist, J., dissenting).
90 Perry Educ. Ass'n v. Perry Local Educators' Ass'n, 460 U.S. 37, 45–46 (1983).
91 *See* Christian Legal Society v. Martinez, 561 U.S. 661, 678–81 (2010).
92 *Perry Educ. Ass'n*, 460 U.S. at 45 n.7.
93 *Christian Legal Soc'y*, 561 U.S. at 678–79, 679 n.11.
94 *Perry Educ. Ass'n*, 460 U.S. at 39–40.
95 *See id.* at 47–48.
96 383 U.S. 131, 139–43 (1966).
97 *See Perry*, 460 U.S. at 60–62 (Brennan, J., dissenting).
98 *Id.* at 61–62.
99 *See id.* at 63–66.

100 *See* Cornelius v. NAACP Legal Def. & Ed. Fund, Inc., 473 U.S. 788, 800, 806 (1985).

101 United States v. Kokinda, 497 U.S. 720, 725, 729–30 (1990).

102 *See* Int'l Soc'y for Krishna Consciousness, Inc. v. Lee, 505 U.S. 672, 679–81 (1992).

103 *See* Hague v. C.I.O., 307 U.S. 496, 515–16 (1939).

104 *See Kokinda*, 497 U.S. at 724–25.

105 *Int'l Soc'y for Krishna Consciousness, Inc.*, 505 U.S. at 678.

106 *See* MAGARIAN, *supra* note 49, at 228–35 (discussing and critiquing a regime of "managed speech" that tends to entrench existing powerful voices and to marginalize the impact of dissenting speech by outsiders).

107 *See* Cornelius v. NAACP Legal Def. & Ed. Fund, Inc., 473 U.S. 788, 805 (1985) ("The Government did not create the CFC [Combined Federal Campaign] for purposes of providing a forum for expressive activity. That such activity occurs in the context of the forum created does not imply that the forum thereby becomes a public forum for First Amendment purposes.").

108 *See Int'l Soc'y for Krishna Consciousness, Inc.*, 505 U.S. at 680 (observing that "the tradition of airport activity does not demonstrate that airports have historically been made available for speech activity. Nor can we say that these particular terminals, or airport terminals generally, have been intentionally opened to such activity").

109 *See* Ward v. Rock Against Racism, 491 U.S. 781, 790–91 (1989).

110 *Id.* at 791 ("A regulation that serves purposes unrelated to the content of expression is deemed neutral, even if it has an incidental effect on some speakers or messages but not others.").

111 *Id.* (internal citations omitted).

112 Hill v. Colorado, 530 U.S. 703, 719–20, 725–30 (2000). The *Hill* majority bizarrely claimed that a speech ban near abortion clinics was "not a regulation of speech" but instead "a regulation of the places where some speech may occur." *Id.* at 719. Similarly, in *Turner Broadcasting System, Inc. v. FCC*, the Supreme Court ignored a clear congressional purpose to help propagate particular kinds of programming – namely local programming, educational programming, and news and public affairs programming – over other kinds of content and used local television stations as a de facto proxy for entities that will create and distribute programming of the sort that Congress favored. *See* Turner Broad. Sys., Inc. v. FCC, 512 U.S. 622, 644–48 (1994). *But cf. id.* at 677–78 (O'Connor, J., concurring in part and dissenting in part) (arguing that the preference for locally-based, educational, and news and public affairs programming constituted a government preference for this kind of content and rendered the must carry provisions of the Cable Act content-based regulations of speech).

113 KROTOSZYNSKI, *supra* note 65, at 27–28.

114 *See id.* at 27–39.

115 *Id.* at 31.

116 MAGARIAN, *supra* note 49, at 235–39, 252–53.

117 *See* POST, *supra* note 49, at 237–47 (discussing the dangers of First Amendment jurisprudence undermining the government's ability to attain legitimate, managerial goals).

118 Forsyth County v. Nationalist Movement, 505 U.S. 123, 133–36 (1992). Writing for the *Forsyth County* majority, Justice Harry Blackmun observed that "[t]his Court has held time and again: Regulations which permit the Government to discriminate on the basis of the content of the message cannot be tolerated under the First Amendment." *Id.* at 135 (internal quotations and citations omitted).

119 Ward v. Rock Against Racism, 491 U.S. 781, 791 (1989).

120 167 U.S. 43, 48 (1897).

121 *See supra* text and accompanying notes 100 to 116.

122 *See* United States v. Kistner, 68 F.3d 218, 221–22 (8th Cir. 1995).

123 *See supra* text and accompanying notes 50 to 69.

124 Cox v. Louisiana, 379 U.S. 536 (1965) *and* Cox v. Louisiana, 379 U.S. 559 (1965).

125 *Cox*, 379 U.S. at 562, 569–70, 574–75.

126 *See* Flower v. United States, 407 U.S. 197, 197–98 (1972).

127 Greer v. Spock, 424 U.S. 828, 836 (1976).

128 *See supra* text and accompanying notes 79 to 88.

129 Pell v. Procunier, 417 U.S. 817, 822 (1974).

130 *See* Williams v. Wallace, 240 F. Supp. 100, 109 (M.D. Ala. 1965).

131 *See id.* at 106–12.

132 *But cf.* Oberwetter v. Hilliard, 639 F.3d 545, 552–54 (D.C. Cir. 2011) (upholding a government ban on protest within the interior of the Jefferson Memorial because it does not constitute a "public forum" and the National Park Service's regulations were content and viewpoint neutral and otherwise "reasonable").

133 Dr. King gave his iconic *I Have a Dream* speech at the mass outdoor rally on the National Mall – a rally that served as the capstone for this event and which constituted a pivotal moment in the nation's long struggle to secure basic civil rights and equal citizenship for all. *See* OFFICIAL PROGRAM FOR THE MARCH ON WASHINGTON (1963), www.ourdocuments.gov/doc.php?flash=true&doc=96 (last visited Oct. 10, 2017); *see also* Martin Luther King, Jr., I Have a Dream Address at the Lincoln Memorial (Aug. 28, 1963), *reprinted in* A TESTAMENT OF HOPE: THE ESSENTIAL WRITINGS OF MARTIN LUTHER KING, JR. 217, 217–20 (James M. Washington ed., 1986).

134 *See* Cox v. Louisiana, 379 U.S. 559, 568–75 (1965).

135 *See* United States v. Kokinda, 497 U.S. 720, 726–27, 737 (1990).

136 *Compare* City of Ladue v. Gilleo, 512 U.S. 43, 54–55 (1994) (invalidating a ban on the placement of lawn signs on private residential property bearing political or ideological messages) *with Kokinda*, 497 U.S. at 727–30 (upholding a postal service regulation banning leafletting on postal service property).

137 Perry Education Ass'n v. Perry Local Educators Ass'n, 460 U.S. 37, 45–46 (1983).

138 Int'l Soc'y for Krishna Consciousness, Inc. v. Lee, 505 U.S. 672, 678–79 (1992) (holding that airport concourses do not constitute public forums and, accordingly, that government may adopt and apply any reasonable restrictions on speech activity on airport grounds).

139 *See* Brown v. Louisiana, 383 U.S. 131, 141–42 (1966).

140 *See, e.g.*, Hess v. Indiana, 414 U.S. 105, 108–09 (1973) (per curiam); Terminiello v. Chicago, 337 U.S. 1, 4–5 (1949).

141 *Terminiello*, 337 U.S. at 4 (observing that "a function of free speech under our system of government is to invite dispute" and holding that although its exercise may cause "a condition of unrest" or "stir[ ] people to anger," under the First Amendment speech "is nevertheless protected against censorship or punishment, unless shown likely to produce a clear and present danger of a serious substantive evil that rises far above public inconvenience, annoyance, or unrest").

142 *See* Gey, *supra* note 36, at 1573–78.

143 Williams v. Wallace, 240 F. Supp. 100, 109 (M.D. Ala. 1965).

144 Forsyth Cty. v. Nationalist Movement, 505 U.S. 123, 134–36 (1992).

145 *See Terminiello*, 337 U.S. at 4–6; *see also* Forsyth County v. Nationalist Movement, 505 U.S. 123, 133–36 (1992); Gregory v. City of Chicago, 394 U.S. 111, (1969); *see generally* Note, *Freedom of Speech and Assembly: The Problem of the Hostile Audience*, 49 COLUM. L. REV. 1118, 1118, 1122–23 (1949) (describing, discussing, and analyzing the then "relatively neglected" problem of permitting a hostile audience's reaction to serve as a basis for silencing speech and proposing that speech should not be proscribed if it is otherwise "independently lawful").

146 *See* Grayned v. City of Rockford, 408 U.S. 104, 116–17 (1972) (using a functional approach focused on "the nature of a place" to determine whether it may be used for public protest activity). Justice Marshall emphasized that "[t]he crucial question is whether the manner of expression is basically incompatible with the normal activity of a particular place at a particular time." *Id.* at 116.

147 *See* Gey, *supra* note 36, at 1566–76 (advocating the imposition of strict rules of necessity for government denials of access to public property for speech activity and also a more critical approach to evaluating time, place, and manner restrictions in public spaces otherwise suitable for First Amendment activities).

148 *See Grayned*, 408 U.S. at 116–17. It also bears noting that Justice Kennedy has argued strongly in favor of using a functional approach to public forum analysis rather than a rigid historical approach. *See* Int'l Soc'y for Krishna Consciousness, Inc. v. Lee, 505 U.S. 672, 693–94 (1992) (Kennedy, J., concurring) ("[o]ur public forum doctrine ought not to be a jurisprudence of categories rather than ideas or convert what was once an analysis protective of expression into one which grants the government authority to restrict speech by fiat"). Kennedy posited that "the Court's public forum analysis in these cases is inconsistent with the values underlying the Speech and Press Clauses of the First Amendment." *Id.* at 694. He objected that the majority's approach "leaves the government with almost unlimited authority to restrict speech on its

property by doing nothing more than articulating a non-speech-related purpose for the area, and it leaves almost no scope for the development of new public forums absent the rare approval of the government." *Id.* at 695. In his view, the determination of whether government property constitutes a public forum "must be an objective one, based on the actual, physical characteristics and uses of the property." *Id.* Thus, Justice Kennedy's approach would consider the actual day-to-day uses of government property rather than the label that government attaches to particular property. Applying this approach, he concluded that an airport concourse constitutes a public forum. *See id.* at 697–703. Justice Kennedy's approach is consistent with the approach of the Warren and Burger Courts in cases like *Brown*, *Pell*, and *Greer*. *But cf.* Gey, *supra* note 36, at 1536–38, 1566–71 (acknowledging that Justice Kennedy's approach would appropriately shift the burden of justification for denials of access to public property for speech activity from would-be speakers to the government, but positing that Justice Kennedy's approach still vests too much unfettered discretion with government officials to squelch speech activity on public property).

149 *See* Gey, *supra* note 36, at 1566–76, 1634.

150 *But cf.* Hodge v. Talkin, 799 F.3d 1145, 1157–62 (D.C. Cir. 2015) (declaring a large plaza in front of the US Supreme Court a "non-public forum" and sustaining, against a First Amendment challenge, a federal law banning all First Amendment activity within the plaza).

151 *But see id.* at 1160–62 (holding constitutionally irrelevant the Supreme Court's tolerance of expressive activity on the plaza by lawyers and litigants presenting oral arguments to the Supreme Court, in addition to selective enforcement of the ban with respect to some protests by non-litigants because the Supreme Court's approach to doling out access to a non-public forum need only be "reasonable" and these practices of limited use were not self-evidently unreasonable).

152 *Cf.* Davis v. Commonwealth of Massachusetts, 167 U.S. 43, 46–47 (1897) (upholding a ban on protest activity within the Boston Common, even though the property was generally open to members of the public).

153 *See* Ashutosh Bhagwat, *Producing Speech*, 56 Wm. & Mary L. Rev. 1029, 1061–64 (2015) (discussing the reasons for applying strict scrutiny to content-based speech regulations, noting that "content-based laws are of greater constitutional concern than content-neutral laws," and explaining that "strict scrutiny generally applies to content-based laws because the Court is highly suspicious of the proposition that particular messages can cause social harm"). Professor Bhagwat argues that even when a valid regulatory interest seems to justify a content-based speech regulation, such as Los Angeles County, California's ban on the production of so-called bareback pornography, *see id.* at 1044–46, 1070–72, courts should still be skeptical about the government and its actual motives for seeking to suppress speech. *See id.* at 1064 (arguing that even under intermediate scrutiny review of regulations that burden speech "it is important that such scrutiny not be excessively deferential to the government,"

with careful consideration of whether "the effect of the law is to completely eliminate particular content, as opposed to merely limit its creation").

154 *Compare* U.S. Railroad Retirement Bd. v. Fritz, 449 U.S. 166, 179 (1980) (declining to assess Congress's real purposes in enacting a statute when the statute's language bears a clear plain meaning because of the difficulties in ascertaining legislative purpose and explaining that "we have historically assumed that Congress intended what it enacted") and Palmer v. Thompson, 403 U.S. 217, 224–26 (1971) (claiming, contrary to well-established case law, that "no case in this Court has held that a legislative act may violate equal protection solely because of the motivations of the men who voted for it" and arguing that "there is an element of futility in a judicial attempt to invalidate a law because of the bad motives of its supporters") *with* Church of the Lukumi Babalu Aye, Inc. v. City of Hialeah, 508 U.S. 520, 534, 540–41 (1993) (explaining that "facial neutrality is not determinative" of a law's constitutionality and holding that a reviewing court must consider "among other things, the historical background of the decision under challenge, the specific series of events leading to the enactment or official policy in question, and the legislative or administrative history, including contemporaneous statements made by members of the decisionmaking body") and Hunter v. Underwood, 471 U.S. 222, 228–32 (1985) (invalidating a facially race-neutral 1901 Alabama state constitutional provision that stripped certain felons of their voting rights because "zeal for white supremacy ran rampant at the convention" that enacted the provision and this improper discriminatory motive rendered the provision inconsistent with the Equal Protection Clause).

155 *See generally* Timothy Zick, Speech Out of Doors: Preserving First Amendment Liberties in Public Places (2008).

156 Brown v. Louisiana, 383 U.S. 131, 141–43 (1966).

157 *See id.* at 142–43.

158 240 F. Supp. 100 (M.D. Ala. 1865).

159 *See* Krotoszynski, *supra* note 65, at 185–207.

160 *Id.* at 200 (noting that "[t]he proportionality principle permits courts to make rational distinctions between proposed uses of public forums for speech activities," explaining that this principle "permits most groups to be relegated to less busy corridors but holds out the possibility of using major highways and byways under sufficiently compelling circumstances," and positing that it "permits courts to match venues for speech activities with the speaker's need to speak and the community's need to hear").

161 *Williams,* 240 F. Supp. at 107–09.

162 *See id.* at 107–11.

163 Krotoszynski, *supra* note 65, at 186; *see* Ronald J. Krotoszynski, Jr., *Celebrating Selma: The Importance of Context in Public Forum Analysis,* 104 Yale L.J. 1411, 1414 (1995) (noting that "[a]lthough the specific circumstances that led Judge Johnson to embrace the proportionality principle in 1965 are, thankfully, long gone, the problem of ensuring that adequate public space is available to accommodate meaningful social protest remains" and suggesting

that "[p]roperly understood and carefully limited, the proportionality principle can continue to help vindicate democratic values today, just as it did … in Selma").

164 *See* Rosenberger v. Rector & Visitors of the Univ. of Va., 515 U.S. 819, 829 (1995).

165 *See* Christian Legal Soc'y v. Martinez, 561 U.S. 661, 679, 685 (2010); *Rosenberger*, 515 U.S. at 829.

166 *Compare* Snyder v. Phelps, 562 U.S. 443, 452–53 (2011) (holding that "speech on public issues occupies the highest rung of the hierarchy of First Amendment values, and is entitled to special protection"); *and* Citizens United v. Fed. Elec. Comm'n, 558 U.S. 310, 339 (2010) (opining that "[t]he First Amendment has its fullest and most urgent application to speech uttered during a campaign for political office") (internal quotations omitted) *with* Central Hudson Gas & Elec. Corp. v. Pub. Serv. Comm'n, 447 U.S. 557, 562–63 (1980) (noting that multiple precedents "have recognized the commonsense distinction between speech proposing a commercial transaction, which occurs in an area traditionally subject to government regulation, and other varieties of speech" and holding that such speech is "therefore accord[ed] a lesser protection … than other constitutionally guaranteed expression") (internal quotations omitted); Miller v. California, 413 U.S. 15, 23–24 (1973) (observing that "the First and Fourteenth Amendments have never been treated as absolutes" and upholding the constitutional power of the state and federal governments to regulate, or even proscribe, obscene speech).

167 *See, e.g.,* Jordan v. Jewel Food Stores, Inc., 743 F.3d 509, 513–15 (7th Cir. 2014).

168 *See id.* at 517–20, 522.

169 *See* Vincent A. Blasi, *The Pathological Perspective and the First Amendment*, 85 COLUM. L. REV. 449, 452–56 (1985) (arguing that the federal courts should seek to protect jealously the central "core" of the First Amendment to ensure that it functions effectively as a check on the suppression of dissent – and dissenters – in times of national crisis); William W. Van Alstyne, *Remembering Melville Nimmer: Some Cautionary Notes on Commercial Speech*, 43 UCLA L. REV. 1635, 1640–43, 1646–48 (1996) (arguing that First Amendment doctrine can and should be nimble enough to draw meaningful distinctions between different kinds of speech and to afford political speech related to the process of democratic self-government a higher measure of constitutional protection than other kinds of speech). Both Professors Blasi and Van Alstyne argue that courts can and should use content-based metrics to afford some speech differential, favorable treatment because the speech relates to the central purposes of the First Amendment. I do not mean to minimize the real risks associated with judicial discretion and the protection of unpopular speakers and speech. Even so, however, if one posits that existing access to public spaces for expressive activity would remain in place, the risks associated with providing enhanced access to public property in some instances should be manageable. Moreover, as previously noted, see *supra* text and accompanying notes 64 to 69, existing First Amendment doctrine, particularly the limited purpose public

forum doctrine, already relies on speaker- and content-based metrics – but does not seem to cause federal courts serious difficulties with implementation.

170 Fiss, *supra* note 5, at 1408.

171 *See* Police Dep't of the City of Chicago v. Mosley, 408 U.S. 92, 95–96 (1972).

172 *See* Martin v. City of Struthers, 319 U.S. 141, 143–45 (1943); Schneider v. State, 308 U.S. 147, 162 (1939).

173 *See, e.g.*, Gerald Korngold, *Land Use Regulation as a Framework to Create Public Space for Speech and Expression in the Evolving and Reconceptualized Shopping Mall of the Twenty-First Century*, 68 CASE W. RES. L. REV. 429, 464–65 (2017) (positing several reasons for why live, in-person protest activity still matters in the age of Facebook, Twitter, YouTube, and Instagram, including the immediacy of in-person dialogue, the higher credibility of attributed speech relative to anonymous speech on the web and, perhaps most important, the ability to reach a particular audience with a particular message).

174 Timothy Zick, *Property, Place, and Public Discourse*, 21 WASH. U. J. L. & POL'Y 173, 204 (2006).

175 *See* CASS R. SUNSTEIN, REPUBLIC.COM 7, 51–86 (2001) (noting that the proliferation of information on the internet has led users to find sources that tend to confirm a person's existing views and biases – rather than challenge them).

176 Zick, *supra* note 174, at 205.

177 *Id.* at 205–06.

178 *See id.* at 206–07.

179 *Id.* at 207.

180 Zick, *Expressive Topography*, *supra* note 15, at 504 (emphasis in the original).

181 Zick, *Speech and Spatial Tactics*, *supra* note 15, at 647.

182 *Id.* at 648.

183 *Id.* (emphasis in the original).

184 *Id.* at 650.

185 530 U.S. 703 (2000).

186 *See id.* at 719–20. The *Hill* majority went so far as to claim that a ban on protest outside abortion clinics was not even a regulation of "speech" but merely of "conduct." *Id.* at 719 ("Rather, it is a regulation of the places where some speech may occur."). This approach has the effect of rendering any and all TPM regulations content neutral because they too only seek to regulate "the places where some speech may occur."

187 *See* Hunter v. Underwood, 471 U.S. 222, 228–32 (1985).

188 *See* Church of the Lukumi Babalu Aye, Inc. v. City of Hialeah, 508 U.S. 520, 534, 540–41 (1993).

189 *See* KROTOSZYNSKI, *supra* note 65, at 28–30.

190 *See id.* at 31–50 (discussing the many cases in which the lower federal courts have reflexively credited the government's claim that draconian limits on public protest were necessary for reasons of public safety and security); *see also* Citizens for Peace in Space v. City of Colorado Springs, 477 F.3d 1212, 1217–21 (10th Cir. 2007).

191 *Citizens for Peace in Space*, 477 F.3d at 1221 ("While an extremely important government interest does not dictate the result in time, place, and manner cases, the significance of the government interest bears an inverse relationship to the rigor of the narrowly tailored analysis").

192 *See id.* at 1217–20.

193 *See* Bl(a)ck Tea Soc'y v. City of Boston, 378 F.3d 8, 10, 13–14 (1st Cir. 2004).

194 KROTOSZYNSKI, *supra* note 65, at 34 ("The key doctrinal point here is that the Free Speech and Free Assembly Clauses apparently do not afford *any* protection to a would-be speaker's interest in speaking to a particular audience in real time, even if he seeks to do so by utilizing a classic traditional public forum, such as a street, sidewalk, or park."); *see* Enrique Armijo, *The "Ample Alternative Channels" Flaw in First Amendment Doctrine*, 73 WASH. & LEE L. REV. 1657 (2016).

195 *See supra* text and accompanying notes 164 to 172.

196 For a relevant discussion of the "managerial First Amendment" and access to public property for speech activity, see MAGARIAN, *supra* note 49, at 227–53.

197 *See* Int'l Soc'y for Krishna Consciousness, Inc. v. Lee, 505 U.S. 672, 693–96, 701–03 (1992) (Kennedy, J., concurring) (rejecting a categorical, historical approach to analyzing whether government property constitutes a public forum and proposing instead an open-ended, contextual, functional approach that would consider the actual day-to-day uses of particular property); *see also* Gey, *supra* note 36, at 1576, 1634 (arguing for a functional approach to making public property available for speech activity and advocating a stricter approach to scrutinizing time, place, and manner regulations as well).

198 *See supra* note 2.

199 *See* ARISTOTLE, THE NICOMACHEAN ETHICS 42–53, paras. 1106a5–1109b (Terence Irwin trans., Hackett Publishing Co. 1985); *see also* Dan M. Kahan & Martha C. Nussbaum, *Two Conceptions of Emotion in Criminal Law*, 96 COLUM. L. REV. 269, 286–88 (1996) (discussing the Aristotelian notion of the virtuous mean that lies between problematic extreme forms of behavior that reflect either a surfeit or a shortage of a particular character trait).

3 THE FIRST AMENDMENT AS A SOURCE OF POSITIVE RIGHTS

1 *See, e.g.*, Brown v. Louisiana, 383 U.S. 131 (1966). Chapter 2, *supra*, discusses in some detail the Warren Court's practical, functional approach to mandating access to government-owned property for First Amendment activities, which was considerably more generous than the current, rather speech-hostile, rules governing such access under the public forum and time, place, and manner doctrines.

2 *See* Amalgamated Food Employees Union Local 590 v. Logan Valley Plaza, Inc., 391 U.S. 308 (1968) (holding that the owner of a private shopping mall complex generally open to the public had to permit the exercise of First Amendment activities on its property).

3 Hague v. Comm. for Indus. Org., 307 U.S. 496, 515–16 (1939) (holding that a city government could not ban expressive activity from a city park – or any other public property traditionally used for public protest).

4 *See* Louis Michael Seidman, *The* Dale *Problem: Property and Speech under the Regulatory State*, 75 U. CHI. L. REV. 1541, 1563–67 (2008).

5 *Logan Valley Plaza, Inc.*, 391 U.S. at 317–20. *But see* RICHARD A. EPSTEIN, TAKINGS: PRIVATE PROPERTY AND THE POWER OF EMINENT DOMAIN 64–66 (1985) (arguing that private property owners should enjoy the legal authority to decide whether and how third parties may access their real property, regardless of the precise reason for which a private third party seeks access to privately owned land); Richard A. Epstein, *Takings, Exclusivity and Speech: The Legacy of* PruneYard v Robins, 64 U. CHI. L. REV. 21, 35–36 (1997) (objecting to judicially-created free speech easements to private property and positing that cases like *Logan Valley* and *PruneYard* "strip[ ] away the exclusive right of use and convert[ ] a private shopping center into a limited commons") [hereinafter Epstein, *Takings, Exclusivity and Speech*].

6 391 U.S. 308 (1968).

7 PruneYard Shopping Center v. Robins, 447 U.S. 74 (1980).

8 In fact, in the context of the National Labor Relations Act (NLRA), the Rehnquist Court went out of its way to reject a statutory right of access to private property for union-related speech activity by non-employees. *See* Lechmere, Inc. v. NLRB, 502 U.S. 527 (1992). However, the Supreme Court held two years later that if state or local law created a right of access to an employers' property, neither the First Amendment nor the NLRA prevented the enforcement of a positive statutory right of access for union organizing activities. *See* Thunder Basin Coal Co. v. Reich, 510 U.S. 200, 217 n.21 (1994) ("The right of employers to exclude union organizers from their private property emanates from state common law, and while this right is not superseded by the NLRA, nothing in the NLRA protects it.").

9 *See supra* Chapter 2; *see also* GREGORY P. MAGARIAN, MANAGED SPEECH: THE ROBERTS COURT'S FIRST AMENDMENT 91–94 (2017) (arguing that the Roberts Court's public forum decisions "largely apply the tenets of managed speech," meaning that they reflect great deference to the government's claims of managerial necessity over its property); ROBERT C. POST, CONSTITUTIONAL DOMAINS: DEMOCRACY, COMMUNITY, MANAGEMENT 12–17, 199–267 (1995) (noting that a legitimate "managerial domain" exists and that government must be free to use its resources to achieve programmatic objectives, but cautioning against undue or reflexive judicial deference to claims of managerial necessity when government attempts to leverage its ownership to stifle dissenting voices).

10 MAGARIAN, *supra* note 9, at 94.

11 *See* Brentwood Academy v. Tennessee Secondary School Athletic Association, 531 U.S. 288 (2001); *see also* Ronald J. Krotoszynski, Jr., *Back to the Briarpatch: An Argument in Favor of Constitutional Meta-Analysis in State Action Determinations*, 94 MICH. L. REV. 302 (1995).

12 *But cf.* Jack Balkin, *Free Speech Is a Triangle*, 118 COLUM. L. REV. 2011, 2025 (2018). ("Nevertheless, the best alternative to this autocracy [by privately owned social media and search engine companies] is not the imposition of First Amendment doctrines by analogy to the public forum or the company town."). Professor Balkin posits that self-regulation, coupled with regulatory programs to create a more diverse and competitive social media universe and the creation of mandatory "due process" rights for users (adopted presumably through positive law or administrative regulation) would constitute better solutions than applying the First Amendment to dominant social media platforms and search engine providers. *See id.* at 2033–36, 2040–47, 2054–57. I address these arguments in some detail in Part III. The short version: We can obtain better, faster results if the federal judiciary applies a less strict version of the First Amendment to these entities – a "junior varsity" First Amendment of the sort that Justice Thurgood Marshall proposed for the owners of shopping centers in *Logan Valley. See* Amalgamated Food Employees Union Local 590 v. Logan Valley Plaza, Inc., 391 U.S. 308, 318–25 (1968). The real issue here is permitting private companies to exercise an unlimited power to corner the political marketplace of ideas in circumstances where no effective alternative forums exist for citizens to use in lieu of the private space (whether a physical or virtual space). *See infra* text and accompanying notes 157 to 191.

13 326 U.S. 501 (1946); *see also* Evans v. Newton, 382 U.S. 296, 301 (1966) (holding that a privately owned park that functioned for all intents and purposes as a public park could not constitutionally be operated on a racially segregated basis because it was "municipal in nature").

14 345 U.S. 461, 468–69 (1953) (imposing Equal Protection Clause and Fifteenth Amendment obligations on an ostensibly private political organization because "[t]he only election that has counted in this Texas county for more than fifty years" was conducted among the members of the "private" organization).

15 Seidman, *supra* note 4, at 1565.

16 *Id.*

17 *Logan Valley Plaza, Inc.*, 391 U.S. at 319–21.

18 *See* Pickering v. Board of Educ., 391 U.S. 563, 568–72 (1968).

19 Tinker v. Des Moines Indep. Cmty. Sch. Dist., 393 U.S. 503, 506–07 (1969).

20 Brown v. Louisiana, 383 U.S. 131 (1966).

21 Lamont v. Postmaster General, 381 U.S. 301, 306–07 (1965).

22 *See* ALEXANDER MEIKLEJOHN, FREE SPEECH AND ITS RELATION TO SELF-GOVERNMENT 24–27, 88–91 (1948).

23 *Id.* at 25.

24 *See id.* at 25–27; *see also* ROBERT C. POST, CITIZENS DIVIDED: CAMPAIGN FINANCE REFORM AND THE CONSTITUTION 73–74 (2014) (arguing that we should value freedom of expression because democratic deliberation is essential to maintaining an electoral process that conveys meaningful legitimacy on the government and its institutions).

25 MEIKLEJOHN, *supra* note 22, at 27.

26 *See* Loren F. Selznick & Carolyn LaMacchia, *#Mall Ruckus Tonight: Should Mall Owners Be Forced to Provide a Stage for Expression in the Virtual Age?*, 53 Willamette L. Rev. 239, 267–69 (2017) (arguing that "[t]he novelty of the shopping mall experience has worn off and mall purchases are gradually being replaced by more convenient e-commerce purchases" and positing that "[t]he idea that malls are the new town square is a late-twentieth century notion contrary to more recent experience").

27 *Id.* at 269–70.

28 *Id.* at 274.

29 *See id.* at 274 n.184.

30 For example, a growing number of conservative voters believe that both social media companies and search engine providers routinely discriminate against them and their content. *See* Cecelia Kang & Sheera Frenkel, *Republicans Accuse Twitter of Exhibiting Bias*, N.Y. Times, Sept. 6, 2018, at A1; Dustin Volz, Deepa Seetharaman & John D. McKinnon, *Sessions Vows to Examine 'Stifling' by Social Media*, Wall St. J., Sept. 6, 2018, at A1, A6. Conservative provocateur Alex Jones claims that "[t]hey [Facebook and Google] are outright banning people and they are blocking conservatives involved in their own First Amendment political speech." Kang & Frenkel, *supra*, at A15.

31 Owen M. Fiss, The Irony of Free Speech (1996); Owen M. Fiss, Liberalism Divided: Freedom of Speech and the Many Uses of State Power (1996); Owen M. Fiss, *Free Speech and Social Structure*, 71 Iowa L. Rev. 1405, 1415–17 (1986) [hereinafter Fiss, *Free Speech and Social Structure*].

32 *See* Jerome A Barron, Freedom of the Press for Whom?: The Right of Access to Mass Media (1973); Jerome A. Barron, *Access to the Press: A New First Amendment Right*, 80 Harv. L. Rev. 1641 (1967).

33 Fiss, *Free Speech and Social Structure*, *supra* note 31, at 1416.

34 Cass R. Sunstein, Republic.com 51–86 (2001).

35 Cass R. Sunstein, Democracy and the Problem of Free Speech xvi–xx, 21–23, 34–46 (1993).

36 *Id.* at 21.

37 *Id.*

38 *Id.*

39 *Id.* at 22.

40 *See* Hudgens v. Nat'l Labor Rel. Bd., 424 U.S. 507, 543 (1976) (Marshall, J., dissenting) ("As far as these groups are concerned, the shopping center owner has assumed the traditional role of the state in its control of historical First Amendment forums. *Lloyd* and *Logan Valley* recognized the vital role the First Amendment has to play in such cases, and I believe that this court errs when it holds otherwise.").

41 *Id.* at 539.

42 *See* Terry v. Adams, 345 U.S. 461 (1953); Smith v. Allwright, 321 U.S. 649 (1944).

43 *See infra* text and accompanying notes 175 to 191.

44 *See generally* Stephen G. Gey, *Reopening the Public Forum – From Sidewalks to Cyberspace*, 58 Ohio St. L.J. 1535, 1611 (1998) ("It does not require much creativity to characterize the Internet as a public forum. … Indeed, it is not unreasonable to suggest that the *Reno* majority opinion itself treats the Internet as a public forum without actually making the designation explicit."). Of course, it is now clear that simply limiting the *government's* power to censor content distributed over the internet will not be sufficient to ensure that information and ideas can flow freely. When privately owned social media platforms, such as Facebook and Twitter, claim an unlimited power to censor content, via their terms of service policies, the problem of censorship simply gets shifted from the government to the companies that control these critical spaces for democratic deliberation. Even if the internet is free of government-imposed content- and viewpoint-based censorship, the problem of pervasive and unlimited *private* censorship of content remains.

45 *See* Terry v. Adams, 345 U.S. 461, 468–70 (1953).

46 *See* Gerald Korngold, *Land Use Regulation as a Framework to Create Public Space for Speech and Expression in the Evolving and Reconceptualized Shopping Mall of the Twenty-First Century*, 68 Case W. Res. L. Rev. 429, 460–62 (2017) (discussing the emergence of large-scale shopping malls as "commercial and social focal points"). *But cf.* Selznick & LaMacchia, *supra* note 26, at 245–50, 267–69 (discussing the rise and subsequent decline of shopping malls as "the new town square" and noting that "[t]he novelty of the shopping mall experience has worn off and small purchases are gradually being replaced by more convenient e-commerce purchases").

47 326 U.S. 501 (1946).

48 PruneYard Shopping Center v. Robins, 447 U.S. 74 (1980).

49 *Marsh*, 326 U.S. at 502–03.

50 *Id.* at 503–04.

51 *Id.* at 504.

52 *See id.* at 510–511, 517. Justice Robert H. Jackson did not participate in the *Marsh* decision. *Id.* at 510.

53 *Id.* at 504.

54 *Marsh*, 326 U.S. at 505.

55 *Id.* at 506.

56 *Id.* at 507.

57 *Id.* at 508–09.

58 *See* Meiklejohn, *supra* note 22, at 25–27, 89–91; *see also* Post, *supra* note 24, at 68–74 (arguing that elections can serve as an effective means of legitimating government institutions only if the process of democratic deliberation is free, open, and unfettered).

59 Post, *supra* note 24, at 73.

60 *Id.*

61 *Marsh*, 326 U.S. at 509.

62 *Id.* at 516 (Reed, J., dissenting).

63 *See id.* at 516–17.

64 Amalgamated Food Employees Union Local 590 v. Logan Valley Plaza, Inc., 391 U.S. 308, 310 (1968).

65 *Id.* at 310–11.

66 *Id.* at 311–12.

67 *See* Logan Valley Plaza, Inc. v. Amalgamated Food Employees Union Local 590, 227 A.2d 874 (Pa. 1967), *rev'd*, 391 U.S. 308 (1968).

68 *Id.* at 876–77.

69 *Id.* at 877.

70 *Id.* at 878.

71 *Logan Valley Plaza, Inc.*, 277 A.2d at 879 (Cohen, J., dissenting).

72 *Id.*

73 *Id.*

74 *Logan Valley Plaza, Inc.*, 391 U.S. at 313.

75 *Id.* at 317.

76 *Id.* at 319.

77 *See id.* at 319–25.

78 *Id.* at 325.

79 *See id.* at 324.

80 *Id.* at 319.

81 *Id.* at 319–20.

82 *Logan Valley Plaza, Inc.*, 391 U.S. at 320.

83 *Id.* at 320–21.

84 *See id.* at 324 ("However, unlike a situation involving a person's home, no meaningful claim to protection of a right of privacy can be advanced by respondents here."); *id.* at 325 (describing the Logan Valley Mall as "the functional equivalent of a 'business block'" or town square). The Supreme Court has held that protecting residential privacy in the home constitutes a compelling government interest sufficient to justify substantial limitations on freedom of expression – for example, a flat ban on maintaining a fixed picket of a private residence is consistent with the First Amendment. *See* Frisby v. Schultz, 487 U.S. 474, 484–86 (1988). Writing for the *Frisby* majority, Justice Sandra Day O'Connor described with abject horror "[t]he devastating effect of targeted picketing on the quiet enjoyment of the home" and observed that "[t]he type of picketers banned by the Brookfield ordinance generally do not seek to disseminate a message to the general public, but to intrude upon the targeted resident, and to do so in an especially offensive way."

85 *Logan Valley Plaza, Inc.*, 391 U.S. at 331 (Black, J., dissenting).

86 *Id.*

87 *Id.*

88 *See id.* at 332.

89 *Id.*

90 *Id.* at 333.

91 *Logan Valley Plaza, Inc.*, 391 U.S. 320 n.8.

92 Professor Richard Epstein is a particularly vociferous critic of the concept of uncompensated, mandatory, third party access to private property for speech

activity. See Epstein, *supra* note 5, at 65–66 (questioning the constitutional legitimacy of free speech easements to private property and characterizing such First Amendment easements as a kind of regulatory taking); Epstein, *Takings, Exclusivity and Speech, supra* note 5, at 56 (arguing that the Takings Clause requires compensation to be paid to land owners "[w]hen government forces the holders of private property to surrender their right to exclude," for whatever reasons, and positing that in forced access cases like *PruneYard* and *Logan Valley* "these principles were neglected").

93 407 U.S. 551 (1972).

94 *See* Amalgamated Food Employees Union Local 590 v. Logan Valley Plaza, Inc., 391 U.S. 308, 320 n.9 (1968) ("We are, therefore, not called upon to consider whether respondents' property rights could, consistently with the First Amendment, justify a bar on picketing which was not thus directly related to its purpose to the use to which the shopping center property was being put.").

95 *See Lloyd Corp.*, 407 U.S. at 564 ("The handbilling by respondents in the malls of Lloyd Center had no relation to any purpose for which the center was built and being used.").

96 *Id.* at 553–54, 556.

97 *Id.* at 556–67.

98 Tanner v. Lloyd Corp., 308 F. Supp. 128, 131–33 (D. Or. 1970), *aff'd*, 446 F.2d 545 (9th Cir. 1971), *rev'd*, 407 U.S. 551 (1972).

99 Lloyd Corp. v. Tanner, 446 F.2d. 545, 545 (9th Cir. 1971), *rev'd*, 407 U.S. 551 (1972). The Ninth Circuit affirmed in a brief, one paragraph, per curiam opinion. *See id.* (holding that "the judgment is affirmed upon the basis of the District Court's Findings of Fact and the reasoning logically followed therefrom, set forth in the court's Opinion").

100 *Lloyd Corp.*, 407 U.S. at 566.

101 *Id.* at 567 (emphasis in the original).

102 *Id.* at 569.

103 *Id.*

104 Marsh v. Alabama, 307 U.S. 501, 507–09 (1946).

105 Cleveland Bd. of Educ. v. Loudermill, 470 U.S. 532 (1985); Perry v. Sindermann, 408 U.S. 593 (1972); Roth v. Bd. of Regents, 408 U.S. 564 (1972).

106 *But cf. Marsh*, 307 U.S. at 504–10 (failing to suggest that the Gulf Shipbuilding Company had an obligation to respect constitutional rights other than those protected under the First Amendment). Under current constitutional standards, a state actor may not use gender classifications either to impose burdens or withhold benefits absent an "exceedingly persuasive justification," which requires the government to show that its use of a gender-based classification bears a substantial relationship to an important government interest. United States v. Virginia, 518 U.S. 515, 524, 531–34, 545–46 (1996); Mississippi Univ. for Women v. Hogan, 458 U.S. 718, 724–25, 731 (1982).

107 *Lloyd Corp.*, 407 U.S. at 569.

108 *Id.* at 551 (Marshall, J., dissenting).

109 *Id.* at 576.

110 *Id.* at 578.

111 *See id.* ("If the property of Lloyd Center is generally open to First Amendment activity, respondents cannot be excluded.").

112 *Id.* at 580.

113 *Lloyd Corp.*, 407 U.S. at 580 (Marshall, J., dissenting).

114 *Id.* at 581.

115 *Id.* at 581 n.5.

116 *Id.*

117 *Id.* at 586.

118 *Lloyd Corp.*, 407 U.S. at 586.

119 *Id.*

120 *Id.*

121 424 U.S. 507 (1976).

122 *Id.* at 508–09.

123 *See id.* at 510–11; *see also* Hudgens v. NLRB, 501 F.2d 161, 169 (5th Cir. 1974), *rev'd*, 424 U.S. 507 (1976).

124 *Hudgens*, 424 U.S. at 513.

125 *Id.*

126 *Id.* at 517–18 (acknowledging that "a substantial portion of the Court's opinion in *Lloyd* was devoted to pointing out the differences between the two cases" and, more specifically, that "the picketing in *Logan Valley* had been specifically directed to a store in the shopping center and the pickets had no other reasonable opportunity to reach their intended audience").

127 *Id.* at 518.

128 *Id.*

129 *Id.*

130 *Hudgens*, 424 U.S. at 539–40 (Marshall, J., dissenting).

131 *See id.* at 540–43.

132 *Id.* at 542.

133 *Id.* at 543.

134 *See id.* at 521–23.

135 *Id.* at 523 (remanding the case to the NLRB "so that the case may be there considered under the statutory criteria of the National Labor Relations Act alone").

136 447 U.S. 74 (1980).

137 *Id.* at 77–78.

138 *Id.* at 77.

139 Cal. Const., art. I, § 2 ("Every person may freely speak, write and publish his or her sentiments on all subjects, being responsible for the abuse of this right. A law may not restrain or abridge liberty of speech or press.").

140 Robins v. PruneYard Shopping Center, 592 P.2d 341, 347 (Cal. 1979).

141 *Id.*

142 *Id.* (holding that the state constitution "protect[s] speech and petitioning, reasonably exercised, in shopping centers even when the centers are privately owned").

143 *PruneYard Shopping Center,* 447 U.S. at 76–77.

144 *Id.* at 81.

145 *Id.*

146 *Id.* at 83.

147 *Id.* at 85 n.8.

148 Seidman, *supra* note 4, at 1564.

149 *Id.*

150 Bock v. Westminster Mall Co., 819 P.2d 55, 58 (Colo. 1991); N.J. Coal. Against War in the Middle East v. J.M.B. Realty Corp., 650 A.2d 757, 778–79 (N.J. 1984). For a discussion of state supreme courts both recognizing and refusing to recognize free speech easements to privately owned property after *PruneYard,* see Selznick & LaMacchia, *supra* note 26, at 254–60.

151 Batchelder v. Allied Stores Int'l, Inc., 445 N.E. 2d 590, 595 (Mass. 1983).

152 Alderwood Assoc. v. Wash. Envt'l Council, 635 P.2d 108, 113–16 (Wash. 1981), *overruled by* Southcenter Joint Venture v. Nat'l Democratic Party Comm., 780 P.2d 1282 (Wash. 1989).

153 Southcenter Joint Venture v. Nat'l Democratic Policy Comm., 780 P.2d 1282 (Wash. 1989).

154 Korngold, *supra* note 46, at 475–76.

155 *See* Thunder Basin Coal Co. v. Reich, 510 U.S. 200, 217 n.21 (1994) ("The right of employers to exclude union organizers from their private property emanates from state common law, and while this right is not superceded by the NLRA, nothing in the NLRA expressly protects it.").

156 *See id.* (noting that "this Court consistently has maintained that the NLRA may entitle union employees to obtain access to an employer's property under limited circumstances"). *But cf.* Lechmere, Inc. v. NLRB, 502 U.S. 527, 533–38 (1992) (holding that the NLRA does not generally create a right of access for "nonemployee union organizers" to enter an employer's property when such organizers "have reasonable access to employees outside an employer's property").

157 Selznick & LaMacchia, *supra* note 26, at 267.

158 *Id.*

159 *Id.* at 277.

160 Korngold, *supra* note 46, at 464.

161 *Id.*

162 *Id.* at 465.

163 *Id.*

164 *Id.*

165 *See id.* at 476–89. Other legal scholars have made this point as well. *See* Curtis J. Berger, PruneYard *Revisited: Political Activity on Private Lands,* 66 N.Y.U. L. REV. 633, 674 (1991) (proposing "that development permission be conditioned upon the owner's willingness to provide for expressive entry" and

suggesting that "linking approval [of major retail developments] to a satisfactory arrangement for expressive activity would not increase significantly community power over a developer's land-use autonomy").

166 Korngold, *supra* note 46, at 490.

167 *See* Sarah Schindler, *The "Publicization" of Private Space*, 103 IOWA L. REV. 1093, 1096 (2018) ("More recently, as malls have grown out of favor in some areas, developers are now building new 'lifestyle centers' that often resemble stylized, traditional main streets, but are effectively outdoor malls on private property.").

168 Korngold, *supra* note 46, at 490.

169 *See* Terry v. Adams, 345 U.S. 461, 468–70 (1953); Smith v. Allwright, 321 U.S. 649, 662–65 (1944).

170 www.cnn.com/2014/12/21/us/mall-of-america-black-lives-protest/index.html (reporting that "[t]he mall bills itself as the nation's largest with more than 500 businesses" and that "[i]t is big enough to hold seven Yankee Stadiums") (last visited Sept. 7, 2018). For a thoughtful discussion of why the Mall of America should be open to expressive activities, see Jennifer Niles Coffin, *The United Mall of America: Free Speech, State Constitutions, and the Growing Fortress of Private Property*, 33 U. MICH. J.L. REFORM 615 (2000).

171 *But cf.* State v. Wicklund, 589 N.W. 2d 793, 799 (Minn. 1999) (holding that the Minnesota state constitution does not create free speech easements to private property, including large-scale retail shopping complexes otherwise open to the general public). As one commentator explains, "in Minnesota, mall visitors cannot assert free speech rights against mall owners because mall owners are private actors." Coffin, *supra* note 170, at 627.

172 *See* Brown v. Louisiana, 383 U.S. 131 (1966).

173 *See* Flower v. United States, 407 U.S. 197 (1972).

174 As one academic commentator explains, a property owner retained the right to ensure that the property could be used for its intended purposes by regulating speech activity on site. *See* David A. Thomas, *Whither the Public Forum Doctrine: Has This Creature of the Courts Outlived Its Usefulness?*, 44 REAL PROP. TR. & EST. L.J. 637, 708 (2010) ("Whether the property is public property or private property treated as public property, First Amendment rights only may be limited to prevent interference with the ordinary use of the property.").

175 Coffin, *supra* note 170, at 627; *see also* Berger, *supra* note 165, at 633–34, 672–75 (arguing that because public marketplaces have constituted quintessential public forums in the United States since time out of mind, the private ownership of a public marketplace should be deemed irrelevant to the property's availability for expressive activities).

176 Coffin, *supra* note 170, at 627.

177 Jason K. Levine, *Defending the Freedom to Be Heard: Where Alternate Avenues Intersect Empty Public Spaces*, 36 U. MEM. L. REV. 277, 322 (2006). Mr. Levine asks a highly relevant question, namely, "What will become of our national and local discourse when all of our town squares are malls and all of our sidewalks are gated?" *Id.*

178 Roberts v. United States Jaycees, 468 U.S. 609, 625 (1984) (citing PruneYard Shopping Center v. Robins, 447 U.S. 72, 81–88).

179 *See* Levine, *supra* note 177, at 318–22 (noting that California, Colorado, Massachusetts, New Jersey, and Oregon have recognized free speech easements to large-scale retail developments).

180 Timothy Zick, *Space, Place, and Speech: The Expressive Topography*, 74 GEO. WASH. L. REV. 439, 504 (2006) (emphasis in the original).

181 *Id.* at 505.

182 Timothy Zick, *Property, Place, and Public Discourse*, 21 WASH. U. J. L. & POL'Y 173, 204 (2006).

183 *See* Balkin, *supra* note 12, at 2021–28, 2032–33, 2054–55.

184 376 U.S. 254 (1964).

185 *See* Ronald J. Krotoszynski, Jr., *Fundamental Property Rights*, 85 GEO. L.J. 555, 556–57, 590–97, 610–11 (1997); *see also* Laura S. Underkuffler, *On Property: An Essay*, 100 YALE L.J. 127 (1990) (discussing how the founding generation understood "property" to encompass not merely land and chattels, but also essential attributes that are constitutive of a person's personality and being). In point of fact, "[r]eputation provides an excellent example of a 'fundamental' property interest." Krotoszynski, *supra*, at 590.

186 *See* Philadelphia Newspapers, Inc. v. Hepps, 475 U.S. 767, 772–77 (1986) (setting forth the constitutional rules for imposing liability on a media defendant for a libel claim involving a public official, public figure, or private figure involved in a matter of public concern); Bose Corp. v. Consumers Union of United States, Inc., 466 U.S. 485, 508–11 (1984) (requiring that a plaintiff in a case governed by *Sullivan* prove malice aforethought by clear and convincing evidence and holding that because malice aforethought is a question of constitutional fact, a non-prevailing media defendant may seek and obtain independent appellate review of whether the actual malice standard was met at trial); *see also* RONALD J. KROTOSZYNSKI, PRIVACY REVISITED: A GLOBAL PERSPECTIVE ON THE RIGHT TO BE LEFT ALONE 96 n.211, 146–47 (2016) (discussing and describing the First Amendment-based rules that constrain libel recoveries under the Supreme Court's *Sullivan* jurisprudence).

187 *Sullivan*, 376 U.S. at 270.

188 Miami Herald v. Tornillo, 418 U.S. 241 (1974). *Tornillo* holds that the First Amendment prohibits legislation that requires a newspaper or magazine to print content that it would prefer not to print. *See id.* at 254–58. In this decision, the Supreme Court squarely held that "[e]ven if a newspaper would face no additional costs to comply with a compulsory access law and would not be forced to forgo publication of news or opinion by the inclusion of a reply, the Florida statute fails to clear the barriers of the First Amendment because of its intrusion into the function of editors." *Id.* at 258. Chief Justice Burger, writing for a unanimous bench, explained:

The choice of material to go into a newspaper, and the decisions made as to limitations on the size and content of the paper, and treatment of public issues and public officials – whether fair or unfair – constitute the exercise of editorial control and judgment. It has yet to be demonstrated how governmental regulation of this crucial process can be exercised consistent with First Amendment guarantees of a free press as they have evolved to this time.

Id. Accordingly, if an entity creates and publishes its own content, the First Amendment's Press Clause would prevent the government from requiring it to publish particular content against its will. However, social media platforms serve as conduits for the speech of others and do not generally produce and distribute their own original content – accordingly, they should not be eligible to claim the benefit of the *Tornillo* rule.

189 Cable Television Consumer Protection and Competition Act of 1992 (Cable Act), Pub. L. 102-385, 106 Stat. 1460.

190 Turner Broad. Sys., Inc. v. Fed. Commc'n. Comm'n, 520 U.S. 180 (1997) (Turner II); Turner Broad. Sys., Inc. v. Fed. Commc'n. Commc'n, 512 U.S. 622 (1994) (Turner I).

191 *See* Stuart Minor Benjamin & James B. Speta, Telecommunications Law and Pol'y 289–93, 303–05, 320–58 (4th ed. 2015).

192 *See* Deepa Seetharaman & Kirsten Grind, *Facebook Gave Out User Data Despite Pledge*, Wall St. J., June 9–10, 2018, at A1, A8.

193 *See id.* at A8.

194 Anna Maria Andriotis & Emily Glazer, *Facebook Sought Users' Financial Data for Years*, Wall St. J., Sept. 19, 2018, at B1-B2.

195 *See* Jane Bambauer, *Is Data Speech?*, 66 Stan. L. Rev. 66 (2015).

196 *See* Toni Massaro & Helen Norton, *Siri-ously?: Free Speech Rights and Artificial Intelligence*, 110 Nw. U. L. Rev. 1169 (2016).

197 Balkin, *supra* note 12, at 2040–47, 2054–55.

198 *See id.* at 2025–28. As Balkin states his position, "the best alternative to this autocracy is not the imposition of First Amendment doctrines by analogy to the public forum or the company town." *Id.* at 2025.

199 *See* Georgia Wells, *Farewell, Google+. Deep Pockets Weren't Enough*, Wall. St. J., Oct. 9, 2018, at A2.

200 *See id.* ("Few tears were shed Monday over the death of Google+, the search giant's oft-derided effort at challenging Facebook Inc. in social media.").

201 Douglas MacMillan & Robert McMillan, *Google Hid Data Breach for Months*, Wall St. J., Oct. 9, 2018, at A1; Daisuke Wakabayashi, *Google Plus Shutting Down After User Data Was Exposed*, N.Y. Times, Oct. 9, 2018, at B1.

202 Wells, *supra* note 199, at A2.

203 *See* United States v. AT & T, 552 F. Supp. 131 (D.D.C. 1982).

204 *See* Richard H. Thaler & Cass R. Sunstein, Nudge: Improving Decisions about Health, Wealth, and Happiness (2008).

205 9 U.S.C. §§ 1–16, Pub. L. 68–401, 43 Stat. 883 (1925).

206 *See* Balkin, *supra* note 12, at 2025–28. Professor Balkin assumes that *any* application of First Amendment values to privately-owned social media platforms would necessarily imply a flat ban on content-based rules. *See id.* at 2027–28. However, this need not be so. A "junior varsity" version of the First Amendment might only proscribe speaker-based and viewpoint-based censorship, but permit a social media platform's owner to maintain and enforce mandatory civility norms that incorporate content-based restrictions on users' speech.

207 *See* Adamson v. California, 332 U.S. 46, 71–75, 89–92 (1947) (Black, J., dissenting); *see also* Hugo L. Black, *The Bill of Rights*, 35 N.Y.U. L. REV. 865, 865–66, 874–79 (1965); Tinsley E. Yarbrough, *Justice Black, the Fourteenth Amendment, and Incorporation*, 30 U. MIAMI L. REV. 231 (1976).

208 *See* Palko v. Connecticut, 302 U.S. 319, 324–25 (1937) (explaining that provisions of the Bill of Rights may be applicable to the states when "immunities that are valid as against the federal government by force of the specific pledges of particular amendments have been found to be implicit in the concept of ordered liberty, and thus, through the Fourteenth Amendment, become valid as against the states").

209 *See* Duncan v. Louisana, 391 U.S. 145, 171–83 (1968) (Harlan, J., dissenting).

210 Barron v. Mayor & City Council of Baltimore, 32 U.S. (7 Pet.) 243, 247–48 (1833).

211 U.S. CONST. amend. VI (providing that "[i]n all criminal prosecutions, the accused shall enjoy the right to a speedy and public trial, by an impartial jury of the State and district wherein the crime shall have been committed, which district shall have been previously ascertained by law, and to be informed of the nature and cause of the accusation; to be confronted with the witnesses against him").

212 U.S. CONST. art. III, § 2, cl. 3 ("The Trial of all Crimes, except in Cases of Impeachment, shall be by Jury; and such Trial shall be held in the State where the said Crimes shall have been committed; but when not committed within any State, the Trial shall be at such Place or Places as the Congress may by Law have directed.").

213 *See* Williams v. Florida, 399 U.S. 78, 129–38 (1970) (Harlan, J., dissenting).

214 *See* PruneYard Shopping Center v. Robins, 447 U.S. 74, 96–101 (1980) (Powell, J., concurring in part and concurring in the judgment); *see also* Epstein, *Takings, Exclusivity and Speech, supra* note 5, at 34–36. In *PruneYard*, Justice Powell found that on the facts presented, the "appellants have not shown that the limited right of access held to be afforded by the California Constitution burdened their First and Fourteenth Amendment rights." *Id.* at 101. Justice Powell also cautioned, however, that "[o]ne easily can identify other circumstances in which a right of access to commercial property would burden the owner's First and Fourteenth right to refrain from speaking." *Id.* at 100–01.

215 Berger, *supra* note 165, at 648.

216 *Id.*

217 *See id.* at 688 ("Once again, the mall owner's ability to impose reasonable restrictions should satisfy any constitutional objection of these nonpatron groups.").

218 Jody Freeman, *Extending Public Law Norms Through Privatization*, 116 HARV. L. REV. 1285, 1285 (2003).

219 *Id.*

220 In this respect, ISPs might stand on different policy ground because they commonly require access to public rights of way for their wires and cell towers. The need to secure permission to occupy public property for an indefinite period of time would provide the kind of leverage that Professor Freeman believes could secure voluntary compliance with rules designed to advance and secure public goods (like democratic deliberation).

221 Schindler, *supra* note 167, at 1149. Professor Schindler argues that "privately owned public open spaces" or "POPOS" should be subject to obligations not applicable to other kinds of private property. *See id.* at 1095–99. More specifically, she posits that "POPOS should be viewed differently from typical privatized public space" and, if so viewed, be subject to "different laws and norms" than non-POPOS. *Id.* at 1098.

222 *Id.* at 1149.

223 *Id.* at 1149 n.359.

224 *See supra* Chapter 1.

225 *See id.*

4 WHISTLEBLOWING SPEECH AND DEMOCRATIC ACCOUNTABILITY: THE GROWING PROBLEM OF REDUCED FIRST AMENDMENT PROTECTION FOR GOVERNMENT EMPLOYEE SPEECH

1 *But see* Lyrissa Barnett Lidsky, *Not a Free Press Court?*, 2012 B.Y.U. L. REV. 1819, 1830–34 (2012) (arguing that the Roberts Court appears "deeply suspicious of the claim that the media play a special constitutional role in our democracy," bordering on outright "hostility," and positing that the conservative majority "treats the differences between media and non-media corporations as nonexistent").

2 For an excellent and comprehensive overview of the purposes and function of both the Free Press Clause and a free press in a democratic polity more generally, see David A. Anderson, *The Origins of the Press Clause*, 30 UCLA L. REV. 455 (1983). Professor Anderson posits that, for the Framers, "[f]reedom of the press – not freedom of speech – was the primary concern." *Id.* at 533; *see also* Sonja R. West, *Awakening the Press Clause*, 58 UCLA L. REV. 1025, 1032–33, 1043, 1069–70 (2011) (noting "the common intuition that there does exist a press that performs a special role in our democracy and is deserving of constitutional status outside the shadow of the Speech Clause" and arguing that "[t]he Press Clause needs a distinct definition to truly fulfill its unique functions in our society and our democracy"). Of course, if one embraces the point of view that the mass media play an integral role in the process of democratic deliberation, it might

necessarily follow that vesting such power in unregulated private hands constitutes a problematic public policy – as opposed to using government power to ensure access to the mass media. *See* JEROME A. BARRON, FREEDOM OF THE PRESS FOR WHOM?: THE RIGHT OF ACCESS TO MASS MEDIA (1973); Jerome A. Barron, *Access to the Press – A New First Amendment Right*, 80 Harv. L. Rev. 1641 (1967). If the mass media are an essential component of the democratic process, like the political parties themselves, one could conceive of the press as having constitutional obligations, as do the political parties, when they undertake an essential role in the electoral process. *See* Terry v. Adams, 345 U.S. 461, 469–70 (1953). *But cf.* Miami Herald Pub. Co. v. Tornillo, 418 U.S. 241, 254–58 (1974) (invalidating on First Amendment grounds a Florida law that required a newspaper to afford a candidate for public office a "right of reply" if a newspaper opposed the candidate's election).

3 Jim Rutenberg, *"Alternative Facts" and the Costs of Trump-Branded Reality*, N.Y. TIMES (Jan. 22, 2017), www.nytimes.com/2017/01/22/business/media/alternative-facts-trump-brand.html [https://perma.cc/UJE9-BSVL] (discussing the Trump administration's efforts to peddle to the press and body public so-called "alternative facts," which are verifiably false, but self-serving, factual claims). The Trump administration's routine flouting of government ethics rules presents another need for whistleblowing speech to ensure that high government offices are not used for personal pecuniary gain – perhaps at the expense of the national interest. *See* Eric Lipton, *White House Moves to Block Ethics Inquiry into Ex-Lobbyists on Payroll*, N.Y. TIMES (May 22, 2017), www.nytimes.com/2017/05/22/us/politics/trump-white-house-government-ethics-lobbyists.html [https://perma.cc/U8MC-VQ8X]. Other examples of the potential abuse of power have come to light only because of internal leaks to the press. *See, e.g.*, Sari Horwitz, Ashley Parker & Ed O'Keefe, *Trump Angrily Calls Russia Investigation a "Witch Hunt," and Denies Charges of Collusion*, WASH. POST (May 18, 2017), www.washingtonpost.com/world/national-security/deputy-attorney-general-rod-rosenstein-will-brief-the-full-senate-in-a-closed-session/2017/05/18/41de8548-3bd4-11e7-8854-21f359183e8c_story.html [https://perma.cc/MW6A-5JAW]; Devlin Barrett & Matt Zapotosky, *Russia Probe Reaches Current White House Official, People Familiar with the Case Say*, WASH. POST (May 19, 2017), www.washingtonpost.com/world/national-security/russia-probe-reaches-current-white-house-official-people-familiar-with-the-case-say/2017/05/19/7685adba-3c99-11e7-9e48-c4f199710b69_story.html [https://perma.cc/AY7H-BE23]. The Trump administration consistently denies growing reports of both financial self-dealing with the Russian government and efforts to block or impede investigation of its political and financial ties to the Russian government; nevertheless, investigators seem to have established that senior leaders in the campaign were on the Russian government's payroll. Mark Mazzetti & Matthew Rosenburg, *Michael Flynn Misled Pentagon About Russia Ties, Letter Says*, N.Y. TIMES (May 22, 2017), www.nytimes.com/2017/05/22/us/politics/michael-flynn-fifth-amendment-russia-senate.html [https://perma.cc/JHG4-28LC]. Even so, however, President Trump himself has admitted, after leaks from White House staffers to the national press corps, that he casually shared classified Israeli

intelligence with senior Russian government officials at an Oval Office meeting. *See* Adam Goldman, Eric Schmitt & Peter Baker, *Israel Said To Be Source of Secret Intelligence Trump Gave to Russians*, N.Y. TIMES (May 16, 2017), www.nytimes.com/2017/05/16/world/middleeast/israel-trump-classified-intelligence-russia.html [https://perma.cc/RHH4-8KFK]. To be sure, all presidential administrations seek to suppress damaging information that calls into question the administration's honesty, competence, and discretion. However, the scale of malfeasance, and possibly corruption, in the current White House may well rival that of the Grant administration, which arguably held the record on these fronts until now. *See* Michael A. Genovese, *Presidential Corruption: A Longitudinal Analysis*, in CORRUPTION IN AMERICAN POLITICS 135, 140–42 (Michael A. Genovese & Victoria A. Farrar-Myers eds., 2010) (noting that that the Grant administration was "victimized by widespread political corruption" that involved the highest levels of government, including the Vice President and several members of the cabinet, and positing that Grant's political inexperience, poor personnel choices, lax management style, and tendency to place personal loyalty over competence were the root causes of it); SCOTT JOHN HAMMOND, ROBERT NORTH ROBERTS & VALERIE A. SULFARO, CAMPAIGNING FOR PRESIDENT IN AMERICA: 1788–2016, at 526–27 (2016) (observing that "Grant led what was far and away the most corrupt administration to date," discussing various scandals that occurred on President Grant's watch, notably including the infamous Crédit Mobilier scandal, and noting that "[b]ecause of the extensive corruption, a new term, 'Grantism,' was coined both to describe the condition of corruption that gripped the administration and to claim the location of its source directly in the president himself rather than in the Republican Party"). Although it is probably too early to draw any firm conclusions, an analogy between the Trump administration and the Grant administration with regard to their ethical standards may well prove to be apt. *See, e.g.*, Nicholas Confessore & Kenneth P. Vogel, *Trump Loyalist Mixes Businesses and Access at "Advisory" Firm*, N.Y. TIMES (Aug. 1, 2017), www.nytimes.com/2017/08/01/us/politics/corey-lewandowski-trump.html [https://perma.cc/NSB8-8TAE] (noting the existence of "ethical quandaries surrounding the Trump White House, where the president has given significant access and power to friends and loyalists who are not on the government payroll but work as lobbyists or retain significant outside business interests" and observing that "Mr. Trump's 'kitchen cabinet' includes Washington lobbyists, a variety of so-called strategic advisers who provide advice on government policy making but are not registered as lobbyists, and a panoply of wealthy friends with extensive business interests before the [federal] government").

4 Anderson, *supra* note 2, at 537.

5 Sonja R. West, *Press Exceptionalism*, 127 HARV. L. REV. 2434, 2434–37 (2014).

6 *Id.* at 2446–47; *see* West, *supra* note 2, at 1032–33, 1041–47, 1069–70 (noting the need for press access to information in order to facilitate using the electoral process to secure government accountability).

7 *See* Ronald J. Krotoszynski, Jr., *Transparency, Accountability, and Competency: An Essay on the Obama Administration, Google Government, and the Difficulties of Securing Effective Governance*, 65 U. MIAMI L. REV. 449, 454, 469 (2011) (observing that "systemic failures of governance are not particularly rare, which

is a very good reason indeed to spend considerable time and energy thinking about issues associated with administrative competence" and positing that "all presidential administrations, regardless of political party, are prone to suppress bad news whenever possible").

8 ALEXANDER MEIKLEJOHN, FREE SPEECH AND ITS RELATION TO SELF-GOVERNMENT 22–27, 36–38 (1948).

9 *See* Editorial, *Edward Snowden, Whistle-Blower,* N.Y. TIMES (Jan. 1, 2014), www.nytimes.com/2014/01/02/opinion/edward-snowden-whistle-blower.html [https://perma.cc/9GSK-YRC5]; *see also* Siobhan Gorman, Carol E. Lee & Janet Hook, *Obama Proposes Surveillance-Policy Overhaul,* WALL ST. J. (Aug. 9, 2013), www.wsj.com/articles/obama-to-unveil-new-plans-for-surveillance-transparency-1376063621 [https://perma.cc/B2MX-LGK6].

10 *See* Margaret Hu, *Taxonomy of the Snowden Disclosures,* 72 WASH. & LEE L. REV. 1679, 1686–93 (2015).

11 *See* Neil M. Richards, *The Dangers of Surveillance,* 126 HARV. L. REV. 1934, 1952–58 (2013).

12 *See* OFFICE OF THE DIR. OF NAT'L INTELLIGENCE, ICA 2017-01D, INTELLIGENCE COMMUNITY ASSESSMENT: ASSESSING RUSSIAN ACTIVITIES AND INTENTIONS IN RECENT U.S. ELECTIONS (2017) (reporting on the Russian government's intentional and sustained activities to damage the presidential campaign of Hillary Rodham Clinton and to advance the electoral prospects of Donald Trump); *see also* Eric Lipton, David E. Sanger & Scott Shane, *The Perfect Weapon: How Russian Cyberpower Invaded the U.S.,* N.Y. TIMES (Dec. 13, 2016), www.nytimes.com/2016/12/13/us/politics/russia-hack-election-dnc.html [https://perma.cc/8NFJ-TTC5] (reporting on how the Russian government used sophisticated cyberattacks to damage Hillary Rodham Clinton's credibility and, in the process, enhanced Donald Trump's electoral chances); Michael D. Shear & David E. Sanger, *Putin Led a Complex Cyberattack Scheme to Aid Trump, Report Finds,* N.Y. TIMES (Jan. 6, 2017), www.nytimes.com/2017/01/06/us/politics/donald-trump-wall-hack-russia.html [https://perma.cc/S98M-WN74] (reporting on the US intelligence community's conclusion that Russia's cyber hacking efforts were intended to advance Donald Trump's candidacy and injure the Clinton campaign's credibility with the electorate).

13 Joined Cases C-293/12 & 594/12, Digital Rights Ireland Ltd. v. Minister for Commc'ns, Marine and Nat. Res., 2014 EUR-Lex CELEX LEXIS 238, ¶ 28 (Apr. 8, 2014), http://curia.europa.eu/juris/celex.jsf?celex=62012CJ0293&lang1=en&type=TXT&ancre= [http://perma.cc/DJ5C-8VJB] (observing that "it is not inconceivable that the retention of the data in question might have an effect on the use, by subscribers or registered users, of the means of communication covered by the directive and, consequently, on their exercise of freedom of expression"); *see also* Opinion of Advocate General Cruz Villalón, Joined Cases C-293/12 & 594/12, Digital Rights Ireland Ltd. v. Minister for Commc'ns, Marine and Nat. Res., 2013 EUR-Lex CELEX LEXIS 845, ¶ 52 (Dec. 12, 2013), http://curia.europa.eu/juris/celex.jsf?celex=62012CC0293&lang1=en&type=TXT&ancre= [http://perma.cc/

DJ5C-8VJB] (observing that the European Union's massive data collection and retention program gave rise to "the vague feeling of surveillance" and that such surveillance could be "capable of having a decisive influence on the exercise by European citizens of their freedom of expression and information" and, accordingly, produced an unacceptable chilling effect on the exercise of freedom of speech).

14 See Opinion of Advocate General Cruz Villalón, 2013 EUR-Lex CELEX LEXIS 845, ¶ 52; *see also* NEIL Richards, INTELLECTUAL PRIVACY: RETHINKING CIVIL LIBERTIES IN THE DIGITAL AGE 105–07, 165, 179–80 (2015). Professor Richards observes that "[a]t one level, it would seem obvious that surveillance chills and deters free thought, reading, and communications," but surveillance also leads people to "change their behavior toward the ordinary and the inoffensive" too. *See* Richards, *supra*, at 106. In sum, "[w]hen we feel we are being watched, we act differently." *Id.*

15 See MEIKLEJOHN, *supra* note 8, at 37 ("In the last resort, it is not our representatives who govern us. We govern ourselves, using them. And we do so in such ways as our own free judgment may decide.").

16 *Id.* at 88.

17 *Id.*

18 See Julian W. Kleinbrodt, Note, *Pro-whistleblower Reform in the Post-*Garcetti *Era*, 112 MICH. L. REV. 111, 113 (2013) (arguing that "[w]histleblower speech is critically important because it helps ensure a well-functioning democracy" and observing that information provided by government employees can be crucial to securing accountability); Diane Norcross, Comment, *Separating the Employee From the Citizen: The Social Science Implications of* Garcetti v. Ceballos, 40 BALT. L. REV. 543, 570–72 (2011) (noting the value of whistleblowing speech to securing government accountability); Julie A. Wenell, Note, Garcetti v. Ceballos: *Stifling the First Amendment in the Public Workplace*, 16 WM. & MARY BILL RTS. J. 623, 635–37 (2007) (noting the importance of government employees engaging in whistleblowing speech to securing reform and quoting a *Garcetti* brief for the proposition that "[n]either the public nor the government itself can hold officials accountable for abuse unless public employees can disclose government misconduct without fear of reprisals.").

19 See Louis Michael Seidman, *Powell's Choice: The Law and Morality of Speech, Silence, and Resignation by High Government Officials, in* SPEECH AND SILENCE IN AMERICAN LAW 48, 78–80 (Austin Sarat ed., 2010). Professor Seidman notes that *Garcetti* creates perverse incentives to ignore the chain of command and features a doctrinal framework that "sharply favors those who are willing to make a clean break." *Id.* at 80. This result obtains because "the [government] employer has no employment needs when the speaker is no longer a government employee." *Id.* Accordingly, "the more an employee is willing to break with her patron, the greater her protection." *Id.* This is undoubtedly true. Even so, however, most employees seek to retain, rather than shed, their current employment. *Cf. id.* at 79–81

(offering reasons and rationales that would incent a government employee to make a noisy exit).

20 The need for encouraging such disclosures should be self-evident. *See, e.g.,* Emily Wax-Thibodeaux, *VA Removes Sharon Helman, Manager at Center of Phoenix Health-Care Scandal,* WASH. POST (Nov. 24, 2014), www.washington post.com/news/federal-eye/wp/2014/11/24/va-removes-sharon-helman-man ager-at-center-of-phoenix-health-care-scandal [https://perma.cc/LP4S-RE7C]. Employees who engage in whistleblowing activity, even using protected internal channels, and in theory under the protection of laws like the federal Whistle Blower Protection Act of 1989, Pub. L. 101–12, 103 Stat. 16 (codified at 5 U.S.C. §§ 1201–1222 (2016)), face a serious prospect of retaliation by their government employers. *See* Emily Wax-Thibodeaux, *Whistleblowers Say VA Has Not Changed,* WASH. POST, Apr. 30, 2015, at A19 [hereinafter Wax-Thibodeaux, *VA Has Not Changed*] (reporting on "widespread reports of retaliation against whistleblowers" within the Department of Veterans Affairs, including demotions followed by being "moved into windowless storage rooms, or basements," for their work spaces); *see also* Emily Wax-Thibodeaux, *Isolated. Harassed. Their Personal Lives Investigated. That's Life as a VA Whistleblower, Employees Tell Congress,* WASH. POST (Apr. 14, 2015), www.washingtonpost.com/news/federal-eye/wp/ 2015/04/14/isolated-harassed-their-personal-lives-investigated-thats-life-as- a-va-whistleblower-employees-tell-congress [https://perma.cc/U5HW-TZQK] (reporting on various forms of targeted retaliation against VA whistleblowers, including having "their medical backgrounds scrutinized, and even their mental health and personal lives investigated" and observing that "those who retaliate against [VA whistleblowers] were rarely if ever punished") [hereinafter Wax-Thibodeaux, *Isolated. Harassed.*].

21 We should also consider whether threatening whistleblowing government employees with treason or espionage charges is fundamentally consistent with our "profound national commitment to the principle that debate on public issues should be uninhibited, robust, and wide-open, and that it may well include vehement, caustic, and sometimes unpleasantly sharp attacks on government and public officials." New York Times Co. v. Sullivan, 376 U.S. 254, 270 (1964). *But cf.* Wax-Thibodeaux, *VA Has Not Changed, supra* note 20 (noting that "[t]he poor and punishing treatment of whistleblowers inside the Department of Veterans Affairs has been described as part of a 'corrosive culture,'" but observing that more than a year after the Secretary of Veterans Affairs "vowed to change" this sorry situation, the promised reforms had not yet been implemented). Current First Amendment law routinely taxes the cost of speech activity against private citizens, even on facts where a meaningful and cognizable legal harm has unquestionably occurred. *See, e.g.,* Snyder v. Phelps, 562 U.S. 443, 458–61 (2011); Hustler Magazine, Inc. v. Falwell, 485 U.S. 46, 54–56 (1988). Why should the government itself be immune from having to incur costs associated with the protection of freedom of expression? If the grieving family of a dead soldier, killed while on active duty, must submit to

an outrageous and offensive targeted protest of their dead relative's funeral and burial services because we must "protect even hurtful speech on public issues to ensure that we do not stifle public debate," *Snyder*, 562 U.S. at 461, then, by parity of logic, the government should have to incur costs that it would rather avoid in order to facilitate the process of democratic deliberation. Unfortunately, however, contemporary First Amendment law does not routinely require the government itself to shoulder the costs of speech when national security or military affairs are at stake. Collective social costs matter – but so do individual social costs. First Amendment theory and doctrine should reflect this basic fact; nevertheless, it currently does not.

22 Rosalie Berger Levinson, *Silencing Government Employee Whistleblowers in the Name of "Efficiency,"* 23 OHIO N.U. L. REV. 17, 25, 51–52, 63 (1996) (noting that both statutory and constitutional protections for government employees who engage in whistleblowing speech are weak and convey uncertain protection and, accordingly, "[t]he uncertainty in this area means that no government employee, regardless of the significance of the communication, can be ensured that her speech will be protected"); Toni M. Massaro, *Significant Silences: Freedom of Speech in the Public Sector Workplace*, 61 S. CAL. L. REV. 1, 65 (1987) (observing that "the government office is *expected* to tolerate more 'deviance' and 'outspokenness' than the private office and many people already assume that it does so" and, in consequence, "[t]ermination from a government job therefore may send a profoundly and disproportionately negative message to other, potential employers" (emphasis in original)). As Professor Levinson explains, "whistleblowers will sometimes be penalized for their speech and speech will be chilled because employees will not know in advance whether their disclosures will be protected." Levinson, *supra*, at 20 n.6. And, as Professor Massaro has argued, "[t]he difficult truth is that an employee who is willing to say things that rankle an employer, however accurate, may also be hard to tolerate." Massaro, *supra*, at 64.

23 *See infra* notes 141–64 and accompanying text.

24 *See* Kleinbrodt, *supra* note 18, at 118–28 (discussing and critiquing the shortcomings and limitations associated with the contemporary *Connick/ Pickering* doctrine in the context of whistleblowing government employee speech).

25 *See* Kathleen Clark & Nancy J. Moore, *Financial Rewards for Whistleblowing Lawyers*, 56 B.C. L. REV. 1697, 1698–1701 (2015).

26 Connick v. Myers, 461 U.S. 138 (1983); Pickering v. Bd. of Educ., 391 U.S. 563 (1968).

27 Kleinbrodt, *supra* note 18, at 113–14; Wenell, *supra* note 18, at 636–37.

28 *See infra* notes 41–56 and accompanying text.

29 *See* Cent. Hudson Gas & Elec. Corp. v. Pub. Serv. Comm'n, 447 U.S. 557 (1980). *But cf.* Alex Kozinski & Stuart Banner, *Who's Afraid of Commercial Speech?*, 76 VA. L. REV. 627 (1990) (questioning the rationales offered to justify lower free speech protection for commercial speech over other kinds of speech).

30 *See* Miller v. California, 413 U.S. 15 (1973). *But cf.* Amy Adler, *The Perverse Law of Child Pornography*, 101 COLUM. L. REV. 209 (2001) (questioning the basic

rationales offered to exclude nude images of children from any First Amendment protection and suggesting that this doctrinal approach places unjustifiable burdens on artistic freedom); Andrew Koppelman, *Does Obscenity Cause Moral Harm?*, 105 Colum. L. Rev. 1635 (2005) (questioning whether the government has any legitimate interest in regulating obscenity because it causes moral harms to those who peruse such materials).

31 Again, it bears noting that government employees speak out about a wide variety of matters of public concern, and many – indeed most – examples of government employee speech do not involve whistleblowing activity. *See infra* notes 151–59 and accompanying text. When a government employee speaks out about a matter of public concern wholly unrelated to her government employment, and which does not facilitate the process of democratic accountability through elections, the speech would not constitute "whistleblowing speech." *See id.*

32 *See, e.g.*, McAuliffe v. Mayor of New Bedford, 29 N.E. 517, 517 (Mass. 1892) (observing without irony that a city policeman "may have a constitutional right to talk politics, but he has no constitutional right to be a policeman").

33 Pickering v. Bd. of Educ., 391 U.S. 563, 568 (1968).

34 Mary-Rose Papandrea, *The Free Speech Rights of Off-Duty Government Employees*, 2010 B.Y.U. L. Rev. 2117, 2119 (2010) ("Under this framework, a public employee's speech is not entitled to any First Amendment protection unless it is determined, as a threshold matter, that the speech involves a matter of public concern, and, even if that requirement is satisfied, the speech is protected only if the value of the speech outweighs the government employer's interests in restricting or punishing it."); *see* Garcetti v. Ceballos, 547 U.S. 410, 419 (2006) (discussing the matter of public concern threshold requirement for First Amendment protection of a government employee's speech and the balancing test federal and state courts should use for determining whether government employee speech about a matter of public concern enjoys First Amendment protection in light of the managerial imperatives of the government employer).

35 *Pickering*, 391 U.S. at 564–66.

36 *Id.* at 575–78 (appendix reprinting Mr. Pickering's letter to the editor).

37 *Id.*

38 *Id.* at 566–67.

39 *Id.* at 564–65 (internal quotations and citation omitted).

40 *Id.* at 565.

41 *See id.* at 565, 574–75.

42 *But cf.* McAuliffe v. Mayor of New Bedford, 29 N.E. 517, 517 (Mass. 1892) (observing that "[t]he petitioner may have a constitutional right to talk politics, but he has no constitutional right to be a policeman"). *McAuliffe* equates the rights of public sector and private sector employees; accordingly, a government employee, just like an employee working for a private employer in an employment-at-will state, "takes the employment on the terms which are offered" and "[t]he servant cannot complain" about those conditions. *Id.* at 518. *Pickering* constitutes a clear break with *McAuliffe's* assumption that

government, as an employer, is no more obliged to respect constitutional constraints than is a private employer. *See Pickering*, 391 U.S. at 568, 571–73.

43 *Pickering*, 391 U.S. at 568.

44 *Id.; see also* Robert C. Post, *Subsidized Speech*, 106 YALE L.J. 151, 164–65, 178–80 (1996) (discussing the "managerial domain" of the government as an employer and steward of public resources and also the need to take legitimate managerial goals and objectives into consideration when determining the proper scope of First Amendment rights in the context of government-created environments, including government employment).

45 *Pickering*, 391 U.S. at 568.

46 *See* Levinson, *supra* note 22, at 25, 51–52. As Professor Levinson observes:

> To hold that a government employee's speech can be proscribed no matter what the content of the speech and no matter what the specific employee/employer situation, is to cut off public debate on speech that lies at the core of the First Amendment – speech which is necessary to democratic self-government.

Id. at 51.

47 *See generally* Kleinbrodt, *supra* note 18, at 113–14 (noting that the value of information provided by a whistleblowing government employee might not be available through other means); Wenell, *supra* note 18, at 635–37 (noting that engaging in whistleblowing speech is likely to lead to retaliation if the information embarrasses a government employer). *But cf.* Massaro, *supra* note 22, at 40–42 (citing Alexander Meiklejohn and arguing that the value of information necessary to facilitate government accountability through the process of democratic self-government should, in most cases, overbear the cost associated with disruption allegedly caused by the whistleblowing speech).

48 *See* Wax-Thibodeaux, *Isolated. Harassed.*, *supra* note 20 (reporting on pervasive forms of retaliation visited on VA hospital employees who reported on shocking failures to meet the medical needs of injured veterans in places like Phoenix, Arizona). Despite assurances by the Secretary of Veterans Affairs that this systematic pattern of retaliation against whistleblowing employees would be stopped, it continued to occur – and on a widespread basis. *See id.*

49 *See generally* Seidman, *supra* note 19, at 56–61 (discussing the practical and political significance of resignations by government officers to the operation of government agencies and observing that resignations can both facilitate and also frustrate public accountability).

50 *Pickering*, 391 U.S. at 571–75.

51 *Id.* at 571–72.

52 *Id.* at 572.

53 *See id.* at 570–73. The *Pickering* Court extended the *New York Times Co. v. Sullivan* "actual malice" standard to government employee speech about a matter of public concern. *See id.* at 574–75; *see also* New York Times Co. v. Sullivan, 376 U.S. 254, 284–85 (1964) (requiring a public official plaintiff to prove that a media defendant published false statements of fact with "actual

malice," meaning with actual knowledge of falsity or reckless indifference to the truth or falsity of a factual assertion of and concerning the plaintiff, and that this showing of actual malice must be supported with "clear and convincing evidence").

54 *Pickering*, 391 U.S. at 571–75.

55 *Id.* at 572–73.

56 *Id.* at 573.

57 *See, e.g.,* Givhan v. W. Line Consol. Sch. Dist., 439 U.S. 410, 414–15 (1979); Mt. Healthy City Sch. Dist. Bd. of Educ. v. Doyle, 429 U.S. 274, 284 (1977); Perry v. Sindermann, 408 U.S. 593, 598 (1972).

58 461 U.S. 138, 145–48 (1983).

59 *See id. But cf.* Snyder v. Phelps, 562 U.S. 443, 451–55 (2011) (defining a "matter of public concern" very broadly to encompass very bizarre claims linking the deaths of US military personnel with God's wrath over a permissive attitude toward sexual minorities in contemporary US society).

60 *Connick*, 461 U.S. at 140.

61 *Id.*

62 *Id.* at 141; *see also id.* at 155–56 (reproducing, as an appendix, the entire office questionnaire that Myers prepared and circulated on October 7, 1980).

63 *Id.*

64 *See id.* at 141–42.

65 *Id.* at 142, 154.

66 *Id.* at 149.

67 *Id.* at 146.

68 *Id.*

69 *Id.*

70 *Id.* at 146–47.

71 *See id.* at 147 ("Our responsibility is to ensure that citizens are not deprived of fundamental rights by virtue of working for the government; this does not require a grant of immunity for employee grievances not afforded by the First Amendment to those who do not work for the State.").

72 *Id.*

73 *Id.* at 147–48.

74 Rankin v. McPherson, 483 U.S. 378, 380 (1987).

75 *See id.* at 381 ("But then after I said that, and then Lawrence said, yeah, he's cutting back medicaid and food stamps. And I said, yeah, welfare and CETA. I said, shoot, if they go for him again, I hope they get him.").

76 *Compare Connick*, 461 U.S. 138 (finding a question related to compelled political activity by employees of a district attorney constituted a matter of public concern and triggered First Amendment protection), *and* Pickering v. Bd. of Educ., 391 U.S. 563, 572–75 (1968) (holding that a letter to the editor about a referendum on public school bonds constitutes a matter of public concern and triggered First Amendment protection against the discharge of the government employee who wrote the letter), *with* Garcetti v. Ceballos, 547 U.S. 410, 419–21 (2006) (acknowledging the importance and value of disclosures

by government employees, notably including "the importance of promoting the public's interest in receiving the well-informed views of government employees engaging in civic discussion," but nevertheless denying First Amendment protection to comments made within the scope of a government employee's work-related duties, even if they relate to a matter of public concern), *and* Waters v. Churchill, 511 U.S. 661, 671 (1994) (plurality opinion) (acknowledging the potential social value of employee speech but concluding that "the government as employer indeed has far broader powers than does the government as sovereign" and this authority extends to firing an employee based on a misattributed comment that, if actually made, could cause workplace disruption).

77 HARRY KALVEN, JR., THE NEGRO AND THE FIRST AMENDMENT 140–41, 145 (1965) (coining the phrase "heckler's veto," and arguing that the hostile reaction of an audience to a speaker, or heckler's veto, cannot consistent with the First Amendment serve as an acceptable basis for government censorship of speech); *see* Owen M. Fiss, *Free Speech and Social Structure*, 71 IOWA L. REV. 1405, 1416–17 (1986) (discussing the concept of the heckler's veto and attributing the concept's creation to Professor Kalven).

78 *See* HARRY KALVEN, JR., A WORTHY TRADITION: FREEDOM OF SPEECH IN AMERICA 89–93, 96–105 (Jamie Kalven ed., 1988) (discussing in some detail the concept of "heckler's veto," which entails using an adverse public reaction as a justification for the government silencing an unpopular speaker). The hostility of a government employee's coworkers, based on her speech, clearly constitutes a form of heckler's veto because the government's power to fire the worker is contingent on the hostile reaction of an audience, in this instance, the speaker's coworkers in the government agency or office. *See* Papandrea, *supra* note 34, at 2165 ("Another problem with the *Pickering* balancing test as most courts have applied it is that it permits adverse public reaction to the expressive activities to be considered on the government's side of the balance. As a result, it theoretically matters very little what an employee says.").

79 *See Connick*, 463 U.S. at 151–53.

80 McAuliffe v. Mayor of New Bedford, 29 N.E. 517, 517 (Mass. 1892) (holding that the government, in its capacity as an employer, has the same right to retain or discharge an employee that a private employer enjoys). Justice Oliver Wendell Holmes, then on the Supreme Judicial Court of Massachusetts, explained that

> [t]here are few employments for hire in which the servant does not agree to suspend his constitutional rights of free speech as well as of idleness by the implied terms of his contract. The servant cannot complain, as he takes the employment on the terms which are offered him. On the same principle the city may impose any reasonable condition upon holding offices within its control. This condition seems to us reasonable, if that be a question open to revision here.

Id. at 517–18. In other words, a government employee, as an employee, does not possess any right to freedom of speech that his employer is not inclined to recognize. *See id. But cf.* Helen Norton, *Constraining Public Employee Speech: Government's Control of Its Workers' Speech to Protect Its Own Expression,* 59 DUKE L.J. 1, 49–50 (2009) (arguing that "requiring public employees to relinquish their free speech rights as a condition of employment suppresses expression at a great cost to key First Amendment values in promoting individual autonomy, contributing to the marketplace of ideas, and facilitating citizen participation in democratic self-governance").

81 511 U.S. 661 (1994) (plurality opinion).

82 *See id.* at 674–75.

83 *See id.* (conceding that "[g]overnment employees are often in the best position to know what ails the agencies for which they work; public debate may gain much from their informed opinions," but nevertheless granting government employers broad authority to fire based on mistaken factual assumptions about an employee's speech because "where the government is employing someone for the very purpose of effectively achieving its goals, such restrictions may well be appropriate"); *see also* Bruce Bodner, Note, *Constitutional Rights – United States Supreme Court Gives Public Employers Greater Latitude to Curb Public Employee Speech* – Waters v. Churchill, 114 S. Ct. 1878 (1994), 68 TEMP. L. REV. 461, 462–63 (1995) (noting that *Waters* advanced managerial control principles at the expense of government employees' First Amendment rights and predicting that "[t]his expansion of management rights will discourage critical public employee speech and undermine efforts to improve the delivery of public services through the promotion of employee participation and identification of inefficient management practices in the workplace").

84 *Waters,* 511 U.S. at 672.

85 *Id.*

86 *Id.* at 680–81.

87 *Id.* at 680.

88 547 U.S. 410 (2006).

89 *See id.* at 412–13, 420.

90 *Id.* at 414–15.

91 *Id.* at 415–16.

92 *See id.* at 414–18, 421.

93 *Id.* at 418. The *Garcetti* majority noted that this rule might not apply in the context of speech by professors employed at a public college or university. *See id.* at 425. Justice Kennedy explained that "[t]here is some argument that expression related to academic scholarship or classroom instruction implicates additional constitutional interests that are not fully accounted for by this Court's customary employee-speech jurisprudence." *Id.* Nevertheless, he concluded that "[w]e need not, and for that reason do not, decide whether the analysis we conduct today would apply in the same manner to a case involving speech related to scholarship or teaching." *Id.* However, as Justice David H. Souter observed in dissent, the majority plainly failed to address this question, and the Supreme Court has not yet issued a definitive ruling on this question. *See id.* at 438–39 (Souter, J., dissenting) (arguing that the *Garcetti* rule does not apply to college

and university professors at state-operated institutions of higher learning and expressing the "hope that today's majority does not mean to imperil First Amendment protection of academic freedom in public colleges and universities"). *But cf.* Grutter v. Bollinger, 539 U.S. 306, 329 (2003) ("We have long recognized that, given the important purpose of public education and the expansive freedoms of speech and thought associated with the university environment, universities occupy a special niche in our constitutional tradition."); Keyishian v. Bd. of Regents, 385 U.S. 589, 603 (1967) ("Our Nation is deeply committed to safeguarding academic freedom, which is of transcendent value to all of us and not merely to the teachers concerned. That freedom is therefore a special concern of the First Amendment, which does not tolerate laws that cast a pall of orthodoxy over the classroom.").

94 *Garcetti*, 547 U.S. at 421.

95 573 U.S. 228 (2014).

96 *Id.* at 238–39.

97 *Id.* at 238 ("Truthful testimony under oath by a public employee outside the scope of his ordinary job duties is speech as a citizen for First Amendment purposes.").

98 *Id.*

99 *See id.* at 238–41.

100 *Id.* at 238.

101 For thoughtful critiques of *Garcetti*'s shortcomings, see Erwin Chemerinsky, *Not a Free Speech Court*, 53 ARIZ. L. REV. 723, 725–27 (2011); Papandrea, *supra* note 34, at 2118–20, 2136–39.

102 Garcetti v. Ceballos, 547 U.S. 410 (2006).

103 Waters v. Churchill, 511 U.S. 661 (1994).

104 *See* Papandrea, *supra* note 34, at 2122 ("Since *Pickering*, however, the Court has cut back dramatically on the free speech rights of public employees, especially with its most recent decision in *Garcetti v. Ceballos*.").

105 *See infra* notes 142–58 and accompanying text.

106 *See infra* notes 152–54 and accompanying text.

107 *See* Post, *supra* note 44, at 164–65, 171–76.

108 *See* ZOOTOPIA (Walt Disney Pictures 2016) (presenting DMV offices in Zootopia, an otherwise paradisiacal urban metropolis populated by peacefully coexisting anthropomorphic animals, as being staffed entirely with slow-talking, slow-moving, and slow-acting sloths).

109 *See* ROBERT C. POST, CONSTITUTIONAL DOMAINS: DEMOCRACY, COMMUNITY, MANAGEMENT 234–40 (1995) (discussing and explaining the "government's need to manage speech within its institutions" and positing that some regulation of employee speech is essential because it is necessary "in order to achieve the institution's legitimate objectives"). Post argues persuasively that "[m]anagerial authority is controlled by First Amendment rules different from those that control the exercise of the authority used by the state when it acts to govern the general public." *Id.* at 240. Accordingly, "[w]hen it exercises the authority of management, the state can constitutionally control speech so as to

facilitate the institutional attainment of organizational ends." *Id.; see also id.* at 247–55 (discussing and defining the boundary that separates managerial authority from more general regulatory authority).

110 Post, *supra* note 44, at 171; *see also* Robert C. Post, *Between Governance and Management: The History and Theory of the Public Forum*, 34 UCLA L. REV. 1713, 1788–89 (1987) (describing and discussing the "managerial domain" of government action that affects speech).

111 *See* Elrod v. Burns, 427 U.S. 347, 355–60, 372–73 (1976) (plurality opinion).

112 *See* Branti v. Finkel, 445 U.S. 507, 517–19 (1980).

113 *Elrod*, 427 U.S. at 372–73.

114 *See* O'Hare Truck Serv., Inc. v. City of Northlake, 518 U.S. 712, 720–21 (1996).

115 Heffernan v. City of Paterson, 136 S. Ct. 1412, 1417–19 (2016).

116 For descriptions and thoughtful discussions of the problem of government regulations or policies producing a "chilling effect," see Frederick Schauer, *Fear, Risk, and the First Amendment: Unraveling the "Chilling Effect,"* 58 B. U. L. REV. 685, 689–705 (1978); Monica Youn, *The Chilling Effect and the Problem of Private Action*, 66 VAND. L. REV. 1473, 1481–85 (2013).

117 *Heffernan*, 136 S. Ct. at 1418.

118 *Id.* at 1419.

119 *Id.*

120 *See id.* at 1418–19.

121 The government employer cannot rely on vague claims of potential disruption in the workplace, but, instead, must mount a necessity defense that involves demonstrating an operational need to use a partisan screen for the position; to date, however, the Supreme Court has validated only operational needs based on a policymaking authority and the regular receipt and possession of confidential information as sufficient to overcome the employee's First Amendment rights against forced association and coerced speech. Arch T. Allen, III, *A Study in Separation of Powers: Executive Power in North Carolina*, 77 N.C. L. REV. 2049, 2097–98 (1999); Martin H. Brinkley, Note, *Despoiling the Spoils*: Rutan v. Republican Party of Illinois, 69 N.C. L. REV. 719, 720–21 (1991); Christopher V. Fenlon, Note, *The Spoils System in Check? Public Employees' Rights to Political Affiliation & the Balkanized Policymaking Exception to § 1983 Liability for Wrongful Termination*, 30 CARDOZO L. REV. 2295, 2313 n.68 (2009). Beyond serving these interests, a government employer would be hard pressed to justify requiring a particular partisan identity, or lack of one, as a condition of government employment.

122 *See* Branti v. Finkel, 445 U.S. 507, 517–519 (1980).

123 *Id.* at 518.

124 *See supra* note 121.

125 *Heffernan*, 136 S. Ct. at 1418.

126 *Id.* at 1419.

127 *Id.*

128 *See id.* at 1417–19; *see also* Brinkley, *supra* note 121, at 720 (observing that the "*Elrod*, *Branti*, and *Rutan* holdings" effectively "bar officials from

conditioning" public employment on partisan loyalty and thereby "checkmated a weakened, but tenacious, political tradition"); Fenlon, *supra* note 121, at 2297 (noting that "in order to justify a political patronage dismissal, the government must demonstrate a significant interest in replacing public employees with individuals who are politically loyal to their employer" and that under this rule "termination of public employees because of their political affiliation [usually] fails under heightened scrutiny and violates the First Amendment"). To provide a concrete example, suppose that a non-confidential, non-policymaking employee in a government office, say a clerk in a county tax assessor's office, runs unsuccessfully for the elected county tax assessor's position – but loses in the general election to another candidate for the office, who subsequently assumes the office. Under the *Elrod/Branti* doctrine, her new boss, the person against whom she contested the general election, would not be permitted to fire her even if the campaign was highly contentious and bitterly contested, thus rendering the losing candidate's mere presence in the tax assessor's office highly disruptive.

129 *See* Papandrea, *supra* note 34, at 2118–20 (discussing the very weak scope of First Amendment protection that the *Pickering/Connick* doctrine conveys on government employees and arguing that "[e]mployees do not stop being citizens when they are at work; likewise, they do not stop being employees when they are not"). Professor Papandrea persuasively argues that "*Pickering's* balancing test, which weighs the value of the employee's speech against the government-employer's interest in restricting it, fails to limit government control over its employee's speech activities sufficiently." *Id.* at 2120.

130 *See* MARTIN & SUSAN J. TOLCHIN, PINSTRIPE PATRONAGE: POLITICAL FAVORITISM FROM THE CLUBHOUSE TO THE WHITE HOUSE AND BEYOND 5–6, 24–28 (2011).

131 West Virginia Bd. of Educ. v. Barnette, 319 U.S. 624, 642 (1943).

132 *See* Kathleen M. Sullivan, *Unconstitutional Conditions*, 102 HARV. L. REV. 1413, 1459–61, 1503–05 (1989).

133 *See* KALVEN, *supra* note 77, at 140–41, 237 n.327 (positing a serious First Amendment problem arising from government's invocation of an audience's hostile reaction to a speaker as a constitutionally acceptable basis for requiring the speaker to cease and desist from speaking because such an approach essentially makes the speech rights of a political minority seeking lawful change contingent on the goodwill of a potentially hostile majority); *see also* Robert C. Post, *The Constitutional Concept of Public Discourse: Outrageous Opinion, Democratic Deliberation, and* Hustler Magazine v. Falwell, 103 HARV. L. REV. 601, 632 (1990) (arguing that the First Amendment should preclude the use of tort law and civil juries to censor highly offensive speech because the use of a liability standard based on the offensiveness or outrageousness of speech "would enable a single community to use the authority of the state to confine speech within its own notions of propriety").

134 To be sure, if a government employee engages in misconduct or fails to perform her duties reliably, alleging that discipline or discharge reflects an impermissible partisan motive will not necessarily save the employee from an

adverse employment action. In such a case, the question would turn on whether the government's motive was a permissible one (misconduct) rather than an impermissible one (a partisan purge). *See* Mt. Healthy City Sch. Dist. Bd. of Educ. v. Doyle, 429 U.S. 274, 286–87 (1977); *see also* Massaro, *supra* note 22, at 17–20, 68 (discussing the pernicious effects of *Mt. Healthy City Sch. Dist. Bd. of Educ. v. Doyle* in the context of government employee speech).

135 Connick v. Myers, 461 U.S. 138, 142 (1983) (applying a balancing test that weighs a government employee's interest in speaking about a matter of public concern against the workplace disruption that the speech either causes or might cause); Pickering v. Bd. of Educ., 391 U.S. 563, 568 (1968) (using potential disruption in the workplace as a permissible basis for firing a government employee who speaks out about a matter of public concern); *see* Randy J. Kozel, *Free Speech and Parity: A Theory of Public Employee Rights*, 53 Wm. & Mary L. Rev. 1985, 2019 (2012) ("Through its contemplation of scenarios in which the disruption caused by speech provides a lawful basis for discipline, the *Pickering* test can be understood as constitutionalizing a 'heckler's veto' for controversial expressions."); Norton, *supra* note 80, at 47 (warning that "unexamined deference to government's fears about onlookers' reactions to workers' off-duty speech threatens to institutionalize the long-maligned 'heckler's veto'"). *But see* Papandrea, *supra* note 34, at 2156 (noting disagreement in the lower courts regarding "whether any actual or expected external disruption resulting from an offended public can play a role in the *Pickering* balancing" and observing that "[s]ome courts have held that only actual or potential disruption of internal operations could outweigh an employee's right to engage in otherwise protected expressive activities").

136 *See* Kozel, *supra* note 135, at 2019–20; Levinson, *supra* note 22, at 17–19, 59–61; Massaro, *supra* note 22, at 4, 20–25. Massaro notes that efforts to engage workplace colleagues regarding problems in the workplace are particularly perilous because engaging one's coworkers could be deemed intrinsically "disruptive" of the workplace. *Id.* at 24 (observing that "if a worker engages others to join in the chorus he or she may pose a threat, and thus can be removed" and, moreover, "that worker can be removed when an employer merely anticipates that the chorus might get too large and disruptive"). Massaro correctly concludes that the *Pickering/Connick* framework permits an employer to "prevent a grievance from spreading and, as it gains support, from capturing the public's interest." *Id.*

137 Tolchin & Tolchin, *supra* note 130, at 5–6, 24–28.

138 Post, *supra* note 109, at 254–61, 282–90; *see* Post, *supra* note 44, at 164–67, 170–75.

139 *See* Gorman, et al., *supra* note 9.

140 *See* Hu, *supra* note 10, at 1686–93; Megan Blass, Note, *The New Data Marketplace: Protecting Personal Data, Electronic Communications, and Individual Privacy in the Age of Mass Surveillance Through a Return to a Property-Based Approach to the Fourth Amendment*, 42 Hastings Const. L.Q. 577, 579–82 (2015); Bruce Ackerman, *Breach or Debate*, Foreign Pol'y (Aug. 1,

2013), http://foreignpolicy.com/2013/08/01/breach-or-debate/ [https://perma.cc/ J4W2-LCAF] (last visited Mar. 29, 2019). For a comprehensive and thoughtful treatment of the government's reasons for resisting disclosure of national security surveillance programs – and also the reasons why transparency about such programs is necessary, see David E. Pozen, *The Leaky Leviathan: Why the Government Condemns and Condones Unlawful Disclosures of Information*, 127 HARV. L. REV. 512 (2013).

141 *See* Massaro, *supra* note 22, at 44; Norton, *supra* note 80, at 21–22, 49–50; Kleinbrodt, *supra* note 18, at 113–14.

142 562 U.S. 443 (2011).

143 Post, *supra* note 133, at 668–69 (noting that "[a]lthough the 'public concern' test rests on a clean and superficially attractive rationale, the Court has offered virtually no analysis to develop its logic" and positing that, "as matters now stand, the test of 'public concern' 'amounts to little more than a message to judges and attorneys that no standards are necessary because they will, or should, know a public concern when they see it'" (internal citation omitted)). Post explains that because free and open public deliberation is essential to the functioning of democratic self-government, "every issue that can potentially agitate the public is also potentially relevant to democratic self-governance," and, accordingly, "[t]he normative conception of public concern, insofar as it is used to exclude speech from public discourse, is thus incompatible with the very democratic self-governance it seeks to facilitate." *Id.* at 670.

144 *Snyder*, 562 U.S. at 448–49. Westboro congregants brandished signs bearing slogans including "God Hates Fags," "God Hates the USA/Thank God for 9/11," and "Thank God for Dead Soldiers." *Id.* at 448.

145 *See id.* at 458–61.

146 RONALD J. KROTOSZYNSKI, JR., PRIVACY REVISITED: A GLOBAL PERSPECTIVE ON THE RIGHT TO BE LEFT ALONE 271 n.169 (2016); *see also* Post, *supra* note 133, at 678–80 (positing that "the criterion of 'public concern' lacks internal coherence" and is entirely dependent on "a wide array of particular variables inherent in specific communicative contexts").

147 William Van Alstyne, *Remembering Melville Nimmer: Some Cautionary Notes on Commercial Speech*, 43 UCLA L. REV. 1635, 1640–43, 1646–48 (1996). Professor Van Alstyne argues, with some persuasive force, that if one defines speech in very broad and inclusive terms, the social costs of accommodating speech will increase correspondingly, rendering it less difficult for the government to justify regulating, or even banning, speech activity on government property. In the specific context of the *Discovery Network* decision, he posits that "[i]n 'leveling up' commercial speech ... the Court has done less leveling up than leveling down." *Id.* at 1648. The result is arguably perverse: "For an increasing number of limitations that may make reasonable sense in restraining commercial vendors now tend to be sustained even if (and sometimes, according to *Discovery Network*, *only if*) applied 'equally' to political and social advocacy uses as well." *Id.* (emphasis in original); *see* Frederick Schauer, *Commercial Speech and the Architecture of the First*

Amendment, 56 U. Cin. L. Rev. 1181, 1187 (1988) (arguing that low value speech, such as commercial speech, "is not a central theoretical concern of the [F]irst [A]mendment" and should be subject to government regulation more readily than core political speech). *But cf.* City of Cincinnati v. Discovery Network, Inc., 507 U.S. 410, 424–28 (1993) (holding that Cincinnati could not treat commercial publications less favorably than non-commercial publications unless commercial periodicals containing nothing but advertising contributed in a distinctive way to creating the problem that the city's regulation sought to address).

148 *See, e.g.*, Brown v. Entm't Merchs. Ass'n, 564 U.S. 786, 790–92 (2011); United States v. Playboy Entm't Grp., Inc. 529 U.S. 803, 811–12, 818 (2000); R.A.V. v. City of St. Paul, 505 U.S. 377, 394–95 (1992). As Professor Post explains, the need to maintain the open and free-flowing debate required to sustain the process of democratic self-governance should lead us to be very cautious before excluding "speech from public discourse, particularly if, as a normative matter, the content of the speech at issue cannot definitively be excluded as irrelevant to matters of self-governance." Post, *supra* note 133, at 674.

149 *See* Ashcroft v. ACLU, 535 U.S. 564, 573 (2002) ("[A]s a general matter, ... government has no power to restrict expression because of its message, its ideas, its subject matter, or its content." (alteration in original) (internal quotations omitted)); *see also* Elena Kagan, *The Changing Face of First Amendment Neutrality: R.A.V. v. St. Paul, Rust v. Sullivan, and the Problem of Content-Based Underinclusion*, 1992 Sup. Ct. Rev. 29, 70–71; Martin H. Redish, *The Content Distinction in First Amendment Analysis*, 34 Stan. L. Rev. 113 (1981).

150 *See* Vincent Blasi, *The Pathological Perspective and the First Amendment*, 85 Colum. L. Rev. 449, 449–52 (1985) (arguing that the federal courts should seek to protect dissenting speech most aggressively in times of disorder or perceived threat because such speech possesses particular importance, or value, in such perilous times). Professor Blasi posits that:

> [T]he overriding objective at all times should be to equip the first amendment to do maximum service in those historical periods when intolerance of unorthodox ideas is most prevalent and when governments are most able and most likely to stifle dissent systematically. The first amendment, in other words, should be targeted for the worst of times.

Id. at 449–50.

151 *See* Van Alstyne, *supra* note 147, at 1639–40.

152 *See* U.S. Const. amend. VI ("In all criminal prosecutions, the accused shall enjoy the right to a speedy and public trial, by an impartial jury of the State and district wherein the crime shall have been committed ...").

153 *See* Duncan v. Louisiana, 391 U.S. 145 (1968).

154 Apodaca v. Oregon, 406 U.S. 404 (1972).

155 Williams v. Florida, 399 U.S. 78 (1970)

156 Ballew v. Georgia, 435 U.S. 223 (1978).

157 *See* Blasi, *supra* note 150, at 452–56 (arguing that the federal courts should seek to protect jealously the "central core" of the First Amendment to ensure that it functions effectively as a check on the suppression of dissent – and dissenters – in times of national crisis).

158 *See* Sullivan, *supra* note 132, at 1416, 1503–04. Professor Sullivan cautions that the *Connick/Pickering* line "present[s] the obvious danger that courts will find justification for requiring public employee silence or conformity too lightly." *Id.* at 1504 n.390. She posits that government claims of managerial necessity to restrict government employee speech, including partisan or ideological speech, "should be treated as infringing speech and thus in need of strong justification, but as arguably justified by the need for an efficient or depoliticized bureaucracy." *Id.* at 1504.

159 Sally Yates, the Acting Attorney General who refused to defend President Donald Trump's anti-Muslim immigration order provides an example of a government employee who chose courage – and was summarily dismissed from her position as a result of this choice. *See* Anemona Hartocollis, *Sally Yates Tells Harvard Law Students Why She Defied Trump*, N.Y. TIMES (May 24, 2017), www.nytimes.com/2017/05/24/us/sally-yates-trump-travel-ban-harvard-law.html [https://perma.cc/2A3D-6B5A]; Sarah Posner, Opinion, *Sally Yates Just Publicly Confirmed Important Facts About the Trump-Russia Story*, WASH. POST: THE PLUM LINE (May 8, 2017), www.washingtonpost.com/blogs/plum-line/wp/2017/05/08/sally-yates-just-publicly-confirmed-important-facts-about-the-trump-russia-story [https://perma.cc/4772-QL3V].

160 The government employee speech doctrine already draws a distinction between speech regarding a matter of public concern and other kinds of speech. Connick v. Myers, 461 U.S. 138, 145–48 (1983). Moreover, the *New York Times Co. v. Sullivan* line of cases also relies on a distinction between speech related to a matter of public concern and other kinds of speech – as well as distinctions based on the subject of the speech – namely whether the subject of the allegedly false speech is a public official, a public figure, or a private figure involved in a matter of public concern. *See* Ronald J. Krotoszynski, Jr., *The Polysemy of Privacy*, 88 IND. L.J. 881, 889–90, 901–02, 901 n.96, 912 n.146 (2013); *see also* Dun & Bradstreet, Inc. v. Greenmoss Builders, Inc., 472 U.S. 749, 755–61 (1985) (discussing how the First Amendment limits the scope of defamation law to ensure robust and wide-open public debate about public officials, public figures, and matters of public concern).

161 Tiffany Smiley, Opinion, *Our Postwar Trauma at the VA*, WALL ST. J. (Dec. 28, 2016), www.wsj.com/articles/make-the-va-great-again-1482882642 [https://perma.cc/QR3B-QT5U] (discussing the inefficiencies and pathologies associated with obtaining medical services through the Department of Veterans Affairs and asking "[i]n a world where technology is making almost all aspects of life easier, why isn't there a website, a liaison, or an advocate" to assist veterans seeking medical benefits for service-related injuries). The myriad dysfunctions that currently plague the Department of Veterans Affairs medical

care system are known only because VA employees had the courage to speak out – and many have suffered direct forms of retaliation as a result. *See* Tori Richards, *Whistleblowers Claim Retaliation for Revealing VA Horrors*, NBC NEWS (Jan. 29, 2017, 4:01 EST), www.nbcnews.com/news/us-news/whistle blowers-claim-retaliation-revealing-va-horrors-n707996 [https://perma.cc/ F4M7-PQUU] (reporting on the failure of the VA to provide timely treatment to veterans at multiple facilities and on targeted retaliation against VA employees who disclosed the agency's systematic failures to provide care to veterans entitled to receive it).

162 *See* Vincent Blasi, *The First Amendment and the Ideal of Civic Courage: The Brandeis Opinion in* Whitney v. California, 29 WM. & MARY L. REV. 653, 692–96 (1988) (arguing that First Amendment theory and doctrine presuppose the necessity of individual citizens taking risks, thereby displaying "civic courage," in order to ensure that the process of democratic self-government functions effectively).

163 *See* Blasi, *supra* note 150, at 474 (arguing that "[i]n crafting standards to govern specific areas of first amendment dispute, courts that adopt the pathological perspective should place a premium on confining the range of discretion left to future decisionmakers" and that "[c]onstitutional standards that are highly outcome-determinative of the cases to which they apply are thus to be preferred").

164 *See id.* at 452–56 (discussing the "pathological perspective," under which federal courts should protect speech most aggressively in times of national tumult and crisis).

165 Dennis v. United States, 341 U.S. 494, 510 (1951). *Dennis* sustained convictions under the Smith Act based on membership in the Communist Party. To be sure, Chief Justice Fred M. Vinson's majority opinion in *Dennis* is generally reviled because it permits government to criminalize political beliefs in the absence of any concrete criminal behavior based on those beliefs. *See* Thomas I. Emerson, *Toward a General Theory of the First Amendment*, 72 YALE L.J. 877, 877, 911–13 (1963); Gerald Gunther, *Learned Hand and the Origins of Modern First Amendment Doctrine: Some Fragments of History*, 27 STAN. L. REV. 719, 752–55 (1975); Kenneth L. Karst, *The First Amendment and Harry Kalven: An Appreciative Comment on the Advantages of Thinking Small*, 13 UCLA L. REV. 1, 11 (1965). On the other hand, however, the Hand formula does have its fans. *See, e.g.*, Richard A. Posner, *Free Speech in an Economic Perspective*, 20 SUFFOLK U. L. REV. 1, 8 (1986). I cite *Dennis* not to endorse the decision's outcome or precise reasoning, but instead to illustrate that a cost/benefit analysis that balances the social value of speech is feasible. Vinson wrote that:

Chief Judge Learned Hand, writing for the majority below, interpreted the phrase as follows: "In each case [courts] must ask whether the gravity of the 'evil,' discounted by its improbability, justifies such invasion of free speech as is necessary to avoid the danger." 183 F.2d at 212. We adopt this statement of the rule. As articulated by Chief Judge Hand, it is as succinct and

inclusive as any other we might devise at this time. It takes into consideration those factors which we deem relevant, and relates their significances.
More we cannot expect from words.

Dennis, 341 U.S. at 510 (alterations in original); *see also* United States v. *Dennis*,
183 F.2d 201, 212 (2d Cir. 1950), *aff'd*, 341 U.S. 494 (1951). In the context of
whistleblowing speech, a reviewing court would consider the gravity of the
wrongdoing exposed by the government employee's whistleblowing speech
discounted by the probability of it being reported or discovered by another
source. To the extent that the government employee's speech was the only
means of exposing the alleged wrongdoing, it should receive greater protection
than identical speech that would probably have come to light absent the
whistleblowing speech.

166 *See, e.g.*, Whistleblower Protection Act of 1989, Pub. L. 101–12, 103 Stat. 16
    (codified at 5 U.S.C. §§ 1201–1222 (2016)); Miriam A. Cherry, *Whistling in the
    Dark? Corporate Fraud, Whistleblowers, and the Implications of the
    Sarbanes-Oxley Act for Employment Law*, 79 WASH. L. REV. 1029, 1087–120
    (2004) (providing a comprehensive compendium of state whistleblower
    protection laws and describing their scope of application); *id.* at 1121–23
    (listing and summarizing federal whistleblower protection laws); Robert
    G. Vaughn, *State Whistleblower Statutes and the Future of Whistleblower
    Protection*, 51 ADMIN. L. REV. 581, 589–91, 597–601 (1999). A wide variety of
    federal and state laws confer highly targeted and limited protection on
    whistleblowers; variations in such laws include "the standard for disclosure,
    whether internal disclosure is required, whether disclosures for violation of
    federal laws are protected, and the entities to which disclosures may be made."
    Robert G. Vaughn, *America's First Comprehensive Statute Protecting Corporate
    Whistleblowers*, 57 ADMIN. L. REV. 1, 68 (2005); *see id.* ("A variety of state laws
    protect whistleblowers. The character and content of these laws vary.").

167 Professor Cherry observes that most states do not provide comprehensive
    protection for whistleblowers – regardless of whether an employee works for
    the government or for a private employer. Cherry, *supra* note 166, at 1045–46.
    Moreover, she also cautions that "the current federal regulatory approach is
    piecemeal." *Id.* at 1121.

168 Both federal and state statutory protections for whistleblowing inevitably
    protect only employees who rely on internal reporting procedures, rather
    than releasing information about wrongdoing to the press or other outside
    parties. *See* Gerard Sinzdak, Comment, *An Analysis of Current Whistleblower
    Laws: Defending a More Flexible Approach to Reporting Requirements*, 96
    CALIF. L. REV. 1633, 1633, 1638–39 (2008) (noting that "[m]ost state
    whistleblower statutes restrict the parties to whom a whistleblower may report
    in order to receive protection from retaliation" and that the main federal law,
    the Whistleblower Protection Act of 1989, does not protect employees who
    make external disclosures either). Accordingly, "[i]f an employee blows the
    whistle on a specific type of violation, then that employee is protected from

retaliation by federal law," but, on the other hand, noting that such "piecemeal," incomplete protection quite often leaves an employee with "no remedy whatsoever." Cherry, *supra* note 166, at 1121; *see* Sinzdak, *supra*, at 1633–34 (noting that virtually no whistleblower protection laws convey protection on employees who "choose to report to the media or other non-governmental third parties").

169 5 U.S.C.A. §§ 7321–326 (West 2007 & Supp. 2017). The first federal effort to cabin the practice of using federal jobs to animate a partisan spoils system was the Civil Service Act. *See* Civil Service Act, ch. 27, § 2, 22 Stat. 403, 403–04 (1883). The Supreme Court has generally sustained civil service laws that proscribe partisan political activity by government employees. *See* United Public Workers of America v. Mitchell, 330 U.S. 75, 95–103 (1947). In *Mitchell*, Justice Stanley Reed explained that "[t]o declare that the present supposed evils of political activity are beyond the power of Congress to redress would leave the nation impotent to deal with what many sincere men believe is a material threat to the democratic system." *Id.* at 99.

170 *See* Elrod v. Burns, 427 U.S. 347, 379–80 (1976) (Powell, J., dissenting) (arguing that maintaining the health and vibrancy of the political parties is a sufficient justification for a patronage system for government employment, noting the existence of federal and state civil service protections, but observing that "the course of such reform is of limited relevance to the task of constitutional adjudication in this case").

171 *See id.* at 370–73.

172 *Id.* at 371–73; *cf. id.* at 386–87 (Powell, J., dissenting) (arguing that the existence of statutory civil service protection against patronage-based hiring decisions adequately protects the First Amendment rights of government employees and objecting that the majority's "*ad hoc* judicial judgment runs counter to the judgments of the representatives of the people in state and local governments, representatives who have chosen, in most instances, to retain some patronage practices in combination with a merit-oriented civil service").

173 *See, e.g.*, U.S. Civil Serv. Comm'n v. Nat'l Ass'n of Letter Carriers, 413 U.S. 548, 556, 564–67 (1973); *Mitchell*, 330 U.S. at 95–103.

174 MEIKLEJOHN, *supra* note 8, at 25–27, 36–38, 70, 88–89.

175 Texas v. Johnson, 491 U.S. 397, 414 (1989) ("If there is a bedrock principal underlying the First Amendment, it is that the government may not prohibit the expression of an idea simply because society finds the idea itself offensive or disagreeable."); Police Dep't of Chicago v. Mosley, 408 U.S. 92, 96–98 (1972) (holding invalid a viewpoint-based regulation of speech and explaining that viewpoint-based regulations of speech are presumptively inconsistent with the First Amendment); *see* CASS R. SUNSTEIN, DEMOCRACY AND THE PROBLEM OF FREE SPEECH 12–13, 169 (1995) (noting that viewpoint-based regulations of speech are particularly objectionable because they represent efforts by government to tilt the marketplace of ideas in one direction, thereby foreclosing the normal operation of democratic politics, and arguing that "[w]hen government regulates on the basis of viewpoint, it will frequently be

acting for objectionable reasons"). Justice Thurgood Marshall explained the
rule against viewpoint discrimination in these terms:

> Necessarily, then, under the Equal Protection Clause, not to mention the
> First Amendment itself, government may not grant the use of a forum to
> people whose views it finds acceptable, but deny use to those wishing to
> express less favored or more controversial views. And it may not select
> which issues are worth discussing or debating in public facilities. There is
> an "equality of status in the field of ideas," and government must afford all
> points of view an equal opportunity to be heard. Once a forum is opened up
> to assembly or speaking by some groups, government may not prohibit
> others from assembling or speaking on the basis of what they intend to say.

Mosley, 408 U.S. at 96 (internal citation omitted); *see* Perry Educ. Ass'n v. Perry
Local Educators' Ass'n, 460 U.S. 37, 57 (1983) (Brennan, J., dissenting) ("The
First Amendment's prohibition against government discrimination among
viewpoints on particular issues falling within the realm of protected speech
has been noted extensively in the opinions of this Court.").

176 *See* Waters v. Churchill, 511 U.S. 661, 680–81 (1994).
177 *See* Garcetti v. Ceballos, 547 U.S. 410 (2006). If applied literally, the *Garcetti*
rule would essentially eliminate any protection for college and university
professors because their employment encompasses their teaching and
writing. *Garcetti* notes, but does not decide, the question of whether
a different rule would apply in this context because of the First Amendment's
protection of academic freedom in the area of higher education. *Id.* at 425. *But
cf.* Keyishian v. Bd. of Regents, 385 U.S. 589, 603–04 (1967); Shelton v. Tucker,
364 U.S. 479, 487 (1960); Sweezy v. New Hampshire, 354 U.S. 234, 250 (1957).
178 *See* Chemerinsky, *supra* note 101, at 725–27 (noting the narrowing of
protections for government employee speakers under the Roberts Court).
179 *See* Papandrea, *supra* note 34, at 2122 (observing that the Rehnquist and Roberts
Courts "ha[ve] cut back dramatically on the free speech rights of public
employees").
180 *See* MEIKLEJOHN, *supra* note 8, at 22–27, 36–41, 88–89, 91.
181 *Id.* at 25–27. Professor Meiklejohn argued forcefully that "public intelligence"
is required for democratic self-government to function, *see id.* at 70, in addition
to the citizenry possessing the information necessary to reach sound collective
judgments about the government on election day. *See id.* at 88.

5 SHEDDING THEIR CONSTITUTIONAL RIGHTS AT THE SCHOOLHOUSE GATE

1 J. Peter Byrne, *Academic Freedom: A "Special Concern of the First Amendment,"*
99 YALE L.J. 251, 251 (1989).
2 *See* William W. Van Alstyne, *Academic Freedom and the First Amendment in the
Supreme Court of the United States: An Unhurried Historical Review*, 53 LAW &
CONTEMP. PROBS. 79, 87–88, 112–18, 153–54 (Summer 1990); William W. Van

Alstyne, *The Specific Theory of Academic Freedom and the General Issue of Civil Liberties*, THE ANNALS OF THE AM. LEGAL ACADEMY 140 (1972).

3 *See* Board of Educ. v. Pico, 457 U.S. 853, 863 (1982) (plurality opinion) ("The Court has long recognized that local school boards have broad discretion in the management of school affairs.").

4 The Burger Court did recognize that, with respect to curricular speech, school officials enjoy a broad power to regulate speech to advance legitimate educational objectives. *See* Bethel School Dist. No. 603 v. Fraser, 478 U.S. 675 (1986) ("The process of educating our youth for citizenship in public schools is not confined to books, the curriculum, and the civics class; schools must teach by example the shared values of a civilized social order. ... The schools, as instruments of the state, may determine that the essential lessons of civil, mature conduct cannot be conveyed in a school that tolerates lewd, indecent, or offensive speech and conduct such as that indulged in by this confused boy."). Whether public school faculty and students possess "academic freedom" as such is also a question that remains unclear; one could characterize *Tinker* as simply recognizing a more generic right to speak about matters of public concern while on a public school campus. For a relevant discussion regarding university students, as opposed to faculty, see William W. Van Alstyne, *The Judicial Trend Toward Student Academic Freedom*, 20 FLA. L. REV. 290 (1968).

5 *See infra* text and accompanying notes 80 to 101.

6 Tinker v. Des Moines Indep. Cmty. School Dist., 393 U.S. 503, 506 (1969).

7 *Id.*

8 Meyer v. Nebraska, 262 U.S. 390 (1923) and Pierce v. Society of Sisters, 268 U.S. 510 (1925), *Lochner*-era substantive due process cases, recognized that the freedom of contract secured by the Due Process Clauses of the Fifth and Fourteenth Amendments encompasses the right to learn a foreign language (*Meyer*) and to seek primary and secondary education in pervasively religious K-12 schools (*Pierce*). Both cases focus primarily on the constitutional right of fit, custodial parents to oversee the education of their children – rather than on the speech rights of the children themselves within the school environment. Accordingly, neither of these decisions represents a recognition of the speech rights of school-age children inside the public schools.

9 *See* West Virginia State Bd. of Educ. v. Barnette, 319 U.S. 624, 641 (1943) ("National unity as an end which officials may foster by persuasion and example is not in question. The problem is whether under our Constitution compulsion as here employed is a permissible means for its achievement."). *Barnette* vindicated the free speech claims of Marie and Gathie Barnett to refuse to participate in a daily flag salute in their West Virginia elementary school. *See id.* at 642 ("We think the action of the local authorities in compelling the flag salute and pledge transcends constitutional limitations on their power and invades the sphere of intellect and spirit which it is the purpose of the First Amendment to our Constitution to reserve from all official control."). However, *Barnette* as a legal precedent did not lead to judicial recognition of a more generalized right to freedom of speech by students – as opposed to

freedom from compelled speech in the context of a flag salute. *Tinker* represents the Supreme Court's first endorsement of the proposition that elementary and secondary school students possess a general right to freedom of speech while on school grounds.

10 Sweezy v. New Hampshire, 354 U.S. 234, 250 (1957) ("The essentiality of freedom in the community of American universities is almost self-evident. No one should underestimate the vital role in a democracy that is played by those who guide and train our youth. To impose any strait jacket upon the intellectual leaders in our colleges and universities would imperil the future of our Nation."); *see also* Barenblatt v. United States, 360 U.S. 109, 112 (1959) ("When academic teaching-freedom and its corollary learning-freedom, so essential to the well-being of the Nation, are claimed, this Court will always be on the alert against intrusion by Congress into this constitutionally protected domain.").

11 Keyishian v. Bd. of Regents, 385 U.S. 589, 603 (1967) ("Our Nation is deeply committed to safeguarding academic freedom, which is of transcendent value to all of us and not merely to the teachers concerned. That freedom is therefore a special concern of the First Amendment, which does not tolerate laws that cast a pall of orthodoxy over the classroom.").

12 *See* Emily Suski, *A First Amendment Deference Approach to Reforming Anti-Bullying Laws*, 77 LA. L. REV. 701, 710–721 (2017) (describing and discussing current state anti-bullying laws). *But cf.* Terri R. Day & Danielle Weatherby, *Speech Narcissism*, 70 FLA. L. REV. 839, 882 (2018) (arguing that "in the name of political correctness, universities have prioritized the heckler's veto with little regard to the traditional First Amendment values of individualism, liberty, human dignity, or equality and have ignored the damage such abrogation does to their students" and also that "[d]espite their pure intent, political correctness measures intended to promote more vigorous speech have resulted in less speech"). Professor Suski observes that "[a]t the risk of making a large understatement, bullying among students is a complicated problem." Suski, *supra*, at 701. Bullying "can take multiple forms: physical, verbal, relational, which includes imposing social isolation on another, and cyberbullying." *Id.* Bullying in public schools is clearly a major problem affecting many students – some surveys estimate that as many as one in three middle school students will experience some form of school bullying. *See id.* at 701, 706–09 (discussing social science data on the ubiquity of bullying). Suski notes that "the effects of bullying on victims are equal to, or more severe than, child maltreatment and are longer lasting." *Id.* at 709.

13 Sarah Kellogg, *Free Speech: The Campus Battlefield*, WASH. LAWYER 18, 19 (Sept. 2017).

14 *See id.* at 20–21 (discussing multiple instances of university administrations permitting a "heckler's veto," which involves a university administration's invocation of a campus audience's probable hostile response to a speaker's message as a basis for canceling an on-campus event featuring the controversial would-be speaker).

15 *See* Gene Nichol, *Keynote Address: Academic Activism and Freedom of Speech*, 39 SEATTLE U. L. REV. 1111, 1112–17 (2016).

16 Kellogg, *supra* note 13, at 21.

17 Douglas Belkin, *Colleges Face High Security Expenses*, WALL ST. J., Oct. 23, 2017, at A3.

18 *Id.*

19 *Id.*

20 Matt Pearce & Sarah Parvini, *Universities Show Resolve on Fraternity Transgressors*, L.A. TIMES, Mar. 19, 2015, at A8; Adam Kemp, *National SAE Leader Disputes OU President David Boren's Statement in Facebook Post*, DAILY OKLAHOMAN (Oklahoma City), Mar. 31, 2015, at A4.

21 Kimberly Hefling & Jesse J. Hollan, *USC N-Word Snapchat Is One in a Number of College Incidents*, POST & COURIER (Charleston, SC) (Apr. 2, 2015, 9:10 PM), www.postandcourier.com/article/20150403/PC16/150409764; Hudson Hongo, *South Carolina Student Suspended for Racist and Dumb WiFi Complaint*, GAWKER (Apr. 4, 2015, 4:30 PM), http://gawker.com/south-carolina-student-sus pended-for-racist-and-dumb-wi-1695718047. University of South Carolina President Harris Pastides immediately suspended the student from her studies and the university would not comment on whether it was initiating expulsion proceedings against her. *See* Associated Press, *South Carolina College Student Suspended Over Racial Slur*, YAHOO NEWS, Apr. 4, 2015, www.yahoo.com/news/ south-carolina-college-student-suspended-over-racial-slur-155117568.html.

22 Fredrik deBoer, *Closed Campus*, N.Y. TIMES, Sept. 13, 2015, at MM64–66; Derek Draplin, *Mixed Reactions as UM Screens "Sniper,"* DETROIT NEWS, Apr. 11, 2015, at A5.

23 *See, e.g.*, Morse v. Frederick, 551 U.S. 393 (2007).

24 *See, e.g.*, Barry P. McDonald, *Regulating Student Cyberspeech*, 77 MO. L. REV. 727 (2012) (providing a relevant discussion of the conflicting lower federal court precedents).

25 *See infra* text and accompanying notes 134 to 184.

26 *See* GREGORY P. MAGARIAN, MANAGED SPEECH: THE ROBERTS COURT'S FIRST AMENDMENT 69–79, 89–90, 133–34, 227–39 (2017).

27 *But cf.* Kathleen Sullivan, *Unconstitutional Conditions*, 102 HARV. L. REV. 1413, 1452–53 & 1453 n.60 (1989) (observing that the government's near monopoly over K-12 education raises a problem with coercion, particularly with respect to speech rights). Professor Sullivan cautions that "[e]ven if it is agreed that a condition on public education is coercive, of course, deep disagreement over its unconstitutionality may remain." *Id.*

28 *See* Day & Weatherby, *supra* note 12, at 848–52 (discussing the greater willingness of university administrators to permit students offended by speech to prevent it from occurring, discussing a number of relevant examples, and also observing that "[s]tudents on college campuses have increasingly begun demanding that professors issue 'trigger warnings' before discussing material in the classroom that may be offensive or trigger past trauma"); *see also* MAGARIAN, *supra* note 26, at 240, 252–53 (positing that "[t]he key institutional speech cases

Beard, Morse, and *Garcetti* diminish public debate by denying First Amendment protection to entire classes of speakers who live, study, or work under government institutional control" and arguing that the regime of "managed speech" deployed by the Roberts Court "encourages a public discussion where a limited number of speakers exchange a limited range of ideas"). To be sure, some universities, such as the University of Chicago and Washington University in St. Louis, have taken the opposite approach and broadly endorse the importance of freedom of speech on campus. *See* Day and Weatherby, *supra* note 12, at 853–54.

29 *See* Tinker v. Des Moines Indep. Cmty. School Dist., 393 U.S. 503, 508–09 (1969) (noting that protecting student and faculty speech on campus creates a risk of disruption but holding that "our Constitution says we must take this risk" and explaining that "our history says that it is this sort of hazardous freedom – this kind of openness – that is the basis of our national strength and of the independence and vigor of Americans who grow up and live in this relatively permissive, often disputatious, society"); *see also* Terminiello v. Chicago, 337 U. S. 1, 4–5 (1949) (holding that a hostile audience reaction to speaker's message is not a permissible basis for silencing a speaker because "a function of free speech under our system of government is to invite dispute").

30 *See* Wieman v. Updegraff, 344 U.S. 183, 196–97 (1952) (Frankfurter, J., concurring). *Wieman* involved an Oklahoma statute that required state employees to take a loyalty oath; the Supreme Court unanimously invalidated the state law. *See id.* at 191–92. The majority opinion did not address the question of academic freedom in the university context. However, in his concurrence, Justice Frankfurter observed that:

> To regard teachers – in our entire educational system, from the primary grades to the university – as the priests of our democracy is therefore not to indulge in hyperbole. It is the special task of teachers to foster those habits of open-mindedness and critical inquiry which alone make for responsible citizens, who, in turn, make possible an enlightened and effective public opinion. Teachers must fulfill their function by precept and practice, by the very atmosphere which they generate; they must be exemplars of open-mindedness and free inquiry. They cannot carry out their noble task if the conditions for the practice of a responsible and critical mind are denied to them. They must have the freedom of responsible inquiry, by thought and action, into the meaning of social and economic ideas, into the checkered history of social and economic dogma. They must be free to sift evanescent doctrine, qualified by time and circumstance, from that restless, enduring process of extending the bounds of understanding and wisdom, to assure which the freedoms of thought, of speech, of inquiry, of worship are guaranteed by the Constitution of the United States against infraction by National or State government.

Id. at 196–97. However, Justice Frankfurter wrote only for himself and Justice Douglas; Frankfurter's broad view of the First Amendment's protection of academic freedom did not command a majority of the Supreme Court in *Wieman.*

31 Sweezy v. New Hampshire, 354 U.S. 234, 250 (1957) ("The essentiality of freedom in the community of American universities is almost self-evident. No one should underestimate the vital role in a democracy that is played by those who guide and train our youth."). Chief Justice Earl Warren added that "[t]o impose any strait jacket upon the intellectual leaders in our colleges and universities would imperil the future of our Nation." *Id.* Accordingly, "[t]eachers and students must always remain free to inquire, to study and to evaluate, to gain new maturity and understanding; otherwise our civilization will stagnate and die." *Id.* Professor Byrne notes that "never before had the Court suggested that academic freedom was protected by the First Amendment." Byrne, *supra* note 1, at 290.

32 Barenblatt v. United States, 360 U.S. 109, 112 (1959) ("When academic teaching-freedom and its corollary learning-freedom, so essential to the well-being of the Nation, are claimed this Court will always be on the alert against intrusion by Congress into this constitutionally protected domain."). Shelton v. Tucker, 364 U.S. 479 (1960), also merits mention. *Shelton* invalidated an Arkansas law that required all public school teachers to provide an annual list of all organizations to which they belonged for the preceding five years – on pain of discharge for failing to disclose this information. *See id.* at 480–81. The Supreme Court invalidated the statute on First Amendment grounds because of its extreme chilling effect on associational freedom. *See id.* at 489–90. Along the way, in dicta, Justice Potter Stewart observed that "[t]he vigilant protection of constitutional freedoms is nowhere more vital than in the community of American schools." *Id.* at 487. *Shelton* does not, however, involve direct government efforts to limit or punish instructional speech and, in consequence, seems less directly related to academic freedom than *Sweezy* and *Barenblatt.*

33 *But cf.* Urofsky v. Gilmore, 216 F.3d 401, 410 (4th Cir. 2000) (en banc) (holding that "[o]ur review of the law, however, leads us to conclude that to the extent the Constitution recognizes any right of 'academic freedom' above and the beyond the First Amendment rights to which every citizen is entitled, the right inheres in the University, not in individual professors"); *id.* at 412 (holding that "[t]he Supreme Court, to the extent it has constitutionalized a right of academic freedom at all, appears to have recognized only an institutional right of self-governance in academic affairs"). In my view, Judge William W. Wilkins, Jr. writing for the *Urofsky* en banc majority, grossly mischaracterized the Supreme Court's academic freedom decisions. In point of fact, the Supreme Court has recognized *both* institutional academic freedom and individual academic freedom for professors with respect to their research, writing, and teaching. *Compare* Board of Regents v. Southworth, 529 U.S. 217, 237 (2000) ("Our understanding of academic freedom has included not merely liberty from restraints on thought, expression, and association in the academy, but also the idea that universities and schools should have the freedom to make decisions

about how and what to teach.") *with id.* at 238 n.4 (observing that "[o]ur university cases have dealt with restrictions imposed from outside the academy *on individual teachers' speech or associations*") (emphasis added); Keyishian v. Board of Regents, 385 U.S. 589, 603 (1967) ("Our nation is deeply committed to safeguarding academic freedom, which is of transcendent value to all of us and *not merely to the teachers concerned.*") (emphasis added). The Supreme Court's precedents make clear that academic freedom encompasses the institutional right of colleges and universities to operate free and clear of direct forms of government-imposed political controls and also the right of individual academics to pursue their research, writing, and lecturing without university-imposed controls wholly unrelated to the academic legitimacy of the faculty member's work. *See infra* text and accompanying notes 34 to 56. As Professor Robert Post argues, academic freedom relates to a joint project of universities as institutions and individual academics to "facilitate the application and improvement of professional standards to advance knowledge for the public good." Robert C. Post, Democracy, Expertise, Academic Freedom: A First Amendment Jurisprudence for the Modern State 78 (2012). I find Professor Post's functional predicate for academic freedom, based on the process of knowledge creation, highly persuasive – academic freedom exists because "government control over factual truth is in tension with the value of democratic legitimation." *Id.* at 29. Moreover, "[a] state that controls our knowledge controls our minds." *Id.* at 33.

34 Keyishian v. Bd. of Regents, 385 U.S. 589, 591–96 (1967).

35 *Id.* at 593–96.

36 Byrne, *supra* note 1, at 295.

37 *Keyishian*, 385 U.S. at 603.

38 *See id.* at 604, 608–09.

39 Byrne, *supra* note 1, at 298.

40 *Id.* at 257.

41 *Id.; see also* Katheryn D. Katz, *The First Amendment's Protection of Expressive Activity in the University Classroom: A Constitutional Myth*, 16 U.C. Davis L. Rev. 857, 858 (1983) (observing the Supreme Court's "eloquent rhetoric on 'academic freedom' … creates the impression that the university classroom provides the professor with a higher order and greater quantum of first amendment protection than is available to those who follow less exalted callings in less sacrosanct workplaces" but cautioning that "[t]his impression, however, does not conform to the reality of the Court's first amendment jurisprudence"); Frederick Schauer, *Is There a Right to Academic Freedom?*, 77 U. Colo. L. Rev. 907, 912–13 (2006) (positing that "[t]he individual right to academic freedom that now exists … turns out to be far less grounded in Supreme Court doctrine than is often maintained, and significantly more limited than is commonly understood and even more commonly promoted").

42 *See* Dan Frosch, *Professor's Dismissal Upheld by Colorado Supreme Court*, N.Y. Times, Sept. 11, 2012, at A12 (reporting on the Colorado Supreme Court's decision upholding the University of Colorado's decision to fire Churchill "for

academic misconduct" rather than his public statements about persons killed in the 9/11 attacks, despite Churchill's contention that the university's academic misconduct charges were entirely pretextual); *see also* Jennifer Elrod, *Critical Inquiry: A Tool for Protecting the Dissident Professor's Academic Freedom*, 96 CALIF. L. REV. 1669, 1670–71, 1673–78, 1691 (2008). Professor Elrod argues that "[i]n my view, the decision by CU's Chancellor and Board of Regents to fire Churchill was a patently obvious attempt to punish Churchill's expression of his personal view of a national political matter." *Id.* at 1670.

43 *See* McKennon v. Nashville Banner Publishing Co., 513 U.S. 352 (1995).

44 Byrne, *supra* note 1, at 301.

45 *Nashville Banner Publishing Co.*, 513 U.S. at 361–62 ("We do conclude that here, and as a general rule in cases of this type, neither reinstatement nor front pay is an appropriate remedy. It would be both inequitable and pointless to order the reinstatement of someone the employer would have terminated, and will terminate, in any event and upon lawful grounds.").

46 *Id.* at 361.

47 *Id.*

48 *Id.* at 361–62.

49 *Id.* at 362.

50 *Id.* at 362–63.

51 As it happens, this proposition is actually open to some serious doubts; many lower federal courts have sustained a university's assertion of authority to regulate the curriculum and how courses within the curriculum are taught. For illustrative examples, see Edwards v. California Univ. of Pa., 156 F.3d 488, 491–92 (3rd Cir. 1998) and Bishop v. Aronov, 926 F.2d 1066, 1076–77 (11th Cir. 1991). *But cf.* Parate v. Isibor, 868 F.2d 821, 827–28 (6th Cir. 1989) (observing that "even as a nontenured professor, [Parate] retains the right to review each of his students' work and to communicate, according to his own professional judgment, academic evaluations and traditional letter grades" and holding that "Parate's First Amendment right to academic freedom was violated by the defendants because they ordered *Parate* to change Student 'Y's' original grade").

52 *See* Elrod, *supra* note 42, at 1670–72, 1677, 1681–83, 1691 (noting that current law permits university administrators to investigate controversial faculty members, such as former University of Colorado faculty member Ward Churchill, and to fire them for violations of university policy discovered incident to such investigations). In fact, lower federal courts reached this conclusion well before the Supreme Court decided *Nashville Banner Publishing Co.*, which was its first major pronouncement on whether after-acquired evidence could serve as a basis for terminating an employee who complained of violations of her constitutional or statutory rights. *See* Starsky v. Williams, 353 F. Supp. 900 (D. Ariz. 1972), *aff'd in part, rev'd in part*, 512 F.2d 109 (9th Cir. 1975). Morris J. Starsky, an untenured assistant professor of philosophy at Arizona State University, was an outspoken advocate of "marxist, socialist, trotskyist social revolution" and made multiple public calls for "social revolution at some future time." *Starsky*, 353 F. Supp. at 926. Starsky's public advocacy became

a matter of considerable public controversy. *See id.* at 924. His employer, Arizona State University, in Tempe, Arizona, fired him – not based on Starsky's teaching or advocacy of Marxist-Leninist political philosophy, but ostensibly for multiple violations of university policies, such as failing to meet regularly his scheduled class sessions. *See id.* at 906–15 (setting forth and discussing the administrative charges filed against Professor Starsky). Judge Carl Muecke held "if judged by constitutional standards, there are valid as well as invalid reasons for the discipline or discharge of a teacher, such discipline or discharge will not be set-aside by the federal court so long as the invalid reasons are not the primary reasons or motivation for the discharge." *Id.* at 916. Thus, "[a] claim of 'free speech' should not excuse actions by a teacher that would normally evoke the kind of discipline applied in this case," but "the employer should not selectively enforce rules, or use minor infractions as an ostensible reason for discipline or discharge in a case where the unprotected conduct complained of would normally evoke only mild disciplinary action or perhaps no discipline at all but for the protected conduct or speech." *Id.* The Ninth Circuit squarely affirmed this approach. *Starsky*, 512 F.2d at 111. Moreover, Judge Muecke's constitutional analysis more or less tracks *Nashville Banner Co.* exactly – the employer must shoulder the burden of showing that the infractions, rather than the protected conduct, motivated the discharge and that the conduct otherwise merited discharge. A problem, however, remains: In many cases of this sort, the investigation into the wrongful conduct is motivated by antipathy toward the university instructor's exercise of her First Amendment rights; the bill of indictment would never have come into existence but for the professor exercising her academic freedom. In sum, the federal courts will not require a university, much less a K-12 public school, to retain a faculty member if it discovers information that would justify discharge despite the information coming to light for retaliatory reasons.

53 Katz, *supra* note 41, at 859.

54 *Id.* at 883.

55 *See* Nichol, *supra* note 15, at 1112–13 & 1112 n.4.

56 Katz, *supra* note 41, at 882–83.

57 Garcetti v. Ceballos, 547 U.S. 410 (2006). As Professor Oren Griffin observes, "[a] review of post-*Garcetti* jurisprudence suggests that lower courts are prepared to determine that academic speech outside of teaching or scholarly functions, but within the scope of a faculty member's professional duties, may be beyond the protective reach of the First Amendment." Oren R. Griffin, *Academic Freedom and Professional Speech in the Post-*Garcetti *World*, 37 SEATTLE U. L. REV. 1, 41 (2013). Griffin argues that "the *Pickering-Connick* analytical framework [should] remain applicable" to cases involving "scholarship or teaching." *Id.* This is a very sensible argument, but the lower federal courts have not always embraced it. *See infra* text and accompanying notes 63 to 74.

58 *See supra* Chapter 4.

59 *See Garcetti*, 547 U.S. at 424 ("Proper application of our precedents thus leads to the conclusion that the First Amendment does not prohibit managerial

discipline based on an employee's expressions made pursuant to official responsibilities. Because Ceballos' memo falls into this category, his allegation of unconstitutional retaliation must fail.").

60 *Id.* at 425.

61 *Id. But cf. id.* at 438 (Souter, J., dissenting) (noting concerns about the *Garcetti* majority's holding on faculty members at public colleges and universities and expressing "hope that today's majority does not mean to imperil First Amendment protection of academic freedom in public colleges and universities").

62 *But see* Kristi L. Bowman, *The Government Speech Doctrine and Speech in Schools*, 48 WAKE FOREST L. REV. 211, 254 (2013) (arguing that "it seems much more likely that the *Garcetti* caveat applies, if at all, in the higher education context because courts historically have been extremely reluctant to recognize academic freedom rights for elementary and secondary teachers" whereas "the concept of academic freedom has become fairly robust in the college and university setting").

63 Mayer v. Monroe County Cmty. School Corp., 474 F.3d 477, 479 (7th Cir. 2007).

64 *Id.* (emphasis in the original).

65 *Id.*

66 *Id.* at 480.

67 *Id.*

68 *Id.*

69 In fact, some lower federal courts had rejected academic freedom claims related to classroom instruction well before *Garcetti*, making the potential extension of *Garcetti* to professors in public colleges and universities a relatively easy doctrinal conclusion. *See* Edwards v. California Univ. of Pa., 156 F.3d 488, 492 (3rd Cir. 1998) (holding that "caselaw from the Supreme Court and this court on academic freedom and the First Amendment compel the conclusion that Edwards does not have a constitutional right to choose curriculum materials in contravention of the University's dictates"); Bishop v. Aronov, 926 F.2d 1066, 1076–77 (11th Cir. 1991) (holding that "[t]he University must have the final say" over curricular matters "when [a professor] is acting under its auspices as a course instructor" because "[t]he University's conclusions about course content must be allowed to hold sway over an individual professor's judgments"). With respect to administrative positions within the university, it is clear that academic freedom principles apply very lightly, if at all. *See* Faghri v. Univ. of Connecticut, 621 F.3d 92, 97–98 (2d Cir. 2010) (holding that "the management of a public institution, such as a university, is not required to retain in a management or policymaking position a person who publicly opposes its policies" but also observing that "[w]e do not suggest that a public university can fire a teacher for voicing opposition to university policy").

At least two US Courts of Appeals have concluded that *Garcetti* does not apply to professors at public colleges and universities. *See* Demers v. Austin, 746 F.3d 402, 411–12 (9th Cir. 2014); Adams v. Trustees of the Univ. of N.C.-Wilmington,

640 F.3d 550, 562 (4th Cir. 2011). On the other hand, however, the US Courts of Appeals for the Sixth and Seventh Circuits have applied *Garcetti* to speech associated with university-related duties by faculty members. *See* Savage v. Gee, 665 F.3d 732, 738–39 (6th Cir. 2012); Renken v. Gregory, 541 F.3d 769, 773–75 (7th Cir. 2008); *see also* Gorum v. Sessoms, 561 F.3d 179, 186 n.6 (3rd Cir. 2009) (observing that "federal circuit courts differ over whether (and, if so, when) to apply *Garcetti*'s official duty test to academic instructors"). Even if *Garcetti* does not apply, lower federal courts have applied *Pickering* instead and balanced the university professor's interest in speaking out about a matter of public concern against the disruption caused by her speech. *See Demers*, 746 F.3d at 412–13. In addition, lower federal courts have held that universities possess broad authority to regulate the curriculum and to limit in-class speech to matters falling within the assigned subject matter. *See* Piggee v. Carl Sandburg College, 464 F.3d 667, 673 (7th Cir. 2006) (holding that "we see no reason why a college or university cannot direct its instructors to keep personal discussion about sexual orientation or religion out of a cosmetology class or clinic").

70 *See* Parate v. Isibor, 868 F.2d 821, 826–27 (6th Cir. 1989) (noting "the problems inherent in resolving clashes between the academy and individual academics when both parties claim a constitutional right to academic freedom" and observing that "[a]lthough judicial concerns have been expressed for the academic freedom of the university, the courts have also afforded substantial protection to the First Amendment freedoms of individual university professors"). Professor Byrne helpfully observes that the Supreme Court itself "has been unclear about whether academic freedom is an individual or community right." Byrne, *supra* note 1, at 257; *see also* Schauer, *supra* note 41, at 919 (arguing that "[t]he strongest argument against creating genuinely distinct individual academic freedom rights, however, is based on the proposition that granting individual academics enforceable rights against their academic supervisors would inevitably restrict the academic autonomy of the institution itself" and positing that "there is no avoiding the conflict between a view of academic freedom that views individual academics as its primary and direct beneficiaries, and a contrasting view that locates the right in academic institutions").

71 Katz, *supra* note 41, at 899.

72 *Id.* at 900.

73 *See Bishop*, 926 F.2d at 1076–78; *see also Piggee*, 464 F.3d at 671–72 (upholding the imposition of limits on a community college instructor's speech with enrolled students because "the college was entitled to insist on a professional relationship between the students and the instructors," which encompassed ensuring "the instructor's adherence to the subject matter of the course she has been hired to teach"). As the Eleventh Circuit stated the matter, a university professor's "interest in academic freedom and free speech do not displace the University's interest inside the classroom." *Bishop*, 926 F.2d at 1076. Moreover, "[t]he University necessarily has dominion over what is taught by its professors

and may so manage them." *Id.* at 1078; *see also* Schauer, *supra* note 41, at 921 (arguing that "an institutional right of academic freedom is best understood as a right of academic institutions against their political and bureaucratic and administrative supervisors, whether those supervisors be elected legislatures or appointed administrators"). It bears noting that the US Court of Appeals for the Tenth Circuit has applied a "legitimate pedagogical concerns" test to determine whether a university's regulation of a faculty member's classroom behavior violates the First Amendment. Vanderhurst v. Colorado Mountain College Dist., 208 F.3d 908, 914–15 (10th Cir. 2000). This is obviously a particularly weak First Amendment standard of review – it is essentially a test of mere reasonableness. *See* Hazelwood School Dist. v. Kuhlmeier, 484 U.S. 260, 273 (1988) (holding that censorship of a high school newspaper, published incident to a journalism class, did not violate the First Amendment provided that the decision to censor student-authored stories was "reasonably related to legitimate pedagogical concerns"); *see also* Pompeo v. Bd. of Regents, 852 F.3d 973, 983–84 (10th Cir. 2017) (holding that the federal courts owe "substantial deference" to a university professor's classroom assignments and evaluations, even if viewpoint-based, and only evaluative decisions unrelated to "legitimate pedagogical concerns" and completely lacking any "valid educational purpose" violate the First Amendment).

74 One could posit that academic freedom does not exist to protect either individual academics or institutions per se, but rather that academic freedom merits constitutional protection because "[t]he Constitution privileges the pursuit of knowledge." Owen M. Fiss, *The Democratic Mission of the University*, 76 ALB. L. REV. 735, 750 (2013). Professor Fiss emphasizes, however, that "in the struggle between the professor or student and the university, there is a First Amendment right that belongs to the individual and that properly falls within the bounds of the principle of academic freedom," namely "the right to be judged exclusively on the basis of professional standards – the norms of the discipline – not on the basis of political allegiances or personal predilections." *Id.* at 746–47; *see* Emily Goldman Waldman, *University Imprimaturs on Student Speech: The Certification Cases*, 11 FIRST AMEND. L. REV. 682 (2013); R. George Wright, *Standards of Professional Conduct as Limitations on Student Speech*, 13 FIRST AMEND. L. REV. 426 (2013).

75 Tinker v. Des Moines Indep. Cmty School Dist., 393 U.S. 503, 511–14 (1969). As Professor Bowman observes, "*Tinker* has been lauded as the 'highwater mark' of students' speech rights." Bowman, *supra* note 62, at 211. Moreover, "none of the Court's post-*Tinker* student speech decisions have protected students' rights as broadly as *Tinker*." *Id.*

76 *Tinker*, 393 U.S. at 511.

77 *Id.* at 514.

78 *Id.* at 511.

79 *Id.* at 514.

80 478 U.S. 675 (1986).

81 *Id.* at 680.

82 *Id.* at 685.
83 *Id.* at 685–86.
84 484 U.S. 260 (1987).
85 *See id.* at 270–73.
86 *Id.* at 270.
87 *Id.* at 271.
88 *Id.* at 273. It bears noting that this language tracks rather closely the First Amendment test used to assess speech regulations in jails and prisons. *See* Pell v. Procunier, 417 U.S. 817, 822 (1974) (holding that "a prison inmate retains those First Amendment rights that are not inconsistent with his status as a prisoner or with the legitimate penological objectives of the corrections system"). There is more than a little irony in the same burden of justification – mere reasonableness – applying to restrictions on the First Amendment rights of both public school students and prisoners.
89 Morse v. Frederick, 551 U.S. 393, 397 (2007).
90 *Id.* at 398.
91 Frederick v. Morse, 439 F.3d 1114, 1121–23 (9th Cir. 2006), *rev'd*, 551 U.S. 393 (2007).
92 *Morse*, 551 U.S. at 397.
93 *Id.* at 400.
94 *Id.* at 400–01.
95 *Id.* at 403.
96 *Id.* at 408.
97 *Id.*
98 *Morse*, 551 U.S. at 410.
99 551 U.S. at 422 (Thomas, J., concurring).
100 *See, e.g.,* Keefe v. Geanakos, 418 F.2d 359 (1st Cir. 1969); Parducci v. Rutland, 316 F. Supp. 352 (M.D. Ala. 1970); Vought v. Van Buren Pub. Schools, 306 F. Supp. 1388 (E.D. Mich. 1969).
101 William Van Alstyne, *The Constitutional Rights of Teachers and Professors,* 1970 DUKE L.J. 841, 858.
102 316 F. Supp. 352 (1970). I should probably acknowledge at this juncture that I served as a law clerk to Judge Johnson in 1991–1992. It was, without a doubt, the best job that I have ever had – or am likely to ever have.
103 *Id.* at 353–54.
104 *Id.* at 354.
105 *Id.*
106 *Id.*
107 *Id.* at 356–58.
108 *Parducci*, 316 F. Supp. at 356.
109 *Id.* at 356 ("Since the defendants have failed to show either that the assignment was inappropriate reading for high school juniors, or that it created a significant disruption to the educational processes of this school, this Court concludes that plaintiff's dismissal constituted an unwarranted invasion of her First Amendment right to academic freedom.").

110 *Id.* at 358.

111 *See id.* at 357–58.

112 Mayer v. Monroe County Cmty. School Corp., 474 F.3d 477, 479–80 (7th Cir. 2007) (holding that a high school teacher has absolutely no protected First Amendment interest in her pedagogical choices in the classroom because she literally has "sold" her speech rights to the public school district); *see also* Evans-Marshall v. Board of Educ., 624 F.3d 332, 340 (6th Cir. 2010) (holding that "[o]nly the school board has ultimate responsibility for what goes on in the classroom, legitimately giving it a say over what teachers may (or may not) teach in the classroom").

113 Academic freedom, in its classic formulation, derives from the German concept of *lehrfreiheit*, which was understood to encompass the ability to make free intellectual inquiries and report, either in writing or by lecture, one's conclusions to others. *See* Richard Hofstadter & Walter P. Metzger, The Development of Academic Freedom in the United States 386–87 (1955).

114 *See* Keefe v. Geanakos, 418 F.2d 369, 361–63 (1st Cir. 1969).

115 *Id.* at 361–62. *But cf.* Brown v. Chicago Bd. of Educ., 824 F.3d 713, 716–18 (7th Cir. 2016) (holding that the Chicago public schools could maintain and enforce strictly a policy against teachers using racial slurs in the classroom and could suspend an elementary school teacher "for using a racial slur while attempting to teach his students why such language is inappropriate," noting that the teacher's "frustration is understandable, but it is not legally actionable," and concluding that "Brown made his comments as a teacher, not a citizen, and so his suspension does not implicate his First Amendment rights").

116 *Keefe*, 418 F.2d at 362–63. Judge Aldrich explained that "no less than five books, by as many authors, containing the word in question were to be found in the school library." *Id.* at 362. He added that "[i]t is hard to think that any student could walk into the library and receive a book, but that his teacher could not subject the content to serious discussion in class." *Id.*

117 *See* Bradley v. Pittsburgh Bd. of Educ., 910 F.2d 1172, 1176 (3rd Cir. 1990) (observing that "no court has found that teachers' First Amendment rights extend to choosing their own curriculum or classroom management techniques in contravention of school policy or dictates"). Professor Byrne notes that "courts have denied relief to teachers sanctioned for unusual teaching methods, for receiving poor student evaluations, and for straying from prescribed coverage." Byrne, *supra* note 1, at 301. In other words, "as far as the courts are concerned, administrators may exercise extensive control over curricular judgments so long as they do not penalize a professor solely for his political viewpoint." *Id.*; *see also* Bowman, *supra* note 62, at 256 (arguing that whatever rights of academic freedom public school teachers in the K-12 classroom might once have enjoyed, "as a practical matter, this deference to individual teachers – at least as compared to entities such as school boards and state boards of education – is a thing of the past").

118 Stephen R. Goldstein, *The Asserted Constitutional Right of Public School Teachers to Determine What They Teach*, 124 U. PA. L. REV. 1293, 1320 (1976).

119 *Id.*

120 *Id.* at 1355–56. To be sure, some prominent academics, such as Marty Redish, have argued that school teachers and students must enjoy some claim on the First Amendment, even in the context of curricular activities. *See* Martin H. Redish & Kevin Finnerty, *What Did You Learn in School Today?: Free Speech, Values Inculcation, and the Democratic-Educational Paradox*, 88 CORNELL L. REV. 62, 67 (2002) (arguing that "by means of the public educational process, the state is able to engage in a dangerous form of political, social, or moral thought control that potentially interferes with a citizen's subsequent exercise of individual autonomy").

121 *See* Boring v. Buncombe County Bd. of Educ., 136 F.3d 364, 371 (4th Cir. 1998) ("Someone must fix the curriculum of any school, public or private. In the case of a public school, in our opinion, it is far better public policy, absent a valid statutory directive on the subject, that the makeup of the curriculum be entrusted to the local school authorities who are in some sense responsible, rather than to the teachers, who would be responsible only to the judges, had they a First Amendment right to participate in the makeup of the curriculum."); *see also* Evans-Marshall v. Board of Educ., 624 F.3d 332, 341 (6th Cir. 2010) (holding that "[t]he Constitution does not prohibit a State from creating elected school boards and from placing responsibility for the curriculum of each school district in the hands of each board" and warning that a contrary rule "would transform run-of-the-mill curricular disputes into constitutional stalemates").

122 Redish & Finnerty, *supra* note 120, at 101.

123 *But cf. Evans-Marshall*, 624 F.3d at 342 (holding "that the First Amendment does not protect primary and secondary school teachers' in-class curricular speech" and observing that "[t]he key insight of *Garcetti* is that the First Amendment has nothing to say about these kinds of decisions"). Judge Jeffrey Sutton emphasized that "[a] [public school] teacher's curricular and pedagogical choices are categorically unprotected." *Id.*

124 The Supreme Court has held that lawyers, as professionals, may not be silenced simply because they happen to be employed by the government – lawyers have the professional discretion to inform clients about potential causes of action, even if the government would prefer the lawyer to hold her tongue. *See* Legal Servs. Corp. v. Velazquez, 531 U.S. 522 (2001). This same zone of professional autonomy should extend to instructors in public schools, colleges, and universities. Even if public educational institutions may decide what shall be taught and even how it shall be taught, see Edwards v. California Univ. of Pa., 156 F.3d 488, 491–92 (3rd Cir. 1998) (holding that "a public university professor does not have a First Amendment right to decide what will be taught in the classroom" and that a professor "does not have a constitutional right to choose curriculum materials in contravention of the University's dictates"), there remains a zone of informed professional discretion that inheres in the

teaching of a class. *See* Van Alstyne, *supra* note 101, at 857 (arguing that, under the First Amendment right of academic freedom, instructors must not "endure ... arbitrary restrictions in the course of their own inquiries or *upon their own communicated classroom references*" because "[o]ne may not, as a condition of his employment, be made an implement of governmental practices which are themselves violative of the First Amendment") (emphasis in the original).

125 *See* Perry v. Sindermann, 408 U.S. 593, 599–602 (1972) (holding that a community college could not fire a faculty member without providing meaningful pre-deprivation process because the community college had adopted a de facto system of tenure that limited discharge to cause after seven years of employment); *see also* Katz, *supra* note 41, at 880–82 (discussing the importance of procedural due process rights in protecting faculty members from arbitrary dismissal); Van Alstyne, *supra* note 101, at 860–62 (same).

126 Van Alstyne, *supra* note 101, at 860.

127 *Id.*

128 *See generally* DANA GOLDSTEIN, THE TEACHER WARS: A HISTORY OF AMERICA'S MOST EMBATTLED PROFESSION (2015) (discussing the various forms of statutory and contract protection that have evolved over time to provide public school teachers with security of position).

129 POST, *supra* note 33, at 35–43, 61–62.

130 *Id.* at 33.

131 *Id.*

132 Letter from Thomas Jefferson to Colonel Charles Yancey, Jan. 6, 1816, *reprinted in* 9 PAPERS OF THOMAS JEFFERSON, RETIREMENT SERIES, SEPTEMBER 1815 TO APRIL 1816, at 328, 330 (J. Jefferson Looney ed., 2013).

133 *See* Redish & Finnerty, *supra* note 120, at 101 (arguing in favor of some degree of meaningful instructor autonomy in the classroom as part of "a strategic desire to diffuse power over the educational process and thereby reduce the danger of monolithic and authoritarian values inculcation by the government" and observing, wryly, that "in Communist educational systems teachers are closely monitored by their superiors"). Redish cautions, however, that an approach that "dilutes the government's ability to provide a monolithic analysis of value choices" could "cause considerably more trouble than it is worth." *Id.* at 102. Nevertheless, despite some lingering doubts about the potential for "chaos developing as a result of including students and parents in the decision-making process," Redish concludes that the First Amendment should be deployed to advance an "anti-indoctrination" project that limits direct political controls over the curriculum in the nation's public schools, colleges, and universities. *See id.* at 102–09.

134 *See* Lochner v. New York, 198 U.S. 45 (1905). Both the majority and dissenting opinions in *Lochner* apply exactly the same standard of review: reasonableness. The majority applies the test in a demanding way that mirrors contemporary strict judicial scrutiny, whereas Justices Oliver Wendell Holmes and John Marshall Harlan, in dissent, apply the test of reasonableness in a much more

deferential fashion. *Compare id.* at 58 ("There is, in our judgment, no reasonable foundation for holding this to be necessary or appropriate as a health law to safeguard the public health or the health of the individuals who are following the trade of a baker.") *with id.* at 76 (Holmes, J., dissenting) ("I think that the word liberty in the Fourteenth Amendment is perverted when it is held to prevent the natural outcome of a dominant opinion, unless it can be said that a rational and fair man necessarily would admit that the statute proposed would infringe fundamental principles as they have been understood by the traditions of our people and our law.") & *id.* at 68, 70 (Harlan, J., dissenting) (opining that "liberty of contract is subject to such regulations as the State may reasonably prescribe for the common good and the well-being of society" and, accordingly, reviewing courts should not invalidate a state police power enactment unless "the regulation prescribed by the State is utterly unreasonable and extravagant or wholly arbitrary").

135 Tinker v. Des Moines Indep. Cmty School Dist., 393 U.S. 503, 510 (1969) (observing that "[t]he record shows that students in some of the schools wore buttons relating to national political campaigns, and some even wore the Iron Cross, traditionally a symbol of Nazism").

136 *See id.* ("It is also relevant that the school authorities did not purport to prohibit the wearing of all symbols of political or controversial significance.").

137 *Id.*

138 *See, e.g.,* West v. Derby Unified School Dist. No. 260, 206 F.3d 1358, 1362–63, 1365 (10th Cir. 2000) (holding that a school district "did not violate T. W.'s First Amendment right to free speech when it suspended him from school for three days after he drew a picture of the Confederate flag during class in violation of the school district's harassment and intimidation policy"). In reaching this conclusion, the court acknowledged that the drawing did not cause any actual disruption, but credited the school district's claim that it "had reason to believe that a student's display of the Confederate flag might cause disruption and interfere with the rights of other students to be secure and let alone." *Id.* at 1366.

139 Katz, *supra* note 41, at 910 (arguing that "[a] moment's reflection reveals . . . that under the Court's analysis constitutional protection is extended [under *Tinker*] only to that classroom speech which is ineffective and fails to stir up the controversy deemed so essential to the health of the republic"). Professor Katz is essentially positing that student speech most relevant to the project of democratic self-government also happens to be the kind of speech most like to prove controversial – and hence potentially disruptive.

140 *See* Day & Weatherby, *supra* note 12, at 849 (discussing the pro-Trump chalking at Emory University and the university administration's response to it).

141 *Id.* ("Students at the school said they 'no longer fe[lt] safe' after seeing the messages of support for a candidate who they considered to be 'the figurehead of hate, racism, xenophobia, and sexism in America.'"). Similar events took place at DePaul University, in Chicago, Illinois. *See id.*

142 *See* Byrne, *supra* note 1, at 299–300 (discussing how the state action requirement affects the potential scope of constitutionally protected academic freedom under the First Amendment). As a private university, of course, Emory University has no obligation to observe the First Amendment. *See* Katz, *supra* note 41, at 863–74 (discussing how the state action doctrine limits the scope of First Amendment rights to public schools, colleges, and universities and excludes private educational institutions, even if they are highly regulated and accept public funds to finance their operations). On the other hand, however, as a major research university that promises faculty and students alike academic freedom, a contractual obligation might exist for Emory University to observe free speech rights that more or less parallel the speech rights protected at public institutions of higher learning under the First and Fourteenth Amendments.

143 *See* Meritor Savings Bank v. Vinson, 477 U.S. 57, 64–68, 72 (1986). Of course, some First Amendment scholars object to hostile work environment liability under Title VII precisely because it can create civil liability for speech alone. Kingsley R. Browne, *Title VII as Censorship: Hostile-Environment Harassment and the First Amendment*, 52 Ohio St. L.J. 481 (1991); Eugene Volokh, *How Harassment Law Violates Free Speech*, 47 Rutgers L. Rev. 563 (1995). To date, however, the federal courts have uniformly rejected this argument and sustained civil liability against employers based on the creation and maintenance of a hostile work environment that effectively precludes employment based on race, sex, religion, or disability. No obvious reason exists that would preclude the adoption of a hostile learning environment theory in the context of public schools, college, and universities. The key to the constitutionality of such a theory would be in narrowly tailoring the regulations to cover only relatively serious forms of harassment and intimidation (as opposed to so-called "micro-aggressions"). A policy drawn up with the necessary precision – that more or less mirrors hostile work environment liability in the workplace context under Title VII – would be perfectly constitutional.

144 Day & Weatherby, *supra* note 12, at 862.

145 *Id.* Day and Weatherby express concern about the chilling effects of such campus speech regulations, arguing that "[i]t is the antithesis of First Amendment principles to make offensiveness the touchstone of speech restriction." *Id.* at 873.

146 To be sure, *Tinker* itself strongly suggests that school district officials must proffer more than a mere "there could be trouble" hunch in order to silence student speech. Justice Fortas explains that:

> Any word spoken, in class, in the lunchroom, or on the campus, that deviates from the views of another person may start an argument or cause a disturbance. But our Constitution says we must take this risk, *Terminiello v. Chicago*, 337 U. S. 1 (1949); and our history says that it is this sort of hazardous freedom – this kind of openness – that is the basis of our national

strength and of the independence and vigor of Americans who grow up and live in this relatively permissive, often disputatious, society.

Tinker v. Des Moines Indep. Cmty School Dist., 393 U.S. 503, 508–09 (1969). The *Tinker* majority's invocation of *Terminiello* is significant because *Terminieillo* plainly requires that the government demonstrate with convincing clarity that speech is "likely to produce a clear and present danger of a serious substantive evil that rises far above public inconvenience, annoyance, or unrest" before silencing a speaker. Terminiello v. Chicago, 337 U.S. 1, 4 (1949). Justice Douglas explained that this rule is essential because "the alternative would lead to standardization of ideas," an outcome for which "[t]here is no room under our Constitution." *Id.* at 4–5. However, when applying *Tinker*, neither the Supreme Court nor the lower federal courts have consistently held public school administrators to the *Terminiello* standard of risk. *See infra* text and accompanying notes 150 to 184.

147 HARRY KALVEN, JR., A WORTHY TRADITION: FREEDOM OF SPEECH IN AMERICA 89–93, 96–105 (Jamie Kalven ed., 1988) (providing a definition and overview of the concept of the "heckler's veto," which entails using an adverse public reaction as a justification for the government silencing an unpopular speaker); HARRY KALVEN, JR., THE NEGRO AND THE FIRST AMENDMENT 140–41, 145 (1965) (coining the phrase "heckler's veto" and positing that the First Amendment cannot be reconciled with permitting the hostile reaction of an audience to justify government censorship of a speaker); *see* Owen E. Fiss, *Free Speech and Social Structure*, 71 IOWA L. REV. 1405, 1416–17 (1986) (discussing the concept of a heckler's veto, noting the fundamental incompatibility with the First Amendment of permitting a hostile public reaction to speech to serve as a basis for the government prohibiting it, and crediting Professor Kalven with authorship of the concept of the heckler's veto).

148 *See Tinker*, 393 U.S. at 508–09; *see also Terminiello*, 337 U.S. at 4–5 (holding that "freedom of speech, though not absolute … is nevertheless protected against censorship or punishment, unless shown likely to produce a clear and present danger of a serious substantive evil that rises far above public inconvenience, annoyance, or unrest" because "the alternative would lead to standardization of ideas either by legislatures, courts, or dominant political or community groups").

149 Texas v. Johnson, 491 U.S. 397, 414 (1989) ("If there is a bedrock principal underlying the First Amendment, it is that the Government may not prohibit the expression of an idea simply because society finds the idea itself offensive or disagreeable."); Police Dep't of Chicago v. Mosley, 408 U.S 92, 96–98 (1972) (invalidating on First Amendment grounds a municipal ordinance that granted access to public property based on the subject and content of the would-be speaker's message because "[o]nce a forum is opened up to assembly or speaking by some groups, government may not prohibit others from assembling or speaking on the basis of what they intend to say"); *see* CASS R. SUNSTEIN, DEMOCRACY AND THE PROBLEM OF FREE SPEECH 169 (1995)

(observing that "[w]hen government regulates on the basis of viewpoint, it will frequently be acting for objectionable reasons").

150 *See* ROBERT C. POST, CONSTITUTIONAL DOMAINS: DEMOCRACY, COMMUNITY, MANAGEMENT 234–40 (1995) (defining the "managerial realm," noting "the government's need to manage speech within its institutions," and positing that speech regulations within government institutions, including workplaces and schools, are necessary "in order to achieve the institution's legitimate objectives"). Post explains that "[w]hen it exercises the authority of management, the state can constitutionally control speech so as to facilitate the institutional attainment of organizational ends." *Id.* at 240.

151 It bears noting that "[p]ublic universities have begun requiring that political student groups pay high prices for security at events at which they expect other students to protest." Day & Weatherby, *supra* note 12, at 854–55.

152 *See, e.g.,* Taylor v. Roswell Indep. School Dist., 713 F.3d 25, 30–31 (10th Cir. 2013) (holding that distribution of small rubber human fetus dolls at two public high schools in Roswell, New Mexico caused substantial disruptions to the schools' educational program and contrasting the contemporaneous distribution of "Valentine's Day-related items such as candy, cards, and stuffed animals," which was not associated with any disruption or disturbance). The high school students used the two and a half inch plastic fetus dolls, distributed as part of an anti-abortion protest, both creatively and destructively:

> Many students pulled the dolls apart, tearing the heads off and using them as rubber balls or sticking them on pencil tops. Others threw dolls and doll parts at the "popcorn" ceilings so they became stuck. Dolls were used to plug toilets. Several students covered the dolls in hand sanitizer and lit them on fire. One or more male students removed the dolls' heads, inverted the bodies to make them resemble penises, and hung them on the outside of their pants zippers.

Id. at 31. The doll-related antics "disrupted classroom instruction" with dolls and doll parts being thrown as projectiles "across classrooms, at one another, and into wastebaskets." Abortion-related disputes also resulted in "name calling and insults." *Id.* A campus "security officer described the day as a 'disaster.'" *Id.* In light of this overwhelming record, the US Court of Appeals for the Tenth Circuit quite properly held that the school district's refusal to permit subsequent plastic fetus distributions at the high schools was entirely consistent with *Tinker* and the First Amendment. *See id.* at 37–39. As Judge Scott Matheson, Jr., observed, "[t]he record is replete with reports of doll related disruptions throughout the day." *Id.* at 38. No predictive judgment was required because actual disruption occurred – although a prediction of disruption would have been reasonable because the "dolls' small size made them tempting projectiles and toilet-clogging devices." *Id.*

153 To provide a somewhat silly example, an anti-Tom Brady t-shirt in a Boston public high school will present a risk of disruption, whereas a t-shirt celebrating

Tom Brady's athletic efforts on the gridiron as the quarterback of the New England Patriots NFL team would not. Because of this difference in real world effects, a school administrator could forbid a student from wearing a t-shirt emblazoned with the message "Tom Brady = Cheater," even while permitting other students to wear t-shirts featuring a more positive message, for example, "Tom Brady = Champion." This hypothetical shows how easily a test calibrated to a risk of substantial disruption could produce results that resemble outright viewpoint discrimination. Morse v. Frederick, 551 U.S. 393 (2007), the most recent student-speech decision from the Supreme Court, confirms this analysis. Had Joseph Frederick, the student who displayed a banner with the message "BONG HiTS 4 JESUS," *id.* at 397, instead held up a banner with the message "Say 'NO!' to Drugs," he would never have been subjected to discipline by school officials. *Morse* plainly holds that, consistent with the First Amendment, public school officials could proscribe the dissemination of a message that seemed to endorse the use of marijuana even at an off-campus community event. *See id.* at 409–10.

154 *See* Peter Singer, *Justifying Infanticide in* WRITINGS ON AN ETHICAL LIFE 186–93 (2000); PETER SINGER, HOW ARE WE TO LIVE?: ETHICS IN AN AGE OF SELF-INTEREST 84–105 (1993); *see also* Harrie McBryde Johnson, *Unspeakable Conversations*, N.Y. TIMES MAGAZINE (Feb. 16, 2003), www.nytimes.com/2003/02/16/magazine/unspeakable-conversations.html (observing that Singer "insists he doesn't want to kill me" but rather "simply thinks it would have been better, all things considered, to have given my parents the option of killing the baby I once was, and to let other parents kill similar babies as they come along and thereby avoid the suffering that comes with lives like mine and satisfy the reasonable preferences of parents for a different kind of child").

155 Day & Weatherby, *supra* note 12, at 875–78. Day and Weatherby explain that "state legislatures have proposed more than twenty bills that restrict university control over campus speech in higher education" with the goal of "preserv[ing] the freedom of expression on college campuses." *Id.* at 875. Seven states have enacted laws that designate college and university campuses as public forums, *see id.* at 875 n.266, and six states have enacted laws that ban the creation of free speech zones the limit where expressive activity may take place on campus, *see id.* at 876 n. 267. Most of these laws are based in whole or in part on a model statute that the Goldwater Institute has drafted. *Id.* at 876 & 876–77 n.271.

156 *Id.* at 877.

157 *See, e.g.*, Ponce v. Socorro Indep. School Dist., 508 F.3d 765, 772 (5th Cir. 2007) (holding that "when a student threatens violence against a student body, his words are as much beyond the constitutional pale as yelling 'fire' in a crowded theater … and such specific threatening speech to a school or its population is unprotected by the First Amendment"); *see also* LaVine v. Blaine School Dist., 257 F.3d 981, 987 (9th Cir. 2001) (observing that "we live in a time when school violence is an unfortunate reality that educators must confront on an all too frequent basis" and noting that "[a]fter Columbine, Thurston, Santee and other school shootings, questions have been asked about how teachers or

administrators could have missed telltale 'warning signs,' why something was not done earlier and what should be done to prevent such tragedies from happening again").

158 See S. Elizabeth Wilborn, *Teaching the New Three Rs – Repression, Rights, and Respect: A Primer of Student Speech Activities*, 37 B.C. L. Rev. 119, 143–44 (1995) (arguing against a "one-size-fits-all approach" to applying the First Amendment to on-campus student speech and in favor of evaluating such speech claims on a "content-specific basis" that takes into account "the strength of a student's speech claims"). Wilborn argues that "[b]y developing a content-sensitive system of evaluating students' speech rights in the schools, the federal courts could select and apply a level of judicial scrutiny appropriate to the nature and content of the students' expression." *Id.* at 146. She suggests three main categories of student speech on campus: political speech, scholastic speech, and obscene/indecent speech. *See id.* at 147–51.

159 BH ex rel. Hawk v. Easton Area School Dist., 725 F.3d 293 (3rd Cir. 2013) (en banc).

160 *See id.* at 320 (holding that the "bracelets are not plainly lewd" and that "[t]he slogan bears no resemblance to Fraser's 'pervasive sexual innuendo' that was 'plainly offensive to both teachers and students.' *Fraser*, 478 U.S. at 683").

161 *See id.* at 319–20 (observing that "plainly lewd speech cannot, by definition, be plausibly interpreted as political or social commentary because the speech offends for the same reason obscenity offends and thus has slight social value" and, accordingly, may be treated as presumptively disruptive to school operations).

162 *See id.* at 336–37 (Hardiman, J., dissenting) (arguing that the bracelets were lewd for purposes of applying *Fraser* because "'I ♥ Boobies!' can reasonably be interpreted as inappropriate sexual double entendre" and that the educational and informational purpose did not "undermine the plausibility of a sexual interpretation of the bracelets").

163 *See* LaVine v. Blaine School Dist., 257 F.3d 981, 983–85 (9th Cir. 2001) (involving a poem, *Last Words*, authored by a high school student in his class-related journal that included a mass-killing fantasia theme featuring the phrase "As I approached the classroom door, I drew my gun and, threw open the door, Bang, Bang, Bang-Bang" and "[w]hen it was all over, 28 were, dead, and all I remember, was not felling, any remorce, for I felt, I was, clensing my soul [sic]").

164 *See id.* at 988, 991–92.

165 *See id.* at 989–90 (upholding the emergency expulsion of a high school student who wrote a poem "filled with imagery of violent death and suicide" because "[t]aken together and given the backdrop of actual school shootings" the public school officials had reasonably "forecast substantial disruption of or material interference with school activities"); *see also* Bell v. Itawamba County School Dist., 799 F.3d 379, 393–98 (5th Cir. 2015) (en banc) (holding that *Tinker* applies to a rap/poem posted on Facebook and YouTube from an off-campus location but "intentionally directed" at an audience comprised of public high

school students, faculty, and staff and that threats of violence contained in the rap lyrics presented a credible risk of substantial disruption that supported the school district's decision to take disciplinary action).

166 *See* Dennis v. United States, 183 F.3d 201, 212 (2d Cir. 1950), *aff'd*, 341 U.S. 494 (1951) (proposing that the nature of the risk created by speech, discounted by its probability of occurring, should determine the protected or unprotected status of the speech). As Judge Learned Hand described his proposed test, "In each case [courts] must ask whether the gravity of the 'evil,' discounted by its improbability, justifies such invasion of free speech as is necessary to avoid the danger." *Id.*

167 *Bell*, 799 F.3d at 383–85.

168 *See* Watts v. United States, 394 U.S. 705, 707–08 (1969) (holding that only "true threats" may be punished consistent with the First Amendment but observing that government possesses "an overwhelming" interest in proscribing true threats of violence).

169 *See id.* at 708 (holding that "political hyperbole," even if it is "vituperative, abusive, and inexact" enjoys First Amendment protection as speech, but that a genuine, or "true" threat, may be the subject of criminal charges without violating the Free Speech Clause). It seems reasonably clear that the constitutional standard for imposing criminal punishment for speech should be considerably more demanding than the standard applicable to a public school official's decision to temporarily remove a student from a public high school for his own safety or that of other students, faculty, and staff).

170 It bears noting that the *Bell* majority clearly relied on the threat of a substantial disruption, and *Tinker*, as a result of the rap being disseminated to an audience comprised of students, faculty, and staff at Itawamba County High School – rather than on the lyrics constituting a true threat. *Bell*, 799 F.3d at 400 (holding that "having affirmed summary judgment for the school board under *Tinker*, it is unnecessary to decide whether Bell's speech also constitutes a 'true threat' under *Watts*").

171 *Id.* at 394 (holding that "Bell's admittedly intentionally directing at the school community his rap recording containing threats to, and harassment and intimidation of, two teachers permits *Tinker's* application in this instance").

172 Layshock v. Hermitage School Dist., 650 F.3d 205, 207–08 (3rd Cir. 2011) (en banc).

173 *Id.* at 208.

174 *Id.*

175 *Id.*

176 *Id.* at 209–10.

177 *Layshock*, 650 F.3d at 216 ("It would be an unseemly and dangerous precedent to allow the state, in the guise of school authorities, to reach into a child's home and control his/her actions there to the same extent that it can control that child when he/she participates in school sponsored activities.").

178 *Id.* at 219; *see also* J.S. Ex. Rel. Snyder v. Blue Mountain School Dist., 650 F.3d 915, 920, 928 (3rd Cir. 2011) (en banc) (holding that the First Amendment

protected a vulgar fake parody MySpace profile of a public middle school principal, featuring "crude content and sexual language," because the student's speech "did not cause a substantial disruption in the school" and the facts did "not support the conclusion that a forecast of substantial disruption was reasonable").

179 *See* Ponce v. Socorro Indep. School Dist., 508 F.3d 765, 772 (5th Cir. 2007).

180 *See* Tinker v. Des Moines Indep. Cmty. School Dist., 393 U.S. 503, 508–09 (1969); *see also* Terminiello v. Chicago, 337 U.S. 1, 4–6 (1949).

181 *Tinker*, 393 U.S. at 508.

182 *Id.*

183 *Id.*

184 *Id.* at 508–09.

185 Byrne, *supra* note 1, at 338; *see also id.* at 340 ("Constitutional protection can preserve the possibility that academics might attain the goals of learning and scholarship. It cannot do more; it should not do less.").

186 POST, *supra* note 33, at 32–33.

187 Indeed, *Garcetti's* failure to recognize a special rule for academics as government employees constitutes a very worrisome negative signal about the current Supreme Court's commitment to using the First Amendment to protect academic freedom. *See* Garcetti v. Ceballos, 547 U.S. 410, 425 (2006). Moreover, several lower federal appellate courts have not hesitated to apply *Garcetti* to speech related to academic duties. *See* Savage v. Gee, 665 F.3d 732, 738–39 (6th Cir. 2012); Renken v. Gregory, 541 F.3d 769, 773–75 (7th Cir. 2008).

188 *See supra* text and accompanying notes 80 to 101.

189 United States v. Kahriger, 345 U.S. 22, 38 (1953) (Frankfurter, J., dissenting) ("However, when oblique use is made of the taxing power as to matters which substantively are not within the powers delegated to Congress, the Court cannot shut its eyes to what is obviously, because designedly, an attempt to control conduct which the Constitution left to the responsibility of the States, merely because Congress wrapped the legislation in the verbal cellophane of a revenue measure."). In other words, the technical form of a government action should not trump the substance of the government's action.

190 *See, e.g.*, Tatro v. University of Minnesota, 816 N.W. 2d 509, 517–20 (Minn. 2012) (declining to extend *Tinker* to off-campus Facebook posts made by an undergraduate mortuary sciences student). The *Tatro* Court did permit the university to create and enforce regulations governing off campus student speech on social media platforms, such as Facebook, Twitter, and YouTube, when particular student speech "violates established professional conduct standards." *Id.* at 521. To be consistent with the First Amendment, such standards must be "narrowly tailored" and "directly related to established professional conduct standards." Id.

191 Tinker v. Des Moines Indep. Cmty. School Dist., 393 U.S. 503, 511 (1969). Moreover, "[s]chool officials do not possess absolute authority over their students." Id.

6 TRANSBORDER SPEECH: USING THE ACCIDENT OF GEOGRAPHY
AS A MAKEWEIGHT JUSTIFICATION FOR SUPPRESSING
EXPRESSIVE FREEDOMS

1 *See* TIMOTHY ZICK, *Territoriality and the First Amendment: Free Speech at – and Beyond – Our Borders*, 85 NOTRE DAME L. REV. 1543, 1544 (2010) (observing that "we live in a world characterized by extraordinary advances in communications technology, widespread global travel, increasing cross-border commerce, and frequent transnational involvements" and "[i]nformation flows at great speed, and in remarkable quantity, across our national borders").

2 *See* TIMOTHY ZICK, THE COSMOPOLITAN FIRST AMENDMENT: PROTECTING TRANSBORDER EXPRESSIVE AND RELIGIOUS LIBERTIES 66–68, 199–227 (2013).

3 Citizens United v. Fed. Elec. Comm'n, 558 U.S. 310, 339 (2010) ("Speech is an essential mechanism of democracy, for it is the means to hold officials accountable to the people. ... The right of citizens to inquire, to hear, to speak, and to use information to reach consensus is a precondition to enlightened self-government and a necessary means to protect it.").

4 *But cf.* Holder v. Humanitarian Law Project, 561 U.S. 1, 33–39 (2010) (upholding a federal statute that, as applied, banned any contact with proscribed organizations abroad on the theory that such contact inevitably constituted "material support" of them and despite any evidence that the actual speech and associational activity at issue advanced unlawful aims or objectives and notwithstanding Congress's failure to narrowly tailor the proscription in any way, shape, or form).

5 ZICK, *supra* note 2, at 215.

6 Burt Neuborne & Steven R. Shapiro, *The Nylon Curtain: America's National Border and the Free Flow of Ideas*, 26 WM. & MARY L. REV. 719, 765 (1985).

7 *Id.*

8 *See, e.g.*, United States v. Alvarez, 567 U.S. 709 (2012) (holding intentionally false speech about military honors to be protected under the First Amendment); Brown v. Entm't Merchs. Ass'n, 564 U.S. 786 (2010) (holding that the First Amendment protects the distribution of violent video games to minors); Snyder v. Phelps, 562 U.S. 443 (2011) (holding outrageous and offensive protest of a deceased US marine's funeral service and burial to be protected speech about a matter of public concern); United States v. Stevens, 559 U.S. 460 (2010) (holding that the First Amendment protects graphic depictions of animal cruelty); Hustler Magazine, Inc. v. Falwell, 485 U.S. 46 (1988) (holding intentionally outrageous and offensive parody of a public figure constitutes protected speech absent the inclusion of a false statement of fact made with malice aforethought).

9 *See* Kent v. Dulles, 357 U.S. 116, 125, 129–30 (1958) (holding that Congress did not convey authority to deny passports to US citizens "because of their beliefs or associations" and noting that such authority, if granted, would raise "important constitutional questions"); Dayton v. Dulles, 357 U.S. 144, 150 (1958) (holding that denial of a passport because of membership in a Communist-affiliated domestic organization would be unconstitutional and declining to find statutory authority for such action); Aptheker v. Sec'y of State, 378 U.S. 500, 505, 514, 517 (1964)

(holding unconstitutional, on Fifth Amendment due process grounds, revocation of a US citizen's passport because of membership in a Communist Party-affiliated organization and observing that foreign travel "is a constitutional liberty closely related to rights of free speech and association"); Lamont v. Postmaster General, 381 U.S. 301, 307 (1965) (invalidating on First Amendment grounds a federal statute that required postal service customers to request, in writing, delivery of "communist political propaganda" in order to receive materials from abroad that Post Office employees deemed to constitute such material and holding that "[t]he regime of this Act is at war with the 'uninhibited, robust, and wide-open' debate and discussion that are contemplated by the First Amendment") (quoting N.Y. Times Co. v. Sullivan, 376 U.S. 254, 270 (1964)). The Warren Court did not, however, always or invariably vindicate transborder speech claims. *See* Zemel v. Rusk, 381 U.S. 1, 16–17 (1965) (upholding the US government's ban on travel to Cuba and holding that the policy constituted merely "an inhibition of action" rather than "speech" and observing that "[t]here are few restrictions on action which could not be clothed by ingenious argument in the garb of decreased data flow"). Nevertheless, the passport cases and the foreign mail case, *Lamont*, afforded transborder speech non-trivial First Amendment protection.

10 *See* Haig v. Agee, 453 U.S. 280, 306–09 (1981) (assuming that the First Amendment protects a US citizen's interest in speaking in foreign venues to foreign audiences, but holding that Agee's prior unlawful leaking of CIA classified material justified the federal government's decision to revoke Agee's passport); Kleindienst v. Mandel, 408 U.S. 753, 762–70 (1972) (recognizing that US citizens have a cognizable First Amendment interest in interacting, in person, with a foreign journalist who advocated Marxist ideologies, but sustaining the federal government's refusal to issue a visa for Mandel to travel to the United States because the decision rested on "a facially legitimate and bona fide reason" ostensibly unrelated to Mandel's politics or ideology).

11 *See* Clapper v. Amnesty Int'l USA, 568 U.S. 398, 422 (2013) (holding that US citizens and corporations that communicate electronically with persons in other countries lacked standing to challenge the federal government's mass surveillance program under the Foreign Intelligence Surveillance Act); Holder v. Humanitarian Law Project, 561 U.S. 1, 40 (2010) (upholding as consistent with the First Amendment the application of criminal sanctions against the provision of "material support" of terrorist organizations based on the Humanitarian Law Project's efforts to teach peaceful and non-violent conflict resolution techniques to members of the PKK); Reno v. American-Arab Anti-Discrimination Comm., 525 U.S. 471, 488 n.10, 490–91 (1999) (rejecting a First Amendment objection to deportation proceedings that were allegedly initiated because of the government's antipathy toward the deportees' First Amendment activities); Meese v. Keene, 481 U.S. 465, 480–85 (1987) (upholding, against a First Amendment compelled speech objection, a federal law that required the labeling of three Canadian films as "political propaganda" distributed by "foreign principals and their agents").

12 Neuborne & Shapiro, *supra* note 6, at 721.

13 *See* ALEXANDER MEIKLEJOHN, FREE SPEECH AND ITS RELATION TO SELF-GOVERNMENT xiii–xiv, 24–27, 91 (1948) (arguing that voters need all relevant information in order to hold government accountable through the electoral process and arguing that foreign speakers and ideas are no less potentially relevant to the process of democratic deliberation than domestic speakers and ideas). Professor Meiklejohn posited that "[t]o be afraid of ideas, any idea, is to be unfit for self-government." *Id.* at 27.

14 The paucity of writing on the status of transborder speech is startling. As Professor Zick observes, "[s]cholars, courts, and government officials have considered the First Amendment's domestic domain in exhaustive detail," but "far less attention has been paid to the manner in which First Amendment liberties intersect with and relate to international borders." ZICK, *supra* note 2, at 1. In fact, only a handful of articles have been written that address the question of how to map the First Amendment on to speech and speakers that originate outside the United States. Professors Zick and Neuborne have authored the most comprehensive works on the subject. *See generally* ZICK, supra note 2; Neuborne & Shapiro, *supra* note 6. Other works that discuss transborder speech include: David Cole, *The First Amendment's Borders: The Place of* Holder v. Humanitarian Law Project *in First Amendment Doctrine*, 6 HARV. L & POL'Y REV. 147 (2012); Aziz Huq, *Preserving Political Speech from Ourselves and Others*, 112 COLUM. L. REV. SIDEBAR 16 (2012); Jeffrey Kahn, *International Travel and the Constitution*, 56 UCLA L. REV. 271 (2008); Robert D. Kamenshine, *Embargoes on Exports of Ideas and Information: First Amendment Issues*, 26 WM. & MARY L. REV. 863 (1985); John A. Scanlan, *Aliens in the Marketplace of Ideas: The Government, the Academy, and the McCarran-Walter Act*, 66 TEX. L. REV. 1481 (1988); Steven R. Shapiro, Commentary, *Ideological Exclusions: Closing the Border to Political Dissidents*, 100 HARV. L. REV. 930 (1987). Remarkably, these works comprise the existing scholarly oeuvre. The failure of the US legal academy to address issues associated with government efforts to regulate or proscribe transborder speech is telling; the subject is sufficiently foreign (so to speak) to contemporary concerns about expressive freedom that the body of literature addressing it pales in comparison to the ink spilled analyzing the First Amendment protection afforded to low value speech, such as advertising, child pornography, and obscenity.

15 ZICK, *supra* note 2, at 212.

16 *See infra* text and accompanying notes 110 to 234.

17 *See infra* text and accompanying notes 193 to 234.

18 *See, e.g.*, Holder v. Humanitarian Law Project, 561 U.S. 1, 36 (2010) ("Given the sensitive interests in national security and foreign affairs at stake, the political branches have adequately substantiated their determination that, to serve the Government's interest in preventing terrorism, it was necessary to prohibit providing material support in the form of training, expert advice, personnel, and services to foreign terrorist groups, even if the supporters meant to promote only the groups' nonviolent ends."); Kleindienst v. Mandel, 408 U.S. 753, 770 (1972) ("We hold that when the Executive exercises this power [to control the

entrance of foreign nationals into the United States] negatively on the basis of a facially legitimate and bona fide reason, the courts will neither look behind the exercise of that discretion, nor test it by balancing its justification against the First Amendment interests of those who seek personal communication with the applicant."); Zemel v. Rusk, 381 U.S. 1, 16–17 (1965) ("There are few restrictions on action which could not be clothed by ingenious argument in the garb of decreased data flow. ... The right to speak and publish does not carry with it the unrestrained right to gather information."). *But cf. id.* at 24 (Douglas, J., dissenting) ("The ability to understand this pluralistic world, filled with clashing ideologies, is a prerequisite of citizenship if we and other peoples of the world are to avoid the nuclear holocaust.").

19 *Humanitarian Law Project*, 561 U.S. at 39.

20 *Id.* at 10–11, 14.

21 *See id.* at 33–40.

22 *Id.* at 40.

23 *See* Cole, *supra* note 14, at 148–50; *see also* text and accompanying notes 215 to 234 text (discussing and critiquing *Humanitarian Law Project* and its unusually weak application of strict judicial scrutiny).

24 Cole, *supra* note 14, at 149.

25 *See* ZICK, *supra* note 2, at 61–76, 126–31, 156, 215, 303.

26 50 U.S.C. §§ 1801-1885c (2012).

27 *See* Clapper v. Amnesty Int'l USA, 568 U.S. 398, 418–22 (2013). For a discussion of how the federal government conducts dragnet surveillance of US citizens' transborder communications (without obtaining a warrant), see James Purce, Comment, *Push It to the (Constitutional) Limit: Strengthening the National Security Agency's Section 702 Surveillance Program*, 70 ADMIN. L. REV. 743 (2018).

28 *See* Neil M. Richards, *The Dangers of Surveillance*, 126 HARV. L. REV. 1934, 1945–47, 1950–52 (2013).

29 *Id.* at 1951.

30 *See generally* Christina E. Wells, *Fear and Loathing in Constitutional Decision-Making*, 2005 WIS. L. REV. 115.

31 *See* Timothy B. Lee, *Here's Everything We Know About PRISM to Date*, WASH. POST, WONKBLOG (June 12, 2013), https://washingtonpost.com/news/wonk/wp/2013/06/12/heres-everything-we-know-about-prism-to-date/?utm_term=161c000cbfe5.

32 *See* 50 U.S.C. §§ 1861–1863 (2012).

33 Digital Rights Ireland Ltd. v. Minister of Communications, Marine, and Natural Resources, Joined Cases C-293 & C-594/12, 2014 E.C.R. 239, paras. 58–62, 69–71 (2014), http://curia.europa.eu/juris/document/document.jsf?text=&docid=150642&pageIndex=0&doclang=en&mode=req&dir=&occ=first&part=1&cid=404289 [http://perma.cc/54C5-A8WLf (invalidating EU Directive 2006/24, which required the collection and storage of literally *all* electronic communications, because of the lack of adequate procedural and administrative safeguards, and observing that "retention of the data in question might have an effect on the use, by subscribers or registered users, of the means of

communication covered by that directive and, consequently, on their exercise of freedom of expression").

34 *See* Richards, *supra* note 28, at 1948 (observing that "surveillance inclines us to the mainstream and the boring" and "menaces our society's foundational commitments to intellectual diversity and eccentric individuality"). Professor Richards persuasively posits that "[i]f we care about the development of eccentric individuality and freedom of thought as First Amendment values, then we should be especially wary of surveillance activities through which those aspects of the self are constructed." *Id.* at 1950.

35 *See* Clapper v. Amnesty Int'l USA, 568 U.S. 398, 401–02, 422 (2013) ("We hold that respondents lack Article III standing because they cannot demonstrate that the future injury they purportedly fear is certainly impending and because they cannot manufacture standing by incurring costs in anticipation of nonimminent harm.").

36 *See id.* at 418–22.

37 *See generally* Kal Raustiala, Does the Constitution Follow the Flag?: The Evolution of Territoriality in American Law 83–90, 209–10 (2009) (discussing the "plenary power" doctrine, which gives Congress very broad authority to regulate persons and territory outside the boundaries of the fifty states and, with respect to the First Amendment, observing that "[o]nly a few cases have ever considered the extraterritorial reach of the First Amendment" and noting that "American judges have tended to deny its extraterritorial reach"). Professor Zick points out, however, that "[s]ince the 1950s, the territorial domain of constitutional liberties, including those set forth in the Bill of Rights, has steadily expanded with respect to both citizens and aliens." Zick, *supra* note 1, at 1593.

38 Meiklejohn, *supra* note 13, at 24–27.

39 Shapiro, *supra* note 14, at 942 ("The Bill of Rights, after all, was adopted to limit the exercise of sovereign powers that are inconsistent with transcendent national values.").

40 *See infra* text and accompanying notes 52 to 109.

41 *See, e.g.,* Lamont v. Postmaster General, 381 U.S. 301, 305–07 (1965) (invalidating a statute that significantly burdened the receipt of "communist political propaganda" mailed from outside the United States because the law constituted "an unconstitutional abridgment of the addressee's First Amendment rights").

42 *See infra* text and accompanying notes 110 to 163.

43 *See, e.g.,* Haig v. Agee, 453 U.S. 280, 308–09 (1981) (assuming "that First Amendment protections reach beyond our national boundaries" but holding that "Agee's First Amendment claim has no foundation").

44 *See id.* at 309 ("To the extent the revocation of his passport operates to inhibit [the owner of a U.S. passport], 'it is an inhibition of *action*,' rather than of speech. *Zemel*, 381 U.S., at 16–17 (emphasis supplied).").

45 *See, e.g.,* Holder v. Humanitarian Law Project, 561 U.S. 1, 36–40 (2010).

46 *See* Meese v. Keene, 481 U.S. 465 (1987).

47 *Humanitarian Law Project*, 561 U.S. at 39–40.

48 Citizens United v. Fed. Elec. Comm'n, 558 U.S. 310, 339–41 (2010).

49 *See id.* at 342 ("The Court has recognized that First Amendment protection extends to corporations."); *see also* First Nat. Bank of Boston v. Bellotti, 435 U.S. 765, 778 n.14, 784 (1978) (holding that the First Amendment protects corporate speech and noting the existence of "many decisions holding state laws invalid under the Fourteenth Amendment when they infringe protected speech by corporate bodies") In *Bellotti*, the Supreme Court held that speech does not lose its First Amendment protection "simply because its source is a corporation." *Bellotti*, 435 U.S. at 784.

50 *See infra* text and accompanying notes 252 to 280.

51 *But cf.* Reid v. Covert, 354 U.S. 1, 10–14 (1957) (holding that the Bill of Rights protects US citizens located abroad and overruling *In Re Ross*, 140 U.S. 453 (1891), a decision that held to the contrary). Justice Hugo L. Black explained that unacceptable consequences would necessarily flow from holding the Bill of Rights to be inapplicable to US citizens when they are outside the United States:

> The concept that the Bill of Rights and other constitutional protections against arbitrary government are inoperative when they become inconvenient or when expediency dictates otherwise is a very dangerous doctrine and if allowed to flourish would destroy the benefit of a written Constitution and undermine the basis of our Government. If our foreign commitments become of such nature that the Government can no longer satisfactorily operate within the bounds laid down by the Constitution, that instrument can be amended by the method which it prescribes.

Id. at 14.

52 As a matter a matter of historical record, foreign travel did not require a passport. *See* Kahn, *supra* note 14, at 316 ("For most of American history, travel abroad was as unencumbered as travel at home. Passports were optional.").

53 *See* Lamont v. Postmaster General, 381 U.S. 301 (1965).

54 357 U.S. 116 (1958).

55 *Id.* at 117.

56 *Id.* at 117–19.

57 *See id.* at 129 (noting that "we do not reach the question of constitutionality").

58 *Id.* at 130.

59 *Id.*

60 Denial of a passport obviously raises serious constitutional questions and reflects efforts to control domestic politics as much as efforts to protect foreign relations and national security concerns. *See* Louis L. Jaffe, *The Right to Travel: The Passport Problem*, 35 FOREIGN AFF. 17, 18 (1956) ("Nearly every passport denial has been a decision to keep the citizen here within the high walled fortress where he can be isolated, neutralized, kept, let us say, to his accustomed and observable routines of malefaction. It has been simply one facet of our tactic of domestic security, and only incidentally a matter of foreign policy.").

61 *Kent*, 357 U.S. at 130.

62 Dayton v. Dulles, 357 U.S. 144, 154 (1958) (Clark, J., dissenting); *see also Kent*, 357 U.S. at 131, 143 (Clark, J., dissenting) (objecting to the majority's conclusion "that the Secretary has not been authorized to deny a passport to a Communist whose travel abroad would be inimical to our national security" and arguing that the State Department possessed statutory authority "to deny petitioners' applications for passports").

63 378 U.S. 500 (1964).

64 64 Stat. 993, 50 U.S.C. § 781 (2012); *Aptheker* 378 U.S. at 501–02.

65 *Aptheker*, 378 U.S. at 501–02.

66 *Id.* at 503–04 & 504 n.4.

67 *Id.* at 504–05.

68 *Id.* at 505.

69 *Id.* at 514.

70 *Id.*

71 *Aptheker*, 378 U.S. at 515.

72 *Id.* at 511–12 n.10.

73 *Id.* at 512 n.10.

74 *Id.* (reporting that Flynn sought to travel for, among other things, "study" and "to observe social, political and economic conditions abroad, and thereafter to write, publish and lecture about her observations").

75 *Id.* at 517.

76 *Aptheker*, 378 U.S. at 520 (Douglas, J., concurring).

77 *Id.*

78 *Id.* at 521.

79 381 U.S. 301 (1965).

80 Postal Service and Federal Employees Salary Act of 1962, Pub. L. No. 87–793, § 4008(a),76 Stat. 840, § 305(a) (codified at 39 U.S.C. § 4008(a)).

81 *Id.*

82 *Id.*

83 *Lamont*, 381 U.S. at 305.

84 *Id.* at 307.

85 *Id.*

86 *Id.*

87 *Lamont*, 381 U.S. at 307–08 (Brennan, J., concurring).

88 *Id.* at 308.

89 *Id.*

90 *Id.*

91 *Id.* at 307 (majority opinion) (quoting New York Times Co. v. Sullivan, 376 U.S. 254, 270 (1964)).

92 *Id.* at 309 (Brennan, J., concurring).

93 See Mike Isaac & Daisuke Wakabayashi, *Russian Influence Reached 126 Million Through Facebook Alone*, N.Y. TIMES (Oct. 31, 2017), www.nytimes.com/2017/10/30/technology/facebook-google-russia.html ("Russian agents intending to sow discord among American citizens disseminated inflammatory posts that reached 126 million users on Facebook, published more than 131,000 messages

on Twitter and uploaded over 1,000 videos to Google's YouTube service …");
Greg Miller, et al., *Obama's Secret Struggle to Punish Russia for Putin's Election
Assault*, WASH. POST (June 23, 2017), www.washingtonpost.com/graphics/2017/
world/national-security/obama-putin-election-hacking/ (reporting that the
Russian President Vladimir Putin issued "specific instructions" aimed at
achieving "[an] audacious objective[ ]," namely to "defeat or at least damage
the Democratic nominee, Hillary Clinton, and help elect her opponent, Donald
Trump"). It bears noting that the advertising buys undertaken by the Russian
government on Facebook, Google, and Twitter constituted a minute portion of
the total paid political advertising related to the 2016 presidential election –
perhaps $100,000 in total on Facebook and about $60,000 in Russian-related ad
buys on Google (with only around $5,000 in purchases by the Russian Internet
Research Agency). *See* Isaac & Wakabayashi, *supra*. Russian-related political
communications also comprised a "minuscule amount" of the total political
communications related to the 2016 presidential election circulating on
Facebook, Google, and Twitter. *See id.*

94 *See* MEIKLEJOHN, *supra* note 13, at 91 (arguing that, under the First Amendment,
"such books as Hitler's *Mein Kampf*, or Lenin's *The State and Revolution*, or the
Communist Manifesto of Engels and Marx, may be freely printed, freely sold,
freely distributed, freely read, freely discussed, freely believed, throughout the
United States" not to safeguard "the financial interests of a publisher, or a
distributor, or even of a writer" but rather because intense ongoing
examination of our government is essential to its proper functioning).

95 *Id.*

96 *See* Cohen v. California, 403 U.S. 15, 24–26 (1971) (invalidating Cohen's
conviction for disturbing the peace based on his public display of a jacket
emblazoned with the word "fuck" and explaining that "we cannot indulge the
facile assumption that one can forbid particular words without also running a
substantial risk of suppressing ideas in the process" and that permitting such
regulation of speech as offensive conduct would encourage governments to
"seize upon the censorship of particular words as a convenient guise for
banning the expression of unpopular views"); *see* Ronald J. Krotoszynski, Jr.,
Cohen v. California: *"Inconsequential" Cases and Larger Principles*, 74 TEX. L.
REV. 1251, 1254 (1996) ("By distinguishing the question of full and free public
debate from the particular content of the message (or the nature of the
messenger), Justice Harlan vindicated the individual citizen's right to hold
and share political views within the marketplace of ideas, and to
communicate those ideas in unconventional – or even patently offensive –
ways.").

97 *See* RAUSTIALA, *supra* note 37, at 83–87. It bears noting, however, that the plenary
power doctrine does not imply the constitutional authority to violate the
constitutional rights of lawfully present aliens. *See id.* at 54 ("The result is a
system that permits largely unfettered discretion in the process of admitting or
expelling aliens, but requires fair treatment while the aliens are within the
United States.").

98 *See* Boutilier v. Immigration and Naturalization Serv., 387 U.S. 118, 123–24 (1967) ("It has long been held that the Congress has plenary power to make rules for the admission of aliens and to exclude those who possess those characteristics which Congress has forbidden."); Galvin v. Press, 347 U.S. 522, 531 (1954) (positing that "[p]olicies pertaining to the entry of aliens and their right to remain here are peculiarly concerned with the political conduct of government" and observing that the principle that "the formulation of these policies is entrusted exclusively to Congress has become about as firmly imbedded in the legislative and judicial tissues of our body politic as any aspect of our government"); Harisiades v. Shaughnessy, 342 U.S. 580, 589 (1952) (holding that Congress's powers over immigration and the national border "are so exclusively entrusted to the political branches of government as to be largely immune from judicial inquiry or interference").

99 381 U.S. 1 (1965).

100 *Id.* at 3.

101 *Id.* at 4.

102 *Id.* at 4.

103 *Id.* at 16.

104 *Id.* at 16–17.

105 *Id.* at 17. It bears noting that "[g]overnment restrictions on travel abroad have a long and unfortunate history in this country." Neuborne & Shapiro, *supra* note 6, at 733.

106 *Zemel*, 381 U.S. at 24 (Douglas, J., dissenting).

107 *Id.*

108 *Id.*

109 *Id.* at 26.

110 Kleindienst v. Mandel, 408 U.S. 753, 762 (1972).

111 Haig v. Agee, 453 U.S. 280 (1981).

112 *Mandel*, 408 U.S. at 756–60, 770.

113 *Id.* at 756.

114 *See id.* at 756–57.

115 *Id.* at 757.

116 *Id.* at 758–59.

117 The relevant statutory provisions actually created a shared responsibility for a waiver from a federal law that barred the admission of persons advocating communist ideologies. *See* 8 U.S.C. § 1182. The relevant language authorizes a waiver of the ban against issuing an entry visa to any alien who advocates, writes, or publishes "the economic, international, and government doctrines of world communism" on the recommendation of the State Department, and with the concurrence of the Attorney General. In Mandel's case, the State Department actually recommended that a waiver be granted for the visit, but the Department of Justice refused to approve this recommendation. *Mandel*, 408 U.S. at 759.

118 Mandel v. Mitchell, 325 F. Supp. 620, 630–34 (E.D. N.Y. 1971), *rev'd sub nom.*, 408 U.S. 753 (1972).

119 *Id.* at 630.

120 *Mandel*, 408 U.S. at 762–63.

121 *Id.* at 763.

122 *Id.* at 765.

123 *Id.*

124 Shapiro, *supra* note 14, at 942 n.75; *see* Zick, *supra* note 1, at 1553 ("In a portion of the opinion that may come to have particular salience in the digital era, the Court noted that the mere possibility that the message could be delivered by means other than face-to-face interaction with the speaker did not satisfy First Amendment concerns.").

125 Boutilier v. Immigration and Naturalization Serv., 387 U.S. 118, 123 (1967).

126 Galvan v. Press, 347 U.S. 522, 531 (1954).

127 *See Mandel*, 408 U.S. at 767 ("They argue that the Executive's implementation of this congressional mandate through [the] decision whether to grant a waiver in each individual case must be limited by the First Amendment rights of persons like appellees.").

128 *Id.* at 769.

129 *Id.* at 770.

130 *See id.* ("What First Amendment or other grounds may be available for attacking [the] exercise of discretion for which no justification whatsoever is advanced is a question we neither address nor decide in this case.").

131 *Mandel*, 408 U.S. at 770 (Douglas, J., dissenting).

132 *Id.* at 772.

133 *Id.*

134 *Mandel*, 408 U.S. at 778 (Marshall, J., dissenting); *see* Shapiro, *supra* note 14, at 944–45 ("Every sovereign nation has the right to control its borders. But in a nation premised on the notion that sovereignty flows from the popular will and that the popular will is determined by political debate, ideological exclusions cannot be justified.").

135 *Mandel*, 408 U.S. at 784 (Marshall, J. dissenting).

136 *Id.* at 785.

137 *Id.*; *see* Neuborne & Shapiro, *supra* note 6, at 767 ("Once the focus is shifted from the foreign speaker, who has no first amendment rights, to the American audience, which possesses full first amendment rights, the issue of judicial capacity in national border cases involving content-based censorship largely disappears."); Shapiro, *supra* note 14, at 945 ("The suppression of speech is surely not the answer in a constitutional democracy.").

138 Zemel v. Rusk, 381 U.S. 1, 16–17 (1965).

139 ZICK, *supra* note 2, at 30.

140 453 U.S. 280 (1981).

141 *Id.* at 304–06.

142 *Id.* at 283.

143 *Id.* at 283–85.

144 *Id.* at 286.

145 Agee v. Vance, 483 F. Supp. 729, 732 (D.D.C. 1980), *aff'd sub nom.*, 629 F.2d 80 (D.C. Cir. 1980), *rev'd*, 453 U.S. 280 (1981).

146 Agee v. Muskie, 629 F.2d 80, 87 (D.C. Cir. 1980), *rev'd*, 453 U.S. 280 (1981).

147 *Id.* at 87.

148 *See id.* at 86–87.

149 *See* New York Times Co. v. Sullivan, 376 U.S. 254, 269–70 (1964); *see also* Robert C. Post, *The Constitutional Concept of Public Discourse: Outrageous Opinion, Democratic Deliberation, and* Hustler Magazine v. Falwell, 103 HARV. L REV. 603, 626–46 (1990) (discussing in some detail the concept of a matter of public concern and how discourse about matters of public concern helps to facilitate the project of democratic deliberation).

150 Post, *supra* note 149, at 683.

151 *Id.* at 684.

152 Haig v. Agee, 453 U.S. 280, 302–03 (1981).

153 *Id.* at 303.

154 *Id.* at 303–04.

155 *Id.* at 304.

156 *Id.* at 308.

157 *Id.* at 309.

158 *Id. But cf.* Kamenshine, *supra* note 14, at 894 ("Permission to travel [should] not be denied for the purpose of punishing the traveler for his political views or attempting to skew scientific or political debate.").

159 *Agee*, 453 U.S. at 309.

160 *Id.* at 309 n.61.

161 *Agee*, 453 U.S. at 312–13 (Brennan, J., dissenting) (arguing that Congress must clearly authorize a power to revoke a citizen's passport and observing that "there is no dispute here that the Passport Act of 1926 does not *expressly* authorize the Secretary to revoke Agee's passport").

162 *See id.* at 314–15.

163 Justice Brennan did object to the deferential standard of review that the majority applied to the First Amendment questions raised by State Department's revocation of Agee's passport based on his past speech. In his view, "the Court's responsibility must be to balance the infringement against the asserted governmental interests to determine whether the revocation contravenes the First Amendment." *Id.* at 320 n.10. This might have been a more intellectually honest approach; the majority essentially engages in a such a balancing exercise, but finds the federal government's interests in foreign affairs and national security overbear Agee's interest in exercising his First Amendment rights abroad. Justice Brennan's proposed approach essentially constitutes a call for proportionality analysis. Proportionality analysis involves a reviewing court acknowledging that a fundamental right, in this case, expressive freedoms safeguarded by the First Amendment, has been

burdened, but nevertheless gives the government an opportunity to demonstrate that the burden is justified because it relates to a pressing and substantial government objective, directly advances that objective, and is otherwise narrowly tailored to minimize the adverse effects on the constitutional right at issue. *See* R. v. Oakes, [1986] 1 S.C.R. 103, 112 (Can.); *see also* AHARON BARAK, PROPORTIONALITY: CONSTITUTIONAL RIGHTS AND THEIR LIMITATIONS (Doron Kalir trans., 2012); Vicki C. Jackson, *Constitutional Law in an Age of Proportionality*, 124 YALE L.J. 3094 (2015).

164 Meese v. Keene, 481 U.S. 465, 480–82 (1987).

165 Reno v. American Arab Anti-Discrimination Comm., 525 U.S. 471, 487–92 (1999).

166 Clapper v. Amnesty Int'l USA, 568 U.S. 398, 401–02 (2013).

167 Holder v. Humanitarian Law Project, 561 U.S. 1, 33–40 (2010).

168 481 U.S. 465 (1987).

169 22 U.S.C. §§ 611–621.

170 The films included *If You Love This Planet, Acid Rain: Requiem or Recovery,* and *Acid from Heaven. Keene,* 481 U.S. at 468 n.3.

171 22 U.S.C. § 611(j).

172 22 U.S.C. § 614(b).

173 22 U.S.C. § 611(j).

174 *Keene,* 481 U.S. at 470–71.

175 Keene v. Meese, 619 F. Supp. 1111 (E.D. Cal. 1985), *rev'd,* 481 U.S. 465 (1987).

176 *Id.* at 1124–26.

177 *Id.* at 1126.

178 *Keene,* 481 U.S. at 480.

179 Lamont v. Postmaster General, 381 U.S. 301, 305 (1965).

180 *Keene,* 481 U.S. at 469–70.

181 *Id.* at 480.

182 *Id.*

183 *Id.* at 481.

184 *See, e.g.,* Nat'l Inst. of Family and Life Advocates v. Becerra, 138 S. Ct. 2361, 2372–75 (2018) (invalidating as coerced speech a California law that imposed mandatory disclosure requirements regarding the scope of the reproductive health services actually offered by crisis pregnancy centers operating within the state).

185 *Keene,* 481 U.S. at 481.

186 *Cf. Becerra,* 138 S. Ct. at 2372–75 (holding that coerced speech about controversial issues is always unconstitutional, even if such coerced speech does not impede the ability of a speaker to add an additional, alternative, message of her choosing).

187 McIntyre v. Ohio Elections Comm'n, 514 U.S. 334, 354–57 (1995).

188 *Id.* at 357.

189 *Id.*

190 *Keene,* 481 U.S. at 465 (Blackmun, J., dissenting).

191 *Id.*

192 *Id.* at 482.

193 525 U.S. 471 (1999).

194 *Id.* at 472–73.

195 *See id.* at 473–74.

196 *Id.* at 474.

197 *See id.* at 488 & 488 n.10.

198 *Id.* at 488 n.10 ("Our holding generally deprives deportable aliens of the defense of selective prosecution.").

199 *Id.* at 490–91.

200 *Id.* at 491.

201 *Id.*

202 *Id.* at 491–92. Justice Ginsburg concurred in the judgment, reasoning that "[i]t suffices to inquire whether the First Amendment necessitates *immediate* judicial consideration of their selective enforcement plea. I conclude that it does not." *Id.* at 492 (Ginsburg, J., concurring in part and concurring in the judgment).

203 568 U.S. 398 (2013).

204 50 U.S.C. § 1881a.

205 *Clapper*, 568 U.S. at 404.

206 *See id.* at 404–05.

207 *Id.* at 407

208 *Id.* at 401.

209 *Id.* at 411.

210 *See id.* at 415–18, 422.

211 *Clapper*, 568 U.S. at 431 (Breyer, J., dissenting).

212 *Id.*

213 *See* Lujan v. Defenders of Wildlife, 504 U.S. 555, 561–62 (1992).

214 *See* Baker v. Carr, 369 U.S. 186, 210–17 (1962).

215 561 U.S. 1 (2010).

216 ZICK, *supra* note 2, at 73.

217 *Id.* at 184 ("*Humanitarian Law Project* is a troubling precedent."). More specifically, Zick argues that *Humanitarian Law Project* is "in conflict with traditional First Amendment justifications, which emphasize a commitment to protecting peaceful political speech in the interest of self-governance and the search for truth." *Id.*

218 18 U.S.C. § 2339B(a)(1).

219 *Humanitarian Law Project*, 561 U.S. at 24–25.

220 *Id.* at 32.

221 *Id.* at 36.

222 *Id.; but cf.* Kahn, *supra* note 14, at 333–34 ("Official disapproval of the traveler or his noncriminal purposes in traveling does not entitle the state to restrict the citizen as a 'potential match[ ]' in the 'international tinderbox.'" (quoting Brichl v. Dulles, 248 F.2d 561, 572 (D.C. Cir. 1957), *rev'd on other grounds sub* nom., Kent v. Dulles, 357 U.S. 116, (1958)). Professor Kahn argues that "[s]o long as the citizen's actions are not treasonous, immediately dangerous, or

contrary to some contractual obligation made to the state, a citizen's travel is none of the state's business." *Id.* at 335. Professor Aziz Huq posits that "although the Court framed its analysis around the compelling interest in 'combating terrorism' directed toward the United States, much of what followed turned on the distinct, foreign-affairs related government interest in maintaining cordial relations with countries such as Turkey and Sri Lanka." Huq, *supra* note 14, at 24.

223 *See* United States v. Robel, 389 U.S. 258 (1967); Scales v. United States, 367 U.S. 203 (1961); Yates v. United States, 354 U.S. 298 (1957), *overruled by* Burks v. United States, 437 U.S. 1 (1978); *see also* Cole, *supra* note 14, at 172 (observing that "the Communist Party cases might have been decided differently had Congress imposed restrictions on association with the *Soviet* rather than the *American* Community Party") (emphasis in original). For relevant discussions of the Red Scare prosecutions of individual citizens for mere membership in or association with the Communist Party in the United States – and the Supreme Court's emphatic rejection of such prosecutions – see WALTER GELLHORN, AMERICAN RIGHTS: THE CONSTITUTION IN ACTION 82–83 (1960) and Marc Rohr, *Communists and the First Amendment: The Shaping of Freedom of Advocacy in the Cold War Era,* 28 SAN DIEGO L. REV. 1, 66–97 (1991). Indeed, Professor Marc Rohr observes that "[a]fter the *Scales* and *SACB* [Subversive Activities Control Board] decisions of 1961, every first amendment challenge to 'loyalty' laws that reached the Supreme Court in the 1960's was successful," meaning that even serious advocacy of a proletariat-led revolution could not be the subject of criminal charges. Rohr, *supra,* at 91; *see* Brandenburg v. Ohio, 395 U.S. 444, 447 & 447–48 n.2 (1969) (holding that the government may not "forbid or proscribe advocacy of the use of force or of law violation except where such advocacy is directed to inciting or producing imminent lawless action and is likely to incite or produce such action" and characterizing prior cases, such as *Yates,* as having adopted and applied this approach). After the Warren Court's landmark 1969 decision in *Brandenburg,* in the absence of convincing evidence that a particular call to action will produce imminent unlawful conduct, advocating violent revolution enjoys full First Amendment protection. *Brandenburg,* 395 U.S. at 447–48; *see* Rohr, *supra,* at 97–100 (discussing *Brandenburg* and its effective rejection of criminal prosecutions for advocacy of a violent Communist revolution absent an imminent risk that calls to action would actually precipitate unlawful acts).

224 *Humanitarian Law Project,* 561 U.S. at 30.

225 Cole, *supra* note 14, at 148.

226 *Id.*

227 *Humanitarian Law Project,* 561 U.S. at 39.

228 *See, e.g.,* Al Haramain Islamic Foundation, Inc. v. U.S. Dep't of the Treasury, 660 F.3d 1019, 1051–54 (9th Cir. 2011) (validating First Amendment claim because "[t]he entities in *HLP* were wholly foreign, whereas AHIF-Oregon is, at least in some respects, a domestic organization" and "content-based prohibitions on speech violate the First Amendment" when such speech

relates to "a domestic branch of an international organization"). As Professor Huq has observed, "some commentators have suggested the opinion [*Humanitarian Law Project*] has only small practical significance because it does not reach domestic organizations." Huq, *supra* note 14, at 22. However, this effort to renormalize *Humanitarian Law Project* ignores the importance of transborder speech to the process of democratic self-government. *See infra* text and accompanying notes 235 to 280.

229 *See* Ashutosh Bhagwat, *Associational Speech*, 120 YALE L.J. 978, 1010 n.150 (2011); Cole, *supra* note 14, at 164 ("There is certainly reason to believe that the analysis in *Humanitarian Law Project* is not generally applicable."); *see also* ZICK, *supra* note 2, at 187 (noting that the Supreme Court in *Humanitarian Law Project* "posits a foreign-domestic distinction with respect to First Amendment freedoms that suggests full constitutional protection applies only to intraterritorial communications and associations").

230 *Humanitarian Law Project*, 561 U.S. at 32.

231 *Id.* at 33–34. On the other hand, good cause exists for concern that the political branches' claimed foreign affairs and national security justifications for regulating or banning transborder speech activity could be merely pretextual. *See* Shapiro, *supra* note 13, at 941 ("But when the nature of that foreign policy interest is explored, it becomes clear that the government's concrete worry is that particular speech, pejoratively labeled as 'propaganda' or 'disinformation,' will cause a public reaction in the United States that will complicate implementation of the administration's foreign policy objectives").

232 *Humanitarian Law Project*, 561 U.S. at 36. *But cf.* Cole, *supra* note 13, at 149 ("For the first time in its history, the Court upheld the criminalization of speech advocating only nonviolent, lawful ends on the ground that such speech might unintentionally assist a third party in criminal wrongdoing.").

233 Citizens United v. Fed. Elec. Comm'n, 558 U.S. 310, 412 (2010) (Stevens, J., concurring in part and dissenting in part) ("The total record [Congress] compiled was 100,000 *pages* long.").

234 *See id.* at 339–41.

235 Of course, in the real world, the source of news or information obviously plays an important role in its credibility. A reliable news source, such as the *New York Times* or *Wall Street Journal*, which observes standards of journalistic ethics and relies on maintaining its journalistic credibility to secure its market position, should be deemed a more reliable and trustworthy source of news and information than a Wikipedia entry or an Infowars post. In this sense, then, the identity of a speaker is crucially important to a viewer, listener, or reader. *See* Gia B. Lee, *Persuasion, Transparency, and Government Speech*, 56 HASTINGS L.J. 983, 983–90 (2005) (noting that the identity of a speaker often prefigures the credibility of information to an audience and documenting the problematic practice of the government deploying so-called "sock puppet" identities to obfuscate the government's authorship of messages in order to enhance the credibility of them with the public); Helen Norton & Danielle Keats Citron, *Government Speech 2.0*, 87 DENV. U. L. REV. 899, 935–38 (2010)

(noting that a speaker's identity can often prefigure the credibility of the speech to an audience and noting that government sometimes attempts to hide its identity in order to enhance the credibility of its speech).

236 2 U.S.C. § 441b.

237 2 U.S.C. § 434(f)(3)A).

238 *Citizens United*, 558 U.S. at 319–21.

239 *Id.* at 322.

240 McConnell v. Fed. Elec. Comm'n, 540 U.S. 93, 203–09 (2003).

241 Austin v. Michigan Chamber of Commerce, 494 U.S. 652, 658–60 (1990).

242 *Citizens United*, 558 U.S. at 339.

243 *Id.* at 341.

244 *Id.* at 340–41.

245 *See id. But cf.* Tamara R. Piety, Brandishing the First Amendment: Commercial Expression in America 121–24 (2012) (arguing that government paternalism can protect consumers from false and misleading speech, that unregulated speech markets merely constitute "paternalism of a different stripe, tough love—hard paternalism rather than soft protective paternalism," and that government interventions in speech markets to weed out false or misleading information do not "in any way interfere[ ] with listeners' interests").

246 *See Citizens United*, 558 U.S. at 340.

247 *Id.* at 339. Moreover, it bears noting that in today's marketplace of ideas, "[i]nformation flows at great speed, and in remarkable quantity, across our national borders." Zick, *supra* note 1, at 1544. These global information flows are plainly relevant to the process of democratic deliberation necessary to sustain the project of democratic self-government. *See* Meiklejohn, *supra* note 13, at 25–27. As Professor Meiklejohn argues, under the First Amendment, "[t]he freedom of ideas shall not be abridged," *id.* at 27, and the local or foreign source of an idea is entirely irrelevant to its potential value to the electorate. *See id.* at xiii–xiv, 90–91.

248 *Citizens United*, 558 U.S. at 341.

249 *Id.* at 339.

250 *See* Meiklejohn, *supra* note 13, at xiii–xiv, 88–89.

251 *Citizens United*, 558 U.S. at 340.

252 In fact, the *Citizens United* majority declined to decide whether the federal government would have a compelling interest in banning speech by "foreign individuals or associations." *See id.* at 362 (observing that "[s]ection 441b is not limited to corporations or associations that were created in foreign countries or funded predominantly by foreign shareholders" and accordingly "would be overbroad even if we assumed, *arguendo*, that the Government has a compelling interest in limiting foreign influence over our political process").

253 Meiklejohn, *supra* note 13, at xiii.

254 *Id.*

255 *Id.*

256 *Id.* at xiv.

257 *Id.* at 91.

258 *Id.; see* ZICK, *supra* note 2, at 20 ("Whether we like it or not, we occupy a world where cultures and legal systems are intertwined."); Cole, *supra* note 13, at 170 ("The First Amendment should protect our right to read *The Guardian* (UK), as it does our right to read the *New York Times*, and our right to post blogs on sites immediately accessible in a distant foreign land, as it does our right to hand out a leaflet on a [domestic] neighborhood street corner.").

259 MEIKLEJOHN, *supra* note 13, at 91.

260 *See* Holder v. Humanitarian Law Project, 561 U.S. 1, 33–39 (2010).

261 *See* Zemel v. Rusk, 381 U.S. 1, 16–17 (1965).

262 *See* Kahn, *supra* note 14, at 348 ("To prevent a citizen from leaving the United States because that travel is asserted to be contrary to the country's foreign policy interests is to engage in a form of countrywide house arrest on grounds that sound uncomfortably close to preventive detention on the basis of future dangerousness (which itself has been held to require strict scrutiny)."); Kamenshine, *supra* note 13, at 894 (arguing that the federal courts should "afford foreign travel by United States citizens a significant degree of first amendment protection").

263 MEIKLEJOHN, *supra* note 13, at 88.

264 *Id.*

265 To be sure, Professor Meiklejohn's examples all involved the domestic consumption of foreign books and interactions with foreign, non-citizen speakers inside the United States. *See id.* at 88–91. However, the logic of his position would necessarily have to encompass the ability of a US citizen to go abroad to gather the information necessary to cast a well-informed vote at home on election day. *See id.* at 25–26, 88–89. *But cf.* Zemel v. Rusk, 381 U.S. 1, 16–17 (1965) (rejecting a First Amendment-based right to travel to Cuba to learn first-hand about conditions there under Fidel Castro because "[t]here are few restrictions on action which could not be clothed by ingenious argument in the garb of decreased data flow").

266 *See* Meese v. Keene, 481 U.S. 465, 480–85 (1987).

267 *See* Kleindienst v. Mandel, 408 U.S. 753, 762–70 (1972). *But cf.* Cole, *supra* note 14, at 170 ("Exchange with foreign voices informs citizens about world affairs, and thereby furthers self-government.").

268 N.Y. Times Co. v. Sullivan, 376 U.S. 254, 270 (1964).

269 Cole, *supra* note 14, at 170.

270 MEIKLEJOHN, *supra* note 13, at 25–26; *see* ZICK, *supra* note 2, at 212 (arguing that "U.S. citizens ought to enjoy protection for free speech, press, assembly, and petition rights without regard to frontiers or borders" and positing that "[t]reating expressive rights as portable will facilitate citizens' participation in global conversation and commingling"); Cole, *supra* note 14, at 169 (arguing that "communication and association with foreign organizations is, and should be, protected by the First Amendment").

271 MEIKLEJOHN, *supra* note 13, at 27.

272 *See* Martin H. Redish, The Adversary First Amendment: Free Expression and the Foundations of American Democracy 1–5, 27–41, 56–59, 176–81 (2013) (arguing that the First Amendment exists primarily to facilitate the process of democratic deliberation and positing that scrupulously honoring the principle of audience autonomy constitutes the best way of making the First Amendment facilitate the process of democratic deliberation). Professor Redish argues that "government's decision to insulate citizens from information and opinion because of a paternalistic distrust of citizens' ability to make wise choices is as threatening to core democratic values as the suppression of any speaker." *Id.* at 57.

273 *Cf.* Neuborne & Shapiro, *supra* note 6, at 744 ("Democratic principles are reinforced, not diminished, by judicial review that prevents a transient majority from tampering with the flow of information necessary to assure its continued political accountability.").

274 Citizens United v. Fed. Elec. Comm'n, 558 U.S. 310, 340 (2010).

275 Holder v. Humanitarian Law Project, 561 U.S. 1, 33–39 (2010). It bears noting that the Supreme Court issued both decisions during the same term.

276 *See Citizens United*, 558 U.S. at 339 (positing that free speech constitutes "an essential mechanism of democracy" because it serves as "the means to hold officials accountable to the people").

277 Meiklejohn, *supra* note 13, at 88–89.

278 *See* Kamenshine, *supra* note 14, at 876 ("The business of government does not include using its regulatory power to shape a political viewpoint."); Neuborne & Shapiro, *supra* note 6, at 748 ("Given the danger to a free society created by widespread censorship at the national border, reviewing courts should insist upon proof, not merely that speech *might* damage our foreign policy or even our national security, but that it is reasonably likely to do so."). Kamenshine concludes that "[r]egulation controlling speech directly related to issues of public policy demands strict review." Kamenshine, *supra* note 14, at 878. On the other hand, however, Neuborne and Shapiro think judicial vigilance is unlikely to occur in transborder speech cases because "[i]n national border cases ... the nature of the asserted governmental interest often involves assessments of fact and policy beyond the institutional competence of the judiciary, making judges extremely wary of estimating the importance of an asserted government justification." Neuborne & Shapiro, *supra* note 6, at 747. Because of this reticence to interfere with foreign relations and national security efforts, federal judges feel "bound to defer to any justification that [is] not facially invalid." *Id.* To be sure, the potential social costs of transborder speech could be quite high – but those costs do not seem to affect the willingness of the federal courts to protect *domestic* speech activity that could easily produce very serious adverse effects abroad – such as the infamous fundamentalist Florida preacher Terry Jones – who conducts public Koran burnings. *See* Kevin Sieff, *Florida Pastor Terry Jones's Koran Burning has Far-reaching Effect*, Wash. Post, Apr. 2, 2011, www.washingtonpost.com/local/edu cation/forida-pastor-terry-joness-koran-burning-has-far-reaching-effect/2011/04/

02/AFpiFoQC_story.html?utm_term=.55666dfcb582; *see also* Alan K. Chen, *Free Speech and the Confluence of National Security and Internet Exceptionalism*, 86 FORDHAM L. REV. 379, 386–91, 397–99 (2017) (providing an excellent historical and doctrinal overview of free speech "national security exceptionalism" and positing that national security concerns, including concerns about terrorism, "are somewhat inflated"). Professor Chen argues that "the legal system ought to be skeptical about calls to relax the free speech protections surrounding unlawful advocacy" and cautions against "a tendency to overreact to what are perceived as new types of national security threats." *Id.* at 399.

279 MEIKLEJOHN, *supra* note 13, at 89.

280 *See* Neuborne & Shapiro, *supra* note 6, at 748 (arguing that "a genuine threat to national security must arise before the national border can be used to impede the free flow of ideas"); *see generally* Vincent Blasi, *The First Amendment and the Ideal of Civic Courage: The Brandeis Opinion in* Whitney v. California, 29 WM & MARY L. REV. 653 (1988) (positing that, consistent with the arguments set forth in Justice Louis Brandeis's iconic concurring opinion in *Whitney*, the process of democratic deliberation necessarily requires that society tolerate speech that could impose serious social costs). As Professor Zick has argued, "[e]xtension of First Amendment protections to U.S. citizens located abroad would seem to be supported by text, theory, and precedent." Zick, *supra* note 1, at 1593. Moreover, "[t]he First Amendment's text does not suggest any geographic limitation." *Id.*

281 ZICK, *supra* note 2, at 7.

282 Neuborne & Shapiro, *supra* note 6, at 765.

283 Citizens United v. Fed. Elec. Comm'n, 558 U.S. 310, 341 (2010) ("Premised on mistrust of governmental power, the First Amendment stands against attempts to disfavor certain subjects or viewpoints. Prohibited, too, are restrictions distinguishing among different speakers, allowing speech by some but not others.") (internal citation omitted).

284 New York Times Co. v. Sullivan, 376 U.S. 254, 270 (1964).

7 SYSTEMIC FAILURES TO PROTECT NEWSGATHERING ACTIVITIES
BY PROFESSIONAL JOURNALISTS AND AMATEUR
CITIZEN-JOURNALISTS ALIKE

1 *See supra* Chapter 4.

2 *See* Barry P. McDonald, *The First Amendment and the Free Flow of Information: Towards a Realistic Right to Gather Information in the Information Age*, 65 OHIO ST. L.J. 249, 250–54 (2004).

3 *Id.* at 269–73.

4 *See* Lyrissa Barnett Lidsky, *Silencing John Doe: Defamation and Discourse in Cyberspace*, 49 DUKE L.J. 855, 860–65 (2008). Dean Lidsky argues, with some persuasive force, that "[t]he promise of the Internet is empowerment: it empowers ordinary individuals with limited financial resources to 'publish' their views on

matters of public concern." *Id.* at 860. This makes the web "a powerful tool for equalizing imbalances of power by giving voice to the disenfranchised and by allowing more democratic participation in public discourse." *Id.* at 860–61. In sum, "the Internet allows ordinary John Does to participate as never before in public discourse, and hence, to shape public policy." *Id.* at 861. These observations would seem to apply with full force to citizen-journalism.

5 *See generally* New York Times v. Sullivan, 376 U.S. 254, 270 (1964) (noting that the process of democratic self-government requires that debate about matters of public concern be "uninhibited, robust, and wide-open").

6 Academic commentary on this question is surprisingly sparse. The two leading First Amendment scholars who have written extensively on this question have reached conflicting conclusions. *Compare* Seth F. Kreimer, *Pervasive Capture and the First Amendment: Memory, Discourse, and the Right to Record*, 159 U. PA. L. REV. 335, 370–86 (2011) (arguing that image capture, and other related activities that are integral to subsequent communication, constitute protected First Amendment activity) *with* Ashutosh Bhagwat, *Producing Speech*, 56 WM. & MARY L. REV. 1029, 1035–36, 1078–80 (2015) (arguing that the First Amendment does not protect the right to gather information because "unlike speech production, information gathering often has no relation to speech at all"). Professor Kreimer's approach would broadly deploy the First Amendment to protect activities that are antecedent to communicating, even at the cost of protecting personal privacy. *See* Kreimer, *supra*, at 403–08 (arguing that, in some circumstances, the First Amendment should protect the unconsented-to capture of images in non-public spaces and places). Professor Bhagwat's approach would make it possible for the states and federal government to enact privacy-protecting statutes. *See* Bhagwat, *supra*, at 1075–76. He posits that resolving questions about a right to record versus privacy requires "the weighing of incommensurate values." *Id.* at 1076. In my view, because image capture potentially involves serious invasions of personal privacy, the First Amendment's protection of surreptitious newsgathering must take personal privacy into account. *See* Frisby v. Shultz, 487 U.S. 474, 484–86 (1988). The most pressing problems that this chapter addresses, involving government efforts to suppress newsgathering activities in public places – where no privacy interests exist under current US law – do not implicate significantly privacy values. *But cf.* ACLU v. Alvarez, 679 F.3d 583, 611–12 (7th Cir. 2012) (Posner, J., dissenting) (arguing that permitting the recording of police officers in public places will "impair the ability of police both to extract information relevant to police duties and to communicate effectively with persons whom they speak with in the line of duty").

7 For a relevant discussion, see Bhagwat, *supra* note 6, at 1033–36, 1052–54, 1068–70 (2015).

8 *See id.* at 1052–53.

9 Kreimer, *supra* note 6, at 360–62; Jocelyn Simonson, *Beyond Body Cameras: Defending a Robust Right to Record the Police*, 104 GEO. L.J. 1559, 1561–62 (2016).

10 RonNell Andersen Jones & Sonja R. West, *The Fragility of the Free American Press*, 112 Nw. U. L. Rev. 567, 573 (2017).

11 *But see* Branzburg v. Hayes, 408 U.S. 665 (1972).

12 *See* James Risen, *Trump Can Target Journalists, Thanks to Obama*, N.Y. Times, Jan. 1, 2017, at SR3 (observing that the Obama Administration's "record of going after both journalists and their sources has set a dangerous precedent that Mr. Trump can easily exploit" and positing that "the administration's heavy-handed approach represents a sharp break with tradition"). Erosion of a federal government practice of not attempting to prosecute journalists who refused to cooperate with leak investigations began in the George W. Bush Administration – but accelerated under the Obama Administration. *See id.* This was so because "[t]he Obama administration ... made combating leaks a top priority for federal law enforcement" and targeted journalists as a means of combating leaks. *Id.*

13 *See* Globe Newspaper Co. v. Superior Court, 457 U.S. 596 (1982); Richmond Newspapers v. Virginia, 448 U.S. 555 (1980); Nebraska Press Ass'n v. Stuart, 427 U.S. 539 (1976). The Supreme Court, during the Rehnquist Court era, also held protected the right of a newspaper to publish truthful information regarding the existence of criminal proceedings – including the identities of the victims of sex-related crimes (including rape). *See* The Florida Star v. B.J.F., 491 U.S. 524 (1989).

14 Simonson, *supra* note 9, at 1561.

15 *See id.* at 1561–62.

16 The trend line currently favors recognition of such a right to record, with the Third Circuit recently joining the First, Sixth, Seventh, and Eleventh Circuits by holding that state governments may not categorically forbid the public from recording police officers while on duty in places generally open to the public. *See* Fields v. City of Philadelphia, 862 F.3d 353 (7th Cir. 2017).

17 *See* Bhagwat, *supra* note 6, at 1052 ("The Supreme Court, however, has flatly rejected such a general right in every single case in which it has been argued.").

18 408 U.S. 665 (1972).

19 438 U.S. 1 (1978).

20 RonNell Andersen Jones & Sonja R. West, *The First Amendment Is Not Enough*, N.Y. Times, Jan. 25, 2017, at A25.

21 *Id.*

22 *Id.*

23 *See id.* (positing that "we should be alarmed when Mr. Trump, defying tradition, vilifies media institutions, attacks reporters by name and refuses to take questions from those whose coverage he dislikes" and "when he decides not to let reporters travel with him on his plane, or fails to inform them when he goes out in public").

24 *See Branzburg*, 408 U.S. at 709–10 (1972) (Powell, J., concurring) (positing that the institutional press must enjoy some measure of constitutional protection, as an incident of the First Amendment, for newsgathering and news reporting activities).

25 Victoria Cavaliere, *Charges Dismissed in Last Cases from Occupy Wall Street March*, REUTERS (Oct. 8, 2013, 5:42 PM), www.reuters.com/article/2013/10/08/us-usa-occupy-casesidUSBRE99713H20131008; John Nichols, *The Constitutional Crisis in Ferguson, Missouri*, THE NATION (Aug. 14, 2014, 2:09 PM), www.thenation.com/blog/181145/police-overreaction-has-become-constitutional-crisis-fergusonmissouri#.

26 Jones & West, *supra* note 10, at 573–74.

27 *Id.* at 574.

28 *See* Christina E. Wells, *Protest, Policing, and the Petition Clause: A Review of Ronald Krotoszynski's* Reclaiming the Petition Clause, 66 ALA. L. REV. 1159, 1164–67 (2015). Professor Wells cogently argues that "law enforcement officials thwart protests by engaging in online surveillance to gather information about the protestors, using it to facilitate pretextual arrests, and participating in coercive information gathering through individual interrogations of protestors." *Id.* at 1166. Moreover, "many journalists covering protests have been harassed or arrested." *Id.* Wells is surely correct to posit that "[s]urveillance of protestors and arrests of journalists are likely to chill protest activity or at the very least manipulate the public's access to protestors' messages." *Id.* at 1166–67.

29 The problem of defining "the press" for purposes of such targeted protection has plagued efforts to make the Press Clause do meaningful work free and clear of the more general Free Speech Clause. *See* Sonja R. West, *Press Exceptionalism*, 127 HARV. L. REV. 2434, 2436–42 (2014). If everyone is "the press," then the Press Clause collapses into the Speech Clause in any event. On the other hand, however, if "the press" is defined in a more circumscribed way, then questions arise about denying protection to amateur journalists. *See id.* at 2438–45 (discussing the problem and proposing a framework for defining "the press"). Professor Bhagwat argues that the Press Clause should be used to protect the creation of news stories – this approach would give the Press Clause independent meaning and avoid the pitfalls associated with defining which journalists are entitled to Press Clause protection. *See* Bhagwat, *supra* note 6, at 1056–58. He argues that "it ... seem[s] eminently sensible, if the Press Clause is to have any meaning in the modern, electronic world, that its protections must be extended to all modern technologies that create messages for mass dissemination." *Id.* at 1057. Under this understanding of the Press Clause, "the First Amendment protects not only literal acts of communication but also penumbral conduct associated with the distribution and production of speech." *Id.* at 1058.

30 McDonald, *supra* note 2, at 309.

31 *Id.* at 268.

32 *Id.* at 270. McDonald notes that "the right to receive information and ideas is a fully recognized First Amendment right even though, like the information gathering process, it is difficult to characterize acts of listening, or reading as being expressive in and of themselves." *Id.* at 270–71; *see* Bhagwat, *supra* note 6, at 1056–58 (arguing for First Amendment protection under the Press Clause for newsgathering activity necessary to support reportage).

33 *See* text and accompanying notes 136 to 180.

34 *See* U.S. CONST. amend. I ("Congress shall make no law ... abridging the freedom of speech, or of the press").

35 *See* Seattle Times Co. v. Rhinehart, 467 U.S. 20 (1984).

36 376 U.S. 254 (1964).

37 *See id.* at 268–70.

38 RONALD J. KROTOSZYNSKI, JR., PRIVACY REVISITED: A GLOBAL PERSPECTIVE ON THE RIGHT TO BE LEFT ALONE 5 (2016).

39 *See id.* at 148, 152–54.

40 *See* ALEXANDER MEIKLEJOHN, FREE SPEECH AND ITS RELATION TO SELF-GOVERNMENT 22–27, 36–39, 69–70, 88–89, 91 (1948).

41 376 U.S. 254 (1964).

42 *See infra* text and accompanying notes 55 to 68.

43 *See infra* text and accompanying notes 82 to 90.

44 *Sullivan*, 376 U.S. at 279–80 ("The constitutional guarantees require, we think a federal rule that prohibits a public official from recovering damages for a defamatory falsehood relating to his official conduct unless he proves that the statement was made with 'actual malice' – that is, with knowledge that it was false or with reckless disregard of whether it was false or not.").

45 Harry Kalven, Jr., *The* New York Times *Case: A Note on "The Central Meaning of the First Amendment*, 1964 SUP. CT. REV. 191, 221 n.125.

46 *Id.* at 209.

47 *Id.*

48 *Sullivan*, 376 U.S. at 256.

49 *Id.* at 278 n.18.

50 It bears noting that only 394 copies of the March 29, 1960, edition of the *New York Times* found their way to Alabama, and that perhaps three dozen copies "were distributed in Montgomery County." *Id.* at 260 n.3. Accordingly, Sullivan's claim that the factual errors seriously damaged his reputation ring false – virtually no one in either Montgomery County or in Alabama more generally had access to the edition of the *New York Times* that included the pro-civil rights advertisement. *See id.* at 256–61. One must keep in mind that, in 1960, physical copies of this issue of the newspaper constituted the only means of accessing its content.

51 *See supra* Chapter 2.

52 *See supra* Chapter 4.

53 *See supra* Chapter 5

54 *See supra* Chapter 6.

55 408 U.S. 665 (1972).

56 *Id.* at 667–79.

57 *See id.* at 708–09.

58 *Branzburg*, 408 U.S. at 709 (Powell, J., concurring).

59 *Id.* at 710.

60 *Id.*

61 *Id.*

62 *Id.*
63 *Branzburg*, 408 U.S. at 747 (Stewart, J., dissenting).
64 *Id.* at 707 (plurality opinion).
65 *Id.*
66 *Id.* at 665.
67 *Id.* at 707–08.
68 *Id.* at 708.
69 427 U.S. 539 (1976).
70 *Id.* at 569.
71 *Id.* at 562.
72 *Id.*
73 448 U.S. 555 (1980).
74 *Id.* at 580.
75 *Id.* at 580 n.17.
76 457 U.S. 596 (1982).
77 *Id.* at 604–07.
78 *Id.* at 609.
79 *Id.*
80 *Id.* at 606.
81 *See* The Freedom of Information Act, 5 U.S.C. § 552 (2012). For a relevant discussion of how the Freedom of Information Act works, see U.S. General Services Administration, Your Right to Federal Records: Questions and Answers on the Freedom of Information Act and the Privacy Act (2004).
82 438 U.S. 1 (1978).
83 *Id.* at 9 (plurality opinion).
84 *Id.* at 15.
85 *See id.* at 3–5, 14–16.
86 *Id.* at 16.
87 *Id.* at 16 (Stewart, J., concurring).
88 *Id.* at 17.
89 *Id.* at 17–18.
90 *Id.* at 19.
91 403 U.S. 713 (1971) (per curiam).
92 Nebraska Press Ass'n v. Stuart, 427 U.S. 539, 558 (1976).
93 *New York Times Co.*, 403 U.S. at 714 (internal quotations and citations omitted).
94 460 U.S. 575 (1983).
95 *See id.* at 585–93; *see also* Minn. Stat. §§ 297A.14, 297A.25.
96 *Minneapolis Star & Tribune Co.*, 460 U.S. at 592–93; *see id.* at 592 (holding that "recognizing a power in the State not only to single out the press but also to tailor the tax so that it singles out a few members of the press presents such a potential for abuse that no interest suggested by Minnesota can justify the scheme").
97 McCulloch v. Maryland, 17 U.S. (4 Wheat.) 159, 210 (1819) ("That the power to tax involves the power to destroy; that the power to destroy may defeat and render useless the power to create; that there is a plain repugnance in conferring on one government a power to control the constitutional measures of another,

which other, with respect to those very measures, is declared to be supreme over that which exerts the control, are propositions not to be denied.").

98 *But cf.* Jones & West, *supra* note 10, at 579 ("The United States Supreme Court has also grown less interested in press protections. In the last decade, the Court has issued no major opinions articulating press freedoms and has likewise denied certiorari on several hotly contested press issues."). Just as a serious prospect of judicial review has a constraining effect, the opposite holds true as well: An absence of oversight, and knowledge of the absence of oversight, invites bolder, more aggressive, and less principled behavior by government officials. *See generally* Mark Seidenfeld, *Cognitive Loafing, Social Conformity, and Judicial Review of Agency Rulemaking*, 87 CORNELL L. REV. 486, 508–09 (2002) (arguing that "accountability, if properly structured, can significantly improve the quality of decisionmaking in the sense of minimizing the extent to which individuals unthinkingly rely on inappropriate decisionmaking rules or fall prey to psychological biases" and observing that "[j]udicial review provides accountability").

99 532 U.S. 514 (2001).

100 408 U.S. 665 (1972).

101 Houchins v. KQED, 438 U.S. 1 (1978).

102 Jones & West, *supra* note 20, at A25.

103 *Id.*

104 *See supra* text and accompanying notes 94 to 97.

105 460 U.S. 575 (1983).

106 Grosjean v. American Press Co., 297 U.S. 233, 244–45, 250 (1936) (holding unconstitutional on First Amendment grounds a Louisiana targeted 2% sales tax on larger circulation newspapers that applied only to 13 newspapers of the 137 daily and weekly newspapers operating within Louisiana).

107 *Minneapolis Star*, 460 U.S. at 585, 591–92 (invalidating on First Amendment grounds a Minnesota law that imposed a tax on newsprint and ink on fourteen of 388 paid circulation newspapers in Minnesota and which fell disproportionately on the *Minneapolis Star and Tribune*, which paid around two-thirds of the total tax collected).

108 *See* Arkansas Writers' Project, Inc. v. Ragland, 481 U.S. 221, 227–31 (1987).

109 Ark. Stat. Ann. § 84–1904(f) & (j). Even though the sales tax exemption, on its face, seemed to create an exemption for any "publications printed and published within this State" if "sold through regular subscriptions," the Arkansas Supreme Court held that only periodicals meeting the content requirements were eligible for the sales tax exemption. *See* Ragland v. Arkansas Writers' Project, Inc., 697 S.W.2d 94, 94 (Ark. 1985).

110 *Ragland*, 697 S.W. 2d at 94. Justice George Rose Smith explained that "[w]e think ... that the lawmakers had a single purpose in mind," namely "to exempt the enumerated periodicals if printed and published in Arkansas and sold by subscription and if the particular periodical comes within the term journal or the term publication or the two terms considered together." *Id.* Under this construction of the statute, the *Arkansas Times*, the Arkansas Writers' Project's

periodical, was "not exempt, for it is admittedly not a religious, professional, trade, or sports periodical." *Id.*

111 *Arkansas Writers' Project*, 481 U.S. at 231–32.

112 *Id.* at 227.

113 *Id.* at 228.

114 *Id.* at 229.

115 *Id.* at 233.

116 499 U.S. 439 (1991).

117 *See id.* at 442–43, 447–49.

118 *Id.* at 447.

119 *Id.* at 449.

120 *Id.* at 453.

121 *See Leathers*, 499 U.S. at 454–55 (Marshall, J., dissenting).

122 *Id.* at 455.

123 *Id.* at 458.

124 *Id.* at 465.

125 New York Times v. United States (Pentagon Papers), 403 U.S. 713 (1971).

126 532 U.S. 514 (2001).

127 *See id.* at 533–35.

128 *Id.* at 534.

129 *Id.* at 535.

130 *Bartnicki*, 532 U.S. at 535 (Breyer, J., concurring).

131 *Id.* at 535–36.

132 *Id.* at 541.

133 *Id.*

134 *Bartnicki*, 532 U.S. at 541–42, 554–56 (Rehnquist, J., dissenting).

135 *See* Jones & West, *supra* note 10, at 571–72.

136 Sydney Ember & Michael M. Grynbaum, *After Press Secretary Rebukes News Media, Journalists Offer Criticism of Their Own*, N.Y. TIMES, Jan. 23, 2017, at A15.

137 *See* Adam Liptak, *Barring Reporters From Briefings: Does It Cross a Line?*, N.Y. TIMES, Mar. 1, 2017, at A16. Trump Press Secretary Sean Spicer "barred journalists from The New York Times, BuzzFeed News, CNN, The Los Angeles Times, Politico, the BBC, and The Huffington Post from a daily briefing." *Id.*

138 *See id.* (describing a senior Trump White House staffer's defense of Sean Spicer's dissemination of "'alternative facts' about the inauguration"); *see also* Nicholas Fandos, *White House Pushes "Alternative Facts." Here Are the Real Ones.*, N.Y. TIMES, Jan. 23, 2017, at A15.

139 Alicia Shepard, *First Amendment Isn't Just for Journalists*, USA TODAY, May 30, 2017, at A7.

140 *Id.*

141 Rep. Gianforte subsequently pled guilty to an assault charge. *See* Christopher Mele, *Montana Republican Greg Gianforte Is Sentenced in Assault on Reporter*, N.Y. TIMES, June 14, 2017, www.nytimes.com/2017/

06/13/us/politics/greg-gianforte-sentenced.html. Sadly, it is not entirely clear whether Gianforte's assault and battery on Jacobs damaged or enhanced his electoral prospects.

142 Shepard, *supra* note 139, at A7.

143 *Id.* (noting that President Trump has referred to the news media as "the enemy of the people").

144 *See* Ronald J. Krotoszynski, Jr., *Transparency, Accountability, and Competency: An Essay on the Obama Administration, Google Government, and the Difficulties of Securing Effective Governance*, 65 U. MIAMI L. REV. 449, 469–70 (2011) (discussing the efforts of the Obama Administration to impede live newsgathering in the areas devastated by the Deep Water Horizon oil spill in the Gulf of Mexico).

145 *Id.* at 469.

146 *See* Risen, *supra* note 12, at SR3.

147 Krotoszynski, *supra* note 144, at 449–51.

148 *See, e.g.*, Commonwealth v. Hyde, 750 N.E. 2d 963, 969–71 (Mass. 2001) (upholding a conviction for secretly recording police officers who were on duty, in public and without any allegation or evidence that the secret recording impeded the police in performing their duties).

149 *See* Simonson, *supra* note 9, at 1560–64.

150 *But cf.* City of Houston v. Hill, 482 U.S. 451, 462–63 (1987) (invalidating a Houston, Texas ordinance, as overbroad, where Hill verbally challenged a city police officer's conduct in public and explaining that "[t]he freedom of individuals verbally to oppose or challenge police action without thereby risking arrest is one of the principal characteristics by which we distinguish a free nation from a police state"). *Hill* prohibits the enactment and enforcement of "laws that provide police with unfettered discretion to arrest individuals for words or conduct that annoy or offend them." *Id.* at 465. The problem, of course, is that a general statute that criminalizes impeding or interfering with police may be used pretextually to arrest a citizen-journalist who seeks merely to record police activity from a public street or sidewalk. *See infra* Chapter 9. As Professor Kreimer explains, "[w]here wiretap prohibitions do not apply, officers faced with defiant videographers frequently turn to broader criminal statutes that provide substantial enforcement discretion." Kreimer, *supra* note 6, at 361. Even when lower federal courts have invalidated state laws that prohibit recording police officers, they have taken pains to exclude these general statutes from invalidation on First Amendment grounds. *See, e.g.*, ACLU v. Alvarez, 679 F.3d 583, 607 (7th Cir. 2012) ("Nothing we have said here immunizes behavior that obstructs or interferes with effective law enforcement or the protection of public safety."). As Judge Richard Posner observed, in his *Alvarez* dissent, "[a] fine line separates 'mere' recording of a police-citizen encounter (whether friendly or hostile) from obstructing police officers and upsetting the citizens they are speaking with." *Id.* at 612 (Posner, J., dissenting). Posner was concerned about the underprotection of police discretion, whereas I am concerned with its abuse

(which seems highly likely if such discretion permits police to avoid not only public embarrassment, but also professional sanctions for official misconduct).

151 *See generally* Stephen Rushin, *Using Data to Reduce Police Violence*, 57 B.C. L. REV. 117 (2016); Stephen Rushin, *Federal Enforcement of Police Reform*, 82 FORDHAM L. REV. 3189 (2014).

152 Rebecca G. Van Tassell, Comment, *Walking a Thin Blue Line: Balancing the Citizen's Right to Record Police Officers Against Officer Privacy*, 2013 BYU L. REV. 183, 187–88 (2013) ("The two-party recording statute in Illinois is unique, and undoubtedly the harshest in the country. Containing no explicit expectation of privacy or secrecy requirement, the Illinois recording statute requires the consent of all parties and protects absolutely all conversations.").

153 *Id.* at 183–84.

154 *See* Shepard, *supra* note 139, at A7.

155 Margot E. Kaminski, *Regulating Real-World Surveillance*, 90 WASH. L. REV. 1113, 1122 (2015).

156 *Id.* at 1126.

157 *Id.*

158 *Id.* at 1155.

159 Kreimer, *supra* note 6, at 344.

160 *Id.* at 345.

161 *Id.*

162 *Id.* at 347.

163 *Id.*

164 Kreimer, *supra* note 6, at 366.

165 *Id.*

166 *See infra* Chapter 9.

167 *See generally* Commonwealth v. Hyde, 750 N.E. 2d 963, 969–70 (Mass. 2001) (arguing that a right to record police officers in public could open the door to "electronic 'bugging' or secret audio tape recording ... of virtually every encounter or meeting between a person and a public official"). The Massachusetts Supreme Judicial Court has squarely held that "[t]he value of obtaining probative evidence of occasional official misconduct does not justify a failure to enforce the clear terms of the statute [prohibiting secret recordings]." *Id.* at 969.

168 *See* Alan Blinder & Manny Fernandez, *Residents Trace Police Shooting to a Crime Strategy Gone Awry*, N.Y. TIMES, Apr. 10, 2015, at A1; Michael Eric Dyson, *Racial Terror, Fast and Slow*, N.Y. TIMES, Apr. 17, 2015, at A31.

169 Farhad Manjoo & Mike Isaac, *Right Time, Right Place, Right App for Capturing Interactions with Police*, N.Y. TIMES, Apr. 9, 2015, at A17.

170 *See generally* Jack M. Balkin, *Information Fiduciaries and the First Amendment*, 49 U.C. DAVIS L. REV. 1183, 1194–95 (2016) (warning that "[w]e should not, however, conclude too hastily that there are not First Amendment rights to collect information" and positing that "[a] right to record might conceivably protect a wide range of technologies for collection of public information, with

the limiting case being harassment and violations of the tort of intrusion on seclusion").

171 See MEIKLEJOHN, *supra* note 40, at 25–26, 88–89 (arguing that citizens must be well-informed about the government's policies and actions if the electoral process is to secure effectively and reliably democratic accountability).

172 Caycee Hampton, Note, *Confirmation of a Catch-22: Glik v. Cunniffe and the Paradox of Citizen Recording*, 63 FLA. L. REV. 1549, 1559 (2011). But cf. Commonwealth v. Hyde, 750 N.E. 2d 963, 964, 969–71 (Mass. 2001) (upholding a conviction for secretly recording a police officer in public because "[s]ecret tape recording by private individuals has been unequivocally banned and, unless and until the Legislature changes the statute, what was done here cannot be done lawfully").

173 See Richard Fausset & Richard Perez-Peña, *U.S. Examines Police Killing in Louisiana*, N.Y. TIMES, July 7, 2016, at A1.

174 *But see* Glik v. Cunniffe, 655 F.3d 78 (1st Cir. 2011) (finding police video taping protected under the First Amendment). The lower federal and state courts have been uneven in applying the First Amendment to protect recording police officers in public. *See* David Murphy, Comment, *"V.I.P." Videographer Intimidation Protection: How the Government Should Protect Citizens Who Videotape the Police*, 43 SETON HALL L. REV. 319, 326 ("Despite 'sweeping' decisions like *Glik* that strongly protect videographers' rights, police engage in arrests and intimidation tactics to suppress videographers from filming police conduct in public."). For a general discussion of how generic anti-recording statutes can be used to prevent the public from filming police, and a discussion of court decisions sustaining this practice, see *id.* at 326–38.

175 See Mitch Smith & Matt Furber, *A Plea for Unity as Hundreds Mourn Minnesota Man*, N.Y. TIMES, July 15, 2016, at A17.

176 See Kreimer, *supra* note 6, at 358–66.

177 See Alan K. Chen & Justin Marceau, *High Value Lies, Ugly Truths, and the First Amendment*, 68 VAND. L. REV. 1435, 1439–40, 1466–71 (2015); Larissa U. Liebmann, *Fraud and First Amendment Protections of False Speech: How United States v. Alvarez Impacts Constitutional Challenges to Ag-Gag Laws*, 31 PACE ENVTL. L. REV. 566 (2014). Professors Chen and Marceau observe that "Ag Gag laws provide a timely and straightforward case study of the First Amendment's role in protecting high value lies because a key component of these laws is the criminalization of misrepresentations made in order to gain access to agricultural facilities." *Id.* at 1439; *see also* Cody Carlson, *The Ag Gag Laws: Hiding Factory Farm Abuses from Public Scrutiny*, ATLANTIC ONLINE (Mar. 20, 2012, 9:06 AM), www.theatlantic.com/health/archive/2012/03/the-ag-gag-laws-hiding-factory-farm-abuses-from-public-scrutiny/254674 (discussing an Iowa statute that prohibits undercover investigation of factory farm practices).

178 Chen & Marceau, *supra* note 177, at 1439 n.9.

179 *But cf.* Bhagwat, *supra* note 6, at 1062–66, 1074–75 (arguing that laws prohibiting recording that reflect impermissible content-based motives

should be subject to strict judicial scrutiny and, in most cases, invalidated); Animal Legal Def. Fund v. Herbert, 263 F. Supp. 3d 1193, 1211–13 (D. Utah 2017) (applying strict scrutiny and invalidating, on First Amendment grounds, Utah's legal proscriptions against photographing industrial farming operations and seeking employment at such facilities with the intent to record an employer's operations); Animal Legal Def. Fund v. Otter, 118 F. Supp. 3d 1195, 1202–04, 1207–09 (D. Idaho 2015) (invaliding, on First Amendment grounds, Idaho's ag gag statute as an impermissible content-based restriction of speech that does not advance a compelling state interest in a sufficiently narrowly tailored way), *aff'd in part, rev'd in part sub nom*, Animal Legal Def. Fund v. Wasden, 878 F.3d 1184 (9th Cir. 2018). At present, most of the litigation challenging ag-gag laws remains in early phases before trial courts. It cannot be gainsaid that video recording of the gross mistreatment of animals has moved public opinion in important ways and has led to the adoption of animal protection laws. *See* Stephanie Strom, *Video of Sheep Slaughtering Ignites a Dispute*, N.Y. TIMES, Feb. 3, 2017, at B6 (reporting on the cruel and shocking slaughter of lambs at a California abattoir and alleged violations of the Humane Method of Slaughter Act at this facility).

180 Idaho Code § 18–7042(1)(a)–(e).

181 Animal Legal Def. Fund v. Wasden, 878 F.3d 1184 (9th Cir. 2018).

182 Idaho Code § 18–7042.

183 *See Otter*, 118 F. Supp. 3d at 1200–01.

184 *Id.* at 1200.

185 *Id.* at 1201.

186 *See* Animal Legal Def. Fund v. Otter, 118 F. Supp. 3d 1195, 1207–09 (D. Idaho 2015), *aff'd in part, rev'd in part sub nom*, Animal Legal Def. Fund v. Wasden, 878 F.3d 1184 (9th Cir. 2018).

187 *Wasden*, 878 F.3d at 1190.

188 *Id.*

189 *Id.* at 1203–05.

190 *Id.* at 1203.

191 *Id.* at 1204–05 (holding that "[p]rohibiting only 'audio or video recordings,' but saying nothing about photographs, is suspiciously under-inclusive" and positing that "Idaho is singling out for suppression one mode of speech – audio and video recordings of agricultural operations – to keep controversy and suspect practices out of the public eye").

192 *Id.* at 1205 (holding the Idaho ban on recording agricultural operations "over-inclusive" because the law "suppresses more speech than necessary to further Idaho's stated goals of protecting property and privacy").

193 *See id.* at 1196–99.

194 Idaho Code § 18–7042(1)(a).

195 *Wasden*, 878 F.3d at 1196–97.

196 *See id.* at 1205–12 (Bea, J., concurring in part and dissenting in part).

197 *See, e.g.*, Hunter v. Underwood, 471 U.S. 222, 228–32 (1985) (holding that enactment of an otherwise constitutionally permissible state policy violates

the Constitution when those enacting the policy seek to burden or deny a fundamental right and the policy has the effect of denying or abridging a constitutional right). Thus, even if truly neutral policies seeking to protect an agricultural production facility's property or privacy rights might be constitutional, this particular statute was enacted in an effort to frustrate, and ideally prevent, investigative journalism activities related to their operation. *See* United States v. O'Brien, 391 U.S. 367, 377 (1968) (holding that a conduct regulation violates the First Amendment if motivated by a desire to suppress the exercise of First Amendment rights).

198 *See O'Brien*, 391 U.S. at 376–77 (rejecting "the view that an apparently limitless variety of conduct can be labeled 'speech' whenever the person engaging in the conduct intends thereby to express an idea" and holding that "a government regulation [of expressive conduct] is sufficiently justified if it is within the constitutional power of the Government; if it furthers an important or substantial governmental interest; *if the governmental interest is unrelated to the suppression of free expression*; and if the incidental restriction on alleged First Amendment freedoms is no greater than is essential to the furtherance of that interest" (emphasis added)); *see also* Bhagwat, *supra* note 6, at 1056–58, 1076–77.

199 Justice Powell's concurring opinion in *Branzburg* provides an illustrative example – rather than create a rule that conveyed absolute or minimal protection on the press, he instead fashioned a rule that required government to possess a substantial reason for forcing a journalist to testify against her will about a confidential source or her investigative materials and called for overt balancing between the needs of prosecutors to obtain testimony from journalists and the need of journalists to be able to promise sources confidentiality and honor those promises. *See* Branzburg v. Hayes, 408 U.S. 665, 709–10 (1972) (Powell, J. concurring). Chief Justice Burger's opinion in *Nebraska Press Association* also embraces a balancing approach. *See* Nebraska Press Ass'n v. Stuart, 427 U.S. 539, 562, 569–70 (1976).

200 *See, e.g.,* Houchins v. KQED, 438 U.S. 1, 16–19 (1978) (Stewart, J., concurring); Branzburg v. Hayes, 408 U.S. 665, 725–27, 736–38 (1972) (Stewart, J., dissenting). Justice Stewart strongly criticized his colleagues' "crabbed view of the First Amendment," which reflected "a disturbing insensitivity to the critical role of an independent press in our society." *Branzburg*, 408 U.S. at 725. His central constitutional argument was that "[e]nlightened choice by an informed citizenry is the basic ideal upon which an open society is premised, and a free press is thus indispensable to a free society." *Id.* at 726; *see* Potter Stewart, *Or of the Press*, 26 Hastings L.J. 631, 634 (1975) (setting forth Justice Stewart's theory of press freedom as a necessary condition for democratic self-government to function).

201 *But cf.* Bhagwat, *supra* note 6, at 1056–58 (arguing that the Press Clause should provide general protection for "penumbral" activities associated with the dissemination of news and information). Professor Bhagwat's proposal deftly avoids the problem of defining "the press" for purposes of applying the First

Amendment by conveying to any and all persons constitutional protection for at least some antecedent activities essential to communicating news and information to others.

202 In this regard, adopting an interpretation of the Press Clause that gives the Clause significant purpose and meaning, while completely avoiding the need to resolve the definitional problem, has significant merit – and promise. *See id.* at 1054–58, 1080–81.

203 For an argument that the definitional problems are not insurmountable, see West, *supra* note 29, at 2453–62. Professor West posits that "[t]he problems posed by defining 'the press' are not qualitatively different than the problems posed by defining terms found in other provisions of the Constitution." *Id.* at 2453.

204 *See, e.g.,* Holder v. Humanitarian Law Project, 561 U.S. 1, 33–39 (2010) (applying strict scrutiny to a federal law that prohibited providing "material assistance" to certain proscribed terrorist organizations but concluding that the federal government had demonstrated both a compelling government interest and sufficient narrow tailoring).

205 *See* David A. Anderson, *The Origins of the Press Clause*, 30 UCLA L. Rev. 455, 536–37 (1983); Sonja R. West, *Awakening the Press Clause*, 58 UCLA L. Rev. 1025, 1039–40, 1069–70 (2011).

206 *See* Anderson, *supra* note 205, at 533–37.

207 *See* Bhagwat, *supra* note 6, at 1054–58, 1080–81; Kreimer, *supra* note 6, at 370–86.

208 New York Times Co. v. United States, 403 U.S. 713 (1971).

209 New York Times Co. v. Sullivan, 376 U.S. 254, 270 (1964).

210 *See generally* Dun & Bradstreet v. Greenmoss Builders, 472 U.S. 749 (1985) (holding that the First Amendment does not constrain tort liability for defamation when the plaintiff is not a public official, public figure, or private person involved in a matter of public concern).

211 *Sullivan*, 376 U.S. at 270.

212 Meiklejohn, *supra* note 40, at 88.

213 *Id.*

214 *Id.*

215 *Id.* at 88–89.

216 *Bartnicki* constitutes the exception that proves the rule. *See* Bartnicki v. Vopper, 532 U.S. 514, 534–35 (2001).

217 Citizens United v. Fed. Elec. Comm'n, 558 U.S. 310, 339–41 (2010) (holding that corporate political speech enjoys full First Amendment protection because "the First Amendment stands against attempts to disfavor certain subjects or viewpoints" and "[s]peech restrictions based on the identity of the speaker are all too often simply a means to control content").

218 Snyder v. Phelps, 562 U.S. 443, 455–61 (2011) (holding unconstitutional the imposition of tort liability for a carefully targeted, outrageous, and highly offensive protest of a deceased soldier's funeral services because the First

Amendment "protect[s] even hurtful speech on public issues" to avoid "stifl[ing] public debate").

219 *See, e.g.,* Hustler Magazine, Inc. v. Falwell, 485 U.S. 46, 54–56 (1988) (holding protected an intentionally outrageous and offensive parody of the Rev. Jerry Falwell, Sr. and observing that "'[o]utrageousness' in the area of political and social discourse has an inherent subjectiveness about it which would allow a jury to impose liability on the basis of the jurors' tastes or views, or perhaps on the basis of their dislike of a particular expression").

220 *See* City of Houston v. Hill, 482 U.S. 451 (1987).

221 MEIKLEJOHN, *supra* note 40, at 25–27, 88–89. Meiklejohn posits that, "[t]he welfare of the community requires that those who decide issues shall understand them." *Id.* at 25. In consequence, "[t]hey must know what they are voting about" and this requires that voters have access to "all facts and interests relevant to the problem." Id.

8 THE CITIZEN AS GOVERNMENT SOCK PUPPET AND THE STATE MASQUERADING AS A CITIZEN

1 *See* Timothy Zick, *Professional Rights Speech*, 47 ARIZ. STATE L.J. 1289, 1292 (2015) ("State regulations of professional speech have become more prevalent, more politically tinged, and more likely to structure and dictate the specific content of professional-client interactions."); *see also* Claudia E. Haupt, *Professional Speech*, 125 YALE L.J. 1238, 1240 (2016) (noting that "new forms of regulation go further" than professional speech regulations in the past because "they target the content of the communication between a professional and her client" and observing that "[s]ometimes, such regulation aligns with professional insights, but sometimes it contradicts them").

2 *See* Caroline Mala Corbin, *Compelled Disclosures*, 65 ALA. L. REV. 1277, 1324–28 (2014) (discussing several illustrative examples of such state laws).

3 *See* Firearm Owners' Privacy Act, ch. 2011–112, 2011 Fla. Laws 1776 (2011) (codified at FLA. STAT. §§ 381.026, 395.1055, 456.072, 790.338 (2011)) [hereinafter FOPA].

4 Zick, *supra* note 1, at 1292.

5 *See* U.S. v. Kahriger, 345 U.S. 22, 38 (1953) (Frankfurter, J., dissenting) (arguing that using an empty label, or "verbal cellophane," should not control constitutional analysis). Justice Frankfurter argues that substance, not form, should govern constitutional review in the context of an ersatz tax that was really a statute regulating commercial gambling operations. By parallel logic, simply labeling a compelled silence or coerced speech measure a "professional regulation" should not confer some sort of generalized blanket immunity from meaningful judicial review of the measure's consistency with core First Amendment values. After all, as Justice Robert Jackson sagely observed in *Barnette*:

If there is any fixed star in our constitutional constellation, it is that no official, high or petty, can prescribe what shall be orthodox in politics, nationalism, religion, or other matters of opinion or force citizens to confess by word or act their faith therein. If there are any circumstances which permit an exception, they do not now occur to us.

West Virginia Bd. of Educ. v. Barnette, 319 U.S. 624, 642 (1943). In sum, government efforts to prescribe orthodoxy, rather than the particular form such measures take, should prefigure the appropriate scope of judicial review.

6 *See* Helen Norton, *Constraining Public Employee Speech: Government's Control of Its Workers' Speech to Protect Its Own Expression*, 59 DUKE L.J. 1, 20–28 (2009) (discussing and explaining the government speech doctrine and observing that "[g]overnment speech is . . . both ubiquitous and necessary" but cautioning that "[t]he value of government speech turns primarily on its transparency, rather than on its popularity or even its truthfulness"). It bears noting that the government speech doctrine represents a doctrinal innovation of the Rehnquist Court that has continued to grow and blossom under the Roberts Court. *See* Caroline Mala Corbin, *Mixed Speech: When Speech Is Both Private and Governmental*, 83 N.Y.U. L. REV. 605, 610–11 (2008) ("Ten years ago, however, the question would have been framed differently, as the doctrine of 'government speech' had not yet been developed.").

7 A "sock puppet" is a false identity used on social media platforms to obfuscate the real identity of the speaker. *See* Helen Norton & Danielle Keats Citron, *Government Speech 2.0*, 87 DENV. U.L. REV. 899, 937–38 (2010) (discussing the concept of a "sock puppet" and observing that "[w]hen online collaborations guarantee anonymity, interested individuals, including government actors, can rig 'the crowd,' ensuring the prominence of a particular view"). The speaker seeks to hide or obfuscate its identity because the message will be more credible if it appears to be coming from a different source. *See* Abner S. Greene, *Government of the Good*, 53 VAND. L. REV. 1, 49–52 (2000); *see also* Gia B. Lee, *Persuasion, Transparency, and Government Speech*, 56 HASTINGS L.J. 983, 983–90 (2005) (documenting government use of sock puppet identities and critiquing this practice as fundamentally inconsistent with the government's obligation to be politically accountable for its actions). Professors Norton and Citron warn that "[g]overnment's participation in opaque interactive technologies substantially increases opportunities for such manipulation at the expense of government accountability, as sock puppetry powerfully demonstrates how government might manipulate opaque interactive technologies in unaccountable ways." Norton & Citron, *supra*, at 937–38.

8 *See* Haupt, *supra* note 1, at 1241–42.

9 *Id.* at 1241.

10 By "professional speech," I mean speech made in a clinical or professional setting by a licensed professional, such as a physician, lawyer, or accountant, incident to her professional practice. *See* Daniel Halberstam, *Commercial Speech, Professional Speech, and the Constitutional Status of Social Institutions*, 147 U. PA. L. REV. 771, 843–44 (1999). I do not mean speech by

licensed professionals outside their regular practice activities. The problem this chapter seeks to address is the aggressive use of professional licensing regulations to turn professionals who require state-issued professional licenses into sock puppets. *See* Texas Med. Providers Performing Abortion Servs. v. Lakey, Case No. A-11-CA-486-SS, 2012 U.S. Dist. Lexis 14721 (W.D. Tex. Feb. 6, 2012) (expressing concern that compelled speech requirements related to abortion services in Texas would "make puppets out of doctors").

11 Planned Parenthood of Se. Pa. v. Casey, 505 U.S. 833, 884 (1992) (joint opinion of O'Connor, Kennedy, and Souter, JJ.); *see also* Rust v. Sullivan, 500 U.S. 173, 193–96 (1991) (treating viewpoint-based professional speech limitations on medical professionals as merely regulations of conduct).

12 138 S. Ct. 2361 (2018) [hereinafter *NIFLA*].

13 *See id.* at 2371–72.

14 *Id.*

15 Planned Parenthood of Southeastern Pa. v. Casey, 505 U.S. 833, 884 (1992) (joint opinion of O'Connor, Kennedy, and Souter, JJ.).

16 *NIFLA*, 138 S. Ct. at 2372 (holding that "[s]tates may regulate professional conduct, even though that conduct incidentally involves speech" and citing *Casey* in support of this proposition).

17 *Casey*, 505 U.S. at 844 ("The Act requires that a woman seeking an abortion give her informed consent prior to the abortion procedure, and specifies that she be provided with certain information at least 24 hours before the abortion is performed. § 3205.").

18 *Id.* at 881. Pennsylvania's "informed consent" requirements, sustained by the Supreme Court as constitutional, provided:

> Except in a medical emergency, the statute requires that at least 24 hours before performing an abortion a physician inform the woman of the nature of the procedure, the health risks of the abortion and of childbirth, and the "probable gestational age of the unborn child." The physician or a qualified nonphysician must inform the woman of the availability of printed materials published by the State describing the fetus and providing information about medical assistance for childbirth, information about child support from the father, and a list of agencies which provide adoption and other services as alternatives to abortion. An abortion may not be performed unless the woman certifies in writing that she has been informed of the availability of these printed materials and has been provided them if she chooses to view them.

Id. These provisions were not designed to ensure that women understand the nature of the abortion procedure and its attendant risks and potential medical benefits – instead, they constituted rather naked efforts to lobby women not to go forward with having abortions. In fact, the Supreme Court had invalidated similar coerced speech regulations aimed at shaming women out of abortions in two prior cases – both overruled in *Casey. See id.* at 881–84. *But cf.* Thornburgh v. American College of Obstetricians and Gynecologists, 476 U.S. 747, 762–63 (1986) (invalidating bogus informed consent requirements for an abortion procedure because they constituted "nothing less than an outright attempt to wedge the Commonwealth's message discouraging abortion into the privacy of the informed-consent dialogue between the woman and her physician"); City of Akron v. Akron Center for Reproductive Health, Inc., 462 U.S. 416, 442–45 (1983) (invalidating ersatz "informed consent" abortion regulations because they went "far beyond merely describing the general subject matter relevant to informed consent").

19 Christina E. Wells, *Abortion Counseling as Vice Activity: The Free Speech Implications of* Rust v. Sullivan *and* Planned Parenthood v. Casey, 95 Colum. L. Rev.1724, 1725–26 (1995).

20 *Id.* at 1725.

21 *See, e.g.* S.D. Codified Laws § 34-23A-10.1(1) (2015). For a discussion of state laws that compel physicians who provide abortion services to make medically questionable mandatory disclosures to their patients, *see* Zick, *supra* note 1, at 1311–12.

22 *See* Norton, *supra* note 6, at 21–23, 29–30.

23 *Id.* at 29.

24 *Cf.* McIntyre v. Ohio Elec. Comm'n, 514 U.S. 334, 357 (1995) ("Under our Constitution, anonymous pamphleteering is not a pernicious, fraudulent practice, but an honorable tradition of advocacy and of dissent."). The *McIntyre* Court declined to extend precedents involving corporate political speech and campaign-related expenditures to speech by an individual citizen. *See id.* at 353–54. As Justice John Paul Stevens explained, these precedents sustaining regulations of political speech and activity "involved a prohibition of anonymous campaign literature." *Id.* at 353. *But cf.* Doe v. Reed, 561 U.S. 181, 221 (2010) (Scalia, J., dissenting) ("Our Nation's longstanding traditions of legislating and voting in public refute the claim that the First Amendment accords a right to anonymity in the performance of an act with governmental effect."). On the other hand, the Supreme Court has rejected privacy and speech-related challenges to state laws that require the release of the names of those who sign a referendum petition. *See Reed,* 561 U.S. at 197–201. The *Reed* majority found that Washington State possesses a sufficiently substantial interest in "preserving electoral integrity" to justify the public release of signatories' names. *Id.* at 197–99.

25 *See* Alexander Meiklejohn, Free Speech and Its Relation to Self-Government 22–47, 88–89 (1948). Professor Meiklejohn famously argued that "unabridged freedom of public discussion is the rock on which our government stands." *Id.* at 20.

26 *See McIntyre,* 514 U.S. at 357 (invalidating an Ohio statute that prohibited anonymous electioneering activities and explaining that "[a]nonymity is a shield from the tyranny of the majority").

27 *See* Joseph Blocher, *Viewpoint Neutrality and Government Speech,* 52 B.C. L. Rev. 695, 717–19 (2011). Professor Blocher posits that "transparency is, or at least should be, the hallmark of the government speech doctrine," *id.* at 717,

meaning that the government should clearly identify itself as the speaker when it speaks. *See id.* at 717–18.

28 *See* R.A.V. v. City of St. Paul, 505 U.S. 377, 387–88, 391–92 (1992); *see also* Police Dep't of the City of Chicago v. Mosley, 408 U.S. 92, 95–96 (1972) (observing that "government may not grant the use of a forum to people whose views it finds acceptable, but deny use to those wishing to express less favored or more controversial views" and that government "may not select which issues are worth discussing or debating in public facilities").

29 The Trump Administration has been particularly aggressive in coercing the silence of professionals employed by the government itself. For example, it has prohibited government-employed scientists from using words such as "science-based" and "evidence-based" in official government reports. Lena H. Sun & Juliet Eilperin, *CDC Gets a List of Forbidden Words, Including "Diversity" and "Transgender,"* WASH. POST, Dec. 16, 2017, at A4 (reporting on a Trump White House directive forbidding the Centers for Disease Control and Prevention from using the words "vulnerable," "entitlement," "diversity," "transgender," "fetus," "evidence-based" and "science-based" in any documents prepared for the 2018 fiscal year budget). CDC employees were "incredulous" at this directive, with one anonymous CDC source observing that "[i]n my experience, we've never had any pushback from an ideological standpoint." *Id.* The Trump Administration is also using government power to suppress both government-employed and government-funded scientists from using the phrase "climate change" or discussing climate change in their work. *See* Lisa Friedman, *E.P.A. Bars 3 of Its Scientists from a Conference to Discuss Climate Change,* N.Y. TIMES, Oct. 23, 2017, at A16. Moreover, EPA funding, including grants to non-government scientific researchers, must be "in line with [then-Trump EPA Administrator] Pruitt's priorities," which included "challeng[ing] established climate science." *Id.*

30 *See, e.g.,* Planned Parenthood Minn., S.D., N.D. v. Rounds, 686 F.3d 889, 904–05 (8th Cir 2012) (en banc) (holding that "although the record reflects 'medical and scientific uncertainty' . . . as to whether abortion itself is a causal factor in the observed correlation between abortion and suicide, there is nothing in the record to suggest that abortion as a cause per se has been ruled out with certainty" and, accordingly, "the suicide advisory is non-misleading and relevant to the patient's decision to have an abortion").

31 *See Rounds,* 686 F.3d at 899–905; Tex Med. Providers Performing Abortion Servs. v. Lakey, 667 F.3d 570, 576–80 (5th 2012).

32 Stuart v. Camnitz, 774 F.3d 238 (4th Cir. 2014), *cert. denied sub nom.,* Walker-McGill v. Stuart, 135 S. Ct. 2838 (2015). The argument that a mandatory ultrasound coupled with compelled physician speech related to fetal development does not constitute an ideological, viewpoint-based speech regulation, rather than a typical regulation of the medical profession, is remarkably weak. *See* Carol Sanger, *Seeing and Believing: Mandatory Ultrasound and the Path to a Protected Choice,* 56 UCLA L. REV. 351, 376–77 (2008).

33 500 U.S. 173 (1991).

34 *Id.* at 198–200.

35 *See* Wollschlaeger v. Governor of the State of Florida, 814 F.3d 1159, 1182–1201 (11th Cir. 2015) (sustaining, as consistent with strict judicial scrutiny, a Florida law that prohibited physicians from asking patients about gun ownership incident to medical examinations). The US Court of Appeals for the Eleventh Circuit, sitting en banc, rejected the panel's reasoning and outcome, invalidating Florida's gun-related gag rule on physicians. *See* Wollschlaeger v. Florida, 848 F.1293 (11th Cir. 2017) (en banc). Even so, however, the en banc court declined to apply strict scrutiny to a self-evidently content-based regulation of speech. *See id.* at 1311–12 (applying "heightened scrutiny" and declining to decide "whether strict scrutiny should apply").

36 NIFLA v. Becerra, 138 S. Ct. 2361, 2371–76 (2018).

37 *See infra* text and accompanying notes 88 to 145.

38 Citizens United v. Fed. Elec. Comm'n, 558 U.S. 310, 341 (2010) ("Premised on mistrust of governmental power, the First Amendment stands against attempts to disfavor certain subjects or viewpoints. Prohibited, too, are restrictions distinguishing among different speakers, allowing speech by some but not others. As instruments to censor, these categories are interrelated: Speech restrictions based on the identity of the speaker are all too often simply a means to control content." (internal citations omitted)); *see* United States v. Playboy Entm't Group, 529 U.S. 803, 813 (2000) ("If a statute regulates speech based on its content, it must be narrowly tailored to promote a compelling Government interest. If a less restrictive alternative would serve the Government's purpose, the legislature must use that alternative."); Blocher, *supra* note 27, at 702 (observing that the First Amendment "flatly prohibits the government from engaging in viewpoint discrimination, even within classes of speech that could otherwise be completely proscribed").

39 *See* David Orentlicher, *Abortion and Compelled Physician's Speech*, 43 J.L. MED. & ETHICS 9 (2015); Sonia M. Suter, *The First Amendment and Physician Speech in Reproductive Decision Making*, 43 J.L. MED. & ETHICS 22 (2015); *see also* Paula Berg, *Toward a First Amendment Theory of Discourse and the Right to Receive Unbiased Medical Advice*, 74 B.U. L. REV. 201, 202–07 (1994) (discussing government efforts to prescribe the professional speech of medical professionals in government-subsidized medical facilities).

40 *See* Editorial, *Central Florida 100, Our Panel of 100 Influential Leaders Discusses the Most Important Issues Affecting You*, ORLANDO SENTINEL, Dec. 30, 2015, at A13 ("Florida Gov. Rick Scott refuses to allow staff to utter the words 'climate change.' Meanwhile, Florida's southern counties and cities are grappling, planning and addressing preparation for rising oceans as tides flood their cities."); *Governor Is No Scientist, Just a Crafty Linguist*, SUN-SENTINEL (Fort Lauderdale), Mar. 15, 2015, at B1 (noting that "Florida Gov. Rick Scott has unofficially banned the terms 'climate change' and 'global warming,' with state employees and agencies told not to use the phrases in documents and

emails" and reporting that "Scott denied the report, while avoiding the words 'global warming' and 'climate change' in remarks to the media).

41 *See* Friedman, *supra* note 29, at A16.

42 *See* Sun & Eilperin, *supra* note 29, at A4.

43 Firearm Owners' Privacy Act, ch. 2011–112, 2011 Fla. Laws 1776 (2011) (codified at Fla. Stat. §§ 381.026, 395.1055, 456.072, 790.338 (2011)) [hereinafter FOPA]; *see* Wollschlaeger v. Governor of Florida, 760 F.3d 1195 (11th Cir. 2014) (sustaining the FOPA against a First Amendment challenge alleging that it compelled physicians to remain silent when their professional judgment required them to speak).

44 Blum v. Yaretsky, 457 U.S. 991, 1002–03 (1982); The Civil Rights Cases, 109 U.S. 2, 11 (1883); *see* Jackson v. Met. Edison Co., 419 U.S. 345, 349–50 (1974) ("While the principle that private action is immune from the restrictions of the Fourteenth Amendment is well established and easily stated, the question whether particular conduct is 'private,' on the one hand, or 'state action,' on the other, frequently admits of no easy answer."); Ronald J. Krotoszynski, Jr., *Back to the Briarpatch: An Argument in Favor of Constitutional Meta-Analysis in State Action Determinations*, 94 MICH. L. REV. 302, 303 (1995) ("Since at least 1879, the Court has consistently held that the guarantees of both the Fourteenth Amendment and the Bill of Rights protect citizens only from acts committed by the government, and has required plaintiffs asserting claims under these provisions to establish the presence of 'state action' before undertaking an analysis of the merits of a particular claim.").

45 U.S. v. Kahriger, 345 U.S. 22, 38 (1953) (Frankfurter, J., dissenting). *But see* Wollschlaeger v. Governor of Florida, 814 F.3d 1159, 1195, 1201 (11th Cir. 2015) (holding, in its third bite at the apple, that "we find the State's asserted interests in protecting Second Amendment rights and protecting privacy to be compelling" and concluding that the FOPA "withstands strict scrutiny as a permissible restriction of speech"). Judge Gerald Tjoflat's arguments to the contrary notwithstanding, *see id.* at 1201 ("It narrowly protects patients in a focused manner in order to advance the State's compelling interest in protecting the Second Amendment's guarantee to keep and bear arms and patients' privacy rights in their medical records, exactly the sort of tailoring strict scrutiny requires. Those are rights that must always be protected in ways big and small."), a private medical doctor simply cannot violate the Second Amendment because she is not a state actor. *See* The Civil Rights Cases, 109 U.S. 2, 11 (1886); *see also* Krotoszynski, *supra* note 44, at 303–21, 335–36. Moreover, any constitutional privacy rights would also run only against the government itself – and not against a private medical doctor. *See id.* at 303, 335, 346–47. The Eleventh Circuit's effort to characterize the FOPA as an effort to protect constitutional rights accordingly lacks much merit – or persuasive force. Simply put, constitutional rights cannot, absent some conspiracy with a government official, be violated by the actions of a non-state actor. *See* David P. Currie, *Positive and Negative Constitutional Rights*, 53 U. Chi. 864, 884–86 (1986); *see* Krotoszynski, *supra* note 44, at 335 ("The state action doctrine

preserves a sphere of individual freedom of action, a freedom of action that would be reduced significantly were the Supreme Court to jettison the doctrine in favor of some sort of ad hoc rights balancing. The state action doctrine also properly reflects and helps to preserve the theoretical priority of the individual over the state."). Given this, the FOPA simply does not enforce or protect "constitutional rights."

46 *See* Ryan Foley, Larry Fenn & Nick Penzenstadler, *Accidental Shootings Put Kids in Early Graves*, USA TODAY, Oct. 14–16, 2016, at A1–A2 (noting that an empirical study found that "minors died from accidental shootings – at their own hands or at the hands of other children or adults – at a pace of one every other day, far more than limited federal statistics indicate").

47 In fact, the current guidelines issued by the American Academy of Pediatrics expressly require pediatricians, in a clinical setting, to inquire about gun ownership in the child's home. *See* American Academy of Pediatrics, American Academy of Pediatrics Gun Violence Policy Recommendations, at 2 (Jan. 2013), *available at* www.aap.org/en-us/advocacy-and-policy/federal-advo cacy/documents/aapgunviolencepreventionpolicyrecommendations_jan2013. pdf ("Physician counseling of parents about firearm safety has been demonstrated to be an effective prevention measure."). The AAP also has taken a strong stance in favor of more robust gun safety, observing that "the absence of guns from children's homes and communities is the most reliable and effective measure to prevent firearm-related injuries in children and adolescents." *Id.* at 1. My thanks to Dr. Stephen W. Hales, of New Orleans, for bringing to my attention the ethical duty of a treating pediatrician to counsel parents about gun safety in the home and the AAP's advocacy of effective gun safety policies to protect the health and lives of children.

48 *See supra* Chapter 1.

49 Bagget v. Bullitt, 377 U.S. 360, 371–73 (1964); Wiemann v. Updegraff, 344 U.S. 183, 193–94 (1952) (Black, J., concurring).

50 Healy v. James, 408 U.S. 169, 180–87 (1972); Keyishian v. Board of Regents, 385 U.S. 589, 605–10 (1967).

51 430 U.S. 705 (1977).

52 *Id.* at 714–17.

53 *Id.* at 715.

54 *Id.*

55 NIFLA v. Becerra, 138 S. Ct. 2361, 2371–76 (2018).

56 *See* Kathleen Sullivan, *Unconstitutional Conditions*, 102 HARV. L. REV. 1413, 1415–16, 1433–42 (1989).

57 Jack M. Balkin, *Information Fiduciaries and the First Amendment*, 49 U.C. DAVIS. L. REV. 1183, 1207–10 (2016).

58 *Id.* at 1209.

59 *Id.* at 1208.

60 *See id.* at 1209–10.

61 *See* Corbin, *supra* note 2, at 1294 (arguing that "compelled speech can lead to error if its content is inaccurate or misleading or its context fails to make clear

whether the message is the government's or the compelled speaker's" and that such speech "may also distort professional discourse if it causes a breach of professional obligations").

62 See GEORGE ORWELL, 1984 at 2 (1949). The dystopian government of George Orwell's 1984 routinely requires its citizens to engage in organized daily coerced speech events precisely because this activity rendered them if not incapable, then certainly less capable, of speaking authentically as citizens (meaning giving voice, freely and voluntarily, to their own personal thoughts, beliefs, concerns, and points of view).

63 Corbin, *supra* note 2, at 1294.

64 *Id.* at 1298.

65 *Id.*

66 *Id.*

67 *Id.* at 1298 n.127.

68 *Id.* at 1334 ("Coercing doctors to speak in a way that violates their professional code of conduct undermines their individual dignity and autonomy.").

69 Robert Post, *Compelled Commercial Speech*, 117 W. VA. L. REV. 867, 876 (2015).

70 *Id.*

71 319 U.S. 624 (1943).

72 See *id.* at 627–29.

73 *Id.* at 642.

74 *Id.*

75 See *id.* at 640–42.

76 Planned Parenthood of Se. Pa. v. Casey, 505 U.S. 833, 844, 881–84 (1992) (joint opinion of O'Connor, Kennedy, and Souter, JJ.).

77 NIFLA v. Becerra, 138 S. Ct. 2361, 2371–72 (2018).

78 See *id.* at 2372; *see also* Zauderer v. Office of Disciplinary Counsel of Supreme Court of Ohio, 471 U.S. 626, 651 (1985).

79 *NIFLA*, 138 S. Ct. at 2372.

80 See *Casey*, 505 U.S. at 882–84.

81 *Id.* at 884.

82 *NIFLA*, 138 S. Ct. at 2373.

83 *Id.*

84 *Id.* at 2385 (Breyer, J., dissenting).

85 *Id.*

86 *Id.* (citing and quoting Heffernan v. City of Paterson, 136 S.Ct. 1412, 1418 (2016)).

87 See Bush v. Gore, 531 U.S. 98, 109 (2000) ("Our consideration is limited to the present circumstances, for the problem of equal protection in election processes generally presents many complexities.").

88 See Norton, *supra* note 6, at 27–30.

89 See Norton & Citron, *supra* note 7, at 936–39.

90 Johanns v. Livestock Marketing Ass'n, 544 U.S. 550 (2005).

91 See *id.* at 554–55.

92 *Id.* at 578–79 (Souter, J., dissenting).

93 *Id.* at 562–63 (holding that "[c]itizens may challenge compelled support of private speech, but have no First Amendment right not to fund government speech" and this rule "is no less true when the funding is achieved through targeted assessments devoted exclusively to the program to which the assessed citizens object"). *But cf.* Norton & Citron, *supra* note 7, at 916 (positing that "the *Johanns* majority's refusal to require the disclosure of expression's governmental origins as a condition of claiming the [government speech] defense makes no pragmatic sense, in that such transparency demands very little from the government as a practical matter while providing considerable value in ensuring meaningful political accountability").

94 Helen Norton, *Government Speech and Political Courage*, 68 STAN. L. REV. ONLINE 61, 61 (2015) [hereinafter Norton, *Political Courage*]; *see also* Helen Norton, *The Measure of Government Speech: Identifying Expression's Source*, 88 B.U. L. REV. 587, 599–600 (2008) (arguing that requiring government to self-identify as a speaker "maximizes opportunities for undeceived credibility assessments and meaningful political accountability" and suggesting that if "political accountability is not available as a check on the government because the governmental source is obscured, then the safeguards of traditional First Amendment analysis should apply") [hereinafter Norton, *Identifying Expression's Source*].

95 Norton & Citron, *supra* note 7, at 925.

96 Lee, *supra* note 7, at 984.

97 *See id.* at 983–88.

98 *Id.* at 990.

99 Blocher, *supra* note 27, at 718.

100 *Id.*

101 *Id.*

102 Post, *supra* note 69, at 918.

103 *Id.*

104 *See id.*

105 *See id.* at 918–19.

106 *See supra* text and accompanying notes 63 to 68.

107 Balkin, *supra* note 57, at 1214.

108 *Id.* at 1215.

109 *See* Corbin, *supra* note 2, at 1339 (arguing that compelled professional speech distorts information markets, misleads clients and patients, and "undermines [doctors'] autonomy"); *see also id.* at 1351 ("Compelled speech may undermine free speech goals and values by chilling speech, distorting the discourse, or intruding upon the autonomy of speakers or audiences.").

110 Greene, *supra* note 7, at 49 (emphasis added).

111 *See id.*

112 *See id.* at 50.

113 *Id.*; *see* Blocher, *supra* note 27, at 718–19 (advocating a transparency requirement as a prerequisite to government claiming the benefit of the government speech doctrine).

114 *See* Rebecca Tushnet, *The Yes Men and The Women Men Don't See* in A WORLD WITHOUT PRIVACY: WHAT LAW CAN AND SHOULD DO? 83, 86–87 (Austin Sarat ed., 2015) (advocating for anonymous and pseudonymous speech on the Web and positing that "[p]seudonyms offer one way for people to maintain boundaries between different aspects of their identities, but without isolating themselves" and "can create rich communities and interactive works of art").

115 Lee, *supra* note 7, at 988–89 (arguing that "when the government participates in public debate, it should make the fact of its participation transparent" because "the legitimacy of those communications depends on the public's ability to identify what the government says and how it does so").

116 Norton & Citron, *supra* note 7, at 909 (arguing that "because government has no individual autonomy interest in self-expression, government's expressive interests do not include an interest in speaking without identifying itself as the speaker" and positing that mis-identified government speech risks compromising "political accountability").

117 Lee, *supra* note 7, at 989; *see* Norton, *Identifying Expression's Source, supra* note 94, at 591 (arguing that "[a] message's perceived source as governmental ... plays a role in shaping its effectiveness apart from its substantive content").

118 Norton, *Political Courage, supra* note 94, at 67.

119 *Id.*

120 135 S. Ct. 2239 (2015).

121 Tex. Transp. Code §§ 504.602, 504.603, 504.851(a) & 504.6011.

122 43 Tex. Admin. Code § 217.45.

123 *See Walker*, 135 S. Ct. at 2244–45.

124 *Id.* at 2245.

125 *Id.*

126 *Id.* at 2246.

127 *See id.* at 2248–52.

128 *See* Norton, *supra* note 6, at 28–30; *see also* Blocher, *supra* note 27, at 717–19.

129 *See* Norton, *Political Courage, supra* note 94, at 62–63; *see also* Wooley v. Maynard, 430 U.S. 705, 714–17 (1977) (holding that the display of a state-issued license plate on a private motor vehicle constitutes a form of compelled speech by the automobile's owner).

130 Corbin, *supra* note 2, at 1281–82, 1298; *see also* Corbin, *supra* note 6, at 607–08 (discussing the reasons why attributing government speech properly is important to the proper functioning of the political marketplace of ideas).

131 *See* Neil Richards, *The Dangers of Surveillance*, 126 HARV. L. REV. 1934, 1945–52 (2013).

132 555 U.S. 460 (2009).

133 *See id.* at 469–74.

134 *Id.* at 481.

135 *Id.* at 470–74.

136 *See id.* at 467, 481.

137 *Id.* at 472.

138 *Id.*

139 *See id.* at 467 (The Free Speech Clause restricts government regulation of private speech; it does not regulate government speech.").

140 *See* Norton, *Political Courage, supra* note 94, at 65–67.

141 *See supra* text and accompanying notes 93 to 119.

142 *See, e.g.,* Walker v. Texas Division, Sons of Confederate Veterans, 135 S. Ct. 2239 (2015); Johanns v. Livestock Marketing Ass'n, 544 U.S. 550 (2005); Rust v. Sullivan, 500 U.S. 173 (1991). *But cf.* Norton, *Political Courage, supra* note 94, at 67 (positing that the Supreme Court "should demand transparency from the government as a condition of recognizing the government speech defense to Free Speech Clause challenges to the government's expressive choices"); Robert C. Post, *Subsidized Speech,* 106 YALE L.J. 151, 172–76 (1996) (arguing that the First Amendment should protect medical doctors counseling patients about reproductive choices from being coerced into silence because the government happens to fund the medical clinic where they work and observing that "[i]t is far from clear, then, that physicians, even if they have accepted employment in Title X clinics, occupy roles defined by reference to a purely organizational logic, particularly in situations where that logic seems to override the necessary exercise of independent professional judgment").

143 *See* Norton, *The Measure of Government Speech, supra* note 94, at 598–601.

144 *Id.* at 599–600 ("If, however, political accountability is not available as a check on the government because the government source is obscured, then the safeguards of traditional First Amendment analysis should apply.").

145 Hustler Magazine, Inc. v. Falwell, 485 U.S. 46, 56–57 (1988).

146 *See* Discount Tobacco City & Lottery Inc. v. U.S., 674 F.3d 509, 529–30 (6th Cir. 2012); *see also* Central Hudson Gas & Elec. Corp. v. PSC, 447 U.S. 557, 564–65 (1980).

147 United States v. Alvarez, 567 U.S. 709, 720–23 (2012).

148 Barr v. Mateo, 360 U.S. 564, 574–75 (1959).

149 *See* Ronald J. Krotoszynski, Jr., *Afterword: Responding to a World without Privacy: On the Potential Merits of a Comparative Law Perspective* in Sarat, *supra* note 114, at 234, 256–65 (arguing that anonymous or pseudonymous speech by the government or for-profit corporations could distort, rather than enhance, the marketplace of ideas). As I have argued previously, "there's a dark side to anonymous and pseudonymous speech" because "the same anonymity that protects a woman criticizing the failure of the armed forces to deal effectively with sexual assault empowers the government itself to propagandize the population." *Id.* at 257. Moreover, "[t]he presence of anonymous or pseudonymous speech by institutional speakers – whether government agencies or corporations – risks engendering a kind of skepticism toward all such speech on the internet." *Id.* at 262.

150 *See* Krotoszynski, *supra* note 44, at 303–14.

151 *See* Citizens United v. Fed. Elec. Comm'n, 558 U.S. 310, 342–43 (2010) (holding that "First Amendment protection extends to corporations" and

rejecting "the argument that political speech of corporations or other associations should be treated differently under the First Amendment simply because such associations are not 'natural persons'"); *id.* at 341 ("We find no basis for the proposition that, in the context of political speech, the Government may impose restrictions on certain disfavored speakers. Both history and logic lead us to this conclusion."); *see also* Burwell v. Hobby Lobby Stores, Inc., 573 U.S. 682, 708 (2014) (noting that "[w]e see nothing in RFRA that suggests a congressional intent to depart from the Dictionary Act definition [that "person" encompasses for-profit corporations]" and concluding that "no conceivable definition of the term includes natural persons and nonprofit corporations, but not for-profit corporations").

152 *See* Jordan v. Jewel Food Stores, Inc., 743 F.3d 509, 519–20 (7th Cir. 2014).

9 USING CONSTITUTIONALLY PERMISSIBLE STATUTES TO IMPEDE FIRST AMENDMENT ACTIVITY

1 *See, e.g.,* Lozman v. City of Riviera Beach, 138 S. Ct. 1945, 1953 (2018) (observing that "it can be difficult to discern whether an arrest was caused by the officer's legitimate or illegitimate consideration of speech" and noting that "the complexity of proving (or disproving) causation in these cases creates a risk that the courts will be flooded with dubious retaliatory arrest suits"). At the same time, however, police can clearly use discretionary authority in pretextual ways. And, as Justice Anthony M. Kennedy explained in *Lozman*, "[a]n official retaliatory policy is a particularly troubling and potent form of retaliation, for a policy can be long term and pervasive, unlike an ad hoc, on-the-spot decision by an individual officer." *Id.* at 1954.

2 Tabatha Abu El-Haj, *Defining Peaceably: Policing the Line between Constitutionally Protected Protest and Unlawful Speech*, 80 Mo. L. Rev. 961, 981 (2015). (arguing that mass public protest still plays an important role in the process of democratic deliberation and positing that "[o]utdoor assemblies can compensate for the limits of electoral politics").

3 *Id.*

4 *See* Christina E. Wells, *Protest, Policing, and the Petition Clause: A Review of Ronald Krotoszynski's Reclaiming the Petition Clause*, 66 Ala. L. Rev. 1159, 1164–66 (2015).

5 *Id.* at 1164–65.

6 *See infra* text and accompanying notes 72 to 87.

7 *See infra* text and accompanying notes 83 to 87.

8 *See infra* text and accompanying notes 88 to 117.

9 It some respects, we have moved back toward a baseline that is "akin to notions of free speech in the early twentieth century when the Supreme Court considered advocacy of lawlessness to be unprotected." Tabatha Abu El-Haj, *All Assemble: Order and Disorder in Law, Politics, and Culture*, 16 U. Pa. J. Const. L. 949, 1034 (2014) [hereinafter Abu El-Haj, *All Assemble*]. Professor Abu El-Haj posits that "[t]oday, a similar constitutional understanding applies to assemblies." *Id.*

10 Wells, *supra* note 4, at 1165 (positing that "aggressive police responses have a significant effect on protestors regardless of available review" and observing that "courts often have few opportunities to assess whether protestors' *free speech* rights are violated" by such police tactics).

11 *See supra* Chapters 1 and 2.

12 John Inazu, *Unlawful Assembly as Social Control*, 64 UCLA L. Rev. 2, 5 (2017).

13 *See* Neil K. Komesar, Imperfect Alternatives: Choosing Institutions in Law, Economics, and Public Policy 123–28, 134–42, 202–13 (1994) (arguing that courts and the adjudicative process are well-suited to solving some problems but not others) [hereinafter Komesar, Imperfect Alternatives]; *see also* Neil K. Komesar, Law's Limits: The Rule of Law and the Supply and Demand of Rights 8, 12 (2001) (observing that "where numbers and complexity are high, the Rule of Law will be most demanded, but it also will be in the shortest supply" and arguing that "[a]s high numbers and complexity continue to grow, courts, recognizing their own limitations, send matters to the political process").

14 Professors Tabatha Abu El-Haj, John Inazu, and Christina Wells have written recently on the problem of police charging protesters with disorderly conduct, trespass, and unlawful assembly as a means of squelching collective protest in public spaces. *See, e.g.,* Abu El-Haj, *All Assemble, supra* note 9; Inazu, *supra* note 12; Wells, *supra* note 4.

15 Professor Inazu observes that "unlawful assembly restrictions target citizens across the political spectrum, including civil rights workers, antiabortion demonstrators, labor organizers, environmental groups, Tea Party activists, Occupy protesters, and antiwar protesters." Inazu, *supra* note 12, at 5.

16 *See, e.g.,* Lozman v. City of Riveria Beach, 138 S. Ct. 1945, 1950–53 (2018) (finding that liability could exist under section 1983 where police arrested a citizen at a city council meeting in the total absence of probable cause and on a pretextual basis).

17 *See infra* text and accompanying notes 118 to 155.

18 Abu El-Haj, *supra* note 2, at 963.

19 Wells, *supra* note 4, at 1165; *see also* Abu El-Haj, *All Assemble, supra* note 9, at 961 ("Even where permits are not required or have been issued, assemblies may be dispersed for actual and anticipated disorder, including obstructions of vehicular or pedestrian traffic.").

20 Wells, *supra* note 4, at 1165 (quoting Alicia A. D'Addario, *Policing Protest: Protecting Dissent and Preventing Violence Through First and Fourteenth Amendment Law*, 31 N.Y.U. Rev. L. & Soc. Change 97, 110 (2006)).

21 *See id.* at 964 (observing that "law enforcement [officers] routinely use[ ] low-level criminal law to manage the disruptiveness of protests, with judicial approval").

22 Wells, *supra* note 4, at 1165; *see* Abu El-Haj, *All Assemble, supra* note 9, at 962 (noting that police in Denver, Colorado, have used charges such as "obstructing the streets, disobeying a lawful order, impeding traffic, disturbing the peace, and improperly honking car horns").

23 Abu El-Haj, *supra* note 2, at 968.

24 *Id.* at 976.
25 Abu El-Haj, *All Assemble, supra* note 9, at 966 (noting that, in the context of Occupy Wall Street protests, local courts generally accepted permit denials and arrests for unlawful assembly because the would-be protesters could use "the Internet and social media" to disseminate their message effectively and explaining that "courts largely accepted those arguments, asserting that the ability to disseminate a message is an adequate substitute for the ability to gather in order to form and express [their] message").
26 Abu El-Haj, *All Assemble, supra* note 9, at 1035.
27 *See* Ronald J. Krotoszynski, Jr., Reclaiming the Petition Clause: Seditious Libel, "Offensive" Protest, and the Right to Petition the Government for a Redress of Grievances 17–19, 174–76 (2012).
28 *See supra* Chapter 3.
29 Krotoszynski, *supra* note 27, at 12–16, 153–56.
30 *Id.* at 12.
31 Inazu, *supra* note 12, at 30.
32 *Id.*
33 *Id.*
34 *Id.*
35 Hiram Emmanuel Arnaud, Note, *Dismantling of Dissent: Militarization and the Right to Peaceably Assemble*, 101 Cornell L. Rev. 777, 779 (2016).
36 Wells, *supra* note 4, at 1167.
37 Arnaud, *supra* note 35, at 780 (arguing that "these types of police tactics pose the threat of having a 'chilling impact' that undermines the right to peaceably assemble by 'causing individuals to reasonably perceive that they cannot safely protest.'" (quoting Protest and Assembly Rights Project, Suppressing Protest: Human Rights Violations in the U.S. Response to Occupy Wall Street 81 (2012)).
38 Wells, *supra* note 4, at 1166 (observing that "prosecutors often dismiss criminal charges against protestors soon after their arrest" and arguing that "[s]uch dismissals may leave protestors with little incentive to bring time-consuming and burdensome lawsuits challenging the free speech violations"); *see also* Abu El-Haj, *supra* note 2, at 973 (noting that "officers regularly make arrests for these crimes in situations that could not result in a conviction").
39 Wells, *supra* note 4, at 1165.
40 Abu El-Haj, *supra* note 2, at 964.
41 Wells, *supra* note 4, at 1166 (observing that "many journalists covering protests have been harassed or arrested").
42 *See* ACLU v. Alvarez, 679 F.3d 583, 606–07 (7th Cir. 2012) (holding that the First Amendment protects the right to record police officers while on duty in public places and spaces and invalidating, on an as-applied basis, an Illinois law that criminalized recording the police without their consent). The Supreme Court of Illinois subsequently invalidated the statute on First Amendment grounds. *See* People v. Clark, 6 N.E. 3d 154 (2014); Illinois v. Melongo, 6 N.E. 3d 120 (Ill. 2014).

43 *See* Krotoszynski, *supra* note 28, at 11–19, 69–70, 166–69.

44 Alexander Meiklejohn, Free Speech and Its Relation to Self-Government 25–27, 88–89 (1948).

45 Wells, *supra* note 4, at 1165.

46 *Id.*

47 *Id.*

48 *Id.* at 1165–66.

49 *Id.* at 1166.

50 Arnaud, *supra* note 35, at 779.

51 *Id.*

52 *Id.* at 780.

53 Abu El-Haj, *supra* note 2, at 966.

54 *Id.*

55 *Id.* at 977.

56 Abdullah v. County of St. Louis, 52 F. Supp. 3d 936, 940–41 (E.D. Mo. 2014). The keep-moving policy required those on Ferguson's sidewalks to stand for no more than five seconds or face arrest for "refusal to disperse." *See id.*

57 *Id.* at 941.

58 *See id.* at 941–43.

59 Mo. Rev. Stat. § 574.060; *see Abdullah*, 52 F. Supp. 3d at 943.

60 *Abdullah*, 52 F. Supp. 3d at 944.

61 *Id.*

62 *Id.* at 947.

63 *Id.*

64 *Id.*

65 *Id.*

66 *Abdullah*, 52 F. Supp. 3d at 947.

67 *Id.*

68 *Id.*

69 *Id.* at 949.

70 *Id.*

71 *See* Marbury v. Madison, 5 U.S. (1 Cranch) 137, 177 (1803) ("It is emphatically the province and duty of the judicial department to say what the law is. Those who apply the rule to particular cases, must of necessity expound and interpret that rule."); *see also* Komesar, Imperfect Alternatives, *supra* note 13, at 136–37 (noting that courts have comparative advantages in performing some tasks relative to the political branches).

72 In the October 2017 Term, the US Supreme Court was set to decide a case that would have determined whether the existence of probable cause insulates a police officer from any First Amendment liability for an arrest, even if a credible argument exists that the arrest was pretextual and an effort to retaliate for the exercise of First Amendment rights. *See* Lozman v. City of Riveria Beach, 138 S. Ct. 1945 (2018). The case involved disorderly conduct charges brought against Fane Lozman, a citizen who allegedly spoke out-of-turn in a city council meeting. *See id.* at 1949–50. *Lozman* presented the question of

whether a First Amendment claim for retaliatory arrest can be maintained if the police had probable cause for making an arrest. The city argued that the existence of probable cause should completely immunize a city police department from a First Amendment retaliatory arrest claim. Under existing Supreme Court precedent, the existence of probable cause absolutely precludes a First Amendment-based challenge to a wrongful *prosecution* claim. *See* Hartman v. Moore, 547 U.S. 250 (2005). *Lozman* was to determine whether the same rule of claim preclusion also governs a retaliatory arrest claim. The *Lozman* majority, however, punted on this issue. Rather than reach the question of whether probable cause to arrest for an otherwise constitutional criminal offense creates an absolute bar to a First Amendment civil action alleging retaliatory arrest, Justice Anthony M. Kennedy, writing for the majority, found that no probable cause requirement applied to Lozman's claim against the city, which presented a direct First Amendment claim that his right to petition the city government had been abridged by an official policy to silence him. *See id.* at 1954–55. Thus, "[t]he Court need not, and does not, address the elements required to prove a retaliatory arrest claim in other contexts." *Id.* at 1955. Accordingly, we will have to await a future Supreme Court case to learn if the *Hartman* rule applies to allegedly pretextual arrests where probable cause existed. However, even if such lawsuits could be maintained where probable cause to arrest exists, the problem of judges and juries being excessively deferential to the police would almost certainly still remain.

73 Abu El-Haj, *supra* note 2, at 977.
74 372 U.S. 229 (1963).
75 414 U.S. 105 (1973).
76 *Edwards*, 372 U.S. at 230.
77 *See id.* at 230–33.
78 *Id.* at 233.
79 *See id.* at 233–34.
80 *Id.* at 236.
81 *Id.* at 237.
82 *Id.*
83 *See id.* at 237–38.
84 379 U.S. 536 (1965).
85 *Id.* at 551.
86 *Id.* at 552.
87 *See id.* at 549–53.
88 It also bears noting that the Warren Court did not always rule in favor of free speech claimants. In *Walker v. City of Birmingham*, 388 U.S. 307 (1967), for instance, a 5–4 majority upheld five-day jail terms and $50 monetary fines when civil rights protesters intentionally violated an injunction against marching in Birmingham, Alabama without a valid parade permit. *See id.* at 311–12. Writing for the majority, Justice Potter Stewart explained that "[t]his Court cannot hold that the petitioners were constitutionally free to ignore all the procedures of the law and carry their battle to the streets" because "respect for judicial process is

a small price to pay for the civilizing hand of law, which alone can give abiding meaning to constitutional freedom." *Id.* at 321.

89 403 U.S. 15 (1971).

90 414 U.S. 105 (1973).

91 405 U.S. 518 (1972). Other decisions in this line of precedent include *Lewis v. City of New Orleans*, 415 U.S. 130 (1974) and *Rosenfeld v. New Jersey*, 408 U.S. 901 (1972). I discuss *Lewis* below. *Rosenfeld* involved a conviction based on the use of the words "mother fucker" at a public school board meeting "held in an auditorium" and "attended by more than 150 men, women, and children of mixed ethnic and racial backgrounds." Rosenfeld v. New Jersey, 408 U.S. 901, 910 (1972) (Rehnquist, J., dissenting). The majority simply summarily reversed the conviction. *See id.* at 901–02.

92 *Cohen*, 403 U.S. at 24–26.

93 *See* Ronald J. Krotoszynski, Jr., Cohen v. California: *"Insignificant" Cases and Larger Legal Principles*, 74 Tex. L. Rev. 1251 (1996).

94 *Cohen*, 403 U.S. at 16–17.

95 Cal. Penal Code § 415

96 *Cohen*, 403 U.S. at 19.

97 *Id.* at 26.

98 *Id.*

99 *Id.*

100 414 U.S. 105 (1973).

101 *Id.* at 107.

102 *Id.*

103 *Id.*

104 *See* Gooding v. Wilson, 405 U.S. 518, 521–22 (1972) ("The constitutional guarantees of freedom of speech forbid the States to punish the use of words or language not within 'narrowly limited classes of speech.' *Chaplinsky* v. *New Hampshire*, 315 U.S. 568, 571 (1942)."). In *Gooding*, the Supreme Court invalidated a Georgia law that prohibited the use of "opprobrious words and abusive language" that tend to "cause a breach of the peace." *See id.* at 518–19. The specific language involved was "White son of a bitch, I'll kill you." and "You son of a bitch, I'll choke you to death." The words were spoken as police officers attempted to prevent an anti-Vietnam War protest from blocking access to an army induction center. As with *Cohen* and *Hess*, the state sought to punish "only spoken words." *Id.* at 520.

105 415 U.S. 130 (1974).

106 New Orleans Ordinance 828 M.C.S. § 49–7.

107 *Lewis*, 415 U.S. at 131 n.1.

108 *Id.* at 134.

109 *Id.*

110 *Id.* at 135 (Powell, J. concurring).

111 *Id.*

112 *Id.* at 136.

113 *Id.*

114 *See* United States v. Alvarez, 567 U.S. 709 (2012).

115 *See* Snyder v. Phelps, 562 U.S. 443 (2011).

116 *See* Hustler v. Falwell, 485 U.S. 46 (1988).

117 *See* McCullen v. Coakley, 134 S. Ct. 2518 (2014). *McCullen* is an illustrative example. Massachusetts enacted a statute banning protest within thirty-five feet of persons entering or leaving family planning clinics. *Id.* at 2525–26. The Supreme Court invalidated the buffer zone requirement because it unduly restricted speech in a public forum. *Id.* at 2540–41 (invalidating the buffer zone law because the state had pursued its legitimate governmental interests "by the extreme step of closing a substantial portion of a traditional public forum to all speakers" and also without seriously considering "alternatives that leave the forum open for its time-honored purposes"). On the other hand, had the local police simply used trespass, breach of peace, or unlawful assembly, rather than a law that targeted protests proximate to an abortion clinic, it would have been much more difficult for the would-be protesters to challenge their arrests on First Amendment grounds.

118 *See, e.g., id.* at 2541 (invalidating a Massachusetts state law that precluded personal interactions with persons entering or leaving health care facilities, including family planning clinics, because Massachusetts used overbroad means to achieve its legitimate interests, notably including "the extreme step of closing a substantial portion of a traditional public forum to all speakers," and also because the state adopted these measures "without seriously addressing the problem through alternatives that leave the forum open for its time-honored purposes").

119 Wells, *supra* note 4, at 1168.

120 *Id.*

121 Abdullah v. County of St. Louis, 52 F. Supp. 3d 936, 948 (E.D. Mo. 2014) ("This injunction does not prevent defendants or other law enforcement agencies from using all lawful means to control crowds and protect against violence.").

122 *Id.* at 949.

123 Abu El-Haj, *All Assemble, supra* note 9, at 1038–39.

124 *Id.* at 1039.

125 *Id.*

126 *Id.* at 1039.

127 *See id.* at 956, 961–64 (documenting the use of mass arrests for minor crimes in progressive cities including New York City, Boston, Denver, and Madison).

128 *Id.* at 964.

129 Arnaud, *supra* note 35, at 807–08.

130 *See id.* at 806–07 & 807 n.193. Mr. Arnaud explains that "I draw inspiration from the balancing in *Communist Party* in my proposed balancing scheme and weigh the purpose of the product of police militarization against the original meaning and vision for the Assembly Clause." *Id.* at 807 n.193.

131 *See supra* Chapters 1 to 4.

132 Abu El-Haj, *supra* note 2, at 985.

133 *Id.*

134 *See id.*

135 *Id.*

136 Inazu, *supra* note 12, at 30–31.

137 *Id.* at 31.

138 *See id.* at 51

139 *Id.*

140 *Id.*

141 *Id.* at 52.

142 *Id.* at 51.

143 *See id.* at 49–51.

144 Abu El-Haj, *supra* note 2, at 961–62.

145 Stephen Rushin, *Using Data to Reduce Police Violence*, 57 B.C. L. Rev. 117, 132–45, 148–54 (2016); *see* Jason Mazzone & Stephen Rushin, *From Selma to Ferguson: The Voting Rights Act as a Blueprint for Police Reform*, 105 Calif. L. Rev. 263, 309–17 (2017).

146 Stephen Rushin, *Structural Reform Litigation in American Police Departments*, 99 Minn. L. Rev. 1343, 1420 (2015) [hereinafter Rushin, *Structural Reform*].

147 *Id.*

148 *See id.* ("States and the federal government could mandate more data collection on frontline officer behavior.").

149 McCleskey v. Kemp, 481 U.S. 279, 312–19 (1987).

150 *Id.* at 292–97, 314–19. Writing for the majority, Justice Lewis F. Powell, Jr. posited that "McCleskey's arguments are best presented to legislative bodies" because legislatures "are better qualified" to judge the persuasive force of statistical evidence than the federal courts. *Id.* at 319.

151 *See* United States v. Carolene Prods. Co., 304 U.S. 144, 152–53 n.4 (1938) (holding that federal courts should review with skepticism laws that appear to be motivated by animus "against discrete and insular minorities" for whom public prejudice may "tend[ ] seriously to curtail the operation of those political processes ordinarily to be relied upon to protect minorities"); *see generally* John Hart Ely, Democracy and Distrust: A Theory of Judicial Review (1980) (arguing that democratic processes systematically and predictably fail in certain structural ways and positing that judicial interventions are required as part of a structural system of "representation reinforcement").

152 This also held true in the context of securing universal voting rights for African American citizens in the Deep South. *See* David J. Garrow, Protest at Selma: Martin Luther King, Jr., and the Voting Rights Act of 1965, at 4–6 (1978). To be sure, federal courts attempted to address widespread and systematic abuse of discretion with respect to voting registration and ballot access. *See, e.g.*, United States v. Alabama, 192 F. Supp. 677, 682–83 (M.D. Ala. 1961) (issuing an injunction with affirmative, mandatory duties for Alabama voting officials because more traditional, prohibitory injunctions had failed to secure the registration of African-American citizens of Alabama). However, these judicial efforts were not particularly successful at solving the problem of race-

based denials of suffrage. *See* JACK BASS, TAMING THE STORM: THE LIFE AND TIMES OF JUDGE FRANK M. JOHNSON, JR. AND THE SOUTH'S FIGHT OVER CIVIL RIGHTS 254–56 (1993). Instead, federal political oversight of the registration and voting process proved necessary. *See id.* Professor David Garrow explains that the Voting Rights Act of 1965 provided new federal methods of enforcing voting rights and that "[t]hese new methods of enforcement, such as federal registrars, federal poll watchers, and the suspension of the numerous tests and requirements that long had been used to hinder or prevent black registration, proved to be far more effective at protecting the right to vote than had the judicial enforcement employed with little success in the years prior to 1965." GARROW, *supra*, at 5. In other words, national controls and oversight were necessary to overcome local opposition to the vindication of voting rights without regard to race. Similar dynamics require external, political forms of oversight for police abuse of discretionary arrest authority to prevent lawful forms of public protest.

153 *See* COLLEEN LEWIS, COMPLAINTS AGAINST THE POLICE: THE POLITICS OF REFORM 11–16, 31–80 (1999).

154 *Id.* at 76–80.

155 STEPHEN RUSHIN, FEDERAL INTERVENTION IN AMERICAN POLICE DEPARTMENTS (2017); Mazzone & Rushin, *supra* note 145, at 279–83; Rushin, *supra* note 145, at 154–66; Stephen Rushin, *Federal Enforcement of Police Reform*, 82 FORD. L. REV. 3189 (2014); Rushin, *Structural Reform, supra* note 146, at 1366–96.

156 *See* Mark Seidenfeld, *Cognitive Loafing, Social Conformity, and Judicial Review of Agency Rulemaking*, 87 CORNELL L. REV. 486 (2002).

157 *See* JEREMY BENTHAM, PANOPTICON; OR, THE INSPECTION-HOUSE (1791).

158 Seidenfeld, *supra* note 156, at 490–91, 522–26, 543–48.

159 Wells, *supra* note 4, at 1168.

160 *See* KOMESAR, *supra* note 13, at 123–52.

161 Indeed, the political question doctrine includes cases for which there is no judicially discernable standard. *See* Baker v. Carr, 369 U.S. 186, 217 (1962). Justice Brennan explained the political question in these terms:

> Prominent on the surface of any case held to involve a political question is found a textually demonstrable constitutional commitment of the issue to a coordinate political department; or a lack of judicially discoverable and manageable standards for resolving it; or the impossibility of deciding without an initial policy determination of a kind clearly for nonjudicial discretion; or the impossibility of a court's undertaking independent resolution without expressing lack of the respect due coordinate branches of government; or an unusual need for unquestioning adherence to a political decision already made; or the potentiality of embarrassment from multifarious pronouncements by various departments on one question.

Id. Reviewing a police officer's use of discretionary arrest authority presents obvious problems involving "judicially discoverable and manageable standards." A judge was not there and even with the advent of police body cameras, it is unlikely that a judge would confidently be able to second-guess the exercise of police discretion in the context of a chaotic public protest that plausibly presented a risk of disorder, a risk of loss of life or damage to property, or other public harms. And, again, when prosecutors drop charges after the police arrest protesters, no obvious means exist for seeking judicial review of the arrests based on First Amendment concerns or objections.

162 Abu El-Haj, *supra* note 2, at 974.

163 KOMESAR, IMPERFECT ALTERNATIVES, *supra* note 13, at 202–13 (positing that complex problems, such as overseeing the military and foreign affairs, lacking clear legal solutions or implicating strongly conflicting legal values, lead courts to doubt their own institutional capabilities and arguing that "[t]he limited scale of judicial resources alone forces courts to abandon a serious review of the vast majority of government activity" and that courts must "choose between the malfunctioning political process and an adjudicative process that often suffers from ignorance, systemic bias, and limited resources").

10 CONCLUSION

1 Reynolds v. Sims, 377 U.S. 533, 558, 560–63, 568 (1964); *see* Gray v. Sanders, 372 U.S. 368, 381 (1963) ("The conception of political equality from the Declaration of Independence, to Lincoln's Gettysburg Address, to the Fifteenth, Seventeenth, and Nineteenth Amendments can mean only one thing – one person, one vote."). In *Reynolds*, Chief Justice Earl Warren held that "an individual's right to vote for state legislators is unconstitutionally impaired when its weight is in a substantial fashion diluted when compared with votes of citizens living in other parts of the State." *Reynolds*, 377 U.S. at 568.

2 ALEXANDER MEIKLEJOHN, FREE SPEECH AND ITS RELATION TO SELF-GOVERNMENT 25 (1948).

3 New York Times Co. v. Sullivan, 376 U.S. 254, 270 (1964).

4 *Id.* at 91.

5 *Id.*

6 *See* Citizens United v. Fed. Elec. Comm'n, 558 U.S. 310, 339–41 (2010).

7 *See, e.g.*, Forsyth County v. Nationalist Movement, 505 U.S. 123 (1992) (holding that a local government could not seek to shift the cost of protecting unpopular speakers on to the speakers themselves because such a policy would empower popular majorities to impose a heckler's veto on those seeking to disseminate unpopular ideas or messages).

8 *See* Arizona Free Enterp. Club's Freedom Club PAC v. Bennett, 564 U.S. 721, 734–40 (2011) (invalidating an Arizona state public campaign financing law that provided public matching funds to candidates competing with self-funded candidates who spent in excess of specified triggers); Davis v. Federal Election Comm'n, 554 U.S. 724, 738–40 (2008) (invalidating a provision of federal law raising contribution limits for candidates facing self-funded opponents who expended more than $350,000 of their personal funds to promote their candidacy for federal office). *But cf. Arizona Free Enterp. Club's Freedom Club PAC*, 564

U.S. at 765–66 (Kagan, J., dissenting) (arguing that "what petitioners demand is essentially a right to quash other's speech through the prohibition of a (universally available) subsidy program" and that the Arizona public campaign finance program was consistent with the First Amendment because it "restrains no one's speech and discriminates against no idea" but instead "provides more voices, wider discussion, and greater competition in elections").

9 *See supra* Chapter 2.

10 *See supra* Chapter 3.

11 Amalgamated Food Employers Local Union 590 v. Logan Valley Plaza, Inc., 391 U.S. 308 (1968).

12 *See supra* Chapter 4.

13 Garcetti v. Ceballos, 547 U.S. 410 (2006).

14 *See supra* Chapter 5.

15 Tinker v. Des Moines Indep. Cmty School Dist., 393 U.S. 503 (1969).

16 Keyishian v. Board of Regents, 385 U.S. 589 (1967).

17 *See, e.g.*, Morse v. Frederick, 551 U.S. 393 (2007).

18 *See supra* Chapter 6.

19 *See* Holder v. Humanitarian Law Project, 561 U.S. 1, 33–40 (2010).

20 *See* Clapper v. Amnesty Int'l USA, 568 U.S. 398, 422 (2013).

21 *See supra* Chapter 7.

22 *See supra* Chapter 8.

23 167 U.S. 43 (1897).

24 29 N.E. 517 (Mass. 1892).

25 *See* ROBERT C. POST, CONSTITUTIONAL DOMAINS: DEMOCRACY, COMMUNITY, MANAGEMENT 234–40 (1995).

26 *See* MARTIN H. REDISH, THE ADVERSARY FIRST AMENDMENT: FREE EXPRESSION AND THE FOUNDATIONS OF AMERICAN DEMOCRACY (2013).

27 512 U.S. 43 (1994).

28 466 U.S. 789 (1984).

29 *See, e.g.*, Tinker v. Des Moines Indep. Cmty. Sch. Dist., 393 U.S. 503 (1969) (adopting a balancing test to determine whether protest activity by a public school student while on campus enjoys First Amendment protection); Pickering v. Bd. of Educ., 391 U.S. 563 (1968) (adopting a balancing test that weighs a government employee's interest in speaking out about a matter of public concern against the government employer's interest in avoiding material disruption within the workplace).

30 MEIKLEJOHN, *supra* note 2, at 25.

31 *See* Kathleen Sullivan, *Unconstitutional Conditions*, 102 HARV. L. REV. 1413 (1989).

32 *Id.* at 1496.

33 *Id.*

34 *See* Bush v. Gore, 531 U.S. 98 (2000); Reynolds v. Sims, 377 U.S. 533 (1964); Baker v. Carr, 369 U.S. 186 (1962).

35 *See* Owen M. Fiss, *Free Speech and Social Structure*, 71 IOWA L. REV. 1405, 1412–16 (1986).

36 *Id.* at 1415.

37 Owen M. Fiss, *Why the State?*, 100 HARV. L. REV. 781, 791 (1987).

38 *See* David P. Currie, *Positive and Negative Constitutional Rights*, 53 U. CHI. L. REV. 864 (1986). *But cf.* Alexander Meiklejohn, *The First Amendment Is an Absolute*, 1961 SUP. CT. REV. 245, 260 (proposing that "[i]n every village, in every district of every town or city, there should be established at public expense cultural centers inviting all citizens, as they may choose, to meet together for the considerations of public policy").

39 *See* Sullivan, *supra* note 31, at 1496–97, 1503–06.

40 *See* Int'l Soc'y for Krishna Consciousness, Inc. v. Lee, 505 U.S. 672, 695–97 (1992) (Kennedy, J., concurring) (proposing a functional approach to analyzing whether government property constitutes a public forum and arguing that public forum analysis should be "objective," meaning "based on the actual, physical characteristics and uses of the property"); *see also* Grayned v. City of Rockford, 408 U.S. 104, 116 (1972) ("The crucial question is whether the manner of expression is basically incompatible with the normal activity of a particular place at a particular time."). Professor Steve Gey has offered an extended, and highly persuasive, argument in favor of taking this approach. *See* Steven G. Gey, *Reopening the Public Forum – From Sidewalks to Cyberspace*, 58 OHIO ST. L.J. 1535, 1566–76 (1998).

41 *See* Ward v. Rock Against Racism, 491 U.S. 781, 791, 802–03 (1989).

42 *See* Christina E. Wells, *Protest, Policing, and the Petition Clause: A Review of Ronald Krotoszynski's* Reclaiming the Petition Clause, 66 ALA. L. REV. 1159, 1164–68 (2015).

43 *See* MEIKLEJOHN, *supra* note 2, at 25–26 (arguing that government should have the ability to regulate public discussion to ensure that all relevant viewpoints are heard). As Meiklejohn states the point, "what is essential is not that everyone shall speak, but that everything worth saying shall be said." *Id.* at 25.

44 *See, e.g.,* Citizens United v. Fed. Elec. Comm'n, 558 U.S. 310, 339–42 (2010).

45 Of course, a libertarian vision of the First Amendment does not necessarily protect only pro-business interests – George Soros and Jeff Bezos are equally empowered to drown out competing voices by occupying the political marketplace of ideas through lavish political spending. *See* Kathleen Sullivan, Comment, *Two Concepts of Freedom of Speech*, 124 HARV. L. REV. 143, 143–46, 155–63 (2010) (discussing the Roberts Court's *laissez faire* approach to speech markets and reflexive faith in private control of speech markets and criticizing its evident lack of interest in using the First Amendment as a means of empowering the less powerful in contemporary US society to play a greater role in the process of democratic self-government).

46 GREGORY P. MAGARIAN, MANAGED SPEECH: THE ROBERTS COURT'S FIRST AMENDMENT 252–53 (2017).

47 *See Citizens United*, 558 U.S. at 340 ("Premised on mistrust of government power, the First Amendment stands against attempts to disfavor certain subjects or viewpoints."); *id.* at 341 ("Quite apart from the purpose or effect of

regulating content ... the Government may commit a constitutional wrong when by law it identifies certain preferred speakers.").

48 *See, e.g.*, Williams v. Wallace, 240 F. Supp. 100, 106–09 (M.D. Ala. 1965).

49 *See* Branzburg v. Hayes, 408 U.S. 665, 709–10 (1972) (Powell, J., concurring) (arguing that First Amendment protection for a reporter's confidential sources requires the claimed privilege to "be judged on its facts by the striking of a proper balance between freedom of the press and the obligation of all citizens to give relevant testimony with respect to criminal conduct" and proposing that this balancing exercise be undertaken "on a case-by-case basis").

50 *See, e.g.*, Tinker v. Des Moines Indep. Cmty School Dist., 393 U.S. 503 (1969).

51 Brown v. Louisiana, 383 U.S. 131 (1966).

52 Pickering v. Board of Educ., 391 U.S. 563 (1968).

53 *See, e.g.*, Walker v. Texas Div., Sons of Confederate Veterans, 135 S. Ct. 2239 (2015); Morse v. Frederick, 551 U.S. 393 (2007); Garcetti v. Ceballos, 547 U.S. 410 (2006); Johanns v. Livestock Marketing Ass'n, 544 U.S. 550 (2005).

54 MEIKLEJOHN, *supra* note 2, at 25–26.

55 Meiklejohn, *supra* note 38, 260 (proposing government subsidies to support and encourage speech related to the project of democratic self-government).

56 *See* Mathews v. Eldridge, 424 U.S. 319, 334–35 (1976).

57 In much of the wider world, constitutional courts routinely engage in "proportionality analysis," which requires judges to balance the infringement of a constitutional right against the government's justification for the infringement and to assess the overall "fit" between the means used by the government to achieve its constitutionally-permissible objective and the burden on the underlying fundamental right. For a relevant discussion of the salience of proportionality analysis in many constitutional systems featuring judicial review, see Vicki C. Jackson, *Constitutional Law in an Age of Proportionality*, 124 YALE L.J. 3094 (2015).

Index